Mariology

A Guide for Priests, Deacons, Seminarians, and Consecrated Persons

Mark Miravalle, S.T.D., Editor

Nihil Obstat:
Fr. Peter M. Fehlner, F.I.

Imprimatur:
The Most Rev. Raymond L. Burke,
Archbishop of St. Louis, Missouri
September 15, 2007
Feast of Our Lady of Sorrows

© 2007 Mark I. Miravalle, S.T.D.
All rights reserved.

Faith & Family Publications
PO Box 365
Downingtown, PA 19335
faithandfamily.pub

Paperback ISBN: 978-1-965803-01-1

Printed in the United States of America

Dedication

*To the memory
and Mariology
of John Paul II*

Contents

Foreword by His Excellency, Archbishop Raymond L. Burke xiii
Editor's Introduction xvii

I. Mary in Scripture and the Early Church
The Mystery of the Blessed Virgin
Mary in the Old Testament
Fr. Stefano Manelli, F.I. 1
    Prophecies 4
        The "Woman" of the *Protoevangelium* 4
        The "Virgin-Mother" 13
        The Woman in Travail 21
    Figures of Mary 25
        Eve, the "Mother of the Living" 26
        Sarah, the Wife of Abraham 27
        Rebecca, Spouse of Isaac 27
        Miriam, the Sister of Moses 28
        Deborah 29
        Ruth, the "Moabitess" 30
        Judith, the "Intrepid Widow" 30
        Esther, the "Queen" 31
        The Mother in the Book of Maccabees 32
        Abraham and Isaac 33
    Marian Symbols 33
        The Ark of the Covenant 35
        The "Virgin Earth" 35
        The "Paradise of God" 36
        "Closed Door," "Gate of God," "Gate of Heaven" 36
    Liturgical Use of Old Testament Marian Symbols 39
        Among the "Poor of Yahweh" 39
        "Exalted Daughter of Zion" 40

    "Created Wisdom" 41
    "You Are All Fair" 42

The Virgin Mary in the New Testament
  Fr. Settimio M. Manelli, F.I. 45
    Mary in the Accounts of the Origin
    and of the Infancy of Christ 47
      "Born not of Blood" (Jn 1:13) 48
      "The Fullness of Time" (Gal 4:4) 54
      Matthew and Luke 66
      Genealogy of Jesus 66
      The Annunciation (Lk 1:26-28) 69
      St. Joseph's Dream and the Virginal
      Birth of Jesus (Mt 1:28-25) 75
      The Adoration of the Magi (Mt 2:1-12) 79
      Meeting with Elizabeth 82
      The Magnificat (Lk 1:46-55) 87
      Birth and Circumcision (Lk 2:1-21) 89
      The Presentation of Jesus
      in the Temple (Lk 2:22-40) 94
      The Finding of Jesus in the Temple (Lk 2:41-52) 99
    Mary in the Accounts of the Public Life of Jesus 101
      The Marriage Feast at Cana (Jn 2:1-11) 101
      At the Foot of the Cross (Jn 19:25-27) 104
      Acts of the Apostles (Acts 1:14) 109
    Mary in the Glory of Christ 111
      Mary and the Apocalypse 111
    Conclusion 114

Mary and the Fathers of the Church
  Fr. Luigi Gambero, S.M. 115
    Mary in the Ante-Nicene Period 118
    The Apostolic Fathers 118
    The Christian Apologists 121
    The Christian Controversialists 125
    The Golden Age of Patristic Thought 132
    The End of the Patristic Age 143

II. Marian Dogma
The Mother of God
Fr. Manfred Hauke 159
    The Divine Maternity as a Constituent of the
    "Fundamental Principle" in Mariology 159
    Biblical Foundation 162
    The Patristic Tradition until the
    End of the Fourth Century 166
        The Divine Maternity before the
        Technical Term *Theotókos* 166
        A Pagan Origin for the Christian Doctrine
        of the Divine Maternity? 170
        Development in the Fourth Century 173
    The Council of Ephesus (431) 175
    History of the Dogma Following
    the Council of Ephesus 180
        Second Vatican Council
        and the Contemporary Magisterium 183
    Ecumenical Aspects 185
    Systematic Assessment 189
        The Title is Important for Comprehension
        of the Divine Person of Jesus Christ 189
        The Holiness of Mary Prepares Her
        for the Divine Maternity 189
        The Divine Maternity
        Implies a Transforming Relation 192
        As Mother of God, Mary Takes
        an Active Part in the Work of Redemption 194
        The Divine Motherhood Constitutes
        the Beginning of Spiritual Motherhood 194
        The Divine Motherhood Exalts Mary
        Over All Other Creatures 196
        The Divine Maternity Constitutes
        a Special Relation with the Holy Trinity 197

The Predestination of the Virgin Mother and Her Immaculate Conception
 Fr. Peter M. Fehlner, F.I. 203
  Introduction 203
  The Predestination of Mary 206
   Foundation in Sacred Scripture 208
   The Witness of Tradition 209
   Theological Reflection 210
   The Contribution of Bl. John Duns Scotus 211
   The Holy Name of Mary 217
  The Immaculate Conception 218
   The "Fecit" or Fact of the
   Immaculate Conception 221
   Possibility/Fittingness, or the
   Reason of the Immaculate Conception 238
   From "Franciscan Thesis" *(Opinio Minorum)*
   to Defined Dogma 250
   New Light on Theology: Biblical,
   Dogmatic, Moral 253
   Total Consecration to and Triumph
   of the Immaculate Heart 257
  Conclusion 261

Our Lady's Perpetual Virginity
 Msgr. Arthur Burton Calkins 265
  Foundational Principles 266
  The Mystery of the Virginal Conception 272
   Questionable Assumptions 273
   The Biblical Witness 277
  The Mystery of the Virginal Birth 285
   The Magisterium 286
   The Biblical Witness 288
   The Allegorical Sense of Scripture 294
  The Mystery of Mary's Lifelong Virginity 295
  Concluding Considerations 299

The Assumption of Our Lady
 Fr. Paul Haffner 303
  The Close of Mary's Earthly Life 304

The Assumption: Development
Towards the Dogma..313
The Assumption and the Queenship 328

III. Marian Doctrine
Mary Co-redemptrix: The Beloved Associate of Christ
Msgr. Arthur Burton Calkins 335
Mary, the New Eve..335
The *Protoevangelium* (Gen 3:15) 342
Development of Doctrine 347
Papal Teaching on Marian Coredemption
before the Second Vatican Council 360
The Situation on the Eve of the
Second Vatican Council...366
The Second Vatican Council.....................................373
The Contribution of John Paul II..............................376
Conclusion..383

Mary Mediatrix of All Graces
Fr. Alessandro M. Apollonio, F.I. 395
The Problematic of Marian Mediation.....................398
Sacred, Revealed Use of the Term........................400
Profane Usage...404
Mary Mediatrix in the Proper,
Theological Sense of Mediation 406
The Difference between Mediator
and Mediatrix in the One Work of Mediation.......... 410
Mediatrix in the Restricted Sense
of Distributrix of Graces after Calvary....................... 412
Theological Meaning of the Title of Mediatrix:
Sources of the Doctrine 413
Sacred Scripture 414
Teaching of the Church Fathers 420
Theological Development: Medieval,
Post-Tridentine and Neo-Scholastic Epochs 423
Mary Mediatrix of all Graces in the Pontifical
Magisterium: From Benedict XIV to Benedict XVI 426

    The Mediation of the Blessed Virgin Mary
    at the Second Vatican Council 432
    The Nature of the Blessed Virgin Mary's
    Influence in the Application of the Redemption 442
    Conclusion..444

Advocate and Queen
    Edward Sri, S.T.D...447
    Introduction 447
    Biblical Foundations 448
        The Queen Mother and Advocate
        in the Davidic Kingdom 448
        The Queen Mother in Prophecy: Isaiah 7:14............ 452
        Mary as Queen Mother
        and Advocate in the New Testament 453
    Advocate: Foundations in Tradition
    and Magisterium...465
    Queenship: Foundations in Tradition
    and Magisterium... 470
    Theological Conclusions and Applications 479

Mary, Mother and Model of the Church
    Fr. Enrique Llamas, O.C.D................................. 485
    Part One: Mary, Mother of the Church 486
        Mary, Mother of the Church: Theological-
        Spiritual Development.................................... 493
        Mary, Mother of the Church, in the
        Mystery of the Incarnation 497
        Mary, Mother of the Church, on Calvary.................504
        Mary's Ecclesial Motherhood at the
        Wedding Feast of Cana (cf. Jn 2:1-12) 517
        Mary's Spiritual Maternity and
        Patristic Doctrine.. 521
        Mary's Spiritual Maternity in
        Ecumenical Dialogue 522
    Part Two: Mary, Model of the Church....................524
        Problematic..524
        Mary, Model and Example of
        the Church—The Fact..................................529

IV. Marian Liturgy and Devotion

Mary and the Liturgical Year

Fr. Neil J. Roy 539
- First Principles and Goals 539
  - Mary in the Life of the Church 541
  - The Relationship between Liturgy and Doctrine 548
- Mary and the Liturgy 562
  - Mary and the Liturgical Year 565
  - Feasts and Seasons 567
- Conclusion 594

Marian Devotion, the Rosary, and the Scapular

Fr. Etienne Richer 595
- Introduction 595
- Gospel Origin and Divine Institution 597
- Nature and Necessity 604
  - A Special and Absolutely Unique Cultus:
    The Cultus of Hyperdulia 604
  - Necessity of Marian Devotion 613
- Marian Devotion in the Code of
  Canon Law of 1983 615
  - Canon 1186 Addressed to All the Faithful: 616
  - Canons 246.3 and 276.2,5°
    (Seminarians and Clerics): 618
  - Canon 663.4 (Religious): 620
- The Rosary of the Blessed Virgin Mary 622
  - Vatican II and the Rosary 622
  - The Genesis of the Rosary 626
  - From the Magisterial Reception (1569)
    to the Luminous Mysteries (2002) 634
- The Scapular Devotion 638
- By Way of Conclusion 646

Marian Consecration and Entrustment

Msgr. Arthur Burton Calkins 651
- Historical Forms 653
  - Patristic Period 653
  - Medieval Period 658
  - Modern Period 661

The Papal Magisterium	671
A Question of Terminology?	679
The Theological Foundations of Consecration/Entrustment	681
The Principle of Analogy	682
The Principle of Marian Mediation	685

Marian Private Revelation: Nature, Evaluation, Message
Mark I. Miravalle, S.T.D. 691

Discerning Private Revelation	692
Public and Private Revelation	692
Prophecy	696
Visions and Apparitions	705
Locutions	712
Levels of Assent to Private Revelation	713
Contemporary Norms for Evaluation	718
Sequence in the Process of Evaluation	724
The Marian Message to the Modern World	727
The "Miraculous Medal" Apparitions, 1830	728
The Lourdes Apparitions, 1858	736
The Fatima Apparitions, 1917	748

List of Contributors 773

Foreword

On the Solemnity of the Annunciation in 1988, Cardinal William Baum, then prefect of the Congregation for Catholic Education, wrote a letter to all ordinaries, that is bishops, major religious superiors and their equivalents; to all rectors of diocesan seminaries, and to presidents of theological faculties. Entitled *The Virgin Mary in Intellectual and Spiritual Formation*, the letter was inspired by the work of the Second Extraordinary Assembly of the Synod of Bishops, which took up the question of the teaching of the Second Vatican Ecumenical Council and its reception over the time since the closing of the Council. One of the fruits of the Synod of Bishops was a renewed emphasis on the study of the four major constitutions of the Council, namely, *Sacrosanctum Concilium*, "On the Sacred Liturgy" (December 4, 1963); *Lumen Gentium*, "On the Church" (November 21, 1964); *Dei Verbum*, "On Divine Revelation" (November 18, 1965); and *Gaudium et Spes*, "On the Church in the Modern World" (December 7, 1965). With respect to the Dogmatic Constitution *Lumen Gentium*, in particular, special attention was directed to its final chapter, "On the Blessed Virgin Mary, Mother of God, in the Mystery of Christ and of the Church."

The letter of Cardinal Baum was further inspired by the indiction of the Marian Year which began on the Solemnity of Pentecost of 1987 (June 7) and concluded on the Solemnity of the Assumption of the Blessed Virgin Mary in 1988. The Servant of God Pope John Paul II announced the Marian Year in his Encyclical *Redemptoris Mater*, making clear his purpose, namely, "to promote a new and more careful reading of what the Council said about the Blessed Virgin Mary, Mother of God, in the mystery of Christ and of the Church."[1] *Redemptoris Mater* itself was a most significant contribution towards the realization of the noble

---

[1] Pope John Paul II, Encyclical *Redemptoris Mater*, "On the Blessed Virgin Mary in the Life of the Pilgrim Church," March 25, 1987, n. 48.

and most important goal which Pope John Paul II established for the celebration of the Marian Year.

The Virgin Mary in Intellectual and Spiritual Formation, issued during the heart of the Marian Year, on the first anniversary of the publication of *Redemptoris Mater*, reminds us that the promotion of the fuller knowledge of and more fervent devotion to the Blessed Virgin Mary is the constant work of the Church. It reviews briefly the Church's perennial teaching regarding the Blessed Virgin Mary and her irreplaceable vocation and mission in the mystery of the redemptive Incarnation. Special attention is given to the synthesis of Marian doctrine found in *Lumen Gentium*, and to the Marian teaching of Pope Paul VI and Pope John Paul II, in the time following the close of the Council. It then sets forth directives regarding research in Mariology, the teaching of Mariology, and the contribution of Marian devotion to the pastoral life of the Church, especially to the apostolate of evangelization. The letter concludes by setting forth three essential goals of the formation of seminarians in what pertains to their relationship with the Blessed Virgin Mary: 1) the acquisition of a *"complete and exact knowledge* of the Church's doctrine regarding the Virgin Mary," in order to identify authentic doctrine and true devotion, and "to contemplate the supreme beauty of the glorious Mother of Christ"; 2) the development of an *"authentic love"* of the Blessed Mother, expressed in "genuine forms of devotion" and leading to the imitation of the virtues of the Blessed Virgin Mary; and 3) the development of "the *capacity to communicate* such love to the Christian people through speech, writing and example."[2]

What *The Virgin Mary in Intellectual and Spiritual Formation* sets forth for seminary formation applies, *mutatis mutandis*, to the ongoing formation of priests, the formation of permanent deacons, and the formation of consecrated persons. I refer, for example, to n. 35 of the *Directory for the Pastoral Ministry of Bishops*, published by the Congregation for Bishops on February 22, 2004; and to n. 68 of the *Directory for the Life and Ministry of Priests*, published by the Congregation for the Clergy on January 31, 1994. Those who are or will be teachers of the faith and guides for others in the life of faith must have both a sound knowledge of the vocation and

---

[2] Congregation for Catholic Education, *The Virgin Mary in Intellectual and Spiritual Formation*, March 25, 1988, Vatican City State: Libreria Editrice Vaticana, 1989, pp. 21-22, n. 34.

mission of the Blessed Virgin Mary in the work of our salvation and, as a result, a devoted love of the Mother of God.

The vocation and mission of our Blessed Mother relates to every aspect of our life in Christ, for it is she who brings Christ into the world, through the overshadowing of the Holy Spirit, and it is she who, by the work of the Holy Spirit, continues to offer Christ to the world in the Church. Rightly, we invoke her with the title, Mother of Divine Grace. Referring to the relationship of the Blessed Virgin Mary to Eucharistic faith and devotion, Pope Benedict XVI declared:

> In her we find realized most perfectly the essence of the Church. The Church sees in Mary – "Woman of the Eucharist," as she is called by the Servant of God John Paul II – her finest icon, and she contemplates Mary as a singular model of Eucharistic life. ... From Mary we must learn to become men and women of the Eucharist and of the Church, and thus to present ourselves, in the words of Saint Paul, "holy and blameless" before the Lord, even as he wished us to be from the beginning (cf. Col 1:22; Eph 1:4).[3]

It is the Blessed Virgin Mary who faithfully and lovingly leads us to her divine Son with the maternal counsel, "Do whatever he tells you" (Jn 2:5). She is the Mother of the Redeemer who, when he was consummating the work of our salvation, gave his Mother to the Church to be her Mother always: "Woman, behold your son! ... Behold, your mother!" (Jn 19:26-27).

Mariology: A Guide for Priests, Deacons, Seminarians, and Consecrated Persons is an extraordinarily complete and rich tool for coming to a deeper knowledge of the teaching of the Church on the Blessed Virgin Mary, for growing in Marian devotion and for developing the means of communicating knowledge and love of the Mother of God to others. Dr. Mark Miravalle, the editor, has brought together the contributions of highly competent and gifted authors whose own deep knowledge and devoted love of our Blessed Mother is wonderfully evident in what

---

[3] Pope Benedict XVI, post-synodal Apostolic Exhortation *Sacramentum Caritatis*, "On the Eucharist as the Source and Summit of the Church's Life and Mission," February 22, 2007, n. 96

they have written. All of the mysteries of the life and mission of Mary are treated in depth, in accord with the directives set forth in *The Virgin Mary in Intellectual and Spiritual Formation*.

The careful study of the texts of the various authors will aid the reader to achieve the three goals of Marian formation: the integral knowledge of Marian doctrine, growth in authentic and heartfelt Marian devotion, and the development in the capacity to introduce others to Marian teaching and devotion by the way of the various communications media. It is my hope that priests, permanent deacons, seminarians, and consecrated persons will find in this volume a treasured instrument for growth in their own spiritual life and for carrying out the mission of the new evangelization. It is also my hope that it will become a standard textbook in seminaries, programs of diaconal formation and houses of formation of institutes of the consecrated life and societies of apostolic life. At the same time, I commend the text to all who desire to know more fully and to love more ardently the Mother of God.

Grateful to Dr. Mark Miravalle and his collaborators in the writing of *Mariology: A Guide for Priests, Deacons, Seminarians, and Consecrated Persons*, let us pray, through the intercession of the Mother of Divine Grace, that their work will lead to a deeper knowledge of the Blessed Virgin Mary in the mystery of Christ and of his Church. Let us also pray that their work will inspire a renewed devotion to the Mother of God who is also the Mother of the Church.

—The Most Reverend Raymond Leo Burke
Archbishop of St. Louis
August 15, 2007
Solemnity of the Assumption of the Blessed Virgin Mary

Editor's Introduction

> If the place occupied by Mary has been essential to the equilibrium of the Faith, today it is urgent, as in few other epochs of Church history, to rediscover that place. ... Yes, it is necessary to go back to Mary if we want to return to that "truth about Jesus Christ," "truth about the Church" and "truth about man" that John Paul II proposed as a program to the whole of Christianity.[1]
>
> —Joseph Cardinal Ratzinger

Mariology, by its very nature, cannot be studied in isolation. The concept of "mother" presupposes the concept of "child," and in this case, the reality of a son. Mariology connaturally leads to Christology, as the study of the Mother of Jesus presupposes and calls forth a deeper knowledge and assent to the truths about Jesus Christ, the incarnate Son of God and of Mary.

Mariology also organically springs forth into Ecclesiology, since anyone who is spiritually united to Jesus through baptism and filial adoption has also, in a particular way, received the Mother of Jesus as his or her own spiritual mother. This Mother offers an immaculate human model of Christian discipleship to Jesus for the entire People of God, and at the same time intercedes as a mother in the order of grace for her Son's disciples who seek to respond to the Lord's invitation to Christian holiness with their own personal *fiat* of faith.

If Cardinal Ratzinger (Benedict XVI) was correct in directing the entire Church to the program of Pope John Paul II in returning to the "whole truth about Mary" in order to ensure authentic Christology

---

[1] Joseph Cardinal Ratzinger with Vittorio Messori, *The Ratzinger Report*, Ignatius Press (English Edition), pp. 105-106.

and Ecclesiology (not to mention anthropology), how much more quintessential is this call for renewed Mariology from the last two pontiffs for today's clergy, seminarians, and consecrated persons?

While this text is certainly not intended to exclude the laity in any manner, its principal goal is to offer clergy, seminarians, and consecrated persons a solid foundation in a contemporary Mariology that appreciates and builds upon the Church's rich Tradition, and also embodies the inspired Mariological contributions from the Second Vatican Council, the recent Papal Magisterium, and the fruitful postconciliar Mariological developments.

The specific thrust of this anthology is to provide a guide in classical and current Mariology for ongoing clergy and religious education and formation, seminary instruction, and the edification of consecrated persons, all of who possess a special call to benefit fully from a greater knowledge and love of the Mother of the Lord. The international team of renowned contributors to this volume, who collectively represent an extensive number of publications in Mariology (as well as national and international theological societies and honorary associations), sought to author their individual chapters with the specific intention of providing a theologically scientific treatment of their particular topic for clergy and religious, the consecrated, and those in formation, but within the designated framework and style indicative of present Mariological literature (rather than a more manualist or textbook approach). The individual articles fall within the following four general categories: I. Mary in Scripture and the Early Church; II. Marian Dogmas (as defined by the Extraordinary Magisterium); III. Marian Doctrine (as taught by the Ordinary Magisterium); and IV. Marian Liturgy and Devotion.

That Mariology cannot appropriately be studied in isolation and must always be seen in complete subordination to the whole truth about Jesus Christ should not, on the other hand, prevent a dynamic investigation into the revealed truth about Our Lady which should intrinsically foster a generous love for that Mother given from the crucified Lord as a personal gift to each one of us (cf. Jn 19:25-27). The testimony of the former Cardinal Ratzinger as to the present efficacy of Marian truth and devotion for the protection of Christian faith, coupled with his admonition for any who might consider Mariology as no longer necessary for one's own theological approach, remain a helpful reminder:

> In Mary, as figure and archetype, the Church herself finds her own visage as Mother and cannot degenerate into the complexity of a party, an organization or a pressure group in the service of human interests, even the noblest. If Mary no longer finds a place in many theologies and ecclesiologies, the reason is obvious: they have reduced faith to an abstraction. And an abstraction does not need a Mother.[2]

May the celebrated truth and love of Mary, Mother of the Church, sanctify and renew with the abundant gifts and fruits of the Holy Spirit the lives of bishops, priests, deacons, and consecrated persons, and all those in formation for these anointed vocations at the service of the Lord Jesus, as providentially designed and called forth by God, the eternal Father of all mankind.

—The Editor

---

[2] Ratzinger and Messori, *The Ratzinger Report*, p. 108.

I.
Mary in Scripture and the Early Church

The Mystery of the Blessed Virgin Mary in the Old Testament

Fr. Stefano Manelli, F.I.

If Holy Scripture, from an inter-testamental perspective, is the birthplace of the Blessed Virgin Mary in the *history of salvation*, one must also add that the Old Testament was this unique creature's *first* land of birth in the world.

But most accurately, the origins of the Blessed Virgin Mary are transcendent, from eternity, in the *"one and the same decree"* of the Incarnation of the Word, universal Savior and Redeemer,[1] about whom numerous pages of Old Testament revelation speak. For us this revelation constitutes the original source of the creative and saving plan of God.

To know the homeland of the Blessed Virgin Mary, it is in fact enough to know the Mariological texts of the Old Testament, reading them "as they are read in the Church,"[2] according to the norms of biblical-theological exegesis, i.e., "in the light of Christ and of the Church,"[3] to find in them what is called "Mariology in its roots." Such Mariology in the New Testament and "in the Tradition originating with the apostles and developing in the Church under the assistance of the Holy Spirit" (Dei Verbum 8) has come to full maturity in its historical-theological realization.[4]

---

[1] Bl. Pius IX, Apostolic Constitution *Ineffabilis Deus* for the dogmatic definition of the Immaculate Conception of the Blessed Virgin Mary.

[2] *Lumen Gentium*, 55. Cf. J.A. De Aldama, *De valore Magisterii Ecclesiae in interpretatione Sacrae Scripturae*, in *De Maria et Sacra Scriptura*, III (Roma 1967) 199-208.

[3] Pontifical Biblical Commission, *The Jewish People and its Sacred Scriptures in the Christian Bible*, 2001, n. 7. Cf. *Dei Verbum*, n. 10.

[4] Cf. S.M. Manelli, *All Generations Shall Call Me Blessed: Biblical Mariology* (New Bedford, MA 2005, 2nd ed.), pp. 111-120.

For a still more solid Mariological reading of the Old Testament, summary explanations of the criteria used by the Magisterium of the Church for assessing the meaning of the Old Testament texts[5] have been formulated, particularly in relation to what is considered the *hebraica* veritas.[6]

In fact, on the basis of directives and norms of the Pontifical Biblical Commission found in the recent document: "The Jewish People and its Sacred Scriptures in the Christian Bible," it appears firmly established that Mariology, or more exactly the mystery of the Blessed Virgin Mary, is found

> in the texts of the Old Testament explicitly and clearly. The genuine content of every revealed datum "finds its realization in Jesus" (21, 6). As a consequence only "the Christian in the light of Christ and of the Church discovers that surplus of meaning hidden in them" (*Ibid.*). Without this "surplus of meaning," which is accessible only to him who reads the Scriptures "in the light of Christ and of the Church," every other interpretation cannot help but be reductive and indeed misrepresent the genuine and real content of revealed truth.
>
> In view of this the document indicates, in relation to Jewish and more specifically rabbinic hermeneutical rules for interpreting the Old Testament, criteria whereby the very firm link binding Old and New Testaments can be perceived. In such wise a Christian hermeneutic of the Old Testament is set in clear relief, one "very different, certainly, from that of Judaism, one nonetheless corresponding to the potential meaning inherent in

---

[5] Cf. *Ibid.*, p. xii: "But to discern the ineffable reality of Mary All Holy in the Sacred Page, working within the parameters of personal research and a merely literal evaluation of the inspired Word is quite insufficient. Rather, one must seek to portray her in accord with the mind and thought of God as expressed in the written Word and authenticated by the Church. In short, such a portrait must be drawn in terms of the full view afforded by a biblical-theological exegesis, and not merely of that attainable from the analytic canons of a purely biblical-philological exegesis." (See also pp. xvi-xviii.)

[6] Cf. I. Cardellini, *Ancora una nota sulla questione dell'* Hebraica veritas, in *Rivista Biblica*, 52 (2004) 136-137.

the texts themselves" (n. 64). The "potential meaning inherent in the texts themselves" can only be grasped by one who reading the Scriptures "in the light of Christ and of the Church" finds the "surplus of meaning" enabling him to pass from "potential" to "actual" harmonious, consistent realization of that meaning, without recourse to tortured and sometimes downright contradictory reinterpretations.

... It has indeed been remarked that in the final analysis "we Christians, to understand fully the Scripture, not grasping merely the necessarily *reductive* meaning understood by the Hebrews, but their entire historical-theological content, must always read them not as if still Hebrews under the Old Covenant, blind in relation to the New, but as "Christians" enlightened by Christ. This is to say, we must read them "in the light of Christ and of the Church" so as to grasp the entire content, "hidden," but *historic* and *real*, of Divine Revelation contained in them and made manifest to us. This is, precisely, biblical-theological exegesis, which the document cited also calls "theological interpretation, but at the same time fully historical" (n. 21).[7]

Now, in an exegetical examination of the Mariological biblical texts of the Old Testament considered as a whole, we discover among the many to be studied a number of prophecies, a group of figures, a notable number of symbols and some other significant texts. In virtue of these one may, without hesitation, affirm that the Blessed Virgin Mary has

---

[7] S.M. Manelli, *La Mariologia nella storia della salvezza. Sintesi storico-teologica*, in *Immacolata Mediatrix*, 2 (2002) 51-52. In this regard, the clearest and most convincing example is that of St. Matthew, who interprets the text of Isaiah 7:14 *historically and theologically*, relating it totally to the Virgin Mary directly prophesized as Virgin-Mother of the Emmanuel (without the tortuous and contradictory references to the wife of Ahaz, already *pregnant with Hezechiah*, and hence at opposite poles from *"the virgin who will conceive and give birth"*). In regard to the different methods of interpreting Sacred Scripture, see H.G. Reventlow, *Storia dell'interpretazione biblica*, Casale Monferrato 1999, 3 volumes.

been clearly prophesied, luminously prefigured, and richly symbolized in the books of the Old Testament.[8]

The presence of the mystery and of the person of the Blessed Virgin Mary in the pages of Old Testament biblical revelation is, therefore, well founded, significant and suggestive. And it is just in this way that it has been cultivated in enlightened fashion, from antiquity, by the Fathers, by Tradition, by the Magisterium, by the liturgy and by sacred art, from century to century, during the course of two Christian millennia.[9] All this confirms *ad abundantiam* what Vatican II clearly and lucidly teaches about the connatural, unbreakable link between the contents of Sacred Scripture, the contents of Tradition, and the contents of the Magisterium: "It is clear, then, that Sacred Tradition, Sacred Scripture and the Magisterium of the Church, in virtue of the wise dispositions of God, are so connected and joined among themselves that no one of them can subsist without the others, and all together, each in its own way, under the action of the one Holy Spirit, contribute efficaciously to the salvation of souls" (*Dei Verbum*, 10).

Prophecies

The "Woman" of the Protoevangelium: Gen 3:15

"*I will put enmity between you and the woman, and between your seed and her seed; she [ipsa] shall crush your head*"

---

[8] It must be said, however, that in recent times, during the post-conciliar period, a negative attitude and position has arisen in regard to the Mariological texts of the Old Testament, one which has considerably narrowed the area of interest to only the three great prophecies (Gen 3:15; Is 7:14; Mic 5:1-2), thus greatly reducing the Mariological references in the figures and symbols found in the books of the Old Testament. This is to renounce the rich patrimony of Marian, biblical exegesis in the books of the Old Testament in the patristic and ecclesiastical Tradition. For this is a patrimony cultivated by the Church in the course of two millennia of life. The loss would be incalculable. Cf. Manelli, *All Generations...*, p. 115, note 10.

[9] De la Potterie speaks authoritatively when he affirms that to have authentic biblical exegesis "it would be necessary to rediscover 'the patristic *mode* of reading the Bible': we must read it in the spirit of the Fathers. This is how the ancient Tradition did it; and this is what Vatican II recommends for us in *Dei Verbum*, n. 12." (De la Potterie, *La lettura della Sacra Scrittura "nello Spirito": il modo patristico di leggere la Bibbia è possibile oggi?*, in *Communio* n. 87 (1986) p. 40. See also Th. Spidlik-I. Gargano, *La spiritualità dei Padri greci e orientali. Storia della spiritualità*, Rome 1983, vol. 3/a, p. 157.)

This text of Genesis, from the first pages of the Bible, has been justly defined as the *Protoevangelium*, or *first gospel*. For in it is revealed the first and most important announcement of the good news of salvation for mankind.[10]

After the fall of our first parents into original sin, when realistically it seemed as though everything had been irremediably lost by Adam and Eve for themselves and for their descendants, behold, the intervention of a merciful God who promises them salvation through a New Eve and a New Adam. They will save mankind from the fall, ransoming it at the price of the redemptive sacrifice.

In the person of Mary, in fact, the second Eve will, in no manner, be imprudent and foolish as was the first Eve. The second Eve will be prompt to consecrate herself faithfully to the plan of salvation according to the will of God. The second Adam, then, in the person of Jesus will join to himself the second Eve for the sake of a universal salvation, in contrast with the first Adam who was bound by the sin of the first Eve, seduced by the serpent in Eden.

As the Second Vatican Council affirms, the New Eve, namely *Mary of Nazareth*, rooted in the will of God by her personal *Fiat*, "consecrated herself totally as Handmaid of the Lord to the person and work of her Son, under him and with him cooperating in the mystery of redemption" (*Lumen Gentium*, 56). It was precisely she [*ipsa*] who "with the grace of almighty God" (*Lumen Gentium*, 56) and with her "immaculate foot" (Pius IX, *Ineffabilis Deus*) crushed the head of the infernal serpent.

The New Adam, then, Jesus the Christ, in contrast to the first Adam under the influence of the first Eve, who had been tricked and seduced by the serpent tempter, perfectly complied with his mission of universal Redeemer, and accomplished his task with the personal, active cooperation of the New Eve, always united to him as generous, most faithful Co-redemptrix, as Vatican II says, "to the very Cross, where in accord with the divine plan she stood ... associating herself in her maternal heart with his sacrifice, lovingly consenting to the immolation of him whom she had begotten" (*Lumen Gentium* 58).

---

[10] Cf. V. Sardi, *La solenne definizione dell'Immacolata Concepimento di Maria SS. Atti e Documenti*, vol. I, p. 706.

From what has been said, it is already perfectly evident that the "woman" about whom the text of Genesis speaks, can only be Mary, Mother of the Redeemer, taken in the literal sense, which therefore excludes disobedient Eve, a sinner and condemned (Gen 3:16) according to the prophetic-oracular character of the text announcing a future salvation linked to an exceptional future woman. This woman, united with her son in the same enmity with the serpent, will crush the head of the infernal seducer of the first Eve.[11]

> The solemn promise of a woman victorious over the serpent and bearer of the Savior finds no verification in poor Eve, a sinner, who will rather live and die in the obscurity of her days, and who immediately after the divine oracle heard God pronounce these bitter words to her: *I will multiply thy sorrows, and thy conceptions: in sorrow shalt thou bring forth children, and thou shalt be under thy husband's power, and he shall have dominion over thee* (Gen 3:16).
>
> The most *elementary* psychology forbids positing any continuity between passages so brusque and opposite to one another. Immediately after speaking solemnly of the plan of victory of the "woman" with her "seed," God speaks of the constant suffering and humiliation in which Eve must live. How is it possible that God could be speaking of the same "woman"? Nor is it any more admissible the coexistence in Eve herself of a plan of life which would entail contemporaneous development under the standards of victory (Gen 3:15) and of servitude of suffering and of man (Gen 3:16).
>
> This is the point of departure, rather, for the logical development of that powerful and fecund *antithesis* perceived by the first of the early Fathers (St. Justin and St. Irenaeus), and subject of study throughout the

---

[11] Rollo writes well when he affirms that "the *Protoevangelium* has first of all an oracular character, which differentiates it from the general tenor of the narrative. Further, its orientation is *messianic* and *universal*, because it looks to the future" (A. Rolla, *Il Messaggio della salvezza*, Turin 1967, vol. II, p. 126); see also M. Cimosa, *Genesi 1-11. Alle origini dell'uomo*, Brescia 1984, pp. 90-93.

following centuries, immediately perceiving the living reality of the contrast between Eve and the "woman" of Gen 3:15 ... as regards their fundamental mission. St. Jerome formulated this concisely when he wrote: "Per Evam mors, vitam per Mariam [Through Eve death, life through Mary]."[12]

... Now, had God wished Eve as well, or only Eve, to be the triumphant enemy of the serpent, a kind of vindication in reverse, as Fr. Da Fonseca notes, "one would hardly understand from what follows, why when speaking to Eve (Gen 3:16-21) God had nothing but words of reproof and chastisement; and that throughout the entire history of redemption there is found not even a minimal allusion to a fact so important. For every time Eve is mentioned, she is described as the cause of our ruin, never as the beginning of our restoration (Sir 25:33; 2 Cor 11:3; 1 Tim 2:14)."[13]

Nothing, therefore, but an intent for the contradictory or strident polemic, can persuade one to also see Eve in the "woman" of Gen 3:15. Nothing in the entire life of Eve can have any kind of valid reference to the grandiose saving mission expounded in the Protoevangelium with its two new protagonists: the Messiah and his Mother.[14]

It is quite certain, in effect, that under attentive theological analysis Gen 3:15 may really be considered a text so rich in Mariological content as to be, despite its paucity of words, a true and proper *mariologia in nuce* (Mariology in a nutshell), one in which it is possible to grasp the substance of the person and of the extraordinary mission of Mary as the New Eve aside the New Adam.[15]

---

[12] St. Jerome, *Epistula 22 ad Eustochium*, n. 21. On the Eve-Mary antithesis, see the study of L. Cignelli, *Maria Nuova Eva nella Patristica greca*, Assisi 1966.
[13] P.L. Da Fonseca, *L'Assunzione di Maria nella S. Scrittura*, in *Biblica* 28 (1947) 348.
[14] S.M. Manelli, *All Generations...*, pp. 25-27.
[15] This is the position supported, among others, by G. Roschini, *La Madonna secondo la fede e la teologia*, Rome 1953, vol. II, pp. 50 and 72. See also S.M. Manelli, *All Generations...*, pp. 32-37.

Nor is it difficult to discover in Gen 3:15, either by induction or deduction, a very great many truths of faith concerning the mystery of the Blessed Virgin Mary, expressly formulated and implicitly veiled by the few words of the text of Genesis on which the early Church Fathers and theologians, mystics and saints, scholars and simple faithful have meditated and reflected on over the course of two thousand years, "*in lumine fidei, sub ductu Ecclesiae* [in the light of faith, under the guidance of the Church]."

The fundamental truths touching the mystery of Mary, in effect, are these: the Immaculate Conception, the divine, messianic, and virginal maternity, the coredemption and universal mediation, the Assumption, and queenship in the Kingdom of heaven. Now, the *root* of these truths is already found, in seed-form, in the passage of Gen 3:15, as it has thus been read, and is still read, by the Magisterium of the Church, for our guidance and enlightenment along the saving path to be followed by all mankind.

The Immaculate

In particular, and, as it were, on center stage, Gen 3:15 presents the "woman" as the New Eve, Immaculate, Virgin-Mother, Co-redemptrix.

The New Eve is above all the Immaculate, because she was predestined to be the enemy of Satan, proclaimed as such in relation to the serpent. It is God who speaks thus: "I will put enmity between you and the woman." Enmity is opposition. The New Eve, in fact full of grace (cf. Lk 1:26), will be in opposition to the enemy and hostile to sin in her maternal mission of universal salvation.

The New Eve is also the "Virgin Mother." She is "Mother," because God speaks of her "seed," that is, of her son, and of her offspring (in the collective sense: cf. Rev 12:17): "I will put enmity ... between your seed and her seed." She is Virgin, because there is not even a hint here of a husband of the *"woman,"* who might be the father of the son of the *"woman."* The New Eve is *Co-redemptrix* as well, because this is implicit in her enmity to Satan, the very same enmity which she shares with her Son, the New Adam, Redeemer in relation to Satan's seed: "I will put enmity between you and the woman, and between your seed and her seed." Such enmity entails hard struggle and victory for the Redeemer and Co-redemptrix against the serpent: "*She shall crush your head, while you shall lie in wait for her heel,*" God said to the serpent.¹⁶

In these words from God, it becomes evident that the New Eve is so united to her Redeemer son, is associated and conjoined with him in the redemptive work in a manner so direct and immediate, that she herself ("*ipsa*") by the grace and power of her Son, crushes the head of the serpent tempter with her "*immaculate foot,*" as written in the papal document *Ineffabilis Deus*, where this is repeated four times.

In recent times, there has been considerable discussion over the authenticity of the pronoun *ipsa* in the feminine in Gen 3:15. But the discussion notwithstanding, the feminine *ipsa*, chosen by St. Jerome, continues to enjoy first place as the preferred translation of the text of Genesis in Church and magisterial Tradition.¹⁷

---

16 On the truth concerning *Marian coredemption* in the text of the *Protoevangelium* in Genesis there exists an immense bibliography. We cite here only a few of the many fundamental studies: S.M. Manelli, *Maria Corredentrice nella Sacra Scrittura*, in AA.VV., *Maria Corredentrice. Storia e Teologia*, Frigento 1998, vol. I, pp. 37-114, here 53-65; Idem, *Mary Coredemptrix in Sacred Scripture*, in *Mary Coredemptrix, Mediatrix, Advocate. Theological Foundations II*, Santa Barbara, CA, 1997, pp. 59-104, here 71-80; T. Gallus, *Die "Frau" in Gn 3, 15*, Klagenfurt 1979; R. Rabanos, *La Corredención de Maria en la Sagrada Escritura*, in *Estudios Marianos* 2 (1943) 10-24; W.G. Most, *Mary Coredemptrix in Scripture. Cooperation in Redemption*, in *Mary Coredemptrix, Mediatrix, Advocate. Theological Foundations I*, Santa Barbara, CA, 1995, pp. 147-171; G.M. Roschini, *Problematica sulla Corredenzione*, Rome 1969, here 93-99; B. Gherardini, *La Corredentrice nel mistero di Cristo e della Chiesa*, Rome 1998, pp. 159-172; Settimio Manelli, *Genesis 3:15 and the Immaculate Coredemptrix*, in *Mary at the Foot of the Cross V*, New Bedford, MA, 2005, pp. 263-322; T.M. Sennott, *Mary Coredemptrix*, in *Mary at the Foot of the Cross II*, New Bedford, MA, 2002, pp. 49-63; J. Ferrer Arellano, *The Immaculate Conception as the Condition for the Possibility of the Coredemption*, in *Mary at the Foot of the Cross V*, New Bedford, MA 2005, pp. 74-185; P.D. Fehlner, *Redemption, Metaphysics and the Immaculate Conception*, in *Mary at the Foot of the Cross V*, New Bedford, MA, 2005, pp. 186-262, here 229-243.

17 Cf. Manelli, *All Generations…*, p. 21: "…according to more recent philological studies, it is now admitted to be certain that the translation of the pronoun *ipsa*, chosen by St. Jerome, must be regarded as quite legitimate, because as Donatella Scaiola affirms 'from the philological standpoint the reading in the feminine is possible in so far as in the Pentateuch we find many masculine pronouns (*q're*) to be understood in the feminine sense'" (D. Scaiola, *Testi tradizionali rivisitati (Gn 3, 15; Is 7, 14)*, in *Theotokos* 8 (2000) 563. In the note Scaiola cites P. Jouon, *Grammaire de l'hébreu biblique*, Rome 1947, #16f., 39c; see also U. Vanni, *La Donna della Genesi*

As frequently observed, the seriousness and competence of St. Jerome cannot but guarantee the validity of the translation in the feminine (*ipsa*). For it is well known that to assure the most exact translation and most faithful interpretation of Sacred Scripture, St. Jerome, as P.L. Ferrari writes, "underscores the importance of a knowledge of Hebrew and Aramaic to understand the Scriptures and the superiority of the original text over the Greek Septuagint translation." And as a confirmation of his extremely serious scholarship, St. Jerome himself "bought from the Jews the best Hebrew manuscripts for purposes of comparison, using methods of textual criticism to select those readings which seemed to him closest to the original."[18]

In regards to this Genesis pronoun translation of St. Jerome in the feminine (*ipsa*), according to the most recent exegetical study of the biblicist, Settimio Manelli,[19]

> There is a need, indeed an obligation once again to return to the adoption of the feminine version which has presided over Old Testament biblical study from the days of Philo and Josephus Flavius, i.e., from the first century after Christ. That adoption, moreover, was celebrated in luminous texts of the poet Prudentius, of the apologist Tertullian, of the great teachers, the Fathers of the Church such as St. Ambrose, St. Jerome and St. John Chrysostom, cited in his day by Cornelius a Lapide, the great exegete of the seventeenth century, who wrote the *Commentaria in Scripturam Sacram* (Paris, 1948). He also resolved the problem of the verb in the masculine (*yashuph*, *conteret*, or crush) citing the "frequent exchange" of gender in Hebrew: the masculine being used in place of the feminine and vice-versa, especially when there is present some cause or mystery, as is the

---

(3, 15) e la Donna dell'Apocalisse (12, 1) nella "Redemptoris Mater," in *Marianum* 50 (1988) 428-429, nt. 14.

[18] P.L. Ferrari, *Due millenni di lettura cristiana della Bibbia*, in AA.VV., *Guida alla lettura della Bibbia. Approccio interdisciplinare all'Antico e al Nuovo Testamento*, Cinisello Balsamo 1995, p. 150. See also I. Cardellini, *Ancora una nota...*, cit.

[19] Settimio Manelli, *Genesis 3: 15...*, cit.

case here. ... This observation is also confirmed by more recent grammatical studies.[20]

This is the plan of universal redemption signaled, on the one hand, by the complete victory of Christ and of Mary with the crushing of the head of the infernal serpent, and on the other hand by the insidiousness of the serpent, who will present himself as having won an apparent victory on Calvary, based on the Passion and death of Christ the Redeemer, and on the compassion and mystical death of Mary Co-redemptrix.

The Blessed Virgin Mary, then, in Gen 3:15, is presented as being associated with the entire redemptive work of Christ, "united to him by a strict and indissoluble bond," according to the expression found in *Lumen Gentium* 53, supplying a cooperation so direct and immediate that she herself (*ipsa*), with her "*immaculate foot*," will crush the head of the serpent, by the power of her divine Son, becoming the universal Mother,[21] the true Mother of all the living.[22]

The first Fathers of the Church have presented this redemptive plan as a plan of *recirculation*, or of *reversal*, or of *recapitulation*, with the double antithesis *Adam-Christ, Eve-Mary*, i.e., with the two couples placed in diametrical opposition: *Adam-Eve* is the first couple, the evil-bearing couple who brought about the ruin of the entire human race through the joint fall of Adam, "sinner," and Eve, "co-sinner"; instead, *Christ-Mary* is the second couple, the couple bearing the blessing of universal salvation through the joint action of the *Redeemer*, Christ and *Co-redemptr*ix, Mary.[23]

---

[20] Settimio Manelli, *Ibid.*, pp. 314-315: "In support of these arguments in favor of the validity of *ipsa*, one should also keep in mind the great antiquity of the Vulgate in relation to the MT and the use made of it by the Church for about 1600 years."

[21] Cf. B. Gherardini, *The Coredemption and Mary's Universal Maternity*, in *Mary at the Foot of the Cross IV*, New Bedford, MA, 2004, pp. 17-28.

[22] Cf. P.D. Fehlner, *Mater Coredemptrix. Mater Viventium (Gen 3: 20)*, in *Mary at the Foot of the Cross IV*, New Bedford, MA, 2004, pp. 1-16.

[23] On the antithesis Adam-Christ, Eve-Mary, it suffices to examine the Fathers of the East: St. Justin, St. Irenaeus, St. Ephrem, St. John Chrysostom; and the Fathers of the West: Tertullian, St. Ambrose, St. Augustine, St. Peter Chrysologus (cf. Th. Spidlik, *Eva-Maria nella Tradizione dei Padri*, AA.VV., *Maria Corredentrice. Storia e Teologia*, Frigento 1998, vol. I, pp. 115-140; L. Cignelli, *Maria Nuova Eva nella Patristica greca*, Assisi 1966; Idem, *Maria, Vergine volontaria nell'esegesi patristica*, in *Studi Biblici Francescani. Liber Annuus* 22 [1972] 169-263).

This interpretation of the redemptive plan formulated in Gen 3:15 has been infallibly guaranteed by Pope Pius IX, with the Apostolic Constitution *Ineffabilis Deus* concerning the dogmatic definition of the Immaculate Conception,[24] and by Pope Pius XII with the Bull *Munificentissimus Deus*, regarding the dogmatic definition of the Assumption of the Blessed Virgin Mary, soul and body into heaven.[25]

According to *Ineffabilis Deus*, in fact, on the basis of the constant faith of the Church with its roots in biblical revelation and its organic development in Tradition by the Fathers and ecclesiastical writers,[26] by the liturgy, by the *sensus fidelium* of the people of God, and by sacred art, the truth of the Immaculate Conception has developed over the nearly two millennia of Christianity *"in lumine fidei, sub ductu Ecclesiae,"* to be finally crowned with the dogmatic definition solemnly proclaimed by the Pope, Bl. Pius IX, in Rome, December 8, 1854, to the exultant jubilation of the entire Church.

The truth of the Immaculate Conception, in effect, is truly linked *"in radice"* (in its roots) to the *Protoevangelium*, Gen 3:15, where "clearly and openly," as *Ineffabilis Deus* affirms, the Redeemer and his Mother are foretold, both involved in the identical *"enmities"* with the serpent, whose head will be crushed by the foot of the Mother, through the power of her Son.[27]

In summation, according to the exegesis of the Pontifical Magisterium, the "woman" of the victorious struggle with the serpent of Eden is precisely the Blessed Virgin Mary, the Immaculate, and not Eve. This exegesis stands in perfect continuity with the constant or

---

[24] Cf. B. Mariani, *L'Immacolata nel Protoevangelio: Gen 3, 15*, in *Virgo Immaculata*, Rome 1955, vol. III, pp. 29-99; A.B. Calkins, *The Immaculate Conception in the Life and Teaching of Blessed Pius IX*, in *Mary at the Foot of the Cross*, vol. V, New Bedford, MA, 2005, pp. 508-541.

[25] A. Bea, *La S. Scrittura "ultimo fondamento" del domma dell'Assunzione*, in *La Civiltá Cattolica*, 101 (1950) IV, 554-558; M. Peinodor, *De argomento scripturistico in Bulla dogmatica*, in *Ephemerides Mariologicae* 1 (1951) 27-43, 395-404; Jason A. Jones, *The Assumption of the Blessed Virgin Mary and It's Foundation in Her Role as the Coredemptrix*, in *Mary at the Foot of the Cross I*, New Bedford, MA, 2001, pp. 41-60.

[26] Cf. D. Unger, *Patristic Interpretation of the Protoevangelium*, in *Marian Studies* 12 (1961) 111-164.

[27] *Ineffabilis Deus* explicitly states that "the all glorious Virgin ... was foretold by God when he said to the serpent: 'I will put enmities between thee and the woman,' who without doubt will crush the poisonous head of that serpent."

"traditional" interpretation of the Church,[28] as the biblicist, Settimio Cipriani, expressly writes, affirming that one may maintain as "exegetically based the 'Mariological' interpretation of the passage, one traditional in Christian exegesis."[29] This "Mariological" interpretation of Gen 3:15 has been consistently present in the Ordinary Papal Magisterium. Pope John Paul II, for example, in his homily for the feast of the Nativity of Mary, spoke decisively as follows: "This very child, still so tiny and fragile, is the 'woman' of the first announcement of the future redemption, opposed by God to the serpent tempter: 'I will put enmities between thee and the woman.'"[30]

Seen concisely as a whole, the teaching of the Church on the Mariological sense of Gen 3:15 must be acknowledged as the keystone of the truth of faith concerning the Immaculate Conception, in relation not only to the person of the Virgin Mary, but also to her mission as Mother Co-redemptrix and Mother of the Church,[31] and to her final exaltation with her Assumption into heaven, there crowned Queen Mother beside her Son, universal King.[32]

The "Virgin-Mother": Isaiah 7:10-14

Again the Lord spoke to Ahaz, "Ask a sign of the Lord your God; let it be deep as Sheol or high as heaven." But Ahaz said, "I will not ask, and I will not put the Lord to the test." And he said,
"Hear then, O house of David! Is it too little for you to weary men,
that you weary my God also?

---

[28] Cf. D. Unger, *Mary in the Woman of the First-gospel (Gen 3,15)*, in Marianum 18 (1956) 62-79. See also the Bible of Navarre, *Antico Testamento [I] Pentateuco*, Milan 2002, pp. 81-83.

[29] S. Cipriani, in *Come leggere nella Bibbia il mistero di Maria*, Rome 1989, p. 155.

[30] John Paul II, homily of September 8, 1980, given during a pastoral visit to Frascati. Cf. D. Bertetto, *Maria nel Magistero di Papa Giovanni Paolo II*, Rome 1981, p. 86.

[31] Cf. J. Ferrer Arellano, *Ecclesiologia latente en el "Protoevangelio,"* in *Actas XV Simposium Teologico*, 1996, University of Navarre, pp. 539-564.

[32] Fr. T. Gallus in his last work justifiably laments that in spite of the fact that tradition, scholarship (including Protestant exegesis from Luther to the Enlightenment) and the Magisterium have been in favor of ascribing to Gen 3:15 a messianic and Mariological sense, today not only Protestant exegetes, but some Catholics as well lightly and rashly refuse to acknowledge Gen 3:15 as the '*Protoevangelium*' (cf. T. Gallus, *Die "Frau" in Gen. 3: 15*, Klagenfurt 1979, p. 167)": S. Manelli, *All Generations...*, p. 36, note 36.

> *Therefore the Lord himself will give you a sign.*
> *Behold, a virgin shall conceive and bear a son,*
> *and shall call his name Emmanuel."*

Historically, this passage of the Prophet Isaiah, 7:10-14, describes the dramatic conditions in which Ahaz, king of the House of Judah, found himself, as he ran the risk of being annihilated by the kings of Syria and Israel.

The prophet Isaiah, therefore, sought to encourage the king, Ahaz, not to lose heart and to turn to God and ask for a "sign" to safeguard the line of David, from whom must be born the awaited Messiah.

But the king refused to obey the prophet and ask a "sign" of God, and thought rather to seek help from the Assyrians. Then Isaiah, indignant, prophesied the fall of the kingdom of Judah on the one hand, while on the other foretold the stupendous "sign" guaranteeing the descent of the Messiah from the House of David: He foretold that a *"virgin shall conceive and bear a son, and shall call his name Emmanuel, God with us,"* who would enjoy the divine attributes of *"Wonderful Counselor, Mighty God, Everlasting Father, Prince of Peace"* (Is 9:6).

The Emmanuel, the Virgin-Mother

The two extraordinary personalities contained within the prophecy of Isaiah are: 1. the *Emmanuel*, or Jesus Christ, the Messiah, Savior; 2. the *pregnant Virgin giving birth*, or Mary, the Virgin-Mother of Jesus.

This is the content of the prophecy of Isaiah according to biblical-theological exegesis, that is to say according to the practically unanimous and perennial *interpretation* both of the Fathers and ecclesiastical writers of East and West, of the constant Magisterium of the Church, and of the liturgy and sacred art throughout two millennia of Christian faith.[33]

The unshakable foundation for this interpretation of the text, the only true one, is given inerrantly and infallibly by the Evangelist Matthew, who, inspired and guided by the Holy Spirit, has presented this passage

---

[33] Cf. S. Manelli, *All Generations...*, pp. 38-53; W.G. Most, *New Light on the Messianic-Marian Character of Isaiah 7:14*, in *Miles Immaculatae* 25 (1989) 54-67: a well documented study also of Jewish Targums; F. Ceuppens, *De Mariologia Biblica*, Turin 1951; M. Peinador, *Los temas de Mariologia biblica*, Madrid 1963; F. Spadafora, *Il vaticinio della Vergine e dell'Emanuele*, in *Marianum* 41 (1979) 67-75.

of the prophet Isaiah as a prophecy literally and integrally realized in Jesus, the divine Messiah, and in the Virgin Mary, made Mother of God "by the working of the Holy Spirit" (Mt 1:18).

In fact, the Evangelist Matthew describes St. Joseph as anxious over the mystery of his virgin spouse's maternity and is thinking of *"divorcing her in secret"* (Mt 1:19). But "behold, an angel of the Lord appeared to him in a dream, saying, 'Joseph, son of David, do not fear to take Mary your wife, for that which is conceived in her is of the Holy Spirit; she will bear a son, and you shall call his name Jesus, for he will save his people from their sins'" (Mt 1:20-21).[34]

As St. Matthew explains, in this event is expressly realized what was *"said by the Lord"* according to the prophecy of Isaiah on the Virgin-Mother of the Emmanuel, the divine Messiah descending from the House of David. St. Matthew writes: *"All this took place to fulfill what the Lord had spoken by the prophet: 'Behold, a virgin shall conceive and bear a son, and his name shall be called Emmanuel' (which means, God with us)"* (Mt 1:22-23).

In the interpretation of St. Matthew we find, then, the clarity of that divinely inspired exegesis, at once literal and spiritual, historical and theological, which for nearly two millennia has been sustained firmly and consistently by "the unanimous and constant Tradition of the Church which sees in the prophecy of Isaiah Mary exclusively, the virgin who conceives and gives birth virginally to the Emmanuel, the Son of God and Messiah, Jesus Christ."[35]

---

[34] St. Luke the Evangelist also clearly alludes to the prophecy of Isaiah in the words spoken by the Angel Gabriel to the Virgin Mary: *"And behold, you will conceive in your womb and bear a son, and you shall call his name Jesus. He will be great, and will be called the Son of the Most High; and the Lord God will give to him the throne of his father David, and he will reign over the house of Jacob forever; and of his kingdom there will be no end"* (Lk 1:31-33).

[35] Manelli, *All Generations...*, p. 40. Cf. Ph. Lefevre, *La Vierge au Livre. Marie et l'Ancien Testament*, Paris 2004, pp. 143-149. On the well nigh unanimous agreement of Catholic exegetes, Rolla says this: "Catholic exegetes are in agreement in interpreting this passage as a prophecy of the virginal birth of Mary Most Holy. They are persuaded of this by its citation in the Gospel (Mt 1:22-23) and by the unanimous consent of the Fathers. The greater number of them [the exegetes] defend the literal and exclusive messianic sense" (A. Rolla, *Il messaggio della salvezza*, Turin 1967, p. 596). Still more concisely is the judgment of F. Ceuppens, *De Mariologia Biblica*, Rome 1951, p. 31, where he affirms: "The

At the very beginning of the Church some commentators from the Jewish tradition who were openly contesting the Christian faith immediately set themselves against St. Matthew's brilliant interpretation of Isaiah 7:10-14. According to them, the prophecy, in substance, could be effectively reduced to the prevision of a son conceived normally: not by a virgin, but by the wife of King Ahaz, already pregnant with Hezekiah.[36] This son, even though a good man, was hardly a king with divine attributes. To the contrary, he was a "disappointment,"[37] a king whom the prophet Isaiah himself accused of "inconsideration and imprudence."[38]

This interpretation sought to destroy the entire extraordinary content of the prophecy of Isaiah, denying both the miracle of the virgin birth, and the divine messianic character of the Son of the Virgin Mother. That meant, in effect, to strike at the heart of the prophecy of Isaiah. This interpretation of the Jews against that of the Christians was immediately battled by St. Justin (*Dialogue with Trypho the Jew*, nn. 66, 68, 71, 77), was refuted by St. Jerome (*Commentary on Isaiah*, PL 24, 111 ff.), came to be marginalized, and was never more considered by patristic exegesis and by the 2,000-year-old Tradition of the Church.

Recently, however, some scholars have desired to resurrect this erroneous interpretation, proposing it anew by way of "reformulations," the fruit of analyses and counter-analyses apparently rich in nuances of thought, of contradictory transitions from the real to the unreal,

---

entire Catholic tradition has unanimously taught that Isaiah 7:14 foretold the virginal conception and birth of Mary."

[36] But it seems now certain that Hezekiah had already been born at least 7-8 years before: which means that the prophecy of Isaiah concerning a *future* conception and birth could have nothing to do with the aforesaid Hezekiah. Yet, in order to defend their "unsupportable" opinion, resource is made to historical-chronological falsehoods, claiming Hezekiah's birth to have occurred *after the prophecy of Isaiah, whereas he had been born at least 7-8 years before!* Cf. A. Penna, *Isaia*, in *La Sacra Scrittura*, Maarietti, Turin 1964, pp. 103-104; A. Rolla, *Il Messaggio...*, p. 597; J. Rosenbaum, *Hezekiah King of Judah*, in D.N. Freedman, *The Anchor Bible Dictionary*, III, New York-London 1992, pp. 190-193; Settimio Manelli, *La nascita di Ezechia in rapporto alla profezia messianica di Isaia 7: 14*, in *Immacolata Mediatrix*, 7 (2007) 137-140.

[37] Cf. R. Laurentin, *La Vergine Maria*, Rome 1983, p. 266.

[38] Cf. Rolla says, *Il messaggio...*, p. 597; cf. also see nt. 35 above.

of utopian travels from the historical to the mythological.³⁹ Still other scholars, including Catholic, propose interpretations of this passage of Isaiah denying its exclusive messianic-Mariological content. Their hypotheses, referring the prophecy to other persons as well as Jesus and Mary, rest on an indirect, oblique, typical sense, but all things said, seriously compromise both the "sign" which is the virgin-birth and the human-divine reality of the Emmanuel.⁴⁰

Mattioli perceptively writes that these are positions supported only by a *"modern exegesis rationalistic in character,"* one repudiating the unanimous faith and exegetical tradition of the Church over the course of two millennia of history and doctrine.⁴¹

---

³⁹ Among the scholars against the two millennia old Tradition see: M. Rehm, *Der Koenigliche Messias im Licht des Immanuel. Weissagnungen der Buches Jesaja*, Kevelaer 1968, p. 84, nt. 194; A. Serra, *Maria nel mistero di Cristo secondo l'Antico Testamento*, Rome 1977; D. Scaiola, *Testi tradizionali rivisitati (Gen 3, 15; Is 7, 14)*, in *Theotokos* 8 (2000) 551-568; G. Odasso, *Il segno dell'Emmanuele nella tradizione dell'Antico Testamento*, in *Theotokos* 4 (1996) 151-188: in this article "the author via analysis and allusion clearly seems to conclude by making the prophet Isaiah say *everything exactly the opposite* of revealed facts, whereas the Evangelist St. Matthew writes with a limpid simplicity when, without sophisticated analysis based on hypotheses and counter-hypotheses, he identifies the virgin of Isaiah, *sic et simpliciter*, with the Virgin Mary in the miraculous sign of the virginal motherhood and birth of the Davidic Messiah, God and King. This has been the constant interpretation of the Fathers, of the liturgy, and so of the Church and of the most reliable Catholic exegesis. Unfortunately, this author presumes to ascribe to traditional exegesis an inability "to situate itself within the saving perspective of Scripture (p. 155)." (Manelli, *All Generations...*, p. 42, nt. 8). For other assessments and reservations see *ibid.*, pp. 43-53, *passim*. Thus, a simple woman, the wife of King Ahaz, already pregnant or already mother of Hezekiah, becomes a *virgin who conceives and gives birth virginally* (!); and a son, Hezekiah, accused by Isaiah himself "of inconsideration and imprudence" becomes the *"Emmanuel,"* viz., the *God with us*, with all the heavenly attributes of a God (!). But how?

⁴⁰ On various opinions and questions one may profitably consult the systematic outline of D. Bertetto, *Maria nel dogma cattolico*, Turin 1955, pp. 52-70; J. Coppens, *Le Messianisme royal*, in *Nouvelle Revue Theologique* 100 (1962) 483-490.

⁴¹ A. Mattioli, *Dio e l'uomo nella Bibbia d'Israele*, Turin 1981, p. 393; Idem, *La dottrina di Isaia nella prima sezione del suo libro (1-12)*, in *Rivista Biblica* 12 (1964) 387-388. Cf. A. Feuillet, *De fundamento Mariologiae in prophetiis messianicis Veteris Testamenti*, in *De Mariologia et Oecumenismo*, Rome 1962, pp. 40-41; A. Penna, *Isaia...*, pp. 103-106.

The "Virgin-Birth"

The most delicate and precious point of Isaiah's prophecy concerns the virginal conception and virginal birth of the Mother of the Emmanuel. In it is enclosed the object of the perennial faith of the Church in the perpetual virginity of Mary. Mary's virginity in soul and body remained ever integral, before, during and after the miraculous birth of Jesus. Ceuppens summarized, with utmost clarity and precision, the conclusion of his accurate and profound study: "With regard to Mariological doctrine we may conclude thus: the dogma of our faith in the virginity of the Blessed Virgin Mary, both in the conception and in the birth of her divine Son, has been foretold in this prophecy of Isaiah 7:14."[42]

The term *"virgin"* in the Hebrew text is expressed by the word *"'almah,"* which has the generic meaning of "girl," one who "normally is an intact virgin (cf. Gen 24:16, 43)," as A. Vaccari explains: "the Jews before Christ understood this word in the precise sense of *virgin*, as the Greek translator [of the LXX] who employed the specific term *'parthenos'* [virgin],[43] and the primitive Christian Church (Mt 1:20-25) both testify."[44]

> The special "sign" offered to the king by Isaiah on behalf of God is precisely this: the "pregnant virgin," i.e., the virgin who conceives her son while remaining a virgin, and the "virgin giving birth," i.e., the pregnant virgin who brings the child to light, while still remaining a virgin. The first, like the second, is a miracle. The message of the prophet Isaiah is just this: in the

---

[42] F. Ceuppens, *De Mariologia biblica*, p. 38.

[43] Is it not extraordinarily curious that *before Christ* even the Jews themselves, in translating the Hebrew text into Greek, *sic et simpliciter*, translated the word *"'almah"* by a precise Greek term, *"parthenos,"* that is, *virgin?* In so interpreting the word *'almah* in the proper sense of *virgin* they could hardly have had any other motive than perfect fidelity to the Hebrew text!

[44] A. Vaccari, *La Sacra Bibbia*, Rome 1955, vol. VI, p. 41, nt. 13-14. Rolla also supports the explanation of Vaccari, affirming that the term *'almah* connotes a maiden without husband, "not married and hence normally still a virgin" (Rolla, *Il messaggio...*, p. 394).

conception and in the act of giving birth, the Mother of the Emmanuel is always *"the virgin."*[45]

As a conclusive confirmation, it is sufficient to cite two authoritative testimonies, one of St. Ambrose and the other of *Lumen Gentium*. St. Ambrose writes: "This is the virgin who conceives in her womb, the virgin who gives birth to her son. Thus it is written: 'Behold the virgin will conceive in her womb and bear a son' (Is 7: 14). He did not only say that the virgin would conceive, but also that the virgin would give birth."[46] The Second Vatican Council teaches: "This is the virgin who will conceive and will bear her son, whose name will be Emmanuel."[47]

The "Emmanuel"

In Isaiah's prophecy (cf. 8:8-10; 9:5-6; 11:1-5) and in the Gospel text of St. Luke on the Annunciation of the Angel to Mary (Lk 1:31-33), the attributes of the Son of the "Virgin" are extraordinary properties which really make of him the true *"God with us."* Divine attributes are indeed involved, described in transcendental terms such as these: *Wonderful Counselor, Mighty God, Everlasting Father, Prince of Peace, Son of the Most High, Son of God*, he to whom *the Lord God will give ... the throne of his father David, and he will reign over the house of Jacob for ever; and of his kingdom there will be no end.*

---

[45] Manelli, *All Generations...*, p. 44. The authoritative Fr. Vaccari also confirms that reflection on the miraculous "sign" of which Isaiah speaks in verse 11 makes clear how "there can be absolutely nothing miraculous about this conception if it occurred at the expense of the virginity of the Mother" (*La Sacra Bibbia*, vol. VI, p. 41, nt. 13-14). See also J.L. Basteri de Eleizalde, in *Maria, Madre del Redentor*, Pamplona 2004, pp. 90-92.

[46] St. Ambrose, *Epistula 42*, PL 16, 1125. Against the crystal clear texts of the Fathers are ranged a number of recent Catholic scholars whose exegesis, though well intentioned, "arrives at conclusions utterly lacking in conviction and overly confident not only in its ability to discover and transmit new truths concerning biblical revelation, but in knowing more than the Church Fathers (e.g., St. Justin, St. Irenaeus, St. Ambrose, St. Jerome, St. Augustine ...). One fears such exegesis has forgotten that the Fathers, with Sacred Scripture, are a source of Divine Revelation. Nor is it to be forgotten that the Fathers were surely acquainted with codices and documents existing in their day, but no longer accessible to us." (Manelli, *All Generations...*, p. 46).

[47] *Lumen Gentium*, 55.

It is important to observe how the entire discourse on the Emmanuel, both in the prophet Isaiah and in the Evangelist St. Luke, is exclusively tied to his mother, in the sense that they set in clear relief the *absence* of a human "father" of the Emmanuel. From this we must deduce, in regard to the Emmanuel, a transcendent or divine paternity, which at the same time enables us to intuit the "divinity" of the Emmanuel himself.[48]

Similarly, in regards to the "kingship" attribute of the Emmanuel in Isaiah's prophecy and the Gospel account of Luke, no doubts are possible concerning the Davidic descent of the Emmanuel. Because the virgin of Isaiah, realized in Mary, Virgin-Mother of the Emmanuel, is descended from the root of David, his "royal" descent cannot be other than authentic. She alone, in fact, in virtue of the miracle of the virginal conception, is capable of guaranteeing the birth of Jesus biologically "*from the seed of David according to the flesh*," as St. Paul writes (Rom 1:3).[49]

It is also important to note the link between the prophecy of Isaiah and that which the prophet Nathan made to David, an oracle containing the promise of an eternal kingdom (cf. 2 Sam 7:8-17), and assuring the stock of Jesse a descendant capable of ruling in time and in eternity. This rule is solely a matter of divine power, and it is this that enables him to rule forever on the throne of David.[50]

---

[48] Cf. J. Coppens, *La prophetie de la 'Almah*, in *Ephemerides Theologicae Lovanienses* 28 (1952) 565. Fr. Vaccari also states concerning the prophecy of Isaiah that the entire thought of the prophet in speaking of the Emmanuel without any mention of a father, "insinuates the divinity of the Messiah as well" (*La Sacra Bibbia*, vol. VI, p. 41, nt. 13-14). See also P. Pietrafesa, *La Madonna nella Rivelazione*, Naples 1970, p. 41. For this, an attentive reflection on the Emmanuel, "Messiah Son of God" may simply suffice, after the example of Feuillet. Cf. A. Feuillet, *De Fundamento...*, p. 44.

[49] Also in regard to the royal-davidic descent of the Messiah Savior through Mary of Nazareth as well as through St. Joseph for legal purposes as husband of Mary and putative father of Jesus, there exist studies which speak of a "unanimous" tradition: e.g., see J. Fischer, *Die Davidische Abkunft der Mütter Jesu. Eine Biblischpatristiche Untersuchung*, in *Wiedenauerstudien* 4 (1911) 1-115; D. Jurant, *Maria figlia di Levi o figlia di Davide?*, in *Renovatio* 10 (1975) 303-329, 451-471; La Bibbia di Navarra, *I quattro Vangeli*, Milan 1988, p. 78.

[50] Manelli, *All Generations...*, p. 43.

★ ★ ★

At this point, we may make our own the conclusion of Fr. Ceuppens, who summarizes the essential content of his systematic study on the prophecy of Isaiah:

> After examining critically the single text of the prophecy, Isaiah 7:14 identifies in the literal sense the Messiah and his Mother: Mary will conceive and will give birth to her Son without damage to her virginity. She is a virgin in conceiving, she is a virgin in giving birth. The assertion, then, of those claiming that the faith of the Church in the virginal conception and birth of Christ is based on a false version and interpretation of the text of Isaiah, finds no support, is entirely gratuitous and is devoid of scientific foundation.[51]

The Woman in Travail: Micah 5:2-3

But you, O Bethlehem Ephrathah, who are little to be among the clans of Judah, from you shall come forth for me one who is to be ruler in Israel, whose origin is from of old, from ancient days.
Therefore he shall give them up until the time when

she who is in travail has brought forth;
then the rest of his brethren shall return to the people of Israel.

The prophecy of Micah 5:2-3 came into primary focus when the Magi from the Far East arrived in Jerusalem, guided by a mysterious star. On their arrival in Jerusalem the Magi no longer saw the star and so they made recourse to King Herod to learn the exact place of the birth of the Messiah, according to indications they had received by way of the star. King Herod, quite unaware of any of this, immediately summoned the high priests and scribes to learn what answer he should give to the Magi concerning the place of birth of the Messiah.

---

[51] F. Ceuppens, *De Mariologia Biblica*, p. 32.

The priests and scribes answered by citing precisely the prophecy of Micah 5:2-3 concerning Bethlehem, quoting it word for word, with its rich content pointedly dealing with so many important and significant things of messianic-Mariological value in the strictest sense (cf. Mt 2:3-6).[52]

The prophecy of Micah, though brief, contains five distinct points: 1) the place of birth of the Messiah, viz., of him who will be the "*ruler in Israel*"; 2) the primary origin of the Messiah: not temporal, but eternal; 3) the exile to which the chosen people were condemned, forced to live dispersed in Babylonia; 4) the sign of the arrival of the Messiah, when the woman "*who is in travail has brought forth*"; 5) the fruit of the return from exile when the "*rest of his brethren shall return to the people of Israel.*"

In Micah's prophecy, then, it is expressly said that the messiah who liberates will be born in little Bethlehem in the land of Ephrathah, located a few miles from Jerusalem, birthplace of King David, quite distinct, therefore, from Bethlehem of Galilee, and far more important than the latter.

As regards the *origin* of the messiah, however, the prophet Micah traces this to *the days of old* and to *ancient days*, viz., to the antiquity of the House of David. The Latin version of the Hebrew text, however, does not mention *ancient days* (as in the Hebrew original), but *eternal days*, textually "*a diebus aeternitatis.*" According to the Vulgate, in Micah's prophecy both the ancient, Davidic origin of the Messiah and the eternal, divine origin of the Messiah, that of the man-God, the Word made man, are affirmed.[53] The Fathers of the Church, however, although they

---

[52] St. John the Evangelist, in reporting the question raised by the Jews concerning the origin of Christ, also holds that Bethlehem, according to the prophecy of the Old Testament, is the birth place of the Messiah: "*Can the Christ come from Galilee? Does not the Scripture say that it is of the offspring of David, and from Bethlehem, the village where David lived, that the Christ is to come?*" (Jn 7: 41-42). Fr. Testa writes: "The rabbis of the second and third centuries also interpret our text in the messianic sense, and medievals such as Rasi and Kinki repeat their explanation" (E. Testa, *I Salvatori apocalittici di Israele: la Partoriente e il suo nato*, in *Marianum* 40 [1978] 39).

[53] Cf. F. Lucani, *Michea*, in *La Sacra Scrittura*, Turin-Rome 1969, vol. III, p. 53, where he writes that "The words, *his origin*, etc., present the case of a text 'open' on the future, as a source of light in relation to the places which it illumines, and in them the evangelists (Mt 2:6; cf. Jn 7:42) and Christian tradition have recognized a prophecy of the mysterious eternal origin of the Messiah. That here are present distinctive elements of a superhuman personality is acknowledged,

are unanimous in admitting the messianic sense of Micah's prophecy, are not unanimous in holding that the phrase *eternal days* connotes the eternal origin of the Word made flesh in the Virgin Mary.[54] It is quite legitimate, however, to accept the teaching of those Church Fathers and those eminent biblicists, e.g., A. Vaccari and G.M. Allegra, who maintain the validity of the exegetical interpretation of *a diebus aeternitatis* in the Latin version of Micah's prophecy as a genuine reading of the Jewish *remote days*, and so indicating the divine origin of the Messiah.[55]

Fr. Vaccari, in fact, clearly affirms that "the Hebrew expression may include a divine origin (cf. Is 9:5) prior to all time, that is, eternal."[56] This interpretation accords quite well with the divine origin of Christ. Fr. Allegra states:

> With this phrase the prophet [Micah] intends to indicate not only the human origin of the Messiah ... but above all an origin transcending the human. This parallels nicely, as close observation reveals, the prophecy about the Emmanuel, where the prophet indicates the divine nature of the Messiah. This prince will be of the family of David and hence will be born in Bethlehem, but will enjoy a more ancient origin: he will in fact be eternally born of God the Father.[57]

"When She Who is in Travail has Brought Forth"

The most extraordinary point of Micah's prophecy is linked to a typical, concise hebraism: the woman *"in travail has brought forth."* The prophet effectively and expressly foretells the "Mother," along with the "Messiah." He employs an expression from Isaiah's prophecy which

---

although with somewhat different an explanation (cultic, mythical), by a non-Catholic commentator (S. Mowinckel, *He That Cometh*, pp. 175-176)"

[54] Cf. E. Testa, *I Salvatori*..., p. 40; A. Skrinjar, *Origo Christi temporalis et aeterna. Mich 5, 2. 3 – Hebr. 5, 1.2*, in *Verbum Domini* 13 (1933) 8-16.
[55] Cf. Manelli, *All Generations*..., pp. 56-57.
[56] A. Vaccari, *La Sacra Bibbia. I Profeti 2*, Florence 1958, vol. VII, p. 307, nt. 1.
[57] G.M. Allegra, *Vaticini Mariani dell'Antico Testamento e dell'Apocalisse*, Castelpetroso 1996, p. 17.

would be very clear and recognizable to the Jewish people: "*Behold, a virgin shall conceive and bear a son.*"

Fr. Vaccari teaches the same, when he writes: "With the words *has brought forth* ... Micah certainly refers to the celebrated prophecy concerning the virgin ... in Isaiah 7:14, a prophecy which he presupposes is well-known to his contemporaries."[58] And Luciani confirms this, asserting that the prophet Micah "borrows the phrase from Is 7:14, as scholars commonly admit today[59] ... and relives the psychological moment of Isaiah himself, who coined the expression."[60]

To this expression, "*when she who is in travail has brought forth,*" are also linked both the reflections on "*the remnant of Israel,*" which through the redemptive work of the Messiah will be brought together in unity,[61] and the reflections bearing on the prophecy of Genesis 3:15. Like Isaiah 7:14 and Micah 5:2, the *Protoevangelium* presents the Mother alone with her son, that is without a father, which in Micah seems to contain the root of a "miraculous birth" as well, hence the miracle of the *virgin birth* which conserves inviolate and integral the virginity of the Mother.[62]

With particular regard to the value and importance of virginity, it is indeed certain that in the three great messianic-Mariological prophecies of the Old Testament, "the Mother always appears a virgin mother. The 'virginity' of the Mother forms the radiant background for the annunciation and birth of the Messiah. This is the evident sign that the

---

[58] A. Vaccari, *La Sacra Bibbia, I Profeti 2*, p. 307. See also P. Pietrafesa, *La Madonna...*, pp. 53-54. D. Ryan writes that "The majority of commentators see a reference to Is 7:14 and the Mother of the Immanuel. Through the birth of her child she brings to an end a period of distress, and by giving birth to the Prince (Is 9:6; Mic 5:4), she is most intimately associated with his work": in *A New Catholic Commentary on Holy Scripture*, New York 1984, p. 711.

[59] Cf. H. Junker, in *Volume du Congres*, Leiden 1957, p. 194.

[60] F. Luciani, *Michea*, p. 34.

[61] In regard to the "remnant of Israel" see the study of O. Carena, *Il resto di Israele*, Bologna 1985, with rich bibliography. Also not to be overlooked is the Mariological dimension of the "remnant of Israel" set in relief by S. Cavalletti, *Maria come "resto" di Israele* (in reference to the texts of Isaiah 4:3; 6:3; 10:20 ff.; 11:1 ff.), in *Nuovo Dizionario di Mariologia*, Rome 1996, p. 463.

[62] Cf. R. Vulleumier-A. Keller, *Miche, Nahoum, Habacuc, Sophonie*, Genova 1990, p. 61 (the authors base their comments on the thought of O. Porcksch).

Messiah is truly a new creation, the new mankind, the beginning of the era of salvation: the redemption."[63]

For a brief overview of the messianic-Mariological content of the three most important Old Testament prophecies, surely authoritative is the mind of Pope John Paul II, set forth so explicitly in a homily for the Nativity of the Blessed Virgin Mary:

> This very child, still so tiny and fragile, is the "woman" of the first announcement of the future redemption, opposed by God to the serpent tempter: "I will put enmities between you and the woman, between your seed and her seed; she will crush your head and you shall lie in wait for her heel" (Gen 3:15).
>
> This very child is the "Virgin" who "conceived and gave birth to a son, who will be called Emmanuel, which means: God with us" (cf. Is 7:14; Mt 1:23).
>
> This very child is the "Mother" who will give birth in Bethlehem to "him who must be the ruler of Israel" (cf. Mic 5:1ff.).[64]

Figures of Mary

In the Old Testament, Mary has been prefigured, as well as foretold and prophesied. In the pages of the Old Testament it is not, in fact, infrequent to encounter in female figures, virgins, wives, mothers, and widows, who typify the Blessed Virgin Mary in one way or another, in this or in that virtue. From the totality of all these images one can effectively form a stupendous mosaic of the person and mission of Mary. Here one may verify the reality of that adage according to which what all other women share only partially, Mary instead has entirely in every way and throughout all: *"Quod alii in partibus, illa in toto."*

Brief reflections on a select group of feminine figures (to which are added two male figures, Abraham and Isaac) will serve to make known the value and the beauty of these biblical types and models of Mary

---

[63] Manelli, *All Generations...*, pp. 58-59.
[64] John Paul II, homily of September 8, 1980, given during a pastoral visit to Frascati. Cf. D. Bertetto, S.D.B., ed., *Maria nel Magistero di Giovanni Paolo II*, (Rome, 1981), p. 86.

throughout the pages of the Old Testament: acknowledged by the Fathers of the Church and in Tradition, frequently adopted, in ages past and today, for use in celebrations of the sacred liturgy and art.[65]

Eve, the "Mother of the Living"

Eve was the first woman, and with Adam our first parent at the inception of human history. According to the original plan of God, she should have transmitted to her children a human nature sanctified by grace, by divine filiation. Through the fall into original sin, she instead passed on to each of her offspring that horrible "stain" which caused the birth of dead children, *"children of wrath"* of God (Eph 2:3). Thus, in fact, Sirach writes: *"From a woman sin had its beginning, and because of her we all die"* (Sir 25:24).[66]

In view of the fall into original sin, one may therefore say that Eve has prefigured Mary only in a negative or antithetical sense, becoming effectively a *counter-figure* of Mary. In fact, Eve was redeemed by Mary, according to St. Irenaeus in his teaching on "recirculation" of grace.[67] Thus, the *fiat* of Eve to the solicitation of the serpent/Satan (Gen 3:1-6) was redeemed by the *fiat* of Mary to the requests of the Angel Gabriel (Lk 1:30-38). In this way, the personal cooperation of Eve in the fall with Adam into original sin (Gen 3:6) was redeemed by the personal, active and immediate cooperation of Mary in the redemption wrought by Christ.[68]

---

[65] On the Marian figures of the Old Testament see: H. Cazelles, *Les figures des Marie dans l'Ancien Testament*, in *Bull. Franc. D'Etudes Mariales* 30-31 (1973-1974), Paris 1976; D. Barsotti, *Le Donne dell'Alleanza*, Turin 1967; G. Boggio, *Donne nell'Antico Testamento*, in *Parole di vita* 30 (1985) 337-344; G. Ortensi, *I grandi Credenti della Bibbia*, Casale Monferrato 1987; E. Green, *Dal silenzio alla parola. Storie di donne nella Bibbia*, Turin 1992; P. Maiberger, *Le grandi figure dell'Antico Testamento*, Brescia 1995; C. Biestro, *Biblical Type-Figures of Mary: Immaculata & Coredemptress*, in *Mary at the Foot of the Cross V*, New Bedford, MA, 2005, pp. 323-343.

[66] Cf. T. Gallus, *A muliere initium peccati et per illam omnes morimur (Sir 25, 33)*, in *Verbum Domini* 23 (1943) 272-277.

[67] St. Irenaeus, *Adversus Haereses*, III, 22, 4.

[68] "By reason of this one may say that the first woman was '*Eve co-sinner*' with Adam '*sinner,*' whereas for our salvation the second woman was the '*Eve co-redemptrix*' with the second Adam '*redeemer,*'" Manelli, *All Generations...*, p. 63. In note 7 are cited the studies of E. Zolli, *Da Eva a Maria*, Frigento 2004, and of Fr. G.M. Allegra, *Il Cuore Immacolato di Maria*, Arcireale 1991. Both these great biblicists

Sarah, the Wife of Abraham (Gen 17:15-16; 18:9-15)

Sarah was the "*free*" wife of Abraham, in contrast with Hagar, the "*slave*" wife. Sarah was sterile, but became fruitful through an extraordinary intervention of God.[69]

On both points, Sarah prefigures Mary. Mary, in fact, is the "*free*" spouse in the truest sense, because conceived immaculately, without any stain of original sin, the sign of the truest and most serious slavery, because "*everyone who commits sin, is a slave of sin*" (Jn 8:34). Further, Mary is a spouse, not *sterile*, like Sarah, but *virginal*, and miraculously becomes Virgin Mother by the work of the Holy Spirit.

In addition, Sarah became mother of Isaac, her only son, who constitutes the old Israel. Mary is the Mother of Jesus, her only Son, who is the "*firstborn among many brethren*" (Rom 8:29) in order to constitute the new Israel, the Church universal: "Sarah is the *shadow* of the New Covenant sanctioned by God with Abraham and sealed with the blood of the circumcision. The Virgin Mary, instead, is the *reality* of the New Covenant between God and his people, established by Jesus, who sealed it by his immolation as crucified victim for a mankind to be redeemed."[70]

Rebecca, Spouse of Isaac (Gen 24)

The prefiguration of Mary on the part of Rebecca is linked to many particular events, about which we can here only consider a few of the more significant aspects. In the life of Rebecca, God's providence that disposed all things so that she might become the wife of Isaac and mother of Jacob, is clearly apparent. At the same time and in a still more evident fashion, one perceives how a special providence ordered events in such a way that Mary became the ever-virginal spouse of St. Joseph, so as to be the virginal Mother of Jesus.

The most important task of Rebecca was that of vesting her son Jacob with the clothes of his brother Esau, so as to obtain from their father

---

speak expressly of *Eve-co-sinner* in contrast to *Eve-coredemptrix*. On the entire figure and work of Eve, cf. the two basic studies: T. Carizzi, *La Madre di Dio nell'Antico Testamento*, Cerreto Sannita 1938, vol. II, p. 390; and L. Cignelli, *Maria Nuova Eva*, Assisi 1966.

[69] For a biblical profile of Sarah see: G. dell'Orto, *Sara*, in *Parole di vita*, 1995, n. 1, pp. 24-29.

[70] Manelli, *All Generations...*, pp. 63-64.

Isaac the blessings for himself and his descendants (even though Esau had already sold the privileges of being firstborn to his brother Jacob: cf. Gen 25:31-33). As Roschini explains: "Mary, with the consent given to the angel, induced the Word of God to clothe himself with human flesh, taking upon himself our iniquity and offering himself to the eternal Father to obtain an eternal blessing."[71]

This last event also manifests that Rebecca, placing herself between father and son, prefigures the role of *Mediatrix* which Mary will exercise between men and Jesus Christ, for the new Israel.

Miriam, the Sister of Moses (Ex 15: 20-21)

Miriam is the sister of Moses, the liberator of the chosen people from slavery in Egypt, and the sister of Aaron as well, the high priest of the Old Covenant. With Moses (the legislator) and with Aaron (the priest), Miriam was also present in the "tent of the assembly," where the Lord came down to speak with them. These relationships prefigure well those between Mary and Jesus, given that Mary is the Mother of Jesus, who is the divine Legislator and Priest.[72]

The sister of Moses, moreover, is called *prophetess*, and it was she who led the chorus of women in the triumphant canticle of Moses after the passage through the Red Sea. But who is more a *prophetess* than Mary in her sublime canticle, the *Magnificat*? Ruotolo writes:

> The first Mary is introduced as a privileged prophetess by God; the second Mary, the blessed among women, is invoked by the Church as the "Queen of Prophets." The first repeats the refrain; with her canticle the second magnifies the greatness of the Omnipotent

---

[71] G. Roschini, *La Madonna secondo la fede e la teologia*, vol. II, p. 102.

[72] Especially important is the exegesis of a former rabbi, the convert E. Zolli, in his *Da Eva a Maria*, cit., pp. 47-49, on the prefiguration "of Miriam as *coredemptrix* of the people of Israel alongside Moses. Miriam prefigures Mary quite well as *Coredemptrix* of the new people of Israel alongside Jesus. Also interesting are his particular reflections on Miriam who 'effectively from the day she saved the life of the baby Moses conducted a work of national coredemption to the benefit of Israel'" (Manelli, *All Generations...*, p. 68, nt. 16). Also interesting are considerations bearing on the sister of Moses found in the article of G. Paximadi, *L'importanza salvifica della donna nell'Antico Testamento*, in *La donna e la salvezza. Maria e la vocazione femminile* (ed. by M. Hauke), Lugano 2006, pp. 15-16.

and prophesizes, in the most literal sense of the term, her future glorification by all human generations.[73]

Deborah (Judg 4:4-24)

Deborah was the energetic woman who cooperated actively and decisively with Barak in conducting war and in achieving, with the help of another woman warrior, Jael, the triumph over the powerful army of Sisera, thus delivering her people from the assault of the Canaanites.[74] In particular, Deborah directly prefigures Mary as *Co-redemptrix* with Christ, because Mary cooperates personally and actively with the Redeemer in accomplishing the work of salvation through universal redemption. Pietrafesa writes: "Deborah cooperated in the liberation of Israel from the oppression of Sisara and of Canaan; Mary cooperated with Christ in the deliverance of the entire human race from the slavery of the Devil, meriting and satisfying with him."[75]

Deborah also specifically prefigures Mary as prophetess and mother of mercy in the place known as the "palm tree of Deborah," between Ramah and Bethel, in the land of Ephraim: it was there, in fact, that the children of Israel went when they were in trouble, to obtain grace and justice. With her canticle, the *Magnificat*, Mary is the greatest prophetess, and in the Church has always been invoked and venerated as "Mother of mercy," maternal and omnipotent "Mediatrix" and Advocate, Patroness of all graces to be distributed to her children who have recourse to her, confident of being heard.[76]

Ruth, the "Moabitess"

This humble and generous woman, who had the courage to leave her own country to follow the pious Naomi, her sister-in-law, ended, according to the designs of providence, by becoming the wife of Boaz,

---

[73] D. Ruotolo, *Maria...chi mai se tu?*, Naples 1975, p. 82. See also R. Le Deaut, *Miryam soeur de Moise, et Marie, mère du Messie*, in *Biblica* 45 (1964) 198-219.
[74] On Deborah, and on her ally, Jael, see V. Scippa, *Due donne forti dell'Antico Testamento*, in *Parole di vita*, 1955, n. 5, pp. 12-16.
[75] P. Pietrafesa, *La Madonna...*, p. 81. See also S.M. Manelli, *Maria Corredentrice nella Sacra Scrittura*, cit., pp. 67-68. See also the important points of reflection in the study of G. Paximadi, *L'importanza salvifica...*, pp. 16-20.
[76] Cf. D. Ruotolo, *Maria...*, pp. 93-97.

and therefore mother of Obed, the grandmother of King David, for which reason she is mentioned in the genealogy of Christ.[77]

She prefigures Mary in this, that Mary as a child was also consecrated to God and enclosed in the Temple, far from her home and from her parents. There she prepared to become, according to the inscrutable designs of God, Spouse of the Holy Spirit, in order to beget the Messiah, Redeemer of the human race.

Ruth is introduced to Boaz as a humble maiden, and hence was chosen by him as wife, thus becoming "the woman who prepares the way to the Messiah."[78] Similarly, Mary concludes her conversation with the Angel Gabriel at the Annunciation by proclaiming herself "handmaid" of God, chosen by him to be the Spouse of the Holy Spirit and to cooperate in the work of the redemptive Incarnation of the Word of God.

Ruth is customarily depicted with sheaves of corn on her arm, as she gleans behind the reapers. In this as well she prefigures Our Lady, who gathers graces and prayers to assist the most desperate and needy. Fr. Mauri writes: "The Fathers of the Church agree in affirming that Ruth, who gleans the corn left behind by the reapers, is a figure of Mary who gathers to herself and brings to God the souls even of the most abandoned and desperate sinners."[79]

Judith, the "Intrepid Widow"

Judith was another woman who was engaged in the mission to save her people. Here we treat of an engagement not merely patriotic, but also religious. G. Paximadi writes: "That Judith brings to completion a plan which has as its immediate result the salvation of the people, and hence includes a profoundly religious resonance as well as patriotic, is perfectly clear in the account."[80]

For this reason Judith, cutting off the head of the enemy Holofernes, very closely prefigures Mary, the Immaculate Virgin who crushes the head of the infernal serpent, saving mankind as Co-redemptrix united to

---

[77] Cf. C. Falchini, *Ruth: una donna*, in *Parole di vita*, 1995, n. 5, pp. 6-8.
[78] *Ibid.*, p. 8.
[79] P. Mauri, *Maria SS. Nella Sacra Scrittura e nei Padri*, Milan 1912, p. 90. On the figure of Ruth one can profitably consult C. Lepre, *Il libro di Ruth*, Naples 1981; also D. Ruotolo, *Maria...*, pp. 99-111.
[80] G. Paximadi, *L'importanza salvifica...*, p. 23; M. La Posta, *Giuditta: una donna al servizio di Dio*, in *Parola di vita*, 1995, pp. 24-28.

her Redeemer son, and so recalling the celebrated prophecy of Genesis: *"She shall crush your head"* (Gen 3:15). There are those who have read in the intrepid courage of Judith the power of Mary, as the "truly strong woman, particularly on Calvary, such that the history of salvation presents her as Co-redemptrix together with her Son for the salvation of all men."[81]

Purity and beauty, together with courage and audacity, are resplendent in Judith and are the reason why she is celebrated with highest praise by prince and priest: *"O daughter, you are blessed by the Most High God above all women on earth"* (Judith 13:18), *"You are the exaltation of Jerusalem, you are the great glory of Israel, you are the great pride of our nation"* (Judith 15:9).

Indeed, these praises of Judith very exactly prefigure the perennial and universal praises of the *"Blessed among women"* (Lk 1:42), given to the "invincible warrior woman" who crushes the head of the enemy with her virginal foot, to her whom the entire Church exalts thus: *"Thou art all fair, O Mary, and the original stain is not in thee. Thou art the glory of Jerusalem, thou art the joy of Israel, thou art the honor of our people."*[82]

Esther, the "Queen"

Queen Esther has been celebrated for three things above all: 1) for her transparent beauty, so exceptional that she merited to be chosen by King Assuerus as his spouse and queen; 2) for having been excluded, she alone, from the decree of condemnation to death for all her people; 3) for having succeeded in saving her people from the extermination already decreed as a consequence of Haman's intrigue.

It is precisely in these things that Esther fully prefigures Mary. 1) The entire Church, in fact, from *time immemorial*, exalts Mary as the "All Fair" with the chanting of the *Tota pulchra es, Maria!*; 2) Mary was the "only person" excluded from the universal law of contraction of original sin, because conceived "immaculate," without the shadow of any taint, and "full of grace" (Lk 1:28); 3) Mary, with her humble and courageous mediation, saved not only a people, but all mankind, from the sentence of condemnation in Eden, directly and immediately

---

[81] G. Ortensi, *I grandi Credenti...*, p. 44; see also B. Gillard, *Maria, che cose dice di te la Scrittura?*, Turin 1983, pp. 105-109.
[82] Cf. P. Maiberger, *Le grandi figure...*, p. 116.

cooperating with the Redeemer in the work of universal redemption by virtue of her role as Co-redemptrix, to ransom the human race from the domination of Satan.

Ortensi summarizes this well: "Esther is queen: she is clothed with humility and penitence to be heard by the King. Our Lady calls herself the 'handmaid' of the Lord, because thus she takes her rightful place in the plan of God and becomes 'Co-redemptrix,' 'Mother' and 'Queen.'"[83]

The Mother in the Book of Maccabees (2 Mac 7)

The figure of the heroic mother in the second book of Maccabees, who assists each of her sons in the act of martyrdom, cannot but be a splendid prefiguration of Mary, who assists in the martyrdom of her son Jesus, crucified on Calvary.

The mother in Maccabees, torn by sorrow, was not only present, but still more made herself present by her maternal, intrepid exhortation and manly support for each son, that they might go forward to meet martyrdom and generously offer the supreme testimony of faith in the Lord, our Creator and Savior.[84]

On Calvary as well, at the foot of the Cross on which Jesus consummated his total immolation for the salvation of all, "*there stood the Mother*" (Jn 19:25), there stood Mary, the inseparable *Co-redemptrix*, ever united to her Redeemer son "by a close and indissoluble bond," as Vatican II says (*Lumen Gentium*, 53), she who had consecrated "herself totally as handmaid of the Lord to the person and work of her Son, serving the mystery of redemption under and with him" (*Lumen Gentium*, 56).

Pope John Paul II also presented the mother in Maccabees as a clear prefiguration of Mary, sharing as the sorrowful Mother the Passion of her Son and offering him as propitiatory Host to the Father, cooperating and co-immolating herself for the redemption of all "with unshakeable faith, with limitless hope and with heroic courage,"[85] as true "Co-redemptrix of mankind."[86]

---

[83] G. Ortensi, *I grandi Credenti...*, p. 42.
[84] Cf. D. Ruotolo, *La Sacra Scrittura. I e II Libro dei Maccabei*, Naples 1986, vol. XIX, pp. 329-332.
[85] John Paul II, *La Donna, un'alleata preziosa di Dio*, in *L'Osservatore Romano*, April 11, 1996, p. 4.
[86] *Insegnamenti di Giovanni Paolo II*, Vatican City 1985, vol. VIII/1, p. 319.

Abraham and Isaac (Gen 22:1-18)

Abraham, too, with his *fiat* to the sacrifice of Isaac, his son, very exactly prefigures that which will be the coredemptive sacrifice of the Blessed Virgin Mary in offering her son Jesus as crucified Redeemer on Calvary. God himself said to Abraham: "Take your son, your only son Isaac, whom you love, and go to the land of Moriah, and offer him there as a burnt offering upon one of the mountains of which I shall tell you" (Gen 22:2). Mount Moriah is a part of the mountain range on which the city of Jerusalem was later built with its two hills, one for the Temple and one for Calvary. "The typology of Abraham and Isaac, fulfilled in Mary and Christ, is precisely that of *Co-redemptrix-Redeemer*."[87]

In the Magisterium of Pope John Paul II, as earlier in that of popes Leo XIII, Benedict XV, Pius XI and Pius XII,[88] there are many references to Abraham and his sacrifice as *type* of Mary and of her coredemptive sacrifice; and this reference is constant in affirming that Abraham is not a figure of the Father, but is a figure of Mary: it is she who, like Abraham, offers her Son to the Father; not the Father, but she, as Co-redemptrix, suffers the co-crucifixion with her immolated Son.[89] The types and antitypes involved between Abraham-Isaac and Mary-Christ, and revealing the mystery of Co-redemptrix-Redeemer, are sublime and profound. They deserve the most wide-ranging reflection, if the mystery of Mary *prefigured* in them, and becoming bright reality in her person and life, is to be appreciated.

Marian Symbols

One of the richest sources of Marian symbols of the Old Testament in relation to belief in the mystery of the Blessed Virgin Mary from the Papal Magisterium is that found in the Apostolic Constitution *Ineffabilis Deus* for the dogmatic definition of the truth of the Immaculate

---

[87] Cf. Manelli, *All Generations...*, p. 76.
[88] Cf. Leo XIII, Encyclical *Jucunda Semper*, September 8, 1894; Benedict XV, Apostolic Letter *Inter Sodalicia*, March 22, 1918; Pius XI, Encyclical *Miserentissimus Redemptor*, May 8, 1928; Pius XII, Encyclical *Mystici Corporis*, June 29, 1943, and Encyclical *Ad Caeli Reginam*, October 11, 1954; John Paul II, Encyclical *Redemptoris Mater*, March 25, 1987, 14.
[89] Cf. L. Deiss, *Mary Daughter of Sion*, Collegeville, MN, 1972, p. 21, nt. 11. See also Manelli, *All Generations...*, p. 77, notes 34 and 35.

Conception of Mary. Bl. Pius IX, among other convincing arguments adduced in support of the Immaculate Conception as a truth of faith, also includes the testimony of the rich Marian symbolism found in the pages of the Old Testament. In the Apostolic Constitution he cites a discrete number of the more expressive symbols of the Immaculate Conception of Mary. These include the "Ark of Salvation," "Jacob's Ladder," the "Burning Bush of Sinai," the "Impregnable Tower," the "Enclosed Garden," the "City of God," the "Lily Among Thorns," the "Virgin Earth," the "Incorruptible Wood," the "Strong Box of Immortality," among many others.[90]

Pondering the mind of Pope Pius IX in regard to the biblical symbols of the Immaculate Conception, one discovers how, linguistically speaking, biblical symbolism generally "possesses a consistency of content and a characteristic incisiveness of expression which cannot but enlighten the mind, animate the sentiments and enrich the soul with a more concrete understanding of things in their multiple senses and significance: every symbol in reality is a word pregnant with understanding of and enthusiasm for the real."[91] In regard to Mariology in particular, biblical symbolism has the power to better reflect the transcendence of the person and mission of the Mother of God and of men, thus conferring on Mariology "a warmth and a concreteness which is wanting in any merely rational construction."[92] Throughout the two millennia of Christian history, the suggestive treasures of Marian symbolism in the Bible has been employed and set in relief by the Fathers and by Tradition, by the liturgy and by sacred art, in connection with a more efficacious presentation of the truths of faith regarding the mystery of Mary.[93]

---

[90] Cf. Pius IX, *Ineffabilis Deus*.
[91] Cf. Manelli, *All Generations...*, p. 81.
[92] M. J. Lopez Perez, *Simbolos naturales asociados a la figura de Maria*, in *Ephemerides Mariologicae* 45 (1995) 378. On Marian symbols in the Bible see the studies of L. Bartoli, *Lessico di simbologia mariana*, Padua 1988; F. Elizondo, *Simbolos aplicados a Maria*, in *Ephemerides Mariologicae* 45 (1995) 387-394; Ch. Bernard, *Simbolismo*, in *Nuovo Dizionario di Mariologia*, cit., pp. 1163-1174; S. Babolin, *Il linguaggio simbolico in Mariologia*, in *Theotokos* 2 (1994) 135-162; M. Lurker, *Dizionario delle imagini e dei simboli biblici*, Cinisello Balsamo 1990.
[93] See in particular the essay of S.M. Manelli, *Maria nella simbologia biblica*, Castelpetroso 1999, in which is set in relief the expressive character of a group of biblical symbols in relation to each truth of the ineffable mystery of Mary.

Here follows now a rapid, summary sampling of a group of particularly significant Marian symbols of the Bible.

The Ark of the Covenant

One of the most prominent Marian symbols is the *Ark of the Covenant*. It is a biblical symbol employed in the renewed liturgy of Vatican II for the solemnity of the Assumption of Mary into heaven. It is also a symbol found for centuries in the Litany of Loreto: *Foederis Arca*. Many, in fact, are the links between the Ark of the Covenant and the Blessed Virgin Mary.

The Ark was the place par excellence of the presence of God, being kept therein the tablets of the Law, the flowering rod of Aaron, and a vase full of manna. Now, the Blessed Virgin Mary is the *reality* of all that the Ark contained in figure, because Mary is she "who bears in herself not the word of God written 'on stone' (the tablets of the Law), but the very Word of God, the *Logos*, made flesh, become her son; who carries in herself not 'the flowering rod of Aaron, but the flower of Jesse';[94] who carries in herself not the manna, figure of the Eucharist, but the very Body, Blood, Soul and Divinity of the Eucharistic Christ, adored by the golden cherubim!"[95]

The "Virgin Earth"

The *Virgin Earth*, from which was made the New Adam, Jesus, is the virginal womb of Mary, rendered divinely fecund by the Holy Spirit. The early Fathers of the Church apply the symbol of the *Virgin Earth* to Mary, who transcends the first Eve precisely because the first Eve was taken from the side of Adam.[96] Mary, in effect, was the *Virgin Earth*, conceived as a new creation without shadow of sin, all immaculate and "*full of grace*" (Lk 1: 28), to carry out the divine mission of conceiving in her virginal womb the New Adam, Christ Jesus, the Word of God made flesh by the work of the Holy Spirit.[97] Mary, as the *Virgin Earth* of

---

[94] M. Lurker, *Dizionario...*, p. 20.
[95] Manelli, *Maria nella simbologia biblica*, p. 13.
[96] See, for example, St. Irenaeus, *Adversus Haereses I*, c. 21; Tertullian, *De Carne Christi*, c. 17; Methodius, *Convivium decem virginum*, c. 4; St. Ephrem, *Evangelii concordantis exposition*, c. 2.
[97] Cf. A. Feuillet, *L'Esprit Saint et la Mère du Christ*, in *Etudes Mariales* 25 (1968) 40-45.

Christ and with Christ, also expresses, according to St. Bonaventure, "the absolute primacy of the New Adam and of the New Eve in relation to our first parents,"[98] in order to realize the primary purpose of the Incarnation, namely the highest glory of God via the work of universal redemption. From the first Earth, Adam came forth; from the second Virgin Earth, the New Adam came forth.

The "Paradise of God"

St. Germain, eighth-century bishop of Constantinople, in his passionate homilies, repeatedly calls the Blessed Virgin Mary: *"Paradise of God."*[99] In the Tradition of the Church, "paradise" has indeed become a Marian symbol "eminently patristic," as Fr. Gabriele Roschini affirms. In support and confirmation of his conviction he cites a number of the great Fathers, such as St. Leo the Great, St. Proclus, St. Andrew of Crete and St. John Damascene,[100] and many others as well.[101]

The earthly paradise, lost because of the original sin committed by our first parents, tricked by the serpent in Eden, the ever merciful God desired to restore in full, projecting another earthly Paradise through the redemptive Incarnation of the Word, and hence preparing the ever virginal womb of Mary as the "paradise" of her Son made man *"in the fullness of time"* (Gal 4:4).

"Closed Door," "Gate of God," "Gate of Heaven"

For centuries now, Our Lady has been invoked by the faithful as *Gate of Heaven* (*"Janua Coeli"*) in the Litany of Loreto. The Immaculate is indeed the *Gate of Heaven*, through which the Word incarnate, Jesus Christ, has come to us and through which we pass to God in paradise.

The passage of the prophet Ezekiel, 44:1-2, speaks of the mystery of a *"closed door"* which "shall remain shut; it shall not be opened, and

---

[98] Cf. P.D. Fehlner, *Immaculata Mediatrix—Toward a Dogmatic Definition of the Coredemption*, in *Mary Coredemptrix, Mediatrix, Advocate. Theological Foundations II*, Santa Barbara CA 1997, p. 294, nt. 51.

[99] St. Germain of Constantinople, *Oratio in Praesentatione Deiparae*, 15: PG 98, 306.

[100] G.M. Roschini, *Maria Sanctissima, "Paradiso di Dio,"* in *Miles Immaculatae* 13 (1977) 37-44.

[101] St. Louis-Marie Grignion de Montfort also holds that "she is the paradise of God, his ineffable world" (*The Secret of Mary*, n. 19).

no one shall enter by it; for the Lord, the God of Israel, has entered by it; therefore it shall remain shut." According to the most accredited exegetical Tradition, this door is the intact virginity of Mary, which before, during and after divine childbirth "has always kept intact the virginal seal, as a door sealed, to remain always closed,"[102] all the more so because, as St. Ambrose says, "Christ has passed through it, but not opened it."[103]

It is also certain that the Blessed Virgin Mary is also the "Gate of Heaven," through which the elect enter paradise. Thus, the Psalmist says: *"This is the gate of the Lord, the just shall enter through it"* (Ps 117:20); so too does the liturgy in the antiphon for the Gospel of the Mass of the Blessed Virgin Mary, "Gate of Heaven": "The gate of paradise, shut by the sin of Eve, has been reopened by you, O Virgin Mary."

★ ★ ★

In addition to these more significant biblical symbols, there are numerous other Old Testament Marian symbols, suggestively enriching the mosaic which is the ineffable mystery of Mary, which include the two symbols, the *"the rod from the root of Jesse"* (Is 11:1) and *"the woman shall compass the man"* (Jer 31:22). A discrete number of the Church Fathers, ecclesiastical writers and Catholic exegetes have interpreted these two texts in a Mariological sense. In perceiving Mary in both texts, in the *"root of Jesse,"* from which the Davidic Messiah germinates, and in the *"woman who compasses the man,"* i.e., who will carry the Messiah in her virginal womb, they ascribe to them an *implicit* Marian sense.

Among the other numerous secondary Marian symbols of the Old Testament, we list here only a few in rapid review: the *Dove with the olive branch*: symbol of Mary who brings and gives to us the olive of peace, Jesus Christ, the *"Prince of Peace"* (Is 9:5);[104] the *Rainbow*: symbol of Mary

---

[102] Manelli, *All Generations...*, p. 88. In notes 69 thru 71 are given references to the Church Fathers and to the two studies of Spadafora and Toniolo (*Ibid.*, pp. 88-89).
[103] St. Ambrose, *De institutione virginis*, 8. 57: PL 16, 334. Cf. Manelli, *All Generations...*, where are found between pages 90-93 references to other testimonies of the Church Fathers and of the Marian Liturgy, both on the "closed gate" as symbol of Mary's virginity, and on the "Gate of Paradise" by which the elect enter the Kingdom of heaven.
[104] Gen 8:8 ff. Cf. G. Roschini, *La Madonna...*, pp. 132-133.

who signals the end of sin and the beginning of the redemption, which circles the globe with the dew of peace;[105] the *Burning Bush*: symbol of the virginity of Mary who received and bore the incarnate God, keeping that virginity ever inviolate and immaculate;[106] the *Rod of Aaron*: symbol of the virginity of Mary who flowered and was fecund with the "*Lily of the Valley*" (Song 2:1), remaining ever intact, by the working of the Holy Spirit;[107] The "*Cloud*," symbol of Mary who "*full of grace*" (Lk 1:28) brought redemptive grace, the Word incarnate, to restore life to the desert of the world; the *Golden Candlestick* (Ex 25:31-40); the *Fleece of Gideon* (Judg 6:36-40); the *Tower of David* (2 Sam 5:17); the *Throne of Solomon* (1 Kings 10:18-20); the *Golden Crown* (Ps 20:4); the *Crown of Stars* (Rev 12:1), and the *Moon* (Song 6:10).[108]

The symbols referring to Mary which are found in the Psalms would merit a separate chapter. These have been, and are employed, in the liturgy, pre-conciliar and post-conciliar. The Greek and Latin Fathers, from the very beginning, and thereafter from century to century, have found in the Psalter significant lines of Mariological thought.[109] For this reason, "the patient work of referencing the 'Mariological verses' of the Psalter is without doubt one of the more important contributions which the Fathers have given to the development of Marian piety."[110] In particular, it has been observed that "the vocabulary used in the Marian verses, and the images contained in them, contribute to enriching the ecological terminology and Marian symbolism (*land, cloud, bridal chamber, sun, tabernacle, city, valley, hall, seat, rod* ...) of the liturgy, of literature and of art."[111]

---

[105] Gen 9:11-17. Roschini, *La Madonna*..., pp. 134-135.
[106] Ex 3:1-11. Cf. L. Cubillo, *Figuras Marianas en el Antiguo Testamento. La zara ardente (Ex 3, 3 sq)*, in *Cultura Biblica* 11 (1954) 271-274.
[107] Num 17:16-24. Cf. Roschini, *La Madonna*..., pp. 141-142.
[108] 1 Kings 18:42-45. Cf. Roschini, *La Madonna*..., pp. 143-144.
[109] Cf. R. Masson, *L'interpretation mariale des psaumes chez les Grecs Pères*, in *De primordiis cultus mariani*, Rome 1970, vol. III, pp. 242-262; I.M. Calabuig, *Repertorio di interpretazioni mariologiche del Salterio presso i Padri Latini*, in *De primordiis cultus mariani*, Rome 1970, vol. III, pp. 263-290. On particular Psalms and verses see R. Cavedio, A. Serra, E.M. Peretto, *I canti dell'umile serva. Salmi 44 (45), 84 (85), 95 (96), 112 (113), 131 (132), 146 (147); I Samuele 2, Giuditta 16, Luca 1, 46-55*, in *Lezionario Mariano*, Brescia 1975, pp. 174-213.
[110] Cf. I.M. Calabuig, *Repertorio*..., pp. 289-290.
[111] *Ibid.*, p. 290.

Liturgical Use of Old Testament Marian Symbols

The privileged expression wherein the best use of biblical Marian texts from the Old Testament can surely be made is within the sacred liturgy. This constitutes a *"locus theologicus"* of special importance, for it enables us to get beyond the tendency to reduce use of Old Testament texts in liturgical celebrations to the category of pious accommodation. In the renewed liturgy of Vatican II we also find a discrete number of Marian biblical texts from the Old Testament.[112]

Le Deaut claims that "Mariology cannot be satisfied in considering the Old Testament as a treasury of images to be applied to the Virgin in a rather elastic, accommodated sense. Concerning the Mother of the Messiah it contains an authentic revelation, even if only in outline, a revelation fully disclosed in the New Testament, the revealer of the Old, and in the traditional interpretation of the Church."[113] For this reason one may rightly assert, along with Roschini, that "the liturgical interpretation of scriptural texts has first-class theological importance,"[114] from the moment that "the faith begets the liturgy."[115]

There are at least four Old Testament texts employed by the liturgy in Marian celebrations, of which two, "among the poor of Yahweh" and "exalted Daughter of Zion," are interpreted in a Marian sense by the Second Vatican Council.[116]

Among the "Poor of Yahweh"

"She [Mary] stands out among the humble and poor of the Lord, who confidently await and receive from him their salvation" (*Lumen Gentium* 55). This is a biblical recollection of the "anawim" of God, considered the true "poor of Yahweh," humble and God-fearing children of God, trusting in the Lord who saves them from the oppression of men. From these poor "anawim," the poorest of the poor, is made up precisely that

---

[112] Cf. A. Morelli, *L'uso della Scrittura nelle feste liturgiche mariane*, Turin 1968: AA.VV., *Lezionario Mariano*, Brescia 1975.
[113] R. Le Deaut, *Marie e l'Ecriture dans le Chapitre VIII*, in *Etudes Mariales* 22 (1965) 61.
[114] I.H. Dalmais, *La Liturgia testimonianza della tradizione*, in *La Chiesa in preghiera*, Grottaferrata 1963, p. 244.
[115] G. Roschini, *Il valore teologico e l'efficacia pastorale del Culto mariano*, in *Marianum* 39 (1977) 86.
[116] *Lumen Gentium*, 55.

"remnant of Israel" who will form the new chosen people, the Church of Christ in saving pilgrimage toward the Kingdom of heaven.[117]

The Blessed Virgin Mary, as we know, is already shown at the Annunciation as the poor *"handmaid of the Lord"* (Lk 1:38), and in her canticle, the *Magnificat*, she counts herself among the humble and poor of the Lord, who *"has looked upon the lowliness of his handmaid"* (Lk 1:48) and *"has lifted up the lowly"* (Lk 1:52). On the basis of this, Pope John Paul II, in his Encyclical *Redemptoris Mater*, could affirm that the Blessed Virgin Mary was "profoundly permeated by the spirit of the 'poor of Yahweh'" (*Redemptoris Mater*, 37).

"Exalted Daughter of Zion"

"After the long expectation of the promise, with Mary, the exalted Daughter of Zion, comes the fullness of times, and a new economy is inaugurated, when the Son of God assumed a human nature to free man from sin through the mysteries of his flesh" (*Lumen Gentium*, 55). Mount Zion is the figure of the eternal kingdom of Yahweh renewed into a new people, the New Israel. Mary is the "exalted Daughter of Zion" who, among the poor of Yahweh, inaugurates the "new economy" of redemption with the ransom of mankind from sin through a return to the *"sovereignty of old."*[118]

Originally, Zion was the rock of Jerusalem on which David built his palace and where he also brought the Ark of the Covenant. Later, Solomon began to call "Zion" the mountain on which he built the new Temple. Finally, "Zion" came to denote all Jerusalem and the entire people of Israel. The "exalted Daughter of Zion," Mary, "carries in herself the fulfillment of the saving plan of God and herself becomes the very personification of the new Israel, the truest 'abode of Yahweh,' through the Incarnation of the Son of God, who restores the kingdom of Israel with a rule which will have no end."[119] For this reason Zephaniah

---

[117] See Psalms 9, 10, 11, 12, 34, 37. On the theme see A. Gelin, *The Poor of Yahweh*, Collegeville, MN, 1964, pp. 121-123.

[118] Cf. Joel 2:21-27; Zeph 3:14-17; Zach 9:9.

[119] Manelli, *All Generations...*, p. 104. On this important theme see N. Lemmo, *Maria "Figlia di Sion," a partire da Lc 1: 26-38. Bilancio esegetico dal 1939 al 1982*, in *Marianum* 45 (1983) 175-258; I. de la Potterie, *Mary in the Mystery of the Covenant*, New York 1992; Ortensio da Spinetorli, *Eccelsa Figlia di Sion*, in *Theotokos* 8 (2000) 499-512.

exultantly foretells the "exalted Daughter of Zion": "Sing aloud, O daughter of Zion" (Zeph 3:14), and St. Luke in turn echoes that cry of joy: "*Hail, full of grace ...*" (1:28).

"Created Wisdom"

Among the more sublime pages of the Old Testament are to be counted those treating of Wisdom (Sir 24:3-21; Prov 8:22-35), "presented as the divine Person, the Word of the Father, who pre-exists and presides over the entire work of creation."[120]

Now, these sublime pages have been used by the Church as liturgical texts for the Marian feasts of the Assumption (since the seventh century) and of the Nativity of Mary (since the tenth century), and hence inserted into the *Lectionary* of the Masses for the *Common of the Blessed Virgin Mary*, under the heading "*Mary, Seat of Wisdom.*"[121] Since the liturgy for over a millennium (from the seventh century) has applied these texts to the Blessed Virgin Mary, it is hardly credible that this came about merely by way of a simple "accommodation." Rather this happened on the basis of the genuine meaning of the texts, which "evidently is found in the letter of the text, but at the same time surpasses it, widens it, enriches it."[122]

Thus it becomes perfectly evident that in the sublime composition of the sacred writer, *Wisdom* "by way of reflection and participation is ascribed to Mary, the Mother of the Word of God,"[123] who *from eternity* was predestined, as *Ineffabilis Deus* says, "in one and the same decree with the Incarnation of divine Wisdom."[124] For this reason, taken in the "full sense" postulated by the ineffable mystery of the Incarnation, Mary "takes on in a certain measure the mission and the prerogatives of

---

[120] Manelli, *All Generations...*, pp. 104-105.

[121] *Lexionario*, section for *Commune della Beata Vergine Maria*, ed. CEI [= Italian Bishops' Conference], Rome 1972, pp. 511-563. [English: *Lectionary for Mass, Common of the Blessed Virgin Mary*, New York 1976].

[122] P. Pietrafesa, *La Madonna...*, p. 64. See also E. Catta, *Sedes Sapientiae*, in *Maria, Etudes sur la Sainte Vierge*, vol. VI, Paris 1961, pp. 688-866; D. Colombo, *Maria nei libri sapienziali*, Vercelli 1979.

[123] A. Romeo, *Maria e il Verbo Incarnato nei libri poetici e sapienziali del V.T.*, in *Tabor* 23 (1958) 323. Cf. M. Gilbert, *Lecture mariale et ecclesiale de Siracide 24 (10), (15)*, in *Marianum* 47 (1985) 539-540; P. Sorci, *Testi biblici non mariani applicati alla Vergine nella Liturgia*, in *Theotokos* 8 (2000) 644.

[124] Cf. Th. Plassmann, *Uno eodemque decreto*, in *Virgo Immaculata*, Rome 1955, vol. III, pp. 174-197.

hypostatic Wisdom who 'has dwelt among us' (Jn 1:14) ... Uncreated Wisdom, become incarnate in Mary, makes of her the center of Truth and of Life (*Sedes Sapientiae*)."[125]

"You Are All Fair"

The *bride* in the Song of Songs,

> according to the soundest interpretations of modern exegesis, confirmed by patristic and medieval tradition, designates metaphorically both the *Daughter of Zion* and the people of Israel in their relations of love and fidelity with Yahweh as bridegroom. Also designated are the Catholic Church which continues the people of God of the Old Testament, and also every faithful soul, member of the Church, and in a particular way Mary Most Holy, to whom are applied and are referred on the basis of a biblical typical sense, illustrated in the patristic and theological tradition, a number of verses of the Canticle: *hortus conclusus, fons signatus* [enclosed garden, fountain sealed up] (Song 4:12), in favor of the virginity of Mary; and *tota pulchra es* [you are all fair] (Song 4:7), in favor of the absence of sin in Mary.[126]

The *sensus fidei* of the Church, which in the liturgy applies these suggestive texts concerning the *bride* in the Song of Songs to the Blessed Virgin Mary, has its roots in the Mariological interpretation of such

---

[125] A. Romeo, *Maria...*, pp. 327-328.

[126] D. Bertetto, *La Madonna oggi*, Rome 1975, p. 66. One cannot but be astounded how anyone, in contradiction of the view of so eminent a Mariologist as Fr. Bertetto, could declare the end of the allegorical-metaphorical interpretation of the Song of Songs. Thus, Mazzinghi writes: "The allegorical interpretation which for centuries has dominated both rabbinical and patristic exegesis, seeing in the bridegroom now God, now Christ, and in the bride now Israel, now the Church, now the soul, seems now definitively outdated" (L. Mazzinghi, *Quanto sei bella, amica mia! Il Cantico dei cantici e la bellezza del corpo*, in AA.VV., *La Bellezza*, in *Parole, Spirito e Vita*, 2001, n. 2, p. 36). With this "pronouncement" Mazzinghi takes no notice that he has declared *annihilated* the biblical interpretation of the Canticle according to a *source* of revelation (Tradition, especially the Fathers), substituting in its place private judgment.

Church Fathers and ecclesiastical writers as St. Hippolytus, St. Ephrem, St. Ambrose, St. Jerome, St. Epiphanius, St. Sophronius, St. John Damascene, St. Germain, St. Peter Damian, Rupert of Deutz, Alan of Lille, and many others.[127]

> The *sensus fidei* of the patristic tradition and of the liturgy enable us to read the Song of Songs along Mariological lines, bringing us to contemplate Mary transparently in the "bride" all fair and without stain. With her original purity, contrasted with the adulterous infidelity of Israel, Mary recapitulates, reflects and sublimates in herself the "new Israel," viz., the Church, and every soul as bride of the Lord.[128]

Laurentin remarks, correctly, that in fact the *bride without spot* "is realized to the letter in this new creation which begins with the Immaculate Conception of Mary."[129] Hence, the identification which Tradition (especially the medieval) has established between Mary and the *"all fair"* bride of the Canticle, between Mary and the *"woman clothed with the sun"* of Revelation (12:1), is well grounded.[130]

★ ★ ★

It is impossible to justify the refusal to accept the Mariological reading of the prophecies, the figures, the symbols and other texts of the Old Testament, as the Church has read and interpreted them *from antiquity*, nourishing the People of God in particular with the teachings of the Fathers, the liturgy, catechesis and pastoral ministry, sacred art and popular religious belief as well. Any biblical exegesis which *minimizes or rejects* the Mariological reading of the prophecies, of the figures and of the

---

[127] On this important and delicate theme see A. Rivera, *Maria Sponsa Verbi en la tradición biblico-patristica*, in *Ephemerides Mariologicae* 9 (1959) 461-478; A. Piolanti, *Sicut Sponsa ornata monilibus suis*, in *Virgo Immaculata*, Rome 1955, vol. V, pp. 183-193.
[128] Manelli, *All Generations...*, p. 109.
[129] R. Laurentin, *La Vergine Maria*, Rome 1983, p. 179, nt. 3. See also A. Romeo. *Maria...*, pp. 318-323.
[130] Cf. Manelli, *All Generations...*, p. 110; P. De Ambrogi, *Il Cantico dei cantici*, Rome 1952, p. 211; G. Nolli, *Cantico dei cantici*, Rome 1968, p. 34.

symbols of the Old Testament, cannot be the exegesis "recommended most highly by the Council," as *Dei Verbum*, 10, asserts, because it is an exegesis which departs from the living Tradition and constant Magisterium of the Church, in opposition to "the bond uniting Bible and Church."[131]

We may therefore conclude this study of the revelation of the Blessed Virgin Mary in the Old Testament by affirming that according to biblical-theological exegesis, one integrating the literal and spiritual interpretation of the Word of God, the Mariological reading of the three prophecies: Genesis 3:5, Isaiah 7:14, and Micah 5:2-3, of the figures, symbols, and other passages of the Old Testament analyzed in the course of this study, have enjoyed and will continue to enjoy, in the Church and in the faith of the people of God, the right of perennial place and citizenship. The Mariological reading of these texts, cultivated by the Church over the centuries, genuinely reveals the essential characteristic of true exegesis, described by Laurentin as "an interior penetration of the text, written for believers and by believers who were inspired according to their experience of God."[132]

---

[131] P. Toinet, *Pour une Théologie de l'éxegese*, Paris 1983, p. 40; see also I. de la Potterie, *La lettura della Sacra Scrittura "nello spirito": il modo patristico di leggere la Bibbia è possibile oggi?*, in *Communio* n. 87 (1986) p. 26; Manelli, *All Generations...*, pp. 115-120.

[132] R. Laurentin, *Come riconciliare l'esegesi e la fede*, Brescia 1985, p. 10; and cf. I. de la Lotterie, *La lettura...*, pp. 37. 40.

The Virgin Mary in the New Testament

Fr. Settimio M. Manelli, F.I.

The love, the veneration and the singular interest which the Church has taken and constantly takes in the Virgin Mary have their basis in the very will of God, made manifest by Revelation and the saving works of God throughout the history of mankind. These works were never an imposition from without, nor are they a pious invention, fruit of an overheated imagination of some self-proclaimed *man of God*, or of the sentimentalism of others run riot.

The scope of the present study is to help Christian faithful to know and better understand the roots of their own faith, in such wise as to become aware of the solidity of what has been proclaimed to them (cf. Lk 1:1-4). We are occupied with the arduous, but rewarding task of an in-depth study of Divine Revelation on Mary, as this is found in the New Testament: difficult for its sublimity and rewarding for its rich content, and importance. We are dealing here with the biblical roots of the Church's faith in the Mother of Jesus, the Mother of God and of mankind. It is truly a particular challenge to seek to summarize everything revealed about the Mother of Jesus that is contained in the New Testament, given the character of this particular publication, in a few pages and at the same time in the clearest and most thorough manner possible.[1]

---

[1] The specialized literature in this field is immense. For in-depth study cf. bibliographical reference works in the fields both of biblical and Marian study. In particular we call attention to P. Pietrafesa, *La Madonna nella Rivelazione*, L.E.R. Naples 1970, who dedicates nearly 230 pages to our theme, viz., pp. 89-317; also the more recent study of Fr. Stefano M. Manelli, *All Generations Shall Call Me Blessed: Biblical Mariology*, Academy of the Immaculate, New Bedford, MA, 2005, Second ed.: from p. 121 to p. 424. The large number of specialized monographs and even greater number of articles dedicated to particular pericopes should not

In the Church one speaks, rightly, of the "mystery" of Mary.[2] Thereby, reference is made to how much God has done for the salvation of mankind through his humblest and littlest creature, Mary of Nazareth. It is God who chose her to fulfill a unique and unrepeatable mission: to be the Mother of the Word incarnate and to be his unique, incomparable collaborator in the work of salvation and of redemption. If it is true that we, too, can be mothers of Christ and become participants in his saving mission (cf. Mt 12:50), it is also true that Mary alone, his immaculate Mother and associate, gave him his human nature, really begot him, and assisted him in that hour when he accomplished the redemption.

From the whole of Revelation it is clearly evident that Mary is in all and throughout all relative to Christ. Her role and importance in the history of salvation are subordinated to him, from whom she receives every grace and blessing. Apart from him she would hardly enjoy such importance.

In undertaking this in-depth study it is basic to realize that one does not leap into the study and knowledge of a person of the past by reading an ancient book. Even if Divine Revelation is contained in a

---

be overlooked. For the relative bibliography on single themes confer specialized works. For themes not treated here for lack of space, e.g., genealogy of Luke, slaughter of innocents, flight into Egypt, events during public life of Jesus, cf. Manelli, *All Generations...*, cit.

[2] Cf. John Paul II, *Redemptoris Mater*, n. 4; Italian Episcopal Conference, *Messale Romano*, Preface for Advent II/A, Vatican City 1983, 315. In the new Latin Missal (third typical edition, Vatican City, 2002) the subtitle of the PRAEFATIO III DE BEATA MARIA VIRGINE is *De mysterio Mariae et Ecclesiae*. There also exists a little known note of the International Pontifical Marian Academy (PAMI) entitled: "La Madre di Dio nella ricerca Teologica e nell'insegnamento" [The Mother of God in Theological Research and Teaching], edited by a commission of Mariologists of PAMI and by a number of professors of Mariology in Roman theological faculties, which in many sections deals with the "mystery of Mary": "The mystery of Mary enlightens us about the mystery of the Church and vice-versa. But the mystery of both is none other than the mystery of Christ, in whom all finds its meaning and its significance ... the history of theology attests that knowledge of the mystery of the Virgin contributes to a more profound knowledge of the mystery of Christ, of the Church and of the calling of man. On the other hand, the strict nexus of the Blessed Virgin with Christ, with the Church and with mankind results in the truth about Christ, about the Church and about man illuminating the truth about Mary of Nazareth." (Also *passim*: http://www.accademiamariana.org/archivio/pami/page9.html).

book, nonetheless the Word of God is *living and efficacious*. Here we are beginning a journey leading us to meet a real person living in God, a journey bringing us to meet the very Mother of God, who is also our Mother. From her we come to know the special mission entrusted to her by God, the mission manifested to us in the accounts written by the sacred writers inspired by the Holy Spirit.

The method which we will follow in this study consists in examining, from the historical, literary and theological points of view, what the books of the New Testament tell us of Mary. Our analysis of the texts rests on an initial supposition that the life of Mary finds its profound significance in the light of the life and mission of Christ. For this reason we have chosen to take as our fundamental point of reference Christ, according to the *chronological* order of the events in his life: from his preexistence in the bosom of the Father to his death on the Cross, including what the Acts of the Apostles and the book of Revelation say of these.

Mary in the Accounts of the Origin and of the Infancy of Christ

The accounts of the infancy of Jesus[3] are fundamental for understanding the rest of the Gospel. They provide the keys to interpreting whatever follows. Thanks to them we can correctly explain the identity of Christ and the mission accomplished by him, his words, his actions and his deeds.[4]

Before examining references to the Virgin Mary in the infancy accounts according to Matthew and Luke, we will first analyze a verse of the prologue of the Gospel of St. John, which deals with the eternal preexistence of the Word and his origin in time, and then the passage of Galatians 4:4, which mentions the divine plan concerning

---

[3] For an introduction to the problematics arising out of these accounts, cf. Stef. Manelli, *All Generations ...*, cit., pp. 122-136; S. Muñoz Iglesias, *Lo historico en los Evangelios de la Infancia*, in *Estudios Marianos* 64 (1998) 3-36; I. de la Potterie, *Mary in the Mystery of the Covenant*, New York 1992, pp. 96-141.

[4] M. Grilli writes in regard to Matthew 1:21 (*He will save his people from their sins*): "In this way the reader is prepared to interpret the work of Jesus in the midst of his people: His words, his actions and his Passion, death and Resurrection are the sign of struggle and victory over sin" (M. Grilli, *Maria alla luce della teologia di Matteo*, in *Theotokos* 8 [2000] 719).

Mary. Mary's unique relation to the preexistence of the Word and her singular place in the divine plan of salvation are fundamental to Catholic Mariology; hence the special importance of these two passages in the New Testament. These are not simply dogmatic truths implicit in other Marian assertions of the Bible, but are explicitly affirmed.

"Born not of Blood" (Jn 1:13)

In the first verses of his gospel, St. John solemnly describes the nature and mission of the Word. According to a great many exegetes, ancient and modern, the evangelist-theologian inserts in this context a brief allusion to the virginal conception of Jesus. Hence, this is the first passage in the fourth gospel to make reference to Mary, in particular to the mystery of the Incarnation of the Word in her most pure womb. We will examine this passage first, since its context is exceptionally "original." In fact, this first Marian citation in John is sublimely framed in the eternal origin of the Word of God.

Let us next consider the full text of the prologue under study (Jn 1:12-13), as it is commonly given in critical editions:

12. To those who have accepted him,
    he has given the power to become sons of God:
    to those who believe in his name,
13. who (*plural* = those)/ who (*singular* = his) not of blood,
    nor of the will of the flesh,
    nor of the will of man,
    but of God *are* born/*is* born.

As one can see, verse 13 contains textual variations. It may be read in the plural or singular. Let us immediately explain these differences. To understand this passage correctly, it is important to keep in mind what Ignatius de la Potterie has clearly demonstrated in various articles, but especially in his well-known book, *Mary in the Mystery of the Covenant*.[5] He tells us that "the fourth evangelist knows perfectly well that the Father of Jesus is God himself, that God is 'his very own Father,' as John states explicitly in 5:18," and not Joseph, as was thought in those days (p. 121). The proof of this first assertion is the result of the analysis

---

[5] New York 1992, hereafter cited MMC.

which the aforementioned scholar makes of two passages in the Gospel of John where Joseph is called *father of Jesus* by the crowd. In those two instances the evangelist simply reports the opinion of the Jews who did not know Jesus, without any intention of declaring his own convictions (pp. 101-120).[6]

As noted above, even at the very beginning of his gospel John alludes *expressly* to the mystery of the virginal conception of Jesus (1:12-13). It must, however, also be said that the text in question is the subject of considerable controversy, both from the standpoint of textual criticism and of exegesis. That notwithstanding, our explanation enjoys the support of a good part of the patristic and theological Tradition.

With de la Potterie it should be noted above all that the text of John represents a literary genre different from the accounts of Jesus' origin found in Matthew and Luke. While the latter are historical accounts in the true and proper sense containing much circumstantial detail, that of John in the prologue is primarily concerned with a theological view of the real fact of the Incarnation.[7]

The first point to clarify, then, regards the text. I. de la Potterie tackles the question from two perspectives: the analysis of textual witness extraneous to the Gospel itself (manuscripts, papyrus, citations of the Fathers), and the internal examination of the gospel (vocabulary and the theology of John).[8]

As regards the witness of the textual tradition, "practically all the critical editions and almost all the translations give the plural at the end of verse 13:" *hoi ... ek Theou egennéthesan, who have been born of God.* "So understood, the verse speaks of the spiritual rebirth of Christians."[9] It is true that no Greek manuscript of the gospel gives the reading for verse 13 in the singular. But one should keep in mind that the earliest manuscripts we possess of the fourth gospel all date from the fourth century, with the exception of a papyrus fragment of the second century, one without our text, however.

---

[6] Cf. also J. Willemse, *La Patrié de Jésus selon saint Jean, IV, 44*, in *New Testament Studies* 11 (1965) 360-362.
[7] MMC, 123.
[8] Cf. also J. Galot, *Maternità verginale di Maria e Paternità divina*, in *La Civiltà Cattolica* 139 (1988) 3/209-222.
[9] MMC, 122.

On the other hand, there are other more ancient testimonies to the original reading. These are especially interesting for the critical study of the text, because they show how the gospel was read in the centuries preceding the fourth. Concretely, we are dealing with citations from the Fathers and from the ancient translations. Now, de la Potterie claims that "all the 'witnesses' of the second century support a reading in the singular:" *who was born of God,* and in addition "these witnesses are not all confined to one locality, but are found throughout the Mediterranean basin."[10] This is extremely important, because it means that already in the second century "the text was read in the singular and only in the singular. And this less than a century after the composition of the fourth gospel."[11]

Internal criticism of the Gospel of John (study of its style, of its linguistic character, of its structure, of the theology of the evangelist) confirms what was said above.[12] The verse cannot be read in the plural, because it would then refer to the spiritual rebirth of Christians. But when John speaks of this theme, he always makes use of the present perfect tense (cf. 1 Jn 5:18), never the aorist found in Jn 1:13, were the plural reading to be accepted. But the aorist form found there is appropriate for a reference to the Incarnation of Christ, a historical fact of the past, while the rebirth of Christians is a continuing fact, one therefore best expressed by a verbal form in the present perfect tense (cf. p. 127ff.). Textual comparison, therefore, favors a reading of verse 13 of the prologue in the singular.

If one were to accept the plural reading with its reference to the spiritual rebirth of Christians by faith and baptism, it also becomes

---

[10] Justin in Palestine, Hyppolite in Rome, Irenaeus in Gaul, Tertullian in North Africa, others in Alexandria in Egypt (cf. MMC, 124). Cf. also J. Galot, *Etre né de Dieu. Jean 1:13*, Rome 1968, p. 80; R. Robert, *La Lecon christologique en Jean 1, 13,* in *Revue Thomiste* 87 (1987) 11; B. Escaffre Ladet, *L'Evangile de Jean fait il reference a la conception virginale?*, in *Ephemerides Mariologicae* 43 (1993) 349-365.

[11] MMC, 124. Following our author we may say the most likely thing is that the text immediately following: *ouk eks aimáton*, the genitive plural, which our translations render in the singular: *not of blood* (cf. *Ibid.*, 125ff.). Cf. also R. Robert, *La lecon christologique...*, cit., 5-22, and other citations of de la Potterie in note 42. In addition see S. De Fiores, *Maria. Nuovissimo Dizionario*, EDB, Bologna 2006, 309.

[12] De la Potterie, with his great competence in Johannine literature, made this analysis in his study MMC, to be consulted for in-depth clarifications (pp. 126-132). It is enough here to give his conclusions. Cf. also De Fiores, *Maria*, cit., 309.

difficult to explain the sense of the three following negations: *not of blood, nor of the will of the flesh, nor of the will of man*, reflecting the evangelist's polemic with the Ebionites. In reality John intends a reference to a corporal birth, from which certain modalities are excluded. The three negations cannot be explained on the premise that the spiritual rebirth of Christians is being treated here, a rebirth entirely spiritual (cf. Jn 3:5). Instead, the three negations nicely accord with the corporal birth of Jesus, of which they are the modalities (cf. p. 129ff.).

Verse 13, then, treats of the Incarnation of the Word and "is *par excellence* a Christological verse" (p. 130). From the theological point of view the verse makes explicit reference to the human, temporal birth of Christ, and implicitly to the eternal birth of the Son of God (cf. p. 131).

At this juncture a correct reading of verse 12: "To those, however, who have accepted him, he has given the power to become sons of God: to those who believe in his name," enjoys crucial importance. The name here spoken of refers to Christ. The pronoun preceding it ("his") refers, in fact, to the first part of the verse: "To those who accept him." In turn this pronoun refers to the "true light" in verse 9, recalled in verses 10 and 11 by way of the personal pronoun. Further, one must keep in mind that in John the expression "believe in the name" always refers to Christ (Jn 2:23; 3:18; 20:31; 1 Jn 3:23; 5:13; cf. also Jn 1:18; Mk 16:17; Acts 10:43. cf. p. 128).

Now, in the Gospel of John "the 'name' of Christ is 'the Son'; and the name of God is always 'the Father'" (p. 128). Even at the beginning of verse 14 John speaks of the "only-begotten Son of the Father." The initial pronoun, then, of verse 13, read in the singular, refers to the "only-begotten Son of the Father." Hence, it must be translated thus: "To those, however, who have accepted him, he has given the power to become sons of God: to those who believe in his name; *him who* has been begotten, not of blood ... but of God." Thus read, verse 14 also links better with what precedes it: "And the Word became flesh and dwelt among us and we have seen his glory, the glory of the only-begotten of the Father, full of grace and truth."

Now we may pass on to the three negations of verse 13. The first, *who not of blood*, is the more difficult, in so far as the plural form of blood (*bloods*) was generally employed in the Old Testament and in profane literature to denote the violent shedding of blood, as in the case of massacres in time of war. In our case, however, this is not the meaning to be given to the term. Following in the footsteps of P. Hofrichter,[13] de la Potterie holds instead that the plural, viz., bloods, is used in the text of Leviticus 12 in reference to the laws of purification of the mother, rendered impure by *bloods* lost at the moment of parturition. John 1:13, read in the light of this context, intends to say that at the moment of Christ's birth there was no shedding of blood on the part of his Mother. In other words, at the moment of Jesus' birth there was no need "of ritual purification by the Mother of Jesus, because in her there had been absolutely no loss of blood" (p. 136).

The second negation, *nor of the will of the flesh*, has a more general meaning and excludes from the process of the Incarnation every carnal desire. The third, *nor of the will of man*, excludes in particular the intervention of a man (cf. p. 132).[14] In this way the virginal conception of the Son of God is affirmed. De la Potterie claims to see an ascending progression in the verse:

> At the beginning we find the exclusion of the more material element, "the bloods" (at the moment of birth); next a more general assertion, that of "carnal" desire in an animal nature while conceiving; finally the exclusion of the will of a human being, the male, in this very conception. The finale, put positively rather than negatively, is raised to a transcendent level, underscoring God's role in this generation: God himself is presented as Father of the Word incarnate.

This verse has a strong Christological import: John presents the virginal conception and the virginal birth of Jesus as the most certain *sign* of his divine sonship.[15] At this point we may very well say that

> with this interpretation of the prologue 1:13-14, we have in St. John the most sublime and complete testimony of the mystery of the Incarnation, revealed in its reality as at once both meta-historical–transcendent, and historical–

---

[13] *Nicht aus Blut sondern monogen aus Gott geboren. Textkritische, dogmengeschichtliche und exegetische Untersuchung zu Joh 1, 13-14*, Würzburg 1978.
[14] Cf. also J. Galot, *Etre né de Dieu*, cit., 98.
[15] Cf. MMC, 153-156; also Manelli, *All Generations...*, 153.

physical (corporal). The fatherhood of God and the sonship of the Word, the divine maternity of Mary and the virginal conception and birth of Jesus of her, are shown to be contained explicitly and implicitly in the words of these two verses of the Johannine prologue.[16]

Even if the name of Mary is not cited expressly, it goes without saying that in speaking of the conception and birth John implicitly alludes to the Mother of the Word.[17] The verse, therefore, refers not only to the virginal conception and birth of Jesus, but in so far as he is the only-begotten Son of the Father, also affirms implicitly the divine maternity of Mary. "These two aspects of the mystery of Mary—her *divine maternity* and her *virginity*—are inseparable."[18]

Taking verse 1:12 into consideration as well, one easily grasps how the divine maternity of Mary is implicitly extended by John to all those who believe in the only-begotten Son of the Father. In this regard I. de la Potterie correctly states:

> According to John 1:12-13 we may "become" progressively children of God, in the measure in which we believe in him who is our model, the Son of God. We are "sons in the Son." ... It is necessary, therefore, to say that if Mary is the Mother of the Son of God made man—our model—she will play a role in the repetition of this "incarnation" in the souls of believers. The maternity of Mary which initiated the Incarnation of Jesus, is prolonged in the life of Christians (p. 140).[19]

Following J. Galot, Fr. Stefano Manelli rightly observes that "an important detail to be set in relief regards the active presence of the 'will' of the Virgin Mary, to which the evangelist does not expressly refer,

---

[16] Cf. Manelli, *Ibid.*, 152; S. De Fiores, *Maria...*, cit. 309.
[17] In addition to MMC, 141, cf. also G. Segalla, *La "Madre degli inizi" nel Vangelo di Giovanni*, in *Theotokos* 7 (2000) 774.
[18] MMC, 141.
[19] Cf. also Manelli, *All Generations....*, 153: "Here it is sufficiently clear that the strict nexus between the divine filiation of Jesus and the filiation by faith of the baptized also involves an intimate link with the divine maternity of Mary, which extends from the Son to the sons."

but which is evidently connatural to the dynamism proper to the act of conceiving by a woman, free and conscious under the divine action as Lk 1:26-28 describes Mary."[20]

"The Fullness of Time" (Gal 4:4)

Significant from many points of view is the fact that chapter 8 of *Lumen Gentium*, treating of the Blessed Virgin Mary in the mystery of Christ and of the Church, begins with the citation of Galatians 4:4ff.: "A most merciful and wise God desiring to effect the redemption of the world, 'when the fullness of time had come, sent his own Son, born of a woman ... to make us his adopted sons'" (n. 52). Evidently the Council Fathers were convinced that this verse provided just the right synthesis of all that would be then affirmed in greater detail concerning the Virgin Mary and her role in the history of salvation.

Contemporary Mariologist S. de Fiores in his *Maria. Nuovissimo Dizionario*, begins his presentation of Gal 4:4 with these words:

> Paul breaks the silence on Mary in offering Gal 4:4 as the first Marian text of the New Testament. ... Mary is the woman who inserts the Son of God into history in a condition of abasement, but she is also involved in the fullness of time and in the historical-saving plan for the transformation of men into children of God.[21]

Not all exegetes and Mariologists, however, are so clear and explicit in acknowledging that this passage of Gal 4:4 plays a key role in biblical Mariology. Effectively, the history of the interpretation of this verse illustrates how the approach of exegetes in general, and of Mariologists in particular, has considerably changed over the last decades: They have passed from an interpretation formed in the light of the whole of Revelation to one rigidly literal, or rather *literalistic*, prescinding from the whole.[22]

The first task of the exegete remains always that of illustrating the literal sense of a text on the basis of the context and literary genre adopted

---

[20] Manelli, *All Generations...*, 152; cf. also J. Galot, *Maternitè verginale di Maria e Paternitè divina*, in *La Civiltà Cattolica* 139 (1988) 3/219.
[21] De Fiores, *Maria*, 293-294.
[22] *Ibid.*, 293ff.

by each sacred author. But he must not stop here. It is evident that if St. Paul does not speak, as instead does St. Luke, of the Annunciation of the Angel Gabriel to Mary (cf. Lk 1:26-38), thanks to which we know the divine and messianic identity of Jesus of Nazareth, this is not to say that in reading the Letter to the Galatians one may prescind from the truth of the Incarnation. Similarly, because St. Paul does not mention expressly the virginity of Mary in the conception of Jesus, as instead do Luke and Matthew, it does not follow that one may not prescind from this dogma of faith in the interpretation of his writing. Hence, as it would be a grave error to read into a text what the author (divine and human) did not wish to say, so also it is an error just as grave to deny to the text that meaning which it could well have in the light of the whole of Scripture, read within the unity of the divine plan of salvation.

Now let us enter more deeply into the theme, offering first a brief introduction to the content of the Letter to the Galatians.[23]

---

[23] For further in-depth study cf. the bibliography in commentaries on the Letter to the Galatians. Among the more recent studies on our theme cf. A.M. Buscemi, *Lettera ai Galati. Commentario esegetico* (SBF Analecta, 63), Jerusalem 1994; Idem, *Paolo. Vita, opera, messaggio* (SBF Analecta 43) Jerusalem 1996; M.D. Nanos (ed.), *The Galatians Debate. Contemporary Issues in Rhetorical and Historical Interpretation*, Peabody, MA, 2002; I.G. Hong, *The Law in Galatians* (JSNT SS 81), Sheffield 1993; S. Légasse, *Paul apôtre. Essai de biographie critique*, Paris 2000; L.A. Jervis, *Galatians* (New International Biblical Commentary. New Testament Series), Macon GA 1999; E.M. Watson (ed.), *Galatians* (Bibliographies for Biblical Research. New Testament Series 9), Lewiston, NY, 1999; P.H. Kern, *Rhetoric and Galatians: Assessing an Approach to Paul's Epistle* (Society for New Testament Studies. Monograph Series 101), Cambridge 1998; J.L. Martins, *Galatians: A New Translation with Introduction and Commentary* (The Anchor Bible 33 A), New York 1998; B. Witherington, *Grace in Galatia: A Commentary on St. Paul's Letter to the Galatians*, Grand Rapids, MI, 1998; J. Lambrecht et Alii (ed.), *The Truth of the Gospel (Galatians 1:1-4:11)*, Rome 1993; J.D.G. Dunn, *The Epistle to the Galatians*, Peabody, MA, 1993; F.J. Matera, *Galatians* (Sacra Pagina 9), Collegeville, MI; A. Vanhoye, *La Merè du Fils de Dieu selon Gal 4,4*, in *Marianum* 40 (1978) 237-247; E. De Roover, *La maternità virginale de Marie dans l'interprétation de Gal 4,4*, in AAVV, *Studiorum Paulinorum Congressus Internationalis Catholicus 1961 I*, Rome 1963, 17-37. Among the classic commentaries of particular value cf. H. Schlier, *Der Brief an der Galater*, Göttingen 1965; M.J. Lagrange, *St. Paul. Epitre aux Galates* (Etudes Bibliques), Paris 1918; V. Jacono, *Le Epistole di S. Paolo ai Romani, ai Corinti e ai Galati* (La Sacra Bibbia) Turin-Rome 1951. For the ancient commentaries, cf. St. Thomas Aquinas, "Super Epistolam ad Galatas lectura," in Idem, *Super Epistulas S. Pauli lectura* (P. R. Cai, ed.), Turin, 1953, 563-649.

The Letter to the Galatians

The letter sent by St. Paul to the Christians of Galatia, probably while he was staying at Ephesus,[24] is commonly dated around the year 54 or 55. A few scholars maintain that it was written in the year 49 from Antioch of Syria. A few others, in view of doctrinal affinities between Galatians and Romans, hold that it was written in 57 and should be considered as a first draft of the Letter to the Romans.

The main theme of the letter is the teaching on Christian freedom in regard to the observance of the prescriptions of the Mosaic Law. The occasion for its writing was offered the apostle by the confusion created in the Galatian community by certain "false brethren" (2:4), namely certain Jewish Christians, who sought to introduce "another gospel" (cf. 1:6-9) by convincing the local Christians to acknowledge that observance of the Mosaic Law is necessary for salvation. In such wise they preferred their own national and religious traditions to the liberty of Christians and to the law of grace.

Further, these "false brethren," in order to lend credibility to their position, cast doubt on Paul's claim to be an "apostle."[25] Since Paul could not himself travel to Galatia to resolve the question, he decided to send this decisively strong letter (cf. 1:6-10; 3:1-5; 5:7-12). In it he firmly proclaimed Christian freedom, by explaining the redemptive value of Christ's Passion, accessible to Christians through faith and baptism, quite independently of the Old Law, now abolished by the new and definitive stage of salvation.[26] With great vigor the apostle contrasts the Cross of Christ with circumcision (cf. 5:2-3, 11; 6:12, 15).[27]

---

[24] Cf. A.M. Buscemi, *Paolo*, 168; A. Wiekenhauser-J. Schmid, *Introduzione al Nuovo Testamento*, Brescia 1981, 464ff; P.N. Harrison, *Introduction*, 274-279.

[25] Cf. A.M. Buscemi, *Paolo*, 168; G. Howard, *Paul: Crisis in Galatia* (SNTSMS 35), Cambridge 1990.

[26] Cf. *La Bibbia di Navarra. Nuovo Testamento (2)*, Milan 1993, 350.388. [Trans. note: The English version of the Navarre Bible is not identical with the Italian.]

[27] Cf. A.M. Buscemi, *Libertà e Huiothesia. Studio esegetico di Gal 4, 1-7*, in *Liber Annuus* 30 (1980) 93-136, here 95-109ff. On the history of interpretations of the structure of the Letter to the Galatians, see A. Pitta, *Disposizione e messaggio della lettera ai Galati: analisi retorico-letteraria* (Analecta Biblica 131) Rome 1992, 13-41. With this general context in mind, Galatians may be outlined along the lines proposed by A.M. Buscemi:

Galatians 4:4

According to what can be observed in the foregoing paragraph and from the structure of the letter, verse 4:4 is found in the doctrinal portion of the letter, more exactly in the pericope 4:1-7, for which it is considered the interpretive key.[28] The text of the pericope is as follows:

1. Now I say, as long as the heir is a child, he differs in no way from a slave, though he is the master of all;
2. but he is under guardians and stewards until the time set by his father.

Introduction

1:1-5: initial greeting
1:6-10: warning to Galatians concerning their inconstancy

Apologetic Section (1:11-2:21): Paul's defense of his ministry via a recounting of the principal steps of his call

1:11-24: divine origin of his vocation
2:1-10: voyage to Jerusalem with Barnabas and Titus
2:11-21: incident at Antioch with Peter

Doctrinal Section (3:1-4:31): justification by faith in Christ and not by the Law, or, a new creature in Christ, sharing the blessings promised to Abraham

3:1-6: the Christian experience of freedom vs. the curse of slavery
3:7-4:20: the teaching of Scripture, viz., role of Law ceases* when we are begotten of the Spirit and made sons and heirs of God with Christ, "born of the Woman"
4:21-31: typology of the sons of Abraham, viz., those begotten of the Spirit are children of the free woman (type of Christ's mother)

Moral Section (5:1-6:10): Christian freedom, i.e., living according to Christ's law to bear the fruits of the Spirit**

Conclusion (6:11-18): live according to this teaching always united to Christ

* Cf. A.M. Buscemi, La funzione della legge nel piano salvifico di Dio in Gal 3, 19-25, in Liber Annuus 32 (1982) 109-132; B. L. Martin, Paul and the Law, Leiden 1989.
** J.M.G. Barclay, Obeying the Truth. A Study in Paul's Ethics in Galatians, Edinburgh 1988; C.K. Barrett, Freedom and Obligation. A Study of the Epistle to the Galatians (SPCK), London 1985; T.J. Deidun, New Covenant Morality in Paul (Analecta Biblica 89) Rome 1981.

[28] A.M. Buscemi, *Libertà e Huiothesia*, 111.

3. So we too, when we were children, were enslaved/subjected under the elements of the world.
4. But when the fullness of time came, God sent his Son,
   a. born of a woman,
   b. born under the Law,
5. a. that he might redeem those who were under the Law,
   b. that we might receive the adoption of sons.
6. And because you are sons, God has sent the Spirit of his Son into our hearts, crying, "Abba, Father."
7. So that he is no longer a slave, but a son; and if a son, an heir also through God.

This passage forms part of what is considered to be the "heart" of the Letter to the Galatians. St. Paul openly affirms that "Christ, sent by the Father, has definitively rescued us from subjection to the Law and has made us children and heirs of his promises."[29]

In this part of the letter, St. Paul, to clarify the nature of Christian existence, has recourse to two examples: one taken from ordinary life (4:1-11), the other from Sacred Scripture (4:21-31). In the first he asserts that before Christ, the Jews were like little children, in need of being under guardians or pedagogues; now, by faith in Christ they have become free sons, in condition to inherit, and able to invoke God as Father. In the second, to explain the difference between slavery to the Law and the liberty of faith in Christ he recalls the two sons of Abraham, one son of the slave Hagar, the other the son of the free woman Sarah; the first, Ishmael, represents the Old Covenant, the other, Isaac, represents the New Covenant.[30]

Literary Observations

Clear interpretation of this passage presupposes two points of literary criticism. The first concerns its delimitation: either from 3:26 through 4:7; or from 4:1 through 4:7. Scholars are divided on this issue, but

---

[29] A.M. Buscemi, *Paolo*, 170; cf. also Idem, *Libertà e Huiothesia*, 93-136; A. Sisti, *L'adozione divina (Gal 4, 1-7)*, in *Bibbia e Oriente* 6 (1964) 267-272; S. Zedda, *L'adozione a figli di Dio* (Analecta Biblica 1), Rome 1952.

[30] Cf. *La Bibbia di Navarra (2)*, 396ff.

the more probable view is the second, one in fact setting in higher relief the Marian aspect of Paul's theology.[31] The second point concerns the passage as an argument, signaled by the presence of connectives (introductory and conclusive), antithetical parallelisms, and a chiasm typical of this genre.[32]

Buscemi thus summarizes Paul's argumentation in 4:1-7. It "is based on three main points: man finds himself under a servile regime; God, by sending his Son and the Spirit, has freed him and has conferred on him the *uiothesía* (adoption); the Christian is no longer slave, but son."[33]

We may add that in this pericope the theme of Christian freedom is expanded in comparison to references in 2:4 and 3:13: "it is no longer considered only as a work of Christ, but as a saving act of the One and Triune God."[34]

Interpretation of 4:4

Verse 4:4 affirms: *But when the fullness of time came, God sent his Son, born of a woman, born under the Law.*

The initial phrase of 4:4, *hote dè elthen tò pléroma tou chrónou* (*but when the fullness of time came*), indicates the realization of the time established by God for realizing his plan of salvation for mankind. The verse begins with "but," in this case strongly adversative. This conjunction, united to the aorist *elthen* (came), signals a radical change of situation in respect to the preceding period.

The verse continues with the main clause: "God sent his Son, born of a woman, born under the Law." With these words the divine origin and preexistence of the Son with the Father are affirmed.[35] Further, they set in relief the first concrete act in the work of salvation by God, consisting in the sending of the Son by the Father. The verb *eksapésteilen* (sending

---

[31] In favor the first position: S. Légasse, *Paul Apôtre*. 290-307; B. Byrne, *"Sons of God" – "Seed of Abraham"* (Analecta Biblica 83) Rome 1979, 174. 186; F.J. Matera, *Galatians*, 153; J.D.G. Dunn, *Galatians*, 209-210. In favor of the second, more probable view: J.M. Scott, *Adoption as Sons of God* (WUNT 2. Reihe 48) Tübingen 1992, 121-122; A. Pitta, *Lettera ai Galati*, Bologna 1996, 231.

[32] Cf. Buscemi, *Libertà e Huiothesia*, 95-97. 108ff.

[33] *Ibid.*, 114.

[34] *Ibid.*, 116, who refers to R. Schulte, *L'opera salvifica del Padre in Cristo*, in *Mysterium Salutis*, Brescia 1971, 69-116.

[35] B. Gherardini, *La Madre. Maria in una sintesi storico-teologica*, Frigento 1989, 64.

from, as an "apostle") indicates above all the "mission" of the Son, viz., that the Father sends him with a plan of salvation to accomplish. But the verb also refers to the mode in which the Son has accomplished his mission, i.e., by the Incarnation, which is a redemptive Incarnation. Precisely because of this aspect of the "mission" of the Son, the use of *eksapostéllo* in Gal 4:4 is like, but not identical with, that in Acts 12:11. There the mode of realization, a mission on the part of the liberating angel, is not specified. Instead, in Gal 4:4 St. Paul specifies the mode, viz., how the Son has made us adoptive children *by being born of the woman*.

It now becomes interesting to note how the apostle, once having identified Jesus by the title, "Son of God," adds immediately *genómenon ek gunaikós*, which the Vulgate translates "factum ex muliere" (made or born of woman). Research on the meaning of these words has always been the object of study and debate in the field of exegesis. Nonetheless, we can recognize here two sure Mariological affirmations: the implicit reference to the virginal conception of Mary, and her immediate involvement in the saving work of the Son of God. Despite the position taken by so many modern commentators,[36] there is no more reason to exclude here the person of Mary *qua* Virgin Mother from the inspired sense of this passage than there is to exclude the Incarnation.

Regarding the first theme, as already said, it is sometimes maintained that St. Paul had no intention of speaking about or referring in this passage to the virginal conception of Jesus by the work of the Holy Spirit. Were this the case, he would have spoken more clearly; indeed he may not have known anything of this mystery, having written this before the circulation of the gospels.

To these difficulties the excellent studies of A. Vicent Cernuda gave a clear and definitive reply quite some time ago.[37] The author, in the second part of his research on the human origins of Jesus Christ according to St. Paul, where he accurately examines Pauline thought and vocabulary, makes this claim. If the expression "born of a virgin" is not used, but rather "born of a woman," this does not mean that the

---

[36] Cf. De Fiores, *Maria*, 294.

[37] A. Vicent Cernuda, *La genesis humana de Jesucristo según San Pablo (II)*, in *Estudios Biblicos* 36 (1978) 267-289; cf. also Idem, *El paralelismo de "genno y tíkto" en Lc 1-2*, in *Bib* 55 (1974) 260-264; Idem, *La dialectica "genno y tíkto" en Mt 1-2*, in *Bib* 55 (1974) 408-417.

apostle was not informed about this truth and that he had not wanted to imply it. Revelation 12 also presents a "woman" about to give birth; but without ever mentioning a father, who for the rest is not even present in the context of that passage. Revelation 12 never calls the woman *méter* (mother), but always *guné* (woman). The parallel with Gal 4:4 is surely notable.[38]

To this reflection, developed at great length by the author, another may be added, which sets in relief the value of the term "woman" applied to the Mother of Jesus.

St. Paul did not adopt the formula "born of a virgin," but preferred "born of a woman," because his reasoning was developed according to a progressive parallelism: It begins with a reference to the relation Father-Son and continues with the relation Son-woman. The term "woman" implies the motherhood of Mary, and is in conformity with biblical-messianic usage of the term (cf. Gen 3:15; Jn 2:4; 19:26; Rev 12). In addition, the use of the term "woman" is required by the context of the argumentation: The expression is not only informative, because it asserts a known fact, but also because it has doctrinal import. Here we are treating "of the woman" inserted into the saving plan of God, at the side of, indeed united intimately to the Savior Messiah by bonds of maternity, bonds never merely passive, least of all in the case of the virginal maternity of Mary.

In the commentaries one often reads that the phrase "born of woman" is merely a characteristic expression of the Old Testament, and therefore, as was already mentioned above, not bearing special Mariological significance. It only indicates that Jesus was born of a woman like any other human being, and hence like any other has assumed the weakness of human nature.[39] In fact, the phrase occurs also in Job 11:2, 12; 14:1; 15:14; 25:4; Sir 10:18; and in the New Testament in Mt 11:11; and Lk 7:28, in the last with the added preposition.

This assertion is true, but is partial, insofar as it is limited to a mere literary consideration. True, the phrase "born of woman" is a linguistic commonplace of the Bible. But in Greek the formula normally appears with a verbal adjective: *gennetòs gunaikós* ("begetting woman,"

---

[38] A. Vicent Cernuda, *La genesis humana de Jesucristo (II)*, 280ff.

[39] Cf. H. Balz-G. Schneider, *Dizionario Esegetico*, vol. 1, col. 645; De Fiores, *Maria*, 294.

in Sir 10:18: *gennémasin gunaikon*: womanly begetting); or the formula is structured with the verb *gennáo*.[40] Rare are the examples employing he verb *gínomai* (born, the verb used in Gal 4:4) in the same sense as *gennáo*. In only one instance are these two verbs used in the same sense in two verses of the same context.[41]

Further, it is true that the expression "born of woman" is usual to indicate the common aspect of human nature. But the normal construction in this case employs the verb *gennáo*. St. Paul in Gal 4:4 uses instead the verb *gígnomai*, and this to connote a singular birth. In fact, an examination of the Pauline letters reveals clearly how the apostle never uses the verbs *gennáo* or *tíkto* in reference to the begetting of Jesus, but always the verb *gígnomai* (cf. Rom 9:11; 1 Cor 4:15; Gal 4:23ff., 29; Philemon 10, etc.).[42] In particular one should note that in chapter four itself of Galatians, St. Paul uses the verb *gennáo*, when he speaks of Abraham who had "begotten" Isaac of Sarah and Ishmael of Hagar. This confirms that in 4:4 the apostle deliberately excluded human paternity in the begetting of Jesus.

Evidently, the faith of the Church in the truth of the virginal conception of Mary is not based exclusively on Gal 4:4, where the reference is only implicit. Rather, it rests on what the gospels of Matthew and Luke clearly state. One may not, however, deny, the possibility that Gal 4:4 can be understood in this sense, even if such a meaning be present only implicitly. Hence, as various exegetes have observed, "Pauline theology on the origin of Christ not only does not ignore and

---

[40] In non-biblical Greek this word is used in reference to begetting on the part of the father; rarely, in substitution for *tíkte*, does it refer to begetting on the part of the mother. In the LXX it is often employed to translate the Hebrew for "to be in labor, to give birth." Cf. H. Balz-G. Schneider, *Dizionario Esegetico*, vol. 1, col. 642ff. *Gennáo*: to make in general, includes begetting; *gígnomai* means first to give birth.

[41] This occurs in Ezra 10:3 and 10:44: "And now, let us make a covenant with the Lord our God, to put away all the wives, and such as are born of them, according to the will of the Lord, and them that fear the commandment of the Lord our God: let it be done according to the law. All these had taken strange wives, and there were among them women that had borne children."

[42] Cf. A. Vicent Cernuda, *El paralelismo de "genno" y "tíkto" en Lc 1-2*, 263.

does not deny his virginal conception, but to the contrary also contains surprising aspects perfectly in accord with it."⁴³

In regard to the virginity of Mary, we make our own the clear conclusion of A. Vicent Cernuda. He states that his research shows:

> St. Paul acknowledged the virginal conception and taught it quite naturally as an integrating element of the Incarnation; and if it is true that in itself this mystery does not constitute a characteristic feature of Pauline theology, it is no less true that the stylized allusions to this mystery (analyzed above) suggest how and with what depth the apostle had meditated on this theme to be able to compose these two verses treating of the assumption of a concrete human nature by a divine person and the connatural, but virginal manner in which this was accomplished. ... He thus devised a means for bequeathing to us a fundamental Christology and Mariology coded as it were with marvelous tracery. To tell the truth it is no easy task to imagine how St. Paul might have limited himself in this context to repeating by rote clichés of the community. ... Although many in recent years have accused this ancient view as being contrived, the archaic character of the formulae confirm that the thesis, according to which the virginal conception belongs to the most ancient forms of Christian faith, is not in error.⁴⁴

The second theme touched on in Gal 4:4 deals with Mary's role in the history of salvation. Now, notwithstanding the existence of minimizing interpretations,¹⁵ there remain in the pericope strong evidence of the Father-Son, Son-woman relationships and finally that of sons-Father. If the mode of conception and birth of Christ is not expressly indicated, it is expressly noted that our adoptive sonship passes through the birth of

---

[43] Manelli, *All Generations...*, 138, who cites R. Laurentin, *Tutte le genti mi diranno beata*, Bologna 1986, 22.

[44] A. Vicent Cernuda, *La génesis humana de Jesucristo (II)*, 289.

[45] These present the role of Mary as that of a merely passive instrument. The term "woman" would thus only indicate a natural relation on the part of Mary in the birth of her son. It is not difficult to perceive the Protestant matrix (*Christus solus*) for such a biblical reading.

the Son of God from the woman.[46] This entails an involvement of the woman in the saving plan realized by God in favor of a sinful mankind. We obtain adoptive sonship as a consequence of, and starting from, the fact that the Son is born of the woman.

In this regard we must remark that in accord with the chiastic structure of the pericope, "born of woman" is related to the phrase "that we might receive the adoption of sons," while "born under the law" stands in relation to "that those under the law might be delivered." In the second affirmation there is found a progression between the two elements constituting it (*a* and *b*): the Son is born under the Law for the sake of rescuing those under the Law. Hence, there is a passage from a condition of slavery to one of freedom in Christ, and in this sense the first phrase (*a*) has a negative value, while the second (*b*) signals the end of a state of oppression and the beginning of a state of freedom.[47] The first correlation, "born of woman" and "that we might receive the adoption of sons," also entails a progression: the birth of the woman (the Incarnation) not only had made the Son of God our brother, but even more has effected (*hína ... apolábamen*) adoptive filiation (*tèn uiothesían*). If we can be called "sons of God" and call God "Father," this is because the Son was born of the woman. The motherhood of Mary is, then, not seen here only at the natural level (she gave human nature to the Son of God and so transmitted to him a condition of frailty), because in reality her "natural" motherhood in relation to Jesus is at the origin of the adoptive sonship of all men or all times. Because of this we can be called sons of God thanks to the "divine" maternity of Mary.

This analysis makes clearer the role of Mary in the divine plan of salvation. The Father is at the origin of this saving project, Christ is at its center, but Mary is called to play a part, engaged in first person in the mission of Christ. And on the basis of its explicit affirmation in Gal 4:4, it is not unreasonable to find it implicitly present elsewhere in St. Paul, e.g., in Eph 1:3ff. (as does John Paul II in *Redemptoris Mater*), in Eph 5:21-32;

---

[46] Generally in Hellenistic Greek there is a tendency to eliminate the article before a noun preceded by a preposition. For this reason *genómenon ek gunaikós* may be translated also as "born *from the* woman." And the Christians knew perfectly well who this Woman was, according to the ancient prophecies of Genesis 3:15; Isaiah 7:14; Micah 5:2 and according to the primitive Christian belief recorded in the gospels: Matthew 1:16; Luke 1:26ff.; John 19:25-27.

[47] Cf. A. Pitta, *Lettera ai Galati* (Scritti delle origini cristiane 9), Bologna 1996, 239.

Rom 5:12-21; 8:28-30; Phil 2:5-11; Heb 10:5-10; and Titus 3:4-7. Nor is it unreasonable to suggest that the very "dogmatic" Marian premises of St. Paul's teaching are related to the gospel of the infancy of Jesus according to his good friend and dear physician, the Evangelist, St. Luke.

From the theological point of view it has also been observed that in Gal 4:4 St. Paul refers, even if fleetingly, to the dual origin of Jesus: the eternal origin from the bosom of the Father, as is shown from the theological meaning of the word "sent" or "sent out of:" *eksapésteilen ho Theòs ton huiòn autou* (God sent his own Son); and the temporal origin from the womb of the Virgin Mary: *genómenon ek gunaikós, factum ex muliere* (born of a woman).[48]

A comment almost always made is that St. Paul says little of Mary. Galatians 4:4 is the only reference to her. "Nonetheless, this verse presents her vividly inserted into the mystery of the Incarnation of the Word and of the redemption of men called to *'adoption of sons.'*"[49] In effect, Mary has *made* Jesus to be in "the fullness of time," and this time is that which the Father from eternity has fixed *for the redemption* of men. And the redemption begins properly with the Incarnation of the Son of God, according to the saving designs of God. In these designs, Mary is shown "inseparable from the Son of God by nature and from the sons of God by 'adoption,' from the Redeemer and from redeemed mankind, and lastly from Christ and from the Church. In Gal 4:4 one comes to perceive, precisely, the Virgin Mother of Christ and of the Church."[50] St. Paul here presents an indispensable frame "for understanding the divine plan and the place of Mary in the history of salvation."[51] Another term for this in Tradition is *Mediatrix*.

One may add that in this passage Mary enjoys the specific function of guaranteeing the reality of the Incarnation against the Docetist heresy. But as we have seen, with the expression: *genómenon ek gunaikós*, unusual in this form in biblical Greek, St. Paul, in conformity with Tradition (cf. Mt 1:16, 18-25, and Lk 1:26-38), affirms the exclusion of human paternity in the generation of Jesus. In this way, "implicitly, but unequivocally" he grounds "not only the *maternal virginity* of Mary in regard to Christ,

---

[48] Manelli, *All Generations…*, 142.
[49] *Ibid.*, 141.
[50] *Ibid.*, 142; cf. also C. Pozo, *Maria en la Escritura y en la fe de la Iglesia*, Madrid 1978.
[51] T. Köhler, *Maria nella Sacra Scrittura*, Vercelli 1970, 45.

but also the *divine maternity* in regard to the Son of God and the *spiritual maternity* in regard to the 'adoptive' sons of God."[52]

Matthew and Luke

The gospels of Matthew and Luke are those which have the greatest number of references to the Virgin Mary, strongly concentrated in the first two chapters of each gospel. In these are recounted episodes relative to the infancy and youth of Jesus. Even if few, there are nevertheless references to her during the public ministry of the Lord. These have profound meaning and help to complete the presentation of the exceptional figure of the Mother of God.

M. Grilli writes: "Matthew, in a singular manner, underscores that the *Son of God* (1:21) is at the same time *son of Mary*. This interplay of divine and human action invites the reader not only to inquire about the identity and role of the babe, but also to ask about the presence and role of the mother."[53] In the treatment to follow, we will seek to study exactly this.

Genealogy of Jesus

The scope of the genealogy recorded by St. Matthew is that of affirming more explicitly that Jesus is the Messiah. In particular the evangelist wishes to show how the redemption was foreseen from the beginning and the birth of Jesus brings to completion the promises first made to Abraham and then to David.[54]

To do this the evangelist recounts a long list of names, organized in three groups of 14 ancestors, beginning with Abraham to David, then from Solomon to the Babylonian exile, and finally from the return from Babylon to Jesus.[55] Each link in the genealogy is introduced by

---

[52] Manelli, *All Generations...*, 142; R. Laurentin, *Tutte le genti mi diranno beata*, 22; P. Pietrafesa, *La Madonna nella Rivelazione*, Naples 1970, 106.

[53] M. Grilli, *Maria alla luce della teologia di Matteo*, in *Theotokos* 8 (2000) 718ff.

[54] Cf. M. Grilli, *Ibid.*, 713ff; T. Stramare, *Vangelo dei Misteri della Vita Nascosta di Gesù (Matteo e Luca I-II)*, Bornato in Franciacorta 1998, 43-77.

[55] M. Orsatti, *Gesù Cristo, figlio di Davide, di Abramo...di Maria*, in *Theotokos* 3 (1995) 22. He points out in summary form the anomalies of Matthew's genealogy. Among other things he notes that Matthew's genealogy is different from Luke's. Many solutions have been proposed for this problem. Since the question is beyond the scope of this chapter, we only mention here that St. Matthew, writing for

a set formula of this kind: "Abraham begot Isaac; Isaac begot Jacob; Jacob begot Judah and his brothers" etc. (1:2). Four times the name of a mother is mentioned, as in the case of Judah who begot Peres and Zerah "of Tamar" (1:3), in the case of Salmon who "begot Boaz of Rahab," of Boaz, who "begot Obed of Ruth" (1:5), and of David who "begot Solomon of the former wife of Uriah," namely Bathsheba (1:6).

The final link in the genealogical line is modified in such wise as to create a certain ambiguity.[56] The genealogical list, in fact, does not close with the usual formula of begetting, but with the phrase: "Jacob begot Joseph, the husband of Mary, and of her was born Jesus called the Christ" (v. 16). In contrast with all the other instances, including those where the name of the mother is cited, here it is not said that the father *begot* the son, namely, that Joseph begot Jesus. It is only said that Joseph was the husband of Mary, and that *of her* was born Jesus. Further, in the entire series of generations, the verb appears in the active voice: "Abraham begot (*egénnesen*) Isaac ..., Jacob begot Joseph." In the final instance, in reference to Mary, the same verb is used, but in the passive voice: from her "was born/was begotten Jesus" (*egennéthe*).[57] In this way Matthew "clearly sets in relief the mystery of the virginal maternity of Mary, and implicitly the mystery of the very divinity of Jesus."[58]

Jews, probably gives the legal genealogy of Jesus, whereas St. Luke, writing for pagans gives the natural one. In *Fausset's Bible Dictionary* among many proposed solutions we find this one: "Mary must have been of the same tribe and family as Joseph, according to the law (Num 36:8). Isaiah. 11:1 implies that the Messiah was the seed of David by natural as well as legal descent. Probably Matthan of Matthew is the Matthat of Luke, and Jacob and Heli were brothers; and Jacob's son Joseph, and Heli's daughter Mary, first cousins. Joseph, as male heir of his uncle Heli, who had only one child, Mary, would marry her according to the law (Num 36:8). Thus the genealogy of the inheritance (Matthew's) and that of natural descent (Luke's) would be primarily Joseph's, then Mary also" (1338.04). But compare with T. Stramare, *Vangelo dei Misteri*, 53-57.

[56] This, however, will be clarified by the evangelist immediately after, when he explains how the birth of Jesus came about.

[57] The text of Jn 1:13, according to the reading we have adopted above, also has the same verb form in the aorist passive, notwithstanding the fact that God is pointed out expressly as direct agent of the human generation of Jesus: "he was born of God."

[58] Manelli, *All Generations...*, 147; cf. also M. Masini-G. Antonioli, *Risalendo alle origini*, in M. Masini (ed), *La Madre di Dio*, Brescia 1975, 263; *The Navarre Bible. St. Matthew's Gospel*, Dublin 1988, 29.

This "anomaly" at the end of the genealogical list refers to a direct intervention of God in this concluding generation, as will be stated expressly just a bit further on, in relation to the conception and birth of Jesus by the working of the Holy Spirit (1:18-21). The passive voice used in 1:16, can in fact be considered a theological passive, referring back to God himself, the only agent.

Another "anomaly" noted in this genealogical list is that the third group, in order to reach the number of 14 ancestors, must include Mary in the thirteenth place: a woman instead of a man,[59] as in the rest of the list. As G. Leonardi remarks, this is truly "exceptional in a Hebrew genealogy, where only the father is counted and not the mother; but this is intentional here, given the extraordinary case of the virginal birth of Jesus from Mary by the working of the Holy Spirit."[60]

Scholars have sought to explain the fact that St. Matthew, generally more attentive to male figures, reports the names of four women in his list.[61] True, the role of these four women differs from that of Mary, who alone forms a "link" in the chain, while the other four are only united to their husbands. Nonetheless, the question arises here, specifically how St. Matthew ever came to cite exactly four women all marked by "irregularities," while he does not cite the *mothers* of Israel or other glorious women, such as Sarah, Rebecca, Rachel, Leah, the sister of Moses, the mother of Samuel.[62]

Fr. Stefano Manelli observes on this point:

> One should see in these four women, or at least in some of them, *sinners*, to show that the Messiah would come to save sinners. One should see in these *strangers*

---

[59] Salathiel, Zorobabel, Abiud, Eliacim, Azor, Sadoc, Achim, Eliud, Eleazar, Matthan, Jacob, Joseph (the husband of), Mary, Jesus. On the other hand, according to Hebrew law it was obligatory to marry within the same tribe and family (Num 36:8). Hence, Mary was probably of the same tribe and family of David.

[60] *L'infanzia di Jesú*, Padua 1975, 37; cf. Stef. Manelli, *All Generations...*, 145; R. Laurentin, *The Truth of Christmas beyond the Myths*, Petersham, MA, 1986, 347; A. Ory, *Riscoprire la verità storica dei vangeli*, Milan 1986, 104.

[61] Also interesting is the fact that St. Luke, more attentive in his account to evidence the role of women, does not mention even one in his genealogy of Jesus, not even the Virgin Mary.

[62] Cf. Laurentin, *The Truth of Christmas...*, 340ff.

and *pagans*, who demonstrate the universality proper to the saving plan of the Messiah Redeemer. In particular, one should see in these four creatures women who have become mothers in an irregular manner, but not sinful, inserted into a design directed from on high, to prepare or prefigure the maternity of the Mother of Jesus, who was above every normality.[63]

These four women "have played an extraordinary personal role in the history of Israel and more exactly in the dynastic history."[64] Hence, the probable scope of St. Matthew in inserting these four women in the list is the assurance that God is "faithful to himself and to his promises" of salvation for the people of Israel,[65] notwithstanding the unforeseen which in turn prefigure "the unexpected and *different* role of Mary."[66] In this way it should have become credible to his contemporaries that "she was the sole human origin of Christ."[67]

We may conclude, therefore, by saying that the genealogy offered by Matthew is intended to communicate two inseparable facts: the miraculous, virginal conception of Jesus by Mary, and his belonging to the house of David in accord with the ancient messianic prophecies.

The Annunciation (Lk 1:26-28)

Within the structure of the first two chapters of the Gospel of St. Luke, the account of the Annunciation of the Angel Gabriel to the Virgin Mary is situated in the first diptych, consisting of the announcement made by the Angel Gabriel to Zechariah in the Temple of Jerusalem concerning the conception and birth of John the Baptist (1:5ff.) and of the announcement to Mary, in her home at Nazareth, of the conception and birth of Jesus, also by the Angel Gabriel. The purpose of this comparison is to make plain the superiority of Jesus in relation to the Baptist, who is

---

[63] Cf. Manelli, *All Generations...*, 145. Cf. also Laurentin, *The Truth of Christmas...*, 340-341.

[64] Laurentin, *The Truth of Christmas...*, 341ff; Manelli, *All Generations...*, 144ff; J. Schniewind, *Il Vangelo secondo Matteo*, Brescia 1977, 27.

[65] M. Grilli, *Maria alla luce della teologia di Matteo*, 715; T. Stramare, *Vangelo dei Misteri*, 67ff.

[66] Laurentin, *The Truth of Christmas...*, 341ff.

[67] Ibid., 346.

his precursor, and the superiority of Mary over Zechariah and Elizabeth. Further, the uniting of the two episodes is intended to signal the unity of the divine plan of salvation, heralded by John and brought to completion by Christ.[68]

The initial verse of the account is linked to the preceding episode chronologically: *in the sixth month*, which refers to the conception of John the Baptist, the precursor. At this precise moment the other extraordinary event occurred. The very same Angel Gabriel was sent by God to another creature, Mary, to whom he announced the conception of the Messiah Savior.

Here it should be remarked how "while John was conceived by a sterile mother (1:5, 24) as prophet of the Most High (1:76), Jesus is conceived by the Virgin Mary (1:27, 35) as Son of the Most High. The parents of the Baptist are just and observers of the law (1:5), Mary, instead, is object of God's favor (1:28). Zechariah doubts the word of God and is punished by being struck dumb (1:20), Mary, to the contrary, believes the word of God (1:38) and comes to be praised for her faith (1:45)."[69]

We also note how Luke tells us nothing about the origin of Mary nor does he praise her directly, as he has already done for Zechariah and Elizabeth (1:5ff.). Of them the evangelist says that "they were just before God, walking blamelessly in all the commandments of God and ordinances of the Lord." Not Mary, but the angel who exalts her (1:27), hence, a heavenly creature sent by God himself, is the evangelist.

The core of the angel's message is the virginal conception and birth of Jesus, the Davidic Messiah and Son of the Most High. By way of this episode,[70] then, the evangelist informs his readers of the true identity and saving mission for God's people of Jesus, the central personality of the gospel account.

The message of the angel, however, contains considerably more than this. Indeed, the entire episode makes plain how Mary as well is called to play a fully active and conscious role in the realization of this divine plan of salvation. It is true that God has, in full freedom chosen to do this. But

---

[68] Cf. Manelli, *All Generations…*, 157; De Fiores, *Maria*, 298ff.
[69] De Fiores, *Maria*, 299.
[70] Primary source of this account was most certainly the Virgin Mary herself. Cf. Manelli, *All Generations…*, 155-156; Laurentin, *The Truth about Christmas…*, 569 ; E. Testa, *Maria Terra Vergine*, Jerusalem 1985, vol. 1, 315; A. Guidetti, *Conoscenza storica di Gesù di Nazareth*, Milan 1981, 159.

it is also true that God has not forced Mary to do anything. Like all men, she, too, was free to accept or refuse the gift of grace. The angel simply revealed to her the divine choice of becoming the Mother of the Son of God and Messiah Savior. Mary, on her part, actively accepted with full freedom, after being informed of the modalities according to which she would have to realize the divine will, and only after having pondered and evaluated the words of the heavenly messenger.[71]

The reply of Mary to the angel is object of a certain emphasis[72] in the dynamics of the account. This resembles in some ways other accounts of vocations in the Bible.[73] Seen from the perspective of the outline characteristic in such accounts, the passage dealing with the announcement to Mary "sets in relief the person of Mary called to give her consent, and the work of mother in the birth of the Son of God in the condition of man. Mary enters into the dialogue between God and mankind, offering a reply shaped by exemplary faith."[74]

Other scholars also find in the account of the Annunciation a reference to covenant formularies. "The account is structured along the lines of the literary genre characteristic of the covenant concluded between God and Israel on Mount Sinai. In both scenes we find three elements: the discourse of the mediator, the reply of the people in terms of obedience and service, the return of the mediator to God. ... In the reply of Mary we note the echo of the formula whereby the people gave their assent to the covenant (Ex 19:3ff.)."[75] In the name of the people Mary accepts the New Covenant offered by God via the mediation of the Angel Gabriel and thus becomes the perfect model for acceptance of the Covenant. Mary had faith and obeyed the will of God. All believers are called to imitate her.

---

[71] Cf. Manelli, *All Generations...*, 174-178, with a reference to W. Harrington, *A New Catholic Commentary on Holy Scripture*, New York 1984, 997; H. De Azevedo, *La Vergine e l'Eucaristia*, in *Studi Cattolici* 29 (1985) 164.
[72] De Fiores, *Maria*, 299.
[73] Cf. the account of the call of Gideon in Judges 6:11-24. De Fiores, *Maria*, 299ff.
[74] De Fiores, *Maria*, 300.
[75] De Fiores, *Maria*, 300, who refers to A. Serra, *Dimensioni ecclesiali della figura di Maria nell'esegesi biblica odierna*, in Idem, *E c'era la Madre di Gesù... (Gv 2, 1). Sagagi di esegesi biblico-mariana (1978-1988)*, Cernusco-Roma 1989, 337; cf. also de la Potterie, MMC, 43; B. Prete, *Il genere letterario di Lc 1, 26-38*, in *Ricerche storico-bibliche* 4 (1992/2) 80.

In particular,[76] we note how the angel greeted Mary with these words: *Chaire, kechariomène, ho kúrios metà sou: Hail, full of grace, the Lord is with thee* (1:28). The word *chaire* may signify *rejoice*. If taken in that sense, then the angel would be inviting Mary to rejoice at "the arrival of the long-expected Messiah and in that sense also prophesized by the prophets, Zephaniah (3:14-18), Joel (2:21-27), Zechariah (2:14; 9:9ff.), Micah (4:8-10)."[77] The term may also be the equivalent of the Hebrew greeting, *shalom*, or *peace*. The Vulgate translates by *ave*, viz., *I salute you*, both in Lk 1:28 and in like passages elsewhere (Mt 26:49; 27:29; Mk 15:18; Jn 19:3).

After this greeting the angel addressed Mary, calling her *kecharitoméne*. This word is a perfect passive participle, translated as *full of grace*, or as *fore-loved, privileged, gratified*. As perfect passive participle, the Greek word means "to be enriched by grace in a stable, lasting way." In fact, the Greek perfect denotes an action completed in the past, whose effects perdure. Hence, the angel greets Mary by announcing that she has been enriched by grace in the past and that the effects of this gift remain. Without doubt this is a singular form of address. No one else in the Bible was ever greeted thus. Only Mary has been so addressed, and this in the moment when she was about to accomplish the "fullness of time," to realize the prophecies of old, and when the Word of God stood ready to take of her our human nature.

To this greeting the angel added: "the Lord is with thee." In the Old Testament, this expression is directed to personages who had been chosen to undertake a great mission, absolutely unique, on behalf of the

---

[76] Many other considerations could be added, as for example the meaning of verse 27, where Mary is said to be a *parthénos emnesteuméne*, *a virgin espoused* to Joseph, a descendant of David. The Greek term, *parthénos, virgin*, had already been used in the Greek Bible of the LXX to translate the Hebrew word *'almah*. The word chosen by Luke, then, refers to the celebrated messianic prophecy of Isaiah 7:14, concerning the virgin to conceive and give birth. The second term, *emnesteuméne*, is a participle variously translated. It is presupposed here that for the Jews celebration of betrothal already created very strong bonds between the betrothed at the juridical level, such that their union already had the legal features of a genuine marriage, the only exception being that of cohabitation (cf. Manelli, *All Generations...*, 159). According to some the term refers to the time running from the betrothal to the celebration of the solemn nuptials. According to others, however, it refers to the period following this solemn celebration.

[77] Manelli, *All Generations...*, 162.

people of God (cf. Gen 28:13-15; Ex 3:12; Josh 1:5; Judg 6:12-16; Jer 1:8). The angel, therefore, informs Mary that she has been called to a special mission for the salvation of Israel, as in the past Jacob, Moses, Joshua, Gideon, Jeremiah, etc., were called. But Mary has been called to a still higher one, because she alone has been addressed by God himself with the name *Enriched (or Perfected) by grace*; only she became the Mother of the Messiah and the Mother of God, only she, as the account will say later on, will participate in the redemptive mission of the Son via the oblation of her own maternal suffering (cf. Lk 2:34ff.). In this her mission Mary "has found grace with God," viz., "has at her disposition every kindness and support for carrying out the heavy responsibility entrusted to her" (cf. Gen 6:8; Ex 33:17; Judg 6:17).[78]

After hearing the words of the angel disclosing her mission of becoming Mother of the Messiah, Mary asked the divine messenger how this could come to be, saying: "I know not man" (v. 34). Mary's question would hardly make sense on the lips of a "spouse." In reality, her words reveal something much more profound. Indeed, the word used is in the present, which in Greek suggests continuity.[79] Hence, Mary says to the angel: "I do not know and I do not intend to know man." For this reason many authors, modern as well as ancient, conclude how "obviously one must therefore admit that the embarrassment of Mary arises from a precise commitment—vow or promise—to 'not know man', i.e., to be and to remain a virgin."[80]

The angel replies to Mary, informing her of the virginal conception by the work of the Holy Spirit: "The Holy Spirit will come upon you and the power of the Most High will overshadow you" (v. 35). The entire Trinity intervenes in the Incarnation, yet this intervention is properly

---

[78] Manelli, *All Generations...*, 164-165.
[79] Cf. O. Battaglia, *La Madre del mio Signore. Maria nei Vangeli di Luca e Giovanni*, Assisi 1994, 68ff.
[80] Manelli, *All Generations...*, 171. He adds a celebrated comment of St. Augustine: "Certainly Mary would not have spoken those words, if she had not already offered to God her virginity" (*De Sancta Virginitate*, PL 40, 398; 38, 1096. 1318). In addition Manelli in note 51, p. 172, cites numerous other exegetes supporting this interpretation. Among others he considers the most exhaustive and definitive the doctoral thesis with the Pontifical Biblical Commission of G. Graystone, *Virgin of All Virgins. The Interpretation of Luke 1:34*, Rome 1958, also published in part in *Ephemerides Mariologicae* 21 (1971) 5-20.

appropriated to the Holy Spirit. The verb "overshadow" is part of the Old Testament vocabulary and refers in particular to the divine presence in the tent of assembly, rendered visible by means of the cloud which filled the tent (cf. Ex 40:34ff.).[81]

The consequence of this intervention is something still greater: the divine-virginal maternity of Mary and, wonder of wonders, the Incarnation of the Son of God. "And therefore the Holy One to be born shall be called the Son of God" (v. 35; see also v. 32). It cannot be overstressed that we have no genuine understanding of Mary except in relation to this unique and stupendous miracle which is the Incarnation; nor do we have any grasp of the Incarnation, even minimal, except through the miracle-sign which is the Virgin Mother. What is true in the first moment of our salvation is true in each successive moment.

Mary gave her full and free consent to the divine project, saying: "Behold, I am the handmaid of the Lord, be it done to me according to thy word" (v. 38). Stefano Manelli comments thus on these words:

> Such "consent," given by Mary, is not merely private, but expresses the willing participation of man, of humanity, in the work of salvation. In the freedom of Mary, at that instant, were contained all the desires, fears, and hopes of man in need of redemption. And the New Eve spoke her full, total *yes* to the angel of light, just as the first Eve had once spoken her *yes* to the angel of darkness. Moreover, the response given by Mary to the angel also expresses, in addition to her consent, a humble and unconditional dedication to the plan of God entrusted to her. Such a dedication reveals the incomparable faith of Mary, a faith that would call forth the inspired exclamation of Elizabeth and offers the perfect model of obedience, animated by the noblest charity, for the salvation of others.[82]

The same author makes a further comment, illustrating the link, indeed the identity, of her consent or *fiat* at the Incarnation with her coredemptive oblation on Calvary, a consent matching the *fiat* of her Son

---

[81] Cf. Manelli, *All Generations...*, 173.
[82] Manelli, *Ibid.*, 179.

at his Incarnation (cf. Heb 10:5-10) and in the Garden of Gethsemani (cf. Mt 26:39; Lk 22:41).

> The expression used by Mary, *"handmaid of the Lord,"* explicitly recalls the celebrated passage of Isaiah concerning the Messiah, the "servant of Yahweh." Indeed, it is the exact "feminine equivalent of the expression servant of Yahweh" as Danieli affirms. This reference establishes two important truths: first, the close union of the "handmaid of the Lord" with the "Servant of Yahweh" in the unique work of the "suffering servant;" and second, the sharing of the painful events of the "suffering servant," immolated for the redemption of men (Is 53:2ff.). The Virgin Mary, in using that expression, did not so much accept as give her all to the redemptive work, as the humble associate of the *"man of sorrows pierced for our offenses, bruised for our iniquities"* (Is 53:3-5).[83]

St. Joseph's Dream and the Virginal Birth of Jesus (Mt 1:28-25)

Various authors have remarked on how Matthew 1:18 very closely resembles the account of the formation of the first man (Gen 2:7): in particular how as the breath of God was present in the formation of the first Adam, so the Holy Spirit intervened in the formation of the second Adam.[84]

But apart from this link with the first pages of the Bible, the fundamental declaration of verse 18 refers to the conception, and therefore the divine origin of Jesus: Mary "was found with child by the work of the Holy Spirit." The apostolic Church made this truth its own and proclaimed it. T. Stramare correctly observes:

---

[83] *Ibid.*, p. 180.

[84] Cf. T. Koehler, *Maria nella Sacra Scrittura*, Vercelli 1970, 56; G. Leopardi, *L'infanzia di Gesù*, 54, cited by Manelli, *All Generations...*, 227, nt. 4. R. Laurentin writes: "The use of this word signifies that the Gospel is a new 'beginning,' a book of genesis, like the first book of the Bible known under this name ... Jesus the Messiah realizes the new creation promised by the prophets for the eschatological times." (*The Truth of Christmas...*, pp. 251-252).

> This proclamation is the link joining the genealogy (of Jesus: Mt 1:1-7) to the following account, in so far as the latter takes up and explains verse 16. In that verse the expression "begot Jesus," omitted after the name of Joseph, is substituted by "husband of Mary, of whom was born Jesus, the Christ." The begetting of Jesus was not ascribed to Joseph precisely because the truth that Jesus was conceived virginally by Mary through the work of the Holy Spirit had already been acknowledged by the apostolic community ... as part of its patrimony of faith.[85]

According to some scholars, this episode belongs to a literary genre known as "apparitions in dreams," with parallels in the dreams recorded in Matthew 2. Others, however, class it among a genre known as "announcements of birth."[86]

As to the structure of the episode, this consists of an introduction (vv. 18-19) summarizing the situation: Mary's conception of Jesus through the work of the Holy Spirit, unknown to Joseph, who was caught by surprise and left preoccupied; of the body (vv. 20-23) narrating the dream of Joseph, during which the angel revealed to him the mystery of the divine conception of Mary and the identity and saving mission of the Son conceived by her, adding a citation from Isaiah; and of a conclusion (vv. 24-25), narrating the resolution adopted by Joseph in accord with the angel's orders.

The primary scope, therefore, of Matthew is to present "the origin of Jesus," making clear the *conjugal bond* of Mary and Joseph, so as to demonstrate the legitimacy of the child, and the *virginal conception*, to indicate the divine origin of Jesus and his messianic identity.[87]

Nonetheless, it is also true that "accents are insistently placed on the Mother of the Child: first in indicating her as object of the mysterious action of the Spirit (v. 20), then as Mother of him who will free his

---

[85] T. Stramare, *Vangelo dei Misteri*, 56.
[86] Cf. Gen 18:9-15; Judg 13:2-7; 1 Sam 1:9-18; Is 7:13-17; Lk 1:11-22, 26-28. Thus, M. Grilli, *Maria alla luce della teologia di Matteo*, 719. On the various interpretations cf. T. Stramare, *Vangelo dei Misteri*, 78-87.
[87] Cf. T. Stramare, *Vangelo dei Misteri*, 98.

people from their sins (v. 21), and finally as the Virgin who brings the Emmanuel into the world (vv. 22-23)."[88]

In verse 18b, Mary's virginal conception by work of the Holy Spirit is discussed. What is affirmed here corresponds to what we read in St. Luke, 1:26-38.[89] St. Matthew states that Mary was "betrothed," or was the "promised bride"[90] of Joseph. He further qualifies this statement in next adding that "before they came together she was found to be with child by the Holy Spirit." In this way the Evangelist Matthew removes even the slightest of doubt concerning the divine and supernatural origin of Jesus.

He makes this same affirmation again in verse 20, this time recording the words of the angel of the Lord. It is also an angel (Gabriel) in the account of St. Luke who announces to Mary the conception through the work of the Holy Spirit. Now, angel means messenger of God. Hence, the testimony is absolutely supreme.

Joseph, made aware of the pregnancy of Mary but not yet informed of the miraculous conception (at a subsequent point he will be so informed), found himself face to face with an agonizing choice. For according to the Law of Moses an adulterous woman had to be repudiated and stoned (cf. Deut 22:20ff.).

St. Matthew, however, says that "Joseph her husband, being a just man and not wishing to expose her to reproach,[91] was minded to put her away privately" (v. 19). To be valid, the divorce had to be effected via a "bill of divorce," viz., a written document, hence not in secret. Joseph decided to dissolve his commitment with Mary with a private procedure, because he did not wish to expose her to public disgrace. Being just, he

---

[88] M. Grilli, *Maria alla luce della teologia di Matteo*, 719.
[89] The phrase "to be with child" in the LXX ordinarily indicates a normal birth, except in Is 7:14 and Mt 1:18, 23. In 1:18, however, the expression is idiomatic and preceded by a strange verb: *"was found* to be with child," indicating something mysterious linked to a divine power, as explained shortly on.
[90] The betrothed maiden was considered "sanctified" i.e., "set apart" for her spouse. The wedding took place a year after the espousals. On the day of betrothal the groom, in the presence of two witnesses, consigned to his bride an object of great value, saying as he did so: "By this gift you are consecrated to me according to the Law of Moses:" F. Manns, *Heureuse es-tu, toi qui a cru. Marie, une femme juive*, Paris 2005, 51-54; Idem, *Que sait-on de Marie et de la Nativité?*, Paris 2006, 77ff.
[91] Additionally he did not believe Mary to be guilty in any way.

could not claim paternity of the Child in her womb.[92] So he decided to separate from her and await enlightenment from on high, "an explicit directive of God. This is what came during his dream with the apparition of the angel. ... Thus was indicated the mission of Joseph to take Mary and to adopt Jesus, so making him son of David."[93]

The angel said to Joseph: "Joseph, son of David, do not fear to take Mary your wife, for that which is conceived in her is of the Holy Spirit; she will bear a son, and you shall call his name Jesus, for he will save his people from their sins." With these words the angel enlightened Joseph concerning the divine origin of Mary's maternity, thus removing any cause for anxiety and filling Joseph with peace and joy.[94]

St. Matthew next affirms that all this has come about in fulfillment of what the Lord had promised through the mouth of Isaiah, who proclaimed to King Ahaz and to the entire house of Israel the prophetic sign of the virgin to bear a son, the Emmanuel, the God with us (Is 7:14). Even if, as some hold today, the rabbis did not interpret this sign in a messianic sense, nonetheless the true and profound meaning of the passage is the one given it by St. Matthew under the inspiration of the Holy Spirit.[95]

Matthew concludes his narrative, stating that Joseph did as the angel had commanded him and "took unto him his wife. And he did not know her till she brought forth her first-born son. And he called his name Jesus" (vv. 24-25). Once again Mary's virginal conception and hence the divine origin of Jesus is underscored.

In the structure of St. Matthew's gospel the angel's revelation is basic, because it manifests to its readers the true identity of Jesus. Thus

---

[92] S. Garofano, *La Madonna nella Bibbia*, Milan 1958, 50, cited by Manelli, *All Generations...*, 234.

[93] De Fiores, *Maria*, 298.

[94] Cf. Manelli, *All Generations...*, 236. Note also that the action of the Holy Spirit in Mary is "creative action."

[95] It is a mistake, however, to say that the interpretation of Matthew is only a Christian reading of a passage of the Old Testament in the light of the virginal conception of Mary, in order to refute gossip about the illegitimacy of the conception of Jesus. But it is true that in the light of accomplished fact we can better understand a passage of the Old Testament, such as Is 7:14. The sense is not that a Christian reading of the Old Testament is extraneous to the meaning of a text; rather it is that the Old Testament finds its fulfillment in Christ who is the center of all Sacred Scripture.

the readers already know the identity of the central personage of the account and so enjoy a distinct advantage over outsiders, like the Jews or the Roman authorities, who do not know who truly is the Lord (cf. Mt 16:13ff.).

The Adoration of the Magi (Mt 2:1-12)

The profound meaning of the adoration of the Magi is the call of all people to the salvation brought by Christ. This perspective of salvation is different from that of the Old Testament, where salvation is limited to the Chosen People.

There is no serious reason for calling into doubt the historicity of the fact narrated by Matthew. Whatever the similarities between this account and Psalm 72, they do not justify the position of those who claim, instead, that the words of the Psalm constitute the bases for the construction of this gospel episode. Rather, Laurentin is correct when he writes that "it was the event to suggest the biblical allusions, not extrapolations and not megalomania. ... The account derives normally from the event, from the fact and not from an imaginary projection."[96]

The Magi remain mysterious persons. They come from the East, perhaps from Persia, or from Babylonia, Arabia, the Syrian desert. They probably belonged to a noble priestly or royal caste, experts in astrology, engaged in divinization and other sacred sciences.[97] In Matthew, however, it is certain that the description of the Magi is entirely positive, so excluding the immoral. They represent pagan peoples who under the guidance of the star, arrive in Bethlehem and there meet the King-Messiah.[98]

Before discovering the place where the King of the Jews was born, so as to adore him, they arrived under the guidance of the star in Jerusalem. There they inquired of Herod the Great about that King. Herod, on consulting his advisors and the scribes, learned on the basis of the ancient

---

[96] Laurentin, *The Truth of Christmas*, 369; T. Stramare, *Vangelo dei Misteri*, 237; Manelli, *All Generations...*, 287, citing a passage from A. Ory, *Riscoprire la verità storica dei Vangeli*, Milan 1986, 95.

[97] Cf. F. Manns, *Que sait-on de Marie...*, 47ff.; A. Poppi, *Sinossi dei Quattro Vangeli. Commento*, Padua 1988, 30; T. Stramare, *Vangeli dei Misteri*, 232-234; 253-263; S. Munoz Iglesias, *Los Evangelios de la Infancia. Nacimiento e infancia de Jesus en San Matteo*, Madrid 1990, 217-222.

[98] Cf. F. Manns, *Que sait-on de Marie...*, 47.

prophecies, that the Messiah King would be born in Bethlehem of Judah. The Magi went there and still guided by the star found the place where the Child was. From the gospel text we know that Herod, even if diplomatically respectful to the Magi, was not a little perturbed to learn a king of Judah had been born. From Herod's perspective birth of such a king threatened the stability of his political power. Hence, he told the Magi to return to him after they had found the Child, so that he also might know the place where he was and so go "to adore him."

St. Matthew takes note of the strong contrast between the terror gripping King Herod and all Jerusalem at learning of the birth of the "King of the Jews" (2:3), and the overwhelming joy of the Magi: "When they had heard the king they went their way; and lo, the star which they had seen in the East went before them, till it came to rest over the place where the child was. When they saw the star, they rejoiced exceedingly with great joy" (2:9-10). In regard to this joy F. Manns observes: "The abundance of joy at the birth of kings (cf. 1 Kings 1:40) is deliberately underlined [by St. Matthew], because here we are dealing with the birth of the King-Messiah."[99]

"And going into the house they saw the child with Mary his mother, and they fell down and worshiped him. Then, opening their treasures, they offered him gifts, gold and frankincense and myrrh." The attention of the Magi, one should note, is focused on the Child, whom they find in the arms of the Mother. St. Joseph is not mentioned. In a country and in a society where the father's role is strongly felt, this silence about him in favor of Mary demonstrates "a systematic intention of setting this woman in relief to distinguish her from all others."[100] F. Manns adds that in this silence one may also see another implicit reference to the virginal conception of Jesus.[101]

Earlier the Magi had asked Herod: "Where is he who has been born King of the Jews? For we have seen his star in the East and have come to worship him" (2:2). In this account the Child is called "King of the Jews," a title he will be given again during the days of his Passion. On

---

[99] *Ibid.*

[100] B. Gillard, *Maria, che cosa dice di te la Scrittura?*, Turin 1983ff; cf. Manelli, *All Generations...*, 296; F. Manns, *Que sait-on de Marie...*, 47ff.; T. Stramare, *Vangelo dei Misteri*, 258-261.

[101] F. Manns, *Que sait-on de Marie...*, 48.

finding the Child the Magi express their homage to the newly born King with a prostration and the presentation of precious gifts, gold, incense and myrrh, symbols of royalty, divinity, and redemptive suffering.[102]

Various authors note the connection of this episode with the oracle of the pagan *prophet* Balaam.[103] Like the Magi, he, too, was a pagan and came from the East. Called by the king of Moab, Balak, to curse the army of Israel, he was able only to pronounce blessings. Among these is the famous messianic prophecy, in which Balaam, on the part of God, announces the coming of a glorious leader in Israel who will conquer all his enemies. This oracle had already been interpreted by the Jews as Messianic: "The oracle of Balaam the son of Beor, the oracle of the man whose eye is opened, the oracle of him who hears the words of God, and knows the knowledge of the Most High, who sees the vision of the Almighty, falling down, but having his eyes uncovered: I see him, but not now; I behold him, but not nigh: a star shall come forth out of Jacob, and a scepter shall rise out of Israel" (Num 24:15-17). The Magi seem to have been aware of this oracle which announced the rising of a star in Jacob/Israel. In Matthew the star guided the Magi, as in Luke the angels guide the shepherds to the child Jesus.

Noteworthy is the fact that in St. Matthew's gospel Mary is addressed with the title "Mother" of the King-Messiah, described in this episode as Redeemer and as salvation and light to the pagans as well as to Israel. Mary is his mother, now shown as closely united with her son. The Magi "found the child *with* Mary his mother." For this reason Stefano Manelli can rightly comment: "This encounter is very significant. Where is Jesus to be found if not in the arms of his Mother? The inseparability of the Mother from the Son in the universal saving mission is here recorded as something logical and permanent."[104] And a bit further on, commenting on an affirmation of G. Segalla, he adds: "In the context of the Church Mary is the one who gathers the peoples of East and West, giving them Jesus, their Redeemer. Mary participates, as Mother, in the dignity of her divine Son, sharing in his sorrows and glories."[105]

---

[102] Cf. *Ibid.*; G. Segalla, *Il Bambino con sua Madre in Matteo 2*, in *Theotokos* 4 (1996) 26ff; Manelli, *All Generations...*, 296.
[103] F. Manns, *Que sait-on de Marie*, 48ff.
[104] Manelli, *All Generations...*, 296.
[105] *Ibid.*

All told, this episode demonstrates that

> the pagans enjoy rights of citizenship in the Church. Nor does St. Matthew hesitate to legitimate this universal opening by describing how the Magi had access to Jesus from his birth. It is Jesus himself who gathers the pagan nations. Jesus himself becomes the Light of the nations; in Jesus is God himself who reveals himself.[106]

Meeting with Elizabeth: Visitation and Magnificat

St. Luke relates how after the Annunciation "Mary arose and went with haste into the hill country, to a town of Judah. And she entered the house of Zechariah and saluted Elizabeth" (Lk 1:39-40). The Angel Gabriel had informed her of the miraculous pregnancy of her cousin. Mary entered her house, where "we find her engaged in a service of charity to her cousin Elizabeth, with whom she remained 'about three months' (1:56) to assist her during the terminal phase of her pregnancy."[107]

The arrival and the presence of Mary in the house of Zechariah, in addition to the precious physical and moral support of her cousin Elizabeth, also brought singular gifts of grace. Mary, in fact, gave to her cousin and to her son the presence of the Messiah, for centuries awaited. To this was linked the outpouring of the Holy Spirit and the gift of messianic joy. It is evident that St. Luke considered the recording in his gospel of this episode known as the "Visitation" very important, because this is a significant moment in the history of salvation, and crucial to knowing and understanding the divine project of salvation.

First, with many exegetes, we note how we are face to face with a "protopentecost,"[108] now investing Elizabeth and the child in her womb, and a little later Zechariah as well (1:67), still later Simeon (2:26ff.) and Anna (cf. 2:38). The Holy Spirit gives himself and acts on a sweeping scale. This detail is particularly relevant, because it shows, above all to Hebrews, that the time of the Messiah has arrived. The prophets had foretold in fact, that the days of the Messiah would see an abundant outpouring of the Spirit of God. Throughout the "account of the hidden

---

[106] F. Manns, *Que sait-on de Marie*, 51.
[107] Benedict XVI, *Deus Caritas Est*, 41.
[108] Laurentin, *The Truth of Christmas*, 99.

life" by Luke we find various references to the Holy Spirit (cf. Lk 1:15, 35, 41, 67; 2:26, 27), who with the arrival of the messianic era acts above all in arousing the spirit of prophecy.[109]

It is thanks to the presence of Mary who is carrying Jesus that the Holy Spirit comes to be poured out in abundance. This is not by chance. Rather it is part of a divine design to employ a woman as Mediatrix of the gifts of grace promised from ancient times. As Eve, by way of the forbidden fruit, procured the spiritual death of Adam and of his descendents, so God desired to re-establish supernatural life to mankind through "the blessed fruit" of the womb of Mary.

In effect, Elizabeth *in a loud voice* blessed and proclaimed Mary and the fruit of her womb blessed, the fruit who is the Savior Lord, Jesus, meaning "God is salvation." "And it came to pass, when Elizabeth heard the greeting of Mary, that the babe in her womb leapt. And Elizabeth was filled with the Holy Spirit, and cried out with a loud voice saying: 'Blessed are you among women and blessed is the fruit of your womb!'" (Lk 1:41-42).[110]

In their reflection on Mary's journey to Ain Karem (a village not far from Jerusalem where Elizabeth resided) a number of exegetes discern a strict parallel with the Old Testament episode involving the transport of the Ark of the Covenant from Gabaa to Jerusalem (2 Sam 6:2-16). The comparison permits the establishment of a strict analogy between Mary and the sacred Ark. The Ark was the visible sign of the invisible, but certain, presence of God in the midst of his people, a presence assuring Israel of divine protection and blessing. Mary is the new sacred Ark, because she carries in herself the sensible, corporal presence of the invisible God, whose birth will bring definitive salvation and redemption

---

[109] Cf. G.C. Bottini, *Introduzione all'opera lucana. Aspetti teologici* (SBF Analecta 35) Jerusalem 1992, 81ff. In addition to that of the Presentation (see Lk 2:36-38) Luke elsewhere in his gospel repeatedly recalls the presence of the Spirit in a number of episodes from the public life of Jesus: 3:21-22; 4:14, 18; 10:21-22; and in the promises of Jesus to his disciples: Lk 11:13; 12:11-12; 24:49; Acts 1:8.

[110] P. Colella observes that the perfect passive participle "blessed" has this meaning: "You have been blessed and will remain such forever." This in effect is the Semitic style for expressing a superlative greater than which none can be conceived: *Tu sei la più benedetta delle donne (Lc 1, 28. 42)*, in *Bibbia e Oriente* 41 (1999) 47ff. Manelli, *All Generations...*, 188, says: "Mary is the only blessed, or the blessed par excellence and exemplar of all blessedness among all women." Cf. also J. Ernst, *Il Vangelo secondo Luca*, Brescia 1985, vol. 1, 111.

not only to Israel, but to all mankind.¹¹¹ Mary is the Ark of the new and eternal Covenant, established by God with man in the blood of his Son.

In this parallelism with 2 Samuel, however, a fundamental difference must be remarked. The ancient Ark, in fact, was a simple object, hence absolutely extraneous to the divine presence, of which it was the symbol, and to its distinctive role of blessing for the people of Israel. Mary, instead, is a living person who carries in herself the living God. She collaborates with her whole self, soul and body, in the realization of the divine design of salvation: will, intelligence, sentiments, thoughts, words, actions, all is accomplished in perfect union with the divine will:

> Another luminous lesson of the "Visitation" narrative is the truth about the salvific-missionary aspect of Mary's journey, above all in the person of Mary *associated* with her Son, *entirely one* with him in the work of redemption. Elizabeth and John, receiving Mary into their house, receive the Messiah Savior, who fills them with joy and the Holy Spirit. Mary thus becomes the first "evangelatrix" of the Kingdom of God in the heart of man. ... The mystery of the Incarnation had just been accomplished in her. Mother and Son are totally one. But why was the Word made flesh? To work the redemption of mankind, bringing the Kingdom of God into the heart of every man. The Redeemer wishes to commence the work at once, by bringing his Kingdom into the heart of his precursor. Mary cooperates, always united and active. She moves; indeed "she hastens." She is the bearer of the Messiah Savior. She has within her the fountain of grace. She is already the "dispensatrix" of grace.¹¹²

Elizabeth, as soon as she heard the greeting of Mary, was filled with the Holy Spirit and by his light recognized Mary as *Mother of her Lord*, declaring herself unworthy to receive her into her house: *kai póthen moi touto hina élthe he méter tou kuríou mou pròs emé*, "And why is this

---

[111] De Fiores, *Maria...*, 301ff; Manelli, *All Generations...*, 183ff; Laurentin, *The Truth of Christmas*, 56-58; 154-159; H. Muñoz, *Beata te che hai creduto*, in *Parola, Spirito e Vita* 6 (1982) 96-98.

[112] Manelli, *All Generations...*, 183-184.

granted me, that the mother of my Lord should come to me?" (Lk 1:43). Elizabeth, writes C. Ghidelli, "considered the effects this visit had on her: she felt herself object of a signal favor on the part of God; indeed she professed herself unworthy of such a visit (cf. 2 Sam 6:9; 24:21)."[113]

To grasp the sense of the expression *"Mother of the Lord,"* it is necessary to examine the meaning of the word *kúrios* (Lord) in reference to Christ. Here it is enough to note that this is a title in the Septuagint that referred to God himself, and is employed to translate the sacred tetragram JHWH. Now, in the first chapter of St. Luke's gospel the term "Lord" appears 17 times, always in reference to God. Its meaning on the lips of Elizabeth can only be this. G. Roschini has already noted quite precisely how in St. Luke "the expression 'Mother of my Lord' is perfectly synonymous with the expression 'Mother of God;'" in fact, "if the 'Lord' about whom Mary (echoed by Elizabeth) speaks is 'God,' it follows that 'God' is the 'Lord' about whom Elizabeth herself had spoken."[114] Further in confirmation of this argument in 2 Sam 6:9 the term Lord is certainly in reference to God. Elizabeth, then, enlightened by the Holy Spirit, is the first to recognize the divinity of the Son of Mary and to proclaim Mary's divine maternity.[115]

The gospel text states that Elizabeth, before speaking these words, which are a profession of faith, "was filled by the Holy Spirit:" *eplésthe pneúatos hagíou* (1:41). Hence, it is the Holy Spirit who aroused in Elizabeth a prophetic spirit permitting her to recognize and exalt the *Mother of her Lord*. And it is always in virtue of the Holy Spirit that Elizabeth blesses Mary and Jesus enclosed in her womb: "Blessed are you among women and blessed is the fruit of your womb" (1:42). Just as the old Simeon who on having received Jesus in his arms exploded in a canticle of praise to God, so, too, Elizabeth experienced joy via the child within her, when Mary arrived with Jesus. "Mary's greeting released the joy of the days of salvation; the long-awaited Messiah had arrived."[116]

---

[113] C. Ghidelli, *Luca* (NVB 35) Rome 1981, 74.
[114] G. Roschini, *La Madre del mio Signore*, in *Miles Immaculatae* 7 (1971) 257.
[115] Cf. John Paul II, *Redemptoris Mater*, n. 13; Manelli, *All Generations...*, 190; G. Aranda Perez, *La Visitación: el arca nuovamente en camino*, in *Ephermerides Mariologicae* 43 (1993) 189-211; Laurentin, *The Truth of Christmas*, 185-187; G. Ferraro, *I racconti dell'infanzia nel Vangelo di Luca*, Naples 1983, 45.
[116] G. Rossé, *Vangelo secondo Luca* (Commenti Spirituali del NT), Rome 2003, 24.

Elizabeth concluded her canticle with a blessing addressed to Mary: "And blessed is she who has believed, because the things promised her by the Lord shall be accomplished" (1:45). This blessing will later be addressed by Jesus himself to all who believe. For them, Mary now becomes the perfect exemplar: "My mother and my brothers are those who hear the word of God and act upon it" (Lk 8:21).[117]

What was the content of Mary's faith at the Annunciation? Fr. Stefano Manelli replies in this way:

> The *mystery of the Most Holy Trinity*: the angel "*sent by God*" (the Father) speaks to her of the Son of God and of the Holy Spirit;
>
> The *mystery of the Incarnation*: the angel proposes to her the conception and birth of the Son of God, by the work of the Holy Spirit;
>
> The *mystery of the redemption*: the angel informs her that the son will be called "Jesus," which means "God saves," because he will be the Savior;
>
> The *mystery of the divine maternity*: the angel tells her that the son to be conceived and born is the Son of God; and
>
> The *mystery of the virginal maternity*: the angel explains to her that she shall conceive virginally, "overshadowed," rendered fruitful by the Holy Spirit.[118]

The same author notes further that even if the faith of Mary was "most sublime and profound,"

> Nonetheless, this affirmation of the fundamental content of the faith of Mary is not a reason for denying that she continued to grow in faith through each of the events in the life and mission of her Son. ... If Mary knew the redemptive plan of God over all, she did not, however, know all the "steps" and "details" of the plan,

---

[117] Cf. *Ibid.*, 24.
[118] Manelli, *All Generations...*, 194-195. Cf. also John Paul II, *Mulieris Dignitatem*, n. 3; AA.VV., *La Trinidat y Maria*, in *Estudios Marianos* 67 (2001) *passim*.

on which precisely ... she continued to "meditate in her heart" via what transpired (Lk 2:19, 51).[119]

The Magnificat (Lk 1:46-55)

After the discourse of Elizabeth, Luke records the canticle of exultation rising from the heart of Mary (1:46-55). Elizabeth praised Mary, Mother of the Lord. Now Mary directs her praise to God, her Savior. Very beautifully, Pope Benedict XVI in the Encyclical *Deus Caritas Est* says that the *Magnificat* is "a portrait as it were of the soul" of Mary (n. 41): a soul who praises God, who thanks him, who knows how to be among the little ones and poor of the Lord among the people of Israel and who praises his mercy and the fidelity of his promises. Mary "celebrates the merciful deeds of God along the course of the history of salvation, which now in the fullness of time find their definitive realization."[120]

The canticle reveals the spiritual dispositions characteristic of the *poor of Yahweh* and of the pious of Israel: "*joy* over the acts of God in history, where he discloses his countenance: merciful, powerful, holy and faithful, *solidarity* with his people (passing from the initial *I* to the final *we*), hope in the realization of the promises made to Abraham."[121]

Mary's canticle, rightly considered the canticle *par excellence* of the New Testament, may be divided into three parts. "The Virgin Mary glorifies the Lord for the works of mercy and power accomplished by him in herself (vv 48-50), in the poor and little ones (vv 51-53), and in the people of Israel (vv. 54-55). In this interpretation the *Magnificat* is above all the canticle of praise and hope of the Chosen People through Mary."[122]

To express the sentiments of praise and thanks in her heart, Mary made use of themes and of words drawn from the Old Testament. The *Magnificat*, in fact, embodies a mosaic of biblical texts, reflecting above all from the canticle of Anna, mother of Samuel, and from the Psalms.[123]

---

[119] Manelli, *All Generations...*, 195.
[120] C. Ghidelli, *Luca*, 75.
[121] De Fiores, *Maria*, 303.
[122] Manelli, *All Generations...*, 198. Cf. also Rossé, *Vangelo secondo Luca*, 24ff; Ghidelli, *Luca*, 75.
[123] De Fiores, *Maria*, 303.

To acknowledge this, however, is not to accept the opinion according to which the author of this canticle is the evangelist himself, who simply places it on the lips of Mary. Based on ingenuous prejudices, this is simply gratuitous. Likewise unconvincing is the opinion that the canticle finds its origin in the first Christian communities and then was employed to describe the sentiments of Mary. F. Manns, a highly respected student of Judaism, rightly says: "Certain exegetes want to attribute the paternity of this song to the author of the third gospel, under the pretext that Mary, a woman, could not have enjoyed the knowledge of the Scriptures as this was expounded in the synagogues. Such a view ignores the ancient rabbinic texts which permitted women to attend the synagogues."[124]

Mary proclaims God's greatness: "My soul magnifies the Lord." In the Old Testament the majesty of God was revealed above all in his interventions on behalf of his people Israel, by fighting at their side to save them from their enemies and to assist them in the conquest of the land he had promised them. This greatness of God "now reaches its high point in the womb of Mary: he reveals himself all-powerful, not as the victorious warrior, but through the mystery of the virginal conception. And the power of God is inseparable from his mercy, indeed it is his mercy in operation."[125]

The joy filling Mary is the same as that which filled the psalmist: "But my soul shall rejoice in the Lord, it shall rejoice because of his help" (Ps 34:9).[126] Mary also calls God her *Savior*, a term which had already entered the vocabulary of piety. With this expression Mary certainly did not intend to speak of salvation in the sense of liberation from sin, which she had not contracted. "The salvation conferred on Mary is not to be understood negatively, viz., liberation of Mary from evil, but positively as the actuation in her 'of great things.'"[127]

---

[124] F. Manns, *Que sait-on de Marie*, 83ff; for a more in-depth analysis cf. above all Manelli, *All Generations...*, 198-206. Manns continues, "The synagogues of the first century were rectangular halls with a single entry. The women's synagogue was only introduced in the fourth century, A.D. Mary, while attending the synagogue, could easily have memorized the canticle of Anna and the Psalms. Hence, we may speak of the Magnificat as a prayer by Mary." However, this should never be interpreted as replacing the inspired origin of the Magnificat.

[125] Rossé, *Vangelo secondo Luca*, 25.

[126] *He dè psyché mou agalliásetai epí to kyrío tephthésetai epì to sterío autou.*

[127] J. Leal, *El Evangelio de la infancia* (BAC 207), Madrid 1961, 121.

Mary forms part of the *poor* of Yahweh. This is why she says that the Lord has looked upon her *tapeinosis*, i.e., her poverty (or lowliness), that poverty of spirit which already makes one a possessor of the Kingdom of heaven, as one day Jesus will say while proclaiming the evangelical beatitudes:[128]

> Beginning with v. 50, the thought ceases to deal solely with the personal experience of Mary to assume a broader context. The divine deeds on behalf of the "poor of Yahweh" are praised, those poor of the community who instead of indulging violence trust in God and who now accept the Messiah about to be born: he will be at the origin of the great reversal of fortune awaited in messianic times. By his hand the mighty will be brought low and the humble exalted. Nothing of militarism here. With the coming of Jesus an event is initiated which finds in the beatitudes its manifesto, in the Resurrection its accomplishment, in the Church its realization and hope. ...
>
> With the final verses (54-55), attention is directed to the history of Israel. The reversal of fortune proclaimed by Mary is a testimonial to the faithfulness of God to his promises made to Abraham, father of the Chosen People. The history of Israel is dominated by the fidelity of JHWH to the covenant, by his love of preference for the poor, the disinherited, of whom Mary is the advocate and comforter.[129]

Birth and Circumcision of Jesus Christ (Lk 2:1-21)

Whereas St. Matthew wrote his gospel above all for Jews, St. Luke addresses all men. Hence, he underscores heavily the universal character of salvation, offered not only to Israel, but to all the nations. For this reason this evangelist is careful to record a number of historical details which permit us to situate the events he narrates within universal history.

---

[128] Cf. F. Manns, *Que sait-on de Marie*, 83.
[129] Rossé, *Vangelo secondo Luca*, 25.

In accord with this approach, when he recounts the episode of the birth of Jesus, he places it within the context of profane history, precisely when Augustus was Roman emperor, when Quirinus was governor of the Roman province of Syria. Thus, St. Luke shows how "the birth of the Messiah corresponds to the expectations, not only of the Chosen People, but of all mankind."[130]

The historical occasion bringing Mary to Bethlehem, precisely when she was about to bring her pregnancy to term, was a census decreed by the emperor. A providential occasion, for it permitted the realization of the ancient prophecies concerning Bethlehem as place of birth of the future Messiah (cf. Mic 5:2). Census regulations required that every male citizen be registered in the city of origin of his ancestors. Joseph was of the house and family of David; hence he had to register in Bethlehem. This accent repeatedly placed on the Davidic descent of Joseph by way of the refrain: "of the house and family of David," is a way of accenting the Davidic descent of Jesus. Matthew and Luke as evangelists are at one in making plain that Jesus is the promised Davidic Messiah.[131] Joseph, then, is the person who assures from a *legal* point of view that Jesus is an heir of David, therefore who can very well be the Davidic Messiah foretold and awaited (cf. 2 Sam 7). Mary, however, is the person who assures that Davidic descent *according to the flesh* (cf. Rom 1:3).[132]

The text of Lk 2:5 ("to register, *together with Mary*, his espoused wife") clearly supposes that Mary as well, notwithstanding the advanced state of pregnancy, traveled with Joseph in order to register. Precisely because already married, she was obliged to be present with her husband at the office of registrations.[133] The decree of Augustus was thus put at the service of the history of salvation. Once again God showed himself the Lord of history and of man, who guides history according to the dispositions of the divine will.[134]

One should take note here how St. Luke says that Joseph went to Bethlehem "together with Mary, his *espoused wife*" (2:5). The word used here to indicate Mary is the same used by Matthew 1:18 and by

---

[130] G. Rossé, *Vangelo secondo Luca*, 29; J. Ernst, *Il Vangelo secondo Luca*, 135.
[131] Cf. C. Ghidelli, *Luca* (NVB 35) Rome 1981, 88.
[132] Manelli, *All Generations…*, 248, in particular note 12.
[133] *Ibid.*, 246; C. Ghidelli, *Luca*, 88.
[134] Cf. G. Rossé, *Vangelo secondo Luca*, 29; Manelli, *All Generations…*, 245; R. Laurentin, *The Truth of Christmas*, 172; G. Ferraro, *I racconti dell'infanzia*, 95.

Luke 1:27: *emnesteuméne*, or "betrothed," "fiancée." However, by this time cohabitation had begun for some time, as the text of Matthew 1:24 clearly indicates. Here the evangelist probably makes an implicit reference to the virginal conception of Jesus by the working of the Holy Spirit. In this sense, one may say that the term here parallels the use made of it in Matthew 1:25, where after the dream with the angel, Joseph is said to have taken Mary as his wife, "whom he did not know till she had brought forth her first-born son."[135]

At Bethlehem, writes St. Luke, "And while they were there, the time came for her to be delivered. And she gave birth to her first-born son and wrapped him in swaddling cloths, and laid him in a manger, because there was no place for them in the inn" (2:6-7) The birth of Jesus in Bethlehem is an indisputable historical fact in virtue of the overwhelming abundance of ancient literary testimonials which we possess. It suffices to recall merely the unanimity of the gospels and apocryphal literature, all in accord on this point, notwithstanding their origin at different times and in different places.[136]

Jesus, although the long-awaited Messiah, was born in poverty, so overturning the hierarchy of values among men.[137] He was born in a manger, because "there was no room for them in the inn." Joseph and Mary were unable to find appropriate arrangements, probably because of overflowing crowds of registrants. Bethlehem for all practical purposes was only a more or less large village.[138] Another factor should be kept in mind, one bearing on the particular condition of Mary, almost at the point of giving birth, hence in need of a place of solitude and tranquility. They found this, as one can deduce from the presence of a manger, in a cave equipped as a stall for animals.

---

[135] Laurentin, *The Truth of Christmas*, 360 (It. Ed.) writes: "'Until' does not prejudice what comes after, but according to Semitic usage only indicates the term or limit of interest. Where 2 Sam 6:23 says that Mikal did not have children 'until she died,' it is obviously not meant that she bore children after death."; Manelli, *All Generations...*, 244ff.

[136] Manelli, *All Generations....*, 247; J. Daniélou, *The Infancy Narratives*, New York 1968, 541; C. Perrot, *Les récits d'enfance dans Haggada antérieure au IIe siècle de notre ère*, in *Recherches de Science Religieuse* 55 (1967) 510ff; A. Ory, *Come riscoprire la verità storica dei vangeli*, 82-91.

[137] Cf. Rossé, *Vangelo secondo Luca*, 29.

[138] According to G. Leopardi, at the time of the slaughter of the innocents Bethlehem and its surroundings counted about 2,000 inhabitants: *L'infanzia di Gesú*, 85.

Jesus is called "firstborn" of Mary. So doing St. Luke wishes to indicate that as such Jesus has acquired all the privileges proper to the firstborn, in particular consecration to God (cf. Ex 13:1-16; 34:19; Num 3:12ff.; 18:15).[139] Shortly after, in fact, the evangelist narrates the episode of the presentation of Jesus in the Temple, where he is offered, consecrated to the Lord.[140]

At the same moment, the Virgin Mary exercises her duties toward Jesus as mother: "She wrapped him in swaddling cloths and laid him in a manger" (Lk 2:7). Fr. Manelli comments:

> The parturition was one in which the woman did everything by herself, alone. She took the child, wrapped him in swaddling clothes, and laid him in a poor manger. There is no shadow of labor or pain in this scene so gentle and maternal. Tradition has rightly read therein the mystery of the joyful, virginal birth of him who had come to bring into the world *"superabundant joy"* (Jn 15:11). From this moment, Mary was no longer the "pregnant Virgin," but the "Virgin Mother" who unites and carries in herself the two seals of glory: that of perpetual virginity and of divine maternity.[141]

In the Gospel of St. Luke as well, the birth of Christ was accompanied by an extraordinary event. In Matthew, the Magi arrive, guided by a star to the very place where the babe was to be found (Mt 2:1-11). In Luke, instead, a choir of angels, in the middle of the night, appears to a group of shepherds in the vicinity of Bethlehem, to announce to them the birth "of a Savior, who is Christ the Lord" (Lk 2:11). The shepherds, filled with joy "said to one another: 'Let us go over to Bethlehem, and see this thing that has come to pass, which the Lord has made known to us.' Then, without delay, they went and found Mary and Joseph and

---

[139] Rossé, *Vangelo secondo Luca*, 29. Leopardi, *L'infanzia di Gesú*, 207; Manelli, *All Generations...*, 251 s.

[140] Ghidelli, *Luca*, 88.

[141] Manelli, *All Generations...*, 252 s. Of special importance are the remarks of Pope John Paul II in Capua for the sixteenth centenary of the Council of Capua in *Convegno internazionale di studio per il XVI centenario del Concilio di Capua*, Rome 1993, 632, cited by Manelli. Cf. also P.D. Fehlner, *Virgin Mother, the Great Sign*, Washington NJ 1993.

the babe lying in a manger" (2:15ff.). Contrary to the Jewish mentality and custom of giving great precedence to the husband, and significantly, here Mary is mentioned first. This detail also serves the evangelist to remind us of the virginal conception of Jesus, in which Mary is the lone human protagonist.[142]

St. Luke also records how the shepherds "when they had seen, they understood what had been told them concerning this child. And all who heard marveled at the things told them by the shepherds. But Mary kept in mind all these things, pondering them in her heart" (Lk 2:17-19).

Once more the evangelist sets in relief the figure of Mary. Here, as later on another occasion (2:51), he describes her contemplative dispositions. Mary's in effect were those of a person of genuine wisdom (philosopher), who precisely kept the word of God in her heart, continually reflecting on it, making it her daily nourishment, her guide and strength (cf. Sir 50:27-29).[143] "Mary is the model of the contemplative soul, capable of silent listening and recollected meditation upon the words and events of faith that ought always to be more deeply penetrated."[144] St. Luke uses the term *rhémata*, meaning things, both events and words, concerning Jesus. All this, then, is object of Mary's contemplation. The contemplation of Mary, however, as G. Rossé insists, is an *active* approach:

> Mary does not merely guard the words and events passively so as to be able to recall them later, but in such wise as to penetrate their meaning. This is a process typical of a faith which grows and progresses in the understanding of the divine mystery. Further, Mary "interprets in her heart" (or better "meditates"). She engages all her intellectual energy and her will (heart) to penetrate events and words which surpass her, in such wise as to grasp them ever more profoundly with the help of grace.[145]

---

[142] Cf. Manelli, *All Generations...*, 262ff; Ernst, *Il Vangelo secondo Luca*, 150.
[143] Cf. A. Serra, *Sapienza e contemplazione di Maria secondo Luca 2, 19. 51*, Rome 1982; De Fiores, *Maria*, 307.
[144] Cf. Manelli, *All Generations...*, 263.
[145] Rossé, *Vangelo secondo Luca* 31ff.

These recollections of Luke are at the same time a veiled indication of the primary source of his account of the infancy of Christ.[146]

Eight days after the birth of a male child, Jewish law prescribed the rite of circumcision and of the conferral of a name. St. Luke recounts that Mary and Joseph fulfilled this rite (cf. 2:21). For the Jews, the rite of circumcision held fundamental importance, because by means of it the babe became part of the Chosen People and sharer in the covenant established by God with Abraham and Moses. Thus the Jew bore in his body a concrete sign of his belonging to the Lord God and, as it were, an assurance of participating in the blessings promised to Israel.[147]

St. Luke, however, puts the accent rather on the imposition of the name Jesus, indicated by the Angel Gabriel to the Mother on the day of the Annunciation (cf. Lk 1:31; 2:21). If the evangelist now recalls again that the name was indicated at the time of the divine message, this is because he wishes to underscore how it is a name from on high, from God, a sign of a singular divine project, summarized by this name which St. Matthew candidly explains: "She shall bring forth a son, and thou shalt call his name Jesus; for he shall save his people from their sins" (Mt 1:21).[148]

Jesus, then, received the name indicating:

> the ontological and dynamic constitution of his personality. Jesus is the proper name of the Word incarnate, and means *"the Lord is salvation."* It is composed of two constituent elements, one pertaining to his essence (Lord) and the other to his mission (salvation).[149]

The Presentation of Jesus in the Temple (Lk 2:22-40)

After forty days the child Jesus was taken to the Temple in Jerusalem by Mary and Joseph, there to fulfill the precepts of the Law regarding the purification of the mother and the ransom of the firstborn. Pope Benedict XVI, in a homily for the liturgical feast of the Presentation of Jesus in the Temple and for the Day of Consecrated Life, February 2, 2006, underscored how Christ had become Mediator between God and

---

[146] Cf. G. Ferraro, *I racconti dell'infanzia*, 133; Manelli, *All Generations…*, 263.
[147] Cf. Ghidelli, *Luca*, 79; Stramare, *Vangelo dei Misteri*, 163-178.
[148] Cf. Rossé, *Vangelo secondo Luca*, 32; Ghidelli, *Luca*, 95.
[149] Cf. Manelli, *All Generations…*, 266-267.

man when he trod the path of obedience, pushed to its extreme limits (cf. Heb 5:7-9). The Pope then added that the Virgin Mary was in a unique way united with him, not only in the mystery of the Incarnation, but in that of the redemption as well, by way of a loving and sorrowful participation in his death and Resurrection. Here is how the Holy Father, beginning with the gospel episode of the Presentation, explains this singular role of Mary:

> The first person associated with Christ on the path of obedience, of proven faith and of sorrow shared, is his mother Mary. The gospel text reveals this in the act of offering her Son: an unconditional sacrifice engaging her in her own person. Mary is Mother of him who is "the glory of his people Israel" and "a light of revelation for the nations," but also of him who is "a sign of contradiction" as well (cf. Lk 2:32, 34). And she, too, in her immaculate soul, must be pierced by the sword of sorrow, thus showing how her role in the history of salvation is not finished with the mystery of the Incarnation, but is consummated in the loving and sorrowful sharing in the death and Resurrection of her Son. Carrying her Son to Jerusalem, the Virgin Mother offers him to God as the true Lamb who takes away the sins of the world; she hands him to Simeon and Anna as an annunciation of redemption; she presents him to all as light for a secure journey on the path of truth and love.

From the literary point of view, and that of content, the account of the Presentation in the Temple is intimately linked with the general structure of Luke's "accounts of the hidden life" (chapters 1-2). This pericope encloses two particularly significant oracles: the *Nunc dimittis* (2:29-32), the canticle with which Simeon accepts the child Jesus in the Temple, and the prophecy which he himself addresses to the Mother of Jesus (2:34-35). This last enjoys a special relevance to Mary, in so far as it is formally addressed to her and regards her in person. As can be gathered from the structure of the narrative, the Mariological aspect is united within the Christological one implied by the context, on which the Mariological substantially depends.

One should underline here the strong link, structure-wise, existing between the pericope of Lk 2:34-35, and the entire account of the Presentation of Jesus in the Temple (Lk 2:22-40), a factor permitting us to link the pericope content-wise as well with the same account. This linking, together with the words of Anna "who spoke of him to all who were awaiting the redemption of Jerusalem" (v. 38), reveals the close union between the offering of the child Jesus by his parents and the words with which Simeon announces his identity (vv. 29-32) and the destiny of this babe (vv. 34c-35).

Further, the unity of this pericope makes possible the discovery of the profound significance of the spatial-temporal ambient in which the episode is situated. Everything occurs within the holy city of Jerusalem (which in Luke has special meaning), in the area of the Temple and in the context of certain sacred rites: the purification of the Mother, the presentation of the firstborn and his ransom. Jesus is offered to God. In addition, the manner in which his redemptive offering will be consummated is indicated: by way of contradiction. Finally, the formal inclusion twice of the term *fulfillment* (2:22, 39) compels us to consider the episode as an actuation of the divine plan of salvation.

All this, then, helps us to gather the pregnant sense of the words regarding Mary in the prophecy of Simeon. For Luke such a reference to the destiny of Mary is not simply the description of an agonizing state of mind vis-à-vis the sufferings of her Son, a sentiment perfectly understandable in a mother's heart. The text affirms much more, even if in a manner quite generic. We are face to face with the preview or anticipated announcement of her mission to be united in and collaborator with, by means of the sword to pierce her heart, the mission of her Son, *sign of contradiction*, in *fulfillment* of the divine project of salvation.

What Simeon announces is a prophecy concerning the destiny of Christ, understood as a preview or "annunciation," even if generically outlined, of the future events regarding him. If it is such, and indeed it is, then this prophecy must be read in the light of its fulfillment. That consummation is to be recognized only in the mystery of the saving Passion, death and Resurrection of Christ, and in the collaboration, compassion and sharing of Mary, his Mother, in this mystery, clearly traced out in the whole of Divine Revelation.

The words of Simeon, then, in Lk 2:35c, understood in the context of his entire prophecy (2:34-35) and in the still broader context of the Presentation (2:22-40), in some way announce the participation of Mary in the saving work of her Son. In fact, the pericope attributes a special saving significance to the presence of Mary. The evangelist, directly recording Mary's role within the context of the mystery of Jesus' Presentation in the Temple, shows that he acknowledges her participation in the event important, all the more so when we observe how her participation extends far beyond the father's part.

This saving significance of the presence of Mary goes far beyond this single episode and accompanies the entire existence and mission of Christ as Savior. Indeed, Mary is here addressed with words foretelling the painful destiny of her Son and the participation of his Mother in his saving mission by way of suffering, symbolized by the sword to transpierce her soul. All this is in view of the revelation of hearts, that is, of their choice to be for or against the Messiah Redeemer.

In regard to verse 35a from a narrative point of view, the prophecy concerning the future of the babe is a conversation addressed to the Mother. Simeon, then, directly speaks to her in the second person. This demonstrates how the destiny of the Son determines that of the Mother as well.

The best translation of verse 35a is as follows: "And a sword will also pierce your very soul." The conjunction "also" joins the destiny of Mary to that of her Son. It serves to indicate that if Jesus is destined to be "a sign of contradiction," so his Mother, Mary, will have a destiny of suffering, symbolized by the sword which will transpierce her soul.

Mary is here understood in the personal sense (one person only) rather than collective (including others with her), precisely in view of the double pronoun, viz., the emphatic mode, *sou ... autes: your own soul*, or *soul of you yourself*, within which Simeon expressly addresses Mary as Mother of Jesus (cf. also 2:34b). His prophecy is directed exclusively to her and not to Joseph, present at the scene and together with Mary, blessed by Simeon in the verse immediately preceding (cf. 2:34a: "said to them"), and who in the rite of presentation and of ransom of the firstborn, according to the regulations of the Temple, had the main part.

The term *rhomphaía, sword*, of Lk 2:35a, is to be understood without doubt in the symbolic sense.[150] In the Old Testament, the more common meaning of the word is that of instrument which provokes physical, real, violent, tragic death.[151] Further, the image of the sword evokes struggle, war, spilling of blood; it suggests an arm which inflicts death-dealing suffering.[152] In the metaphorical sense, it indicates a mortal suffering which strikes and wounds the most intimate part of man. In Lk 2:35a the term is united to *tèn psychèn dieleúsetai: will pierce your soul*. The verb denotes the action of the sword, which is to pierce, to pass from part to part; the complement indicates the object to which the action of the sword is directed, namely the soul of Mary. The sword which pierces the soul of Mary indicates, then, the mortal suffering which strikes the depths of Mary's soul, a terrible sorrow, like that provoked by a sword which wounds as it passes, which Mary herself must bear.[153] Simeon, as he foretells the future destiny of Jesus *qua* Messiah, also pre-announces the destiny of Mary, Mother of the Messiah. If on the one hand the Son will not be accepted by many, if there are about him "thoughts" dividing Israel, on the other hand his Mother's soul will be pierced by a sword. By means of this sword and of this suffering, his Mother is all the more one with this destiny and mission of her Son who will find struggle, contestation, opposition about him, until enduring in the end the "contradiction" of death on the Cross (Heb 12:3). All this "that the thoughts of many hearts might be revealed" (Lk 2:35b).

The image of the sword, and therefore of suffering, whereby Mary is associated with her Son, is perfectly in accord with the entire context of the pericope of the Presentation in the Temple in which sacrifice, ransom, purification, victim, presentation of the offering, redemption is mentioned.[154] The sacrificial context is equally present in the immediate

---

[150] Cf. H. Schürmann, *Il Vangelo di Luca. Parte prima* (CTNT III/1) Brescia 1983, 255.
[151] Cf. Gen 27:40; 31:26; Lev 26:6; Deut 32:25; Josh 5:13; Judg 7:14; Is 1:20; Jer 2:30; Ezek 5:1ff.
[152] Cf. Ex 5:21; 32:27; Num 31:8; Hos 7:16; 11:6; 14:1; Amos 4:10; 7:9, 11; 9:1, 4, 10; Nahum 2:13; 3:3, 15; Zeph 2:12; Hag 1:11; Zech 13:7. Cf. S. Garfolo, *Tuam ipsius animam pertransibit gladius (Lc 2, 35)*, in *Maria in Sacra Scriptura* IV, Rome 1967, 176; A. Feuillet, *Jesus and His Mother*, Still River, MA, 1984, 51.
[153] Cf. W. Michaelis, *rhomphaía*, in GLNT, XI, 995.
[154] Cf. Stefano Manelli, *Mary Coredemptrix in Sacred Scripture*, in *Mary Coredemptrix, Mediatrix, Advocate. Theological Foundations II*, Santa Barbara, CA, 1997, 88. Cf.

context of the pericope of 2:34-35. The mission of Christ, indeed, Christ himself, will be "contradicted," will be the object "of contradiction" and will not be accepted by many, will meet rejection and opposition. Mary as Mother of Christ is directly revealed within the destiny of her "contradicted" Son, with whom she shares the suffering and in whose mission she will participate according to a specific role, that of Mother of the Messiah. For this reason, her suffering will be personal and unique. It is not simply a question here of natural suffering, typical of every mother who endures pain on seeing the destiny of a son frustrated. Mary suffers as "Mother of the Christ," therefore suffering because of the rejection of *the Christ* on the part of men. This suffering, prophesized by Simeon to Mary, is not limited, then, to one particular moment, but assumes dimensions far vaster and extending to her entire life. Every rejection endured by Christ will pierce her mother's heart. This suffering clearly finds its high point on Calvary, when Christ is crucified and dies.[155]

The Finding of Jesus in the Temple (Lk 2:41-52)

This episode in St. Luke closes the account of Christ's infancy. It touches the high point, Christologically speaking, when Jesus reveals his identity as Son of the Father. At root this is properly the scope of the entire revelation of the New Testament: the affirmation that Jesus is the only-begotten Son of God.[156]

The episode can be divided into three parts: the *going up* to Jerusalem on the occasion of the Passover; the dialogue between Jesus and his Mother, with the *revelation* of the identity of Jesus and the response/reflection of his Mother; the *departure* and return to Nazareth, where Jesus will live in obedience to his parents.[157]

---

also Gallus, *De sensu verborum*, 230.

[155] Cf. Schürmann, *Il Vangelo di Luca*, 256; De Fiores, *Maria*, 305. Both Paul VI in *Marialis Cultus*, n. 20, and John Paul II in *Redemptoris Mater*, n. 16, have commented on this episode of the Presentation, effectively stressing (without the title) the coredemptive doctrine found there. In particular John Paul II has stressed the character of this episode as a "second annunciation." Whereas the first centered on the Incarnation and the role of Mary as Virgin Mother, the second focuses on the redemptive sacrifice and Mary's active part therein.

[156] Manelli, *All Generations...*, 313ff; De Fiores, *Maria*, 305; G. Ferraro, *I racconti dell'infanzia nel Vangelo di Luca*, Naples 1983, 172. 180; Ghidelli, *Luca*, 105.

[157] De Fiores, *Maria*, 305.

In the first part we are told how the 12-year-old Jesus went up with his parents to Jerusalem for the annual celebration of the Paschal Feast, and how he remained in the Temple unbeknownst to his parents, who departed for Nazareth and after three days of journey became aware that the boy was not with the caravan. They then returned to Jerusalem where they found him in the Temple, in the midst of the doctors of the Law, "not as a disciple, but as a master of wisdom: not sitting at their feet, but in their midst arousing the wonder of all (v. 47) and then the amazement of his parents (v. 48)."[158]

This occasions the dialogue between Mary and Jesus: the Mother manifests her profound sorrow, the anguish of herself[159] and of Joseph when they became aware of his absence. Jesus on his part replied with a choice of words in many ways full of mystery. He openly manifested his true identity as Son, not of Joseph, but of God the Father, in whose house, the Temple, he found himself.[160] In effect, many authors observe that the episode is a clear reference to these facts. De Fiores writes that "the loss/finding of Jesus in the Temple does not seem to be a simple episode, nor is it mere whimsy, but 'an act pregnant with typological meaning.'[161] The actions and words of Jesus are a prophecy of his future Passion and Resurrection."[162] Fr. Manelli is more precise:

> His words and stay in Jerusalem have a prophetic value, projected toward the future, in the sense that he will go to dwell in the house of his Father, of which the material temple is merely a symbol, passing via the three days of his redemptive Passion and death at the end of his earthly sojourn.[163]

---

[158] *Ibid.*, 306; cf. Manelli, *All Generations...*, 317.
[159] Some exegetes underscore how this anxiety is for Mary an anticipation of what she will experience during the days of the Passion and death of Jesus, who will remain in the tomb three days. Thus, F. Manns, *Heureuse es-tu*, 92. Also S. Garofalo, *La Madonna nella Bibbia*, Milan 1958, 128; Manelli, *All Generations...*, 325.
[160] Manelli, *All Generations...*, 325; Ferraro, *I racconti dell'infanzia*, 177.
[161] R. Laurentin, *¿Que enseña sobre Maria el hallazgo de Jesús en el templo?*, in *Maria del evangelio. Las primeras generaciones cristianas hablan de María*, Madrid 1994, 220.
[162] De Fiores, *Maria*, 306.
[163] Manelli, *All Generations...*, 321.

Jesus returned with them to Nazareth and remained there, obedient to his parents and growing "in wisdom, age and grace" (2:52). Here, once again, the evangelist accents the contemplative and sapiential dispositions of Mary, who "kept all these things in her heart" (2:51). The heart is the interior, central nucleus of the person. There Mary kept, i.e., actively reflected on, the words and events regarding her Son, becoming thus the model of contemplatives and of whoever devotes himself to the pursuit of theological knowledge and wisdom.[164]

Mary in the Accounts of the Public Life of Jesus

The Marriage Feast at Cana (Jn 2:1-11)

Jesus decided to leave Bethany where he had been staying and where John was baptizing, and return to Galilee (Jn 1:43). The evangelist writes that "on the third day a marriage took place at Cana of Galilee, and the mother of Jesus was there. Now Jesus too was invited to the marriage, and also his disciples" (2:1-2). These words constitute the immediate context of the episode of Jesus' first miracle. They situate it in a very precise place and at a very exact time, indicating as well the chief personalities whom the evangelist wishes to set in relief: Jesus, his Mother and the disciples.

The importance of this first miracle worked by Jesus is noted by the evangelist at the conclusion of the account, when he writes: "This first of his signs Jesus worked at Cana of Galilee; and he manifested his glory, and his disciples believed in him" (2:11). In this context the figure of Mary occupies front stage. She appears indeed as the one who intervenes with her Son to initiate the revelation of his messianic identity. Through her intervention with Jesus and her sage directives to the servants, she guided the working of the miracle by which her Son publicly initiated the work of salvation.

As verse one indicates, Mary is called "mother of Jesus." This is a gracious title of honor, concentrating attention on the role to be played by Mary in relation to Jesus: she is the Mother of him who is the Son of God, the Mother of the Word incarnate. This title, then, unveils the

---

[164] De Fiores, *Maria*, 307; Ferraro, *I racconti dell'infanzia*, 197ff; Manelli, *All Generations...*, 326.

singular role played by Mary in the history of salvation.[165] This role is one which in the episode of Cana is given summary definition.

St. John relates that with the unforeseen shortage of wine the Mother of Jesus intervened with her Son, to have him resolve the embarrassing situation, which had it continued would have deeply humiliated the two newlyweds. Mary addressed Jesus with a very simple observation: "They have no wine" (2:3). Often John the Evangelist tacitly invites his readers to go beyond the strictly literal meaning of the facts he narrates. Here at Cana Jesus' miracle is a sign of something far more profound. Mary is here presented as someone who asks the help of her divine Son, of the Word incarnate of the Father, through whom the entire world was created. She asks help, not for herself, but for mankind in need of an intervention from on high. Mary "is ever the one who presents our needs to God. This she does with a minimum of words, without adding anything superfluous. This is the essence of mediation. This is direct intercession—one may say 'calculated'—for a precise end."[166]

Mary requests of her Son a miraculous intervention. From the assurance in her words: "They have no wine. ... Do whatever he tells you" (2:3, 5), one can deduce what she expected.[167] The reply of Jesus: "Woman, what is this to you and to me?" (2:4), might seem to indicate, if we take an oft used formulary, both in the Old and New Testament as model, a certain surprise and divergence of views. Nonetheless, this remains an enigmatic phrase, to be interpreted each time as used in its context. In John 2:4 it is not to be understood as though Jesus wanted to distance himself from his Mother's request, treating her as someone barely known. De Fiores correctly states: "The theory that this occasions a distancing and alienation between Jesus and Mary is refuted by the fact that the Son does intervene as requested by his Mother and that after the event they go together to live in Capernaum."[168] Realistically, one must hold that between Mother and Son there exists a higher level of mutual understanding.[169]

---

[165] De la Potterie, MMC, 69-70.
[166] Manelli, *All Generations…*, 331.
[167] Cf. *Ibid.*, 331; C. Spicq, *Il primo miracolo di Gesù dovuto a sua Madre (Gv 2, 1-11)*, in *Sacra Doctrina* 18 (1973) 125-144; U. Vanni, *Maria e l'incarnazione nell'esperienza della chiesa giovannea*, in *Theotokos* 3 (1995) 312; De Fiores, *Maria*, 2311ff.
[168] De Fiores, *Ibid.*
[169] Thus Manelli, *All Generations…*, 332-335.

To this first enigmatic phrase Jesus added another, equally enigmatic: "My hour has not yet come." The hour of which he speaks is the "hour set to begin his activity as Messiah-wonderworker, thus revealing his glory during the redemptive mission culminating finally in the *hour* of Calvary."[170]

Jesus, nonetheless, agrees to do what his Mother asked. She knew quite well he would, and for this reason immediately said to the servants: "Do whatever he tells you to do" (2:5). In this way Mary "determines a crucial step or turn in the execution of the divine plan of salvation," as she had earlier at Nazareth when she gave her *fiat* to that divine plan announced to her by the Angel Gabriel.[171] Hence:

> the reply of the Lord seems to indicate that although the divine plan had not originally intended that Jesus intervene to resolve an embarrassment arising during a wedding, merely the request of Mary Most Holy persuaded Christ to provide for the need. It is also possible to surmise, however, that the divine plan envisioned that Jesus would work this miracle through the intercession of his Mother. In any event, it was God's will that the revelation of the New Testament include this fundamental teaching: the Most Holy Virgin is so powerful that God will always attend to all petitions which reach him through the mediation of Mary. For just such a reason Christian piety, with theological exactitude, has given Our Lady the title "omnipotence at prayer."[172]

The symbolism behind the episode of Cana is very rich. The water turned by Jesus into wine symbolizes the Law, while the new wine is the gospel proclaimed by Christ. The water served for the *purification of the Jews*. Jesus changed it into the wine of the New Law, the law of charity, which purifies and transforms believers.[173] The servants fill the water-jars "to the brim." Even this detail has a deeper sense, indicating "the superabundance of blessings brought by the redemption and, at the

---

[170] *Ibid.*, 335ff.
[171] *Ibid.*, 336.
[172] *The Navarre Bible. St. John's Gospel*, Dublin 1987, 62.
[173] Cf. De la Potterie, MMC, 192.

same time, signals the extreme care of the servants in obeying Jesus."[174] So, too, the excellent quality of the wine offered by Christ is an index of his supreme generosity in working the redemption of the world. The wedding feast as context of the miracle symbolizes the messianic nuptials between God and mankind.[175] There is also a transposition involving the spouses. "If Jesus, in fact, is the divine *Groom* of the new people of God, symbolized in the small group of first disciples, how is Mary's role and position to be understood? Hers is certainly the role of mediation, as already indicated. But there is something more and different. Here Mary is both Bride and Mother. She is Bride of the Word incarnate, Mother of the Church."[176] Mary, in fact, addressed with the title *woman* by Jesus, is not only Mediatrix between Jesus and men, but in the context of the New Covenant is also associate of the Messiah, as *New Eve* aside the *New Adam*. Also rich in meaning is the textual significance of the term *"woman,"* which connects Mary, the *"Woman of Cana,"* with the *"Woman of Genesis"* (cf. Gen 3:15), the *"Woman of Galatians"* (Gal 4:4), the *"Woman of Calvary"* (Jn 19:25-27), and the *"Woman of Revelation"* (Rev 12:1).

At the Foot of the Cross (Jn 19:25-27)

John is the only evangelist to record the presence of Mary, the Mother of Jesus, at the foot of the Cross of her Son. He reports her standing, a position, however, not connoting a cold insensitivity, but compassion and intimate sharing of the suffering of him who for our salvation became a *curse*, as St. Paul tells us (Gal 3:13). Nor could it be otherwise. Mary, at the foot of the Cross, suffered as any mother would have on seeing her Son so treated. Yet she suffered still more, because she knew who her Son really was, the eternal Word, God from God. She knew as well how he had taught the way to salvation, and how sensitive he was. For the mission of Mary was far greater, and her suffering went far beyond, a mere human sentiment.

The essential content of this passage in John's gospel is the *spiritual, universal motherhood of Mary*. On Calvary, at

---

[174] *The Navarre Bible. St. John's Gospel*, 63.
[175] Cf. A. Feuillet, *The Hour of Jesus and the Miracle of Cana*, in *Johannine Studies*, New York, 1973, 26.
[176] Cf. Manelli, *All Generations...*, 344ff; De la Potterie, MMC, 205-206.

the foot of the Cross, Mary's divine motherhood, with the "pangs" of a most painful childbirth, is shown to extend to all the redeemed, brothers of Christ *"the firstborn"* (Rom 8:29).[177]

One should note that there were present at the foot of the Cross other persons. Nonetheless, the evangelist is interested only in the pair, Mother of Jesus-disciple whom Jesus loved.[178] Jesus is about to die, exhausted by uncountable sufferings. Before breathing his last, he turns to his Mother, saying: "Woman, behold, your son!" (19:26). The son whom Mary acquires at the foot of the Cross is John, the beloved disciple of Jesus. To this son Jesus immediately turns and says: "Behold, your mother!" (19:27). These words are effectively a testament of Jesus, fruit of his love pressed to its utmost limits (Jn 13:1). With these two the divine plan of salvation is brought to its conclusion, as can be deduced from the next verse, where the evangelist affirms: "After this Jesus, knowing that all things had been accomplished...." Hence, the entrustment of the disciple to Mary and of Mary to the disciple was a part of the plan of redemption[179] and obliges us to interpret the episode in a profounder sense.

This final gesture is not to be read, therefore, merely as a simple act of filial piety on the part of Jesus, anxious to entrust his Mother, now alone, to John. The entire context (Jn 19:17-37) speaks rather of the realization of the plan of salvation foretold by Scripture.[180] Thus, the gesture has a theological meaning to be discovered. As early as Origen the theological import of Jesus' words have been underscored: John is seen as the representative of every believer. And from the fourth century on, Mary has been considered as the image of the Church. As Mary now becomes spiritual Mother of John, at the same time she becomes spiritual Mother of every believer.[181]

The literary genre of the pericope confirms this interpretation. In fact, since the time of M. de Goedt, nearly every exegete has held that

---

[177] Manelli, *All Generations...*, 366; cf. A. Feuillet, *Maria, Madre del Messia, Madre della Chiesa*, Milan 2004, 42.
[178] G. Segalla, *Giovanni* (NVB 36), Cinisello Balsamo 1998, 449.
[179] Manelli, *All Generations...*, 366ff.
[180] Cf. De Fiores, *Maria*, 312.
[181] Segalla, *Giovanni*, 449.

the account has been composed according to a "structure of revelation," in which one person announces or reveals something about another.[182] With these words:

> Jesus, dying on the Cross, reveals that his Mother, as the "woman," with all the biblical resonance of this word, will now also be the Mother of the "disciple" of Jesus, who will now be the son of his Mother. In other words, he reveals a new role of the Mother of Jesus in the economy of salvation; but in a correlative way he reveals at the same time that the first task of the disciples will consist in being "sons of the Mother of Jesus."[183]

The most coherent interpretation of the text is, then, that which reads the verses in a personal-communal key: Mary is proclaimed by Jesus to be Mother of all believers, represented by John; and in a representative-communal key: Mary, figure of the Church, becomes Mother of believers.

G. Segalla gives a good summary of the arguments in favor of this reading:

> 1) The fact that Jesus turns first to Mary, as if to say, this is your primary responsibility; 2) the relation of this fact with the episode of Cana, where Mary also intervenes (here it is Jesus instead who intervenes); 3) the comparison of John 16:21, a text where in common with 19:26ff. the word "woman" and "hour," the theme of her maternity and Jesus' death, are used.[184]

The theological basis of this spiritual and universal maternity of Mary consists in her participation in the redemptive suffering of her Son dying on the Cross, in such wise that her motherhood becomes a *coredemptive* or sacrificial motherhood, because as *Lumen Gentium* clearly affirms, Mary stood at the foot of the Cross "profoundly suffering with her Only-begotten, with a maternal heart associating herself in his

---

[182] M. de Goedt, *Un schème de révélation dans le quatrième Evangile*, in *New Testament Studies* 8 (1961-62) 142-150.

[183] De la Potterie, MMC, 218.

[184] Segalla, *Giovanni*, 449ff.

sacrifice, lovingly consenting to the immolation of the victim whom she had begotten" (n. 58).[185]

Fundamental in this sense is what John Paul II writes in his Encyclical *Redemptoris Mater*:

> If John's description of the event at Cana presents Mary's caring motherhood at the beginning of Christ's messianic activity, another passage from the same gospel confirms this motherhood in the salvific economy of grace at its crowning moment, namely, when Christ's sacrifice on the Cross, his Paschal Mystery, is accomplished. ...
>
> Undoubtedly, we find here an expression of the Son's solicitude for his Mother, whom he is leaving in such great sorrow. And yet the "testament of Christ's Cross" says more. Jesus highlights a new relationship between Mother and Son, the whole truth and reality of which he solemnly confirms. One can say that if Mary's motherhood of the human race had already been outlined, now it is clearly stated and established. It *emerges* from the definitive accomplishment of the *Redeemer's Paschal Mystery*. The Mother of Christ, who stands at the very center of this mystery—a mystery that embraces each individual and all humanity—is given as mother to every single individual and all humanity. The man at the foot of the Cross is John, "the disciple whom he loved."

---

[185] During the past two decades the bibliography concerning Jn 19:25-27 has grown tremendously along the lines of Council teaching and that of the Ordinary Magisterium, which sees proclaimed there the spiritual and coredemptive maternity of Mary. Cf. M. Miravalle, *Mary Coredemptrix, Mediatrix, Advocate: Foundational Presence in Divine Revelation*, in *Mary Coredemptrix, Mediatrix, Advocate: Theological Foundations I*, Santa Barbara, CA, 1995, 256-269; Stefano M. Manelli, *Maria Corredentrice nella Sacra Scrittura*, in *Maria Corredentrice. Storia e Teologia*, Frigento 1998, 91-101; Idem, *Maria a titolo unico Corredentrice*, in *Immaculata Mediatrix* 2 (2002) 247-264; Idem, *All Generations...*, cit., 364-383; B. Gherardini, *Lo Corredentrice nel mistero di Cristo e della Chiesa*, Rome 1998, 217-220; G. Cottier, *La Mariologia dal Concilio Vaticano II ad oggi*, in *L'Osservatore Romano*, 3-4 June, 2002, 8; Th.M. Sennott, *Mary Coredemptrix*, in *Mary at the Foot of the Cross II*, New Bedford, MA, 2002, 616.

> But it is not he alone. Following tradition, the Council does not hesitate to call Mary *"the mother of Christ and the mother of mankind:"* since she "belongs to the offspring of Adam she is one with human beings. Indeed she is 'clearly the mother of the members of Christ ... since she cooperated out of love so that there might be born in the Church the faithful'" (*Lumen Gentium* 54, 53).
>
> And so this "new motherhood of Mary," generated by faith, is *the fruit of the "new" love*, which came to definitive maturity in her at the foot of the Cross, through her sharing in the redemptive love of her Son (n. 23).

Mary, in addition, "actively cooperates in the universal redemption, both as a single person and as personification of the Daughter of Zion, figure of the Church who begets the new people of God."[186] Mary, however, is not only figure of the Church, but in becoming Mother of all the disciples of Jesus, represented by John, becomes Mother of the entire Church as well.

Pope John Paul II spoke powerfully about this role of the Blessed Virgin's as Co-redemptrix and spiritual Mother of all men:

> Mary goes before us and accompanies us. The silent journey that begins with her Immaculate Conception and passes through the "yes" of Nazareth, which makes her the Mother of God, finds on Calvary a particularly important moment. There also, accepting and assisting at the sacrifice of her Son, Mary is the dawn of redemption; ... Crucified spiritually with her crucified Son (cf. Gal. 2:20), she contemplated with heroic love the death of her God, she "lovingly consented to the immolation of this Victim which she herself had brought forth" (*Lumen Gentium*, 58).
>
> In fact, at Calvary she united herself with the sacrifice of her Son that led to the foundation of the Church; her maternal heart shared to the very depths the will of Christ "to gather into one all the dispersed children of God" (Jn. 11:52). Having suffered for the Church, Mary

---

[186] Manelli, *All Generations...*, 370.

deserved to become the Mother of all the disciples of her Son, the Mother of their unity. ...

In fact, Mary's role as Co-redemptrix did not cease with the glorification of her Son.[187]

One may, then, conclude with I. de la Potterie, that

> As an individual person she (Mary) is the Mother of Jesus, and becomes the Mother of all of us, the Mother of the Church. But her corporeal motherhood in relation to Jesus is prolonged in a spiritual motherhood toward believers and toward the Church. And this spiritual motherhood of Mary becomes the image and the form of the motherhood of the Church. Mary's motherhood and that of the Church are both very important for the filial life of believers. To become children of God we must become children of Mary and children of the Church. Jesus is her only Son, but we become conformed to him, if we become children of God and children of Mary.[188]

Acts of the Apostles (Acts 1:14)

After recording the Ascension of Jesus into heaven, St. Luke inserts into his Acts a brief reference to the life of the disciples of Jesus up to the day of Pentecost. From the Mount of Olives the twelve returned to the Cenacle. According to St. Luke these "with one mind continued steadfastly in prayer with the women and Mary, the mother of Jesus, and with his brethren" (Acts 1:14). All these persons are next found in the same place on the day of Pentecost, when the Holy Spirit came down upon them (2:1ff.). Immediately attracting attention is the fact that Mary is designated with the title "Mother of Jesus" and is by name set apart from the other believing women. Exegetes have recognized in these two details the intention of the author to set in relief the figure of Mary. Further, they demonstrate the existence of a strict analogy between the fact of the Annunciation/Incarnation of Jesus and the birth of the Church on the day of Pentecost. On both occasions the Holy Spirit and Mary are

---

[187] John Paul II, *L'Osservatore Romano*, English edition, March 11, 1985, p. 7.
[188] De la Potterie, MMC, 223ff.

present. Mary is thus shown to have been constituted by God the Mother of Christ and Mother of the Church. For this reason, in relation to the faithful, she enjoys the role of Mother in the order of grace.

This has been nicely accentuated by Pope John Paul II in his Encyclical *Redemptoris Mater*, where the Pontiff writes:

> According to the eternal designs of Providence, the divine maternity of Mary would be poured out upon the Church, as Tradition affirms. In the Church the maternity of Mary is the reflection and prolongation of her motherhood toward the Son of God. The very moment of the birth of the Church and of her public manifestation to the world, according to the Council, permits us to perceive this continuity of the motherhood of Mary: "As it pleased God not to manifest solemnly the mystery of human salvation before having poured out the Spirit promised by Christ, we see the apostles before the day of Pentecost 'of one mind continuing steadfastly in prayer, together with the women and with Mary, the Mother of Jesus, and with his brethren' (Acts 1:14), and with Mary imploring with her prayers the gift of the Spirit, who had already overshadowed her at the Annunciation" (*Lumen Gentium* 59). In the redemptive economy of grace, brought about through the action of the Holy Spirit, there is a unique correspondence between the moment of the Incarnation of the Word and the moment of the birth of the Church. The person who links these two moments is Mary: *Mary at Nazareth* and *Mary in the upper room at Jerusalem*. In both cases her discreet yet essential presence indicates the path of "birth from the Holy Spirit." Thus she who is present in the mystery of Christ as Mother becomes—by the will of the Son and the power of the Holy Spirit—present in the mystery of the Church. In the Church, too, she continues to be a *maternal presence*, as is shown by the words spoken from the Cross: "Woman, behold, your son!"; "Behold, your mother" (no. 24).

Mary in the Glory of Christ

Mary in the Apocalypse: The Woman Clothed with the Sun (Rev 12)

Chapter 12 of the book of Revelation is, under various aspects, very difficult to interpret because of the complexity of the literary genre employed in its composition and because of its numerous references to other texts of Sacred Scripture.[189] The history of its exegesis, with the multiplicity of hypotheses encountered in it, confirms this estimate.

With chapter 12 there begins a series of signs, allegorical-symbolic visions, concerning the conflict between the Kingdom of God and the kingdom of Satan.[190] The chapter is structured via "concentric circles," according to a style typical of the Semitic world. In the first circle are presented the *woman with child*, the dragon ready to devour the son to whom the woman is about to give birth, the son who is rapt up to heaven, the flight of the woman into the desert (vv. 1-6). The second circle presents the victorious combat of Michael and of his angels against the dragon, who is cast down to earth. There follows the canticle of victory (vv. 7-12). In the third circle the dragon pursues the woman, who however flees to a secure place; thereafter the dragon vents his anger on the offspring of the woman (vv. 13-18).[191]

The principal personages are the woman, her son and the dragon. The identification of the last two creates no difficulties. The son of the woman is clearly the Messiah, as is evident from the reference in Revelation 12:5: "And she brought forth a male child, who is to rule all nations with a rod of iron," to Psalm 2:9: "You shall rule them with a rod of iron and break them in pieces like a potter's vessel," where the irresistible power of the future Messiah is exalted.[192]

The *red dragon* is identified by St. John himself in verse 9: "that great dragon, the ancient serpent, he who is called the Devil and Satan, who leads astray the whole world." Clearly, the reference here is to the *serpent* seducer of the first parents of mankind (Gen 3).[193] In Revelation 12 he is presented as the adversary and enemy of all those who are on

---

[189] Cf. Gen 3:15; Is 7:14; Dan 7:7; 10:13; Mic 4:9ff; Jn 2:1-11; 19:25-27; Gal 4:4.
[190] De la Potterie, MMC, 244.
[191] Manelli, *All Generations...*, 396ff.
[192] De la Potterie, MMC, 251.
[193] Cf. F. Manns, *Heureuse es-tu*, 150.

the side of God: he is against the male Child, hence against the Messiah; against Michael and his angels; against the woman, against the rest of her offspring. He has an extraordinary power, for he has "seven heads and ten horns, and upon his head seven diadems. And his tail was dragging along the third part of the stars of heaven, and it dashed them to the earth" (12:3-4). Nevertheless, his destiny is certain: he will be defeated and thrown into the "pool of fire and brimstone" (Rev 20:10).

The identification of the *woman* has, somewhat surprisingly, created more difficulties.[194] Exegetical opinion has been summarized quite well by Fr. Manelli:

> In answering this question with an astounding variety and diversity of opinion, reflecting ancient and modern trends in hermeneutics, exegetes divide into numerous groups. Listed summarily, the views of biblical scholars on the identity of the *"woman clothed with the sun"* fall into these categories. She could be a) Mary; b) Mary and the Church; c) Israel, the Chosen People; d) the people of the Old and New Testament; e) the Church of Christ; f) the Church as eschatological community, with her archetype in heaven.
>
> A more critical analysis of the theories, however, shows that as in past exegesis, so today there are but two basic interpretations of the "woman" of Revelation 12, namely: *Mary* and the *Church*. Traditionally, there has been "a pendulum movement between the two interpretations," writes I. de la Potterie, "and neither of the two aspects can be totally excluded in the interpretation of this mysterious symbol."[195] We would qualify this assessment somewhat to grasp the precise line of development followed by exegetical thought from patristic to medieval tradition. There occurred, in fact, a slow passage from the ecclesiological interpretation (prevalently patristic) to the Mariological (prevalently medieval).[196]

---

[194] On the various interpretations of *Woman* cf. H. Gollinger, *Das "grosse Zeichen" von Apokalypse 12*, Würzburg-Stuttgart 1971, 25-72.
[195] De la Potterie, MMC, 242.
[196] Manelli, *All Generations...*, 400ff.

The same author succeeds in finding the correct balance between the two basic interpretations. He states:

> It is our conviction [as is the most consistent Traditional and papal magisterial interpretation] that the *"woman"* is Mary, *also exemplifying the Church,* that is to say, she is Mary as a physical person, the Mother of Jesus, and she is Mary as a mystical figure, Mother of all the believers, "heavenly model" of the Church (*Lumen Gentium*, 65). The *"woman"* of Revelation recapitulates and expresses the total reality or Mary's divine and ecclesial maternity. The *"woman"* of Revelation recapitulates and expresses the whole reality of the divine motherhood and of the ecclesial motherhood of Mary. She is the Mother of the Messiah, *"the male child"* (v. 5), and she is the Mother of those who believe in Jesus, namely, of the *"rest of her offspring ... those who observe the commandments of God and have possession of the testimony of Jesus"* (v. 17).[197]

Absolutely fundamental is Fr. Stefano Manelli's conclusion:

> The point, then, on which the identification of the *"woman"* hangs, is the dual maternity realized indivisibly and only *in Mary*: she is the real, physical Mother of the Messiah; she is the real, mystical Mother of the Church, the new People of God. This is the thread that, without a break in continuity, starts with Genesis and reaches to Revelation, passing through Cana and Calvary. In Genesis 3:15 and in Revelation 12, in fact, we find the *"woman,"* *"the Son,"* and the *"rest of the offspring"* in victorious combat against the serpent. The picture is substantially neat and linear.[198]
>
> The pains of childbirth of the *"woman"* seem to constitute a particular problem, if they are referred to the virginal childbirth of Mary at Bethlehem. If, instead, they

---

[197] Manelli, *All Generations...* 402-403; more detailed exposition on pages 402-408.
[198] *Ibid.*, 406.

are referred to the childbirth of Mary on Calvary, where she is constituted "truly the mother of the members of [Jesus] Christ," as St. Augustine affirms (quoted by *Lumen Gentium*, 53), then we too can understand with other exegetes, among then D. Squillaci, that to Our Lady "is to be ascribed a double childbirth: one *natural* and virginal, by which, without pain or injury of any kind, she begot the Son of God, the physical Christ; the other *spiritual*, by means of which on Calvary, uniting her sufferings to those of the Redeemer she begot the Mystical Body of Christ."[199]

Conclusion

In retrospect, the outline of New Testament Mariology emerging from this overview quite naturally matches that of the mysteries of the Holy Rosary: Joyful (Mary in the accounts of Jesus' origin and infancy), Luminous-Sorrowful (Mary in the mysteries of Christ's public life), and Glorious (Mary in the glory of Christ). Further, the golden thread binding all these episodes together is the mystery of Mary as basis of our life in Christ: we are brothers and sisters in Christ solely to the degree that we are children of Mary, the "rest of her offspring:" to the degree we consider it our prime obligation as believers "to take her into our home" as did the beloved disciple. The evangelical spirituality of St. Francis of Assisi has well been described in these terms: Mary is our Mediatrix with Christ, as Christ is our Mediator with the Father.[200] Another way of putting this, with St. Bonaventure, is this: "As God comes to us through her, so through her we must return to God."[201] This is expressed still another way in the Litany of Loreto: Mary is the virginal Gate of heaven (for us), and the virginal Gate of God (to us).[202] Without as it were being a prolongation of the Virgin Mother as the "rest of her offspring," we cannot have "God with us," the Emmanuel.

---

[199] *Ibid.*, pp. 408-409.
[200] Henri d'Avranche, *Legenda Versificata S. Francisci*, in *Analecta Franciscana* X, Quaracchi 1941, 445; cf. also St. Bonaventure, *III Sent.*, d 3, p 1, a 1, q 2.
[201] St. Bonaventure, *Commentarium in Lucam*, 1, 70 [Eng. Trans.: *Commentary on Luke*].
[202] Cf. Manelli, *All Generations...*, 87-93, (particularly the biblical basis in Ezek 44:1-2), 88-90.

MARY AND THE FATHERS OF THE CHURCH

Fr. Luigi Gambero, S.M.

Our purpose is to elucidate the doctrine on the Blessed Virgin Mary in the ancient Christian tradition, that is in the time of the Fathers of the Church. We are convinced that from the beginning of our Christian history, Mary occupied a unique place beside Jesus in the evangelical *kerygma* of the Church; and from then on Christians have always paid special attention to her person and her role in the salvific plan of God. Mary is a "witness" of Jesus, as many Protestant theologians like to call her. Clearly she is that; but we ought to add: Mary is a very particular witness, whose presence and participation beside Jesus helps in an absolutely unique way to make his divine person more understandable. We cannot speak of the incarnate Word without referring explicitly or implicitly to his Mother. This is what we learn from the Fathers of the Church and the other ancient Christian writers.

Looking at the early history of Christian faith, we get the impression that the doctrine on Mary is like a river with mysterious springs. After a brief start, however not yet completely explored, little by little it appears majestic and overwhelming. Though this mysterious beginning still continues to pose questions to patristic scholars, we today have at our disposal numerous studies about the historical beginning of Marian doctrine.[1]

---

[1] Even though the very early years of the history of Christianity are still keeping some secrets about the connection between our Christian faith and theology and the apostolic preaching, which is the fundamental source of all subsequent tradition, we are anxious to understand as clearly as possible this absolutely necessary link. For an English translation of the Fathers, cf. the *Ancient Christian Writers* series, Paulist Press, or L. Gambero, *Mary and the Fathers of the Church: The Blessed Virgin Mary in Patristic Thought*, Ignatius, 1999.

To understand the importance of patristics in studying Marian doctrine we need to recognize its role in theology in general. Studying the Fathers of the Church means coming in touch with men who acted in order to establish a link between the apostolic tradition and the subsequent Christian generations. They transmitted to these latter that deposit of faith which the apostles themselves received from the Lord Jesus. St. Athanasius of Alexandria (+373) defines this process very well with a clear-cut statement: "The doctrine of faith is the one that the Lord taught, the apostles preached and the Fathers have kept."[2]

These men were able to draw the truths directly from the wells of the Word of God, thanks to a special mentality and capability of understanding, empowered by the light and the grace of the Holy Spirit. For this reason they provided good foundations to Christian tradition and a strong support to the Church, especially at the occasion of the councils when solemn declarations were issued regarding dogmatic truths.

This fact was confirmed also by John Paul II, who said: "[The Fathers] were the first theologians since they were able to investigate the mystery of Christ having recourse to notions borrowed from the thinking of their time. When it was necessary, they did not hesitate to remodel these notions in order to give them a universal content."[3]

The historical period in which the Fathers lived was closer to the time of the apostles and they may lead us to discover the apostolic origins of our Marian doctrine and devotion. In particular, the Fathers and ancient Christian writers show in their attitude towards Mary a special attention to three Mariological truths: Mary as a mother, Mary as a virgin, and Mary in her "intentional" relationship with Eve. These three doctrinal points were very much emphasized by the Fathers.

The two main patristic dimensions of Marian doctrine, namely the Christological and the ecclesiological, were fully reflected by Vatican II in chapter 8 of *Lumen Gentium*, in which Mary is shown in the context of the mysteries of Christ and the Church. This way of treating the Marian topic clearly recalls the tradition of the Church Fathers, who already in their day felt obliged to find solutions to the problems rising from the theological reflection on these two mysteries.

---

[2] *First Letter to Serapion* 28, PG 26, 594.
[3] *L'Osservatore Romano*, October 31, 1993, p. 5, n. 5.

A Vatican document issued by the Congregation for Catholic Education, November 10, 1989, reminds us again of the importance of the Church Fathers:

> In the flow of living Tradition that continues from the beginning of Christianity over the centuries up to our own time, they occupy an entirely special place which makes them stand out compared with other protagonists of the history of the Church. They laid down the first basic structures of the Church together with doctrinal and pastoral positions that remain valid for all times.[4]

According to this traditional concept, we consider as *Fathers* those Christian writers combining four qualifications: orthodoxy in their doctrine, holiness in their life, approval by the Church, and antiquity.

Following the holy Fathers of the Church, we are sure that we can meet the authentic apostolic tradition, which is not a past event, but is a living phenomenon which never dies out. We read in the document quoted from the Congregation for Catholic Education:

> Tradition, to which the Fathers are witnesses, is a living Tradition that demonstrates unity in variety and continuity in progress... Tradition, therefore, as it was known and lived by the Fathers, is not like a monolithic, immovable and sclerotic block, but a multiform organism pulsating with life.[5]

Pope Benedict XVI believed it was important to again recall the doctrine on Tradition. He did it during two audiences in April 2006. Let me quote a passage from one of his talks:

> Tradition is not a simple transmission of things or words, a collection of dead things. Tradition is like a living river that connects us with the origins; a river in which the origins are ever present. It is the great river which leads us to eternity. Therefore, in this living river

---

[4] Congregatio de Institutione Catholica, *Instructio de Patrum Ecclesiae studio* 18, AAS 82, 1 (1990), 615.
[5] *The Pope speaks,* 35 (1990), 174.

the Word of God (in Matthew's Gospel) becomes always something real again, namely: "I am with you always, until the end of the world" (Mt 28:20).[6]

Mary in the Ante-Nicene Period

The patristic epoch embraces more or less the first eight centuries of our era. Usually it is divided into three periods: the origins, the golden age, and the times of decline. The period of the origins goes from the beginning of Christianity to the Council of Nicea I (325). It is the time of the earliest Christian writers, who did not always have clearly in mind whether there was a distinction between Holy Scripture and Tradition. According to their mentality, there was just one Christian teaching, whether it was written in the books of the Old and New Testaments or handed down orally by the apostles and their immediate disciples. In this time we may distinguish three different groups of Fathers of the Church and other Christian writers: the so-called "Apostolic Fathers," the Christian apologists and the Christian controversialists.

The Apostolic Fathers

The Apostolic Fathers are the most ancient writers of the Church, and are named thus because their teachings directly echo the preaching of the apostles, which is contained especially in their letters. They lived between the end of the first century and the first half of the second. Their Mariological materials, in spite of their paucity, are of great value for later centuries, because the Fathers in this age seem to be the most qualified witnesses to the apostolic tradition, to which the teaching of the Church must in every age refer.

These writers look at Mary as to a person present in the New Testament writings and in the proclamation of the Church (*kerygma*) in the apostolic and sub-apostolic age. This means that Mary was chiefly considered in relation to the mystery of the incarnate Word.[7]

---

[6] *L'Osservatore Romano,* April 27, 2006, p. 4.

[7] Even though scholars usually see in the first kerygma of the primitive Church the proclamation of the risen Lord, very soon this kerygma grows complete and includes other statements, among which we recognize the mention of Jesus' birth from Mary. Cf. A. Harnack, *Lehrbuch der Dogmengeschichte* with English translation by N. Buchanan, *History of Dogma*, vol. I, New York 1961, p. 202. Harnack

We have clear examples in the letters of *St. Ignatius of Antioch* (+c.115). This great bishop of the Syrian church presents some examples of professions of faith where the Virgin Mary is explicitly remembered. In his letter to the Ephesians[8] he calls Jesus "the one and only physician" and continues:

> Both, flesh and spirit; begotten and unbegotten; in man God, in death true life; both from Mary and from God; first passible and then impassible; Jesus Christ our Lord.[9]

We read in his letters three other similar texts:

> For our God Jesus the Christ was carried in the womb by Mary in accordance with the plan of God, of the seed of David and of the Holy Spirit; he was born and baptized in order to purify the water by the Passion.[10]
>
> Be deaf, then, when anyone speaks to you apart from Jesus Christ, who was of the family of David, who was of Mary, who was truly born, ate and drank, was truly persecuted under Pontius Pilate, was truly crucified and died, while heavenly, earthly and subterranean beings looked on. He was also truly raised from the dead when his Father raised him up, as in similar fashion his Father will raise up in Christ Jesus, we who believe him, without whom we have no true life.[11]
>
> Concerning our Lord that he is truly of the family of David as to the flesh, Son of God by God's will and power, truly born of a Virgin, baptized by John so that all righteousness might be fulfilled by him; truly

---

synthesizes the primitive kerygma of the Church in four sentences: the Virgin birth through the power of the Holy Spirit, Jesus' death and Resurrection, his glorification at the right hand of the Father, and his return at the end of time.

[8] See the texts in *The Apostolic Fathers*, vol. 1, The Loeb Classical Library 24, Harvard University Press, Cambridge 2003, pp. 218-321.
[9] *Ad Ephesians* 7, 2.
[10] *Ibid.* 18, 2.
[11] *Trallians* 9, 1-2.

nailed for us in the flesh under Pontius Pilate and the tetrarch Herod.[12]

From these four texts it clearly appears that Ignatius is quoting some early creedal formulations. As J.H. Newman pointed out, we believe that when the ancient Fathers speak of the doctrine of faith, they speak of it as being universally held in the Church. Therefore, we receive the doctrines which they teach, not because they are great personalities, namely endowed with great talents and authority in the Church, but because they bear witness that all Christians everywhere held them.[13]

From the testimony of St. Ignatius we learn that the mystery of Christ's birth from the Virgin entered not only the faith of the Christian people, but also the earliest liturgical tradition of the Church. In fact it has been demonstrated that creedal formulas were mostly used in liturgical celebrations, especially in the dispensing of baptism. In addition, we notice that the Virgin Mary is mentioned in all the four formulas, as if Christians considered it important, while professing their faith in Jesus Christ, to mention his birth from Our Lady.

Certainly Ignatius also had a polemical reason to insist on the real birth of Jesus from the Virgin Mary: fighting against Gnosticism, which taught a Docetic theology of the Incarnation. Hence, according to St. Ignatius, Mary really gave birth to the incarnate Word and this birth was the result of an intervention of the Holy Spirit. The purpose of the Incarnation is the redemption of mankind, according to the plan of God which Ignatius calls *oikonomia*, a word already known in the New Testament and that became common in the language of the Fathers.

To the Ephesians, Ignatius also states that both Mary's virginity and God's Incarnation escaped the notice of the prince of this world, together with another mystery, namely the death of the Lord. He wrote: "Three mysteries worked in the stillness of God."[14] But he does not explain why these three mysteries had to be hidden from the Devil. Nonetheless, this statement shows an evangelical analogy: Jesus himself hid his own divine origin from the Devil. Ignatius does not say how God chose to keep these three mysteries hidden. Later authors who quoted this Ignatian

---

[12] *Smyrnaeans* 1, 1-2.
[13] *Discussions and Arguments on various subjects* II, 1, London 1899, p. 45.
[14] *Ephesians* 19, 1.

text believed that the wedding of Mary and Joseph was the evident way chosen by God in order to keep secret the virginal birth of Christ.

The witness of Ignatius of Antioch on Mary has to be evaluated as very significant. His language, with short and firm statements, without proofs and demonstrations, is in the typical style of the primitive *kerygma*.[15] Besides, Ignatius possesses the doctrinal authority of a bishop and he is very conscious of this fact.[16] Therefore, his testimony on Mary has a particular significance, even though it was not a direct Mariological announcement. In fact, the main concern of the preachers of the Gospel was to proclaim Jesus as God and Savior and not to preach Mary apart from Christ.[17]

Hence, the early *kerygma* of the Church was extremely concentrated in a few enunciations especially related to some basic truths, namely there is only one God who became incarnate in Jesus Christ, who is both Creator and Redeemer of the world. The reference to Mary was a way to demonstrate the reality of the Incarnation and the human nature of the Son of God.

The Christian Apologists

The Christian Apologists lived in the second century and their writings were a defense of Christian faith against the charges made by Jews and pagans. They were the first Christian writers able to establish a contact with the world outside the Church. We have a long list of names: Quadratus, Aristides of Athens, Aristo of Pella, Tatian the Syrian, Miltiades, Apollinaris of Hierapolis, Athenagoras of Athens, Theophilus of Antioch, Hermias, the author of the Epistle to Diognetus, Melito of Sardes and Justin.

As far as Mary is concerned, we are especially interested in St. Justin the Martyr (+c.165), whose Marian doctrine must be understood in his theological context, as it appears from his extant works, namely

---

[15] Cf. E. Neubert, *Marie dans l'Eglise anténicéenne*, Paris 1908, pp. 171-172; A.M. Cecchin, *Maria nell'economia di Dio secondo Ignazio di Antiochia*, in Marianum 14 (1952), 373-383; W.J. Burghardt, *Mary in Eastern Patristic Thought*, in J.B. Carol, *Mariology, Vol. 2*, Milwaukee 1957, p. 101.

[16] Cf. Cf. *Trallians* 3, 1

[17] Further, the religious atmosphere in which the Gospel was preached may have reacted negatively to the announcement of a Virgin Mother of God.

two Apologies and a Dialogue with the Jew Trypho. He develops an extensive theory on the divine Logos, the Son of God, through whom the Father created all things and governs the world. Because of the ruse and the trick of Satan, in whom Adam and Eve put their faith and trust, human beings fell into sin and were subjected to the demons, to sufferings and to death. God conceived a salvific plan (*oikonomia*) and entrusted its achievement to his Son, who became incarnate, suffered and died in order to bring us a remedy. The Logos accepted the will of the Father not because the *oikonomia* was unavoidable, but for our sake.

Among the details of this economy, Justin pays special attention to the mystery of Jesus' birth from the Virgin, because through all that Mary did for him as a mother we understand that the Son of God really became the son of man. God, though having many ways to carry out the Incarnation of his divine Logos, had a special reason for performing the miracle of the virgin birth. Justin gives a deep explanation: as Eve, the first virgin, accepted and conceived the word of Satan and gave birth to disobedience and death, in the same way another virgin, believing in the Word of God, through her obedience gave birth to the Son of God, who is himself Life.

Thus we have two women, both virgin and mother. At the beginning of the world's history, Eve is the symbol and the cause of a ruinous economy for all humanity. In opposition to her, God wanted another virgin, one who opens the new economy of redemption and salvation for all human creatures.[18]

Virginity and maternity are the two evangelical and traditional statements on Mary, which Justin also stresses, yet in Christological contexts. These two prerogatives go together in the writings of Justin, because he understands very well that God's economy required a virgin mother for the Incarnation of his Son.

Mary truly gave birth to Jesus, as every human mother gives birth to her children. We should not wonder if Justin does not attribute to Mary the title of mother and still less of Mother of God. The reasons are: first of all he always speaks about Christ and not initially about Mary, who enters the discourse only because of her function regarding the incarnate Word. Secondly the title of Mother of God will become current much later,

---

[18] Cf. *Dialogue with Trypho* 100, *Justini Opera*, in *Corpus Apologetarum*, vol. 1, pp. 356-359.

especially at the time of the Nestorian heresy. Before that time, we do not have many witnesses for the use of this title. However, in the writings of Justin, the objective content of divine maternity is fully expressed. In fact, he insistently affirms that the Son of the unbegotten and invisible God and Creator, eternally begotten by him, but distinct from him, the Word by whom all things were made and left in them his own mark,[19] who appeared and spoke with the patriarchs and prophets, according to the will of his Father, came down into the world and became man of the Virgin Mary, taking a true human flesh. Justin plainly affirms that the incarnate Son of God is one in being, one in substance, one in person. To this one being we refer all his words and all his deeds, both the human and the divine. Therefore we may presume that Justin thought that Mary was really the Mother of God, having conceived, carried in her womb and given birth to the eternal Word of God.

The difficult question could be raised: What was the real contribution which Mary, as Mother, gave to the conception of the Son of God? Did Justin consider Mary's body the material cause of Christ's humanity, namely its carnal root? He denies that the body of Christ was formed by male seed. He very seldom uses the preposition *ek* (from), whereas he very often states that the Son of God was born *dia* (through or by means) of the Virgin Mary. We can understand this terminology if we do not forget that Justin is something of a philosopher. He does not employ the expression: *dia tes Parthenou* (through the Virgin) to diminish or to depreciate Mary's maternal activity in the conception of Christ, but only because this was the teaching of the biology of that time, according to which a woman was completely passive in the conception of babies. The only active principle was the man's seed (Cf. 1 Cor 11:8 and 12).

Of course, in the conception of Christ, male seed was excluded; in fact, Justin speaks of a virginal conception in which the body of the incarnate Word was the result of the intervention of God's almightiness which replaced man's seed. But leaving aside the biological theory of that time, Justin seems very aware of the perfect maternal role played by Mary in the Incarnation. Like every other mother, Mary conceived; but she also carried in her womb and gave birth to the Son of God. Thus, she is indeed the Mother of the Son of God.

---

[19] Cf. *Apologia II*, 6, *Ibid.*, pp. 212-217.

We already said that the virginal motherhood of Mary is firmly defended by Justin; it should be added that it is his main statement on Mary. In fact he was able to understand that virginal maternity was the condition which allowed Mary to enter the divine plan of salvation in a unique way. Differently from any other mother, she is the Virgin-Mother; Mother and Virgin at the same time. Justin had to face pagans and Jews. Pagans did not believe in the miracle of a Virgin-Mother; Jews were scandalized that one could state that God has a mother. Our apologist understands that no human proof is able to demonstrate such a miracle. Therefore, he feels compelled to have recourse to the prophecies of the Old Testament. He rightly identifies Mary with the virgin foretold by the prophet Isaiah (7:14). For him, Mary is the virgin par excellence, so that several times in his writings she is simply called: "the Virgin," without her name; saying "Mary" and saying "the Virgin" is the same thing. We ought not ask Justin whether he believed in the virginity *ante-*, *in-* and *post-partum*. This was not his problem, even though we may guess that his answer on this point would certainly be affirmative.

Between Ignatius of Antioch and Justin we have only a half-century of history, and we can notice how much the image of Mary has gained clearer and more detailed features. We are not yet dealing with a real Marian theology; but we notice that Justin feels the need to pay greater attention to the person of the Mother of Jesus in order to make more understandable the mystery of her divine Son.

Especially in the conception of the *oikonomia*, the teaching of our apologist represents a remarkable progress. In this economy, the Virgin Mary is shown in so active a role that our mind immediately goes to the concept of mediation.[20]

However, the significance of the Marian texts of St. Justin can be compared with the texts of St. Ignatius. Justin was not a bishop like Ignatius, and therefore he was not a qualified witness and preacher of Divine Revelation. He was only a layman, a philosopher, who passionately cultivated Christian truth as it was transmitted by the Tradition of the Church. He is the first author who describes with remarkable extent the figure and the mission of Mary. For the first time, the traditional data are elaborated, developed and compared one with another, though we must not forget that Justin, in elaborating his teaching, is guided by

---

[20] However, we do not feel justified in attributing it to Justin.

apologetic and polemic criteria and not by theological principles. The importance of Justin is still greater if we consider that he knew perfectly the sources of Revelation, both the Old and the New Testament, and he had a considerable respect for them. For instance, he avoids taking away or adding anything to the Holy Scriptures. He searches in the Old Testament for a confirmation of the New; but he also interprets the Old Testament in the light arising from the New and especially from the divine person of the incarnate Word of God.

Moreover, the teaching of Justin can be referred to the entire Church of his time, because as a wandering philosopher he knew both Eastern and Western Christianity. For this reason his teaching about the Virgin Mary appears more universal than St. Ignatius' and testifies that on the Mother of the Lord the unanimity of both the Eastern and Western churches is very ancient. Therefore we also understand why the teaching of the Fathers of the Church can offer a base for today's ecumenical dialogue.

The Christian Controversialists

The Christian controversialists of the third century left more powerful works, not only in order to defend Christian faith, but also to attack the errors of its opponents. In doing so, they had the opportunity to explain also the orthodox doctrine of faith. These authors had a more direct and determinative influence in the process, at the outset of Christian theology. The Fathers and the Christian writers of this period began (however infrequently), to write on Mary to deal with her person and her mission in salvation history. Usually they speak of Mary in other contexts, for instance, explaining and commenting on Holy Scripture, dealing with the mystery of the Incarnation or with the person of Jesus Christ, illustrating the life and mission of the Church.

Among them *St. Irenaeus of Lyons* (+ after 178) was foremost, and we concentrate our attention on him. His origins are from Asia Minor, maybe from Smyrna, because in one of his letters he wrote to the Roman presbyter Florinus that in his early youth he had listened to the sermons of Polycarp. Later, for unknown reasons, he left his country and moved to Gaul where he became a presbyter of the church of Lyons and later on bishop, succeeding Photinus who had died as a martyr.

His masterpiece is a five-volume work entitled *Adversus Haereses*, whose original version in Greek is no longer extant, but of which we have a very ancient Latin version made in Northern Africa, probably before 258. He fights heresy, especially the many branches of Gnosticism; but to these heresies he also presents the orthodox teaching of the Church. Another work we have from him, but only in an Armenian version, is the *Demonstration of the Apostolic Preaching*.[21]

The Marian teaching of Irenaeus does not appear like a kerygmatic proclamation, but rather as a true theological and dogmatic reflection. In fact, his development and deepening of the Eve-Mary parallel can be rightly considered the starting point of the theology on Mary. To enter this question, we have to refer to one of the foundations of Irenaeus' Christology and soteriology, namely the principle of recapitulation (*anakephalaiosis*). This term, meaning "summing up," is used in its verbal form in Ephesians 1:10, where God is said to sum up all things in Christ.

Irenaeus further elaborated on the term and applied it to Christ who, through his obedience, restored fallen humanity to communion with God by taking upon himself all things since the beginning. In other words, God rehabilitates the earlier divine plan of salvation for mankind, which was interrupted by the fall of Adam, and gathers up his entire work from the beginning to renew, to restore, to reorganize it in his Son, who, therefore, through his Incarnation, became the second Adam. This further elaboration is based on other Pauline texts which establish a parallel between Adam and Christ (Rom 5:12-21; 1 Cor 15:21-22, 45-49) and presents the work of salvation as a new creation, a repetition of the first one, and the Savior himself as a New Adam. Since by the fall of man the whole human race was lost, the Son of God had to become a man so that the plan of salvation, or the second creation, could be fulfilled in the same way that the first creation was frustrated.[22] This recapitulation has two great results: a negative one, consisting in the fact that the effects of the disobedience of the first Adam, namely sin

---

[21] During many centuries this work was known through the witness of Eusebius of Caesarea (*Hist. Eccl.* 5, 26). In 1904, Karapet Ter Mekerttschian discovered the entire text in an Armenian version and published the *editio princes* in 1907. In 1913, the Armenian text with an English translation appeared in *Patrologia Orientalis* 12, 654-731.

[22] *Haer* 5, 14, 2, SC 153, 186-188.

and death, are destroyed,[23] because Christ, the second Adam, through his obedience, renewed the ancient conflict against the Devil and overcame him.[24] The positive effect is that the whole of mankind was renewed and restored in the second Adam.[25]

In the framework of the recapitulation of all things in Christ, the role of the Virgin Mary is explained by means of the Eve-Mary parallel. For the first time, Irenaeus gives a theological content to this analogy, so that in it we find the first and most ancient theological reflection on the Mother of God. In his writings, we find three passages asserting this parallelism. By reading the three texts in chronological succession we can better understand the progressive development of his thought.

In the first text the Bishop of Lyons does not touch the parallel casually, as Justin did, but he rather makes of it a source for deep theological reflection. We notice that the parallelism between Eve and Mary is perfectly constructed in the form of a sharp antithesis. Eve and Mary were still virgins when they received God's message, though they already had a husband. Eve disobeyed God; Mary obeyed; and so Eve's disobedience became the cause of death both to herself and to the whole human race, whereas Mary's obedience became the cause of salvation (*causa salutis*) both to herself and to all mankind. Eve's disobedience tightened knots around our liberty; Mary's obedience set us free from such knots. Eve's disobedience follows from her unbelief; Mary's obedience is caused by her faith:

> Even though Eve had Adam for a husband, she was still a virgin.... By disobeying, she became the cause of death for herself and for the whole human race. In the same way, Mary, though she also had a husband, was still a virgin, and by obeying, she became the cause of salvation for herself and for the whole human race. ... The knot of Eve's disobedience was untied by Mary's obedience. What Eve bound through her unbelief, Mary loosed by her faith.[26]

---

[23] *Haer* 3, 18, 7, SC 211, 365-371.
[24] *Haer* 5, 21, 2, SC 153, 272-274.
[25] *Haer* 3, 18, 1, SC 211, 342-345; 4, 34, 1, SC 100, 846-849.
[26] *Haer* 3, 22, 4, SC 211, 438-443.

In the second passage, the Eve-Mary antithesis is set side-by-side with the Adam-Christ parallel. From the antithetic role of Christ in regard to Adam and that of Mary in regard to Eve, Irenaeus draws the conclusion that the Virgin Mary became the advocate (*advocata*) of the virgin Eve, balancing by her obedience the disobedience of Eve, as Jesus through his correction amended the sin of Adam. Thus Irenaeus not only puts the role of Mary within Christ's redemptive plan, but he also clearly explains that Mary has a function strictly joined with Christ's function, as Eve did with Adam:

> Eve was seduced by the word of the [fallen] angel and transgressed God's word, so that she fled from him. In the same way, [Mary] was evangelized by the word of an angel and obeyed God's word, so that she carried him [within her]. And while the former was seduced into disobeying God, the latter was persuaded to obey God, so that the Virgin Mary became the advocate (*advocata*) of the virgin Eve.
>
> And just as the human race was bound to death because of a virgin, so it was set free from death by a Virgin, since the disobedience of one virgin was counterbalanced by a Virgin's obedience.
>
> If, then, the first-made man's sin was mended by the right conduct of the first-born Son [of God], and if the serpent's cunning was bested by the simplicity of the dove [Mary], and if the chains that held us bound to death have been broken, then the heretics are fools; they are ignorant of God's economy, and they are unaware of his economy for [the salvation of] man.[27]

We also notice that the role of Mary does not only parallel the role of Eve; much more, it interferes in the plan of Eve, since Mary directly overcomes the guile of the serpent with her simplicity.

The third text comes from the *Demonstration of the Apostolic Preaching*. Here Irenaeus stresses the concepts both of death and life. Death comes from the disobedience of Eve, life from the obedience of Mary:

---

[27] *Haer* 5, 19, 1, SC 153, 248-251.

> Adam had to be recapitulated in Christ, so that death might be swallowed up in immortality, and Eve [had to be recapitulated] in Mary, so that the Virgin, having become another virgin's advocate, might destroy and abolish one virgin's disobedience by the obedience of another virgin.[28]

Further on, Irenaeus justifies the fact that the Lord took his body from the Virgin Mary, a descendant of Adam, instead of becoming incarnate in a creature extraneous to us, because the work of salvation had to be achieved within the same human race.

Irenaeus' insistence on this parallelism ought to be explained by his concern to refute the error of Tatian, a Christian apologist of Gnostic tendency, former disciple of St. Justin and founder of the sect of the Encratites. He is the author of the *Diatessaron*, a kind of synopsis of the four gospels. Irenaeus argues against him that Adam and Eve, after their sin, recovered grace and the friendship of God. He could not accept that our ancestors were damned, and accused Tatian of being guilty of this heresy. Irenaeus wants to demonstrate that both Adam and Eve were saved by Christ, in anticipation of his redemptive work, in which Mary had her own role to play. In this economy the human race receives a new progenitor, in place of the first Adam. But since the first woman was also implicated in the fall by her disobedience, the work of salvation starts also by the obedience of a woman. Giving life to the New Adam, she becomes the New Eve, the true Mother of the living. Therefore Irenaeus says that Mary is *causa salutis*, as antitype of Eve who was *causa mortis*.

According to Irenaeus, in the economy of salvation Mary's function as second Eve is not limited to a merely negative and physiological cooperation as Virgin and Mother. Her cooperation involves activities of the moral order. Her obedience to the word of God was conscious and free. Moreover, her consent had a soteriological character, because she knew that the Incarnation of the Son of God was in view of the redemption of mankind.

---

[28] *Demonstration of the Apostolic Preaching* 33, SC 406, 128-131. We have this text only in an Armenian translation.

In the other two passages we have quoted, Irenaeus applies to Mary the title of *advocate*. It is the first time in the history of ancient Christian literature that this word is attributed to the Blessed Virgin.²⁹

In what sense can Mary be termed Eve's advocate? Here, Mary did the opposite of what Eve did; and in that way she removed the lamentable effects of Eve's disobedience. So Eve will not be condemned anymore as responsible for the ruin of humankind, because this ruin was removed by means of Mary's obedience. In conclusion we might affirm that the current doctrine of Mary's universal mediation and cooperation in redemption has its most ancient roots in the teaching of the Bishop of Lyons. Many years ago J.M. Bover had already seen in St. Irenaeus a clear defender of the doctrine on Marian mediation,³⁰ and more recently other scholars have come to the same conclusion.³¹ Evidently modern terminology (*mediatio, mediatrix, coredemptio, co-redemptrix*) was not known by Irenaeus; but their content, that is the true doctrine on Marian mediation and collaboration in the salvific economy, seems to have been clearly taught by the Bishop of Lyons.

Irenaeus of Lyons considered the Virgin Mary not only as the subject of a dogmatic formula, but as a person with a specific identity. She is the woman who has to counterbalance Eve, and repair the damages caused by the latter. Theological reflection on the Virgin Mary brought to light some questions regarding her person. Questions were raised about

---

[29] But unfortunately, for both texts, we have only the Latin and Armenian version and therefore some may question the Greek term used by Irenaeus. Perhaps we may receive some light from another text which says: "... *ubi accusatorem habemus, illic habeamus et Paracletum*" (Where we have an accuser, there we may also have an Advocate) (*Haer* 3, 17, 3, PG 7, 930 C.). This sentence seems to indicate that in the case of Mary the original term was also very probably *parakleitos*, whose meaning might be: defender. In the sentence quoted, Irenaeus applies the word *parakleitos* to the Holy Spirit, in opposition to the term *accusatorem* (prosecutor) indicating the Devil.

[30] *La mediación universal de la "segunda Eva" en la tradición patrística*, Estudios Ecclesiasticos 2 (1923), 321-350.

[31] Cf. W. Delius, *Geschichte der Marienverehrung*, München-Basel 1963, S. 63; J.A. de Aldama, *Maria en la Patrística de los siglos I y II*, Madrid 1970, pp. 292-293; L. Cignelli, *Maria nuova Eva nella patristica greca*, Assisi 1966, pp. 32-33; I. Ortiz de Urbina, *Mediatio Mariae estne exclusa ab unico mediatore Christo?*, in *De Maria et Oecumenismo*, Pontificia Academia Mariana Internationalis, Romae 1962, pp. 154-155.

Mary's perpetual virginity, and the reality of her perpetual virginity was quickly affirmed by the Fathers, with the exception of Tertullian. The belief in this truth was transmitted through different traditions: liturgical, dogmatic, apologetic, and also apocryphal. In any case, all these traditions agreed in their purpose of defending Mary's perpetual virginity. People denying this truth became more and more rare in the Church, and by the time of Origen (+c.253), only heretics refused to accept Mary's perpetual virginity. A few authors, following the Protoevangelium of James, identified the "brothers of the Lord" with children born of a former marriage of Joseph. Others gave more credit to the explanation of Hegesippus, a Christian author of the second century, whose fragments are quoted by Eusebius of Caesarea, and whose explanation seems to be closer to Palestinian traditions. Hegesippus said that the brothers of the Lord must be identified with his cousins. If the *virginitas ante partum* and *in partu* could directly affect the person of Jesus, the *virginitas post partum* seemed more directly related to the person of Mary, to her glorification and to the desire of the faithful, who liked to look at Mary as a perfect pattern of virginal life.

In the third century, and especially in the fourth, several elements testify that Mary was indeed the object of devotion in earlier times. One of these elements would be the famous prayer, *Sub Tuum Praesidium*. This prayer, known for many centuries in a Latin version, was originally believed to belong to the Middle Ages; but in 1917 the original Greek text, probably of the third century, was discovered in a papyrus acquired by the John Rylands Library of Manchester. Many are the documents testifying that the Mother of God was already venerated in previous centuries, such as the numerous accounts of the virgin birth, the symbols and pictures found in the Roman catacombs, and the homilies of the Fathers of the Church. All these elements cannot be interpreted as a sudden phenomenon. Certainly they presume a preceding tradition.

Reflecting on the personal and special relationship between Mary and her Son, ecclesial tradition also became aware of her special association with God's salvific economy. On this particular point the writings of Justin and Irenaeus opened a long tradition lasting up to our day. The Fathers of the Church usually came to this conclusion by considering three facts. First, Mary's personal relationship with the Redeemer required a partnership with him in his work, as Eve was

Adam's partner in sin. Secondly, the Adam-Christ parallelism led to the opposing of Eve with another woman whose attitude and behavior would neutralize Eve's attitude and behavior, the cause of our sin. Thirdly, the Fathers saw Jesus' virgin birth as the *type* of our new birth in Christ through the sacrament of Baptism. Hence, Mary was not a mere passive instrument for the Incarnation. The active and responsible aspect of Mary's cooperation in the redemptive work of Jesus, which was intuited by Justin and Tertullian, was clarified and deepened by Irenaeus, whose doctrine exerted a tremendous influence on future generations.

In the famous Alexandrian school of theology, the great Origen is renowned, even for his Marian thought. He shared in the New Testament teaching on the Virgin Mary as Mother of God and ever-Virgin. But he formulated a curious theory about Mary's holiness. He understood Christian sanctity as a continual journey that makes progress toward higher forms of the spiritual life. According to this dynamic concept of Christian perfection, he thought that Mary could not have been totally holy from the beginning of her life; she also had to make progress in holiness. For this reason Origen incorrectly posited that Mary had some defects and imperfections; for instance, she suffered doubt and scandal on Calvary.[32] However, the great thinker of the Alexandrian school did not avoid exalting Mary's sanctity and virtues.

The Golden Age of Patristic Thought

In the controversies of the fourth century, some heretics were unable to understand how two different natures could be united to the point of forming one unique being. Against them, the Church presented her teaching on Mary's divine maternity, understood in a Christological sense more than in a Mariological one. In fact the statement that Mary was the Mother of God implied that Christ was only one being, one subject; that in him human and divine nature were distinct but not separated. Tertullian, elaborating on the theory of the hypostatic union (*unio hypostatica*), and Origen, introducing the concept of the communication of idioms (*communicatio idiomatum*), created the premises for the dogmatization of the term *Theotókos*. Perhaps Origen himself,

---

[32] *Homily on Luke 17*, 6-7, PG 13, 184; SC 87, 256-258.

as we already said, used this word.[33] However, we cannot quote any author before Nicaea using it in his writings. Any statement concerning Mary's motherhood, because of its relationship with the Christological dogma, was able to guarantee the orthodox doctrine on the incarnate Word. It is noteworthy that Mary entered the many liturgical formulas that Christians used in order to express their own faith in the Incarnation of the Son of God. This is evident in the creedal formulas of Ignatius of Antioch.

This subsequent period goes from the councils of Nicea (325) to Chalcedon (451). During this time, patristic literature reaches its climax both in its literary form and in its contents. The Fathers are very strongly involved in the long-lasting and harsh Trinitarian and Christological controversies; and they contributed much to the growth of theology in all its branches and especially to the confirmation of the truths of faith. During this period, Marian doctrine continues to develop with the entrance of specifically Marian homilies and further Mariological development in light of the crucial Christological discussions of the period.

Mary is first introduced as the woman who plays the extraordinary role of the Virgin Mother of our Savior; and this role is considered in the light of biblical texts, in particular Isaiah 7:14 and the first two chapters of Matthew and Luke. In the Eastern Church, the title of *Theotókos* (the God-bearer) becomes more and more frequent and better rooted in the doctrine of the incarnate Word. The evangelical titles of *Virgin* and *ever-Virgin*, coined by the Fathers, begin to signify not only the mysterious intervention of God in the event of the Incarnation of his eternal Son, but also an admirable prerogative of Mary's person. These two terms are very soon understood as synonymous with *panaghia* (all-holy), since the Fathers looked at the practice of virginity as the equivalent of a holy life. Mary ought to be the holiest creature just because she is the Virgin-Mother of God. In such a perspective, it is understandable that the two dogmas of the divine motherhood and the perpetual virginity became

---

[33] In fragment 49 on the Gospel of Luke the term appears, but the authenticity of the fragment is not certain (Cf. SC 87, 449). In the *History of the Church*, the historian Socrates, mentioning Origen, writes: "Origen also, in the first tome of his commentary on the letter of St. Paul to the Romans, explaining the reasons why Mary is called *Theotókos*, treated this question extensively" (cf. PG 67, 812 B).

conveyed as only one truth: Mary is the Virgin-Mother of God. In fact the Fathers believed that a faithful Christian could not conceive a divine maternity without virginity. An amazing confirmation of this popular belief is available in the Christmas homily of St. Basil of Caesarea. After quoting the Gospel's statement: "He knew her not until she had borne a son" (Mt 1:25), the Cappadocian Father of the Church adds the following remark:

> This could cause the supposition that Mary, after having done her part in all purity in the birth of the Lord, accomplished thanks to the intervention of the Holy Spirit, in the future may not have refused normal conjugal relations. This would not damage any doctrine of religion, because virginity was only necessary until the service of the Incarnation was achieved; and what she might have done afterwards need not be investigated as to any effects on the doctrine of the mystery. But since the lovers of Christ cannot bear to hear that the Theotókos at a certain moment may have ceased to be a virgin, we deem their testimony as sufficient.[34]

Therefore, because of her virginity and holiness, Mary was proposed as the pattern *par excellence* of that life of perfection that thousands of virgins, belonging to both sexes, embraced in the Christian communities of that time.

Furthermore, the relationship between Mary and the mystery of the Church becomes more and more clear. On this point, Western Fathers like Ambrose and Augustine supplied us with a splendid doctrine which became normal teaching in the Church throughout the centuries, down to the Second Vatican Council. Thanks to the preaching of the Church Fathers, the presence of Mary in the liturgical life of the Church also became more and more explicit. In this period, homilies which may be called Marian homilies made their first appearance. They are either explicitly related to Mary or they are extensive treatments of Marian subjects. This is the case with the Christmas homily of St. Basil, the

---

[34] *Christou ghennesis* 5, PG 31, 1468 B. Cf. L. Gambero, *L'omelia sulla generazione di Cristo di Basilio di Cesarea. Il posto della Vergine Maria*, Marian Library Studies 13-4, Dayton, Ohio 1981-1982, pp. 188-191.

homilies on the same subject by Gregory of Nazianzus and Gregory of Nyssa, and the homily for the feast of Jesus' Presentation in the Temple (*Hypapante*) by Amphilochius of Iconium.

After the Council of Ephesus (431) the homiletic literature on Mary had an extraordinary development. Let us recall some names like Cyril of Alexandria, Theodotus of Ancyra, Proclus of Constantinople, Esichius of Jerusalem, and in the West the immense production of St. Augustine. Some of these Fathers were acknowledged as endowed with a special authority. In fact they have been quoted by ecumenical councils, and their writings were even included in the acts of the councils themselves. The three great *Cappadocian Fathers*, Basil of Caesarea, Gregory of Nyssa, and Gregory Nazianzus, contributed significantly to the increase of Marian doctrine.[35]

St. *Basil*, metropolitan bishop of Caesarea Cappadocia (+379), sees in the Son of Mary the Emmanuel foretold by Isaiah and calls the womb of Mary the workshop (*ergasterion*) in which the mysterious event of the Incarnation of God took place. The power of the Most High and the Holy Spirit are shown to be the agents of this indescribable phenomenon. In the passage quoted above, Basil applies the famous term *Theotókos* to Mary. He praises Mary's holiness; nonetheless he erroneously speculates that her moral figure was not totally without shadow, referring to the doubt that, according to him, the Blessed Virgin suffered under the Cross of her Son.[36]

St. *Gregory of Nyssa* (+c.394), Basil's brother, in order to defend Christ's complete and perfect humanity against Apollinaris of Laodicea, stresses the real motherhood of Mary, who, therefore, has to be called the Mother of God (*Theotókos*). Gregory proposes this term as a criterion of orthodoxy. He expresses all his admiration before the wonder of Mary's virginity, and interpreting her answer to the angel at the Annunciation, maintains that she had previously made a kind of vow of virginity.[37]

St. *Gregory of Nazianzus* (+390), anticipating the declaration of Ephesus, pronounces a sharp anathema against those who refuse to call

---

[35] Cf. G. Söll, *Die Mariologie der Kappadozier im Lichte der Dogmengeschichte*, in *Theologische Quartalschrift* 131 (1951), 163-188, 288-319, 426-457.

[36] *Letter 260*, PG 32, 965-968.

[37] He also shares in the opinion that Zechariah, Elizabeth's husband, was martyred in the Jerusalem Temple because he let Mary stay in the area reserved for the virgins.

Mary *Theotókos*. He also condemns two other kinds of heresy connected to Mary's divine motherhood: the belief that Jesus merely passed through Mary and was not formed in her womb; and that the Son born of Mary is not the same Son eternally begotten by the Father.[38] For Gregory, an admirable exchange between God and Mary occurred in the mystery of the Incarnation: God purified her in advance (*prokatharsis*) to make her fit for her role in the Incarnation;[39] Mary offered God the gift of her undefiled virginity. Gregory is one of the first Christian authors to mention the custom of the faithful addressing prayers to the Mother of God. In fact he recounts the story of a virgin named Justine who addressed Mary directly, requesting her help in particular difficulties. From the Church historian Sozomen (early fifth century), we know that Gregory was called to Constantinople to serve as pastor of the small community faithful to the dogma of Nicea that gathered in the church of the *Anastasis* (Resurrection). Sozomen adds that the Mother of God performed miracles in response to the invocations addressed to her by the faithful in that church.[40]

St. Ephrem the Syrian (+373), from Nisibis, was a biblical exegete and a prolific ecclesiastical writer of the Syrian Church. In his poetry, he combines solid Marian doctrine with expressions of sublime beauty. Eastern tradition called him "Harp of the Holy Spirit." From his writings we may assume that he was indeed in love with the Virgin Mary. Addressing Jesus, he wrote: "Only you and your Mother are more beautiful than every thing. For on you, O Lord, there is no mark; neither is there any stain in your Mother."[41] This beauty is not only of an esthetic dimension; it belongs to the great deeds operated by God in his Mother. He wrote:

> A wonder is your Mother; the Lord entered her and became a servant; he entered able to speak and he became silent in her; he entered her thundering and his voice grew silent; he entered shepherd of all and in her a lamb he became; he emerged bleating.[42]

---

[38] *Letter 101*, to Chledonius, PG 37, 177-180.
[39] *Sermon 38*, 13, PG 36, 325 B.
[40] *Historia Ecclesiastica* 7, 5, PG 67, 1424-1425.
[41] *Carmina Nisibena* 27, 8, CSCO 219, 76.
[42] *Hymns on the Nativity* 2, 6, CSCO 187, 62.

St. Ephrem contemplates with enthusiasm the unique spectacle of Mary's virginity, praising God's wisdom and love for this treasure given to Mary. Another peculiar condition that he mentions in the Mother of God is her relationship with the Church of which she is a prophetic figure, a symbol. But he goes even so far as to identify the Church with Mary, interpreting John 19:25-27, when Jesus on the Cross entrusted his Mother to the beloved disciple. He wrote that Jesus entrusted to the apostle John his Mother, the Church, as Moses consigned his flock to Joshua.[43] Ephrem also deals with the Eve-Mary parallelism, applying to the two women the contrasting concepts of light and darkness, death and life, the good triumphing and evil perishing.[44] Ephrem not only spoke and wrote about the Virgin Mary; he also nourished a deep and passionate devotion toward her. He is one of the first Fathers of the Church to express in his writings sentiments of love and devotion to the Mother of the Lord.

Several other Fathers of the Eastern Church deserve to be mentioned. *Athanasius* proposed the life of Mary to consecrated virgins as a very high pattern of spiritual life; the author who introduced the name of Mary in the 24 catecheses attributed to *Cyril of Jerusalem* (+386); *Epiphanius of Salamis* (+403), transmitted to later Christian generations a Marian doctrine which is one of the best developed in his time and is undoubtedly the most copious. *St. John Chrysostom* (+407) left many homilies on the Mother of God for the celebration of her feasts.

Special mention is due the patriarch *Cyril of Alexandria* (+444). St. Cyril played a decisive role in the proclamation of the orthodox doctrine of faith on Jesus Christ as one in being, and on Mary as Mother of God.[45] Pope Celestine approved his behavior and doctrinal teaching, so that the theological position of the Constantinopolitan patriarch *Nestorius* (+c.451) was officially condemned and Mary recognized as *Theotókos*, since she generated the human nature of Christ's divine person.

In this historical period, Latin Christianity was also rich in names of eminent Fathers of the Church. Some of them exerted a strong influence on the development of Marian doctrine and devotion.

---

[43] *Diatessaron* 12, 5, SC 121, 216.
[44] *Ibid.*, 2, 2, SC 121, 66.
[45] But his thought on the duality of Christ's natures was not clear and was later interpreted as supporting monophysitism.

St. *Hilary of Poitiers* (+367) was one of them. He became the leading theologian of his age and was a tenacious and formidable adversary of Arianism. For this reason he was deposed from his episcopal see and sent into exile by the Emperor Constantius. In his writings, he reserved a significant place to the Mother of God, regarding her as an exceptional person who was outstanding in the primitive Church because of her role and her glorious virginity and holiness. Hilary likes to speak of Mary in the frame of the New Testament. To defend Mary's virginity in the Incarnation, he introduces a distinction between marriage (*sponsalia*) and matrimony (*coniugium*). Conceiving Jesus, Mary was still a *sponsa* or fiancée; only afterwards did Joseph recognize her as a *coniux*, namely a wife.[46]

From the second half of the fourth century on, the authority and teaching of the three greatest Fathers of that time, Sts. Ambrose, Jerome, and Augustine, grew more and more influential in the Western Church. *Ambrose*, bishop of Milan (+397) could be considered the founder of Marian doctrine in the West. His Marian texts are remarkable not only because of their number, but especially for their quality. He mentions Mary most frequently in his writings dealing with virginity. At the beginning of his treatise to the virgins (*De virginibus*), Ambrose tries to sketch a kind of biography of the Blessed Virgin, but his purpose is not to elaborate an impossible historical work, but to provide consecrated virgins with the highest pattern of perfect Christian life.[47] Mary is the Mother of God and "what could be nobler than the Mother of God? What could be more splendid than the one who chose Splendor himself? Who could be more chaste than the one who gave birth to a body without the corruption of her own body?"[48] Perpetual virginity was a requirement of her divine motherhood. Ambrose also faced the question of the relationship between Mary and the Church. He is the first Christian writer to call Mary the type (*typus*) of the Church, and knowing his thought on this point is an indispensable premise for

---

[46] *In Matthaeum* 1, 3, PL 9, 921. Following the apocryphal *Gospel of James*, he explains that the brothers of Jesus were sons of Joseph from his first marriage; *Ibid.*, 1, 4, PL 9, 922.
[47] *De virginibus* 2, 2-3, PL 16, 208-212.
[48] *Ibid.*, 2, 2, 7, PL 16, 209.

understanding the development of this doctrine in the later tradition of the Church. He writes:

> [Mary was] of course married but a virgin, because she is the type of the Church, which is also married but remains immaculate. The virgin (Church) conceived us by the Holy Spirit and, as a virgin, gave birth to us without pain. And perhaps this is why holy Mary, married to one man, is made fruitful by another (the Holy Spirit), to show that the individual churches are filled with the Spirit and with grace, even as they are united in the person of a temporal priest.[49]

Ambrose also made a definitive contribution to a portrayal of the Mother of God as completely devoid of any moral shadow, radiant with extraordinary greatness and holiness.

Another influential Father of the Church was *St. Jerome* (+419), the most outstanding biblical scholar in the ancient Latin Church. He greatly contributed to the growth of a Marian mentality in the Church both East and West. Like Hilary of Poitiers, he happened to write about Mary in the context of the Holy Scriptures; but he is also famous because of his engagement in the controversy on Mary's virginity, that in his time was primed by the spreading of the heretical pamphlets of Jovinian and Helvidius.

Jerome was endowed with a formidable polemic strength, and if somebody was destined to fall under his controversial stylus, he certainly risked being slain. This is what occurred to Jovinian and Helvidius, the two unlucky deniers of Mary's perpetual virginity. For instance, in his treatise against Helvidius, Jerome confutes the interpretation of his opponent on Matthew 1:18, "Before they came together, she was found to be with child by the power of the Holy Spirit." He responds to Helvidius in this way:

> I don't know whether to laugh or cry. Should I accuse him of lack of experience or just carelessness? Suppose someone should say: "Before eating lunch at the harbor, I set sail for Africa." Would this mean that his statement

---

[49] *Expositio in Lucam* 2, 7, PL 15, 1555.

could not be valid unless he had to eat lunch at the harbor some day? Or if we wished to say: "The apostle Paul, before departing for Spain, was put in chains in Rome?" Or to say—which is quite likely—"Helvidius, before repenting, was struck down by death?"

And he concludes:

> Therefore, it is not necessary that the things one was planning to do should really happen, should something else intervene to prevent them from happening. Thus, when the evangelist says: "Before they came together," he means that the time of the wedding is near and that things have reached the point that she who had been considered engaged was about to become a wife.[50]

Jerome likes to discover the image of Mary in the prophecies of the Old Testament and to consider her as the woman promised by God. Like St. Ambrose, he has a great esteem for Mary's complete holiness.

St. Augustine (+430) is undoubtedly the most genial Father of the Western Church, and his extraordinary genius is also evident in the texts in which he deals with the Virgin Mary, especially in the sermons he preached at Christmas and in his exegetical writings, commenting on passages where Mary is mentioned. Many factors, such as his engagement in the Christological controversy, his lively sense of the Church, his zeal in the ministering to the people of God, and the very original experience of his personal conversion, exerted an undeniable influence in his approach to the mysteries of the Mother of God. If his Marian doctrine appears very open to the problems of his time, it is also oriented to the future of Christianity. In fact, he anticipates intuitions and perspectives that are considered topical even today. All this might explain the reasons why Augustine is the Father of the Church most quoted or mentioned in the documents of Vatican II, especially in chapter 8 of *Lumen Gentium*.

In order to understand the peculiar attitude of the Bishop of Hippo toward the mystery of the Mother of the Lord, it may be useful to refer to a truth which is fundamental in Augustine's thought, namely the mystery of predestination. He started from this conviction to defend the

---

[50] *Ad versus Helvidium* 4, PL 23, 195-196.

absolute gratuity of divine grace in the controversy against Pelagius. The first grace in the process of salvation cannot be deserved by a creature. It is simply given gratuitously by God. From such a universal law, not even the incarnate Word, in so far as he is a creature, was dispensed. Let us read Augustine: "I repeat: there is no more outstanding example of predestination than the Mediator himself. The faithful Christian who wishes to understand this well, should pay attention to this example, for in it he shall find himself."[51]

Neither could Mary escape such a divine plan. She could not deserve to be chosen by God; her choice was absolutely gratuitous. Augustine explains this truth when commenting on the scene of Calvary (Jn 19:25-27): "Then he recognized her; yet, he had always known her. Even before he was born of her, he knew his Mother in her predestination. Before he, as God, created her from whom he would be created as man, he knew his Mother."[52] According to Augustine, Mary's call to divine maternity and all its consequences was not determined by any foreseen merit of hers; it was just a pure grace. Her merit is subsequent, in as much she responded to such grace.

Following the tradition of the preceding Fathers (and in particular of his master St. Ambrose), he attributes to Mary a total holiness that excluded in her any kind of imperfection, or stain and moral shadow. Famous is the statement in which he is explicit about her personal sinlessness: "Except the holy Virgin Mary, concerning whom, for the honor of the Lord, I will have no question of sin; for we know how much to conquer in every way was given to her who merited conceiving and bringing forth him who certainly had no sin."[53]

In the context of Mary's holiness, Augustine emphasizes her perpetual virginity: "As a virgin she conceived; as a virgin she brought forth; a virgin she remained."[54] In one of his statements he seems to present this prerogative of the Mother of God as a dogma of faith: "It is allowed to say, without endangering faith, that Mary had a face like

---

[51] *De dono perseverantiae* 24, 67, PL 45, 1033.
[52] *In Joannem*, tr. 8, 9, PL 35, 1455.
[53] *De natura et gratia* 36, 42, PL 44, 267.
[54] *Sermo 51*, 11, 18, PL 38, 343.

this or that. But nobody could say, without endangering Christian faith: Perhaps Christ is born of a virgin."[55]

A significant point of Augustine's Marian doctrine is the relation of Mary with the Church. Imitating St. Ambrose, he also calls Mary type (*typus*) of the Church, since Mary already is what the Church will be in her eschatological fulfillment. He wrote: "Nevertheless it is true; the Church is the mother of Christ. Mary preceded the Church as its type."[56] Mary is not excluded from the Church. She is a member of the body of Christ: "Mary is part of the Church, a holy member, an outstanding member, a super eminent member, but a member of the whole body, nonetheless."[57]

The Bishop of Hippo urges consecrated virgins to take Mary as their own model of Christian life. Without Mary, consecrated virginity would not even exist in the Church. But he presents Mary as a pattern of Christian life for married women also, because she was a most upright and loving wife of St. Joseph.[58]

Augustine died on the eve of the Council of Ephesus, to which he had been invited because of his prestigious reputation. The 20 years between Ephesus and Chalcedon constitute for the Church a period of intense theological activity. Many ecclesiastical personalities were involved in the doctrinal debate beside the two main protagonists, Cyril of Alexandria and Nestorius.

In the East, we may recall *Proclus of Constantinople* (+446) and *Theodotus of Ancyra* (+ before 446); in the West *Peter Chrysologus* (+c.450), and *Pope Leo the Great* (+461), who assured the happy conclusion of the Council of Chalcedon through his famous document, the *Tomus ad Flavianum*. In this period Christian poetry flourished in the verses of *Caelius Sedulius* (+450), who reserved an important place to Mary in the *Carmen Paschale*, which is his masterpiece.

---

[55] *De Trinitate* 8, 5, 7, PL 42, 952.
[56] *Sermo Denis* 25, 8, *Miscellanea Agostiniana*, p. 164.
[57] *Sermo Denis* 25, 7, *Miscellanea Agostiniana*, p. 163.
[58] Cf. *Contra Faustum* 23, 8, PL 42, 470.

The End of the Patristic Age

The third patristic epoch is a time of decadence, and is conventionally considered as lasting until the death of John Damascene (+c.750) in the East, and Isidore of Seville (+636) in the West.

This decline was caused especially by two historical phenomena: the invasions of the Barbarians in the West; and, in the East, the authoritarian and despotic politics of the imperial court of Constantinople that presumed to interfere in the life and in the organization of the Church. Nevertheless, even in this very difficult period, we find some Fathers and Christian authors endowed with great personality and extraordinary genius, who were able to sail upstream. In the East, they fought against the imperial abuse of power, as happened for instance during the somber years of the iconoclastic persecution. In the West, they fixed the presuppositions for the subsequent Medieval culture and civilization.

In the Mariological field, this period is characterized by a very abundant homiletic literature. Marian truths, already preached and explained by the Fathers of the previous centuries, are again presented, not as needing better formulations or a necessary defense against opponents, but as treasures able to affect Christian life and devotion.

A significant phenomenon of this time is a greater attention paid to the person of Mary herself, to her moral image and her perfect virtues. All these spiritual and moral elements, along with the holiness of the Mother of God, brought about in Christian authors pages of admiration, praise and exaltation. The reactions of the faithful assumed the form of increasing expressions of liturgical cult and popular devotion. The first Marian feasts arose and started to spread all over the Christian world. Marian hymnography reached extraordinary heights of artistic beauty and theological richness, especially in the poetry of *Romanos the Melodist* (+c.560), in the Syrian hymnographer *James of Serugh* (+521), and especially in the admirable *Akathistos Hymn*, whose author remains unknown. In the East, the custom of publicly reading the homilies of the Fathers during liturgical celebrations contributed to consolidating in the people of God the sense of Tradition. The Fathers, in fact, were considered dogmatic authorities, especially in the East, because they were regarded as depositaries of the apostolic tradition. All these religious phenomena deeply marked the life of the Church, as well as the Marian cult and devotion of the Christian people, in subsequent centuries.

Another phenomenon which began during this time deserves to be mentioned for its significance in relation to the history of Marian dogmas. Devotion and reflection on Mary's perfect virtues and admirable holiness caused rise, little by little, to the awareness that she had to be free from any sin, both actual and original. This kind of sense of faith in the Christian people, after many centuries eventually led to the proclamation of the dogma of the Immaculate Conception in 1854.

In Jerusalem where, according to a very ancient tradition, the tomb of the Blessed Virgin is kept in a church located in the neighborhood of Gethsemane, the celebration of a feast in honor of the Mother of God on August 15 led people to ask the question: Where does the body of the Mother of God lie, since her tomb was found empty, according to the tradition of the apocrypha of the *Transitus*, which was also the position of many Fathers? The answer came through an increasing faith in the bodily Assumption of Mary into heaven, and through the institution of the feast of the *Koimesis* by the Emperor Maurice in 600 for the church of Constantinople, and soon extended to all the Eastern Church. Pope Sergius did the same for Western Christianity in the second half of the same century. Even in this case, the proclamation of the dogma by the solemn Magisterium of the Church would come many centuries later.

We already mentioned that the end of the patristic age occurred diversely in the East and in the West. In Latin Christianity the period of the Fathers ended at the beginning of the seventh century, and *Gregory the Great* (+604) is generally considered the last Father of the Western Church. In one of his writings, he presents an interesting account of the apparition of Mary to a little girl named Musa, showing that by this time even a pope considered it normal to write about a religious phenomenon like a Marian apparition.[59] Some other Christian writers emerge in this atmosphere of declining society. *St. Gregory of Tours* (+594) is the first author in the West who witnesses to the mystery of Mary's Assumption into heaven.[60] In his work *Libri miraculorum*, he collects popular traditions about miracles attributed to the intercession of the Blessed Virgin. The Latin poet *Venantius Fortunatus* (+c.600) gives an attractive voice to popular devotion toward the Mother of God through his hymns and other kinds of poetic composition. In the choir of Marian

---

[59] *Dialogorum liber IV,* 17, PL 77, 348–349.
[60] His testimony may be based on a Greek apocrypha.

piety that Spanish Christianity offered at the end of the sixth century, the voice of *Isidore of Seville* (+636) is surely remarkable. He deals with several Marian topics, such as the dignity and holiness of the Mother of God, the meaning of her name, the end of her earthly life, and the relationship of Mary to the mystery of the Church. He also contributed to the spreading of Marian cult and devotion.

In Eastern Christianity the names of the last three Fathers of the Church, Germanus of Constantinople, Andrew of Crete, and John Damascene brought some positive light to the gloomy horizon of the iconoclastic crisis that officially started with the decree of 730 by Emperor Leo III the Isaurian, in which he attacked and prohibited the veneration of sacred icons. The situation grew worse when Leo's son, Constantine V Copronymus, succeeded his father in the government of the empire (741). In fact, the iconoclastic politics of the imperial court soon became a real religious persecution, since many persons, especially among the monks, lost their lives to be faithful to the Christian Tradition. These three Fathers of the Church did not only intervene in defense of this veneration with their preaching and writing, they were able to support and enrich the liturgical cult as well as the personal devotion toward the Mother of God, who was related to the persecution, since her icons were indeed numerous in Eastern Christianity.

Germanus of Constantinople (+733) was forced to resign from the patriarchal see by Emperor Leo III, because he refused to sign the iconoclastic decree of the emperor. Three of his letters were addressed to various Eastern bishops in order to convince them that the cult of the sacred images was orthodox and in line with the Tradition of the Church. He wrote many works belonging to various literary genres; but not all of them have reached us or are known to us. Seven of his nine homilies treat Marian subjects: Mary's Presentation in the Temple, the Annunciation, the Dormition (*Koimesis*), the dedication of the Marian shrine of the Blacherna, where the relics of Mary's garments and the swaddling clothes of the child Jesus were kept. One homily was delivered on the celebration of the *Akathistos Hymn*.

From his writings, Germanus appears to be one of the most eminent Marian doctors of the eighth century, as well as a fervent devotee of the Blessed Virgin. He exalts her as the ever-Virgin and all-holy Mother of God, and gives her marvelous titles: Throne of God, House of Glory,

Beautiful Splendor, Chosen Jewel, Universal Propitiator, Heaven which narrates the Glory of God, Dawn that brings Unfailing Light, Dove that Announces to us the Good Tidings of Salvation, Golden Urn that contains the Sweetness for our soul. He calls her "full of grace," "holier than the saints," "higher than the heavens."[61]

Because of her spiritual richness she was received into heaven soon after her death. Germanus witnesses that in the eighth century the belief in Mary's Assumption into heaven, body and soul, was peacefully accepted in the Eastern Church. Pius XII quotes Germanus among the testimonies of the Tradition of the Church in favor of the dogma.[62] St. Germanus proposes an interesting explanation for this Marian privilege. Jesus, in a certain way, wanted to repay his Mother for all that he received from her during his earthly life: "I want to repay the dwelling in the maternal womb, the penny of lactation, the compensation for the education."[63] Germanus finds another explanation in Jesus' filial love for his Mother:

> Since a son seeks and longs for his mother and a mother likes to live together with her son, so it was right that you who possessed a heart filled with maternal love toward your Son and God, could return to him; and it was quite fitting that God, who had for you that feeling of love which everyone experiences for his mother, made you share in his communion of life.[64]

But Mary had to be assumed into heaven also for our sake. She had to play a role of mediation and intercession for us. Germanus has Jesus talk to his Mother thus:

> I will build you up as a rampart for the world, as a bridge for those tossed about by the tides, as an ark for those who are saved, as a staff for those who are led by the hand, as the intercessor for sinners, and as the ladder that can conduct men to heaven."[65]

---

[61] Cf. *Homilia I in Praesetationem* 17-18, PG 98, 308 A-C.
[62] Cf. *Munificentissimus Deus*, AAS 42 (1950), 761.
[63] *Homilia III in Dormitionem*, PG 98, 361 C.
[64] *Homilia I in Dormitionem*, PG 98, 348 A.
[65] *Homilia III in Dormitionem*, PG 98 361 D.

Mary's mediation is a theme on which Germanus offers abundant reflections. We find a significant text in his homily commemorating the liberation of Constantinople from the siege of the Arabs:

> May the ever-Virgin Mary, radiant with divine light and full of grace, Mediatrix first through her supernatural birth and now because of the intercession of her maternal assistance, be crowned with never-ending blessings.[66]

As for Mary's death, our author considers it normal that she should have gone to heaven after passing through bodily death, and he suggests two reasons. First, Mary, as a creature, could not escape the universal law of death ruling all human kind: "You shared in our bodily condition, so that you could not avoid meeting with death (which is common to all human beings), just as your own Son, the God of all, also tasted death."[67] From this passage it is possible to draw out a second reason for Mary's death, namely the sharing in the destiny of her Son. In fact, the criterion of the so-called *analogia Christi* was commonly used in the theological tradition of the Church to investigate and clarify the mysteries of the Mother of the Lord.

In one of his letters, Germanus reports the case of a miraculous icon of the Blessed Virgin, venerated at Sozopolis, a town in the region of Pisidia, which emitted oil from the palm of the Virgin's hand. This kind of miracle is still celebrated in the Byzantine Church.

Andrew of Crete (+c.740), a native of Damascus, gave a tremendous contribution to the Byzantine liturgy through his copious production of hymns, canons, and other poetic compositions. Unfortunately a complete critical edition of his works is lacking, and some of them are available only in manuscripts. As far as the Blessed Virgin is concerned, Andrew was deeply attracted by the moral beauty and holiness of the Mother of God, and in this respect he may be considered a remarkable witness to the faith of the people of God in the absolute holiness of Mary. He repeatedly writes that throughout her life her soul was never contaminated by any moral stain. His insistence on this point led some scholars to make of him a supporter of the development leading to the

---

[66] *Homily for the liberation of Constantinople* 23, edited by V. Grumel, *Revue des Etudes Byzantines* 16 (1958), 198.

[67] *Homilia I in Dormitionem*, PG 98, 345 D.

dogma of the Immaculate Conception. It cannot be denied that Andrew shared in the highest understanding of Mary's sinlessness and sanctity. Already at the beginning of her earthly life, Mary appears to be the first fruits of humankind, who was born as the consequence of the prayers and holy life of her parents, the first of all humanity blessed by God's grace and salvation. Therefore Andrew dares to write:

> It was right, then, that the admirable Joachim and his spouse Anna, inspired by divine thoughts, did obtain her as the fruit of their prayer; her, I say, the queen of nature, the first fruit of our race, whose birthday we celebrate, whose swaddling clothes we honor, and whom we venerate as the source of the restoration of our fallen race.[68]

The Bishop of Crete tends to see in Mary's holiness that sanctity which God returned to the human race through his saving economy:

> Today pure human nature receives from God the gift of our original creation and reverts to its original purity. By giving our inherited splendor, which had been hidden by the deformity of vice, to the Mother of him who is beautiful, human nature receives a magnificent and divine renovation, which becomes a complete restoration. The restoration, in turn, becomes deification, and this becomes a new formation, like its pristine state.[69]

Andrew places the initial gift of an extraordinary holiness given to Mary at the moment of her birth, since he is preaching on the feast of her nativity.[70]

In response to Mary's death and Assumption into heaven, Andrew expounds a somewhat nuanced doctrine. He clearly believes in Mary's death because, like Germanus, he posits the principle of the analogy with the destiny of her divine Son; at the same time he touches on a question never mentioned before by anyone. Is it reasonable to think that an all-holy creature like Mary might have suffered death which was

---

[68] *Homilia III in Nativitatem*, PG 97, 860 B-C.
[69] *Homilia I in Nativitatem*, PG 97, 812 A.
[70] There is no reference which would lead us to think that he refers to the instant of her passive conception.

introduced by God as a punishment for Adam and Eve's sin? Could Mary also be punished? The answer needs a *distinguo*: she had to die because the law of death is universal; but for her death was not a punishment, a condemnation, or a curse; it was only a way to enter the eternal glory and live with her Son and God. On the contrary, through the mystery of her death this condemnation and curse were overcome:

> Death, natural to men, also reached her; not, however, to imprison her, as is the case with us, or to overcome her. God forbid! It was only to secure for her the experience of that sleep (*Dormition*) which comes from on high, leading us up to the object of our hope.[71]

While Andrew has no doubt that Mary's soul definitely rose to heaven, he is not clear about the specific destiny of her body. Perhaps it was reunited with her soul in the glory of heaven, or it might have been transferred to some suitable place on earth to wait for the final resurrection. He was only sure about one detail: Mary's tomb remained empty.[72]

St. Andrew also tries to find reasons why the ancient tradition of the Church kept a total silence about the end of the earthly life of the Blessed Virgin. He formulates some hypotheses. Perhaps the books of the New Testament were already completed when Mary died; or because it was not suitable to treat events like this during a period when the concern of the Church was concentrated on the announcement of the economy of salvation through Christ. However, he considers trustworthy an account of Mary's death and Assumption that he attributes to Dionysius the Areopagite.[73] Andrew quotes as authentic the work *De divinis nominibus*.[74]

The Bishop of Crete beautifully praises Mary for her glorious queenship and her role as Mediatrix. These two prerogatives are usually framed in the context of Mary's Assumption into heaven. About Mary's queenship, he writes: "Today Jesus carries the Queen of the human race out of her earthy dwelling: she, who is his ever-Virgin Mother, and in

---

[71] *Homilia I in Dormitionem*, PG 97, 1052 C-1053 A.
[72] Cf. *Homilia II in Dormitionem*, PG 97, 1081 D-1084 B.
[73] *Homilia I in Dormitionem*, PG 97, 1061-1064.
[74] For the text of the *De divinis nominibus* 3, 2, cf. PG 3, 689. Today it is attributed to the unknown Pseudo-Dionysius, a mystical theologian of the sixth century.

whose womb he assumed a human form without ceasing to be God."[75] In his homilies, Andrew frequently addresses Mary with titles such as: "New Queen," "Immaculate Queen," "Queen of the Human Race," "Queen of All Men," and "Queen of Nature." Commenting on the greeting of the Angel Gabriel, *Chaire!*, he noted that it was fitting for the angel to address such a greeting to a Queen (*Basilida*).[76] In his homily on Mary's birth, Andrew presents a long discourse to explain that she was born as a royal descent of King David.[77] Moreover, he considers the feast of her nativity to be like a joyful banquet offered to the Queen of heaven and to her devotees: "Royal is the banquet of the Queen, who descends from a royal seed."[78] Elsewhere he addresses an amazing paean of praise which shows how far Marian devotion had progressed: "Queen of the whole human race, faithful indeed to the meaning of your name, you are over all things, except God."[79]

In the writings of the Bishop of Crete, the emphasis on Mary's role as Mediatrix of human beings before God is also frequent and significant. Exalting the marvel of the Incarnation, he explains that in virtue of this event, a kind of kinship came to exist between God and humanity. In such a context, he illustrates the function of Mary thus: "What a marvel! She acts as Mediatrix between God's sublimity and the lowliness of the flesh and becomes the Mother of the Creator."[80] Another text greets Mary as Mediatrix between "law and grace, Old and New Testament."[81] In his canons, used for liturgical celebrations, he continuously invokes Mary's intercession. Let us take an example:

> You, who deserved to carry God in your womb, O spouse of God and his immaculate Virgin Mother, do not cease interceding for us, so that we may be free from all misfortunes, since we always take refuge under your protection."[82]

---

[75] *Homilia II in Dormitionem*, PG 97, 1080 B.
[76] *Homilia in Annuntiationem*, PG 97, 893 B.
[77] Cf. *Homilia in Nativitatem*, PG 97, 848-853.
[78] *Homilia III in Nativitatem*, PG 97, 844 C.
[79] *Homilia III in Dormitionem*, PG 97, 1100 A.
[80] *Homilia II in Nativitatem*, PG 97, 808 C.
[81] *Homilia IV in Nativitatem*, PG 97, 865 A.
[82] *Canon in Mediam Pentecostem*, ode 4, PG 97, 1425B.

In the thought of Andrew of Crete, Mary's mediation is obviously linked with her great role as Mother of God, and ever respectful of the primacy of Christ's role as mediator between God and man, unique on his level. From a mere Mariological point of view, Andrew's doctrine seems to be less significant than Germanus', but he greatly contributed to improving the presence of Mary in the liturgy and piety of the Byzantine Church.

Andrew left us a short treatise on the veneration of sacred icons. He confirms that this religious practice belongs to the ancient tradition of the Church and proves it through some interesting examples of icons venerated from Christian antiquity related to Jesus and Mary. He first mentions the famous image of Jesus:

> ... image of our Lord Jesus Christ, sent to King Abgar. This image on a wooden tablet showed the outlines of his bodily form.
>
> The second example is that of the image not painted by human hands (*acheropita*) of her who gave birth without seed: it is found at Lidda, a city also called Diospolis. The image is painted in very bright colors and shows the body of the Mother of God, three cubits in height. It was venerated in the time of the apostles on the western wall of the Temple that they built. It is so finely done that it appears to have been produced by the hands of a painter. It clearly shows her purple habit, her hands, her face, and all of her outward form, as can still be affirmed today. They say that when Julian, that apostate and enemy of Christ, heard about the painting, he wanted to know more about it. So he sent some Jewish painters [to examine it], who informed him that it was genuine; Julian dumbfounded, had no desire to investigate further.
>
> It is told that the Temple was constructed when the Mother of God was still living. Going up to Sion, where she lived, the apostles said to her: "Where were you, Lady, when we have built you a house at Lidda?" Mary answered them: "I was with you, and I am still with you." Returning to Lidda and entering the Temple, they found her complete image painted there, as she had told

them. This is what an ancient local tradition has testified from the beginning, and the tradition lives today.

...Everyone witnesses to the fact that Luke, apostle and evangelist, painted the incarnate Christ and his immaculate Mother with his own hands and that these images are conserved in Rome with fitting honor. Others assert that these images are kept at Jerusalem. Even the Jew Josephus tells that the Lord looked just like the picture: eyebrows meeting in the middle, beautiful eyes, long face, somewhat oval, of a fair height. This was undoubtedly his appearance when he dwelt among men. Josephus describes the appearance of the Mother of God in the same way, as it appears today in the image that some call the Roman woman.[83]

In speaking of *John Damascene* (+c.750), we come to the last and one of the greatest of the Greek Fathers. As his own nickname suggests, he was born in Damascus, Syria, from a noble Christian family; but he spent all his life as a monk and priest in the monastery of St. Saba, near Jerusalem, where he went on with his mission of teaching, preaching, and writing. He was an eminent theologian and hymnographer. In the treatise *De fide orthodoxa*, his theological masterpiece, he touches on Marian themes, but he does this especially in his Marian homilies and liturgical hymns. St. John dealt more or less with all Mariological questions that were topical in his time, such as Mary's divine predestination; the images and prophecies of the Old Testament applied to Mary in Christian tradition; the meaning of the name "Maria," which he translated as Lady (*Kyria*), according to Syriac terminology; her perpetual virginity and divine motherhood. He thought that the term of Mother of God (*Theotókos*) expressed the whole mystery of the Incarnation.[84] We will do better to concentrate on some aspects of John's Marian doctrine that are more original, and which even today make him a theological authority quoted in the magisterial documents of the Church.

Frequently he presents Mary as a wonderful creature, filled with spiritual richness. Her conception and nativity were under the prevailing

---

[83] This short treatise is available in PG 97, 1301-1304.
[84] *De fide orthodoxa* 3, 12, PG 94, 1029 C.

influence of divine grace. These two events even conditioned the role played by her parents Joachim and Anne. Their preceding sterility had an explanation: "Since the Virgin *Theotókos* is to be born from Anne, nature did not dare to anticipate the fruit of grace, but remained fruitless until grace brought forth the fruit."[85] Therefore Anne's fruitlessness was a previous condition disposed by God in his divine economy, so that the predominant role of grace in Mary could more clearly appear. John contemplates in Mary a kind of "new heaven": "This heaven is much more divine and marvelous indeed than the first one. In fact, the one who in the first sky created our sun is going to be born in this second heaven as the sun of justice."[86] Mary is like the lofty ladder set by her Son between heaven and earth. This was seen by the Patriarch Jacob in a dream (Cf. Gen 28:12). In fact, the Damascene thought that Mary became the way through which human creatures communicate with their Creator.[87]

John stresses the fact that Mary's spiritual perfection is the result of her special relationship with her divine Son: "She is all beautiful, very near to God, for she, surpassing the cherubim and exalted beyond the seraphim, is indeed near to God."[88]

On the mystery of the end of Our Lady's life on earth, John Damascene dedicated three homilies that he delivered for the celebration of the feast of the Dormition. Sharing in the teaching of his two great contemporaries, Germanus of Constantinople and Andrew of Crete, John shared the idea that death for Mary was just the premise of her imminent glorification:

> O how can the source of life be led to life through death? How can she obey the law of nature, since she in conceiving surpasses the boundaries of nature? How is her spotless body made subject to death? She first must put off mortality in order to be clothed with immortality, since the Lord of nature did not reject the penalty of death. She dies according to the flesh, destroys death by

---

[85] *Homilia in Nativitatem* 2, PG 96, 664 A.
[86] *Ibid.*, 3, PG 96, 664 D.
[87] *Ibid.*, 3, PG 96, 664.
[88] *Ibid.*, 9, PG 96, 676 D.

death, through corruption gives incorruption, and makes her own death the source of resurrection.[89]

Damascene established a connection between this privilege and Mary's virginity during the birth of Jesus: "The body of her, whose virginity remained unspotted in childbirth, was preserved in its incorruption, and was taken to a better and divine place, where there is no death, but eternal life."[90]

Once again, taking inspiration from the biblical image of the ladder of Jacob, John accentuates the concept of Mary's mediation in a text where he directly addresses the Blessed Virgin:

> Just as Jacob saw the ladder bringing together heaven and earth ... so you have become the Mediatrix (*mesiteusasa*) and the ladder through which God descended to take upon himself our weakness, uniting us to himself and enabling man to see God.[91]

St. John considers powerful the function of Mary as Mediatrix, because through her intervention we receive the fruits of the Incarnation that open to us the way to eternal life. The text speaks for itself:

> Through her the old enmity against the Creator is destroyed. Through her our reconciliation with him is strengthened; peace and grace are given to us; human beings are the companions of angels, and we who were in dishonor are made the children of God. From her we have plucked the fruit of life; from her we have received the need of immortality. She is the channel of all our goods. In her God became man and man became God.[92]

The teaching on Marian devotion by John of Damascus is noteworthy indeed, because it was conditioned not only by his interior attitude of respect and love toward Mary, but also by his personal involvement in the iconoclastic controversy, when he had to defend the legitimacy of the

---

[89] *Homilia I in Dormitionem* 10, PG 96, 713 D.
[90] *Ibid.*, 10, PG 96, 716 B.
[91] *Ibid.*, 8, PG 96, 713 A.
[92] *Homilia II in Dormitionem* 16, PG 96, 744 CD.

veneration of icons, many of which were images of the Mother of God. He composed three discourses against the calumniators of sacred icons and was able to elaborate a precise doctrine about cult and devotion. He speaks of *latreia* (or *latria*) when he refers to the cult due to God alone. As for devotion toward the saints (which includes Mary), he applies the concept of relation: the saints are related to God as his friends and servants. Mary is the greatest servant of God, because she is his Mother, and, therefore, she deserves a special cult among the saints.

Marian devotion can grow to the point of inspiring an act of very special dependence on Mary, which typically is referred to as Marian *consecration*. To express this attitude, the Damascene uses the verb *anatithemi*, which among its many significations in a religious context means dedicating, consecrating, and offering something acceptable to God. He writes:

> O Queen, O Virgin Mother of God, we bind our souls to your hope, as to a most firm and totally unbreakable anchor, consecrating (*anathemenoi*) to you mind, soul, body, and all our being and honoring you, as much as we can, with psalms, hymns, and spiritual canticles."[93]

According to his biography, written in the tenth century by a certain John, patriarch of Jerusalem, St. John of Damascus received a Marian apparition in a very special circumstance, which reveals his deep and tender love toward the Mother of God. In the period of the iconoclastic controversy, he came into conflict with the emperor, Leo III, because he had taken up the defense of sacred icons. The emperor devised a plan to take revenge against John, who at that time was living at the court of the Caliph of Damascus, and therefore out of his jurisdiction. Leo sent to the Caliph letters in which John was accused of plotting against the Caliph himself. This latter took the accusation seriously and had John's right hand cut off and hung in the public square to dissuade others. St. John went to the church and, crying, addressed the Blessed Virgin with the following prayer:

---

[93] *Homilia I in Dormitionem* 14, PG 96, 720 C-D.

> O Lady, most pure Mother, who gave birth to my God, it is because of the sacred icons that my right hand has been cut off. You are not unaware of the cause of Leo's rage. Hurry then, show your help, and give back my hand to me. The right hand of the Most High, who took flesh from you, performed innumerable wonders through your intercession. May he heal my right hand through your prayers and it will compose for you and for the one who took flesh from you, hymns and harmonious melodies, and will become an instrument of the orthodox faith. You can in fact what you will, because you are the true Mother of God.

Afterwards the saint fell asleep and had a dream. Mary appeared to him saying: "Your hand is healed; keep the vow you made in your prayer." Waking up, John realized that he was healed. Then standing with uplifted arms, he sang the following hymn: "Your right hand, O Lord, has been greatly magnified! Your right hand healed my cut hand! Through it you throw into confusion the enemies who refuse to venerate your image and the image of the one who gave you life. In your multiform glory, you will through my hand destroy the enemies of the icons." John had a silver hand made and put it in front of the icon of the Mother of God as an *ex voto*.[94]

---

[94] This incident can be read in the biography mentioned, PG 94, 456–457. Though this story may not be able to be confirmed by other historical evidence, it may explain a Marian iconographic type called *Tricherousa*, namely the Mother of God of Three Hands, also called the Madonna of St. John Damascene, known and venerated in all Orthodox worlds. It may also be an amazing way to emphasize the Marian piety of this great theologian, with whom we consider the patristic period of the Eastern Church to be closed.

II.
Marian Dogma

The Mother of God

Fr. Manfred Hauke

The Divine Maternity as a Constituent of the "Fundamental Principle" in Mariology

> The Virgin Mary ... is acknowledged and honored as being truly the Mother of God and Mother of the Redeemer. Redeemed by reason of the merits of her son and united to him by a close and indissoluble tie, she is endowed with the high office and dignity of being the Mother of the Son of God, by which account she is also the beloved daughter of the Father and the temple of the Holy Spirit. Because of this gift of sublime grace she far surpasses all creatures, both in heaven and on earth.[1]

These words, taken from the Second Vatican Council, show very well the central importance of Mary as the Mother of God. The most relevant Marian dogma, the divine maternity, is essentially linked to the most important Christological dogma, the hypostatic union: in the person, or hypostasis, of the eternal Son of God are united the divine and the human nature of Christ. The definition of the title *Theotókos* (God-bearer) at the Council of Ephesus (431) underlines the unity of the two natures of Christ in the same personal subject: as Jesus Christ is one person, the Son of God who assumed a human nature from the Virgin Mary, she must be the Mother of God. Obviously Mary does not generate God in his divinity, but she generates the Son of God in his humanity, because he takes his human nature from her. For this reason her dignity is above that of the whole of creation. She is truly "Mother of God."

---

[1] *Lumen Gentium* 53.

Every Christian who wants to develop a balanced view about Mary must consider the divine maternity at the beginning of his reflections. In modern theology, the centrality of this belief manifests itself in the discussion about the so-called "fundamental principle" in Mariology.[2] There are different answers to this question which should be the foundational truth for any systematic reflection about the Holy Virgin. The various reflections, in any case, have to integrate the divine maternity into this fundamental truth. The discussion about the "fundamental principle" does not mean that every doctrine of faith about Mary can be deduced from this basic truth in a "geometrical" way. But there is a kind of center to which these single doctrines "move" and from which they "come." Already by the twelfth century, Eadmer, a famous theologian from the Middle Ages, deduces affirmations about Mary from the fact that she is the Mother of God,[3] whereas a Greek theologian, John the Geometer (tenth century), praises the perpetual virginity as the basic Marian truth.[4] A more systematic discourse begins after the Council of Trent and uses the terms "first principle" and "fundament." Lawrence of Brindisi (+1619) calls the divine maternity the "first principle of the nobility and dignity of Mary."[5] Also Francis Suarez, S.J. (+1617), "the founder of systematic or scholastic Mariology,"[6] thinks that the dignity of being the Mother of God is the fundament from which can be developed everything about the Blessed Virgin.[7]

Systematic discussion concerning the "fundamental principle," with various solutions, was only begun in the twentieth century; the

---

[2] Cf. Michael O'Carroll, *Theotokos. A Theological Encyclopedia of the Blessed Virgin Mary*, Eugene, OR, 2000, 152-153; Leo Scheffczyk, *Fundamentalprinzip, mariol.*, in Marienlexikon 2 (1989) 565-567; Stefano De Fiores, *Maria Madre di Gesù*, Bologna 1992, 189-197; J.L. Bastero de Eleizalde, *María, Madre del Redentor*, Pamplona 1995, 29-35; Anton Ziegenaus, *Maria in der Heilsgeschichte. Mariologie* (Katholische Dogmatik V), Aachen 1998, 28-43; Manfred Hauke, *La questione del "Primo principio" e l'indole della cooperazione di Maria all'opera redentrice di Cristo: due temi rilevanti nella mariologia di Gabriele M. Roschini*, in Marianum 64 (2002) 569-597.

[3] Eadmer, *Liber de excellentia Virginis Mariae* (PL 159, 557-580).

[4] John the Geometer, *Hymni in SS. Deiparam* (Analecta Byzantina, Poznan 1931); cf. L. Scheffczyk (note 2) 566.

[5] Lawrence of Brindisi, *Mariale*, Padova 1929, 479; cf. S. De Fiores (note 2) 189.

[6] M. O'Carroll (note 2) 334.

[7] Cf. Francis Suarez, *Mysteria vitae Christi*, Venice 1605, disp. I, p. 2; cf. S. De Fiores (note 2) 189.

most important starting point, still valuable, is an article by the Belgian theologian Jacques Bittremieux in 1931.[8] Bittremieux, already famous for his systematic study on the universal mediation of Mary,[9] proposed a double basic principle: Mary as "Mother of God and Helpmate of the Redeemer" (*mater Dei et consors Filii sui Redemptoris*). According to him, the divine maternity and Mary's association with the redemption are linked to one another: Mary's role as Helpmate of the Redeemer is based on her divine maternity, whereas her divine maternity leads to Mary being the companion of our Savior in redemption. Bittremieux makes a comparison with the mystery of Christ discussed in the *Summa Theologiae*: Thomas Aquinas distinguishes between the Incarnation of the Son of God and the mysteries of his life (what Christ has accomplished and suffered for us).[10] As Christology and soteriology were later distinguished from one another, so it is possible to present Mary as the Mother of God (oriented to the incarnated Son of God) and as the Helpmate of the Redeemer.

The theological discussion after Bittremieux did not arrive at a conclusion accepted by all specialists in Mariology but the various proposals tended towards this dual structure: accentuating the divine maternity (which prolongs itself into the spiritual motherhood for the Church) and Mary's cooperation in the work of salvation, with the culminating points at the Annunciation and under the Cross. "This dual structure corresponds to the order of redemption with the Incarnation and the death on the Cross; neither in this order can be reduced to a single principle."[11] Proposals which do not integrate the divine maternity into the fundamental principle of Mariology risk ruining the whole systematic approach to the figure of Mary, as happens, for example, with the theory of Karl Rahner who presents the fact that Mary has been perfectly redeemed as the fundamental principle of Mariology; according to him, the divine maternity is also included in this reception of redemption.[12] Here the active cooperation of Mary in redemption is

---

[8] Jacques Bittremieux, *De principio supremo Mariologiae*, in Ephemerides Theologiae Lovanienses 8 (1931) 249-251; cf. M. Hauke, *Primo principio* (note 2) 572-575.
[9] Jacques Bittremieux, *De Mediatione universali B.M. Virginis quoad gratias*, Bruges 1926.
[10] Cf. Thomas Aquinas, *Summa Theologiae* III, prologus.
[11] L. Scheffczyk (note 2) 567.
[12] Cf. A. Ziegenaus (note 2) 39.

not taken seriously, a defect typical for approaches which only present the Holy Virgin as the type of the Church it its receptivity, without putting any value on her association with the redemptive work of Christ. Matthias Joseph Scheeben, the most renowned German theologian of the nineteenth century, tries to describe this duality as a single principle, speaking of a "bridal mother" and a "maternal bride." With her *fiat* at the Annunciation, her divine maternity takes on a "bridal" aspect: Mary consents to the proposal of God the Father, Son and Holy Spirit to become the Mother of the Savior. Her cooperation at redemption, on the other side, is totally determined by her being the Mother of God: it is a maternal mediation in Christ.[13]

Biblical Foundation[14]

Holy Scripture does not contain the explicit title, "Mother of God," but offers the doctrinal basis for this expression. The correct understanding of the figure of Mary depends on a true understanding of the person of Jesus Christ, the incarnate Word of God (Jn 1:14). When discussing the biblical foundation for calling Mary Mother of God, we have to take into consideration all the affirmations which link the divinity of Jesus with the maternity of Mary.

The most important scriptural passage comes from the Letter of the Apostle Paul to the Galatians: in the fullness of time, "God sent his Son, born of a woman, born under the law, to redeem those who were under the law, that we might receive the adoption of sons" (Gal 4:4-5).[15] It is the only passage of the Pauline letters which contains an allusion to Mary, because the Apostle of the Gentiles does not report many biographical details about the life of Christ. He focuses his attention on

---

[13] Cf. M.J. Scheeben, *Mariology I-II*, St. Louis – London 1946; Manfred Hauke, *Die Mariologie Scheebens – ein zukunftsträchtiges Vermächtnis*, in Idem – Michael Stickelbroeck (eds.), *Donum veritatis*, Regensburg 2005, 255-274 (261-263).

[14] Cf. A.M. Serra, *Madre di Dio I. Fondamenti biblici*, in Stefano De Fiores – Salvatore Meo (eds.), *Nuovo dizionario di Mariologia*, Cinisello Balsamo 1985, 806-812; Brunero Gherardini, *La Madre. Maria in una sintesi storico-teologica*, Frigento 1989, 63-69; Miguel Ponce Cuéllar, *María. Madre del Redentor y Madre de la Iglesia*, Barcelona, 2001, 299-300.

[15] For an exegetical analysis of this passage, see Albert Vanhoye, *La Mère de Dieu selon Gal 4,4*, in Marianum 40 (1978) 237-247; S.M. Manelli, *All Generations Shall Call Me Blessed. Biblical Mariology*, New Bedford, MA, 2005, 137-142.

the Incarnation (especially in Phil 2:5-11), and particularly focuses on the Cross and the Resurrection of Christ (e.g. 1 Cor 15:3-8). This is the reason why Paul gives very little information about the Mother of Christ: he does not even mention her name. The aim of the passage in Galatians is to underline the true humanity of Christ, "born" of a woman and under the law of Moses (cf. Gal 4:4-5). The Son of God has taken upon himself the human condition of a Jew, in order to introduce humanity into the life of God as adopted sons.

Nevertheless, we may consider Galatians 4:4 the most important passage for dogmatic Mariology in the whole New Testament.[16] God (the Father) sends his Son into the world: this formulation presupposes the preexistence of the Son before being born of the woman, that is, we find here a hint of the divinity of Christ (for other references to the divinity of Christ in the Pauline letters, see in particular 1 Cor 8:6; Phil 2:5-11). If the Son of God is born by Mary, she can later on be called "Mother of God." In the most ancient New Testament passage about Mary we find her strictly united to the event of the Incarnation; for this reason it is not possible to separate her from her Son. It should also be noted that Paul, speaking about the human condition of Jesus, does not mention any human paternity in the process of generation; he only indicates the "woman." This fact can be seen as an implicit reference to the virginal maternity of Mary.[17]

The Gospel of Luke, which gives us the most abundant references about the Virgin Mary, also contains a most significant testimony about her divine maternity. In the Annunciation narrative, the evangelist links the maternity of Mary with the divinity of Christ: "Therefore, he who is to be born of you shall be holy and shall be called the Son of God" (Lk 1:35b). Whereas St. John the Baptist is conceived in a normal way, though the sterility of Elizabeth is overcome miraculously (cf. Lk 1:5-25), Jesus is generated from the Virgin Mary by the force of the Holy Spirit without any intervention of a human father. Here we see the difference between the greatest prophet and the Son of God. The Gospel of Luke

---

[16] Cf. Georg Söll, *Mariologie* (Handbuch der Dogmengeschichte III/4), Freiburg i. Br. 1978, 11.

[17] Cf. E. de Roover, *La maternité virginale de Marie dans l'interprétation de Gal 4,4*, in Studiorum Paulinorum Congressus Internationalis Catholicus 1961 (Analecta Biblica 18), Roma 1963, 17-37; S.M. Manelli (note 15) 139-141.

does not speak explicitly of the preexistent divinity of Christ, but this conviction is certainly implicit. Moreover, for Luke, the preeminence of Jesus is not only linked to the virginal conception, but also to his being the Son of God even before assuming human nature in the womb of the Holy Virgin.

We should note that already the hymn to Christ in the Letter to the Philippians, with its formulations taken by Paul from the primitive Christian community, clearly professes the preexistence of the Son of God (Phil 2:5-11). This text is even older than the Gospel of Mark, the first, according to some, in chronological order of the synoptic gospels. For this reason, and on the basis of a historical analysis of New Testament sources, we can exclude the theory that belief in the divinity of Christ is present only in the "late" Gospel of John.[18]

After the Annunciation, the scene of the Visitation also gives a precious reference regarding the divine maternity. Elizabeth proclaims, face to face with Mary: "To what do I owe that the mother of my Lord should come to me?" (Lk 1:43). The Greek word for "Lord" is *Kyrios*, a term used abundantly by the Septuagint (the most important Greek translation of the Old Testament) for referring to God without using his revealed name (*Yahweh*) which, at the time of Jesus, was never pronounced by the Jews. Also, in the immediate context of Elizabeth's question, the term "Lord" clearly refers to God (Lk 1:45-46). The Lord proclaimed by Luke is therefore the divine Lord.[19] Thus it is only a small step from the expression "mother of the Lord" to the title "Mother of God."

The Visitation can be compared with the account of the journey of the Ark of the Old Covenant to Jerusalem (2 Sam 6:1-15). Many exegetes see in these parallels an implicit hint in the Gospel that Mary is the new Ark of the Covenant in which God himself comes to visit mankind and to sanctify John the Baptist in the womb of Elizabeth, who prophesies in the joy of the Holy Spirit.[20] Here we also see a link between Mary's divine maternity and her spiritual motherhood: when Mary is arriving

---

[18] Cf. e.g. Martin Hengel, *Der Sohn Gottes. Die Entstehung der Christologie und die jüdisch-hellenistische Religionsgeschichte*, Tübingen 1975 (English translation *The Son of God*, London – Philadelphia, 1976).

[19] See also S.M. Manelli (note 15) 190-192.

[20] Cf. René Laurentin, *The Truth of Christmas Beyond the Myths. The Gospels of the Infancy of Christ*, Petersham, MA, 1986, 54-56, 154-159.

and greeting Elizabeth, John the Baptist is sanctified and in this way receives a fruit of the mediation of Christ, mediated by the Mother of the Lord.

Whereas the strongest biblical testimonies about the divine maternity can be found in Paul's Letter to the Galatians and in the Gospel of Luke, some discrete hints are also present in Matthew, Mark and John. Matthew, recording the prophecy of Isaiah about the birth of the "Emmanuel" (Is 7:14), mentions that this name signifies "God with us" (Mt 1:23).

> Taken strictly, this expression already indicates the divinity of Christ, that is to say, that Jesus is the Son of God conceived in the womb of a virgin. ... In such wise, Jesus is at the same time Son of God and son of Adam.[21]

The Gospel of Mark does not contain such an explicit hint, although Jesus is called "son of Mary" (Mk 6:3), whereas the parallel passages in Matthew and Luke speak of the "son of the carpenter" (Mt 13:55) or the "son of Joseph" (Lk 4:22) (as the Jews thought him to be). Matthew and Luke can mention Joseph as "father" of Jesus without any problem, because readers already know Christ's divine origin from the infancy narratives. Mark, who begins his account with Jesus' Baptism in the Jordan, calls Jesus "son of Mary," contrary to the normal practice of mentioning children according to their paternal lineage. This procedure hints at the virginal peculiarity of Mary's motherhood.[22] Already Mark is putting the profession of faith that Jesus Christ is the "Son of God" at the very center of his message (Mk 1:1; 9:7; 14:61-62; 15:39, etc.).

The testimony of John for the divinity of Jesus is quite explicit (Jn 1:1; 20:28; 1 Jn 5:20). In the narratives about the miracle of Cana and the death of Christ on the Cross, Mary is not mentioned by her name, but called the "mother" of Jesus (Jn 2:1; 19:25). Given the premise that her Son is the eternal Word made flesh (Jn 1:14), the divine maternity is evidently a truth implicitly present in the Gospel of John. Under the Cross, the maternity of Mary is extended by Christ to the beloved disciple, who represents all believers in him: "Behold your mother" (Jn

---

[21] S.M. Manelli (note 15) 241.
[22] Cf. A. Ziegenaus (note 2) 85-88.

19:27).²³ This spiritual maternity of Mary manifests itself as a consequence of her being Mother of God. This systematical perspective, developed later on in the Church, is hinted at already in the biblical source. Mary is not only the mother of the divine Son, but she also takes care of the adoptive children of God. The divine maternity cannot be separated from her maternal mediation.

The Patristic Tradition until the End of the Fourth Century[24]

The First Testimonies about the Divine Maternity before the Appearance of the Technical Term **Theotókos**

In the beginning of the patristic tradition, the maternity of Mary is emphasized against Gnostic heresies, which denied the true humanity of Jesus. As early as the first century, Ignatius of Antioch (c. 107), one of the Apostolic Fathers, stresses the real birth and death of Jesus Christ against the idea that our Lord was not truly born of Mary and only "appeared" to die on the Cross. This heretical view is called "Docetism" (from *dokein*, "to seem"). Ignatius teaches the true corporality of the incarnate Son of God:

> Be deaf whenever one speaks to you apart from Jesus Christ who was of the race of David, of Mary, who was really born, ate and drank, was really persecuted under Pontius Pilate ... who really rose from the dead.[25]

Together with the real birth of Christ by the Virgin Mary, Ignatius also underlines the unity of Christ, who as the eternal Son of God unites divinity and humanity: "There is but one physician, bodily and spiritual, born and unborn, God who became flesh, true life in death, from Mary,

---

[23] Cf. S.M. Manelli (note 15) 375-380.
[24] For a detailed treatment of the Fathers, see Luigi Gambero, *Mary and the Fathers of the Church: The Blessed Virgin Mary in Patristic Thought*, San Francisco 1999. On divine maternity until the end of the fourth century, see also G. Söll (note 16) 48-49, 60-63; Gerhard Ludwig Müller, *Gottesmutter*, in Marienlexikon 2 (1989) 684-692 (686-688); Marek Starowieyski, *Le titre Theotokos avant le concile d'Ephèse*, in *Studia Patristica XIX* (1989) 237-242; M. Ponce Cuéllar (note 14) 300-307.
[25] Ignatius of Antioch, *In Trall*. 9:1-2 (SC 10bis, 100), translated in M. O'Carroll (note 2) 177.

from God, first suffering and then impassible, Jesus Christ, our Lord."[26] Christ is only one personal subject, but he unites in himself divine and human attributes. Speaking of him as "God who became flesh" reflects the truth that later came to be called "communication of idioms:" the divine and human attributes ("idioms" are the specific proprieties) can be attributed to the same divine person in which they "communicate." The unity of Christ as the divine person, the eternal Son who has assumed a human nature, is the systematical basis from which we can speak of Mary as Mother of God. The technical term "hypostatic union" only comes into use later on, but what it signifies is perfectly present in the Church's teaching from the beginning, as we can see with the example of Ignatius.

The most important Father who combats Gnosticism is Irenaeus, bishop of Lyons at the end of the second century. He was brought up in the circle of Bishop Polycarp at Smyrna, who was himself a pupil of the Apostle John. Irenaeus refutes the Docetism of Marcion: According to his heretical position, Jesus was not born of the Virgin Mary, but came to earth as an adult, first presenting himself in the synagogue of Capernaum. Marcion also held that Jesus' body was not a true body but only an illusion; for this reason Marcion eliminated the infancy narratives in the gospels.[27] The Gnostics from the school of Valentinus accepted the maternity of Mary, but only in an improper way: according to them, the Son of God came to earth with a heavenly body which only passed through the womb of Mary as water passes through a channel.[28] According to these Docetist errors, Jesus "was born *through* a virgin, but not *of* a virgin, and *in* a womb, not *of* a womb."[29] Whereas Marcionites said that Jesus only appeared to have a human body, without becoming human, and Valentinians pretended that he became human without receiving anything from Mary, Irenaeus teaches that Jesus really and truly became man from the Virgin; otherwise his saving Passion would be without any importance for us.[30] "The Son of God was born of the Virgin."[31]

---

[26] Ignatius of Antioch, *In Eph.* 7:2 (SC 10bis, 64), translated in M. O'Carroll (note 2) 177.

[27] Cf. Irenaeus, *Adversus haereses* I, 27 (SC 264, 348-354); Tertullian, *Adversus Marcionem* (SC 365, 368, 399); *De carne Christi* (SC 216-217).

[28] Cf. Irenaeus, *Adv. haer.* III, 17,3; 22,1-2 (SC 211, 334-336. 430-436).

[29] Tertullian, *De carne Christi* XX, 1 (SC 216, 290).

[30] Cf. *Adv. haer.* III, 22, 1 (SC 211, 430-432).

[31] *Adv. haer.* III, 16, 2 (SC 211, 292-294).

Presenting together the birth of Christ from the Virgin Mary and the rebirth of Christians from the "maternal womb" of baptism in the Church, Irenaeus gives a strong hint as to the relation between the divine maternity of Mary and the spiritual maternity of the Church: the Son of God, the "pure one purely opens the pure womb, which regenerates men in God, which he himself had made pure."[32]

The true maternity of the Virgin Mary is also affirmed, against Gnostic errors, in professions of faith such as the catecheses of Cyril of Jerusalem (+387): the Word "became man not apparently or in our fantasy, but really. He did not pass through the Virgin like passing through a channel, but he has really taken flesh from her."[33] For this reason, the professions of faith (like the Apostles' Creed or the creed formulated by the councils of Nicea and Constantinople) do not say that the Son of God is born "by" the Virgin Mary (*per* in Latin, *dià* in Greek), but "from" or "of" the Holy Virgin (*ex Maria Virgine*, in Greek, *ek*).[34]

The maternity of Mary guarantees the true humanity of Jesus Christ. As Mother of the Son of God, Mary also manifests the divinity of Christ. The decisive basis for the divine maternity is the communication of idioms, formulated in the third century by Tertullian: the Son of God is "born" and then "died" on the Cross.[35] This theological foundation is more important than the phrase "Mother of God," which does not yet appear in the works of this theologian. In the same century, the Alexandrian theologian Origen had probably already used the expression *Theotókos*,[36] but his Christology poses some problems as to the communication of idioms.[37]

---

[32] *Adv. haer.* IV, 33, 11 (SC 100, 830); cf. M. O'Carroll (note 2) 190.

[33] Cyril of Jerusalem, *Cat.* IV, 9 (PG 33, 465 B – 468 A). See also the title *Theotókos* in *Cat.* X, 19 (PG 33, 685 A).

[34] Cf. DS 10-30; 150.

[35] Tertullian, *De carne Christi* V,1 (SC 216, 226).

[36] This assertion is not proved because the term appears only in fourth-century Latin translations of Greek sources which have been lost. See G. Söll (note 16) 49. In any case, the Greek historian Socrates (d. after 439) mentions that Origen, in his Commentary on the Letter to the Romans, already used and explained the expression *Theotókos*: *Historia Ecclesiae* VII, 32 (PG 67, 812 B).

[37] Cf. Alois Grillmeier, *Christ in Christian Tradition*, London 1975, 138-149. The appearance of the title in the works of Hippolytus of Rome (d. 235) is a later interpolation: cf. G. Söll (note 16) 48; F. Baumeister, *Hippolyt v. Rom*, in Marienlexikon 3 (1991) 212f; M. O'Carroll (note 2) 172.

The Council of Nicea (325) defends the divinity of Christ against Arius, for whom the divine Word was not God but only a magnificent creature existing from time immemorial. The technical term for "Mother of God," *Theotókos*, which literally means "God-bearer" in Greek, was already being used in Egypt before Nicea. The Greek term which literally means "Mother of God," *mêter theou*, was used later on, and more rarely. The first incontrovertible use of the term *Theotókos* is found around the year 320 in the letter of Alexander, bishop of Alexandria, who announces the deposition of Arius to Alexander, bishop of Constantinople:

> After this we know of the resurrection of the dead, the first-fruits of which was our Lord Jesus Christ, who in very deed, and not merely in appearance, carried a body, of Mary, Mother of God, who at the end of times came to the human race to put away any sin, was crucified and died, and yet without any detriment to his divinity, being raised from the dead, taken up into heaven, and seated at the right hand of Majesty.[38]

In this text, we find the title "Mother of God" as part of a profession of faith promulgated in a circular letter from the Alexandrian Bishop Alexander, head of the Egyptian Church, to his fellow bishops. Its use without need of comment, in such an official text, presupposes that its use had already become commonplace some time before, allowing us to arrive at a date of around the third century for the origin of the term. This provenience is confirmed by an early papyrus of the famous prayer *Sub Tuum Praesidium* found in the desert of Egypt: the text comes from the third or (latest) from the fourth century:[39] "Under your mercy, we take refuge, Mother of God, do not reject our supplications in necessity. But deliver us from danger. (You) alone chaste, alone blessed."[40]

---

[38] Alexander of Alexandria, *Ep. ad Alex. Const.* 12 (PG 82, 908 A-B). For the appearance of the terms *Theotókos* and *Mêter theou* in the Ancient Christian sources see also G.W.H. Lampe, *A Patristic Greek Lexikon*, Oxford 1987, 639. 868.

[39] Cf. M. O'Carroll (note 2) 342; Leo Scheffczyk, *Theotokos*, in Marienlexikon 6 (1994) 390-391.

[40] English translation in M. O'Carroll (note 2) 336; see also, together with the Greek text, Theodor Maas-Ewerd, *Sub Tuum Praesidium*, in Marienlexikon 6 (1994) 327-328.

A Pagan Origin for the Christian Doctrine of the Divine Maternity?

The word *Theotókos*, as such, is even older than Christianity and has a pagan origin. According to testimonies beginning in the second century of the Christian era, the term is given to the divine mother of the gods, who was not normally called *Theotókos*, but *mêter theíon*, "mother of the gods."[41] In the liberal school of the history of religion (*religionsgeschichtliche Schule*) during the nineteenth and beginning of the twentieth centuries, the pagan origin of the word was interpreted as a proof for the thesis that ancient Christianity was a syncretism from diverse religions. These researchers insinuated that the various cults of the mother goddesses were the source of devotion to Mary and the doctrine of divine maternity. They noted that the dogma of the *Theotókos* was proclaimed at the Council of Ephesus (431), a city formerly known as the center of the cult to the goddess Artemis (Diana), who unites in herself maternal and virginal traits. This theory has been "recycled" by feminist publications, but also in the realms of Protestantism. Feminists present Mary as a goddess in early Christianity whose secret cult was suppressed by the patriarchal authority of the Church, and they believe that one should transfer the female traits of Mary to God, who, according to them, is our real mother in heaven.[42]

From the point of view of systematic theology, Mary is also a revelation of the "female" traits of God, but in this she specifically manifests the cooperation of the *creature* in the redemptive work of Christ. Mary is the Mother of God and not the Divine Mother. St. Ambrose gives a brilliant summary of this account, which he formulates thus: "Mary is the temple of God, but not the God of the temple."[43] Mary, as type of the Church and of redeemed humanity, can participate in the salvation process.

From a historical point of view, the thesis of the *religionsgeschichtliche Schule* is plainly false.[44] The origin of the divine maternity of Mary comes

---

[41] Epiphanius, *Panarion* 79 (GCS 37, 475-485); cf. G. L. Müller (note 24) (684).

[42] For a critical presentation of feminist Mariology, see Manfred Hauke, *God or Goddess? Feminist Theology: What Is It? Where Does It Lead?* San Francisco 1995, 180-204.

[43] Ambrose, *De Spiritu Sancto* III, 80 (PL 16, 795 A).

[44] See for instance Jean Daniélou, *Le culte marial et le paganisme*, in Hubert du Manoir (ed.), *Maria I*, Paris 1952, 159-181; G. Söll (note 16) 68-69; G. L. Müller (1989)

from Divine Revelation itself, as has been shown above. The theologians of the Ancient Church were not sympathizers of an indiscriminate reception of pagan elements into the Church, as these elements were seen prevalently as manifestations of the Devil. Tertullian, for instance, calls Cybele, the mother of the gods, *magna mater daemonum* (great mother of the evil spirits).[45] What Marian devotion and the goddess cults have in common is the importance of the feminine in the religious realm. For this reason we can observe a natural esteem for maternity, but also (though less evident) for virginity. In the Ancient Church the religious importance of female symbolism is underlined by accentuating human cooperation: the Church, for example, appears like the moon, which receives its light from the sun, Jesus Christ. It is the "heavenly body with the femininely soft and maternally fecund light, which receives the masculine and powerful rays of the sun and passes them, lovingly softened, down to the earth."[46]

This new accent is already prepared for in the history of Israel, beginning with the divine mission of the prophet Hosea: the love between bridegroom and spouse appears as symbol of the Covenant between God and his people, a relation which becomes the alliance between Christ and his Church in the New Testament (Eph 5:21-33). The Christian faith could assume some traits that stem from natural religiosity, such as statues of a mother giving milk to her child; this type of image could be used to depict a pagan goddess such as the divine mother Isis, but also the Mother of God. Nevertheless, these pagan expressions of religious sentiment have been exposed to a purification, a sanctification, according to the criteria given by the word of God. As to exterior parallels (like the word *Theotókos*), it must be made clear: a linguistic analogy is not identical with a historical origin of doctrine.

The distinction between Christianity and paganism is reflected even on the terminological level: in the first centuries, Christians had been very reticent to use the word "Mother of God" (*mêter theou*), as it was also used in Egyptian religion for various goddesses (especially Isis). The Egyptian Church chose a less current term, *Theotókos*, giving to it a specifically Christian significance. The "word was almost completely

---

(note 24) 690-692; S. De Fiores (note 2) 27-30.

[45] Cf. Tertullian, *De spectaculis* VIII, 5 (SC 332, 162).

[46] Hugo Rahner, *Symbole der Kirche. Die Ekklesiologie der Väter*, Salzburg 1964, 99.

free of the undesirable pagan associations of the explicit vocabulary of 'mother of god/gods.'"[47]

> The differences between Mary and Isis were well clarified: she was also "the handmaid of the Lord," the chaste virgin whose son was true God and true man, whereas Isis was seen as a goddess, one who conceived her son in passion, entirely removed from the mysterious destiny of the Incarnation.[48]

As to the definition of the title *Theotókos* at Ephesus, some Protestant authors suggested that because this city had been the center of the cult of Artemis (Diana) the proclamation of Mary as Mother of God was merely a continuation of the Artemis cult. In fact, as early as the very beginning of the Church, St. Paul was confronted with this cult (Acts 19:28). Artemis, called the Great Mother, was venerated as symbol of fecundity and exaltation of maternal qualities. According to this particular Protestant interpretation, the desire to have a feminine Godhead subsequently entered into Christology. As a "proof" of their theory, the authors indicated the enthusiasm with which the people of Ephesus applauded the definition of the council.

These speculative affirmations are contrary to historical reality. The title *Theotókos* does not come from Ephesus, but from Alexandria. The cult of Artemis was already dead by 263, when the city was plundered by the Goths. The figure of Mary could have been attractive to religious sentiments that desired to honor the feminine, which were present in people before their conversion to Christianity, but Christianity operated a profound transformation of the symbolism present in these pagan religious systems: these feminine attributes became the expression for the cooperation of the creature in the process of redemption. The Mother of God is not a secret goddess, but the most holy created person called to collaborate with God.

A later sign of this transformation is visible, even in the iconography, in the apparition of Mary at Guadalupe. The place where the Mother

---

[47] D.F. Wright, *From "God-Bearer" to "Mother of God" in the Later Fathers*, in R.N. Swanson (ed.), *The Church and Mary* (Studies in Church History 39), Woodbridge (U.K.) – Rochester, NY 2004, 22-30 (23).
[48] M. O'Carroll (note 2) 342.

of God appeared was not far from a destroyed temple of the mother goddess, Tonantzin.

> [The] picture of Mary that arose miraculously on the visionary's cloak contains motifs pertaining to the world of Aztec gods: sun, moon, stars, and serpent. However, through the way that these symbols are arranged, paganism is turned completely upside-down. Mary stands before the sun and is thus more powerful than the feared sun god. She has one foot placed on the half-moon, a symbol of the feared serpent god, to whom thousands upon thousands of humans were sacrificed and whose machinations she has overcome. She is more powerful than all goddesses and gods, than the stars. And yet Mary is no goddess, for she folds her hands together in prayer and bows her head before one who is greater than she. She wears no mask in order to conceal her godly nature—as do the Aztec gods—but quite openly displays her human status.[49]

Development in the Fourth Century

Already in the beginning of the fourth century, *Theotókos* was a term with profound roots in the Christian faith in Egypt. In the Alexandrian realm, the expression was so common that even Arians used it (certainly they cited "God" here, between quotation marks so to speak). In the works of Athanasius (+373) we find the title a dozen times.[50] The fourth century also gives testimonies of the title "Mother of God" in the other regions of the Church besides Egypt. In 324-325, a synod at Antiochia (Syria) against Arius cites the Alexandrian creed and underlines: "The Son of God, the Word, is born from Mary Mother of God (*Theotókos*) and became flesh."[51] The Cappadocian Gregory of Nazianzus (+c.390) explains the concept of the hypostatic union in his famous Letter to Cledonius:

---

[49] M. Hauke, *God or Goddess?* (note 42) 203f.
[50] For instance Athanasius, *De incarnatione Dei Verbi* 8 (PG 26, 696); *In virginitatem* 3 (PG 28, 256); *Contra Arianos* III, 29 (PG 26, 385); cf. G. Söll (note 16) 60.
[51] Cf. G.L. Müller (1989) (note 24) 684.

> If anyone does not believe the holy Mary to be *Theotókos*, he is separated from the Godhead. If anyone should say that Christ passed through the Virgin as through a channel, and was not formed in her at once in a divine and human way, divine because without the help of man, human because subject to the law of human conception, he is equally godless. If anyone should say that first was formed the manhood of Jesus and that the God exists only after it, he too is to be condemned. ... If anyone introduces two sons, one of God the Father, and the other of the Mother, but not the one and the same, he must fall away from the adoption of sons promised to the orthodox. Because there are two natures, God and man, but not two sons.[52]

The title enters even in the realm of Antioch, contrary to the difficulties inherent in Antiochene theology. Antiochene Christology underlined the duality in Jesus Christ and preferred the term "Word-man" (*Logos-anthropos*) when speaking about him. The risk of this description is that the Word and the man Jesus can be presented as two different subjects, united only by their will (a moral, but not an ontological unity). The Alexandrian theologians, on the other hand, were accentuating the unity of Christ with the term "Word-flesh" (*Logos-sarx*). Their risk is to forget the clear distinction between the divine and the human nature in the incarnate Word. Whereas the Alexandrians were more inclined to accept Mary as "Mother of God," the Antiochenes were hesitant to use the phrase, because in their theology they tended to separate the Son of God from the man Jesus Christ, in whom, for them, the Son dwells as in a temple. This tendency comes from the founder of the Antiochene school, Diodor of Tarsus (+394), the teacher of John Chrysostom (who never uses the title *Theotókos*) and of Theodore of Mopsuestia (+428, that is before the Council of Ephesus in 431).[53] Theodore, recognized by the Nestorians as their theological "father," divides the actions of Christ between two distinct subjects, the man and the God who dwells in him. According to Theodore, we could only adore the Word who was

---

[52] Gregory of Nazianzus, *Ep.* 101,4 (PG 37, 177 A – 180 A).
[53] Cf. G. Söll (note 16) 88-89.

incarnate in Christ, but not the man Jesus, and it was only Jesus Christ the man, and not the Word, who was born of Mary. He did not refute the title *Theotókos*, but affirmed: "We cannot say that God was born by the Virgin."[54] Theodore was not inclined to really accept the divine maternity because he did not arrive at the doctrine of the hypostatic union in his Christology.

Even if the Antiochene theology was not favorable to the title *Theotókos*, by the end of the fourth century it was diffused everywhere in the Christian Orient. In the Latin West of the Roman Empire, we find the first occurrence of the term in the Spanish writer Prudentius (+405), who speaks of Mary as *Dei genitrix* (God-bearer).[55] Ambrose uses the expression *mater Dei* ("Mother of God") and affirms: "Mary has generated God."[56]

The Council of Ephesus (431)[57]

At the end of the fourth century, the title *Theotókos* was already widely diffused and was regarded as a part of the deposit of faith, first of all in Egypt. For this reason St. Cyril of Alexandria spoke of a "worldwide scandal" (*skándalon oikumenikón*), when the word was questioned. The controversy began when Nestorius, an eloquent monk from Antioch, was appointed patriarch of Constantinople in 428. He spoke out against the word *Theotókos*, preferring to speak of Mary as *Christotókos* (bearer of Christ). His difficulties, typical for the Antiochene school, came from his position against the communication of idioms, by which Christ's

---

[54] Theodore of Mopsuestia, *In Joh.* (PG 66, 997 B-C).
[55] Prudentius, *Psychomachia* (PL 60, 52 A). Cf. A. Ziegenaus (note 2) 213.
[56] Ambrose, *De virg.* II, 2, 13 (PL 16, 210 C); cf. G. Söll (note 16) 88.
[57] Cf. G. Söll (note 16) 88-96; Salvatore Meo, *Madre di Dio II. Dogma. Storia e teologia*, in S. De Fiores – S. Meo (note 14) 812-825 (815-819); Basil Studer, *Il concilio di Efeso (431) nella luce della dottrina Mariana di Cirillo di Alessandria*, in Sergio Felici (ed.), *La Mariologia nella catechesi dei Padri (età postnicena)*, Roma 1991, 49-67; Christiane Fraisse-Coué, *Die theologische Diskussion zur Zeit Theodosius' II.: Nestorius*, in Luce Piétri etc. (eds.), *Das Entstehen der einen Christenheit (250-430) (Die Geschichte des Christentums. Altertum II)*, Freiburg i. Br. 2005 (= 1996), 570-626 (originally in French: *Histoire du christianisme des origines à nos jours II. Naissance d'une chrétienté (250-430)*, Paris 1995); M. Ponce Cuéllar (note 14) 307-313. The critical edition of the Acts: Eduard Schwarz (ed.), ACO (= *Acta conciliorum oecumenicorum* I/1,1-8), Berlin 1927-30; the essential parts are translated in French: A.J. Festugière (ed.), *Ephèse et Calcédoine. Textes des conciles*, Paris 1982.

human actions and sufferings can be attributed to the divine person. He suspected an influence of Arianism in the use of the title *Theotókos* that presented the divine Word as a creature, subject to the passions. Nestorius spoke of a single "person" in Christ (*prosopon*), but he intended by this word only a moral union between two individual subjects. In Theodore of Mopsuestia and Nestorius a correct appreciation of the Blessed Virgin is blocked by their Christology: for their approach, "the humanity of Christ takes the position attributed in the traditional theology to Mary, 'temple' or bearer of God."[58]

The title *Theotókos* was defended by Cyril of Alexandria: when we say that the divine Word was born and has suffered, we do not intend to say that the divinity was born or has suffered, but we mean the humanity united to God. Mary is the Mother of God because she has born the eternal Son who has assumed human flesh, that is, she has born God according to the flesh.

Nestorius and Cyril both appealed to Pope Celestine, who took the part of Cyril. The Council of Ephesus (431), summoned by the emperor, accepted as its foundation the second letter of Cyril to Nestorius:

> The Word is said to have been begotten according to the flesh, because for us and for our salvation he united what was human to himself hypostatically and came forth from a woman. For he was not first begotten of the holy virgin, a man like us, and then the Word descended upon him; but from the very womb of his mother he was so united and then underwent begetting according to the flesh, making his own the begetting of his own flesh. ... So shall we find that the holy fathers believed. So have they dared to call the holy Virgin, Mother of God (*Theotókos*), not as though the nature of the Word or his Godhead received the origin of their being from the holy Virgin, but because there was born from her his holy body rationally ensouled, with which the Word was

---

[58] Anton Ziegenaus, *Jesus Christus. Die Fülle des Heils. Christologie und Erlösungslehre* (Katholische Dogmatik IV), Aachen 2000, 144. On the Christological doctrine of Nestorius, whom some theologians try to "purify" from heresy, see the balanced treatment, which justifies the condemnation, from Leo Scheffczyk, *Nestorius*, in Marienlexikon 4 (1992) 598f.

hypostatically united and is said to have been begotten in the flesh.[59]

In other words: *Jesus Christ, God and man, is one person, and for this reason Mary must be recognized as Mother of God.* The activity of Mary as "God-bearer" is relevant regarding the human generation of Jesus, but not the divine generation of the Second Person of the Trinity. The Word is born from Mary "according to the flesh." Mary is not the mother of the "Trinity," but of God's eternal Son. The term "God" is referring only to the person of the divine Word. Mary is not called "mother of the Godhead."

Cyril of Alexandria began the council before the arrival of the representatives sent by the Pope and without the Syrian bishops (from the Antiochene region). The representatives of the Holy Father consented to the proclamations of the council, but it was only two years later, in 433, that Cyril could establish an agreement with the Antiochene bishops in which they accepted the title *Theotókos*:

> We confess ... that our Lord Jesus Christ, the only begotten Son of God, perfect God and perfect man ..., generated from the Father before the centuries according to the Godhead, born, for us and for our salvation, at the end of the times by the Virgin Mary according to the humanity, of the same substance of the Father according to the Godhead, and of the same substance as us according to the humanity. As a matter of fact, the union of the two natures came through, and for this reason we confess only one Christ, only one Son, only one Lord. According to this concept of non-confused union, we confess the holy Virgin Mother of God, because the Word of God incarnated himself and became man, uniting to himself from the time of conception the temple assumed from her.[60]

---

[59] N.P. Tanner (ed.), *Decrees of the Ecumenical Councils I*, London 1990, 42-44. See also the excerpt in DS 250f.

[60] DS 272 (our translation).

This dogmatic agreement cleared the terminology, because Cyril had spoken of "one nature of the Word incarnate" and of "one hypostasis" of the Word. The difference between nature and hypostasis had not been evident, whereas by 433 even the patriarch of Alexandria accepted and began to speak of "two natures" in one single subject, the eternal Word, the Son of God.

The creed of reunion in 433 prepared for the definition of the Council of Chalcedon in 451, which accentuated that there are two natures in the hypostatic union of Christ that are neither separated nor mixed. In this context we once again find the title *Theotókos*:

> One and the same Son ... begotten before the ages from the Father as regards his divinity, and in the last days the same for us and for our salvation from Mary, the virgin God-bearer, as regards his humanity.[61]

The intention of the Council of Ephesus to correct the doctrine of Nestorius was renewed by the Second Council of Constantinople in 553, which formally approved the twelve anathemas of Cyril of Alexandria against Nestorius (at Ephesus they had only been collected in the Acts without receiving any formal approval).[62] In the first anathema, we read: "If anyone does not confess that the Emmanuel is God in truth, and therefore not confess that the holy Virgin is the Mother of God (for she bore in a fleshly way the Word of God become flesh), let him be anathema."[63] The council gives some more assessments, especially the following condemnation: "If anyone affirms that the holy glorious and perpetual Virgin Mary is Mother of God only in an improper sense but not truly ... let him be anathema."[64] The synod also speaks of the "two births" of the divine Word, "one before the ages from the Father, above time and incorporeal, and the other in these latest times" from Mary.[65]

The Council of Ephesus was accompanied by the enthusiasm of the faithful (from which Nestorius had to escape):

---

[61] DS 301.
[62] See DS 252-263.
[63] N.P. Tanner (note 54) I 59; cf. DS 252.
[64] DS 427 (our translation).
[65] DS 422 (our translation).

> The night on which the decrees were promulgated, crowds of the faithful took to the streets and shouted enthusiastically, "*Hagia Maria Theotókos*," "Holy Mary, Mother of God." ... The proclamation of Mary as *Theotókos* ... thus caused great joy among the local populace who accompanied the Fathers of the council to their homes with lights and singing.[66]

The Council of Ephesus inspired the most famous Marian homily of antiquity, attributed to St. Cyril of Alexandria. The Egyptian patriarch describes Mary as "scepter of the true faith."[67] In an enthusiastic praise of the Blessed Virgin, the divine motherhood is also shown to have spiritual consequences for our salvation:

> Through thee, the Trinity is glorified; through thee, the Cross is venerated in the whole world ... through thee, angels and archangels rejoice, through thee, demons are chased ... through thee, the fallen creature is raised to heaven ... through thee, churches are founded in the whole world, through thee, peoples are led to conversion.[68]

The invocations of Mary's universal mediation with the formulation "through thee" finish with the words: "through thee ... kings reign, in the name of the Trinity."[69] It seems that Mary is presented here as personal instrument for the operation of the Triune God, similar to the Trinitarian function of the Church.[70] "This is a statement of Mary's

---

[66] Paul Haffner, *The Mystery of Mary*, Chicago 2004, 116, referring to the third letter of Cyril to his Alexandrian church (ACO I, 1, 2, 117-118).

[67] Cyril of Alexandria, *Sermo* 4 (PG 77, 992 B). According to some researchers, this homily was not given by Cyril, but by another bishop; their arguments are not substantiated, according to Hubert Du Manoir, Cyrill, in Marienlexikon 2 (1989) 114-119 (115). Its authenticity is maintained by CPG (= Maurits Geerard [ed.], *Clavis Patrum Graecorum*) III, Turnhout 1979, nr. 5243; M. O'Carroll (note 2) 113 ("fully restored to C. as its author"), with reference to Roberto Caro Mendoza, *La homiletica mariana griega en el siglo V*, vol. II, Roma 1965, 269-278.

[68] *Sermo* 4 (PG 77, 992 B-C); cf. M. O'Carroll (note 2) 113.

[69] *Sermo* 4 (PG 77, 992 C).

[70] Cf. Alois Müller, *Ecclesia-Maria. Die Einheit Marias und der Kirche*, Fribourg 1955, 157.

mediation, an inspired utterance by a man privileged to unite his personal intuition with the revealed truth of God."[71] We find in these words the intrinsic link between the divine maternity and Mary's relation with the Most Holy Trinity, with the mystery of the Church and the universal mediation of grace.

The Council of Ephesus gave a strong impulse for the development of Marian devotion. A typical example is architecture. At the time of the council, some churches were already dedicated to the Blessed Virgin, for instance at Ephesus (the council took place in the church of St. Mary). But after the council, many more churches were consecrated to the Mother of God. The most famous case is the construction of the Basilica of St. Mary Major (Santa Maria Maggiore) at Rome by Pope Sixtus III soon after the council. The mosaics of the triumph arch manifest the Church's faith in the divine motherhood.[72]

History of the Dogma Following the Council of Ephesus

With the Council of Ephesus we already have the essence of Catholic dogma about the Mother of God. The doctrine is maintained as a precious treasure in the years following the council. A good summary of the Fathers' doctrine can be found in the systematic presentation of St. John Damascene at the end of the patristic period:

> Moreover we proclaim the holy Virgin to be in strict truth the Mother of God. For inasmuch as he who was born of her was true God, she who bore the true God incarnate is the true Mother of God. For we hold that God was born of her, not implying that the divinity of the Word received from her the beginning of its being, but meaning that God the Word himself, who was begotten of the Father timelessly before the ages, and was with the Father and the Spirit without beginning through eternity, took up his abode in these last days for the sake of our salvation in the Virgin's womb, and was without change made flesh and born of her. For the holy Virgin did not give birth to mere man but to true God: and not

---

[71] M. O'Carroll (note 2) 113.
[72] Cf. Carlo Pietrangeli, *Santa Maria Maggiore a Roma*, Firenze 1988.

only God but God incarnate who did not bring down his body from heaven, nor simply passed through the Virgin as a channel, but received flesh from her, of like essence to our own and subsisting in himself. For if the body had come down from heaven and had not partaken of our nature, what would have been the use of his becoming man? For the purpose of God the Word becoming man was that the very same nature, which had sinned and fallen and become corrupted, should triumph over the deceiving tyrant and so be freed from corruption.

For John of Damascus, the word *Theotókos* expresses the whole mystery of the work of salvation (*oikonomia*), because it reveals the one divine hypostasis of the Son in two natures.[73]

In the Middle Ages, the divine maternity is most often presented in the systematic context of the Incarnation.[74] Thomas Aquinas, for instance, treats the whole figure of Mary in his *Summa Theologiae* between the questions about the mediation of Christ, God and man, and his birth.[75] The treatment is integrated into the beginning of the redemptive work of Christ.[76] In order to prove the divine maternity of Mary, the *doctor angelicus* uses the analogy of ordinary human birth. Our parents do not generate our soul, which is given directly by God, but only our body. Nevertheless, they are called our father and mother. Since every woman is called "mother" because her child has taken his body from her, then the Blessed Virgin can also be called "Mother of God" because the Son of God has taken his body from her. Who professes that the Son of God has assumed human nature in the unity of his divine person, must also recognize that the Blessed Virgin Mary is the Mother of God.[77]

Another important deepening of the understanding of the doctrine regards the concept of the person. Motherhood, as such, is related not to

---

[73] John Damascene, *De fide orthodoxa* III, 12 (PG 94, 1028 B-1029 A); English translation in P. Haffner (note 66) 117.
[74] For a global treatment, see Luigi Gambero, *Mary in the Middle Ages: the Blessed Virgin Mary in the thought of medieval Latin theologians*, San Francisco 2005.
[75] Thomas Aquinas, STh III q. 27-35.
[76] Cf. Richard Schenk, *Thomas v. Aquin*, in Marienlexikon 6 (1994) 399-405 (404).
[77] Cf. Thomas Aquinas, *Compendium Theologiae*, cap. 222. The idea is developed already by Cyril of Alexandria in various texts, e.g. *Ep. 4 ad Nestorium* (PG 77, 480); cf. H. Du Manoir (note 67) 116.

nature, but to person. Conception and birth are attributed to the person, according to the nature in which the person is conceived or born. A human mother gives birth to a person, not a nature. When the divine person of the Word assumes human nature, it is clear that the Son of God has been conceived and was born by the Virgin. For this reason she must be called truly "Mother of God."[78]

Thomas Aquinas states that the Son of God has been eternally generated by the Father and has been temporally born by the Blessed Virgin. Thus, in Jesus Christ we find two sonships, but there is only one Son. As in God there is no change through the Incarnation, the relation between Mary and her Son is real in Mary (because it constitutes a new reality), but not in the divine Son. There is a real temporal relation of the Son with his Mother only regarding his humanity.[79] This ontological clarification underlines the divine transcendence of the person of Christ and the situation of Mary as a creature.

Other important contributions arrive with Francis Suarez, who speaks of Mary's place in the hypostatic order: the Blessed Virgin cannot be separated from the Son of God who has assumed human nature in his hypostatic union. Mary does not belong to the hypostatic union, but is strictly related to the hypostasis (person) of her Son: she makes part of the "hypostatic order."[80] The most outstanding theological contribution of the nineteenth century comes from Matthias Joseph Scheeben, who speaks about the "personal character" and the "bridal motherhood" of Mary.[81]

Among the magisterial documents, special mention should be made of the Encyclical *Lux Veritatis* of Pius XI, written on the fifteenth centenary of the Council of Ephesus (December 25, 1931).[82] The Holy Father gave an extensive description of the doctrinal importance of this Marian dogma, which should be noted also today. Against recent attempts to rehabilitate Nestorius, Pope Pius XI underlined the traditional verdict:

---

[78] Cf. STh III q. 35 a. 4.
[79] Cf. STh III q. 35 a. 5; Quodlib. 9 a. 2 ad 1. See also Gregorio Alastruey, *Tratado de la Virgen Santissima*, Madrid, 1952, 99-101, and the defense of this doctrine against contemporary criticism in B. Gherardini (note 14) 84-89.
[80] Cf. M. O'Carroll (note 2) 258. 334f.
[81] See later in this chapter, *The Divine Maternity Implies a Transforming Relation*.
[82] AAS 23 (1931) 493-517.

> The Church ... protests against this futile and temerarious attempt; for she has at all times acknowledged the condemnation of Nestorius as rightly and deservedly decreed; and has regarded the doctrine of Cyril as orthodox; and has counted the Council of Ephesus among the ecumenical synods, celebrated under the guidance of the Holy Spirit, and has held it in veneration.[83]

Pope Pius XI also explained the pastoral ramifications of the divine motherhood of Mary. He noted, for instance, the veneration of Mary's dignity as virginal Mother of God outside the Catholic Church, even among Protestants, and expressed the hope that these Christians would return to the one flock of Christ guided by his vicar on earth; the Blessed Virgin embraces all her erring children with motherly love and sustains the prayer for unity with her intercession.[84]

Second Vatican Council and the Contemporary Magisterium

In the Second Vatican Council, the divine motherhood of Mary is treated in the mystery of Christ and the Church. As the "Council of the Church about the Church," this ecumenical synod accentuates the similarity between the Mother of God, who as a Virgin has born the Son of God, and the Church. Mary, according to an expression of St. Ambrose, is "type of the Church" (*typus Ecclesiae*). The Church becomes "mother" through the believing reception of the divine Word. She bears her children, conceived by the Holy Spirit, through the preaching of the Gospel, and through baptism. She is also Virgin because she maintains the promise given to her divine bridegroom, virginally professing an integral faith, a solid hope and a sincere love.[85]

The reform of the liturgical calendar in 1969 introduced the solemnity of Most Holy Mary Mother of God, to be celebrated on January 1. It replaced the feast of divine maternity, introduced by Pius XI in 1931 and collocated on October 11. This date of January 1, which places the feast of Mary Mother of God in relation to the Christmas mystery is well-chosen and corresponds to the most ancient tradition.

---

[83] AAS 23 (1931) 504; English in P. Haffner (note 66) 120.
[84] Cf. AAS 23 (1931) 513.
[85] *Lumen Gentium* 63-64. Cf. S. Meo (note 57) 822-825.

In the Byzantine Church, the solemn feast of the *Theotókos* appears on December 26.[86]

Pope John Paul II, in his Encyclical *Redemptoris Mater* (1987), records that "the dogma of the divine motherhood of Mary was for the Council of Ephesus and is for the Church like a confirmation of the dogma of the Incarnation, in which the Word truly assumes human nature into the unity of his person, without canceling out that nature."[87] In his Apostolic Letter on the dignity of woman in the light of Mary (*Mulieris Dignitatem*, 1988), the Holy Father shows the relation of divine motherhood with the vocation of every woman. The mystery of the Incarnation implies the faithful response of Mary, which is a full participation for her as person and as woman.[88] The Pope also insisted on the perpetual importance of the title *Theotókos* in his Apostolic Letter on the occasion of the 1600th anniversary of the First Council of Constantinople and the 1550th anniversary of the Council of Ephesus (1991).[89] John Paul II, in a general audience, criticized the proposal of some theologians (which renews the old heresies of Arius or Nestorius) to speak of Jesus as a human person; in this case Mary would not be the Mother of God.[90] Last but not least, the divine maternity was underlined in the preparation of the 2000th anniversary of the Incarnation at the Jubilee of the year 2000:

> *The Blessed Virgin* who will be as it were "indirectly" present in the whole preparatory phase, will be contemplated in this first year especially in the mystery of her divine motherhood. It was in her womb that the Word became flesh! The affirmation of the central place of Christ cannot therefore be separated from the recognition of the role played by his Most Holy Mother.

---

[86] Cf. Danilo Sartor, *Madre di Dio III. Celebrazione liturgica*, in S. De Fiores – S. Meo (note 14) 825-828.

[87] *Redemptoris Mater* 4; English translation in P. Haffner (note 66) 121.

[88] Cf. *Mulieris dignitatem* 4. See also Arthur B. Calkins, *Totus tuus. Il Magistero mariano di Giovanni Paolo II*, Siena 2006, 88-94.

[89] Cf. P. Haffner (note 66) 121.

[90] Cf. General audience of April 13, 1988, *Le definizioni cristologiche dei concili e la fede della Chiesa oggi*, nr. 4, in *Insegnamenti di Giovanni Paolo II*, vol. XI/1, Città del Vaticano 1989, 878f. The theological context is explained in M. Ponce Cuéllar (note 14) 316-318; J. L. Bastero de Eleizalde, *Virgen singular. La reflexión teológica mariana en el siglo XX*, Madrid 2001, 17-57.

Veneration of her, when properly understood, can in no way take away from "the dignity and efficacy of Christ the one Mediator" (Lumen Gentium 62). Mary in fact constantly points to her divine Son and she is proposed to all believers as the *model of faith* which is put into practice. "Devotedly meditating on her and contemplating her in the light of the Word made man, the Church with reverence enters more intimately into the supreme mystery of the Incarnation and becomes ever increasingly like her Spouse" (Lumen Gentium 65).[91]

Ecumenical Aspects

The Council of Ephesus, at least in a general sense, contributes to a global consensus between the great Christian denominations. This is evident for the Catholic Church, but also for the Orthodox Churches, which count Ephesus as the third ecumenical council. Ephesus is also accepted by the Coptic churches (Egypt, Ethiopia), which very much honor the tradition of St. Cyril of Alexandria, even if they have been separated from the universal Church since the Council of Chalcedon in 451.

The title *Theotókos*, on the other hand, is not used by the spiritual heirs of the Antiochene tradition, who did not accept the Council of Ephesus and today constitute the Assyrian Church of the Orient, a group that has become very small (about 400,000 members). They call Mary "Mother of the Lord" and "Mother of Christ."[92] On November 11, 1994, the Assyrian Patriarch Mar Dinkha IV and Pope John Paul II signed a Joint Christological Declaration which affirms that Catholic and Assyrians "today are united in the profession of the same faith in the Son of God." The document uses the Christological formulations of Chalcedon: "his divinity and his humanity are united in one person, without mixture and without separation." The Assyrians venerate Mary as "Mother of Christ, our God and Savior." "In the light of the same faith, the Catholic Tradition is calling the Virgin Mary 'Mother of God' and 'Mother of Christ'. We both recognize the justification

---

[91] *Tertio Millennio Adveniente* (1994), 43; English translation in www.vatican.va.
[92] Cf. R. Roberson, *Assira, Chiesa, d'Oriente*, in E.G. Farrugia (ed.), *Dizionario enciclopedico dell'Oriente cristiano*, Roma 2000, 82f.

and correctness of these manifestations of the same faith."[93] In other words: the "ex-Nestorians" now also recognize the Catholic doctrine concerning the Mother of God, even if their liturgical tradition does not use the title *Theotókos*.

In Protestantism (especially among traditional Lutherans), we encounter the reference to the "consensus of the first five centuries" (*consensus quinquesaecularis*), which recognizes the Trinitarian and Christological councils of the Ancient Church. The theologians of the Reformation accepted the title *Theotókos* because it manifests the Christological dogma of the hypostatic union (and of the communication of idioms). Luther, for instance, insisted on the importance of Mary's divine maternity:

> The great thing is none other than that she became the Mother of God; in which process so many and such great gifts are bestowed upon her that no one is able to comprehend them. Thereupon follows all honor, all blessedness, and the fact that in the whole race of men only one person is above the rest, one to whom no one else is equal. For that reason her dignity is summed up in one phrase when we call her Mother of God; no one can say greater things of her or to her, even if he had as many tongues as leaves and blades of grass, as stars in heaven and sands on the seashore. It should also be meditated in the heart what that means: to be the Mother of God.[94]

Nevertheless, the principles of the Reformation lead to a depreciation of Mary's maternal role. Luther, in the same Exposition of the Magnificat text just cited above, criticizes the Marian antiphon *Regina Caeli* which contains the expression *quem meruisti portare* ("whom you merited to bear"). Luther compares the dignity of Mary with the dignity of the Cross whose wood "merited" to carry our Lord: everything is grace,

---

[93] *Joint Christological Declaration of the Catholic Church and the Assyrian Church of the East*, Rome, November 11, 1994, Nr. 1-4, cited here from a German translation in *Una Sancta* 50 (1995) 164-165; the English original is published in *Sobornost* 17 (1/1995) 52-54.

[94] Luther, *Exposition on the Magnificat* (1521) (WA 7, 546); English translation in P. Haffner (note 66) 122f.

and for this reason we cannot attribute to Mary any merit.[95] For Catholic doctrine, the primary factor of divine grace does not exclude human cooperation, whereas the Protestant principle, *sola gratia* ("grace alone"), establishes a justification without any human merit sustained by grace.[96]

The general acceptance of the Council of Ephesus, on the one hand, and the depreciation of Mary's active contribution in redemption, on the other hand, constitutes a profound ambiguity in Protestant doctrine. This problem is visible in recent Protestant theology, especially in that of Karl Barth, the most renowned Calvinist theologian of the twentieth century. According to Barth, the title "Mother of God" is only "an assistant sentence for Christology,"[97] which has a biblical basis (Gal 4:4; Lk 1:43) and shows the true unity between the two natures in the unique subject of Christ. Whereas Barth accepts the title *Theotókos*, many other Protestant theologians abandon this dogmatic attribute. Their attitude is influenced by the liberal branch of Protestantism: He who refutes the true divinity of Christ cannot accept that Mary is called "Mother of God." Sometimes we even find a certain sympathy with Nestorius, such as in an official document of "mainstream" Lutherans in Germany which attests: "we can no longer recognize the condemnation of Nestorius who fought against the misunderstanding that God himself was born by Mary."[98]

The situation is somewhat better in Evangelical theology, which refuses the liberal negation of Christ's divinity:

> Evangelicals affirm Jesus Christ to be true God and true man. For that reason, Evangelical objections to *Theotókos* and "Mother of God" usually soften after a short discussion. ... Certainly it was God whom Mary

---

[95] See Luther, *Exposition on the Magnificat* (1521) (WA 7, 573); Achim Dittrich, *Protestantische Mariologiekritik. Historische Entwicklung bis 1997 und dogmatische Analyse* (Mariologische Studien 11), Regensburg 1998, 29-37.

[96] Cf. C.J. Malloy, *Engrafted into Christ. A Critique of the Joint Declaration*, New York 2005.

[97] Karl Barth, *Kirchliche Dogmatik I/2*, Zürich, 1983, 1938; cf. A. Dittrich (note 95) 305f.

[98] Lutherisches Kirchenamt des VELKD (Vereinigte Evangelisch-Lutherische Kirche Deutschlands), *Maria – Evangelische Fragen und Gesichtspunkte. Eine Einladung zum Gespräch*, in Una Sancta 37 (1982) 184-201 (189); cf. A. Dittrich (note 95) 306.

bore, so we gladly affirm that Mary was indeed the "God-bearer."[99]

But even in Evangelicals we find a strong uneasiness about the terminology of the Fathers because the special honor given to Mary does not fit into their conception of the unique mediation of Christ, which excludes any cooperation of redeemed creatures.[100] According to Luther, not even Christ in his humanity had an active part in redemption (his human nature was only passive, suffering on the Cross as bait for the Devil, who encounters Christ's divinity by which he is defeated).[101]

Modern Protestant theology, in any case, is divided on the title *Theotókos*. Normally, the word is refuted with the argument that it suggests a natural power of Mary to produce the divine nature of her Son. Some authors maintain that the title "Mother of God" is derived from mythology.

> In contrast to the orthodox desire to maintain the Creed of the Ancient Church [that is, of "orthodox" Protestantism, which likes to maintain the tradition of the first ecumenical councils] and also the doctrine of Ephesus about the Mother of God, in Protestant theology [today] we find a manifold and often contradictory evaluation of the Marian doctrine [about divine maternity].[102]

In Anglicanism we find a greater acceptance of the Marian doctrine formulated in the Ancient Church. This fact is evident in the Agreed Statement about "Mary: Grace and Hope in Christ," formulated by the 2004 Anglican-Roman Catholic International Commission (ARCIC). According to this joint statement, the Council of Ephesus

> used *Theotókos* ... to affirm the oneness of Christ's person by identifying Mary as the Mother of God the Word

---

[99] David Gustafson, in: Dwight Longenecker – David Gustafson, *Mary. A Catholic-Evangelical Debate*, Grand Rapids, Michigan 2003, 37.
[100] Cf. D. Longenecker – D. Gustafson (note 99) 43. 189-207.
[101] Cf. Michael Kreuzer, *"Und das Wort ist Fleisch geworden". Zur Bedeutung des Menschseins Jesu bei Johannes Driedo und Martin Luther*, Paderborn 1998.
[102] A. Dittrich (note 95) 305.

incarnate. The rule of faith on this matter takes more precise expression in the definition of Chalcedon: "One and the same Son ... was begotten from the Father before the ages as to the divinity and in the latter days for us and our salvation was born as to the humanity from Mary the Virgin *Theotókos.*" In receiving the Council of Ephesus and the definition of Chalcedon, Anglicans and Roman Catholics together confess Mary as *Theotókos.*[103]

Systematic Assessment

The Title "Mother of God" is Important for the Correct Comprehension of the Divine Person of Jesus Christ

The first intention of the Council of Ephesus was not Marian devotion, but the defense of the faith in Jesus Christ against Nestorius. The title *Theotókos* clearly showed the unity of the personal subject in the Word incarnate. The Nestorian danger is also present in modern theology, when some theologians speak of Jesus as a human person[104] (and not as a divine person, the eternal Son, who assumed human nature from the Virgin Mary).

The Holiness of Mary Prepares Her for the Divine Maternity

For her task to be the Mother of Christ, Mary was prepared according to the eternal plan of God. She was "predestined from eternity as Mother of God together with the Incarnation of the Word."[105] Her preservation from original sin happened in view of the Incarnation. The consent asked of Mary was formed by the theological virtue of faith, which can be compared in some way with divine maternity itself. Augustine explains this relation in a sermon, when he comments on the encounter between Jesus and his relatives: his brother, sister and mother is anyone who obeys the Father in heaven (Mt 12:48-50):

---

[103] ARCIC, *Mary: Grace and Hope in Christ*, nr. 34, cited in www.ecumenism.net/archive/arcic/mary_en.htm.

[104] Such as Piet Schoonenberg: see Jean Galot, *Maria. La donna nell'opera della salvezza*, Roma 1991, 98; M. Ponce Cuéllar (note 14) 316-318; J.L. Bastero de Eleizalde (note 90) 17-57.

[105] *Lumen Gentium* 61.

> Did the Virgin Mary not do the will of the Father? She who believed by faith, conceived by faith and had been elected because our salvation should be born from her in the midst of mankind? She who had been created by Christ before Christ was created in her? Holy Mary plainly did the will of the Father: and for this reason it was more important for Mary to have been a disciple of Christ than to have been the Mother of Christ.[106]

In an analogically wider sense, every virgin consecrated to the Lord and every soul devoted to God is "mother" of Christ, favoring the growth of grace in this world:

> There is … no reason why the virgins of God should be sad, because they themselves also cannot, keeping their virginity, be mothers of the flesh. For him alone could virginity give birth to with fitting propriety, who in his birth could have no peer. However, that birth of the Holy Virgin is the ornament of all holy virgins; and themselves together with Mary are mothers of Christ, if they do the will of his Father … his mother is the whole Church, because she herself assuredly gives birth to his members, that is, his faithful ones. Also his mother is every pious soul, doing the will of his Father with most fruitful charity, in them of whom it travailed, until he himself be formed in them. Mary, therefore, doing the will of God, after the flesh, is only the mother of Christ, but after the Spirit she is both his sister and mother.[107]

The Fathers of the Church describe the spiritual "maternity" of any disciple as a "conception" of the Word.

> Such as conception, faith is, on the spiritual level, the fecund reception of a semen of life. Every Christian, … receiving the word, is conceiving God in his heart. In this perspective, faith implies a kind of spiritual motherhood;

---

[106] Augustine, *Sermo* 72/A, 7 (MA 1, 162; cf. PL 46, 935) (our translation).
[107] Augustine, *De sancta virginitate* (PL 40, 399) (English translation on www.newadvent.org).

the physical divine motherhood of Mary appears as a radiation of her faith to the flesh.[108]

The holiness of Mary is a *gratis* gift of God, as is the grace of divine maternity. Could Mary also merit to become the Mother of God? The idea of a certain merit is present, for instance, in the Marian antiphon *Regina coeli, laetare alleluia. Quia quem meruisti portare, alleluia, resurrexit, sicut dixit, alleluia. Ora pro nobis Deum, alleluia.* As to the kind of merit, we find a classical explanation in Thomas Aquinas, which was later developed by Francis Suarez:

> The Blessed Virgin did not merit the Incarnation, but, assuming that it would take place, she merited that it would be through her, not with condign merit, but with the merit of suitability, in so far as it was fitting that the Mother of God should be a most pure and perfect Virgin.[109]

Mary could not "merit," in a strict sense, becoming the Mother of God. There is no merit of strict justice (*meritum de condigno*) in this case. Nevertheless, we can speak here of a merit of fittingness (*meritum de congruo*): with her sanctity, sustained by the grace of God, Mary responded generously to the intentions of the divine plan. Mary "by the grace bestowed upon her she merited that grade of purity and holiness, which fitted (*congrue*) her to be the Mother of God."[110]

The merit of Mary depended on her free will, sustained by the divine gift of grace. The importance of her "yes," her free consent, is described in an impressive manner by St. Bernard:

> The angel waits for the answer: it is time for him to return to God who sent him. We too, O Lady, are waiting for the word of salvation, we who walk so miserably bent under the sentence of condemnation.

---

[108] René Laurentin, *Breve trattato sulla Vergine Maria*, Cinisello Balsamo 1990, 192 (English translation: *A Short Treatise on the Virgin Mary*, Washington, New Jersey 1991).

[109] Thomas Aquinas, III Sent. d. 4 a. 1 ad 5; cf. M. O'Carroll (note 2) 258.

[110] Thomas Aquinas, STh III q. 2 art. 11 ad 3. About the merit of Mary, see also M. O'Carroll (note 2) 246f.

> Behold the price of our redemption is offered to you; if you agree, we shall be instantly set free. We were all made by the eternal Word of God, and behold, we are dying. By one single word from you we shall be revived and called back to life. Adam with all his grief, Adam with all his wretched offspring implores you to say that word, O gracious Virgin. Abraham, David and all the other holy patriarchs, your ancestors who dwell in the shadows of death, beg you to say that word. The whole world is waiting for it, prostrate at your feet. And they are right, since there depend on your lips the consolation of the wretched, the redemption of prisoners, the freedom of the condemned, and finally the salvation of all Adam's children, of your whole race! Hasten, then! Give the answer that earth and the underworld and even the heavens are expecting from you.[111]

The Divine Maternity Implies a Transforming Relation

The descent of the Holy Spirit on Mary in the narration of Luke, evokes the act of creation (Gen 1:2) and the presence of God in the Ark of the Covenant (Ex 40:34).[112] Through the Incarnation of the Son of God at the Annunciation, Mary arrives at "a higher grade of purity and assimilation to God, something like the last passage to the melting-pot of a metal already pure which finds now its grade of hardness and its splendor."[113]

The divine maternity, as a basic relation of Mary to Christ, can be compared with the character of a sacrament which is distinct from

---

[111] Bernard of Clairvaux, *Super missus est* 1,7 (PL 183, 59 D); English translation according to C.X.J.M. Friethoff, *A Complete Mariology*, London 1958, 23.

[112] Cf. Heinz Schürmann, *Das Lukasevangelium I*, Freiburg i. Br. 1969, 52f; S.M. Manelli, *Biblical Mariology* (note 15) 173.

[113] R. Laurentin, *Breve trattato* (note 108), 203, with reference to the Byzantine theologian Nicholas Cabasilas (fourteenth century). In this way the idea of purification (*kátharsis*) can be interpreted in various oriental authors: see op. cit., 225f; Manfred Hauke, *Heilsverlust in Adam*, Paderborn 1993, 560; Idem, *Die Unbefleckte Empfängnis Mariens bei den griechischen Vätern. Die Hinweise Johannes Pauls II. im ökumenischen Dialog*, in Sedes Sapientiae. Mariologisches Jahrbuch 8 (2/2004) 13-54 (52f).

grace, but given in view of grace.¹¹⁴ The indelible sacramental character constitutes the consecration of the Christian to the Holy Trinity and a conformation with Christ. Similarly, the divine motherhood, prepared in the grace of the Immaculate Conception at the very beginning of Mary's being, consecrates Our Lady to God because of her definite relation to her Son, who takes human nature from her through the power of the Holy Spirit. According to Scheeben, the grace of divine maternity is already present in Mary at the beginning of her life. The most renowned German theologian of the nineteenth century describes the maternal relation of the Holy Virgin to Christ with the expression "personal character," identifying it also as spiritual marriage with the Word. This "personal character" implies, at the same time, her characteristics as mother and as companion or "bride" of Christ, who asked her consent before becoming her Son. Scheeben thus speaks of "bridal motherhood:"

> Mary is as much anointed and made the Mother of God as the flesh taken from her is made the flesh of God, for the Logos is so taken up in her that she herself is taken up in him in an analogous way as the flesh taken from her. Consequently the relation of the Mother to her divine Son appears as a marriage with this divine Person. Here now the Bridegroom gives himself to the Bride as her Son and dwells in her in virtue of this gift.¹¹⁵

The systematic reflection of Scheeben confirms the Catholic conviction that divine motherhood cannot be separated from Mary's mediation, which is not restricted to the physical birth of Jesus. Her whole being is consecrated in its motherhood to Christ forever and this motherhood goes together with her cooperation in redemption. For this concept, we can cite a statement of Thomas Aquinas, finding its foundation in the Fathers and repeated in the teaching of the popes: the event of the Annunciation was suitable

---

[114] Cf. R. Laurentin, *Breve trattato* (note 108), 206.
[115] M.J. Scheeben, *Mariology I*, London – St. Louis 1946, 162f; cf. Manfred Hauke, *Die Mariologie Scheebens – ein zukunftsträchtiges Vermächtnis*, in Idem – Michael Stickelbroeck (eds.), *Donum veritatis*, Regensburg 2006, 255-274 (261f).

to manifest that there is a kind of spiritual marriage between the Son of God and human nature. And hence through the Annunciation the consent of the Virgin was sought in the place of the whole human nature.[116]

Christ also represents all of human nature, but he does so as a divine Person and as head of the Church. Mary represents the whole human race as a created person and in some way as "heart" of the mystical body of Christ. She does so as a woman in her specific "bridal" receptivity, which includes an active response to the initiative of God.

Through Her Vocation as Mother of God, Mary Takes an Active Part in the Work of Redemption

The Incarnation is not only a premise to the work of salvation, but already a basic part of it. For this reason, the consent of Mary has a saving quality made possible by the grace of Christ received after the Immaculate Conception. The cooperation of Mary is orientated towards the redemptive work of Christ, which begins immediately at the Incarnation, as we can conclude from the Letter to the Hebrews: "Christ said, as he came into the world: 'O God, the blood of bulls and goats cannot satisfy you, so you have made ready this body of mine for me to lay as a sacrifice upon your altar'" (Heb 10:5). Whereas Christ is appearing as the "New Adam," Mary is acting as the "New Eve," who together will renew humanity fallen into sin.[117]

The Divine Motherhood Constitutes the Beginning of Mary's Spiritual Motherhood for the Church

The divine maternity is also related to the person of the Word incarnate as the head of the mystical body of the Church.

---

[116] Thomas Aquinas, STh III q. 30 a. 1. The text is cited especially by Pope Leo XIII, Encyclical *Octobri mense* (1891) (DS 3274); Pius XII, Encyclical *Mystici corporis* (1943) (AAS 35 [1943] 247); John Paul II, *Marian Catechesis 33* (18.9.1996), nr. 2, in *Insegnamenti di Giovanni Paolo II*, vol. XIX/2, Città del Vaticano 1998, 373 (= CCC, nr. 511).

[117] Cf. Stefano M. Manelli, *Maria Corredentrice nella Sacra Scrittura*, in Autori vari, *Maria Corredentrice. Storia e teologia I*, Frigento 1998, 37-114 (73-82).

> Through the grace of divine motherhood, Mary has become an excellent member of the ecclesiastical body of Christ, and so her motherhood refers not only to the historical Christ, but also to Christ as head of the Church, and as such to the Church itself, which takes her origin from the operation of Christ, as the new people of God, as temple of the Holy Spirit and body of Christ.[118]

An important step for the development of the doctrine about the spiritual motherhood of Mary can be found in a famous text of St. Augustine, cited by the Second Vatican Council:[119]

> According to the body, Mary is Mother only of Christ. But insofar as she does the will of God, she is spiritually sister and mother. And thus this unique woman is mother and virgin, not only in spirit but bodily—mother in spirit, not of the Savior, our Head, of whom rather she is born spiritually, for all who believe in him—and she is one of them—are rightly called sons of the Spouse, but she is really[120] Mother of the members who we are, because she cooperated by charity so that there might be born in the Church believers, of whom he is the Head.[121]

The cooperation of Mary in the spiritual birth of the members of the Church points to a universal dimension. The spiritual maternity, based on the Incarnation, is confirmed and fully constituted at the foot of the Cross, when Jesus Christ reveals Mary's vocation to become the "mother" of St. John, type of every faithful disciple.[122]

Pope Benedict XVI, during his visit to Ephesus, underlined this relation between Mary's divine maternity and her motherhood for the Church. Mary, "united to her Son in the offering of his sacrifice,

---

[118] G.M. Müller (note 24) 690.
[119] *Lumen Gentium* 53.
[120] Extended quote by St. Augustine added by author.
[121] Augustine, *De sancta virginitate* 6 (PL 40, 399); cf. M. O'Carroll (note 2) 254.
[122] The explication of spiritual motherhood comes forth more fully in the twelfth century. As to this topic, see the treatments of Mary's mediation, for instance the introducing notes in M. O'Carroll (note 2) 238-245. 253-256.

extended her motherhood under the Cross to all men and women, and in particular to the disciples of Jesus."[123]

The Divine Motherhood Exalts Mary Over All Other Creatures

The New Testament already alludes to the highest dignity of Mary as Mother of the Lord. This is evident from the salutation by the angel (Lk 1:26: "Rejoice, full of grace, the Lord is with you"), but also from the praise of Elizabeth (Lk 1:42: "Blessed are you among women, and blessed is the fruit of your womb") and from the Magnificat (Lk 1:48: "For behold, henceforth all generations will call me blessed").

In the third century it is not yet universally clear that Mary's grace is superior to that of the apostles, as we can deduce from a reflection of Origen who interprets the "sword" in the prophecy of Simeon (Lk 2:35) as incredulity and doubt under the Cross. The Alexandrian theologian held this because he wanted to assert that Mary also needed to be redeemed. If even the apostles had some defects, Origen sought a sin also in the Mother of the Lord.[124] In the fourth century, we find a continual maturation of the Church's understanding of the dignity of the Mother of God, which leads to explicit testimonies about the superiority of Mary's dignity over that of all other creatures. Through the Council of Ephesus, this conviction becomes universal. We find an echo of this faith in the Second Vatican Council: through the gift of divine maternity, Mary "far surpasses all creatures, both in heaven and on earth."[125]

The personal relationship to God that comes from divine maternity is the most perfect that can exist between a created person and the Creator. This relation is certainly less profound than the one between the humanity of Jesus Christ and the divine Word: It constitutes the subsistence of the human nature of our Lord in the divine person of the Son of God, according to the explanation of Thomas Aquinas. Nevertheless, Mary has born her own Creator in his humanity, thus receiving a kind of quasi-infinite dignity: "The Blessed Virgin from the fact that she is the Mother of God has a kind of infinite dignity from the

---

[123] Homily from November 29, 2006.
[124] Cf. Origen, *In Lucam hom.* XVII, 6-7 (SC 87, 256-258).
[125] *Lumen Gentium* 53.

infinite good which is God; and for this reason nothing can be better than her, such as nothing can be better than God."¹²⁶

From the time of Suarez (sixteenth century), many theologians express the dignity of the Mother of God with the idea that Mary's divine maternity contributes to the "hypostatic order," that is she cannot be separated from the Word incarnate: "This dignity of the Mother belongs to a higher order and belongs in some way to the order of hypostatic union, because she has an intrinsic relation to it and a necessary bond."¹²⁷

*The Divine Maternity Constitutes a Special Relation with the Most Holy Trinity*¹²⁸

A theological work from the seventeenth century calls Mary "mirror and revelation of the Trinity," when reflecting on the event of Annunciation: The Father sends the Son, whereas the Son is made flesh by the power and operation of the Holy Spirit.¹²⁹ The Second Vatican Council delivers a precise summary of Mary's relation to the Holy Trinity:

> Redeemed by reason of the merits of her Son and united to him by a close and indissoluble tie, she is endowed with the high office and dignity of being the Mother of the Son of God, by which account she is also the beloved daughter of the Father and the temple of the Holy Spirit.¹³⁰

Mary was the "beloved" or "favorite" "daughter of the Father" (*praedilecta filia Patris*) and "temple of the Holy Spirit" even before

---

[126] Thomas Aquinas, STh I q. 25 a. 6 ad 4.
[127] Francis Suarez, *De mysteriis vitae Christi*, sect. 2,4 (Opera omnia 19, Paris 1856, 8). As to this topic, see also S.M. Ragazzini, *La Divina Maternità di Maria nel suo concetto teologico integrale*, Frigento 1986, 214-238. For a wider treatment of Mary's dignity, see G. Alastruey (note 79) 102-138.
[128] For a more explicit treatment, see Manfred Hauke, *Maria und die Trinität. Die trinitarischen Beziehungen Mariens als Urbild der Kirche auf dem Zweiten Vatikanischen Konzil*, in Sedes Sapientiae. Mariologisches Jahrbuch 4 (2/2000) 78-114; Angelo Amato, *Maria e la Trinità*, Cinisello Balsamo 2000; Rosa Lombardi, *Maria Icona della Trinità*, Roma 2003.
[129] Cf. Josephus de la Cerda, *Maria effigies revelatioque trinitatis*, Almeria 1640.
[130] *Lumen Gentium* 53.

becoming the Mother of God. Nevertheless, her relations with the Father and with the Holy Spirit have a strict link with divine maternity, which is the systematic starting point for describing its connection with the Most Holy Trinity.

The title "daughter" is the most frequent one used to describe Mary's relation to God the Father. We find it prefigured in the Old Testament theme, "Daughter of Zion:"[131] it seems that the Lucan infancy narrative alludes to it, especially in the salutation of the angel (*chaire*, "Rejoice"), which prompts comparison with the explicit Daughter of Zion texts.[132] Mary as "daughter" of the divine Father is similar to the adoptive sonship of all baptized Christians, who can pray "Abbà, Father" (cf. Gal 3:26; 4:4-7). The purpose of our life is to "receive the adoption of sons" (Gal 4:5). In this context, the Apostle Paul speaks of the divine maternity of Mary: "God sent his Son, born of a woman" (Gal 4:4).

Certainly Mary is also the "favorite" daughter of the Father. This exclusive relation is reflected by the Fathers of Church, who describe Christ as the common Son of God the Father and the Virgin Mary. This distinction was also formulated by the Council of Chalcedon: "Begotten before the ages from the Father as regards his divinity, and in the last days the same for us and for our salvation from Mary, the virgin God-bearer, as regards his humanity."[133]

In the Ancient Church one also begins to see an awareness of a "bridal" relation of Mary to God the Father, such as in this passage from St. John of Damascus, cited in the Encyclical *Munificentissimus Deus* (1950), in which Pope Pius XII defined the bodily Assumption of Mary to heavenly glory: "It was fitting that the spouse whom the Father had taken to himself should live in the divine mansions."[134] The title becomes more current in the Middle Ages, for instance in Rupert of Deutz, and in the French school of spirituality, notably Bérulle and Olier.[135] According to Olier, the Father chose Mary as his spouse in order that she would become, together with him, the principle of the temporal generation of the Word, his helper in the Incarnation. Nonetheless, the

---

[131] Cf. *Lumen Gentium* 55.
[132] Cf. M. O'Carroll (note 2) 116f; S.M. Manelli, *Biblical Mariology* (note 15), 162.
[133] DS 301.
[134] John of Damascus, *Hom. II in Dormit.*, 14 (PG 96, 741).
[135] Cf. M. O'Carroll (note 2) 333f; K. Wittkemper, *Braut IV. Dogmatik*, in Marienlexikon 1 (1988) 564-571 (568f).

title "spouse of the Father" is not very common, because of the possible misunderstanding that it meant Mary had eternally generated the Son of God, in contradiction to the fact that her contribution stayed in the temporal realm.

The title "daughter" implies some similarity to the Father. For this reason we also find the comparison of divine maternity with the active generation of the Father. The eternal source of the Son from the Father is reflected in the temporal origin of the same Son from Mary as Mother. According to St. Louis-Marie Grignion de Montfort,

> God the Father communicated to Mary his own fecundity in the greatest measure possible for a creature in order to give her the power to generate his Son and all the members of his Mystical Body.[136]

Contemplating the assimilation of divine maternity to the eternal paternity of God, we can better understand the virginity of Mary:

> If one maintains that the divine motherhood is the most perfect possible created assimilation to the divine Paternity, it would seem to indicate that Mary's divine motherhood is necessarily a virginal motherhood.[137]

Mary, in some way, can be called the "female face" of the Father, revealing in particular his mercy and tenderness. This observation is very much emphasized by feminist theologians nowadays, but it should not be exaggerated. "It must be noted ... that Mary does not directly represent the 'maternity' of *God* but is the Mother of God and thus embodies *creaturely* worth at its supreme level."[138]

The basic word to describe Mary's relation with her Son is certainly the title "Mother." Nevertheless, by the time of the Fathers, and still more in the Middle Ages, we already find the description of Mary as "spouse" of Christ. Among the bridal designations that are used for Mary, "Bride of Christ" becomes increasingly prominent, especially as Mary is recognized more clearly and distinctly as Christ's helper in his

---

[136] Louis-Marie Grignion de Montfort, *Traité de la vrai dévotion* ..., nr. 17.
[137] P. Haffner (note 66) 128.
[138] M. Hauke, *God or Goddess?* (note 42) 194. Cf. idem, *Women in the Priesthood?* San Francisco 1988, 309-312.

redemptive work, as a mediatrix of grace.[139] The title "Bride of Christ" becomes more important for the Church when it is seen as already present in Biblical sources (Eph 5:21-33 etc.).[140] This description was already prefigured in the Old Testament, which compared the Covenant between God and his people with the union between the husband and his wife in marriage. The Song of Songs, which sings of the love between man and woman, has been accepted in the canon of holy Scripture because of this profound religious significance. The commentaries on the Song of Songs, prepared by the Fathers and fully developed in the Middle Ages, present the "spouse" in various ways which cannot be separated from one another: the people of God (Israel, which becomes the Church in the New Covenant), the soul of every believer, and the Holy Virgin Mary. The Church, the human soul and Mary are invited to open themselves to the love of the divine "bridegroom."

Nowadays the most frequent use of the title "spouse" does not makes reference to the relation of the Blessed Virgin to Christ, but to the Holy Spirit. The first clear testimony of this custom is St. Francis, who exalts Mary as "daughter and handmaid of the highest kind, the Father in heaven," as "Mother of our Most Holy Lord Jesus Christ" and "spouse of the Holy Spirit."[141]

This attribution is justified in so far as it accentuates Mary's role as "cooperator" with the Third Person of the Trinity. Some of contemporary Mariology is more reticent to use the title, in order to avoid the misunderstanding that there was a common generational act between the Holy Spirit and the Blessed Virgin.[142] In fact, the Holy Spirit is not called "bridegroom" of Mary. He is not the Father of Jesus,[143] and his action in the Incarnation is compared in Luke with the first creation, not with generation. Probably for this reason, the Second Vatican Council did not use the title "spouse of the Holy Spirit," but preferred the designation "temple."[144]

---

[139] Cf. K. Wittkemper (note 135) 564-568.
[140] Cf. M. Hauke, *Women in the Priesthood?* (note 138) 252-256.
[141] Antiphon *Sancta Maria Virgo*, verse 2. Cf. Johannes Schneider, *Virgo Ecclesia facta*, Assisi 2003, 223-272 (the first explicit use: 259). Earlier allusions are given in K. Wittkemper (note 135) 569.
[142] Cf. K. Wittkemper (note 135) 569f.
[143] Cf. 11th Synod of Toledo (DS 533).
[144] Cf. M. Hauke, *Die trinitarischen Beziehungen Mariens* (note 128) 87-90.

On the other hand, the description "temple of the Holy Spirit" does not describe the specific relation of Mary to the Holy Spirit, but only reflects that which is a characteristic of every Christian. The expression "spouse of the Holy Spirit" has the advantage of manifesting a specific trait of the Holy Virgin. As mentioned before, in the works of St. Francis, the title *sponsa Spiritus Sancti* is used exclusively for the Mother of God.[145] John Paul II presents this expression omitted by the Second Vatican Council with a new vigor, especially in his Encyclical *Redemptoris Mater*[146] and in his Marian catecheses. In one of the catecheses he writes:

> And again: every Christian is a "temple of the Holy Spirit." … But this assertion takes on an extraordinary meaning in Mary: in her the relationship with the Holy Spirit is enriched with a spousal dimension. I recalled this in the Encyclical *Redemptoris Mater*: "The Holy Spirit had already come down upon her, and she became his faithful spouse at the Annunciation, welcoming the Word of the true God."[147]

Pope Paul VI, in his Apostolic Exhortation *Marialis Cultus* (1974), has underlined the Trinitarian character of Marian devotion. Mary helps us to orient ourselves to the Father, through the Son, in the Holy Spirit.[148] Pope John Paul II records that the Annunciation brings us a revelation of the Trinity in its relations to Mary.[149] In the Blessed Virgin is thus realized the supreme vocation of the creature. All the members of the Church participate in this vocation, but Mary has a specific role. The title "Mother of God" can be attributed in its full sense only to her.

---

[145] Cf. L.M. Ago, *La "Salutatio Beatae Mariae Virginis" di san Francesco di Assisi*, Roma 1998, 228.

[146] *Redemptoris Mater* 9, 26.

[147] *Marian Catechesis 11* (January 10, 1996), nr. 4, *Insegnamenti di Giovanni Paolo II*, vol. XIX/1, Città del Vaticano 1998, 48 (cf. *Redemptoris Mater* 26). The theological background in John Paul II (the influence of St. Grignion and St. Maximilian Kolbe, but also – for the Marian Catecheses – of Jean Galot) is evidenced by Arthur B. Calkins, *Totus tuus* (note 88) 282-286; Manfred Hauke, *La mediazione materna di Maria secondo Papa Giovanni Paolo II*, in AA. VV., *Maria Corredentrice VII*, Frigento 2005, 35-91 (47-49. 70f).

[148] Cf. Paul VI, *Marialis cultus*, nr. 25.

[149] Cf. John Paul II, *Mulieris dignitatem* (1988), nr. 3.

For this reason the expressions "spouse of the Holy Spirit" and "*favored daughter of the Father*" are appropriate. "Here we see the authentic meaning of Mary's privileges and of her extraordinary relationship with the Trinity: Their purpose is to enable her to co-operate in the salvation of the human race."[150]

---

[150] *Marian Catechesis 11* (January 10, 1996), nr. 5, in *Insegnamenti di Giovanni Paolo II*, vol. XIX/1, Città del Vaticano 1998, 48f.

The Predestination of the Virgin Mother and Her Immaculate Conception

Fr. Peter M. Fehlner, F.I.

Introduction

The two closely related mysteries treated in this chapter are extraordinarily important, indeed, according to the Scotistic-Franciscan view of Mariology, crucially important, for a correct appreciation of Catholic theology on Mary and the Marian character of "our theology," viz., the saving knowledge of God possible to us in a time of pilgrimage.[1]

Since the close of Vatican II, and despite that Council's very firm reaffirmation of both mysteries in the traditional sense,[2] treatment of the predestination of Mary has disappeared from Mariological study. Some expositions of the Immaculate Conception have either 1) minimized its binding dogmatic character with calls for its "dedogmatization," viz., its reduction to the status of a thesis pertaining to an unimportant and perhaps out-dated theological system no longer binding in faith on all Catholics; 2) downplayed or even denied its character as a unique privilege of Mary alone, and so reducing the Mother of God to the status of just another woman; or 3) totally naturalized the privilege (along the

---

[1] The phrase "our theology" is from Bl. John Duns Scotus, *Ordinatio*, Prologue. A listing of my earlier studies on this theme can be found in P. Fehlner, *St. Maximilian M. Kolbe, Martyr of Charity, Pneumatologist. His Theology of the Holy Spirit* (New Bedford MA 2004) pp. 187-189.

[2] *Lumen Gentium*, nn. 56, 61 (predestination); nn. 53, 59 (Immaculate Conception).

lines of the ancient heretic Pelagius) by eliminating any reference in its definition to original sin.³

Closely examined, these trends reflect both the anti-metaphysical, anti-supernatural and ultimately pantheistic character fueling some current theological speculation claiming to offer "new" and "radically different" directions given to Catholic thought and life by Vatican II.⁴ Pope Benedict XVI has recently⁵ described this kind of Vatican II hermeneutic as one of discontinuity, inevitably leading to rupture within the Church. Such a hermeneutic, says the Holy Father, betrays the genuine intentions and meaning of the council texts, which are those of continuity and renewal in harmony with Tradition. Continuity with Tradition in reading Vatican II means not opposing the metaphysical and supernatural character of patristic-scholastic theology, always insisted upon authoritatively by the apostolic Magisterium, to a biblical-historical approach as mutually exclusive alternatives. Rather, continuity with tradition postulates a recognition that the metaphysical and supernatural content of theology is at the very heart of the biblical-

---

3   Proposals concerning "dedogmatization" of the Immaculate Conception and Assumption were initially associated with the name of A. Dulles in the English-speaking world; those concerning the redefinition of the Immaculate Conception without reference to sin are associated with the names of K. Rahner and P. Schoonenberg. Cf. the study of J.L. Bastero de Eleizade, *La Inmaculada Conceptión en el Magistero reciente*, in *Estudios Marianos*, LXXI (2005) pp. 81-107. The post-conciliar Magisterium has not directly condemned any of these "redefinitions," but effectively has rejected them in insisting on defining the Immaculate Conception in relation to original sin. Dulles, first during the 1970s and more recently in an interview published in *The Long Island Catholic*, March 5, 1997 (before being created a cardinal), urged the Church to make belief in the dogmas of the Immaculate Conception and Assumption optional, i.e., "to dedogmatize them," because these dogmas could be "a barrier to ecumenical unity" and are "something less than central to the faith," reasons widely shared since the end of Vatican II by the theological avant-garde. Cf. G. Morrissey, *For the Love of Mary: Defending the Church from Anti-Marianism* (Brooklyn NY 1999) pp. 161-162, note 11. Also valuable for insights into the current Marian scene from an orthodox point of view is V. Messori, *Ipotesi su Maria. Fatti, indizi, enigma* (Milan 2005).

4   Cf. H. Munsterman, *Marie Corédemptrice. Débat sur un titre controversé* (Paris 2006) and my review of this book, *Marian Minimalists on Coredemption*, in *Immaculata Mediatrix* 6 (2006) 397-420.

5   Benedict XVI – Allocution to Roman Curia, Dec. 22, 2005: text in *L'Osservatore Romano*, Dec. 23, 2005.

historical. Both Bl. Pius IX in the bull of definition of the Immaculate Conception, *Ineffabilis Deus*, 1854, and Pope Pius XII in the bull of definition of the Assumption, *Munificentissimus Deus*, 1950, expressly teach the joint predestination of Jesus and Mary: *uno eodemque decreto* (in one and the same decree). Vatican II, in its summary of the Mariology of the Church, has done nothing else but point this out, stressing in particular how 1) the joint predestination of Mary with Christ (*Lumen Gentium* 61 and 62) and 2) the Immaculate Conception as the beginning of her history (*Lumen Gentium* 56), are starting points for understanding the person and unique role of Mary in the mystery of Christ and of the Church, both in the mind of God and in the unfolding of the divine counsels of salvation. And John Paul II reiterates, in *Redemptoris Mater* 8-10, that this doctrine is at the root of the Church's teaching and of our faith concerning the economy of salvation. This is what is meant when Mariology is described as metaphysical, and when our metaphysics is said to be radically Marian-Christic.[6]

Hence, a biblically based theology is radically metaphysical at its core, because in the final analysis the very possibility of an economy of salvation and an order of finite realities outside the Creator and Savior is anchored in the counsels of the divine will, that is, on predestination or the order between various intentions determined by divine mercy and goodness. In turn, a full grasp of theological metaphysics is only possible via Revelation, viz., via Scripture and Tradition. No one has ever seen God or known the counsels of his will except him who is in the bosom of the Father. On entering our world through and from the bosom of Mary, he has told us about this "metaphysics" (cf. Jn 1:18). This is why biblical history is metaphysical, and theological metaphysics is biblical.

Because this is so, the relation between creation and grace, or between creation and predestination to grace and glory in Christ in the order of finite realities outside of God (*ad extra*), becomes central to any understanding of what exists and why it exists. The mystery of grace, viz., of the metaphysical (i.e., "supernatural"), is primarily the mystery of the grace of the Incarnation. Inseparably linked to this mystery is the grace of the Immaculate Conception, or unique personal sanctity of

---

[6] Cf. J. Ferrer Arellano, *The Immaculate Conception as the Condition for the Possibility of the Coredemption*, in *Mary at the Foot of the Cross V* (New Bedford MA 2005) pp. 74-185.

the Mother of the Savior God. For this reason the Virgin Mother as a person belongs not only to the economy of salvation as one of the saved-redeemed, but she alone among the saved also pertains to the order of the hypostatic union, because, as the Immaculate Conception or "Full of Grace," she is capable of being the Virgin-Mother of God.

From these few introductory observations it should be clear that those who claim the authority of Vatican II for something this Council not only did not affirm, but firmly denied, not only reject patristic-scholastic Mariology, but the biblical as well. In doing so they undermine the basis of genuine faith in the Incarnation and redemption.

It is also possible to relate the two mysteries treated in this chapter in terms of a scholastic axiom concerning the divine counsels and their execution outside the mind of God. *Quod primum est in intentione, ultimum est in executione* ("what is first in intention is last in execution"). What is first in the divine counsels concerning Mary is the divine maternity; what is first in the implementation of this first counsel is the Immaculate Conception. This last is the unique personal sanctity of the Virgin, her personal consecration to her Son and Savior. Mary's only reason for existence is to be full of grace and Christ's Mother, and he would come to be incarnate only through her because she is immaculate. All this would come to be, not by necessity of nature, but by the good-pleasure of the Father. This fittingness, the Scotistic *decuit*, far from being irrational and arbitrary, is the font of all rationality in creation.

The Predestination of Mary[7]

This mystery has been implicit in all discussions—biblical, patristic, scholastic—of the divine plan of salvation from its first revelation in the

---

[7] Bibliography: see G. Roschini, *Mariologia* (Rome 1947) vol. II, p. 12. Roschini lists the main patristic texts where mention is made of Mary's predestination. These texts, however, do not deal directly with the precise questions raised concerning this mystery in relation to the absolute primacy of the Incarnation as the grace of graces. On St. Augustine and predestination in general cf. the excellent collection of texts in F. Moriones, *Enchiridion theologicum Sancti Augustini* (Madrid 1961): numbers listed under *Praedestinatio* in the *Index Rerum*, p. 741.

book of Genesis. According to almost all the Fathers of the Church,[8] discussion of this plan is central to the interpretation of the first words of the Bible, "in the beginning" (Gen 1:1), as denoting not a first moment of time, but the first point in his eternal counsels, namely the incarnate Word, Son of Mary. The first point of those counsels is that God created heaven and earth for the sake of Jesus and Mary. This is why the first man and woman, the high point of the work of six days, were formed before the fall in a spousal context. Marriage as a divinely instituted covenant between Adam and Eve typified Christ and Mary, and through Mary, Christ and the Church. The absolute primacy of Jesus and Mary so indicated in the work of the six days constitutes the ontological basis both for the possibility of redemption from the tragedy of the fall and for the perfection of that redemptive work, namely, its character as most perfect (Bl. Duns Scotus) or quasi-infinite (St. Thomas).

An interesting overview of the entire question is to be found in K. Lynch, *The Predestination of Our Lady in the Franciscan School—A Survey*, in *Franciscan Educational Conference*, vol. 38 (1957) pp. 77-165. For a detailed, but very readable introduction to the Scotistic theology which has in great part guided the development of this doctrine, see M. Dean, *A Primer on the Absolute Primacy of Christ. Blessed John Duns Scotus and the Franciscan Thesis* (New Bedford MA 2006); also R. Rosini, *Mariologia del beato Giovanni Duns Scoto* (Castelpetroso 1994) pp. 18-31. The chapter on this doctrine by J. Fr. Bonnefoy, *The Predestination of Our Blessed Lady*, in J. Carol (ed.), *Mariology*, vol. 2 (Milwaukee 1957) pp. 154-176, is tendentious. K. Lynch correctly remarks, *The Predestination...*, pp. 157-160, that Bonnefoy introduces an interpretation of the axiom: *bonum est diffusium sui* (good tends to communicate itself), metaphysically quite contrary to that of Scotus, in fact anticipating on this point the premises of contemporary neo-patripassianism such as that found in B. Forte. Since the end of Vatican II relatively little attention has been given to this mystery. Nonetheless, a passing reference to its importance in relation to the problem of the primary principle of Mariology is made in a work published as Vatican II closed by C. Vollert, *The Theology of Mary* (New York 1965) pp. 67-68 (commenting on a theory of J. Thomas).

[8] The best collections of patristic texts on these and related affirmations of the absolute primacy of Jesus and Mary in Scripture are those of F. Risi and C. Urritibehety, cited in notes 16 and 17 below. On the *Protoevangelium* and its relation to the account of creation in chapters one and two of Genesis see Settimio Manelli, *Genesis 3:15 and the Immaculate Conception*, in *Mary at the Foot of the Cross V* (New Bedford MA 2005) pp. 276-277, note 32; P.D. Fehlner, *Redemption, Metaphysics and the Immaculate Conception*, in *Mary at the Foot of the Cross V* (New Bedford MA 2005) pp. 229-239.

We may call this the fact of Mary's predestination to be the Mother of God, of the incarnate Word, before the foundation of the world. This fore-love of Mary by the Father may not, however, be regarded as arbitrary or capricious, because the will of God is always ordered and wise. Mary in some intrinsic manner pertains as no other person to the order of the hypostatic union, the grace of graces and source of all order and intelligibility both in the economy of salvation and in creation. To this fact and to the special place enjoyed by Mary in the economy of salvation, both in relation to the mystery of Jesus and of the Church (cf. *Lumen Gentium*, ch. 8, title), the whole of revelation affords abundant witness (as sketched out in *Lumen Gentium*, nn. 55ff.).

Foundation in Sacred Scripture

Taking this authoritative witness as the point of departure, we may indicate how the revealed teaching on the fact of Mary's unique place within the predestination of all the saved before the foundation of the world in Christ is shown in Scripture and Tradition. Because the coming of the Messiah is via the divine maternity and therefore always Marian in mode, the messianic revelation of the Old Testament is a progressive realization and unveiling of the Marian mode of the divine counsels of salvation. What is true of the prophecies, is also true of the symbols, figures and types bearing on the Savior and his Mother. Their fulfillment under the New and Eternal Covenant is expressly related by St. Paul to the great mystery of predestination (cf. Eph 1:3-14; Col 1:13-20). Careful examination of Romans 1:3-4 (cf. Rom 9:4-5) and Galatians 4:4-7 shows that the predestination of the Son of God to become incarnate, and so son of David, and the predestination of the saved-redeemed to adoptive sonship of the Father in Christ, both hinge upon the woman who conceives and gives birth by the operation of the Holy Spirit. Hence the importance of generic Pauline texts on the predestination of all in Christ (e.g. Eph 1:3ff.), that he might be the firstborn of many brethren, e.g., Romans 8:28-30. On these generic references depend the more detailed explanation of the order of those predestined to Christ and to each other, reflected in texts such as Romans 5:12-21 (Adam—with Eve, Christ—with Mary; original sin vs. superabundant grace), Philippians 2:5-11 (the *kenosis* of the Son via the virgin birth and Cross is crowned in the glory of the Father), Hebrews 10:4-10 (the assent of Christ to the

Incarnation and counsels of salvation, corresponding to the assent of the Virgin Mother, Luke 1:38), Ephesians 5:21-32 (the Church as bride of Christ to the degree that she is one with the immaculate purity of Mary: *sine macula, sine ruga*—"without spot or wrinkle").

Pondering texts from John 1:13 (belief in the one born virginally of God), 1 John 4:10 (the prior love of God) and Luke 1:30 (Mary found grace with God), we may say that the grace of predestination, viz., the prior love of God for us, is concretely our predestination with that of the incarnate Son. It is a mystery only brought to pass through the unique grace found by Mary to be chosen before the foundation of the world to be the immaculate, virginal Mother of the Savior God.

The Witness of Tradition

The predestination of Mary as a fact is frequently mentioned or clearly alluded to by the Fathers from the earliest days of the Church, and so is clearly a doctrine taught by the apostles and their immediate successors. St. Ignatius of Antioch tells us[9] that the virgin birth is one of the three principal mysteries of salvation hidden in the silence of the divine counsels, and inaccessible therefore to the Devil. The basic method of our theology, that of recirculation and recapitulation as set forth by St. Justin and St. Irenaeus, ultimately is grounded in the mystery of predestination. Among the many texts cited in the repertoire of Fr. Roschini[10] are these very explicit affirmations of Mary's predestination:

> St. Augustine: "Before he was born of her, he knew his Mother in her predestination" (*Tractatus in Joannem*, 9).
> St. John Damascene: "Mary was predestined before all time in the foreknowing counsel ..." (*De fide orthodoxa*).
> St. Bernard: "The angel was sent to the Virgin ... not found recently or by chance, but chosen before the ages, foreknown by the Most High" (*Homilia II super Missus est*).

---

[9] St. Ignatius of Antioch, *Letter to the Ephesians*.
[10] Cf. note 7 above. As an example of the many riches on this theme still to be unearthed in the Fathers of the Church, cf. the study of A. Kerrigan, *The Predestination of Mary According to St. Cyril of Alexandria*, in *Alma Socia Christi*, vol. 3 (Rome 1952) pp. 34-58.

To these should be added the testimony of the liturgy, for instance in these verses from the hymn *O Virgo Mater*,[11] used in the office of readings for Our Lady on Saturday:

O Virgo Mater, Filia tui beata Filii	O Virgin Mother, blessed daughter of thy Son
Sublimis et humilisima prae creatures omnibus,	Sublimest of all creatures and humblest,
Divini tu consilii fixus ab aevo terminus,	*Thou from eternity preset goal of God's saving counsels,*
Tu decus et fastigium naturae nostrae maximum.	Highest glory of our nature and zenith.

A long text of St. Augustine from *The Predestination of the Saints*, ch. 15, 30-31, provides an excellent summary of Catholic Tradition on predestination, stressing the simultaneous predestination of all the saints in that of Christ, the grace of graces. This is the point of departure for the systematic elaboration of Scotus, perhaps the profoundest ever achieved.

Theological Reflection

Systematically, however, the unique manner in which Our Lady alone enters the order of the hypostatic union and so occupies after Christ the highest place in the saving counsels of God, and the one closest to us (cf. *Lumen Gentium*, 54), came to be studied consequent to discussion of the absolute predestination or primacy of Christ as set forth by Bl. John Duns Scotus and his disciples, a discussion closely bound up with the theological justification of the Immaculate Conception. In fact, Scotus himself does not directly treat of the predestination of Mary. But he laid down the principles on the basis of which Mary's predestination has been treated ever since. Hence, the best way to grasp the sense of the theme, to appreciate its importance and why the Catholic concept of predestination does not lead to predestinationism or Calvinism, is to organize our exposition along the lines of Scotus himself.[12]

---

[11] Immortalized by Dante in *The Divine Comedy*, Paradiso, XXXIII, 3: "termine fisso d'eterno consiglio."

[12] The principle texts on which this summary is based are these: *Ordinatio* III, d. 7, qq. 3 & 4; d. 13, q. 4; d. 32, q. un., and the parallel distinctions in the various

The Contribution of Bl. John Duns Scotus

1. By predestination Scotus means God's gratuitous or gracious fore-choice of creatures for glory. It is the prior love of God for us, before we have loved him, viz., gained any merit, of which St. John speaks in his first letter (1 Jn 4:10). This act of love is absolutely gratuitous, viz., is prior to and independent of any consideration of personal worth or merit, not only in the case of created persons, but also in case of the Incarnation or hypostatically assumed humanity of Jesus. This prior act of the Father no more deprives the creature so predestined to glory, viz., to the sharing of the divine nature and beatific vision, of his personal freedom than does the act of creation and of formation of Adam preclude Adam's freedom and personal activity. Quite the contrary: the formation of spiritual or rational creatures in the image and likeness of God is the very basis of their freedom and its presupposition, justice. So, too, in the higher order of glory which does not follow automatically from the fact of creation, the prior love of God is the presupposition of the very possibility of merit or cooperation in the work of salvation.

Set in this context, the many references of St. Paul to the absolute predestination of Jesus, and with him of the elect, as a pure gift of grace, antecedent to any considerations of merit or demerit (cf. Rom 9:6-13), hardly preclude, but constitute the very basis for the possibility of human freedom and merit. Ephesians 1:3ff. and 2 Timothy 1:9 are examples, but hardly the only ones, of the classic Pauline doctrine on which rests the articulation of the predestination of Mary.

This predestination to glory, at the very core of the theology of grace, is commonly considered a matter of faith. Further, this concept of predestination to grace and glory is, in the order of divine intentions, prior to any consideration of sin, either on the part of the angels or on the part of Adam and Eve and their offspring. On the very possibility of the grace of the Incarnation or absolute primacy of Christ rests the possibility both of creation and of a redemption from sin.

2. The second point on which Scotus insists is that of St. Paul in the Letter to the Ephesians. On the part of God, acts of predestination are not multiplied in relation to the number of persons predestined to glory;

---

reportationes. The best summary exposition of these Scotistic texts in relation to Our Lady is in Rosini, *Mariologia*, cit., pp. 18-31. The exposition here reflects that of Fr. Rosini.

all are predestined simultaneously in the predestination of the Head of the saints, viz., Jesus Christ, the incarnate Word. Predestination is a joint affair within which the place or order of single persons to Christ the Savior is situated, not simply by divine *fiat*, but in view of the merits of Christ or in short, of his human *fiat*. The notion of headship implicates above all this truth. The conferral of the blessings of salvation occurs in and through the body of Christ according to the mutual ordering of the members therein. The grace of headship is precisely the power to do this in the context of the Mystical Body. The blessings of salvation are dispensed, not aside from or independently of the merits and satisfaction of Christ, but through him, nor according to a certain subordination to Christ as Head through the merits of the elect themselves. The elect can indeed merit eternal glory, but neither the first grace nor the grace of perseverance, for these are merited for them by the merits and satisfaction of the Savior-Redeemer. This teaching is also commonly acknowledged as a matter of faith.

3. The third point of Scotus, often known as the "Franciscan thesis," but hardly exclusive to Franciscan theologians, concerns the absolute primacy of Christ as Head of those predestined jointly in him. The Incarnation of the Savior is willed absolutely prior to any consideration of sin or of creation, in that sense independently of both. On the other hand both creation, and afterwards the redemption of mankind, are willed dependently in view of the Incarnation, the central mystery of salvation effected through the divine-virginal maternity. Hence, within the one act of jointly predestining all in Christ, there is a more restricted sense of joint predestination, viz., that of one of the elect to be Mother of the incarnate Head-Savior, and so Mediatrix of all graces, viz., the person through whom the Mediator comes to us and through whom we are incorporated into Christ. On this basis later theologians will distinguish, within the divine counsels of salvation, between the order of the hypostatic union and the order of the saved-redeemed. Mary by reason of her singular role as Mother of God, a role resting on her unique personal state of holiness (Immaculate Conception), pertains to both orders, so making possible the realization of the Incarnation and the cooperation of the Church and faithful in the work of salvation.

The predestination of all the elect in Christ before the foundation of the world is in view of their cooperation in the work of salvation.

Whereas the creation of the world depends solely on the *fiat* of the Father, that of its salvation depends also on the world's cooperation.[13] Here we see most clearly the root of the differences between a Catholic and Protestant soteriology, the Catholic insisting that the mediation of Christ does not exclude, as Protestant soteriology asserts in the famous *Christus solus*, but includes in a certain order a subordinate mediation of the redeemed. This is clearly affirmed by *Lumen Gentium* 62, precisely after ascribing the title *Mediatrix* to Mary. Just as clearly this implies that in the order of divine providence such cooperation hinges on the *fiat* of Mary. This point is fundamental to any grasp of the possibility, unique in Mary, to be actively involved not merely in the distribution of divine blessings once acquired by the Redeemer, but to be associated with him in their acquisition, in the so-called "objective redemption" or *redemptio ad sufficientiam*.[14] Hence, Mary's capacity, under and with Christ, to merit the conferral of grace on others. Without the Immaculate Conception, Mary's maternal mediation, and so our cooperation in the work of salvation (cf. Col 1:24), would not be possible. Lacking that cooperation, a perfect redemption could not be realized. Whence, the crucial importance of the mystery of the Immaculate Conception as foundation for the actualization of all Mary's other privileges in the order of history, culminating in the consummation of her maternal mediation in Christ and in the Church (divine and spiritual maternity).

---

[13] The classic formulation, found in St. Anselm, *Oratio* 52, still read during the Office of Readings for the solemnity of the Immaculate Conception, is a commonplace of Catholic theology, and is particularly stressed by Bl. John Duns Scotus in his soteriology, viz., that this cooperation achieved through the preservative redemption of the Mother of God accounts for the perfection, not only of her redemption, but of the redemption of all saved in and through the Church. A most perfect redemption (or quasi-infinite in the terminology of St. Thomas: S.T. I, q. 25, a. 6, ad 4) postulates the Immaculate Conception of the Virgin Mother as Mediatrix of all grace. St. Thomas, like Scotus, insists on this point, stating (S.T. III, q. 30, ad 1) that the prior consent of Mary to the Incarnation was given not only personally, but for all mankind. The common teaching on cooperation with the one Mediator, based on the joint predestination of Jesus and Mary is confirmed by Vatican II, *Lumen Gentium*, nn. 61-62.

[14] Cf. St. Bonaventure, *Breviloquium*, p. IV, ch. 10. What is today called subjective redemption is termed *redemptio quoad efficaciam* by the Seraphic Doctor. The current terminology (objective-subjective) seems to have first been used by the seventeenth century Franciscan Scotist of Naples, Angelo Vulpes, *Sacrae Theologiae Summa*, Tome III, p. 4, to translate that of St. Bonaventure.

Is this merely a theological theory or is it revealed truth? The disciples of Scotus[15] have always insisted that the theological discussion is rooted precisely in Revelation. Anyone who considers the evidence assembled in such works as those of F. Risi[16] and C. Urritibehety[17] will understand why more and more scholars, including biblicists, agree that the Scotistic reading is the correct one.[18] It is this fact or "*fecit*" of the old axiom: *potuit, decuit, ergo fecit* (he was able, it was fitting, therefore he did it), associated with Scotus' defense of the Immaculate Conception, which grounds the "*decuit*" and "*potuit*."[19] Our redemption is most perfect precisely because it follows upon the absolute primary of Christ, rather than acting as exclusive condition-motive for the Incarnation.[20]

4. Our fourth point concerns the relation between predestination and conferral of the graces whereby the predestined come to enjoy all the blessings of paradise. Precisely because their predestination to glory is in Christ, therefore all of them attain these blessings *in facto esse* through the merits and mediation of Christ the Head: one way in Mary and another way in all the rest. Whereas the fullness of grace in Mary is in view of the foreseen merits of her Son, the participation in grace by all others is in view of the mediation of Jesus and Mary. Because of the fact of sin

---

[15] Among the better known Franciscan disciples of Scotus: Petrus Thomae, Bartholomew of Pisa, Bernadine of Siena, Robert of Carraciola, St. Lawrence of Brindisi, Angelo Vulpes, Carlo del Moral, Bl. Lodovico di Castelplanio, may be cited; but not only Franciscans: St. Antonine of Florence, O.P., St. Francis de Sales, Francisco Suarez, S.J., St. Alphonsus Liguori, C.Ss.R., John Henry Newman, F.W. Faber, M. Scheeben, G. Roschini, O.S.M., all underscored the importance of this mystery, very often sharing the premises for this teaching found in Scotus.

[16] F. Risi, *Sul motivo primario dell'Incarnazione del Verbo, ossia Gesu Cristo predestinato di primo intento per fini indipendenti della caduta dell'uman genere e dal decreto di Redenzione*. 4 vols. (Brescia-Roma 1897-1898); cf. also the more recent studies in substantial agreement with Risi: J.Fr. Bonnefoy, *La Primauté du Christ selon l'Ecriture et la Tradition* (Rome 1959); R. Rosini, *Il Cristo nella Bibbia, nei Santi Padri, nel Vaticano II* (Venice 1980).

[17] C. Urritibehety, *Christus alpha et omega seu de Christi universali regno* (Lille 1910). Cf. also E. Longpre, *The Kingship of Christ* (Paterson NJ 1942).

[18] J.B. Carol, *Why Jesus Christ?* (Manassas VA 1986).

[19] On this axiom cf. Rosini, *Mariologia...*, cit., p. 80, note 16.

[20] Cf. my essay: *Immaculata Mediatrix: Toward a Dogmatic Definition of the Coredemption*, in M. Miravalle (ed.), *Mary Coredemptrix, Mediatrix, Advocate: Theological Foundations II* (Santa Barbara CA 1997) pp. 259-329.

on the part of Adam and Eve, that mediation of Christ, when realized historically after the tragic event of original sin and the fall of the angels, is in fact redemptive as well as saving: preservatively in Mary (and in a subordinate way in the angels who did not fall) and libertatively in all others. In Mary redemption is her Immaculate Conception; in us it is our liberation from sin. In both cases redemption is the term of divine mercy: more perfectly, however, in Mary than in us, and in us dependently on its realization in the Immaculate.

This brings us to the final point, not expressly discussed by Scotus, but taken up by his immediate disciples, the predestination of Mary to be the Mother of God, the Savior-Head of the saved. Does this postulate in her a unique relation to Christ? St. Bonaventure calls[21] her relation to Jesus a singular sacred order (hierarchy), above all other orders, such that the mystery of the Incarnation and divine maternity constitute a single indivisible mystery of salvation,[22] or as later theologians are accustomed to say the order of the hypostatic union. The Scotistic answer, reflecting Bonaventure, is affirmative, both in relation to the original holiness of the angels and in relation to Adam and Eve before the fall. Hence, it is the basis in Mary of her Immaculate Conception or preservative redemption. Precisely because Mary is predestined to be Mother of God in the joint predestination of all in Christ, therefore she is also Mother of the Church and so the pre-eminent member of the Church, because maternal Mediatrix of all grace. For in a manner beyond our comprehension she is actively involved in the conferral on Jesus of the grace of the Incarnation by the power of the Holy Spirit, i.e., she is the instrument of the Holy Spirit at the Incarnation in forming the Body of Christ, which includes the Church, just as the formation of the body of the first Adam included in some way the entire human family.[23]

Here we must underscore a point overlooked by all the critics of Scotus. In the joint predestination of Jesus and Mary, the distinctive personal roles of Jesus and Mary are not confused, nor does their

---

[21] St. Bonaventure, II Sent., d. 9, q. 7: "Cum… (Beata Virgo) sit supra omnes ordines, per se constituit ordinem."

[22] Idem, III Sent., d. 2, a. 2, q. 2: "Sive dicamus (Verbum) fieri hominem, sive dicamus mulierem fieri Matrem Dei, utrumque est super statum qui debetur creaturae."

[23] S. Ragazzini, *La Divina Maternita di Maria nel suo concetto teologico integrale* (Frigento 1986).

coordination within a single work of mediation put Mary on a par with Jesus, any more than the capacity of the blessed to think and love in the mode of divine persons (a kind of coordination, anticipated in the divine indwelling by grace) put them on a par with the divine persons. Such coordination, heart of the supernatural order of grace, rests ever on a radical subordination. In this joint predestination Jesus is ordained absolutely for his own sake, and Mary for the sake of Jesus and no other, not even herself. Yet in virtue of the very grace of the Immaculate Conception whereby she totally belongs to Jesus and to the Church as Mother, she is ennobled in a most personal way, thereby revealing how grace transforms and perfects the person.[24]

The logical corollary of this is the assertion that Mary would not have existed except that the Incarnation was *de facto* decreed as the reason for creation. That means that Mary in her being and in her activity is totally related to Christ and to the work of salvation and redemption. The perfection of human existence and personal freedom is directly proportionate to its assimilation within the totality of Mary's relation to Christ and to his work. This is what it means to be full of grace: so holy that one can contribute to the sanctification of others, even if sanctified by the merits of Christ. Mary is in some true manner the maternal Mediatrix of all persons: as Christ's Mother bringing him to us; as Mother of the Church and of believers bringing us to Christ. On this rests the meaning and importance of total consecration to Mary Immaculate.

---

[24] On the meaning of the phrase *uno eodemque decreto* first used in a pontifical document by Bl. Pius IX, in relation to the teaching of Scotus on predestination, cf. R. Rosini, *La Mariologia...*, cit., pp. 21; 28-31. As K. Lynch notes, *The Predestination...*, pp. 163-164, this phrase is not to be found as such in most Scotists before 1854, yet without canonizing the Scotistic position certainly provides support for it. For the central inspiration of St. Francis on the thought of Scotus, particularly as regards the absolute primacy of Christ and the Immaculate Conception, cf. J. Schneider, *Virgo Ecclesia Facta. The Presence of Mary in the Crucifix of San Damiano and in the Office of the Passion of St. Francis of Assisi* (New Bedford MA 2004). As Fr. Schneider notes, two well-known works of St. Francis: his *Salute to the Virgin* and the *Marian Antiphon, Office of the Passion*, read in this light are particularly important for the subsequent theological development of the theology both of the predestination and of Immaculate Conception of Mary.

The Holy Name of Mary

It is has been objected that such a total consecration nullifies the meaning of personality. Quite the contrary is true. Such a consecration is the basis of a most perfect personhood in Christ, none so perfect as that of being Mother of the Savior God, Jesus. The discussion of the name of Mary,[25] like that of Jesus (which she confers on him) is intimately linked to Mary's unique place in the predestination of Jesus. The discussion of the meaning of her name, which reaches back to the beginning of the Church, is implicitly a discussion of her predestination.[26] This is what is meant when her name, like that of her Son, is said to have been chosen by the Blessed Trinity before the foundation of the world for the first-born daughter, Mother of the Son and Spouse of the Holy Spirit. The conclusion shared by many students of the name of Mary is this: Mary means "Full of Grace," Immaculate Conception, a name of the woman foretold from the beginning, revealed in the fullness of time. With the Marian teaching of Pope John Paul II (*Redemptoris Mater*, nn. 8-11) this conclusion appears to have entered expressly into the Papal Magisterium on Mary, just as the joint predestination of Jesus and Mary by one and the same decree entered that Magisterium with the solemn definition of the Immaculate Conception by Bl. Pius IX, to be confirmed by Pius XII in the definition of the Assumption, and repeated by Vatican II in its presentation of the role of Mary as unique participant with Jesus in the work of salvation decreed before the foundation of the world (*Lumen Gentium* 61).

How much the direction of this recent reflection was in fact guided by Our Lady's reply to St. Bernadette's question: who are you or what is your name?, viz., "I am the Immaculate Conception," is hard to say. The conclusion, however, underscores the correctness of St. Maximilian Kolbe's insights into the name of the Holy Spirit and of Mary, respectively the Uncreated Immaculate Conception and created Immaculate Conception.[27] That is why Mary became Mother of the

---

[25] One of the best summary introductions to the mystery of Mary's name is to be found in Roschini, *Mariologia*, cit., vol. II, pp. 12-57.

[26] Roschini, *Mariologia*, cit., Vol. II, pp. 58-66.

[27] *Scritti di Massimiliano Kolbe* (Rome 1997) 1319, pp. 2328-2331. Cf. also H. Manteau-Bonamy, *The Immaculate Conception and the Holy Spirit. The Marian Teachings of Fr. Kolbe* (Kenosha WI 1977).

Lord. This mystery of the Immaculate Conception provides the key to the relation between person and role in the Mother of God and of the Church.

By way of conclusion to our reflections on Mary's predestination, and as an introduction to those on her Immaculate Conception, we may well ponder these two citations from *Redemptoris Mater*, nos. 8 and 10 (a commentary primarily on Ephesians 1:3ff.):

> In the mystery of Christ Mary is *present* even "before the creation of the world," as the one whom the Father "has chosen" as *Mother* of his Son in the Incarnation… In this way, from the first moment of her existence she belonged to Christ, sharing in the salvific and sanctifying grace and in that love which has its beginning in the "Beloved."

Thus, the grace she receives in fact through the saving-redemptive merit of her Son she receives not by way of liberation from sin, but by way of preservation, a preservation that is the connatural corollary of her predestination with her Son prior to, and not dependently, on the prevision of Adam's sin.

The Immaculate Conception[28]

It is commonplace today to encounter theologians who dismiss the auto-definition of Mary at Lourdes as an impossibility, typical of an over-excited mystical imagination and without theological, much less doctrinal, value.[29] Such skepticism is but an aspect of a general

---

[28] For general overviews: A. Carr – G. Williams, *Mary's Immaculate Conception*, in J.B. Carol (ed.), *Mariology*, vol. I (Milwaukee 1954) pp. 328-394; E.D. O'Connor (ed.), *The Dogma of the Immaculate Conception* (Notre Dame IN 1958); *Mary at the Foot of the Cross V. Redemption and Coredemption under the Sign of the Immaculate Conception* (New Bedford MA 2005); D. Calloway (ed.), *The Immaculate Conception in the Life of the Church* (Stockbridge MA 2004). For a focus more on apologetic considerations and answers to objections cf. H.F. Davis, *Immaculate Conception*, in K. McNamara (ed.), *Mother of the Redeemer* (New York 1960) pp. 84-103. For biblical aspects cf. Stefano Manelli, *All Generations Shall Call Me Blessed. Biblical Mariology* (New Bedford MA, 2nd ed., 2005) *passim*, especially the synthesis, pp. 415-424.

[29] Cf. Fehlner, *St. Maximilian… Pneumatologist…*, cit., pp. 45-46, n. 82.

minimizing of the Immaculate Conception as a doctrine without any immediate biblical foundation, or as a late blooming *theologoumenon*, coefficient of an outdated scholastic system of metaphysics and tributary to a questionable Augustinian theory of original sin, since Vatican II historical relics of a bygone age. Assertions of this kind form the basis for proposals to "dedogmatize" the Immaculate Conception and thereby reduce Mariology to the status of a marginal part of theology, dealing with truths on the lower rungs of the "hierarchy of truths," belief in which is not absolutely necessary for salvation.[30]

Careful, honest and objective examination of these claims does not require much time to recognize the unsustainable structure of this kind of argumentation and the gratuitous character of so many of its erroneous assertions.[31] Let us focus our attention on one of the most gratuitous, viz., that the mystery now known as the dogma of the Immaculate Conception made a late appearance in the Church, long after the close of public revelation and formation of the deposit of faith. This is simply false. And the demonstration of its falsity not only undermines the credibility of most of the other assertions in modern arguments against the Immaculate Conception, but makes plain the central importance of this mystery within the economy of salvation. The development or process culminating in the dogmatic definition

---

[30] This position is commonly linked with proposals first aired some 35 years ago by A. Dulles: see n. 3 above. Behind these proposals, however, there lurks a still more radical theological orientation whose true character is only discerned in its total opposition to the Immaculate Conception and absolute primacy of her incarnate Son. This orientation, radically naturalistic and pantheistic, appears under two forms apparently contradictory to each other. One would divorce the Immaculate Conception from any reference to sin, which is essentially the position of Pelagius. The other form would relate grace in Mary only to sin and in no way primarily to the most perfect realization of human nature via its divinization, essentially the position of Calvin. The first position has been resurrected by K. Rahner and those theologians who would set the Immaculate Conception in an evolutionary context. The second position is that of Marian minimalists who would exclude any possibility that the Mother of Jesus might actively cooperate in the work of redemption, and as the Immaculate Conception set concrete limits on the frontiers of moral decadence and the powers of the prince of this world. On Marian minimalism and its dangers for the Church cf. Morrissey, *For the Love of Mary...*, cit. For a contemporary defense of Marian minimalism, cf. Munsterman, *Marie Corédemptrice...*, cit.

[31] Cf. my critique of Munsterman, *Marian Minimalists on Coredemption*, cit.

of 1854, rather than creating a new truth, clarified one always believed because always included in the deposit of faith formed by our Lord. It is by first studying this Tradition as it is proclaimed by the living Magisterium of the Church that we come to master a theological (and not merely philological-historical) exegesis of the Scriptures. In studying the Immaculate Conception as framed by Tradition we come to realize what St. Bonaventure means when he says[32] that we find in Scripture not merely a treatise on Mariology, but somehow the presence of Mary in every verse of Scripture from Genesis to Revelation. For it is impossible to speak of the incarnate Word without including some reference to the Marian mode of the Incarnation. Appreciation of how the biblical affirmation of the all-holiness of Mary, her blessedness, her absolute immunity from the Devil's influence, comes to be expressed as the Immaculate Conception, and how this formulation is basic to an understanding of the mysteries of grace and of the Church, arises precisely out of study of this mystery in Tradition.

The witness of Tradition[33] to the character of the Immaculate Conception as a revealed truth may best be appreciated by considering it under three headings: 1) the grounds of the dogma in Revelation; 2) assertions (explicit and implicit) of the stainless conception as such; and 3)

---

[32] St. Bonaventure, *Collationes in Hexaemeron*, c. 13, n. 20. The little-known, but profoundly Marian German Jesuit, Wilhelm Klein (1889-1996) held the same position, especially in regard to Sts. John and Paul: cf. G. Trentin, *In Principio. Il "mistero di Maria" nei manoscritti di Wilhelm Klein* (Padua 2005).

[33] For introductory studies cf. M. Jugie, *L'Immaculée Conception dans l'Ecriture sainte et dans la Tradition orientale* (Rome 1952); G. Jouassard, *Marie a travers la patristique: maternité divine, virginité, sainteté*, in H. du Manoir (ed.), *Maria. Etudes sur la Sainte Vierge*, vol. I (Paris 1949) pp. 19-157. In addition the following studies in the volume of O'Connor, *The Dogma of the Immaculate Conception*, are most helpful: C. Journet, *Scripture and the Immaculate Conception*, pp. 1-48; G. Jouassard, *The Fathers of the Church and the Immaculate Conception*, pp. 51-85; F. Dvornik, *The Byzantine Church and the Immaculate Conception*, pp. 87-112; C. Balić, *The Medieval Controversies over the Immaculate Conception to the Death of Scotus*, pp. 161-212; W. Sebastian, *The Controversies after Scotus to 1900*, pp. 213-270; C. De Koninck, *The Immaculate Conception and the Divine Motherhood, Coredemption and Assumption*, pp. 303-412. An English version of pertinent patristic and medieval texts is easily available in two volumes edited by L. Gambero: *Mary and the Fathers of the Church. The Blessed Virgin Mary in Patristic Thought* (San Francisco 1999); and *Mary in the Middle Ages. The Blessed Virgin Mary in the Thought of Medieval Latin Theologians* (San Francisco 2005).

explanations of its possibility and appropriateness. The first two headings are a commentary on the *fecit* of the old axiom: *potuit, decuit, ergo fecit*, and will be treated together. The last deals with the *potuit* and *decuit*. We know God preserved Mary pure at conception, because he has told us so.

The "Fecit" or Fact of the Immaculate Conception

In revealing her inclusion in the absolute primacy of his Son, the Christ, God has revealed her state of all-holiness, clearly signaled in the title *Panhaghia* (All Holy); *Sanctissima* (All Holy); *Beatissima* (All Blessed). This title of Mary has been used of her from the first days of the Church. Indeed, it is present in the address of Gabriel at the Annunciation, in that of St. Elizabeth at the Visitation and in the very practice of Christ himself. Her state from the first moment of her personal existence, and throughout it, contrasts with that of the first Eve, before as well as after the fall. It is also revealed in the *terra virgo* from which the first man was formed, a figure of Mary from whom and by whom the last Adam was formed. This is a type of Mary dear to the ancient Jewish Christians and to many Fathers and theologians well into the thirteenth century, as with St. Bonaventure. It is also revealed in the figure of the wholly innocent *Agna* (she-lamb) from whom comes the sinless *Agnus* (Christ) led to the slaughter for our redemption. The title is found in Melito of Sardis and is employed in the liturgy of the sacred triduum.[34] The celebration of Mary's conception as immaculate, or all-holy, both in the feast and in the title, is not simply the celebration of a moment, but of a moment determining the sense of the name by which the angel addresses the future Mother of God, viz. "Full of Grace," or Immaculate Conception, therefore blessed among women as no other. The mystery of the Immaculate Conception explains why Mary is the "Full of Grace," and therefore incomparably blessed among women precisely in relation to the central attribute of woman: being Mother of Christ the Head and

---

[34] For references cf. Stefano Manelli, *All Generations Shall Call Me Blessed. Biblical Mariology* (New Bedford MA, 2nd ed., 2005), pp. 85-86; Fehlner, *Immaculata Mediatrix...*, cit., pp. 286-302 More extensive discussion of the early Christian literature on these points can be found in E. Testa, *Maria terra vergine* (Jerusalem 1985), vol. I. Fr. Testa maintains that the title *Terra Virgo* is the equivalent of Immaculate Conception.

Mediatrix between him and the rest of his brethren, as Eve between Adam and all other men.

In brief, the fact of the Immaculate Conception is implicitly rooted in the truth of the absolute primacy of Christ and revealed in all those texts such as Genesis 3:15, Luke 1:28 and Revelation 12:1ff., which deal with the fulfillment of a precise promise of salvation involving a woman in no way, however slightly, tainted by the dominion of the serpent. That primacy, as with the sacred humanity of Jesus, entails in the Mother a kind of "substantial holiness," a unique moral state, holier than which none can be conceived,[35] so that the Virgin so consecrated to God may be uniquely and actively associated with the New Adam in the work of recapitulation and restoration of the human family. The Immaculate Conception is not merely a first instance of the restoration of the redeemed to the holiness entailed in the state of original justice before the fall. It is the realization of the most perfect holiness in Mary, and through Mary in the Church, only partially and typologically reflected in that of the state of original justice. This is the heart of preservative redemption: to be constituted maternal Mediatrix through whom Jesus comes to us and through whom we approach Jesus and are united with him. This is the first reason why the conception of Mary was celebrated as a feast in the East: it was recognized as the first dawn of a new order, the order or economy of salvation, of a new humanity, as the indispensable (because divinely willed) introduction to the Incarnation, to the knowledge and love of the Savior and of his Cross. So contemplated, even the dogmatic title of the mystery has its evident roots in the deposit of faith. Immaculate is but another form of St. Paul's *sine macula* in the Letter to the Ephesians, 5:27. Conception is but a reference to the mystery celebrated in the feasts of the Conception-Nativity of the Virgin Mother.

At the time of Scotus, as often enough today, the statement was made that because God could have made Mary holy at conception, and had a reason for doing so, therefore he had to do this. Hence, the dogma is a fact to be believed. As Peter of Candia (Crete), a Franciscan and later the Pisan Pope Alexander V, observed, this is a foolish argument,

---

[35] The formulation is that of St. Anselm, *De conceptione Virginis*, but the reality is confessed from the Church's birth at Pentecost in the title *Panhaghia*.

thinly veiling a rationalist mind-set.[36] We can never demonstrate from theological analysis a mystery of the economy of salvation, except God reveal what he has freely and graciously chosen to do. In showing how God might have worked the Immaculate Conception, and that he had a reason for so doing, the theologian in the footsteps of Scotus confirms and illustrates the truth of a fact antecedently known to be true because founded on Scripture and witnessed by Tradition, and prepares the way for a profounder contemplation of that truth as mystery.[37]

Grounds of the Dogma in Revelation

The truth proclaimed so precisely in the dogma is none other than the focus of the mystery of the "all-holiness" of the Virgin of virgins, the reason she is addressed reverently and devoutly as the *Panhaghia*. It is what defines her unique and permanent moral state, both 1) in relation to Christ, the Savior-Redeemer (Virgin Mother, therefore like the fruit of her womb, all blessed; like us in all things but sin, as St. Elizabeth confessed calling her blessed among women: cf. Luke 1:42), and 2) to the rest of mankind (spiritual Mother), for whom, before the trial of angels and of Adam and Eve she was their Mediatrix in relation to their original justice (*quoad statum naturae institutae*—as regards the original state of human nature), and after the sin of our first parents she was Co-redemptrix of fallen mankind (*quoad statum naturae lapsae*—as regards the fallen state of human nature), precisely because without sin.[38] The focal point of this moral state is her conception, not simply as a first biological moment, but as the beginning of a person, found in and determining the personal worth of every subsequent moment in the life of that person. We may discern three great truths explicit in Revelation handed down to us by Christ through the Church and the apostles, which as it were contain the dogma expressing this mystery:

---

[36] Cf. S. Cecchin, *L'Immacolata Concezione. Breve storia del dogma* (Vatican City 2003) p. 60. Cf. also Rosini, *Mariologia…*, cit., p. 80, note 16.
[37] Cf. Bonaventure on the three modes of theological understanding: symbolic, proper (academic) and mystical (infused contemplation), in his *Itinerarium Mentis in Deum*, ch. 1, n. 7, and *Christus unus omnium Magister, passim*.
[38] The distinction here between Salvatrix and Co-redemptrix reflects the concept of Immaculate Mediatrix seen in the context of the absolute primacy of Christ according to Scotus. Cf. Dean, *A Primer on the Absolute Primacy*, pp. 101-119.

1) Mary's unique condition as the *Panhaghia*;

2) Her inclusion in the primacy of Christ in virtue of their joint predestination to constitute the order of the hypostatic union;

3) Her descent from Adam and solidarity with our human family in need of redemption from sin.

Mary, therefore, is the rose among thorns; she is the New Eve, from the New Adam, not as his wife, but as his Mother, coming after the first Eve historically, but before her in the divine counsels and above her morally. She is, finally, the maternal Mediatrix who gives our humanity to the Son of God and is the Mother of divine and eternal life in us, i.e., the Mother of divine grace. Any one of these points taken singly would not prove the Immaculate Conception to be an object of divine faith on the part of believers. Together, the Marian mystery they proclaim is the Immaculate Conception. The witness of Tradition illustrates 1) how when given occasion the believing mind quite naturally recognized that the celebration of the mystery of the Virgin's holiness (immaculate or without any stain) centered on the celebration of the feast of her conception-birth; and 2) that her all-holiness or Immaculate Conception, setting her above but not apart from the rest of creation for the sake of God's glory and our salvation, should be understood and professed so as to avoid the basic pitfalls to salvation, the twin heresies of Pelagianism and Manichaeism.[39]

The All-Holy Virgin in the Earliest Days of the Church

Each of these three points is well documented in the earliest ages of the Church.[40] The use of the title *Panhaghia* dates at least from the end of the second century in Egypt.[41] When we link this usage to the continuous public devotion to Our Lady from the very first days of

---

[39] Cf. E. Testa, *Maria terra vergine* (Jerusalem 1985) vol. 1, book 4, pp. 281-409, concerning the original polarity—Ebionite-Gnostic—in relation to Christ and Mary reflected in subsequent generations as Nestorian-Monophysite, Pelagian-Manichean.

[40] Cf. the studies listed in note 26 above. More recent studies listed in the various volumes of the *Bibliographia Mariana* confirm these conclusions.

[41] Cf. M.F. Perillo, *Sub Tuum Praesidium. Incomparable Marian Praeconium*, in *Mary at the Foot of the Cross IV* (New Bedford MA 2004) pp. 138-169.

the Church after Pentecost in Palestine, Egypt and Syria, a devotion imitating the *Ave* of the Angel Gabriel, it is perfectly obvious that the title is a recognition of the uniqueness of the person of Mary, viz., of her unique moral condition within the family of Adam, as well as of her role as Mother of God.

As the all-holy Virgin, she is the woman who undoes the tragedy stemming from the disobedience of the first Eve (St. Justin and St. Irenaeus), as the hymn *Ave maris stella* says, reversing the name of Eva to read *Ave*. In his reply to the strictures of Pusey on the dogma of the Immaculate Conception as an illicit addition to the revealed content of faith, Cardinal Newman states that the Immaculate Conception was professed by the earliest Fathers in their discussion of Mary's title, New Eve.[42] Newman's insight is a valid one, not because the Immaculate Conception can be deduced from the title of New Eve, but because the New Eve, Mary, is precisely such in virtue of being the *Panhaghia*, the all-holy Virgin whose moral condition is unique in virtue of her inclusion in the primacy of the last Adam, the Christ predestined before the foundation of the world to be the Head and King of all creation.

Finally, the solidarity of Mary with the family of Adam was always known to be essential to the solidarity of Christ with us in virtue of the Incarnation effected by his virginal conception in Mary's womb. So early and famous an ecclesiastical writer as Tertullian (end of second, beginning of third century), preoccupied with the need to defend this solidarity and the authenticity of Christ's human nature against Gnostic and Docetist tendencies to deny these because Christ was conceived and born virginally, rejected the virginity of Mary *in partu* (during the birth). So doing he left the maternity of Mary no different from that of other women, with the consequence that the person of her Son was regarded as no different from that of other human beings.[43] It suffices to note that the Church, in the face of even slight errors concerning the dogma of Mary's perpetual virginity as the basis of her solidarity with Jesus and with us, has always reacted quickly to reaffirm the virginal character of Mary's maternity and the maternal character of her virginity. She alone

---

[42] J.H. Newman, *A Letter Addressed to the Rev. E.B. Pusey, D.D., on Occasion of His Eirenicon*, in *Difficulties of Anglicans* (London 1910) vol. II, pp. 1-170.

[43] Cf. my *The Great Sign. The Virgin Mother—The Birth of Our Lord Jesus Christ* (Washington, NJ 1993).

as perpetual Virgin is shown to be absolutely sinless, and so the only member of our race able to be Mother of our Savior and so "Salvatrix" of Adam and Eve and of their human family. She descends truly from Adam, but as a rose among thorns, as the "virgin earth" from whom and by whom is formed the New Adam. Because she is overshadowed by the Holy Spirit, she is the *Panhaghia*, with a purity greater than which none can be conceived. Therefore she is invoked as no other saint associated with Christ in the work of redemption. For, the enmity between her and the serpent being total and unconditional, she is totally on the side of Christ, and in no wise, even minimally, of his adversary. Lack of holiness is inconceivable in the Mother of God, a given of Tradition which will ultimately lead to a definition of the holiness of the Virgin of virgins in terms of her conception, a holiness greater than which none can be conceived.

Affirmations of the Holiness of Mary in Terms of Her Conception

Until the fourth century we encounter no affirmations of the Fathers or ecclesiastical writers concerning the all-holiness of Mary formulated in terms of her conception or first moment of existence. But neither do we encounter any denials of her Immaculate Conception. When we do, whether these denials be direct or indirect, they are invariably consequent on affirmations, direct or indirect, of the Immaculate Conception. In the West such denials only begin after the time of St. Augustine; and in the East no direct denials are met until after the fifteenth century.

It is true that certain situations and actions involving Mary in the gospels (e.g., her need to fulfill the law of purification for women giving birth; her lack of understanding on finding the child Jesus in the Temple; her apparent boldness and reproof at Cana; her need for support at the foot of the Cross) were incorrectly explained by some Eastern Fathers as imperfections, as lack of perfect faith, as a kind of doubt, in a word, as venial sins.[44] But such examples of "naturalistic exegesis," almost completely confined to the East from the third to fifth centuries (Origen, St. John Chrysostom, St. Athanasius and even St. Cyril of Alexandria),

---

[44] The pertinent texts can be found in Jugie, *L'Immaculée Conception*..., cit. pp. 55-93. Major responsibility for this false direction is ascribed by Jugie to Origen (see *op. cit.*, p. 474), who to show why Our Lady needed redemption erroneously imputed to her a venial sin of doubt at the foot of the Cross!

were never used systematically (as they are today by those who would "dedogmatize" the Immaculate Conception) to deny the fact of Mary's all-holiness or to deny her initial sanctity as such.

After the Council of Ephesus (431) defined the title *Theotókos*, these difficulties ceased to be mentioned anywhere in the Church until the Protestant Reformation began, a sure indication that they touched not the problem of the Virgin's initial sanctity, but only occasional questions concerning the course of her life after the Annunciation. Eventually the principle that Mary, once sanctified, was always holy, always in the state of grace, impeccable, was adopted. The reason for the adoption of such a principle excluding a "naturalistic exegesis" of incidents during the course of her life, is to be found in the definition of Ephesus. That definition is the realization that anything less that the "all holy" cannot be reconciled with a central feature of the economy of salvation, the divine maternity and the Marian mode of our incorporation into the body of Christ virginally conceived. This is the basis for that cooperation in the work of salvation which the Father desires from the Church, one and holy. The quasi-unlimited praise for the dignity of the Mother of God in Eastern homiletic literature, dating precisely from the latter half of the fifth century, quite naturally leads to a recognition of the unique sanctity of Mary from conception as the basis for her consecration and exalted dignity as Mother of God and Queen of the universe.[45]

The principle of Mariology known as the principle of excellence-uniqueness, and the basis for the axiom *De Maria numquam satis* ("Enough can never be said of Mary"), so harshly criticized by some today, was already clearly accepted before any doubts were formally raised about Mary's initial holiness. Such doubts when raised could have, and in fact did have, only one principle source: an erroneous explanation of the *infectio carnis* (infection of the flesh) as the cause of the transmission of original sin in all descending from Adam by carnal intercourse. They were reinforced later by a restriction of the absolute primacy of Christ, limiting the purpose of the Incarnation to a redemption from original sin and from its consequences.

Indeed, Mary's unique, habitual, and by implication initial sanctity from the first moment of conception, soon came to be celebrated in the East on the feast of her nativity (dating at least from the fifth century in

---

[45] Cf. Jouassard, *The Fathers of the Church...*, cit.

Jerusalem), from which another feast had been derived by the seventh century, that of the conception by St. Ann, to which the earlier feast was subordinated. The feast of the conception, though called "of Ann" because the Greek word for conception suggests active rather than passive conception, had in fact as its object not the action of the mother Ann in conceiving, but the unique fruit of that action, the all-holy Mary, the *Theotókos*. It is the child, Mary, who is from conception the worthy subject of liturgical veneration, because unlike all other children of Eve she is holy from conception as well as birth, in no wise under the possession and control of Satan.

The celebration of this feast, not without links to the popularity of the apocryphal gospel of James, is not, however, the origin of the belief; it is rather a witness to the truth of the mystery already confessed by faith in the unique sanctity of the Virgin. Popular reminiscences and devotions, not without their own value, function as the occasion, the catalyst for giving more exact expression to a faith whose grounds are quite independent of the occasion conditioning that expression. In this case, first in the East and later in the West in England and Northern France, and wherever Byzantine Greeks were found, as in Southern Italy, the norm of prayer to the all-holy Virgin (liturgical celebration as well as devotional) determines the norm of faith in the all-holiness of Mary in so far as prayer gives proper expression to the content of that faith. This ultimately justifies defining the all-holiness of Mary by way of Immaculate Conception.

Such was the religious climate in the East after the councils of Ephesus and Chalcedon, forming the backdrop for the first hints, theologically speaking, that the title *Panhaghia* means Immaculate Conception. Thus there began a way of talking about the *Panhaghia* including explicit references to that first moment of conception as crucial in defining the uniqueness of Mary's moral state, determined not by her descent from the first Adam, but by her virginal motherhood in relation to the second Adam. Scholars continue to dispute whether any reference to the Immaculate Conception can in fact be found in the writings of saints like Ephrem and Ambrose before the Council of Ephesus, or in any contemporary of those councils, e.g., Atticus of Constantinople, Severin of Gabala, Hesychius of Jerusalem, and Maximus of Turin. But with Sophronius of Jerusalem (+638, just as the Muslims conquered Palestine) we encounter statements far more unequivocal as incipient expressions of a sinless conception.

By the time of St. Andrew of Crete (660-740), a native of Damascus and monk in Jerusalem and Constantinople before becoming bishop of Gortyna in Crete, and of his younger contemporary St. Germain, Patriarch of Constantinople, the sanctity of Mary at conception, viz., her total exemption from the power of Satan, is being expressly affirmed. But even before their time no more mention is made by Eastern theologians of Mary's full sanctification at the Annunciation, or at her birth, or in her mother's womb after conception. Thereafter in the East this approach would continue expressly and without question for nearly a thousand years. Jugie[46] summarizes the position of St. Andrew of Crete, one of the most prolific of the Fathers on Mary, as follows:

> a) Though conceived and born in normal fashion, the conception and birth of Mary are holy as those of no other person, except her Son, Jesus, the fruit of her womb;
>
> b) Mary is the daughter of God (theopais: in St. Francis' Antiphon for the Office of the Passion, "first-born daughter of the Father") on unique grounds, because God intervened in a special way at the moment of her conception;
>
> c) She is thereby at that moment the first fruits of a redeemed humanity, and endowed with the original beauty of mankind, viz., without original or inherited sin;
>
> d) Though she died, it is not for the reason that other men die, viz., as penalty of original sin in them personally.

When it is rendered explicit for the first time in the Eastern Church, the sinless conception of the Virgin is linked with an equally express inclusion of Mary in the absolute primacy of Christ, and in no wise is conditioned by the resolution of problems surrounding the doctrine of original sin, or inherited sin as it is commonly known in the East, and its universal extension. Mary is saved, viz., holy by the merits of Christ, but prior to any consideration of the universality of original sin

---

[46] Jugie, *L'Immaculée Conception...*, cit., pp. 105-114.

and its possible extension to her. Or by implication the potency and universality of original sin is limited by the inclusion of Mary in the absolute primacy of Christ. This is all that the Scotist school means by the absence of any *debitum peccati originalis*, debt or necessity to contract original sin at conception in Mary. The fullness of sanctifying grace in her is conditioned only by the fact of her joint predestination with Christ prior to any consideration of creation and redemption. That this fullness should be actually conferred via a preservative redemption explains how the tragedy of original sin is no obstacle to the realization of the Father's original design for his beloved daughter.

Other well-known Eastern Fathers and theologians associated with this position according to Jugie[47] are: St. John Damascene, Photius, Theodore Studite, Joseph the Hymnographer, John the Geometer, Nicephoros Callistus, Gregory Palamas, Theophane of Nicea, Nicholas Cabasilas, Demetrius Kydones, and George Scholarios.

During the fourteenth and fifteenth centuries, through acquaintance with discussions of the Immaculate Conception in Western Europe and because of a danger of Pelagian interpretations infiltrating their tradition (via certain features associated with the teaching and spiritual practice of Gregory Palamas), Eastern theologians, such as George Scholarios, began to study how to reconcile the unique sanctity of Mary with the universality of redemption from original sin. Generally these Eastern theologians reached the same conclusions as Scotus, even when they were sympathetic to the synthesis of St. Thomas, as was Demetrios Kydones. With the fall of Constantinople to the Turks in 1453, the advent of the Protestant Reformation in 1517, and the rise of anti-papal nationalism throughout Europe, Byzantine theologians began to question their own tradition in reaction to the papal championing of the immaculatist position at the end of the fifteenth century and thereafter (Sixtus IV, the Council of Trent, Paul V, Alexander VII).

Unfortunately, contemporary Orthodox theologians, not all, yet nonetheless a large proportion claiming to be a majority, insist that refusal of Orthodox Church authorities to accept the definition of 1854 is the equivalent of denial of the doctrine as traditional.[48] The equivalency

---

[47] Jugie, *L'Immaculée Conception*..., cit. pp. 164-301.
[48] On contemporary Eastern Orthodox theologians and the Immaculate Conception see J. Likoudis, *The Immaculate Conception of the Mother of God and the Doctrine of*

is not at all evident, because 1) the main reason for the refusal to accept is an ecclesiological one, not Mariological, and 2) the Eastern tradition of the Church, before 1500, shows even stronger support for what the Western Church now calls the Immaculate Conception than does that of the Latin West. Contemporary Orthodox theologians reject the dogma and in the process misrepresent the tradition, because they do not admit, as the ancient tradition of the East did, the absolute primacy of the Incarnation and joint predestination of Jesus and Mary (treated previously in this essay), from which the doctrine of the Immaculate Conception and correct understanding of the *Panhaghia* logically flow. In other words, these theologians do not accept the theological distinction between preservative and liberative redemption.

Non-acceptance is one thing, claiming traditional support for explicit denial of the distinction as an "erroneous rationalization" is quite another. Aside from systematic maculism in the medieval West after Anselm, there is no such explicit tradition as distinct from occasional erroneous opinion concerning the sins of Mary. This point alone is sufficient to engender a suspicion that contemporary Orthodox theologians have imbibed a goodly dose of the Protestant *solus Christus Mediator* to the exclusion even of the Virgin Mother, a *solus* with its roots in the Western medieval maculism between St. Bernard and Bl. Scotus.

Texts adduced to prove the "undivided Church" before 1054 knew no such doctrine, viz., that it is a later invention of the West, are texts either dealing with the heresy which represents Mary as a goddess (such as that of Epiphanius in his treatise *Against the Antidikomarionites*), or texts such as those of Ambrose in his *Commentary on Luke*, ch. 2 where he appears, like St. Paul in Romans 3:23 (the favorite citation of Protestants to prove the dogma of the Immaculate Conception anti-biblical), to describe all but Christ as in need of liberative redemption, above all from original sin, no exceptions allowed.

To the first we may reply that the question of the Immaculate Conception has nothing to do with the Antidikomarionite heresy

---

Mary as Coredemptrix in Eastern Orthodoxy, in *Mary at the Foot of the Cross III*, New Bedford MA 2003, pp. 295-315. See also Likoudis, *The Divine Primacy of the Bishop of Rome and Modern Eastern Orthodoxy: Letters to a Greek Orthodox on the Unity of the Church*, Montour Falls, NY, and *Eastern Orthodoxy and the See of Peter: A Journey Toward Full Communion*, Montour Falls, NY.

claiming Mary a goddess. It is one thing to deny a doctrine, another to misrepresent its definition. The dogma defined in 1854 clearly does not present or understand Mary as a goddess, either expressly or implicitly or by way of inference-deduction. It emphatically ascribes this privilege to a human person at conception, not the act of St. Ann *conceiving*, but the term of her maternal conceiving in a distinct and new human person *conceived*, the daughter of St. Ann. This daughter is Mary, conceived in a human way as a daughter of Adam, predestined to belong intrinsically to the order of the hypostatic union. In being conceived immaculately, Mary initiates historically the order of the hypostatic union, an initiation completed with the virginal conception of Jesus. This is what Scripture and the liturgy mean in calling Mary "dawn" of salvation, viz., dawn of the Incarnation. Being all holy, or without sin, does not make Mary a goddess, any more than being without sin before the fall made Adam and Eve gods. Or, if with the Greek and Latin Fathers we speak of sanctifying grace as "deifying" the just, we do not mean the just have ceased to be creatures.

Hence, in reply to the exegesis making Paul and Ambrose opponents of preservative redemption, we may say that their affirmation concerning the universality of sin applies to all who do not pertain to the order of the hypostatic union: first Christ and then by implication Mary, his Mother. Christ pertains to that order on the basis of the hypostatic union; his Mother does so on the basis of the grace of the Immaculate Conception. Preservative redemption explains why Mary does not hear the good news of salvation from John as do others to be freed from sin, but announces this to John at the Visitation (cf. Lk 1:41, 56).

This brings us to the so-called theological objection, claimed by some to be even more important. This objection arises from the truism that the Immaculate Conception would render Mary sinless, to the point of being impeccable. Therefore, it deprives her of her personal freedom, and renders her nature unlike ours. We may cheerfully agree the Immaculate Conception does render Mary impeccable from the first moment of her conception. But this does not mean her human nature is different from ours, for she, too, is a child of Adam in the ordinary sense of that term. It means rather that her human nature is more perfect because more holy, or more human because more holy, just as is that of her Son without being a human nature different from ours. Being impeccable in virtue of the Immaculate Conception, Mary is no more lacking in personal freedom than is her Son by virtue of the hypostatic union, nor is either exempt from trial, far more difficult than our temptations, viz., that of Calvary and the Cross, of Passion and compassion. Being impeccable, Jesus and Mary suffered more in enduring trials to save us. Precisely because Jesus and Mary are impeccable, we can aspire to overcome temptation and reach the same blessed state.

Behind the objection is the unspoken assumption that freedom necessarily entails the possibility of sinning, and that is particularly the case in a theory of salvation which entails merit and suffering. If this assumption excludes Mary from active cooperation in the redemptive sacrifice because not impeccable and so sinful, ultimately it also excludes Christ as man. In soteriology, *substitutionalism* does exactly that. Christ the man at best is only a passive bait or snare for the Devil; Christ alone is Mediator, because Christ is Mediator actively as God. Or if Christ as man is capable of sinning and so can redeem, so can Mary, and so can each of us. This is soteriological *Pelagianism*, where Mary is immaculate and peccable, therefore holy. Both theories are contrary to vicarious satisfaction, either because they exclude any active human element based on genuine freedom, or because they deny any distinction between Jesus and Mary based on holiness.

Hence, it is this assumption about freedom entailing, as such, the possibility of sinning, which must be carefully critiqued, indeed denied. The so-called possibility of sinning is not a characteristic of freedom as such, viz., as a simple perfection. The possibility of offending God is but an index of *limited* freedom, not of freedom itself. The greater the impossibility of sinning, the greater the freedom, the greater in a time of pilgrimage to merit, to satisfy by suffering for the sins of others, viz., exactly what is meant by the theory of vicarious satisfaction for the sins of all by a sinless Mediator. This is a common teaching of the "undivided Church," against quite opposite heresies which share one thing in common: denial of a redemption via vicarious satisfaction as the joint work of Jesus and Mary.

This common teaching about the integrity of the human will of Christ vis-à-vis his divine will, the freedom and perfect sanctity-impeccability of the human will, is at the heart of the controversies over monothelitism (an early form of the *solus Christus Mediator*) during the seventh century, a teaching defined at the Lateran Synod of 649, called by Pope St. Martin I, and at the third Council of Constantinople in 681.[49] The teaching and influence of St. Maximus Confessor was particularly strong during the Lateran Synod. What is to be noted is the intimate relation between the defense of the integrity of the human will of Jesus, both free and all holy, as essential to the work of redemption, and the defense of the virgin-birth: truly human, yet miraculous because of the holiness of the Mother: impeccable. The unique sanctity of the Mother no more deprives her of her personal dignity and freedom as Virgin Mother, than does the Incarnation deprive the man Jesus of a genuine human will.

If this "more important reason," viz., that the Immaculate Conception is incompatible with personal freedom in Mary, is shown to be theologically "unreasonable," then it would seem highly plausible that the current interpretation (in Eastern Orthodox scholarly circles) of the ancient Eastern tradition, viz., before 1054, as against the Immaculate Conception, is quite mistaken. This current opinion, also influential in Western theological circles, represents a radical departure from Tradition, fully guaranteed in the solemn definition of 1854 by Bl. Pius IX.

The Panhaghia in the West and the Problem of the Immaculate Conception

Between the councils of Nicea and Ephesus, a period when the sanctity of Our Lady was relatively little studied by theologians in the East, it was in the Western part of the Church a theme enjoying considerable prominence, especially in some of the greatest Fathers such as Jerome, Ambrose and Augustine. Their reflections on her virginal holiness were occasioned 1) by denials of Mary's virginity during childbirth; 2) by denials of the superiority of the virginal state to the married, such as those of Jovinian toward the end of the fourth century; by the need 3) to defend the divinity of the child of Mary; and 4) the essence of grace as distinct from nature. All four points, linked to the mystery of the Virgin of virgins, brought these Fathers close to a recognition of the mystery of her sinlessness, viz., that of the *Panhaghia*, at conception. This inner thrust of their thought is an indication that 1) the unique moral state of

---

[49] On the nexus between monothelitism and denial of the virgin birth cf. P. Fehlner, *The Great Sign: The Virgin Mother – The Birth of Our Lord Jesus Christ*, Washington NJ 1993.

Mary from conception and 2) her exceptional virginity as Mother—she is the Virgin of virgins who in becoming Mother does not lose her virginity—are both intimately linked not merely with her work, but with her very person as the divinely willed preparation and basis for the maternal mediation of Mary in the universe. Certainly none of these Western Fathers denied the mystery of the Immaculate Conception expressly and directly; but neither did they affirm it unambiguously.

The reason for this is to be found not in the naturalism of Jovinian directly opposed to the Incarnation as such, but in that of Pelagius aimed at a denial of original sin and of the need for redemption on the part of all members of the family of Adam. The Pelagians affirmed the Immaculate Conception in Mary not as a privilege, but as a perfect example of what occurs at any human conception. As Augustine saw so clearly, perhaps more so than any of his contemporaries, this form of naturalism at once 1) relativizes, indeed banalizes the redemptive sacrifice of Jesus, and 2) radically alters the meaning of grace from that of being the basis for an elevation to the very order of divine life, to that of an ethical utility in the building of mature character. The Pelagian theory is still very much alive and can easily be discerned as the motivation behind much Marian minimalizing today, as in the days of Augustine. While it is true that an immaculate conception with no relation to original sin is a radical denial of redemption and grace, it is also true, as the subsequent history shows that original sin not set in the perspective of the Immaculate Conception entails some form of Calvinism or Jansenism.

Of these three great Fathers, the views of Augustine on the subject of the Immaculate Conception have for centuries been most controversial. Whatever may be the final verdict on what Augustine held or did not hold, without doubt he became, during the course of his controversy with the Pelagians, the first great theologian to face directly the problem of Mary's sanctity and the universality of the redemption from original sin.

Two texts of Augustine are commonly cited to show that if he did not unequivocally affirm the Immaculate Conception, neither did he deny it.[50] In his critique of Pelagianism Augustine was explicit about Mary's personal sinlessness. All are sinners,

---

[50] See the detailed discussion in Jouassard, *The Fathers of the Church...*, cit., pp. 69-74.

> except… the holy Virgin Mary, concerning whom, for the honor of the Lord, I will have no question of sin; for we know how much to conquer sin in every way was given to her who merited to conceive and bring forth him who certainly had no sin.[51]

The formulation of the exception, reflecting the primordial tradition of Mary's transcendent holiness, is certainly broad enough to encompass the first moment of conception and so point to a logical explanation of her singular holiness, so honorable to the Lord, the perfect Redeemer, whom she merited to conceive first, as Augustine notes, in her mind and then in her womb.[52]

The thrust of Augustine's thought here is identical with that which would soon become explicit in the East: the all-holiness of Mary is not limited by any sin, even original, and hence represents first a datum of Revelation, not a theological conclusion consequent upon a theory of redemption. But the ambivalence of his formulation, viz., in not specifying whether "question of sin" includes or excludes original sin, led Bishop Julian of Eclanum, perhaps the most brilliant of Augustine's Pelagian opponents, to accuse Augustine thus: "He [Jovinian] undermined the virginity of Mary by the condition of her childbearing; you [Augustine] deliver her to the Devil by the condition of her birth."[53] This heretical tactic is the same as that of many theological sophists, that of presenting the genuine orthodox view as one of two heretical extremes (naturalism and Manichaeism) and his own heresy as the happy middle ground of reasonable orthodoxy.

In his reply, the Doctor of Hippo is less than clear. Julian obviously posed the problem not simply in terms of Mary's sinlessness in general, but of her conception and birth in particular, which the Pelagians held to be unaffected by any sin inherited from Adam. They could say this, because, denying original sin, they held every human conception by that fact was both good and holy. Augustine, of course, rightly denied this identification of grace with nature at conception. But his reply to the specific point does not say that Mary is stainless at conception; rather he leaves the door open to a "liberative sanctification" in the womb.

---

[51] From *De natura et gratia*, XXXVI, 42.
[52] St. Augustine, *De sancta virginitate*, ch. 3; *Sermo 25*, 7-8.
[53] From *Opus imperfectum adversum Julianum* IV, 122.

He wrote: "We do not deliver Mary to the Devil by the condition of her birth; for this reason, that her very condition finds a solution in the grace of rebirth."[54]

Linked with this reply is the saint's theology of the transmission of original sin through concupiscence (the *infectio carnis*) inherent in conjugal intercourse, in this question as in that concerning the origin of the human soul (traducianism vs. creationism).[55] And like his position on the Immaculate Conception, it is not without ambiguity, although its underlying thrust is not toward the view subsequently associated with the Jansenist reading of Augustine, but toward those in fact canonized by the Church. Elsewhere Augustine also seems to lean to a maculist solution: "And thus it appears that the concupiscence through which Christ did not wish to be conceived, has propagated evil in the human race, for the body of Mary, though it came from this, nevertheless did not transmit it, for she did not conceive in this way,"[56] i.e., by intercourse, but rather virginally. It is plain from this text that the Pelagian formulation of the problematic in ethical-pragmatic rather than metaphysical-contemplative terms dominated the fifth century discussion, thus for a moment obscuring in the resolution of the problem the primary importance of absolute rather than relative sinlessness in the person of the Mother of the God-Savior, an importance only to be made clear in the affirmation by Scotus of the absolute primacy of Christ and the subsequent joint predestination of Jesus and Mary.

With the collapse of the Western Roman Empire in the fifth century, conditions favorable to the consistent development of speculative theology so deteriorated that the question of the Immaculate Conception of Mary was not often mentioned in the West until the end of the eleventh

---

[54] *Ibid.* For a balanced assessment of the pros and cons in the long debate over the position of Augustine on the sanctity of Mary at her conception see Moriones, *Enchiridion...*, cit., pp. 348-350, notes 3-4. In affirming the *Panhaghia*, Augustine also affirms in principle, or radically, the Immaculate Conception, an interpretation seemingly confirmed by his support for the absolute primacy of Christ (Moriones, *Enchiridion...*, cit., pp. 340-342); and in affirming the universality of the redemption he does not exclude the Immaculate Conception, even if his theory of the transmission of original sin points to an exclusion.

[55] On traducianism and the position of St. Augustine cf. A. Michel, *Traducionisme*, in *Dictionnaire de Théologie Catholique*, v. 15, 1351-1358.

[56] St. Augustine, *Contra Julianum*, Book V; Cf. Jouassard, *The Fathers of the Church...*, cit., p. 73.

century with St. Anselm. One or another writer such as Paschasius Radbert asserted it; but others, such as St. Anselm, quite clearly denied it on the basis of the transmission of original sin via intercourse infected by concupiscence. On the other hand, Anselm clearly asserted a purity of Mary greater than which none can be conceived under God. A sanctity so defined must logically include as well the sanctity of the first moment of conception; otherwise it would not be the greatest conceivable. This is the logical opening of which Scotus will take advantage in resolving the major objection to the Immaculate Conception, viz., that it cannot logically be reconciled with the universality of redemption and solidarity of the human family with Adam. That opening is intended by the great Marian Doctor to provide a logically valid escape from the horns of a dilemma more or less explicit since the time of Augustine: either the universality of the redemption of the entire family of Adam (an article of faith) includes Mary or it is not universal. Hence, to be included in the redemption, Mary must have contracted original sin before her sanctification, or if immaculately conceived her sanctity has nothing to do with Christ or us.

Possibility/Fittingness, or the Reason of the Immaculate Conception

St. Anselm is considered the first of the great Western scholastics. With him begins a systematic discussion of the possibility and fittingness of the mystery of the Immaculate Conception: not the fact of Mary's all-holiness, but *how* this could be in view of the dilemma arising from the universality of original sin. It is Anselm who first set forth[57] a theory of original sin centered on the privation of original justice rather than the *infectio carnis* of St. Augustine as the cause (and not merely condition) of its universality, an exposition capable of illustrating how Mary could descend from Adam, yet not contract original sin. This, too, will be the point of departure for the classic theory of Scotus. In the Scotistic development of this theory the *infectio carnis* is the condition for, not cause of, contracting original sin at conception. Because the children of Adam after Adam's sin are conceived without the state of original justice, therefore they are lacking in the necessary prerequisite ordained by God for the conferral of sanctifying grace. The absence of original justice, otherwise called the debt of contracting original sin, not the

---

[57] St. Anselm, *Cur Deus Homo*.

infectio carnis, is reason for the non-conferral of sanctifying grace. Without sanctifying grace the newly conceived find themselves in the state of sin. Mary does not fall under this arrangement touching all who come under the moral headship of the first Adam, because the grace of the Immaculate Conception merited for her by her Son constitutes a moral state higher than that of original justice, and so brings with it not merely sanctifying grace, but a fullness of that grace constituting Mary under Christ a mediatrix of grace for others.

It is worth noting also, that the structure of argumentation concerning the all-holiness of the Virgin in Anselm, a purity greater than which none can be conceived and only God can conceive, exactly parallels that of his basic argument[58] for the existence of God: a being greater than which none can be conceived and which only God can conceive. Both arguments are developed by Scotus[59] to the full, and are at the heart of his exposition of the two great parts of theology: that of the Trinity and that of the economy of salvation (*theologia de necessariis; theologia de contingentibus*—theology of necessary being; theology of contingent being).

Anselm, then, stands at a juncture in the development of the witness of Tradition to this great mystery of faith. He initiates a new discussion of the holiness of Mary's conception. Though he denies that this conception is immaculate, at the same time he clearly testifies to the received Tradition, Western as well as Eastern: Mary is the *Panhaghia*. Anselm himself may not have been aware of the implications of that maximal purity he assigned to Mary, as this was expressly understood in the East. Anselm does not tell us whether or what might be the limits on devotion to Mary: her need of redemption, or simply her dignity as Mother of the incarnate Savior prior to any consideration of the fall and redemption of the human family.

In any case it is important to note that on the eve of the medieval controversies in the West over the feast of the conception of Mary, the

---

[58] In the *Monologion* and *Proslogion*.
[59] Especially in III Sent., d. 3, q. 1; and in *De primo principio*, where he subtly revises and perfects Anselm's notion of divine being, as he does that of Mary's purity, thus deepening the relation between divinity, purity and our deification or elevation to the supernatural order (cf. 2 Pet 1:4).

mystery of her initial sanctity at conception was commonly affirmed in the East in a manner presupposing the absolute primacy of Christ:[60]

> 1) explicit affirmations in proper terms: exempt from all stain of original sin from the first moment of conception; Mary never contracted original sin or inherited Adam's sin;
>
> 2) explicit affirmations in equivalent terms: Mary was always in grace, i.e., pleasing or acceptable before God; Mary was justified in the first moment of her conception; Mary escaped the curse, the judgment and condemnation accompanying the sin of Adam; among all the descendants of Adam, Mary alone is blessed; Mary was always blessed;
>
> 3) implicit affirmations: Mary is holier than any other creature; Mary is holier than the seraphim and cherubim, so holy one could conceive of no one holier; Mary is the intermediary through whom the human race is reconciled to God, through whom the ancient curse is withdrawn, through whom original sin is erased; Mary is all holy (*Panhaghia*), all immaculate (*Panachranta*); Mary is the pure virgin earth from whom and by whom the New Adam is formed all pure.

These affirmations may be arranged in terms of their positive and negative formulations:

> 1) explicit affirmations in negative form (which the eventual dogmatic definition took): Mary is exempt from original sin, from death, from concupiscence, from slavery to the Devil;
>
> 2) explicit affirmations in positive form: Mary was always just, always in grace before God, was clothed with

---

[60] Jugie, *L'Immaculée Conception...*, cit., pp. 39-41, lists the various possible ways of formulating the truth of the Immaculate Conception, all of which by the end of the first millennium could be found in the writings of one or another of the Eastern Fathers.

original justice from conception, was created similar to Eve before the sin of Adam, was always in paradise;

    3) implicit affirmations in positive form: Mary is all-holy, all-beautiful, the ideal of humanity;

    4) implicit affirmations in negative form: Mary is immaculate, without stain.

Explanation of the Possibility and Fittingness (Reason) of the Mystery

Although the first assertions (at least plausible) of the sinless conception of Mary occur almost simultaneously both in the East and West (Ephrem and Ambrose), it is in the West that difficulties concerning both the possibility and appropriateness of an immaculate conception were raised and its truth systematically denied.

Previous to the appearance of twelfth century maculism—the theory claiming to explain the feast of Mary's conception in terms of a sanctification in the womb after conception in original sin—the fact of the Immaculate Conception had been denied in the West sporadically rather than systematically. This is to say, it was denied only when it was perceived to contradict the commonly accepted theory for the transmission of original sin via carnal generation infected by concupiscence. This is what Augustine seems to have claimed for concupiscence after the fall: an all pervading presence of concupiscence in its consequences (*actu*) in the baptized after Baptism, even if no longer linked to a state of guilt (*reatu*). The Augustinian explanation of the transmission of original sin by carnal descent from Adam, not only as a condition for, but as the cause of the contraction of original sin in each of his descendants, has since the time of Scotus gradually come to be recognized as defective, not because Augustine's theory of concupiscence was necessarily false, but because he failed to account for an important distinction, which the contemplation of the Immaculate Conception across history has made clear.

Augustine did not clearly affirm the Immaculate Conception; neither did he deny it directly and systematically, so limiting her absolute sinlessness. What we find in the West until the rise of systematic maculism is an affirmation of theological contradictories: the inclusion of Mary in the absolute primacy of Christ and consequent on that her unique holiness as a state of life prior to and independent of that of the first

Adam; and her descent by carnal generation from Adam or conception in original sin. The distinction of these last two points: carnal generation from Adam and conception in original sin was either not made or was denied. Hence to say, as faith requires, that Mary is a daughter of Adam by carnal descent, seems also to say that she was conceived in original sin. Or, if she is immaculate, then she is not a descendant of Adam and consequently neither the mediation of her Son nor her own are relevant to our redemption.

This is the dilemma we meet in Anselm as well,[61] a monastic theologian who, as already noted, may be called the first of the scholastics. He affirmed with the whole of tradition the absolute all-holiness of Mary as the New Eve, rooted ultimately in her inclusion in the absolute primacy of Christ. A purity greater than which none is conceivable would not logically be such, should it be shown that an immaculate conception is impossible, incompatible *de facto* with a salvation only accomplished via a redemptive sacrifice. Apparently Anselm did think this impossible in virtue of the received explanation for the contraction of original sin. He did not advert, so it seems, to the serious doubt cast on this impossibility by his own explanation for the existence of original sin in the descendents of Adam: the privation of original justice by coming under the moral headship of Adam.

It would be the merit of Scotus to point out clearly for the first time that the contraction of original sin is caused in each of us by coming under the moral headship of the first Adam before coming under that of the second Adam. Were we not under that headship and so deprived of original justice, the condition for the infusion of sanctifying grace at conception, we would not contract original sin, no matter how infected by concupiscence the process of carnal generation and descent. Generation is but the condition for coming under the moral headship of Adam, not the reason for contracting original sin. That reason is simply the fact that the moral headship of Adam after his sin no longer includes the state of original justice, the condition decreed by God for conception in the state of grace. Mary, in virtue of a preservative, more excellent form of redemption, comes under the headship of Christ in

---

[61] On the Immaculate Conception in English theology before Scotus see T. Finnigan, *Belief in and Devotion to the Immaculate Conception in Medieval England*, in *Mary at the Foot of the Cross V* (New Bedford MA 2005) pp. 344-359.

a manner logically prior to becoming a descendent of the first Adam, and so although truly descending from him by carnal generation, does not contract original sin, because in her a higher form of justice not dependent on Adam is verified.[62]

Eadmer, the secretary of St. Anselm and author of the first theological treatise[63] dealing directly with the conception of the Virgin, expressly supported the sinless character of Mary's conception. He denied quite clearly that she was conceived in the state of original sin. But he did not explain how such could be possible in descending carnally from Adam. Rather he insisted once again on the revealed fact of the Virgin's unique

---

[62] For the texts of Scotus see Rosini, *La Mariologia...*, cit., pp. 84ff.; Dean, *A Primer...*, cit. Closely related to the question of original justice and grace is that of the so-called *debitum*, generally denied in Scotistic theories of the Immaculate Conception, and affirmed in Thomistic. Thus C. Journet says that Mary was preserved from contracting the guilt of original sin, not the *debitum* (*Scripture and the Immaculate Conception*, pp. 45-46). From the Scotistic viewpoint original justice in Adam was established by God as a condition for sanctifying grace, because it reflected what was more perfectly realized in Mary predestined to be Immaculate, the perfect harmony of her will with the divine in respect to the Incarnation. Hence her preservation is from contracting both guilt and *debitum*, taken in the original sense of "subject to sins" (cf. Wis 1:4). Denial of the *debitum* is a radical affirmation of Mary's never having been subject to sin and to the prince of this world. Such a denial is radically an affirmation of Mary's unqualified personal impeccability on the basis of the grace of the Immaculate Conception, whence her "fullness of grace" as new name (cf. Lk 1:28) and definition of her person.

Some have argued in recent times, particularly in the context of the preparations for the dogmatic definition of the Assumption, that Mary, in virtue of the Immaculate Conception, enjoyed the gift of immortality of the body because she was in the state of original justice. This does not follow, anymore than the hypostatic union excludes suffering and mortality in Christ *in carne passibili* (in flesh subject to suffering). The passible mode of the Incarnation and Immaculate Conception is consequent upon original sin. The Incarnation and Immaculate Conception as such are not; rather the perfection of the actual redemption is consequent on the prior predestination of Incarnation and Immaculate Conception jointly. The Immaculate Conception is the basis of the Coredemption and compassion of Mary, as a rose among thorns. For the history of the question cf. J.B. Carol, *A History of the Controversy over the "Debitum Peccati"* (St. Bonaventure NY 1978). On the meaning of *debitum*, cf. Rosini, *Marologia...*, cit., p. 88; and on the *debitum* in Mary *ibid.*, pp. 95-100.

[63] *De conceptione Sanctae Mariae*, in former times sometimes ascribed to St. Anselm, whence the confusion over his position on the Immaculate Conception.

sanctity qua New Eve, jointly predestined with the Christ before the ages.

Some have said that Eadmer's treatise is a reply to the denial of the Immaculate Conception by St. Bernard in his letter to the cathedral canons of Lyon. This, however, does not seem to be the case, particularly because Eadmer does not deal with the principal reason adduced by Bernard for not celebrating the feast of the Conception: Mary's necessary contraction of original sin via carnal descent from Adam. An event cannot be celebrated liturgically unless it be holy, which conception via ordinary sexual intercourse is not. Evidently, neither could the Nativity of Mary be celebrated unless there occur an intervening "sanctification in the womb of St. Ann."

Eadmer rather insists on the primacy of Christ (Prov 8) as the basis for explaining the distinctive moral state of the woman foretold in Genesis 3:15—not Eve, but the Mother of the Savior as pure beyond compare. Hence the crucial importance of these two biblical passages in all subsequent discussion of Scotistic immaculatism. The question of the Immaculate Conception is linked not only to the mystery of redemption (Gen 3:15), but even more to that of the absolute primacy of Christ (Prov 8, to which may be joined Sir 24). And hence the importance of Marian maximalism for Scotus as the methodological corollary of addressing Mary as Panhaghia, all-holy, Beatissima, most blessed, as Mary foretold in her Magnificat: "all generations shall call me blessed" (Lk 1:48). The Marian "metaphysic" of Scotus is to be located at the very center of a revealed tradition unbroken from apostolic times, and so is not the discovery of a new truth, but the illustration of one already believed in a formulary providentially appointed for the good of the Church as she prepares for the final coming of her Founder and Head. In the preparation of this formulary the contribution of Scotus is a decisive one.

As in the East, so in the West the liturgical celebration of the feast of the Conception of Mary served as catalyst for this formulation.[64] That celebration, as distinct from literary reminiscences, leaves no record earlier than a prayer found in the Book of Cerne dating from the first half of the ninth century. At the beginning of the eleventh century English liturgical books for Canterbury (1023) and Exeter (Leofric Missal, 1050-

---

[64] Cf. T. Finnigan, *Belief in and Devotion to the Immaculate Conception in Medieval England*, cit., pp. 344-359.

1073) assign the feast of the Conception to December 8. The celebration, though neither universal nor permanent, especially after the Norman conquest in 1066, nonetheless was popular and no doubt pre-existed the written record, as seems to be indicated by a reference to Mary as "spotless" in an early eighth century Anglo-Saxon poem, *Crist*, by Cynewulf. As with the celebration of that feast in Naples and Sicily, the feast in England had no doubt been introduced from the East. By the time of Eadmer (after the death of St. Anselm) the feast had been revived and had spread into France, where it encountered the opposition of St. Bernard. Although the earliest liturgical texts leave the precise object of the celebration ambiguous, there was no doubt in St. Bernard's mind what objectively that celebration must entail: the admission of a stainless conception. And so he concluded, erroneously, that this included a necessary denial of original sin, all of which constitutes the position of Pelagius. Forceful and persuasive as was St. Bernard's argumentation, it failed to carry the day. Indeed, the weakness of his argument was noted in a contemporary witticism of Nicholas of St. Albans: Our Lady's soul was pierced by the sword of sorrow twice; the first time on Calvary when her Son was crucified for our sins, and a second time when St. Bernard denied her Immaculate Conception.

The opposition of Bernard resulted neither in the suppression of the feast nor in the loss of its popularity. Instead, unlike what happened in the East after the seventh century when doubt among theologians about the sanctity of Mary at conception simply disappeared, Western opposition to the feast occasioned the rise of a maculist theology systematically denying the Immaculate Conception. As a consequence of this, the purpose of the Incarnation came to be limited to the reparation of Adam's fall. Without this limitation, the maculist theory, defended by some even on the eve of the solemn definition of 1854, could not demonstrate why Anselm's principal of maximal purity in Mary should not logically tend to an assertion of the Immaculate Conception. This limitation, however, has in fact no demonstrable basis in Tradition. It is merely a hypothesis to justify a denial of the Immaculate Conception. Whereas the absolute primacy of Christ is a revealed fact which amply justifies belief in the Immaculate Conception.

Thus arose the paralogism: the Immaculate Conception detracts from the work of Christ as Savior of all, because it withdraws Mary from any dependence on him as Redeemer. To be redeemed, it was said, one must first have been a sinner. The impossibility of an Immaculate Conception was thus linked to the question of its appropriateness in view of the redemption. In the paralogism the only reason for the Incarnation is redemption from sin. Hence, not only is it impossible for any child of Adam to be free of original sin, it is appropriate that they should not be so in order to enhance the greatness of the Redeemer.[65]

The Contribution of Scotus

Scotus[66] linked his explanation of the possibility of an Immaculate Conception with a resolution of this objection, precisely by retorting the argument, an extraordinarily powerful move, since the perfection of the redemption wrought by Christ, and not only its universality, was commonly acknowledged to be a matter of faith. Far from detracting from the merit of Christ's work on the Cross, a preservative[67] rather than liberative redemption of Mary, argued Scotus, enhances the greatness of the redemptive work *qua* redemptive. For had Christ not preserved his Mother from contracting original sin, his redemptive work would not have been the most perfect redemption by a most perfect Redeemer, that is, it would in some way have been defective. Grace would not have absolutely "superabounded" over sin (cf. Rom 5:12-21). In what consists concretely the superabundance of grace, is contemplated in the Immaculate Conception. With his substitution of "preservation from sin" in the place of "purification or liberation from sin" as key to resolving the dispute over the perfection of Christ's redemptive work,

---

[65] This is the argument, in substance, curiously resurrected in our times by Bonnefoy, *Christ and the Cosmos*, cit., and other neo-Scotists.

[66] III Sent., d. 3, q. 1 (both in the *Ordinatio* and in the *Lectura completa* as cited by C. Balić, *Theologiae Marianae Elementa*, Sebenico 1933).

[67] The distinction between preservative and liberative redemption was not an invention of Scotus. It had been used by Fathers of the Church in connection with the redemption by Christ of the angels who did not sin. Cf. Rosini, *Mariologia...*, cit., pp. 93-94. The concept of a grace preserving from sinning arises in the discussion of the impeccability of the created will, e.g., of the angels and saints in heaven, and in relation to the concept of efficacious grace given to those still in pilgrimage. Among the Fathers cited by Rosini are Sts. Jerome, Augustine and John Damascene. The originality of Scotus consists in applying the concept of preservation to the contraction of original sin rather than commission of personal sin.

Scotus revolutionized the entire discussion and opened the road to a dogmatic definition. With that he also opened the door to a profounder understanding of the key biblical passages touching on the maximal sanctity of Mary and its practical role in the economy of salvation.

It has been objected, even in recent times, that the argument of Scotus either proves nothing (Roschini)[68] or is incomplete, indicating as formulated that all should be preserved to realize the most perfect redemption (Galot).[69] In fact, Scotus' argument is neither; rather it is cryptic. The most perfect redemption consists, not in the fact that all are sanctified in the first moment of conception (essentially a restoration of a moral state on a par with that of original justice, but not superior), but its perfection rests in the fact that one woman foreseen as the Mother of God and of the Church is preserved from the contagion of original sin and all others redeemed share that same holiness through her maternal mediation. Preservative redemption in the case of Mary Immaculate connotes not simply preservation from falling into sin, as in the case of the good angels, but a fullness of grace defining her personal state, metaphysically and spiritually, and hence her unique place in the order of the hypostatic union.

Thus, being placed in an absolutely perfect moral state, the state postulated by her joint predestination as Mother Co-redemptrix with the incarnate Savior, the Christ and Redeemer, she makes possible for the Church and for all believers a most perfect cooperation in the work of salvation. For this reason our liberation from original sin concludes in a state of grace more perfect than that of our first parents before the fall, and more perfect even than that which might have resulted from the sanctification of each person at conception instead of after birth. The Church *sine macula* of which St. Paul speaks (cf. Eph 5:22-31) implies this very truth about Mary as Immaculate Mediatrix, because the redemption of the Church is by way of corporate solidarity, the solidarity achieved through maternal mediation. This is what predestination in Christ ultimately implies.

---

[68] On the controversial position taken by Roschini cf. P. Parrotta, *Father Roschini and the Contribution of Blessed John Duns Scotus to the Dogma of the Immaculate Conception*, in *Mary at the Foot of the Cross V* (New Bedford MA 2005) pp. 360-392.

[69] J. Galot, *L'Immaculée Conception*, in *Maria. Etudes sur la sainte Vierge*, vol. VII (Paris 1964) pp. 9-116.

Scotus summarized[70] his thought by observing that three possible positions might be adopted as regards the moral state of Mary at conception. The first is the maculist theory, viz., of her conception in sin, and at some moment subsequent to this her sanctification within or without the womb. The second is a form of "semi-maculism," a theory which held that Mary, in one and the same first moment of conception, was simultaneously conceived in original sin and then with logical, but not chronological succession, was purified, and so her conception was immaculate. This theory, first proposed by Henry of Ghent, was a way of justifying the feast of the Immaculate Conception without denying the need to be purified from sin: all-pure, yet not preserved from contraction.[71] Finally, there is the immaculatist position, eventually confirmed by the Church as correct. Scotus himself awaited the judgment of the Church, but also indicated his personal preference or belief: the immaculatist, because in the absence of contrary indications (either touching the possibility or appropriateness of a Marian title) we should always predicate of Mary what is objectively most to her honor and God's glory in Christ. Nothing so much redounds to her honor and Christ's glory (and ours) than to ascribe to her conception a holiness beyond compare. The theological application by Scotus of Anselm's principle concerning the purity of Mary is, as we shall see, fully in accord with the biblical foundations of Mary's singular and exalted moral-spiritual condition throughout her life, and with the consistent witness of tradition.

The Contribution of the Saints

It is often said that Scotus, coming from a land where the feast of the Virgin's conception was celebrated, and teaching mostly in northwestern Europe where that feast was likewise commonly celebrated, was

---

[70] III Sent., d. 3, q. 1.
[71] Cf. J.-Fr. Bonnefoy, *Le Ven. Jean Duns Scot, Docteur de L'Immaculée-Conception: son milieu, sa doctrine, son influence* (Rome 1960). The theory of semi-maculism as an explanation of the Immaculate Conception was considered a contradiction in terms by Bonaventure and Thomas. For Scotus, the theory Fr. Bonnefoy calls "semi-maculism" is that of Henry of Ghent (pp. 92-98), from which Scotus carefully distinguishes his own. On a number of key issues the teaching of Scotus, as Bonnefoy notes, differs from that of his master, William of Ware, who later in life fully adopted the views of his one-time student.

influenced by liturgical considerations in his defense of the Immaculate Conception against almost all the great theological names of the thirteenth century. This may be so, but it is not an entirely satisfactory explanation, because the precise object of the feast and its great prestige as a celebration of the stainless conception, and not merely a purification from original sin within the womb of St. Ann, came only after Scotus had made his great contributions to the elucidation of the mystery.

Rather, a second factor ought also to be considered along with that of "symbolic" theology in the formation of his theological convictions: namely, that of the "mystical" theology or spirituality of the founder of his Order, St. Francis of Assisi. St. Francis is not known to have ever used the title Immaculate Conception, though that of Spouse of the Holy Spirit could well have been an equivalent. Neither is he shown to have ever celebrated the feast, though he often visited places where it was celebrated in Southern Italy and could hardly have been ignorant of this. Apart from this historical discussion, it is a fact that his spirituality is centered on the mystery of the Cross and of the Church, the link between these two being the maternal mediation of the Sorrowful Mother or Immaculate Co-redemptrix. This fits well with his documented affirmation of the absolute primacy or kingship of the Word incarnate. Any such affirmation must logically lead to an affirmation of the all-holiness of Mary, the moral state defined by the Immaculate Conception or espousal of the Holy Spirit, the ontological premise of the divine and spiritual maternity by the power of the Holy Spirit. Many scholars hold that St. Francis knew the mystery without the dogmatic terminology, or that he used titles such as Spouse of the Holy Spirit to designate what this mystery meant concretely. They also hold that the Scotistic reflection on the concrete excellence of the redemption wrought by Christ to the glory of God and triumph of the Church, given formulation in the dogma of the Immaculate Conception, is inspired by St. Francis, specifically by Francis' view of Mary as our Mediatrix with Christ as Christ is our Mediator with the Father. In Scotus such Marian mediation is a direct corollary of the Immaculate Conception.

The point is crucial, for it makes perfectly evident that the Holy Spirit and his bride, the Immaculate Virgin Mother and teacher of the apostles, are primarily responsible for doctrinal development, not the academic theologians. Nowhere is this truer than in the case of the

Immaculate Conception. That mystery could have been defined, had a pope desired this, once the work of Scotus was acknowledged by the Church under Sixtus IV. In fact it was only defined after a crucial apparition of Mary in Paris (in 1830, to St. Catherine Labouré), one indication that the only viable basis for a renewal of the Church after the disaster of the French Revolution was the mystery of the Immaculate Conception, illustrated in the medal of the Immaculate Conception, or miraculous medal.[72] More importantly, the apparition and the medal commemorating it universally confirm the mystery of the Immaculate Conception as the basis of Mary's role as maternal Mediatrix: at the Incarnation, on Calvary and in the Church.

From "Franciscan Thesis" (Opinio Minorum) to Defined Dogma

With the contribution of Scotus to a precise theological understanding of the mystery of the all-holiness, incomparable blessedness, most perfect graciousness and acceptability to the heavenly Father of his first-born daughter, Mary, the subsequent development of the doctrine known now as the Immaculate Conception up to its solemn definition in 1854, though drawn out, is relatively simple and easy to summarize. For from 1308 (year of the death of Scotus in Cologne) the problematic ultimately assumed in the Bull *Ineffabilis Deus* remained essentially the same. The power fueling that subsequent development first appears clearly in the explanation of Scotus, an explanation that relates the universal need of redemption to the absolute primacy of Christ (so including both Mary who descended from Adam but did not contract original sin,

---

[72] Cf. P.D. Fehlner, *Fr. Juniper Carol: His Mariology and Scholarly Achievement*, in *Marian Studies* 43 (1992) 17-59. The complementary character of a primarily academic approach to the mystery of Mary, as exemplified in the approach of Frs. Balić and Carol, with one accenting the contemplative and charismatic as exemplified in St. Maximilian M. Kolbe should not be underestimated. Cf. also P.D. Fehlner, *Mariae Advocatae Causa. The Marian Issue in the Church Today*, in *Maria "Unica Cooperatrice alla Redenzione"* (New Bedford MA 2005) pp. 529-577, and also by him *The Other Page*, in *Miles Immaculatae* 24 (1988) 512-531. The very interesting book of S. Cecchin, *L'Immacolata Concezione. Breve storia del dogma*, cit., takes little or no account of the contemplative-charismatic aspect of this history. Extraordinarily important on this point is the study of J. Schneider, *Virgo Ecclesia facta...*, cit.

and the angels who did not sin) rather than to descent from Adam and contraction of original sin or the so-called *debitum*.

In establishing a distinctive link between the Immaculate Conception and the headship of Christ, Scotus has effectively defined the redemption in terms of the mediation of Christ, not the mediation in terms of the work of redemption. That mediation includes Mary Immaculate as Mediatrix; hence, her inclusion under Christ in the work of redemption, not to be purified but in being "preserved" to actively cooperate in the purification or liberation of the rest of his brethren and of her offspring (cf. Rev 12:17). Conversely, the Immaculate Conception is not merely an isolated, arbitrary exception to a universal rule, the debt of contracting original sin; it is the Marian mode of the absolute primacy of Christ, a mode found in each of the saving mysteries of Christ's life and work: in his conception and birth, his public life, his Passion, death and Resurrection, his glorification of the Church.

By the pontificate of Sixtus IV (1471-1484) the feast of the Immaculate Conception was being celebrated by the Roman Church, and the collect for the Mass, composed personally by the Pope (Francesco della Rovere, a Franciscan and Scotist) contains the essentials of the definition of 1854. The implications of these decisions of Sixtus IV (cf. *Cum praecelsa*, 1477, on the celebration of the feast in Rome; and *Grave nimis*, 1483, prohibiting that the "pious opinion" of the Immaculate Conception be called heretical) were confirmed by the Council of Trent in exempting Our Lady by name from the decree on the universality of original sin (Session V, 6 – DS 1516), in effect a move which effectively confirmed that her redemption was not liberative, but preservative. Paul V in 1617 prohibited public discussion of the maculist position, and in 1622 Gregory XV extended the prohibition to private discussion. With the brief *Sollicitudo omnium ecclesiarum* in 1661 (DS 2015-2017), Alexander VII ended a nearly 40-year-old prohibition of the Holy Office of preaching that the object of the feast was the Immaculate Conception. This pope's definition of the Immaculate Conception as object of the feast is nearly identical with that used by Bl. Pius IX, except for two particulars. Where Alexander speaks of an Immaculate Conception at the moment of creation and infusion of the soul, Pius speaks of the first moment of conception as that of the person of Mary as a whole, thus approximating the definition of Mary at Lourdes: "I am the Immaculate

Conception," not merely in one moment of existence, but in her personal existence. And where Alexander speaks of a preservation from all stain of original sin, Pius speaks of preservation from all stain of original guilt, according to many interpreters an allusion to the question of a *debitum peccati*.[73]

Here is the text of Alexander VII:

> ... *eius animam in primo instanti creationis et infusionis in corpus fuisse speciali Dei gratia et privilegio, intuitu meritorum Jesu Christi eius filii, humani generis Redemptoris, a macula peccati originalis praeservatam immunem...* [...her soul, from the first moment of its creation and infusion into the body was by a special grace and privilege of God, in view of the merits of Jesus Christ, her Son, Redeemer of the human race, preserved immune from the stain of original sin...]

And here is the text of the solemn definition of Bl. Pius IX:

> ... *beatissimam Virginem Mariam in primo instanti suae Conceptionis fuisse singulari omnipotentis Dei gratia et privilegio, intuitu meritorum Christi Jesu Salvatoris humani generis, ab omni originalis culpae labe praeservatam immunem, esse a Deo revelatam...* [...that the Blessed Virgin Mary from the first moment of her Conception, by a singular grace and privilege of almighty God, in view of the merits of Christ Jesus, Savior of the human race, was preserved immune from every taint of original sin, has been revealed by God...]

Use of the term "preserved" and reference to the first instant of conception clearly indicates the Scotistic provenance of the argumentation. Yet reference to the foreseen merits of Christ clearly incorporates the concerns of St. Thomas and St. Bonaventure and avoids any Pelagian-inspired attempts to define the Immaculate Conception without reference to redemption and sin, or to her solidarity with the family of Adam. Mary truly is, in the famous line of Wordsworth,

---

[73] Rosini, *Mariologia...*, cit., pp. 84ff.

"our fallen nature's solitary boast." Far from being isolated from us by the Immaculate Conception, Mary in virtue of it is our maternal Co-redemptrix, the reason the Church in the paschal *Praeconium* describes original sin as the *felix culpa* (O happy fault). Mary who descends from Adam, yet is above Adam and Eve by virtue of her joint predestination with Christ, is thereby, as immaculate, their *Salvatrix*, reversing or recirculating our initial fortune in Adam so as to enable us to participate in the recapitulation of all creation in the New Adam, Son of Mary.

Set in the context of this history, the solemn definition of 1854 is clearly seen as a profound declaration of a mystery fundamental to the life of the Church. That mystery, always believed implicitly because part of the deposit of faith entrusted to the Church, hence not the conclusion of a theological argumentation, was eventually defined to the glory of God, the prosperity of the Church and the salvation of souls in these perilous times.

New Light on Theology: Biblical, Dogmatic, Moral

Indeed, the text of the dogma, though not without implications for questions of theology, apologetics and philosophy-science, is hardly linked to their resolution, as the differences of the two texts above, viz., those of Alexander VII and Bl. Pius IX, illustrate. Thus, affirmation of the mystery is not to be dependent on the resolution of problems involving the biology of conception and the creation and infusion/quickening of the soul, but is directly related to the unique status of Mary in relation to Christ as Mediatrix of all graces. The change was introduced not to deny the point of Pope Alexander, or as an implicit denial that the truth of the Immaculate Conception has no bearing on the solution of these questions, but to eliminate any loopholes which semi-maculists might find to equate immaculate conception with sanctification in the womb. But this clarification, though seemingly a minor detail, in fact is particularly relevant both to the subsequent opposition to the Immaculate Conception and to its practical bearing on the life of the Church and her preparation for the final coming of Christ, a point stressed by Pope John Paul II throughout his pontificate.

Opposition to that mystery after the brief of Alexander VII, and still more so after the solemn definition, takes the form not of theological argumentation, but of a minimizing of the person of the Mother of

God as Immaculate, a minimizing ultimately undermining faith both in Christ's person and in his redemptive work. Adam Widenfeld's *Monita Salutaria* (1673) is the great prelude to this tune, echoed in the writing of L.A. Muratori, so ably refuted by St. Alphonsus in his *Glories of Mary*. It is now being resurrected[74] in current minimizing of the Mother of God, and in opposition to the practice of "total consecration to the Immaculate Heart" as the effective basis for securing the life of the Church and of the believer, indicated especially by Our Lady herself at Fatima.

The apparitions of the Immaculate at Lourdes, precisely under that title, a kind of crowning of earlier apparitions at Rue du Bac, Paris (the Miraculous Medal or Medal of the Immaculate Conception, 1830), La Salette (Co-redemptrix, 1846), and later at Castelpetroso (Co-redemptrix, 1890), was not so much a confirmation of the definition as it was an indication of its practical import for the directions to be taken by the Church as a whole, what St. Maximilian M. Kolbe called the incorporation of the mystery into the life of the Church and into the lives of each and every actual and potential member of Christ's Mystical Body.[75] Some of these indications are given by St. Pius X in his Encyclical *Ad diem illum* (1904, golden jubilee of the definition) and Pius XII in the Encyclical *Fulgens corona* (1953, for the centenary celebrations of the same). Vatican II, in the Dogmatic Constitution on the Church, *Lumen Gentium*, 56, not only indicates the major biblical bases for the dogma, but sets the dogma in the context of salvation history, as it were a major key to that history along lines already indicated by St. Bonaventure in his *Collationes in Hexaemeron*: all history is about the conflict between Christ and his Body the Church on the one hand, and on the other the anti-Christ and the anti-Church.[76] At the center of that conflict and of the victory of the Lamb stands the woman whose name we know to be Mary, or Immaculate Conception.

This very traditional exegesis is further clarified by Pope John Paul II in his 1987 Encyclical *Redemptoris Mater*. His lengthy discussion of the mystery of the Immaculate Conception as the basis for her maternal mediation at Nazareth, on Calvary and in the Church from Pentecost, may be summarized under these points:

---

[74] E.g., Munsterman, *Marie Corédemptrice...*, cit.
[75] *Scritti di Massimiliano Kolbe* (Rome 1997) n. 486.
[76] St. Bonaventure, *Collationes in Hexaemeron*, c. 14, n. 17.

1) The "glory of grace" (of our predestination in Christ) mentioned in chapter one of the Letter to the Ephesians (1:7) is most perfectly manifested in the Mother of God by the fact that she has been redeemed in a "more sublime manner," being preserved by reason of the redemptive merits of her Son from the inheritance of original sin, being thus constituted in a state of belonging entirely to Christ from the first moment of her conception or existence. She is thereby "Daughter of the Father's Son" and so able to be "Mother of the Creator."

2) As Mother of the incarnate Word-Savior she is placed at the very center of the enmity between him and the serpent: foretold in the *Protoevangelium* and confirmed in the book of Revelation under the sign of the woman (11:19 -12:1ff.).

3) In this central place, most of all the place of the Cross (Jn 19:25-27), stands one belonging to our weak and poor family, yet whose whole being is permeated by a greatness and beauty determined by the "glory of grace" bestowed on her at her conception. Hence, the new name: Full of Grace (or Immaculate Conception) by which the heavenly messenger (Lk 1:28) salutes her, a name given to her alone and no other before or after the Annunciation.

We could not desire a clearer identification of the woman of Genesis 3:15 and Revelation 12:1 with the Mary espoused to a man named Joseph in Luke 1:28.[77] These are the three classic texts adduced as the scriptural basis for the Immaculate Conception. What is still more astounding is the linking of the Mariology of Luke centering on the angelic salutation and effectively interpreting the new name of Mary as "Full of Grace," or Immaculate Conception, with the Pauline theology of grace, above all in Ephesians, the letter so much concerned with grace and the mystery of the Church, and regarded by Scotists and the majority of contemporary exegetes as teaching the absolute primacy of Christ. This teaching on

---

[77] An excellent, detailed overview of biblical Mariology is to be found in Stefano Manelli, *All Generations Shall Call Me Blessed...*, cit. On the Immaculate Conception in particular see the concluding synthesis, pp. 415-425.

the name of Mary clearly leads us to read St. Paul in Philippians 2:5-10 in a Marian vein: the kenosis of Christ is his conception by Mary and the glorification of Christ's name is inseparably linked to that of Mary, because they are joined in a single oblation on Calvary and at the altar of the Eucharistic sacrifice. That linking leads to an acknowledgement, as Pope Benedict XVI notes,[78] of the coincidence of Mary's *Fiat* at the Annunciation with the "I come to do your will," or *Fiat*, of Christ accepting his Incarnation ordained to sacrifice in becoming flesh in the immaculate womb of Mary. She it is who fitted him with a body subject to suffering and death (cf. Heb 10:5-10). To this coincidence St. Elizabeth alludes in addressing Mary: "Blessed art thou among women and blessed is the fruit of thy womb" (Lk 1:42). Read as a synonym for Immaculate Conception, *Kecharitomene* ("Full of Grace") as the name of Mary defines the character of Mary's response to the salutation, *Chaire, Ave*, Hail, Rejoice: My spirit rejoices in God my Savior (Lk 1:47).

But at the same time this contextualization of the mystery of the Immaculate Conception also provides a foundation for the ecclesial dimensions of Mariology. St. Paul himself strongly hints at this in Ephesians 5:27 where he states that Christ sacrificed himself for the Church that she might be "without spot and without wrinkle," viz., exactly like his Immaculate Mother. Precisely in Mary *qua* Immaculate we perceive how and in what measure grace superabounds over sin (cf. Rom 5:12-21). In pursuing these lines of thought we also see how the Woman of Apocalypse is not either Mary or the Church or the soul espoused to Christ, but that in a very real, but mystical, way, Mary *is* the Church, or the Church in the first instance is Mary, and how no soul is the bride of Christ except to the extent it is, in the words of St. Maximilian M. Kolbe, transubstantiated into the Immaculate, as the Immaculate is transubstantiated into the Holy Spirit.[79] For it is only by

---

[78] Homily, Feast of the Annunciation, March 25, 2006, in *L'Osservatore Romano*, March 26, 2006. The perfect harmonization of these two wills is the work of the Holy Spirit, who, in the happy formula of St. Maximilian Kolbe, is the "uncreated Immaculate Conception." For text and commentary cf. Fehlner, *St. Maximilian... Pneumatologist...*, cit., pp. 108-115; also for relevant Kolbean texts in English translation cf. H. Manteau-Bonamy, *The Immaculate Conception and the Holy Spirit*....

[79] For texts and commentary see Fehlner, *St. Maximilian...Pneumatologist...*, cit., pp. 146-150.

the overshadowing of the Holy Spirit that Christ becomes present as bridegroom of the Church. Revelation 12 must be read in conjunction with Revelation 21, viz., the new and glorious Jerusalem descending from heaven.[80] What that New Jerusalem is in the first instance is revealed in the Immaculate, present in the midst of the Church from the day of Pentecost.

Total Consecration to and Triumph of the Immaculate Heart

What we perceive in this summary of Catholic Tradition and belief concerning the Immaculate Conception is an explanation of the scriptural roots of this mystery, a mystery which pervades every page of Scripture and every aspect of the mystery of Christ and of the Church. The mystery of Mary Immaculate is the key to the central mystery of Revelation, viz., that of the incarnate Savior and our incorporation into his Mystical Body, a salvation which, according to St. Anselm, St. Thomas and Bl. John Duns Scotus, could not be more perfect in any possible world.[81] In his *Conferences on the Hexaemeron*, in treating of the illumination of the mind through the Scriptures, St. Bonaventure has an inspired perception of this key when he tells us that Mary is the second of the four fundamental mysteries of faith illustrated by the Bible. Wonderful things are told of Mary in every passage of Scripture, because in every passage she is included in relation to her Son. And what some claim in asking (as much today as in the Middle Ages): "why is so little said of Mary in the Bible?" is of no import, for the simple reason that everywhere in Scripture Mary is spoken of. For to speak everywhere of Mary far transcends even the most detailed treatise on her, whether biblical or doctrinal.[82] Guided by a study of

---

[80] Cf. H. Rahner, *Our Lady and the Church* (New York 1961).
[81] On the concept of *perfect redemption* (with texts of the three great Doctors just cited), its bearing on the doctrines of coredemption, Immaculate Conception and absolute primacy of Christ as Redeemer cf. Fehlner, *Immaculata Mediatrix...*, cit., pp. 286-302.
[82] St. Bonaventure, *Collationes in Hexaemeron*, c. 13, n. 20: "secunda est Mater Dei Maria, quia mira dicuntur de ipsa in Scripturis, quia in omnibus Scripturis refertur in relatione ad Filium. Et quod dicunt aliqui: quare ita pauca dicuntur de beata Virgine?, nihil est; quia multa dicuntur, quia ubique de ipsa et plus est dici de ipsa ubique, quam si unus tractatus fieret"; "the second point concerns the Mother of God, Mary, because wonderful things are said of her in the Scriptures, and in the

the living Tradition of the Church we are able to grasp the passages of Scripture dealing with the Immaculate Conception in the literal sense as keys to the whole of theology.

With this we may ponder the suggestion of some contemporary scholars[83] that the position of the ancient Scotistic school on the content of the *Protoevangelium* be reconsidered, viz., that it not be restricted to Genesis 3:15. Instead, the promise of the Redeemer after the fall should be included within the framework of the absolute primacy of Christ and Mary as set forth in Genesis, chapters one and two, where this is given as the reason for the original creation culminating in the formation of Adam and Eve as male and female. Such an approach is not merely the one of Scotus; it is also affirmed both by St. Bonaventure and St. Thomas as the common view of Tradition, even if these two Doctors try to explain why the absolute primacy cannot be demonstrated thereby as fact.[84]

Here a point underscored by St. Maximilian M. Kolbe[85] may be fruitfully pondered. The Immaculate Conception may not be divorced from considerations reflecting the reality of sin, in particular original sin and the involvement of the Devil in this, and the need of redemption in order to attain salvation. But even if Adam had not sinned, the mystery of the Immaculate Conception, like that of the Incarnation, would have involved considerations of this kind, viz., in relation to the nature of the trial, or proving, both of the angels and of mankind in the persons of our first parents. A great many doctors and theologians of the past, indeed the letter to the Hebrews and the book of Revelation,[86] appear to suggest

---

Scriptures she is always spoken of in relation to her son. And some ask: why is so little said of Mary in the Bible? This is a pointless question, for the simple reason that a very great deal is said of her there, because everywhere in Scripture she is spoken of [as is her son, Christ], and it is much more to speak of her everywhere than merely compose a treatise about her."

[83] Cf. Settimio Manelli, *Genesis 3:15 and the Immaculate Coredemptrix*, in *Mary at the Foot of the Cross V* (New Bedford MA 2005) pp. 263-322; and P. Fehlner, *Redemption, Metaphysics and the Immaculate Conception*, in *Mary at the Foot of the Cross V* (New Bedford MA 2005) pp. 186-262.

[84] Cf. the two essays cited in note 58.

[85] *Scritti... Kolbe*, nn. 1293; 1311.

[86] Still a good résumé of the doctrinal tradition on this point is that of the Benedictine Archbishop of Birmingham and friend of Cardinal Newman, Bernard Ullathorne, *The Immaculate Conception* (New York 1904, 2nd ed.) pp. 64-80.

strongly that at the heart of those trials was a willingness to accept and revere the incarnate Son and the Immaculate Mother, to prefer the fruit of the tree of life to that of the tree of the knowledge of good and evil. Preservative redemption, as distinct from liberative, can only be grasped when we see how the Immaculate Conception is the key, not only to our *de facto* liberation from sin, but also 1) to the trial by which we were to merit heaven even before any consideration of redemption, and 2) after original sin to our good fortune (unlike the fallen angels)[87] to have a Savior-Redeemer, because the Son of God still wanted our Mother as his Mother, notwithstanding our infidelity.

Clearly, the Immaculate Conception is not a privilege, as some claim, which isolates the Mother of God from us. Quite the contrary, being the singular grace whereby one of our family can be the Mother of God, the associate of the Redeemer in crushing the head of our accuser and enemy (cf. Gen 3:15; Rev 12:10), we too can come to participate via our liberation from sin what she lives by her preservation from original sin. Here is the ultimate implication of that first promise-prophecy (Gen 3:15) of a Redeemer whose Immaculate Mother would crush the head of the serpent. Its fulfillment is sketched synthetically in the grand vision of the Ark of the Covenant in heaven, who is the woman clothed with the sun.[88]

May we give more concrete, practical formulation to the significance of lived faith in the Immaculate Conception, or devotion to the Immaculate Heart based on total consecration and wholehearted support for the triumph of that Heart, as requested by Jesus himself? Indeed, this may be done on two scores.

The first concerns the relation between the Immaculate Conception and the divine maternity, more exactly divine because virginal. Why a virginal maternity might be possible, and if activated should entail a virginal conception and virginal birth of a divine person—or in reverse, how a divine person might be born of a woman and so identified as divine—becomes clear in pondering the mystery of the Immaculate Conception, created and uncreated. The mystery of the uncreated Immaculate Conception is the mystery of the spousal love of the Holy

---

[87] *Scritti… Kolbe*, n. 1305.
[88] Cf. Stefano Manelli, *All Generations Shall Call Me Blessed…*, cit. (2 ed.), pp. 415-424 (synthesis).

Spirit: all the love of the Father and Son. The mystery of the created Immaculate Conception is that of the spousal love of the Father and incarnate Son in Mary. That mystery is her unique union with the Holy Spirit and how it shaped both her body and soul to be the prime worthy dwelling place of the incarnate Word (cf. Collect of the Mass of the Immaculate Conception). Nothing could underscore so well the value of perfect virginity and every other form of chastity subordinate to it. It is the key to God being with us, as the angel so concisely explained to Mary at the Annunciation. It is the key to the divinization of man. The high point of such divinization in this time of pilgrimage is the celebration of the Eucharist. We can only enjoy fully the fruits of that mystery as sacrifice and sacrament if our own hearts are one with the Immaculate Heart. For Mary made the Eucharist possible, because she first brought the Word into our world and into our lives. To deny this or minimize this is ultimately to preclude sharing in these stupendous blessings.

The second concerns the reality of the Church here and now as one and holy. It is the Immaculate Mother's dynamic presence at the center of the Church. This explains why the Church is one and holy here and now, despite so many sinners or half-saints and so much quarreling and division among her members. As the Immaculate Conception, Mary is the Church, personally rather than collectively. And to the degree the mystery of the Immaculate Conception is incorporated into the Church collectively and into each of her members singly, the Church will more and more be without spot and without wrinkle (cf. Eph 5:27). This is the praise of the glory of his grace (cf. Eph 1:6) which the Father desires. Much has been said since the Council on the need to relate Mary more to the Church, but often those saying this have tended to minimize the crucial importance of the Immaculate Conception, viz., that genuine ecclesio-typology can only rest on the mystery of the Immaculate Conception, and the only effective ecumenism will be that rooted in and ending with the praise of all the baptized for "our fallen nature's solitary boast."[89]

The doctrine of the Immaculate Conception is, then, simply the most radical, personal and social specification of what it means to address Mary as the *Panhaghia*, the all-holy, all-blessed among women (cf. Lk

---

[89] Cf. A. Livi, *Marian Co-redemption in the Ecclesiology of Charles Journet*, in *Mary at the Foot of the Cross VII* (New Bedford MA 2007, in course of publication).

1:28. 42), the reason why he who is the Holy One of God, the Son of God (cf. Lk 1:35; Jn 6:70), like us in all things but sin (Jn 8:44, 46; 14:30; 1 Jn 1:5; 1 Pet 2:22; 2 Cor 5:21; Heb 4:15), will make us who are like him in all things but holiness, like him even in that, and so make us sharers in the divine nature (cf. 2 Pet 1:4).

Put practically, this mystery translates as Mediatrix of all grace, clearly depicted without the name in the account of the Presentation of Jesus in the Temple by his most pure Mother, thereby making possible and effecting the encounter of the Church, in the persons of Simeon and Anna, with the Savior and salvation, the light illumining the darkness of sin (cf. Lk 2:22-40). What Christ asks of us, the whole Church and each member, actual and potential, is to "take her into our homes," viz., into our hearts (cf. Jn 19:25-27). In biblical terminology this is what St. Maximilian M. Kolbe means by "incorporation of the Immaculate Conception into the Church and into the lives of men," at once the basis and the goal of all missionary activity.

Conclusion

We may conclude these considerations on the mystery of the Immaculate Conception with an exercise of the *analogia fidei* (analogy of faith), or as St. Paul says *spiritualia spiritualibus comparantes* (1 Cor 2:13): comparing mystery ("spiritual reality") with mystery.

The interconnection of mysteries and their illustration, not the deduction of conclusions implied in the express contents of the deposit of faith, is the heart of theological reasoning, a reasoning ultimately resting on the logic of the divine counsels. The Immaculate Conception is a dogma, not deduced from revealed premises. It is itself revealed. The use of deduction is but one logical method employed to illustrate just how that dogma is contained within the deposit. The closer our theological reflections come to an adequate formulation of a mystery, the greater will be our appreciation of this interconnection, what Vatican II calls the hierarchy (sacred order, not relative certainty or importance) of truths, as this is arranged in the saving counsels of God concerning the predestination of the saints to glory in Christ. Methodologically, the recognition of the signs of the saving will of God (*signa voluntatis Dei*), as for instance in its classic formulation by Scotus, functions as a kind of convergence of considerations, in which each reflects the truth and certainty of the others, and a denial of one, even on a seemingly small point, leads to a repudiation of all. This, mass repudiation, is exactly what is entailed in contemporary calls for the "dedogmatization" the Immaculate Conception, hardly a minor point.

And in the case of the Immaculate Conception this convergence is particularly impressive. The perfection of Our Lady's virginity rests in this, that it is the fullest realization of that moral state defined by the grace of the Immaculate Conception, the complement in Mary of the grace of the hypostatic union and substantial sanctity of Christ's human nature. In turn, it is this perfect espousal of the Holy Spirit which explains, as Gabriel observed at the Annunciation, how a mere creature might become the virginal Mother of God and Mother of the Church. We may say that the mission of the Holy Spirit as complement to that of the Son is realized, or has its term in the Immaculate Virgin *qua* Immaculate, whether we refer this mission to the anointing of the Messiah at the Incarnation, or to the sanctification of the Church beginning with Pentecost. Finally, as the crown of her maternal mediation consummated by her coredemptive role on Calvary and continued in the work of bringing the Church to full glory, the singular grace and privilege of the Assumption at the end of her earthly life is the same as that working the Immaculate Conception at its beginning. In speaking of an Immaculate Conception, we are not speaking of one moment among many others, but of the one moment which determines the fundamental moral character and dignity of all the others, a dignity which underlies the moral worth of conception and of every person conceived by woman. Immaculate Conception is what is meant when a person is named as *Panhaghia*. To call her most blessed among women is to describe her conception as untouched by the prince of this world.

The mystery of the Immaculate Conception is intimately linked to the absolute primacy of Christ, a given of Tradition never questioned until the Immaculate Conception was systematically denied, or qualified until hypotheses concerning an alleged *debitum peccati* were proposed as necessary to insure Our Lady's inclusion in the work of redemption. That link rooted in the joint predestination of Christ and Mary as constituting the "hierarchy" (St. Bonaventure) or sacred order of the hypostatic union, is not only made evident at the first moment of the Incarnation (that of the Annunciation in Nazareth), but above all by a contemplation of that primacy in terms of the preservative redemption of Mary at the moment of Christ's exaltation on the Cross and his ensuing triumph in the Church through the mediation of the Immaculate and the glorification of her Immaculate Heart. In a word, we are talking about her coredemptive role, why the Immaculate Conception makes possible her active role in the sacrifice of Calvary and in the establishment of the objective economy of salvation.

The surpassing excellence of the Immaculate Conception in Mary, type of the Church, is the key to an appreciation of the holiness of the Church and of the excellence of that salvation won for us by Christ through a liberative redemption from sin, and therefore to the dignity and hope of every child conceived, the inestimable value of conception and conversely, the horror of contraception. Incorporation of that mystery into the very life of the Church and into the lives of each of its members, according to St. Maximilian M. Kolbe, is crucial to an appreciation of, and commitment to, the moral and supernatural life of the Church and of the entire human family, at its inception, in its progress and at its conclusion.[90]

Finally, the grace of the Immaculate Conception, as foretold in the *Protoevangelium*, makes of the Virgin the destroyer of every heresy in the whole world, of all that is contrary to and subversive of faith in her Son, in doctrine and in discipline. Here is meant not only each heresy, but what is at the root of every heresy, namely self-will in the place of God's will to believe in his Son. Total consecration to Mary means just this: to make one's own will one with that of the Immaculate, as her will is one with that of the Spirit of the Father and the Son. Quite correctly, refusal of this has been identified as a sign of a lack of balance, that reduces Mary and Christ to the level and condition of all other men in the present state of fallen nature (denial of the divinity of the Son of Mary Immaculate as Messiah: Ebionites, Nestorians, Pelagians); or reduces them to the condition of heavenly symbols (denial of the sacred humanity of Christ and the perfect virginal motherhood of Mary: Docetism, Gnosticism, Monophysitism). Acceptance of total consecration, on the other hand, is the sign and guarantee of the triumph of the Immaculate Heart, the

---

[90] Cf. *Scritti... Kolbe*, no. 486 & 1168. [English Translation: *The Kolbe Reader. The Writings of St. Maximilian M. Kolbe, O.F.M.Conv*, ed. A. Romb (Libertyville IL 1987) pp. 78-84]. Cf. Fehlner, *The Other Page*, cit.

realization of the mission of the Holy Spirit to sanctify the Church, to render it holy, without spot or wrinkle (Eph 5:27). In the Immaculate Conception, in the *Panhaghia*, is revealed the reality of that perfect union of wills, of being one heart and soul (cf. Acts 4:32), which constitutes the tabernacle of God on earth, first in Mary, and then by extension in the Church, as it is marianized or transubstantiated into the Immaculate Conception. We may then join Mary Immaculate responding to the angelic salutation with her canticle, *Magnificat*, and so rejoice forever in God our Savior. Indeed, "All generations will call her blessed," no more so than when they proclaim her in word and deed "the Immaculate Conception."

Our Lady's Perpetual Virginity

Msgr. Arthur Burton Calkins

The mystery of the Incarnation is inseparable in the eternal plans of God from the virginal conception of the Son of God in the womb of the Blessed Virgin Mary. While God could have brought about the enfleshment of the Word in any way that he chose, he concretely willed that the Word should become flesh by the power of the Holy Spirit in the womb of the Virgin Mary (*Et incarnatus est de Spiritu Sancto ex Maria Virgine*). This fact transmitted to us in the gospels of St. Luke (1:26-38) and St. John (1:14) has been an integral part of the Church's creed from the earliest days of her existence,[1] and was solemnly ratified by the First Council of Constantinople in 381 to express, within the limits of human language, the mystery which the Church received, believes and transmits about the Incarnation of the Son of God.[2] It is the Catholic Church's perennial belief in the three facets of this mystery which immediately touch upon the role of Our Lady that is the specific object of this study: the fact that she was a virgin before (*ante partum*), during (*in partu*) and after the birth of Christ (*post partum*). The *Catechism of the Catholic Church* expresses this truth succinctly by stating that "The deepening of faith in the virginal motherhood led the Church to confess Mary's real and perpetual virginity even in the act of giving birth to the Son of God made man."[3]

---

[1] Heinrich Denzinger, S.I., *Enchiridion Symbolorum Definitionum et Declarationum de Rebus Fidei et Morum: Edizione Bilingue* (XXXVII) a cura di Peter Hünermann (Bologna: Edizioni Dehoniane, 2000) [=*D-H*] 10-64; Jacques Dupuis, S.J. (ed.), *The Christian Faith in the Doctrinal Documents of the Catholic Church*, Originally Prepared by Josef Neuner, S.J., and Jacques Dupuis; Sixth Revised and Enlarged Edition (New York: Alba House, 1998) [=*TCF*] 2-11.

[2] *D-H* 150 [*TCF* 12].

[3] *Catechism of the Catholic Church* [= *CCC*] 499.

Foundational Principles

At the very beginning I would like to make my own the declaration of Father John Saward in his excellent book, *Cradle of Redeeming Love*:

> I make no claim to originality. Self-consciously original theology tends always to be heretical theology. Orthodox theology has, by contrast, a blessed familiarity, for it does no more than assist the faithful in understanding what they already believe; its surprises are the outcome not of human ingenuity but of divine infinitude, the sign of a Truth that is ever ancient and ever new.[4]

The best approach to the Scripture texts which we will be considering is *via* the living Tradition of the Catholic Church, and in this regard I would like to cite this fundamental text from *Dei Verbum*, the Second Vatican Council's Dogmatic Constitution on Divine Revelation:

> The apostolic preaching, which is expressed in a special way in the inspired books, was to be preserved in a continuous line of succession until the end of time. Hence the apostles, in handing on what they themselves had received, warn the faithful to maintain the traditions which they had learned either by word of mouth or by letter (cf. 2 Thess 2:15); and they warn them to fight hard for the faith that had been handed on to them once and for all (cf. Jude 3). What was handed on by the apostles comprises everything that serves to make the People of God live their lives in holiness and increase their faith. In this way the Church, in her doctrine, life and worship, perpetuates and transmits to every generation all that she herself is, all that she believes.
>
> The Tradition that comes from the apostles makes progress in the Church, with the help of the Holy Spirit. There is a growth in insight into the realities and words that are being passed on. This comes about in various

---

[4] John Saward, *Cradle of Redeeming Love: The Theology of the Christmas Mystery* (San Francisco: Ignatius Press, 2002) [=Saward] 14.

ways. It comes through the contemplation and study of believers who ponder these things in their hearts (cf. Lk 2:19 and 51). It comes from the intimate sense of spiritual realities which they experience. And it comes from the preaching of those who have received, along with their right of succession in the episcopate, the sure charism of truth. Thus as the centuries go by, the Church is always advancing towards the plenitude of divine truth, until eventually the words of God are fulfilled in her.[5]

In these paragraphs we have two very important assertions: (1) what we have received from the apostolic preaching must be handed on in its integrity and (2) by the assistance of the Holy Spirit "there is a growth in insight into the realities and words that are being passed on." On this matter the *Catechism of the Catholic Church* offers a helpful clarification: "Yet even if Revelation is already complete, it has not been made completely explicit; it remains for Christian faith gradually to grasp its full significance over the course of the centuries."[6]

In the course of this study we will see that there have been many intuitions regarding the virginal conception and birth of Christ in the course of the centuries, but not all of them have been genuine developments of the faith once delivered to the apostles. Some of these intuitions have proven to be aberrations, heresies which have distorted and misrepresented the faith. For this reason the Church has constant need of authoritative guidance in order to distinguish genuine developments from false ones. Hence

> the task of giving an authentic interpretation of the Word of God, whether in its written form or in the form of Tradition, has been entrusted to the living teaching office [Magisterium] of the Church alone. Its authority in this matter is exercised in the name of Jesus Christ. Yet this Magisterium is not superior to the Word of God, but is its servant. It teaches only what has been handed on to it. At the divine command and with the help of the Holy Spirit, it listens to this [Word of God] devotedly, guards it with

---

[5] *Dei Verbum* 8.
[6] *CCC* 66.

dedication and expounds it faithfully. All that it proposes for belief as being divinely revealed is drawn from this single deposit of faith.

It is clear, therefore, that, in the supremely wise arrangement of God, sacred Tradition, Sacred Scripture and the Magisterium of the Church are so connected and associated that one of them cannot stand without the others. Working together, each in its own way under the action of the one Holy Spirit, they all contribute effectively to the salvation of souls.[7]

The magisterial teaching of the Catholic Church as exercised by popes and councils, then, will provide the fundamental framework for this study, and in this regard we are fortunate to have recent authoritative statements of the Papal Magisterium on the three fundamental aspects of Mary's perpetual virginity. Among these I assign a very important place to the discourse given by Pope John Paul II at Capua (near Naples) on May 24, 1992, to commemorate the 16th centenary of the Plenary Council of Capua, a discourse which recapitulates the tradition and offers us at the same time valuable orientations for our investigation. Among the literally thousands of other papal documents, addresses and homilies devoted primarily or partially to Our Lady by John Paul II, I would also signal for special attention the 70 Marian catecheses which he delivered at general audiences from September 6, 1995, to November 12, 1997. These constitute a valuable compendium of Mariology, touching upon all of the major themes and providing a useful summary of his own teaching, and a further consolidation of that of his predecessors and that of the Second Vatican Council. These catecheses may be justly regarded as an important exercise of the Ordinary Magisterium of the Roman pontiff and thus should be received by the faithful "with religious submission of mind and will" (cf. Dogmatic Constitution on the Church *Lumen Gentium* 25).[8]

---

[7] *Dei Verbum* 10.

[8] These 70 discourses are available in English as *Theotókos—Woman, Mother, Disciple: A Catechesis on Mary, Mother of God* with a foreword by Eamon R. Carroll, O.Carm, S.T.D. (Boston: Pauline Books and Media, 2000) [= *MCat*]. The translation varies in only minor details from the translation provided in the English edition of *L'Osservatore Romano* [= *ORE*].

In treating of the Incarnation, which is inseparable from Mary's divine maternity and virginity, we are dealing with a mystery of faith, a truth which admits of rational explanation, but which is so profound that we can never fully exhaust it. Father Saward puts it beautifully:

> The human birth of the Son of God is a mystery in the strict theological sense: a divinely revealed reality that little ones can understand but not even learned ones can comprehend. Theological mysteries are truth and therefore light for the mind, but the truth is so vast, the light of such intensity, that the mind is dazzled and amazed. When a man meets a mystery of the faith, he finds not a deficiency but an excess of intelligibility: there is just too much to understand. Reverence for supernaturally revealed mysteries is therefore not reason's abdication, but reason's recognition, through faith, of a grandeur transcending its powers.[9]

It will be noted that the above quote is in full harmony with what Pope John Paul II said in his magisterial discourse at Capua on May 24, 1992:

> The theologian must approach the mystery of Mary's fruitful virginity *with a deep sense of veneration for God's free, holy and sovereign action.* Reading through the writings of the holy Fathers and the liturgical texts we notice that few of the saving mysteries have caused so much amazement, admiration or praise as the Incarnation of God's Son in Mary's virginal womb. ...
>
> The theologian, however, who approaches the mystery of Mary's virginity with a heart full of faith and adoring respect, does not thereby forego the duty of studying the data of Revelation and showing their harmony and interrelationship; rather, following the

---

[9] Saward 47-48. Happily, the interested reader who would like to pursue the theological concept of mystery in greater depth may refer to the first chapter of *Cradle of Redeeming Love* where the author develops it in a masterly fashion and with particular reference to the mystery of the Incarnation (Saward 47-120).

> Spirit, ... he puts himself in the great and fruitful theological tradition of *fides quærens intellectum*.
>
> When theological reflection becomes a moment of doxology and latria, the mystery of Mary's virginity is disclosed, allowing one to catch a glimpse of other aspects and other depths.[10]

One who is not willing to recognize that in attempting to scrutinize the mystery of the Incarnation he is treading on sacred ground (cf. Ex 3:5) and, therefore, must approach with reverence and awe, is doomed to remain in the darkness of agnosticism or worse. In fact, the concept of sacred ground brings us remarkably close to an allied notion very dear to the Fathers of the Church, viz. that Mary is *terra virgo*, the virgin earth from which emerged the Son of God.[11] Her fruitful virginity cannot be separated from the blessed fruit of which it is the sign.

As we have already noted, the Catholic Tradition always witnesses to an indissoluble link between Mary's virginity and the Incarnation of the Word. This is clearly attested to by John Paul II in his discourse at Capua:

> For a fruitful theological reflection on Mary's virginity it is first of all essential to have *a correct point of departure*. Actually, in its interwoven aspects the question of Mary's virginity cannot be adequately treated by beginning with her person alone, her people's culture or the social conditions of her time. The Fathers of the Church had already clearly seen that Mary's virginity was a "Christological theme" before being a "Mariological question." They observed that *the virginity of the Mother is a requirement flowing from the divine nature of the Son*; it is the concrete condition in which, according to a free and wise divine plan, the Incarnation of the eternal Son took place. ... As a consequence, for Christian tradition

---

[10] *Acta Apostolicae Sedis* [= *AAS*] 85 (1993) 664 [*ORE* 1244:13 (First number = cumulative edition number; second number = page).]

[11] Cf. Emmanuele Testa, O.F.M., *Maria Terra Vergine*, Vol. I: *I rapporti della Madre di Dio con la SS. Trinità (Sec. I-IX)* (Jerusalem: Franciscan Printing Press, 1984) 416-432. On St. Irenaeus' treatment of Mary as the virgin earth for the New Adam, cf. François-Marie Léthel, O.C.D., *Connaître l'amour du Christ qui surpasse toute connaissance: La Théologie des Saints* (Venasque: Éditions du Carmel, 1989) 77-88.

Mary's virginal womb, made fruitful by the divine *Pneuma* without human intervention (cf. Lk 1:34–35), became, like the wood of the Cross (cf. Mk 15:39) or the wrappings in the tomb (cf. Jn 20:5–8), a reason and sign for recognizing in Jesus of Nazareth the Son of God.[12]

The fact that in studying the virginal conception and birth of Jesus Christ we are dealing first of all with a Christological theme is cogently brought home by John Henry Newman in one of his first Catholic sermons entitled "The Glories of Mary for the Sake of Her Son":

> They [the prerogatives with which the Church invests the Blessed Mother of God] are startling and difficult to those whose imagination is not accustomed to them, and whose reason has not reflected on them; but the more carefully and religiously they are dwelt on, the more, I am sure, will they be found essential to the Catholic faith, and integral to the worship of Christ. This simply is the point which I shall insist on—disputable indeed by aliens from the Church, but most clear to her children—that the glories of Mary are for the sake of Jesus; and that we praise and bless her as the first of creatures, that we may duly confess him as our sole Creator.[13]

The link is indeed indissoluble, and further on in the same sermon Newman did not hesitate to draw a very specific conclusion from it which is far more readily verifiable today than when he uttered it: "Catholics who have honored the Mother, still worship the Son, while Protestants, who now have ceased to confess the Son, began then by scoffing at the Mother."[14]

---

[12] *AAS* 85 (1993) 663 [*ORE* 1244:13].

[13] Philip Boyce, O.C.D. (ed.), *Mary: The Virgin Mary in the Life and Writings of John Henry Newman* (Leominster, Herefordshire: Gracewing Publishing; Grand Rapids, MI: William B. Eerdmans Publishing Company, 2001) [= Newman] 131-132.

[14] Newman 37. Cf. the strikingly similar comment made by Matthias Joseph Scheeben quoted in Saward 175.

The Mystery of the Virginal Conception

In his Marian catechesis of July 10, 1996, in which he dealt with the virginal conception as a biological fact, Pope John Paul II made this very straightforward declaration:

> The Church has constantly held that Mary's virginity is a truth of faith, as the Church has received and reflected on the witness of the gospels of Luke, of Matthew and probably also of John. In the episode of the Annunciation, the Evangelist Luke calls Mary a "virgin," referring both to her intention to persevere in virginity, as well as to the divine plan which reconciled this intention with her miraculous motherhood. The affirmation of the virginal conception, due to the action of the Holy Spirit, excludes every hypothesis of natural parthenogenesis and rejects the attempts to explain Luke's account as the development of a Jewish theme or as the derivation of a pagan mythological legend.
>
> The structure of the Lucan text resists any reductive interpretation (cf. Lk. 1:26-38; 2:19, 51). Its coherence does not validly support any mutilation of the terms or expressions which affirm the virginal conception brought about by the Holy Spirit.[15]

The Pope's language is unmistakably clear. He discounts any attempt to explain the virginal conception of Jesus in terms of (1) parthenogenesis (reproduction from an egg without male fertilization),[16] (2) midrash (development of a Jewish theme)[17] or (3) derivation of a pagan

---

[15] *Insegnamenti di Giovanni Paolo II* [= *Inseg*] XIX/2 (1996) 75 [*ORE* 1450:11; *MCat* 112].

[16] Cf. Salvatore M. Perrella, O.S.M., *Maria Vergine e Madre. La verginità feconda di Maria tra fede, storia e teologia* (Cinisello Balsamo: Edizione San Paolo, 2003) [= Perrella] 111-116. As Father Perrella points out on page 12, even though no cases of parthenogenesis can be adduced within the human species, if such were to be the case the sex of the one generated would have to be female. Dr. Catherine Brown Tkacz comes to the same conclusion in her article, "Reproductive Science and the Incarnation," *Fellowship of Catholic Scholars Quarterly* 25 (Fall 2002) 17-19.

[17] Cf. Raymond E. Brown, S.S., *The Birth of the Messiah: A Commentary on the Infancy Narratives in the Gospels of Matthew and Luke*. New Updated Edition (New York:

mythological legend.[18] Further on in the same discourse he explicitly rejects a further, and lethal, hypothesis which undermines belief in the virginal conception of Jesus as the Church has always understood it: "The opinion—that the account of the virginal conception would instead be a theologoumenon, that is, a way of expressing a theological doctrine, that of Jesus' divine sonship, or would be a mythological portrayal of him."[19]

Questionable Assumptions

Referring to the gospel references to the miraculous conception of Jesus as a theologoumenon is the result of the program of radical demythologizing of the gospels championed by Lutheran Scripture scholars Martin Dibelius (1883-1947), Rudolf Bultmann (1884-1976), and their followers.[20] According to them, the belief that Jesus had no human father was a theological fabrication of the early Christian community in order to heighten Jesus' importance, in other words to "mythologize" him. Having established such assumptions, these scholars set about to demythologize the New Testament. Dibelius specifically maintained that the virginal conception is an entirely Christian legend resulting from a theologoumenon of Judeo-Hellenistic provenance. Bultmann went on to insist that it was a late excrescence which is in contradiction to the internal evidence of the gospels.[21]

While I have no desire to judge the intentions of these men, neither, following the lead of the Holy Father, do I have any intention of giving them serious attention: a theory which flies in the face of the New Testament evidence and the unbroken testimony of the great Tradition may be readily dismissed—*gratis asseritur, gratis negatur*. In fact, much subsequent biblical scholarship since Dibelius and Bultmann first advanced their positions demonstrates precisely why the Pope deemed it necessary in that same catechesis to affirm that:

Doubleday, 1993) [= Birth] 557-563.

[18] Cf. Perrella 108-110; Cf. Paul Haffner, *The Mystery of Mary* (Leominster, Herefordshire: Gracewing; Chicago: Liturgy Training Publications, 2004) [= Haffner] 139-140.
[19] *Inseg* XIX/2 (1996) 77 [*ORE* 1450:11; *MCat* 114].
[20] Cf. Haffner 26.
[21] Cf. Stefano De Fiores' preface to Perrella, *Maria Vergine e Madre* 6-9.

> The uniform gospel witness testifies how faith in the virginal conception of Jesus was firmly rooted in various milieus of the early Church. This deprives of any foundation several recent interpretations which understand the virginal conception not in a physical or biological sense, but only as symbolic or metaphorical.[22]

Unfortunately, once the demythologizing currents were in the air, it was only a matter of time before they were passed off as compatible with Catholic belief in the so-called *Dutch Catechism* of 1966 and in the writings of Hans Küng, Piet Schoonenberg, Edward Schillebeeckx and numerous other Catholic theologians.[23]

Even more complex was the approach to the virginal conception of Jesus taken by the late noted American Sulpician exegete, Raymond Brown, S.S. (+1998). In a major essay on this topic he concluded thus:

> My judgment, in conclusion, is that the totality of the *scientifically controllable* evidence leaves an unresolved problem—a conclusion that should not disappoint since I used the word "problem" in my title—and that is why I want to induce an honest, ecumenical discussion of it. Part of the difficulty is that past discussions have often been conducted by people who were interpreting ambiguous evidence to favor positions already taken.[24]

---

[22] *Inseg* XIX/2 (1996) 76-77 [*ORE* 1450:11; *MCat* 114].

[23] Cf. De Fiores in Perrella, *Maria Vergine e Madre* 9-12: Brunero Gherardini, *La Madre. Maria in una sintesi storico-teologica* (Frigento (AV): Casa Mariana Editrice, 1989) [= Gherardini] 93-95.

[24] Raymond E. Brown, S.S., *The Virginal Conception & Bodily Resurrection of Jesus* (New York: Paulist Press, 1973) [= *Virginal Conception*] 66-76. He quoted that conclusion again in the appendix to his second edition of *The Birth of the Messiah* (p. 698) in the course of a further treatment of the "Historicity of the Virginal Conception" (pp. 698-708). I must humbly confess that that treatment baffles me as much as this statement in his earlier essay:

> Please understand: I am not saying that there is no longer impressive evidence for the virginal conception—personally I think that it is far more impressive than many who deny the virginal conception will admit. Nor am I saying that the Catholic position is dependent on the impressiveness of the scientifically controllable evidence, for I have just mentioned the Catholic belief that the Holy

In effect, Father Brown's work in this area seems to have been based on a number of working principles which must be challenged: (1) the assumption that what he considered the "scientifically controllable" study of the Scriptures, largely following the canons of the Bultmannian school, may be separate from, and independent of, the content of Catholic faith; (2) the employment of a reductionistic and minimizing approach to Catholic dogma[25] and following from these (3) an ecumenical methodology which might be described as consensus based on the "lowest common denominator."[26]

> Spirit can give to the Church a deeper perception than would be warranted by the evidence alone. I am simply asking whether for Catholics a modern evaluation of the evidence is irrelevant because the answer is already decided through past Church teaching. The very fact that theologians are discussing the limits of infallibility and how well the criteria for judging infallibility have been applied suggests that further investigation is not necessarily foreclosed (*Virginal Conception*, pp. 37-38).

[25] Similar to that of Francis A. Sullivan, S.J., who, while not directly denying Catholic dogma, was prepared to challenge its weight on the basis of his evaluation of how it was defined (On Father Sullivan's work, cf. Perrella 52-55, 172, 217).

[26] While I appreciate the vast apparatus of Father Brown's critical scholarship and the enormous accumulation of data which his publications have made available to the scholarly world, of which his monumental volume *The Birth of the Messiah* is an outstanding example, I cannot pass over his fundamental assumptions in silence precisely because of his towering influence in the world of biblical scholarship and his membership on the Pontifical Biblical Commission (Cf. John F. McCarthy, "The Pontifical Biblical Commission—Yesterday and Today," *Homiletic & Pastoral Review* (January 2003) 8-13). His name, more than any other, is identified with the acclaimed collaborative assessment by Protestant and Roman Catholic scholars entitled *Mary in the New Testament*. While he was not its sole author, he was a principal participant, coordinator, discussion leader and editor, and, since the conclusions were always arrived at by the consensus of the participants, we may assume that he was in accord with the working hypotheses adopted. Here are some of them:

> While we do not exclude the possibility and even the likelihood that some items of historical information about Jesus' birth have come to Luke, we are not working with the hypothesis that he is giving us substantially the memoirs of Mary. Rather, the possibility that he constructed his narrative in the light of OT themes and stories will be stressed.

Where do such assumptions leave one? The answer, I'm afraid, is "nowhere." This or that datum of the Tradition may or may not be true. About what is true we can have no real certitude. This is the *reductio ad absurdum* which so much post-Bultmannian exegesis leaves us with. This destabilizing approach to the Word of God provides no satisfactory basis for either the study of Scripture or the practice of genuine ecumenism.[27] With regard to this state of affairs Father Saward offers some very astute remarks:

> Sadly, Liberal Protestant and Modernist Biblical scholars have seemed, for a large part of the last two centuries, to be determined to separate the evangelists as far as possible, in space and time as well as in direct contact, from the Jesus whose life and teaching they set forth. First, the critics "prescind" from the dogmatic faith and Tradition of the Church, in order, so they allege, to

> …Our contention, then, is that the Lucan Annunciation message is a reflection of the Christological language and formulas of the post-resurrectional church. To put it in another way, the angel's words to Mary dramatize vividly what the church has said about Jesus after the Resurrection and about Jesus during his ministry after the baptism. Now this Christology has been carried back to Jesus at the very moment of conception in his mother's womb.
> …All of this means that [Lk] 1:32, 33, 35 are scarcely the explicit words of a Divine Revelation to Mary prior to Jesus' birth; and hence one ought not to assume that Mary had explicit knowledge of Jesus as "the Son of God" during his lifetime. … We do not deny the possibility of a revelation to Mary at the conception of her son, but in the Lucan Annunciation we are hearing a revelation phrased in post-resurrectional language.
> …Finally, in interpreting the virginal conception of Jesus as the begetting of God's Son, we recognize that Luke is not talking about the incarnation of a pre-existent divine being (Raymond E. Brown, Karl P. Donfried, Joseph A. Fitzmyer, John Reumann (eds.), *Mary in the New Testament* (Philadelphia: Fortress Press; New York: Paulist Press, 1978) [= *MNT*] 11, 118-119, 122).

[27] For a critique of much of what has passed for ecumenism among Catholics in recent years cf. Brunero Gherardini, "Sulla Lettera Enciclica *Ut Unum Sint* di Papa Giovanni Paolo II," *Divinitas* 40 (1997) 3-12; *Una sola Fede—una sola Chiesa. La Chiesa Cattolica dinanz all'ecumensmo* (Castelpetroso (IS): Casa Editrice Mariana, 2000).

attain a scientific reading of the texts. Secondly, they give prominence to what they take to be contradictions of fact or opinion between the sacred authors, or between the Bible and natural science. Thirdly, they destroy the historical identity of the evangelists. The gospels—so they claim—were written, not by recognized disciples of truth but by unknown and unknowable devisers of myth. The evangelists composed their narratives not in order to tell the honest truth about the Lord but to promote the religious interests (or "theologies," as the critics like to say) of particular communities in the early Church. The Higher Critics are embarrassed by every physical marvel in the life of Jesus—his miracles, his bodily Resurrection, and the virginity of his Blessed Mother; like the Gnostics of old, they seem repelled by the Word's deep descent into the world of matter.[28]

These "Higher Critics," as Father Saward justly concludes, "cannot teach us how to read the Holy Gospels."[29] They have not placed themselves, as the Pope exhorted theologians in Capua, "in the great and fruitful theological Tradition of *fides quærens intellectum*" precisely because they do not approach the mystery "with a heart full of faith and adoring respect."[30] Happily, however, there are exegetes who have acquired the necessary technical skills and who also stand "in the great and fruitful theological tradition." From them we can learn, as we shall see.

The Biblical Witness

Let us turn once again to the Pope's discourse in Capua.

> In our day the Church has deemed it necessary to recall the reality of Christ's virginal conception, pointing out that the texts of Luke 1:26-38 and Matthew 1:18-25 cannot be reduced to simple etiological accounts meant

---

[28] Saward 110.
[29] Saward 113.
[30] *AAS* 85 (1993) 664 [*ORE* 1244:13]. For further reflection on the mystery of the virginal conception in terms of objections and reasons of fittingness, cf. Saward 184-206.

> to make it easier for the faithful to believe in Christ's divinity. More than the literary genre used by Matthew and Luke, they are instead the expression of a biblical tradition of apostolic origin.
>
> To affirm the reality of Christ's virginal conception does not mean that an apodictic proof of the rational sort can be provided for it. In fact, the virginal conception of Christ is a truth revealed by God, which the human person accepts through the obedience of faith (cf. Rom 16:26). Only the person who is willing to believe that God acts within the reality of this world and that with him "nothing is impossible" (Lk 1:37) can, with devout gratitude, accept the truths of the *kenosis* of God's eternal Son, of his virginal conception-birth, of the universal salvific value of his death on the Cross and of the true Resurrection in his own body of him who was hung and died on the wood of the Cross.[31]

In this illuminating statement the Pope makes several important points, among which are the following: (1) the fundamental biblical texts regarding the virginal conception are Luke 1:26-38 and Matthew 1:18-25; (2) they constitute "a biblical tradition of apostolic origin"; (3) these texts do not provide "an apodictic proof of the rational sort," rather they require faith in the God who reveals.[32] This third point is very appropriately made in the light of the presuppositions of the kind of biblical studies represented by the Catholic-Protestant collaborative volume *Mary in the New Testament*. Such a foundational assertion was already made with great clarity in the Profession of Faith of the Eleventh Council of Toledo of 675, which declares that the virginal conception is "neither proved by reason nor demonstrated from precedent. Were

---

[31] *AAS* 85 (1993) 666-667 [*ORE* 1244:14].
[32] Cf. *Dei Verbum* 5. Cf. also the interesting discussion on this point in Vittorio Messori, *Ipotesi su Maria: Fatti, indizi, enigmi* (Milan: Edizioni Ares, 2005) [= Messori] 91-101, in which he asserts that the "Christian God proposes but does not impose, leaving always a margin of penumbra which permits denial and preserves man's liberty (91)."

it proved by reason, it would not be miraculous; were it demonstrated from precedent, it would not be unique."[33]

Father Ignace de la Potterie, S.J., provides a recent insight into Luke 1:31, arguably the first explicit reference to the virginal conception in the Lucan infancy narrative. The angel says to Mary "you will conceive in your womb," but the words "in your womb" are omitted in many modern translations as being redundant.[34] Where else does a woman conceive, except in her womb, many would ask, but Father de la Potterie argues that St. Luke was very particular about his vocabulary:

> "To conceive in your womb" is a paradoxical and new formula which is only found here in the entire Bible. For what reason did Luke introduce this strange, totally new and seemingly redundant expression? The reason is evident enough. To speak of the ordinary conception of a woman the Old Testament habitually employed two formulas: "to receive in her womb," e.g. Gen 25:22, Is 8:3, etc., in reference to the man from whom the woman receives the seed into her womb (the name of the man is sometimes indicated); or else "to have in her womb," after the woman's sexual relationship with the man, but here also, after having "received" the seed from the man; in this way it was indicated that a woman was now *pregnant*, e.g. Gen 38:25, Amos 1:3, etc.[35]

He points out that the expression "conceive in your womb" has an indirect reference to the Greek text of Isaiah 7:14 and Matthew 1:23[36] and he goes on to draw out the implications:

> For Mary, by contrast [with Elizabeth] Luke employs twice the verb "to conceive," but here *with* the addition of "in your womb"; the first text is precisely the one

---

[33] *D-H* 533 [translation in Saward 187].

[34] Ignace de la Potterie, S.J., "'Et voici que tu concevras en ton sein' (Lc 1, 31): l'ange annonce à Marie sa conception virginale," *Marianum* 61 (1999) [= "Et voici"] 100.

[35] De la Potterie, "Et voice," 101-102 (my trans.).

[36] De la Potterie, "Et voici" 101. Interestingly, Raymond Brown duly notes this terminology in *Birth* 145 (footnote 34) and 300 (footnote 11), but draws no conclusion.

under consideration: *"you will conceive in your womb"* (1:31); further on, we read again: "… He was called Jesus, the name given by the angel before he was conceived *in the womb* [of Mary]" (2:21). This formula "in your womb," seemingly useless and pleonastic, is unique in the entire Bible; it is the sign of a particular meaning, a sign which becomes still more clear when we note that it is found uniquely in these two adjacent texts (1:31; 2:21) both of which concern Mary: they announce precisely her virginal conception.

From the perspective of salvation history and theology, these two "linguistic facts" (retaining the verb "to conceive," but *with* the specification "in your womb") must have a double signification in the case of Mary: on the one hand, the use of the traditional verb "to conceive" commonly used for many other women, indicated for Mary also, the physical realism of a real *bodily* conception, not a mythical one as some would maintain (we are not dealing here with a theologoumenon). On the other hand, the expression "in your womb," added *for her alone*, reveals that this physical conception had to be entirely *within* ("in your womb"), without the previous penetration of any "masculine semen" coming from without. Such a totally interior conception would have to be accomplished by a real power, certainly, but a non-physical one; it obviously required a fecundating action, but a *spiritual* one. Moreover, our text thus prepared and anticipated verse 1:35 where it would be explained that the Holy Spirit would descend on Mary, to activate *in her*, that is to say "in the womb" of Mary, a real, but purely *interior* conception. Such a conception, without sexual contact, due to the "power of the Most High," must necessarily be a virginal conception.[37]

… The conclusion of all of this is that the evangelist, in verse 1:31, is rigorously inspired by the formulas of the biblical tradition, but by way of some truly *radical*

---

[37] "Et voici" 102 (my trans.).

modifications he succeeds already here in stating the Christian newness: the *virginal conception* of Mary and the imposition on her son of the *name of Jesus* will henceforth allow the world to understand the mystery of the Incarnation of the Son of God. And this woman who subsequently brings forth her son *Jesus* virginally into the world thus becomes the Mother of God.[38]

Now let us consider Luke 1:34, a text most crucial to our argument, in which Mary asks her question: "How shall this be since I do not know man?" Here is how John Paul II outlined the matter in his catechesis of July 24, 1996:

Such a query seems surprising, to say the least, if we call to mind the biblical accounts that relate the announcement of an extraordinary birth to a childless woman. Those cases concerned married women who were naturally sterile, to whom God gave the gift of a child through their normal conjugal life (1 Sam 1:19-20), in response to their anguished prayers (cf. Gen 15:2; 30:22-23; 1 Sam 1:10; Lk 1:13).

Mary received the angel's message in a different situation. She was not a married woman with problems of sterility; by a voluntary choice she intended to remain a virgin. Therefore, her intention of virginity, the fruit of her love for the Lord, appeared to be an obstacle to the motherhood announced to her.

At first sight, Mary's words would seem merely to express only her present state of virginity. ... Nevertheless, the context in which the question was asked: "How can this be?" and the affirmation that follows: "since I do not know man," emphasize both Mary's present virginity and her intention to remain a virgin. The expression she used, with the verb in the present tense, reveals the permanence and continuity of her state. ...

To some, Mary's words and intentions appear improbable since in the Jewish world virginity was

---

[38] "Et voici" 110 (my trans.).

considered neither a value nor an ideal to be pursued. The same Old Testament writings confirm this in several well-known episodes and expressions.[39]

This entire catechesis is strikingly incisive in its transmission of the Church's Tradition as well as in its grasp of the state of much modern scholarship on this question.[40] Interestingly, the Holy Father's brief analysis of Our Lady's declaration follows what I believe is still the classic and most complete analysis of the matter, that written by Father Geoffrey Graystone, S.M.[41]

The Pope continues with an explanation of Mary's resolve which indicates how the understanding of "full of grace" (κεχαριτωμένη)[42] has continued to develop under the guidance of the Holy Spirit in the Catholic Church:

> However, the extraordinary case of the Virgin of Nazareth must not lead us into the error of tying her inner dispositions completely to the mentality of her surroundings, thereby eliminating the uniqueness of the mystery that came to pass in her. In particular, we must not forget that, from the very beginning of her life, Mary received a wondrous grace, recognized by the angel at the moment of the Annunciation. "Full of grace" (Lk 1:28). Mary was enriched with a perfection of holiness that, according to the Church's interpretation, goes back to the very first moment of her existence. The unique privilege of the Immaculate Conception influences the whole development of the young woman of Nazareth's spiritual life.

---

[39] *Inseg* XIX/2 (1996) 103, 104 [*ORE* 1452:7; *MCat* 116, 117].
[40] Cf. *Birth* 298-309; *MNT* 114-126.
[41] *Virgin of All Virgins: The Interpretation of Luke 1:34* (Rome: Doctoral Dissertation presentation to the Pontifical Biblical Commission, 1968).
[42] Cf. Ignace de la Potterie, S.J., *Mary in the Mystery of the Covenant* trans. by Bertrand Buby, S.M. (New York: Alba House, 1992) [= *MMC*] 17-20. Cf. also Ignace de la Potterie, S.J., "Kecharitoméne en Lc 1,28: Étude philologique," *Biblica* 68 (1987) 357-382; "Kecharitoméne en Lc 1,28: Étude exégétique et théologique," *Biblica* 68 (1987) 480-508; Ernesto della Corte, "Kecharitoméne (Lc 1, 28) Crux interpretum," *Marianum* 52 (1990) 101-148.

Thus, it should be maintained that Mary was guided to the ideal of virginity by an exceptional inspiration of [the] Holy Spirit.[43]

Appropriately, in speaking of Mary's intention of virginity the Pope points to "the uniqueness of the mystery that came to pass" in Mary, and this as a direct consequence of her Immaculate Conception.

Obviously it took time, under the guidance of the Holy Spirit, for the Church as listener to the Word of God and teacher (*Ecclesia discens et docens*) to penetrate ever more deeply into the understanding of Mary's determination to remain a virgin and of her virginal marriage to Joseph. Once again, the Holy Father summarizes the development of this tradition beautifully in his catechesis of August 21, 1996:

> In presenting Mary as a "virgin," the Gospel of Luke adds that she was "betrothed to a man whose name was Joseph, of the house of David" (Lk 1:27). These two pieces of information at first sight seem contradictory. The Greek word used in this passage does not indicate the situation of a woman who has contracted marriage and therefore lives in the marital state, but that of betrothal. Unlike what occurs in modern cultures, however, the ancient Jewish custom of betrothal provided for a contract and normally had definitive value. It actually introduced the betrothed to the marital state, even if the marriage was brought to full completion only when the young man took the girl to his home.
>
> At the time of the Annunciation, Mary thus had the status of one betrothed. We can wonder why she would accept betrothal, since she had the intention of remaining a virgin forever. Luke is aware of this difficulty, but merely notes the situation without offering any explanation. The fact that the evangelist, while stressing Mary's intention of virginity, also presents her as Joseph's spouse is a sign of the historical reliability of the two pieces of information.
>
> It may be presumed that at the time of their betrothal there was an understanding between Joseph and Mary

---

[43] *Inseg* XIX/2 (1996) 105 [*ORE* 1452:7; *MCat* 118].

about the plan to live as a virgin. Moreover, the Holy Spirit, who had inspired Mary to choose virginity in view of the mystery of the Incarnation and who wanted the latter to come about in a family setting suited to the child's growth, was quite able to instill in Joseph the ideal of virginity as well.[44]

The seeming contradiction between Mary's disposition to remain a virgin and her betrothal to Joseph may cause endless difficulties for the "Higher Critics" and lead to strange hypotheses,[45] but it can also lead faithful Christians to an ever more profound appreciation of the multifaceted mystery of the Incarnation, as the Pope indicated. Indeed, as he subsequently affirmed:

> This type of marriage to which the Holy Spirit led Mary and Joseph can only be understood in the context of the saving plan and of a lofty spirituality. The concrete realization of the mystery of the Incarnation called for a virgin birth which would highlight the divine sonship and, at the same time, for a family that could provide for the normal development of the child's personality.[46]

---

[44] *Inseg* XIX/2 (1996) 214-215 [*ORE* 1455:7; *MCat* 127-128].

[45] Cf. *Birth* 303-309; *MNT* 114-115. Manuel Miguens, O.F.M., considers the biblical evidence in responding to Raymond Brown's provocative essay on "The Virginal Conception" in his *The Virgin Birth: An Evaluation of Scriptural Evidence* second edition (Boston: St. Paul Editions, 1981). It is only to be regretted that in the final section of the book he shows himself ready to accept a very "low" Christology.

[46] *Inseg* XIX/2 (1996) 215 [*ORE* 1455:7; *MCat* 128]. It will be noted that in the above citations the Holy Father speaks of Mary's intention of virginity, but not of an explicit "vow of virginity," terminology used consistently in the Church's great Tradition since St. Augustine. In his catechesis of August 7, 1996, however, the Holy Father pointed out that Our Lady's intention became the inspiration for all subsequent consecrated virginity. Cf. *Inseg* XIX/2 (1996) 150-153 [*ORE* 1454:7; *MCat* 123-126]. In consonance with the Tradition, I believe that a vow was not at all beyond the capacity of Our Lady and St. Joseph under the guidance of the Holy Spirit. Cf. Haffner 138.

The Mystery of the Virginal Birth

The words of the Holy Father cited above lead us appropriately to the mystery of the virgin birth which is described in this way in the *Catechism of the Catholic Church*:

> The deepening of faith in the virginal motherhood led the Church to confess Mary's real and perpetual virginity even in the act of giving birth to the Son of God made man. In fact, Christ's birth "did not diminish his Mother's virginal integrity but sanctified it."[47]

Tertullian (+c.200) put it succinctly: "It was necessary for the author of a new birth to be born in a new way."[48] Literally hundreds of similar illuminating statements such as this can be found throughout the entire Tradition.[49] Effectively, this new birth "without corruption" has always been understood to refer to the "birth of the Child without bodily lesion of the Mother, and absence of all pain and afterbirth."[50] In summarizing the patristic, scholastic, and more recent tradition on this matter, Father Saward states:

> According to the Church's Doctors, this freedom from corruption means that the God-man leaves his Mother's womb without opening it (*utero clauso vel obsignato*), without inflicting any injury to her bodily virginity (*sine violatione claustri virginalis*), and therefore without causing her any pain.[51]

Evidently the same questionable assumptions which undermine belief in the virginal conception are at work in this area as well,[52] with the

---

[47] CCC 499. Cf. *Lumen Gentium* 57 which likewise speaks of "the birth of Our Lord, who did not diminish his mother's virginal integrity but sanctified it."
[48] *Nove nasci debebat novæ nativitatis dedicator. De Carne Christi* 17, Corpus Christianorum Latinorum 2, 903.
[49] Cf. Saward 206-217; Haffner 150-156.
[50] Peter Damian Fehlner, *Virgin Mother: The Great Sign* (Washington, NJ: AMI Press, 1993) [= Fehlner] 1-2.
[51] Saward 206.
[52] Cf. Cardinal Leo Scheffczyk, *Maria, Crocevia della Fede Cattolica* trans. from German by Manfred Hauke (Lugano: Eupress, 2002) 88-90.

addition of a major challenge which emerged with the publication of Dr. Albert Mitterer's 1952 study *Dogma und Biologie* which questioned Our Lady's physical integrity and the absence of pain.[53] Mitterer's work and the discussion which it provoked resulted in a *monitum* issued by the Holy Office (now Congregation for the Doctrine of the Faith) stating that "theological works are being published in which the delicate question of Mary's virginity *in partu* is treated with a deplorable crudeness of expression and, what is more serious, in flagrant contradiction to the doctrinal tradition of the Church and to the sense of respect the faithful have" and thus prohibiting the publication of such dissertations in the future.[54] Unfortunately, this prohibition has been effectively ignored by many well-known theologians,[55] including the late Karl Rahner, S.J. (1904-1984).[56]

The Magisterium

The Church's Magisterium has been entirely consistent and unflagging in upholding belief in Mary's virginity in childbirth.[57] In commenting on the restatement of this article of faith made in *Lumen Gentium* 57, and subsequently quoted in the *Catechism of the Catholic Church* 499, Father Fehlner states:

> After the phrase "sanctified it" the Council appended references to indicate the precise sense in which virginal integrity at the time of Christ's birth is to be understood. Three references are given by the Council in note 10: to canon 3 of the Lateran Synod of 649, to the Dogmatic Tome of Saint Leo the Great to Flavian, and to the passage of Saint Ambrose in his work on the education of virgins. ...

---

[53] Cf. Perrella 9, 204-205, 215-216; Fehlner 1-4.

[54] Cf. *Ephemerides Mariologicæ* 11 (1961) 137-138; René Laurentin, *A Short Treatise on the Virgin Mary* trans. Charles Neumann, S.M. (Washington, NJ: AMI Press, 1991) [= *Treatise*] 328-329. Cf. also the commentary in Fehlner 19-21.

[55] Cf. Fehlner 2-4; Perrella 204-218.

[56] "Virginitas in Partu," *Theological Investigations* Vol. 4 (Baltimore: Helicon, 1966) 134-162. Cf. Haffner 157.

[57] Fehlner 6-20.

> From all the references which Vatican II might have chosen to illustrate the faith of the Church in Our Lady's virginal integrity at childbirth these three, utterly unequivocal, are found in the definitive text. No clearer indication could have been given that this mystery, inseparable from the Nativity of the Savior, is of crucial importance to faith as such. Even the slightest question or doubt about the reality of meaning of that mystery, whether it concerns the Mother or the Child, cannot be tolerated.[58]

In his discourse in Capua, Pope John Paul II noted a highly significant correlation with regard to patristic teaching on the *virginitas in partu* and the Resurrection, thus linking his Magisterium with the teaching of the Fathers:

> It is a well-known fact that some Church Fathers set up a significant parallel between the begetting of Christ *ex intacta Virgine* [from the untouched Virgin] and his Resurrection *ex intacto sepulcro* [from the intact sepulcher]. In the parallelism relative to the begetting of Christ, some Fathers put the emphasis on the virginal conception, others on the virgin birth, others on the subsequent perpetual virginity of the Mother, but they all testify to the conviction that between the two saving events—the generation-birth of Christ and his Resurrection from the dead—there exists an intrinsic connection which corresponds to a precise plan of God: a connection which the Church, led by the Spirit, has discovered, not created.[59]

How important it is to grasp in this case—as well as with regard to all that has been conveyed thus far—that, under the guidance of the Spirit, the Church receives and discovers the truth, but does not create it.

---

[58] Fehlner 21-22. Cf. *D-H* 503, 291, 294 [*TCF* 703, 609, 612]; *Patrologia Latina* [= *PL*] 16, 320. Fehlner omits mention of a reference also made in this footnote to the Council of Chalcedon, Mansi 7, 462.

[59] *AAS* 85 (1993) 665 [*ORE* 1244:13].

In that same discourse the Holy Father points out precisely how the insight into this correlation comes about:

> In adoring reflection on the mystery of the Incarnation of the Word, one discerns *a particularly important relationship between the beginning and the end of Christ's earthly life*, that is, between his virginal conception and his Resurrection from the dead, two truths which are closely connected with faith in Jesus' divinity.
>
> They belong to the deposit of faith; they are professed by the whole Church; and they have been expressly stated in the creeds. History shows that doubts or uncertainty about one has inevitable repercussions on the other, just as, on the contrary, humble and strong assent to one of them fosters the warm acceptance of the other.[60]

The Biblical Witness

Two very prominent Old Testament messianic texts point to the mystery of the virginal birth of Christ. The first occurs immediately after Genesis 3:15, known in the Tradition as the *Protoevangelium*, which speaks of the "woman," the "New Eve" through whom redemption will come.[61] In the following verse the Lord God addresses Eve stating "I will greatly multiply your pain in childbearing; in pain you shall bring forth children, yet your desire shall be for your husband, and he shall rule over you." Father Stefano Manelli's comment on these two verses is very insightful:

---

[60] *AAS* 85 (1993) 554-665 [*ORE* 1244:13]. In reflecting on this converging evidence (Cf. Perrella 222-226; Saward 237, 239-240) I cannot help but be struck by the juxtaposition of these same themes in the late Raymond E. Brown's controversial essays published together under the title of *The Virginal Conception & Bodily Resurrection of Jesus*, which raise questions about these truths of faith. Quite evidently there is a profound link between these complimentary mysteries which touch the beginning and end of Christ's earthly life. Those who treat them without "adoring reflection" and as expendable assumptions should not be surprised to arrive at a "shipwreck of the faith" (cf. 1 Tim. 2:19), or to lead others to it. Without any *anathema*, this is, nonetheless, the solemn warning of the Magisterium.

[61] Cf. the Pope John Paul II's catechesis of January 24, 1996, *Inseg* XIX/1 (1996) 115-117 [*ORE* 1426:11; *MCat* 61-63].

The two verses of Genesis 3:15 and 16, so sharply contrasting one another, make it psychologically impossible for them to refer to one and the same person. Immediately after having spoken so solemnly of how the "woman" with her "seed" is to triumph over the serpent, God speaks of how Eve must endure suffering and humiliation for the rest of her life. On what grounds is it possible to understand in each the same "woman"? Nor, similarly, can one, with any kind of consistency, suppose in the same person, Eve, a plan of life to unfold simultaneously under the sign of victory (Gen. 3:15) and the sign of subjection to suffering and man (Gen. 3:16).

Rather, the point of departure for the logical development of this powerful and fruitful *antithesis* between Eve and Mary, noted by the earliest Fathers, such as St. Justin and St. Irenaeus, and commented upon down the centuries since, is the reality of that contrast between Eve and the "woman" of Genesis 3:15.[62]

The Roman Catechism (also known as *The Catechism of the Council of Trent*) draws out the Marian implications of verse 16:

> To Eve it was said: "In pain you shall bring forth children" (Gen. 3:16). Mary was exempt from this law, for preserving her virginal integrity inviolate, she brought forth Jesus the Son of God, without experiencing, as we have already said, any sense of pain.[63]

With a genial intuition which can serve as a way of summarizing what we have just presented, Haymo of Halberstadt (+853) stated: "Just as she conceived without pleasure, so she gave birth without pain."[64]

---

[62] Stefano M. Manelli, F.I., *All Generations Shall Call Me Blessed: Biblical Mariology*, revised and enlarged second edition trans. by Peter Damian Fehlner, F.I. (New Bedford, MA: Academy of the Immaculate, 2005) [= Manelli] 26-27.

[63] Robert I. Bradley, S.J., and Eugene Kevane (eds.), *The Roman Catechism* (Boston, MA: St. Paul Editions, 1985) [= *Roman Catechism*] 50. Cf. also *Treatise* 64, 333, 338.

[64] *Expositio in Apocalypsim* 3, 12; *PL* 117:1081D-1082A [quoted in John Saward, *The Way of the Lamb: The Spirit of Childhood and the End of the Age* (Edinburgh: T&T

The other major Old Testament prediction which sheds light on the mystery of the virgin birth is that of Isaiah 7:14.[65] I believe that John Saward is right in stating that "Isaiah prophesied that the Mother of Emmanuel would be a virgin not only in conceiving him in the womb (*Ecce virgo concipiet*) but also in bringing him forth from the womb (*et virgo pariet*, cf. Is 7:14)."[66]

With regard to the gospel witness, one should not be surprised that the Holy Spirit might continue to bring to light treasures once known to the saints, as well as those which can be acquired by pondering in one's heart after the manner of the Virgin herself (cf. Lk 2:19, 51). In the light of the teaching of the Fathers, I find the reasoning of Ignace de la Potterie on the best translation of Luke 1:35b very cogent:

> We discover, however, since the time of the Fathers up to the present, four different versions. One either makes "*hagion*" ("holy") the subject and translates as Legrand does: "that is why *the holy* (child) who is to be born will be called Son of God"; or one makes of "*hagios*" an attribute of "will be," as in the Jerusalem Bible and the lectionary: "And so the child *will be holy* and will be called Son of God"; or one also reads "holy" an attribute of "called"; this latter is the translation recently proposed by A. Médebielle in his article "Annunciation" in the *Supplément au dictionnaire de la Bible*: "This is why the one to be born *will be called* holy, Son of God." These are the usual three translations. At the same time there is a fourth possibility which modern authors no longer think of, but which was very popular among the Fathers of the Church and during the Middle Ages. This reading, we think, is philologically the only one that is satisfactory; we then consider "holy," not as a complement of "will be" (this word is not found in the Greek text), nor of "will be called"; "holy" is rather to be taken as the complement of "will be born."

Clark, 1999) 153 (footnote 9).
[65] Cf. Manelli 38-53.
[66] Saward 208. Cf. also Saward 210 (footnote 123); Manelli 44-50.

The word "holy," in this instance, informs us about the *manner* in which the child will be born, that is to say in a "holy" manner. We therefore translate it so: "This is why *the one who will be born holy* will be called Son of God." Here it is not a question of the future holiness of Jesus: that is totally outside of the perspective of the Annunciation and of the birth of the child. The child of Mary "will be born holy" in the levitical meaning: it is the birth of Jesus that will be "holy," without blemish, intact, that is "pure" in the ritual sense. If we read the text in this way, we set up here a biblical argument favoring that which the theologians call "*virginitas in partu*," the virginity of Mary while giving birth. The message of the angel to Mary contains then not only the announcement of the virginal *conception*, but also of the virginal *birth* of Jesus.[67]

Father de la Potterie's years of patient study have yielded other fruit in this area as well, especially his extensive analysis of John 1:13. Here I can only hope to indicate some of the major components of his argument, referring the interested reader to de la Potterie's own exposition.[68] In effect, what he proposes is that this controverted verse of the prologue to St. John's Gospel should be translated thus:

He is not born of blood(s),
nor of the will of the flesh
nor of the will of man,
but *he was begotten of* God.[69]

In defending this translation as a reference to the virginal conception and birth of Christ, the first major objection to be overcome is that the Greek manuscripts of St. John's Gospel all give this text in the plural, as a reference to the children of God referred to in John 1.12: they "who were born, not of blood nor of the will of the flesh, nor of the will of man, but of God." Here is de la Potterie's response:

---

[67] *MMC* 31; cf. his entire treatment of this text in *MMC* 30-33 and also Saward 208.
[68] Cf. "Il parto verginale del Verbo incarnato: 'Non ex sanguinibus ... sed ex Deo natus est' (Gv 1,13)," *Marianum* 45 (1983) 127-174; *MMC* 96-122.
[69] *MMC* 98; cf. also 96.

Since the Greek manuscripts are fifty or one hundred years more recent, it is really too simple to want to relate to them, and ignore a period that precedes them. The reality is that *all* the texts from the second century witnessing to our passage have the singular. And in addition, it is interesting to notice that all these witnesses, when they are localized geographically, are not concentrated in one area, but are diffused all over the Mediterranean basin: in Asia Minor, most likely also in Palestine (Justin), at Rome (Hippolytus), in Gaul (Irenaeus), in Northern Africa (Tertullian), and at Alexandria in Egypt. That is a very important fact because it demonstrates that in the second century, during a time in which rapid means of communication did not yet exist, this text was universally read only in the singular. And this within one century of the composition of the fourth gospel.

We find that, for the first time, the plural form occurs only at the end of the second century; and these two or three witnesses are *all* concentrated at Alexandria in Egypt. One could conclude that the plural form took birth in this milieu, where the polemic battles with the Gnostics were in full force. ...

Tertullian maintains then that the Valentinians have falsified the text of John 1:13 in order to be able, after the fact, to base their Gnostic doctrine of the rebirth of the "Spirituals" or "Perfect" on it.

But then, obviously the question arises: how did it happen that the singular original form was lost? This is not easy to answer because there are very few traces available. However, we believe—and this remains partially a hypothesis—that the reason for the change is above all to be looked for in the fact that the earliest Church Fathers, who were still reading the text in the singular, did not know how to explain the first of three negatives in verse 13: "non ex sanguinibus."[70]

---

[70] *MMC* 99-101.

In explaining the original sense of "non ex sanguinibus" de la Potterie has recourse to the doctoral thesis of Peter Hofrichter,[71] who points out that

> in several texts of the Old Testament, and later in the Jewish tradition, the word "blood" is also used in the plural for the loss of blood which is linked with a women's period; that is with menstruation and childbirth, hence of a *birth*. The basic text for this is found in Leviticus 12:4-7.[72]
>
> What conclusion can we make from this text for the interpretation of the first negation in verse 13 of the prologue: "not born of blood(s)"? In the context for the laws of purification it signifies that Jesus, in being born, did not cause an *effusion of blood* in his mother; in other words, at the birth of Jesus there would not have been any ritual impurity in his mother because in her there would not have taken place any shedding of blood. There would then be here a scriptural indication for what the theologians have in mind when they speak of the *"virginitas in partu,"* the virginity of the birthing of Jesus.[73]

The author then goes on to cite the testimonies of Hippolytus, Ambrose, Jerome, John Damascene and Thomas Aquinas in support of his argumentation.[74] Quite evidently, it is this thesis of Ignace de la Potterie which Pope John Paul II had in mind in his Marian catechesis of July 10, 1996:

> This truth [of the virginal conception], according to a recent exegetical discovery, would be explicitly contained in verse 13 of the Prologue of John's Gospel, which some ancient authoritative authors (for example, Irenaeus and

---

[71] *Nicht aus Blut sondern monogen aus Gott geboren. Textkritische, dogmengeschichtliche und exegetische Untersuchung zu Joh 1, 13-14* (Würzburg: "Forschung zur Bible" 31, 1978).
[72] *MMC* 111.
[73] *MMC* 112.
[74] *MMC* 112-113. He cites even more authorities in his article "Il parto verginale del Verbo incarnato: 'Non ex sanguinibus ... sed ex Deo natus est' (Gv 1,13)," *Marianum* 45 (1983) 153-158.

Tertullian) present, not in the usual plural form, but in the singular: "He, who was born not of blood nor of the will of the flesh nor of the will of man, but of God." This version in the singular would make the Johannine Prologue one of the major attestations of Jesus' virginal conception, placed in the context of the mystery of the Incarnation.[75]

It should simply be pointed out that Father de la Potterie's "exegetical discovery" bears as much on the virginal birth as on the virginal conception, whereas the subject of the pope's catechesis of July 10, 1996 was the conception.

The Allegorical Sense of Scripture

Constraint of space does not allow for an exposition of the Fathers on this subject. Here I wish simply to underscore that much of the patristic treatment of the virginal conception and birth of Christ is based on what the *Catechism of the Catholic Church*, following the tradition, calls the allegorical sense of Scripture.[76] It is precisely the allegorical sense of Scripture which the *Roman Catechism* proposes with regard to our subject:

> Since the mysteries of this admirable conception and nativity are so great and so numerous, it accorded with divine providence to signify them by many types and prophecies. Hence the Fathers of the Church understood many things which we meet in the Sacred Scriptures to relate to them, particularly that gate of the Sanctuary which Ezekiel saw closed (see Ezek 44:2). … Likewise the bush which Moses saw burn without being consumed (see Ex 3.2).[77]

It is by means of this allegorical sense, as John Saward tells us:

> The Fathers find types of the virginity *in partu* in Ezekiel's prophecy of the closed gate of the Temple (cf.

---

[75] *Inseg* XIX/2 (1996) 76 [*ORE* 1450:11; *MCat* 113].
[76] *CCC* 115-118.
[77] *Roman Catechism* 50.

Ezek 44:2) and in the "garden enclosed" and "fountain sealed up" of Solomon's canticle (cf. Song 4:12). The reverence and modesty shown by the Fathers towards this beautiful mystery is in stark contrast with the prying crudeness of the heretics.[78]

Suffice it here to quote the monumental reference by Pope St. Leo I to Our Lady's virginity before, during, and after the birth of Christ: "It was decided by God's almighty power that Mary should conceive as a virgin, give birth as a virgin, and remain a virgin."[79]

The Mystery of Mary's Lifelong Virginity

This instinctive reverence and modesty of the Fathers of the Church regarding Our Lady's virginity effectively led them to intuit her virginal union with Joseph. In his catechesis of August 28, 1996, Pope John Paul II enumerated four facts in support of the Church's consistent belief in Mary's virginity *post partum*. Here are the first two:

> As regards her virginity after the birth, it must first of all be pointed out that there are no reasons for thinking that the will to remain a virgin, which Mary expressed at the moment of the Annunciation (cf. Lk 1:34) was then changed. Moreover, the immediate meaning of the words "Woman, behold your son!" "Behold your mother" (Jn 19:26), which Jesus addressed from the Cross to Mary and to his favorite disciple, imply that Mary had no other children.[80]

Father Saward supports the second of the Pope's arguments with this further affirmation:

> One of the signs of the perpetual virginity of Our Lady in Scripture is our Lord's entrusting of his Mother to the care of St. John. From Origen onwards, Catholic exegetes have argued that this shows that, after the death

---

[78] Saward 208. Cf. Saward passim 208-217. On Ezekiel 44:2, cf. Manelli 87-90.
[79] Sermo 22, 2; *PL* 54:195-196.
[80] *Inseg* XIX/2 (1996) 242 [*ORE* 1456:11; *MCat* 131].

of Joseph, there was no one else within the immediate family to look after Mary, and that she therefore conceived no child but Jesus.[81]

Here is it worth noting that Origen's date of death is given as 253[82] by Father Luigi Gambero, who also summarizes Origen's teaching on Mary's perpetual virginity.[83]

The third fact to which the Pope pointed meets a common objection:

> Those who deny her virginity after the birth thought they had found a convincing argument in the term "firstborn," attributed to Jesus in the Gospel (Lk 2:7), almost as though this word implied that Mary had borne other children after Jesus. But the word "firstborn" literally means "a child not preceded by another" and, in itself, makes no reference to the existence of other children. Moreover, the evangelist stressed this characteristic of the child since certain obligations proper to Jewish law were linked to the birth of the first-born son, independently of whether the Mother might have given birth to other children. Thus, every only son was subject to these prescriptions because he was "begotten first" (cf. Lk 2:23).[84]

The fourth fact adduced by the Pope meets an even more common objection:

> According to some, Mary's virginity after the birth is denied by the Gospel texts which record the existence of four "brothers of Jesus": James, Joseph, Simon and Judas (Mt 13:55-56; Mk 6:3) and of several sisters. It should be recalled that no specific term exists in Hebrew and Aramaic to express the word "cousin," and that the terms

---

[81] Saward 218.
[82] Luigi Gambero, S.M., *Mary and the Fathers of the Church: The Blessed Virgin Mary in Patristic Thought*, trans. Thomas Buffer (San Francisco: Ignatius Press, 1999) [= Gambero] 71.
[83] Cf. Gambero 75-77.
[84] *Inseg* XIX/2 (1996) 242-243 [*ORE* 1456:11; *MCat* 131-132]. Cf. Saward 224-225.

"brother" and "sister" therefore included several degrees of relationship. The phrase "brothers of Jesus" indicates "the children" of a Mary who was a disciple of Christ (cf. Mt 27:56) and who is significantly described as "the other Mary" (Mt 28:1). "They are close relations of Jesus, according to an Old Testament expression" (*CCC* 500).[85]

It is, indeed, precisely the argument about the "brothers of Jesus" which has been most frequently invoked to argue against Mary's perpetual virginity. Father Paul Haffner summarizes two major attacks on Mary's virginity after the birth of Jesus that evoked responses which are now part of the Church's doctrinal heritage:

> During the decade between 383 and 392 it became necessary to defend the doctrine of Mary's virginity *post partum*. The key antagonists in this struggle were primarily Helvidius and Bonosus. Helvidius did not make the tactical blunder of affirming that virginity is inferior to marriage and he did not appear to attack the Virgin Mary. He simply asserted that marriage and virginity are equal in honor, that Mary is doubly admirable for having been, in turn, virgin and mother of a family: virgin until the birth of Jesus, then mother of the brothers and sisters of Jesus spoken of is Scripture. St. Jerome defended the faith, and in the year 383 in his work *Adversus Helvidium* developed the thesis that virginity is superior to marriage; his key proof was that Mary would never have dreamed of relations with any man, no matter who. As witnesses to this doctrine, Jerome cited the Fathers Ignatius, Polycarp, Irenaeus, and Justin. For Jerome, the Lord's brethren are children not of Mary but of her sister.[86]
>
> The other adversary, Bonosus, bishop of Naissus ... proposed around the year 390 that Mary had had more than one child. St. Ambrose replied to this error. Adopting several Old Testament symbols of Mary's perpetual

---

[85] *Inseg* XIX/2 (1996) 243 [*ORE* 1456:11; *MCat* 132]. Cf. Saward 225-227.
[86] Haffner 161. For important texts from St. Jerome on this argument, cf. Gambero 205-212.

virginity like the "closed gate" of Ezekiel, the "enclosed garden" and "sealed fountain" of the Song of Songs, he explained the New Testament texts misinterpreted by Bonosus (Mt 1:18-25). The brothers of Jesus are not children of Mary; they may have been Joseph's. In any case, the term "brother" need not be interpreted in the literal modern sense of the word.[87]

One of the principal reasons for convening the regional Council of Capua in 392 was to deal with the error of Bonosus. Mary's perpetual virginity was reaffirmed and defended at this council, and it was precisely in commemoration of the sixteenth centenary of this council that the late Pope John Paul II visited Capua on May 24, 1992, and gave the discourse which I have frequently cited above. The interventions of Sts. Jerome and Ambrose proved definitive and eventually became part and parcel of the Church's teaching on Mary's perpetual virginity. Solemn form was given to this teaching at the Lateran Council held under Pope St. Martin I in 649, with the following canon:

> If anyone does not, according to the holy Fathers, confess truly and properly that holy Mary, ever virgin and immaculate, is Mother of God, since this latter age she conceived in true reality without human seed from the Holy Spirit, God the Word himself, who before the ages was born of God the Father, and gave birth to him without corruption, her virginity remaining equally inviolate after the birth, let him be condemned.[88]

This teaching has been consistently reiterated in successive magisterial declarations encapsulated in the phrase "Blessed Mary ever virgin,"[89] which we also recite in the *Confiteor* recited at Mass.

---

[87] Haffner 162. For major texts of St. Ambrose on this topic, cf. Gambero 190-193, 199-202.

[88] *D-H* 503 [*TCF* 703].

[89] Cf. the Second Council of Constantinople: *D-H* 422 [*TCF* 620/2]; the Fourth Lateran Council: *D-H* 801 [*TCF* 20]; the Second Council of Lyons: *D-H* 852 [*TCF* 23]. Unfortunately there are still those who continue in various ways to undermine the Church's perennial teaching on Mary's perpetual virginity, like Monsignor John P. Meier who, in his book *Jesus: A Marginal Jew*, states:

Concluding Considerations

Why is the Catholic Church's teaching about Mary's perpetual virginity important? First of all, it is important simply because it is the truth and, if received with reverence and faith, it will lead us to a deeper appreciation of the mystery of the Incarnation and the singular role which God assigned to the Mother of God. As the Fathers of the Second Vatican Council told us: "Having entered deeply into the history of salvation, Mary, in a way, unites in her person and re-echoes the most

---

> Nevertheless, if—prescinding from the faith and later Church teaching—the historian or exegete is asked to render a judgment on the NT and patristic texts we have examined, viewed simply as historical sources, the most probable opinion is that the brothers and sisters of Jesus were true siblings (John P. Meier, A Marginal Jew: Rethinking the Historical Jesus, Volume One: The Roots of the Problem and the Person (New York: Doubleday, 1991) 331. This text is cited in Messori 508-509, but his entire last chapter is devoted to the question of the "brothers of Jesus," which is remarkably well-handled; cf. Messori 507-528).

My first comment regards the patristic evidence. Tertullian did hold that the brothers of Jesus were born to Mary and Joseph after the birth of Jesus (Cf. Gambero 62-66), but his position was a minority position which did not prevail in the face of ongoing dogmatic development under the guidance of the Holy Spirit. As Father Haffner tells us, St. Hilary of Poitiers (+367), even before Sts. Jerome and Ambrose, "marked an important watershed in rejecting the errors of those who held that Mary had marital relations with Joseph after Jesus' birth; for Hilary these are 'irreligious individuals, utterly divorced from spiritual teaching'" (Haffner 160; cf. Gambero 184-185).

But, even more importantly, one must question the mentality which believes it possible to "prescind" from the faith and the Magisterium in order to render an opinion that those referred to as brothers and sisters of Jesus were other children of Mary. Here we may detect the same mindset of the late Raymond Brown, who wished effectively to distinguish between the faith and teaching of the Church and the "scientifically controllable evidence." I submit that this approach is not acceptable for a Catholic theologian because it implies that the faith may be at odds with what is "scientifically controllable," whereas in fact one is dealing here with the pseudo-science of Bultmann and his disciples. Further, such a position flies directly in the face of the guidelines which Pope John Paul II outlined at Capua regarding the theologian's task vis-à-vis the Church's teaching on Mary's perpetual virginity.

important doctrines of the faith."[90] The full truth about Mary provides an interpretive key to all Catholic doctrine. In his address at Capua, John Paul II insisted that the mystery of Mary's perpetual virginity "primarily concerns the *mysterium Christi* and the *mysterium Ecclesiae*."[91] Inaccurate teaching about Our Lady's virginity will have deleterious effects on the doctrine about Christ and the Church, whose model is Our Lady. History shows that denial of Our Lady's perpetual virginity has not infrequently led to denial of the divinity of Christ, as Cardinal Newman pointed out. At Capua John Paul II made a particular point of linking "*between the beginning and the end of Christ's earthly life*, that is, between his virginal conception and his Resurrection from the dead, two truths which are closely connected with faith in Jesus' divinity."[92]

Secondly, and as a corollary of the above, our ever-deeper penetration into the mystery of Mary's perpetual virginity will lead us to an ever-deeper veneration for her and, as the Fathers of the Council tell us: "When she is proclaimed and venerated, she prompts the faithful to come to her Son, to his sacrifice and to the love of the Father."[93] As John Paul II put it at Capua, genuine theological reflection on this truth of faith can become "a moment of doxology and latria."[94] Every truth about Mary is useful for leading us to Christ. *Ad Iesum per Mariam*.

Thirdly, our meditation on the mystery of Mary's perpetual virginity can also lead us to a deeper appreciation of the profound meaning of virginity, of which she stands out as an eminent and singular exemplar.[95] In his catechesis of August 7, 1996, Pope John Paul II beautifully drew out some of the most important implications:

> In short, the choice of the virginal state is motivated by full adherence to Christ. This is particularly obvious in Mary. Although before the Annunciation she was not conscious of it, the Holy Spirit inspired her virginal consecration in view of Christ. Mary remained a virgin to welcome the Messiah and Savior with her whole

---

[90] *Lumen Gentium* 65.
[91] *AAS* 85 (1993) 669 [*ORE* 1244:14].
[92] *AAS* 85 (1993) 665 [*ORE* 1244:13].
[93] *Lumen Gentium* 65.
[94] *AAS* 85 (1993) 664 [*ORE* 1244:13].
[95] *Lumen Gentium* 63.

being. The virginity begun in Mary thus reveals its own Christocentric dimension, essential also for virginity lived in the Church which finds its sublime model in the Mother of Christ. If her personal virginity, linked to the divine motherhood, remains an exceptional fact, it gives light and meaning to every gift of virginity.

How many young women in the Church's history, as they contemplated the nobility and beauty of the virginal heart of the Lord's Mother, have felt encouraged to respond generously to God's call by embracing the ideal of virginity! "Precisely such virginity," as I recalled in the Encyclical *Redemptoris Mater*, "after the example of the Virgin of Nazareth, is the source of a special spiritual fruitfulness: It is the source of motherhood in the Holy Spirit" (n. 43).

Mary's virginal life inspires in the entire Christian people esteem for the gift of virginity and the desire that it should increase in the Church as a sign of God's primacy over all reality and as a prophetic anticipation of the life to come.[96]

At Capua the Pope offered a further clarification, insisting that Mary's physical virginity [*virginitas carnis*] is a symbol of her virginity of heart [*virginitas cordis*]:

The integrity of the doctrine requires that holy Mary's *virginitas cordis* be highlighted with due emphasis. If, because of its symbolic values, *virginitas carnis* is important, the Mother of Jesus' *virginitas cordis* is even more so. In her condition as a virgin she is the New Eve, the true Daughter of Zion, the perfect disciple, the consummate icon of the Church. Therefore, she fulfils in herself the ideal of perfect adherence to God's plan, without compromise and without the defilement of falsehood or pride; the ideal of faithful fulfillment of the covenant, the violation of which on the part of Israel is compared to adultery by the prophets; the ideal of

---

[96] *Inseg* XIX/2 (1996) 152 [*ORE* 1454:7: *MCat* 125].

sincere acceptance of the Gospel message, in which the pure-hearted are called blest (cf. Mt 5:8) and virginity for the kingdom is extolled (cf. Mt 19:12); the ideal of rightly understanding the mystery of Christ—the *Truth par excellence* (cf. Jn 14:16)—and his doctrine, because of which the Church is also called virgin since she preserves the deposit of faith whole and incorrupt.

The Church has always taught that *virginitas carnis* has no value if falsehood and pride are nursed in the heart, if it lacks love.[97]

---

[97] *AAS* 85 (1993) 668-669 [*ORE* 1244:14].

The Assumption of Our Lady

Fr. Paul Haffner

In the Old Testament, there were some mysterious departures from this life. God granted a special privilege of not dying to Enoch and Elijah. The first case concerns Enoch, referred to in the book of Genesis: "Enoch walked with God, then was no more, because God took him" (Gen 5:24). The letter to the Hebrews furnishes more information: "It was because of his faith that Enoch was taken up and did not experience death: he was no more, because God took him; because before his assumption he was acknowledged to have pleased God" (Heb 11:5). Significantly, the word *assumption* is adopted.[1] Similarly, the passing of Elijah was extraordinary, since he did not die: "Now as they [Elijah and Elisha] walked on, talking as they went, a chariot of fire appeared and horses of fire coming between the two of them; and Elijah went up to heaven in the whirlwind" (2 Kings 2:11; Cf. Sir 48:9).

In the New Testament, the fate of the last generation who are present at the time of Christ's appearing in glory is sometimes considered to involve a kind of assumption. In two passages in the Pauline letters, the apostle points out that "we are not all going to die, but we shall all be changed" (1 Cor 15:51) and he affirms that "those who have died in Christ will be the first to rise and then those of us who are still alive will be taken up in the clouds, together with them to meet the Lord in the air" (1 Thess 4:16-17). The opinion that the last generation upon the face of the earth will not die is supported by Greek Fathers including St. Gregory of Nyssa and St. John Chrysostom and Latin Fathers including Tertullian and St. Jerome. The Creed follows the

---

[1] The expression used in Greek is *metatithemi*, which carries the sense of being transposed or carried over.

Scriptures by indicating that those who are alive at the Second Coming will not die, for it affirms that Christ will come to judge the *living* and the dead. However, this assumption of a last generation of believers is to be carefully distinguished from the notion of the "Rapture," current in some Protestant and Pentecostal thought.[2]

The Close of Mary's Earthly Life

Where Mary passed the last years of her life on earth is a matter for conjecture, although various traditions propose Ephesus or near Jerusalem as possibilities. Some apocryphal works dating from the second to the fourth centuries are all favorable to the Jerusalem tradition. The letter of Dionysius the Areopagite to the Bishop Titus (363), as well as the *Joannis liber de Dormitione Mariae* (third to fourth century), locate her tomb at Gethsemane. Historically these works have some value despite being apocryphal, since they echo a belief from earlier centuries. The indication of a tomb of the Virgin in the valley of Josaphat dated from about the fifth century, and this tomb became the object of pilgrimage and devotion.[3] St. John Damascene bears witness to a tradition that Our Lady passed from this world from Jerusalem: "Zion is the mother of churches in the whole world, who offered a resting-place to the Mother of God after her Son's Resurrection from the dead. In it, lastly, the Blessed Virgin was stretched on a small bed."[4] He indicated Gethsemane as the place of her Assumption: "Then they reached the most sacred Gethsemane, and once more there were embraces and prayers and panegyrics, hymns and tears, poured forth by sorrowful and loving hearts. They mingled a flood of weeping and sweating. And thus the immaculate body was laid in the tomb. Then it was assumed after three days to the heavenly

---

[2] See C.E. Olson, *Will Catholics Be Left Behind?* (San Francisco: Ignatius Press, 2003), which is a thorough critique of the popular Fundamentalist notion of the "Rapture"—the belief that Christians will be removed from earth prior to a time of tribulation and the Second Coming.

[3] This tradition can be seen for example in the Venerable Bede, *Liber de locis sacris* 2, 5 in *CSEL* 39, 309f.

[4] St. John Damascene, *Homily 2 on the Dormition of the Blessed Virgin*, 4 in *PG* 96, 730. St. Gregory of Tours; St. Sophronius, patriarch of Jerusalem; St. Germanus, patriarch of Constantinople; St. Andrew, bishop of Crete; and the Venerable Bede indicate this same tradition, common to East and West.

mansions."[5] Within this tradition, then, there are various opinions as to whether Mary's tomb was in the Garden of Olives or in the Valley of Josaphat. A pointer towards placing the tomb of Mary in Gethsemane is the basilica erected above the sacred spot, about the end of the fourth or the beginning of the fifth century. The present church was built in the same place in which the old edifice had stood.[6]

Another tradition posits the place of Mary's transition as being in Ephesus. There is no mention made in the Acts of the Council of Ephesus (431) of that city being the one chosen by God for Mary's last days. Only after that Council was there any firm indication placing her tomb in that city. Since St. John had lived in Ephesus and had been buried there,[7] it has been inferred that since he took Our Lady into his care after the death of the Lord, she could have lived there after Christ's Ascension, and then passed from this life in that town. Benedict XIV states that Mary followed St. John to Ephesus and died there. He intended also to remove from the Breviary those lessons which mention Mary's death in Jerusalem, but died before carrying out his intention.[8] Various private revelations indicate Ephesus as the place of Mary's passage from this life.[9]

The question then arises concerning the nature of her passing, and concretely whether she died or not. This issue examines whether she experienced the separation of the soul from the body. The dogma of the Assumption of the Mother of God leaves open the question of whether or not she died. A minority of theologians hold that she did not in fact suffer death. In the late fourth century, we find the earliest known, non-apocryphal mention of the close of Mary's life, in the writings of St. Epiphanius (315-403), bishop of Constantia, on the island of Cyprus:

---

[5] St. John Damascene, *Homily 2 on the Dormition of the Blessed Virgin*, 14 in *PG* 96, 739.
[6] See E.P. Le Camus, *Notre voyage aux pays bibliques*, (Paris: 1894), I, p. 253.
[7] See Eusebius, *Historia Ecclesiastica*, III, 31; V, 24, in *PG* 20, 280; 493.
[8] Cf. D. Arnaldi, *Super transitu Beatae Mariae Virginis Deiparae expertis omni labe culpae originalis dubia proposita* (Genuae: Montaldi, 1879), I, c. I.
[9] According to the meditations of Bl. Anne Catherine Emmerich (+1824), compiled and published in 1852, the Blessed Virgin died and was buried a few miles south of Ephesus. In Panaghia Kapoli, on a hill about nine or ten miles distant from Ephesus, the remains of a house were discovered, in which Mary is supposed to have lived, according to the indications given by Bl. Anne Catherine Emmerich in her life of the Blessed Virgin.

> Whether she died or was buried we do not know … Say she died a natural death. In that case she fell asleep in glory, and departed in purity, and received the crown of her virginity. Or say she was slain with the sword according to Simeon's prophecy. Then her glory is with the martyrs, and she through whom the divine light shone upon the world is in the place of bliss with her sacred body. Or say she left this world without dying, for God can do what he wills. Then she was simply transferred to eternal glory.[10]

St. Epiphanius genuinely may have not known, or else he was being careful not to play into the hands of certain contemporary heretics, the Antidicomarianites and the Collyridians. The former group denied the perpetual virginity of Mary; the latter, erring in the opposite direction, maintained that divine worship should be given to her. To claim that Our Lady died was to give possible fuel to the former heresy (for it was to suggest that the body of Mary was subject to the corruption of the tomb, and thus minimize her prerogatives); to assert that she did not die was to encourage the latter.[11] Around the same time, Timothy of Jerusalem affirmed that Mary did not die: "Wherefore the Virgin is immortal up to now, because he who dwelt in her, assumed her to the heavenly regions."[12]

St. Isidore of Seville (+636) appears to be the first to cast some doubt upon the fact of Mary's death: "Nowhere does one read of her death. Although, as some say, her sepulcher may be found in the valley of Josaphat."[13] Tusaredo, a bishop in the Asturias province of Spain in the eighth century, wrote: "Of the glorious Mary, no history teaches that she suffered martyrdom or any other kind of death."[14] In the early ninth century, Theodore Abou-Kurra likened the death of Mary to the sleep

---

[10] St. Epiphanius, *Adversus Octaginta Haereses* Book 3, Tome 2, Heresy 78, 11 and 24 in *PG* 42, 715-716 and 738.
[11] See G.M. Roschini, "Did Our Lady Die?" in *The Irish Ecclesiastical Record*, 80 (1953), pp. 75-76.
[12] Timothy of Jerusalem, *Homily on Simeon* in *PG* 86, 246-247.
[13] St. Isidore of Seville, *De ortu et obitu Patrum*, 67 in *PL* 83, 150.
[14] Tusaredo, *Epistola ad Ascaricum*, II in *PL* 99, 1239-1240.

of Adam in the Garden, when God formed Eve from one of his ribs.[15] This, obviously, was not a true death.

Most of the Fathers, however, reflecting on Mary's destiny and on her relationship with her divine Son, proposed that since Christ died, it would be difficult to maintain the contrary for his Mother. St. Augustine (354-430), who was not clear concerning the absence of original sin in Our Lady, stated baldly: "Mary, as a daughter of Adam died as a consequence of sin; Adam died because of sin, and the flesh of the Lord, born of Mary, died to destroy sin."[16] The Syriac Father, St. Jacob of Sarug (+521), wrote that when the time came for Mary "to walk the way of all generations," that is the way of death, "the group of the twelve apostles" gathered to bury "the virginal body of the blessed one."[17] St. Modestus of Jerusalem (+634), after a lengthy discussion of "the most blessed dormition of the most glorious Mother of God," ends his eulogy by exalting the miraculous intervention of Christ who "raised her from the tomb," to take her up with him in glory.[18] St John Damascene (+749) asks the basic question: "For how could she, who brought life to all, be under the dominion of death? But she obeys the law of her own Son, and inherits this chastisement as a daughter of the first Adam, since her Son, who is the life, did not refuse it. As the Mother of the living God, she goes through death to him."[19] St. Andrew of Crete (+740) also followed

---

[15] Theodore Abou-Kurra, *Opuscula*, op. 37 in *PG* 97, 1594.

[16] St. Augustine, *Enarratio in Psalmo 34*, 3 in *PL* 41, 501: "Maria ex Adam mortua propter peccatum, Adam mortuus propter peccatum, et caro Domini ex Maria mortua est propter delenda peccata."

[17] St. Jacob of Sarug, *Discourse on the burial of the Holy Mother of God*, 87-99 in *EM* 1493-1494. See also C. Vona, *Lateranum* 19 (1953), p. 188.

[18] St. Modestus of Jerusalem, *Encomium in dormitionem Deiparae semperque Virginis Mariae*, nn. 7 and 14 in *PG* 86 *bis*, 3293; 3311.

[19] St. John Damascene, *Homily 2 on the Dormition of the Blessed Virgin*, 2 in *PG* 96, 726. See also Idem, *Homily 1 on the Dormition of the Blessed Virgin*, 10 in *PG* 96, 714, where St. John Damascene asks: "Why is it that she who in giving birth surpassed all the limits of nature should now bend to its laws, and her immaculate body be subjected to death?" And he answers: "To be clothed in immortality, it is of course necessary that the mortal part be shed, since even the master of nature did not refuse the experience of death. Indeed, he died according to the flesh and by dying destroyed death; on corruption he bestowed incorruption and made death the source of resurrection."

the line of those who affirmed, with very little argumentation, that Mary died because her Son died.[20]

Many Fathers attest to the pious tradition that at least some of the apostles were present at Our Lady's passing from this world. In the East, St. John Damascene wrote:

> When the Ark of God [Mary], departing from Mount Zion for the heavenly country, was borne on the shoulders of the apostles, it was placed on the way in the tomb. First it was taken through the city, as a bride dazzling with spiritual radiance, and then carried to the sacred place of Gethsemane, angels overshadowing it with their wings, going before, accompanying, and following it, together with the whole assembly of the Church.[21]

In the West, St. Gregory of Tours (+593) wrote:

> When finally the Blessed Virgin had fulfilled the course of this life, and was now to be called out of this world, all the apostles were gathered together from each region to her house ... and behold the Lord Jesus came with his angels and, receiving her soul, entrusted it to the Archangel Michael and departed. At the break of day the apostles lifted the body with the couch and laid it in the sepulcher, and they guarded it awaiting the coming of the Lord. And behold the Lord again stood by them, and commanded that the holy body be taken up and borne on a cloud into paradise, where now, reunited with (her) soul and rejoicing with the elect, it enjoys the good things of eternity which shall never come to an end.[22]

Many of the great scholastics taught that Mary died, because they were unable to see how she remained free from original sin. St. Thomas, since he could not see how Our Lady was conceived without original sin,

---

[20] St. Andrew of Crete, *Oratio 12 in dormitione SS. Deiparae* in *PG* 97, 1051-1054.
[21] St. John Damascene, *Homily 2 on the Dormition of the Blessed Virgin*, 12 in *PG* 96, 738.
[22] St. Gregory of Tours, *De gloria beatorum martyrum*, 4 in *PL* 71, 708.

maintained the she suffered the consequences, and in particular, death.[23] St. Bonaventure wrote:

> If the Blessed Virgin was free from original sin, she was also exempt from the necessity of dying; therefore, either her death was an injustice or she died for the salvation of the human race. But the former supposition is blasphemous, implying that God is not just; and the latter, too, is a blasphemy against Christ for it implies that his redemption is insufficient. Both are therefore erroneous and impossible. Therefore Our Blessed Lady was subject to original sin.[24]

Most interestingly, this passage also connects the question of Mary's death with the role which she played in the redemption. Even those authors who accepted the doctrine of the Immaculate Conception did not always deduce that Mary would have remained without death. Even Bl. John Duns Scotus, who was clear on the Immaculate Conception, did not hold that Mary would have been exempted from death. For Scotus, the sentence of death is so general, that neither Christ nor Mary is an exception. The resurrection of the body is, for him, a victory over death, like that of Christ and his Mother.[25]

St. Alphonsus Liguori (1696-1787) held a nuanced position on Mary's death, pointing out that in one sense she should not have died, but in fact did die in order to be like her Son:

> Death being the punishment of sin, it would seem that the divine Mother all-holy, and exempt as she was from its slightest stain should also have been exempt from death, and from encountering the misfortunes to which the children of Adam, infected by the poison of sin, are subject. But God was pleased that Mary should in all things resemble Jesus; and as the Son died, it was

---

[23] See St. Thomas Aquinas, *Summa Theologiae* III, q.14, a.3.
[24] St. Bonaventure, *Commentarius in III Librum Sententiarum Petri Lombardi*, distinction 3, question 2, in *S. Bonaventurae Opera Omnia* (Collegio San Bonaventura: Quaracchi, 1888), vol. III, p.66.
[25] See Bl. John Duns Scotus, *Fragmenta*, in K. Balić (ed.) *Theologiae Marianae elementa* (Sibenik: Kacik, 1933), p. 172.

becoming that the Mother should also die; because, moreover, he wished to give the just an example of the precious death prepared for them, he willed that even the most Blessed Virgin should die, but by a sweet and happy death.[26]

In the seventeenth century, there was renewed interest in the question of Mary's death. An Italian theologian, Beverini, proposed that Mary did not die.[27] After 1854, once Pope Bl. Pius IX had defined the Immaculate Conception, the question of whether Our Blessed Lady died gradually became a subject of wide theological discussion. The impetus for further research, out of which arose the present state of dispute, was given by the writings of Dominic Arnaldi (+1895) of Genoa, who proposed that Our Blessed Lady's complete freedom from sin demanded her immunity from the penalty of death.[28] Later in the twentieth century, the clearest proponents of the thesis that Mary did not die were Roschini and Gallus.[29] Others like Bonnefoy were clear proponents of Mary's death: "the death of the Most Holy Virgin may be considered as historically proved and explicitly revealed: as such (explicitly revealed) it may be the subject of a dogmatic definition: there is no reason why it should not be."[30] John Henry Newman also held that Our Lady died, but it was a special kind of death:

> She, the Lily of Eden, who had always dwelt out of the sight of man, fittingly did she die in the garden's shade, and amid the sweet flowers in which she had lived. Her departure made no noise in the world ... Pilgrims

---

[26] St. Alphonsus Liguori, "Discourse VII. Of the Assumption of the Blessed Virgin Mary" in *The Glories of Mary* (Rockford, Illinois: Tan, 1977), p. 371.

[27] B. Beverini, *De corporali morte Deiparae* (Roma: Academia Mariana, 1950). This work was republished in 1950, under the editorship of K. Balić.

[28] D. Arnaldi, *Super transitu Beatae Mariae Virginis Deiparae expertis omni labe culpae originalis dubia proposita* (Genoa: Montaldum, 1879).

[29] G.M. Roschini, "Il problema della morte di Maria SS. dopo la Costituzione Dogmatica *Munificentissimus Deus*" in *Marianum* 13 (1951), pp. 148-163; T. Gallus, *La Vergine Immortale* (Roma: 1949).

[30] J.F. Bonnefoy, "Définibilité de l'Assomption" in *Congrès Marial du Puy-en-Velay* (Paris: 1950), p. 241; cf. Idem, "La Bulle Dogmatique *Munificentissimus Deus* (November 1, 1950)" in *Ephemerides Mariologicae* 1 (1951), pp. 104-114.

went to and fro; they sought for her relics, but they found them not; did she die at Ephesus? or did she die at Jerusalem? reports varied; but her tomb could not be pointed out, or if it was found, it was open; and instead of her pure and fragrant body, there was a growth of lilies from the earth which she had touched.[31]

Pope John Paul II has come closest to addressing the issue, and he inclined in favor of Mary's participation in death: "The fact that the Church proclaims Mary free from original sin by a unique divine privilege does not lead to the conclusion that she also received physical immortality. The Mother is not superior to the Son who underwent death, giving it a new meaning and changing it into a means of salvation."[32] The Pope went on to ask: "Could Mary of Nazareth have experienced the drama of death in her own flesh?" His response is that reflecting on Mary's destiny and her relationship with her divine Son, "it seems legitimate to answer in the affirmative: since Christ died, it would be difficult to maintain the contrary for his Mother. ... Involved in Christ's redemptive work and associated in his saving sacrifice, Mary was able to share in his suffering and death for the sake of humanity's redemption."[33] Clearly the Pope did not wish to close the question, but indicated the theological weight in favor of the position that Mary participated somehow in death's mystery.

There are two basic reasons in favor of the position that our Blessed Mother actually died. First, that of conformity to Christ. The condition of the Mother should not be better than that of her divine Son. As the Mother of the passible and mortal Redeemer from whom he took his mortal flesh, Mary, too, had to be passible and mortal. This argument seems *post factum*, proposing to explain the fact of Mary's death once that death had been taken for granted. The Second Council of Orange is quite explicit in its teaching that those who hold that the penalty of death is transmitted to the body without the transmission of sin, or the death of the soul, to all the children of Adam, do an injustice to God.[34]

---

[31] J.H. Newman, *Sermon for the Assumption*, 1849 in Idem, *Discourses to Mixed Congregations* (London: Longmans, Green, and Co., 1906), p. 373.

[32] Pope John Paul II, *Discourse at General Audience* (June 25, 1997), 3.

[33] *Ibid.*, 2 and 3.

[34] See Second Council of Orange, canon 2 in DS 372.

Hence, where there is no sin there can be no mandatory death of the body in a child of Adam. A second reason favoring Mary's death would involve voluntary acceptance on her part. Some theologians locate this within the framework of Mary's role of Co-redemptrix of the human race. They would maintain that Mary died, though she had a right to immortality. She, like her Son, freely accepted death in order that she might coredeem the human race together with him. Yet, the objection can then be put that Mary should then have died on Calvary with Christ.

Contrary to the proposition that Mary died, one could say that it seems strange that she should have enjoyed any lesser privilege than Elijah or Enoch from the Old Testament, who seemingly did not die. Moreover, it could be argued that she enjoyed the first fruits of Christ's Resurrection and Ascension, in such a way that she did not die. Furthermore, one may apply to her the words of Jesus to his disciples: "For the Father loves the Son and shows him everything he himself does, and he will show him even *greater things than these*, works that will astonish you. Thus, as the Father raises the dead and gives them life, so the Son gives life to anyone he chooses" (Jn 5:20-21).

Since all theologians are agreed, at least after the definition of the doctrine of the Immaculate Conception, that Mary cannot have died as a penalty for sin, the issue remains as to what was the cause of death. It is clear that she cannot have simply died of illness, a consequence of old age. Neither would she have died of old age, as this is also connected with original sin. Also, a minority thesis that she suffered martyrdom, based on a misinterpretation of the prophecy of Simeon (Lk 2:35), has long since been rejected, among others by St. Ambrose: "Neither the letter [of Scripture] nor history, teach us that Mary departed this life after having been assassinated; whereby not the soul but the body was pierced by a material sword."[35] That leaves various other opinions. One is that she voluntarily gave up her privilege of immortality, in order to be more like her Son. Another position is that she died of sorrow in the aftermath of having seen her Son crucified.[36] Perhaps the soundest approach would be to say, along with St. Francis de Sales, that Mary's death was due to

---

[35] St. Ambrose, *Expositio Evangelii secundum Lucam*, Book 2, chapter 2, 61 in *PL* 15, 1574: "Nec littera, nec historia docet ex hac vita Mariam corporalis necis passione migrasse; non enim anima, sed corpus materiali gladio transverberatur."

[36] This line was taken by St. Peter Damian, *De celebrandis vigiliis*, 1 in *PL* 145, 801.

a transport of love.[37] He pointed out that as Christ's Mother lived her Son's life, she also died her Son's death:

> The Virgin-Mother, having collected in her spirit all the most beloved mysteries of the life and death of her Son by a most lively and continual memory of them, and withal, ever receiving directly the most ardent inspirations which her Child, the sun of justice, has cast upon human beings in the highest noon of his charity; and besides, making on her part also, a perpetual movement of contemplation, at length the sacred fire of this divine love consumed her entirely as a holocaust of sweetness, so that she died thereof, the soul being wholly ravished and transported into the arms of the dilection of her Son.[38]

The saint also explained that this death was not violent, but rather her "death was more sweet than could be imagined, her Son sweetly drawing her after the odor of his perfumes, and she most lovingly flowing out after their sacred sweetness even into the bosom of her Son's goodness."[39]

Finally, it should be remarked that however one conceives of the end of Mary's life, namely whether Mary died or not, she was not subject to the *law of death*, which is the corruption of the body in the grave. If she died, then she was assumed into heaven before her sacred body saw corruption. For, so long as the bodies of the just remain in the dust of the earth, they are under the dominion of death, and they sigh for the ultimate redemption of their bodies.

The Assumption: Development Towards the Dogma

Pope Pius XII, in his *Apostolic Constitution Munificentissimus Deus* that dogmatically defined the Assumption, refers to the *Protoevangelium*, Genesis 3:15, as a prophecy of Mary's victory over sin and death. The New Vulgate (1979) offers this translation: "I shall put enmity between

---

[37] This was the line taken by Pope John Paul II in his *Discourse at General Audience* (June 25, 1997), 4.
[38] St. Francis de Sales, *Treatise on the Love of God*, book 7, chapter 13.
[39] St. Francis de Sales, *Treatise on the Love of God*, book 7, chapter 14. He added (13. 24) that "love at the Cross gave her the supreme sorrows of death. So it was right that finally death should give her the sovereign pleasure of love."

you and the woman, and between your offspring and hers; it will bruise your head and you will strike its heel" (Gen 3:15). This rendering, based on the Vulgate, appears to differ in two respects from the original Hebrew text. First, the Hebrew text employs the same verb for the two renderings, "it will bruise or crush" and "you will strike," while the Greek Septuagint renders the verb both times by the expression "to strike." Some translators, like St. Jerome, interpret the Hebrew verb by expressions which mean to crush or to bruise, rather than to strike or to lie in wait.[40] Nevertheless, in his Latin Vulgate translation, he employed the verb "to crush" (*conterere*) in the first place, and "to lie in wait" (*insidiari*) in the second. Hence the punishment inflicted on the serpent and the serpent's retaliation are expressed by the same Hebrew verb: but in the Vulgate the wound of the serpent is mortal, since it affects his head, while the wound inflicted by the serpent is not mortal, being inflicted on the heel.

The second point of difference between the Hebrew text and the Greek and Latin versions concerns the agent who is to inflict the mortal wound on the serpent. The Hebrew text reads *hu'* (*autos*, *ipse*) which refers to the seed of the woman. "It" refers to the offspring, which is masculine in Hebrew, and Christian tradition has referred this to Christ.[41] The human race is thus opposed to the Devil and his "seed," and a hint is given of humanity's ultimate victory, in a first glimpse of salvation; hence the passage is referred to as the *Protoevangelium*. The Greek version has a masculine pronoun, which ascribes the victory to one of the woman's descendants in particular, rather than just the offspring in general. This allusion to Christ is consonant with the Messianic interpretation of many Fathers of the Church. The Vulgate reads "she" (*ipsa*), which refers to a woman. Thus, according to the Vulgate reading, the woman herself will win the victory; according to the Hebrew text, she will be victorious through her offspring, rendered by "it." In the author's opinion, the reading "she" (*ipsa*) is neither an intentional corruption of the original text, nor is it an accidental error; it is rather an explanatory version

---

[40] See St. Jerome, *Hebraicae quaestiones in Genesim* in *PL* 23, 943.
[41] See R.J. Clifford and R.E. Murphy, "Genesis" in R.E. Brown, J.A. Fitzmeyer, R.E. Murphy, *The New Jerome Biblical Commentary* (Englewood Cliffs, N.J: Prentice-Hall, 2000), p. 12.

expressing explicitly the fact of Our Lady's part in the victory over the serpent, which is contained implicitly in the Hebrew original.[42]

As is quite commonly admitted, the divine judgment is directed not only against the serpent as the originator of sin, but also against the seed of the serpent, denoting its followers, the "brood of vipers," the "generation of vipers," those whose father is the Devil, the children of evil.[43] One may understand the offspring or seed of the woman in a similar collective sense, as embracing all who are born of God. However, seed often denotes a particular person in biblical theology, if the context allows it. St. Paul gives this explanation of the word offspring or "progeny" as it occurs in the patriarchal promises: "Now the promises were addressed to Abraham and to his progeny. The words were not 'and to his progenies' in the plural, but in the singular, 'and to your progeny,' which means Christ" (Gal 3:16). Finally the expression "the woman" in the clause "I will put enmity between you and the woman" is a literal version of the Hebrew text. Peculiar to the Hebrew language is the use of the article in a sentence to indicate a person or thing which is not yet known, but may possibly be described more clearly later, either as present or as to be taken into account within the context.[44] Since our indefinite article serves this purpose, we may translate: "I will put enmity between you and a woman." Hence the prophecy promises a woman, Our Blessed Lady, who will be the enemy of the serpent to a marked degree; besides, the same woman will be victorious over the Devil, at least through her offspring. The completeness of the victory is emphasized by the contextual phrase "on dust you will feed as long as you live" (Gen 3:14), which is a common old Near-Eastern expression denoting the deepest humiliation.[45]

---

[42] For other interpretations of Genesis 3:15 and justification for "ipsa" (She) as the most accurate and appropriate translations, cf. S.M. Manelli, *All Generations Shall Call Me Blessed: Biblical Mariology* (New Bedford, MA: Academy of the Immaculate, 2005), T.M. Sennott, *The Woman of Genesis* (Cambridge, MA: The Ravengate Press, 1984) – Ed. Note.

[43] Cf. Wis 2:25; Mt 3:7; 23:33; Jn 8:44; 1 Jn 3:8-12.

[44] See F.H.W. Gesenius and E. Kautzsch, *Hebräische Grammatik* (Leipzig: F.C.W. Vogel, 1909), p. 402.

[45] Cf. A. Jeremias, *Das Alte Testament im Lichte des alten Orients* (Leipzig: J.C. Hinrichs, 1916), p. 216. See also St. Justin, *Dialogue with Trypho*, 100 in *PG* 6, 712; St. Irenaeus, *Adversus haereses*, III, 23 in *PG* 7, 964; St. Epiphanius, *Haereses*, III, 2, 18 in *PG* 42, 729.

That nothing is found explicitly in the New Testament about Our Lady's Assumption is not surprising, since it is possible that much of it may have been composed before the event. This is clearly a matter of conjecture, especially if many of the apostles were present at her Dormition, as several Fathers propose. No isolated text of the New Testament explicitly affirms the doctrine of the Assumption. However, the Church does not read the Word of God as segmented texts of Scripture alone, but in its fullness in relation to the whole deposit of Revelation as it is also expressed in Tradition.[46] The Church's Tradition shows that Mary's Assumption was at least implicitly revealed. It is false to maintain, along with the rationalists, that the later tradition of the Church expressing belief in the Assumption is an outgrowth of the apocrypha.[47] A concrete indication of belief in the Assumption of Mary is found in the fact that the Church has never looked for the bodily relics of the Blessed Virgin, nor proposed them for veneration.[48] It is probable that the revelation made to the apostles, or to one of them, was even explicit, since otherwise it is difficult to explain the universal tradition of Mary's Assumption in the East and the West from the seventh century at the latest, which is also expressed in the liturgical celebration of the Feast.[49] Nevertheless, "the liturgy of the Church does not engender the Catholic faith, but rather springs from it, in such a way that the practices of the sacred worship proceed from the faith as the fruit comes from the tree."[50]

---

[46] See Vatican II, *Dei Verbum*, 9: "For Sacred Scripture is the Word of God inasmuch as it is consigned to writing under the inspiration of the divine Spirit, while Sacred Tradition takes the Word of God entrusted by Christ the Lord and the Holy Spirit to the apostles, and hands it on to their successors in its full purity, so that led by the light of the Spirit of truth, they may in proclaiming it preserve this Word of God faithfully, explain it, and make it more widely known. Consequently it is not from Sacred Scripture alone that the Church draws her certainty about everything which has been revealed. Therefore both Sacred Tradition and Sacred Scripture are to be accepted and venerated with the same sense of loyalty and reverence." See also Council of Trent, session IV, *Decree on Scriptural Canons* in DS 1501.

[47] For the rationalist position see, for example, E. Renan, *L'Eglise Chrétienne*, in *Histoire des origines du Christianisme*, Vol. 6 (Paris: 1879) p. 513; C. Tischendorf, *Apocalypses Apocryphae* (Leipzig: 1866), p. 34.

[48] See St. Bernardine of Siena, *In Assumptione B. Mariae Virginis,* Sermo 11.

[49] See R. Garrigou-Lagrange, *The Mother of the Saviour and Our Interior Life* (Dublin: Golden Eagle Books, 1948), pp. 164-165.

[50] Pope Pius XII, Apostolic Constitution *Munificentissimus Deus*, 20.

The feast of the Assumption began its life in the East, as did many of the older Marian feasts. At first, Mary was implicitly honored in her Assumption by a celebration known as *The Memory of Mary*, the celebration of which began in the East around the fourth century. Honor was given to Mary's Assumption here because the Church intended to celebrate the "birthday" of Mary, or her entrance into heaven. Later, *The Memory of Mary* liturgy was changed and became the feast of the *Dormitio*, or the "Falling to Sleep" of the Blessed Mother. The feast of the *Dormitio*, or *Koimesis*, celebrated as its object the death, resurrection, and Assumption of the Blessed Mother, and was widely established in the East by the end of the fourth century.

The fact that the feast was even kept by the churches separated from the Catholic Church is an indication of how early the tradition flourished. The Nestorian Churches separated very early from the Catholic Church (after the Council of Ephesus, in 439) and introduced the feast later, under the title of the death or *transitus* of Mary. As regards the *transitus*, normally it was held that Mary remained incorrupt after her death, and that her body awaited the resurrection. The Monophysite Churches marked the 15th of August with a special celebration dating from the patristic period. These churches rejected the Council of Chalcedon in 451, and include the Coptic Church in Egypt today, with a related church in Ethiopia, and the so-called Jacobite Church of Syria, with most of its adherents in South India. However, their theology is far from uniform. While some taught the death and resurrection of Mary, others held that her body remained incorrupt somewhere, awaiting her resurrection from the dead. The Coptic Church normally followed the doctrine of Theodosius, the Monophysite patriarch of Alexandria (+567), and celebrated a double feast, the death of Mary on January 16th, and her glorious resurrection on the 9th of August, 216 days later. Now, since the monks of Gaul adopted many customs from the Egyptian monks this feast is found celebrated in January in sixth-century Gaul. The Gallican Liturgy has it on the 18th of January, under the title: *Depositio, Assumptio, or Festivitas S. Mariae*.[51] This custom was kept up in the Gallican Church to the time of the introduction of the Roman rite.

In the Greek Church, it seems, some kept this feast in January, with the monks of Egypt; others in August, with those of Palestine.

---

[51] See Mabillon, *Notes on the Gallican Liturgy* in *PL* 72, 180.

Uniformity was brought about by the Emperor Maurice (582-602), who ordered that the feast be set for the whole Byzantine Empire on August 15.[52] It is important to note that the emperor did not establish the feast but merely fixed the date of an already well-established event. The earliest witness to the existence of the feast in the West seems to be the Gospel Lectionary of Wurzburg (c. 650) in which the feast for August 15 is found to be *Natale Sanctae Mariae*.[53] Then Pope Sergius I (687-701) decreed that on the feast of the Dormition (as well as on the Annunciation and the Nativity of our Blessed Mother) there should be a procession from the church of St. Adrian to the church of St. Mary Major. Most likely it was this same pope who introduced the feast of the Dormition into the Roman calendar. Pope Sergius was a Syrian by birth, and so was well acquainted with the feast from his homeland. After Pope Sergius introduced the feast into Rome, thereafter it spread rapidly throughout Western Europe. The name of the feast was changed from the *Dormition* to the *Assumption of St. Mary* in the eighth century, probably at the behest of Pope Hadrian I.

There are early glimpses within patristic tradition that Mary's body is incorruptible. St. Hippolytus (172-235) associated the Ark of the Covenant of the book of Revelation (Rev 11:19) with Mary's incorruptible flesh from which Christ's flesh was taken: "Now the Lord was without sin, being in his human nature from incorruptible wood, that is, from the Virgin, and being sheathed inwardly as it were with the pure gold of the Word and by the Spirit outwardly."[54] The earliest clear mention of the doctrine of the Assumption dates from the second half of the sixth century, in a homily preached by Bishop Theoteknos of Livias, in Palestine.[55] Theoteknos spoke as though the doctrine were commonplace, and he affirmed several times that Mary's body was raised

---

[52] Nicephorus Callistus, *Historia Ecclesiastica*, 18, 18, in *PG* 147, 292.

[53] Cf. C. Lee, "The Feast of the Assumption of the Blessed Virgin Mary," in *The Irish Ecclesiastical Record*, 54 (1939), p. 177.

[54] St. Hippolytus, *Sermonum Fragmentum* quoted by Theodoret, *Dialogue I* in *EM* 118. See also Ps 132:8: "Go up, Lord, to the place of your rest, you and the ark of your strength."

[55] Theoteknos, bishop of Livias, Encomium in Assumptionem Beatae Mariae Virginis in A. Wenger, *L Assomption de la Très Sainte Vierge dans la tradition byzantine du VIe au Xe siècle* (Paris: Institut Français d Etudes Byzantines, 1955), pp. 272-291.

to the heavens with her soul.[56] The homily describes how Christ, having ascended into heaven, gathered all the saints round the immaculate and pure Virgin. Mary, because of her exalted position, was to receive more than all the other saints: "She found what Eve lost. She found what Adam had forfeited through his disobedience."[57] Theoteknos recalled the special privileges traditionally accorded to Enoch and Elijah of escaping the normal deathly end of human life, and declared that Mary's end must be more privileged than theirs: "How much more then, will he glorify in body and soul the one who has been his Mother according to the flesh! In truth he has glorified her, and he will glorify her still."[58] Theoteknos propounded the sound principle that the Son cannot forsake his Mother, and the Mother in her mystery cannot be separated from her Son. Significantly, Theoteknos makes much of the link between Mary's being *Theotókos* (God-bearer) and her bodily Assumption:

> For it was fitting that the holy one who begot him should see her Son upon a high throne, raised above all, and should see every knee bend before him of those above the earth and of those upon the earth, and every tongue confess him that will judge the living and the dead. ... It was fitting ... that her all-holy body, her God-bearing body, godlike, undefiled, shining with the divine light and full of glory, should be carried by the apostles in company of the angels, and, after being placed for a short while in the earth, should be raised up to heaven in glory with her soul so loved by God.[59]

Another very rich theological argument was the Trinitarian perspective furnished by Theoteknos: "For, she, the holy one, pleased God the Father. She, the Virgin, pleased the subsistent Word born of the

---

[56] Theoteknos, *Encomium*, 9, 10, 15, 36.
[57] Ibid., 25
[58] Ibid., 17. See also, as a New Testament example of how people shared in Christ's Resurrection, Mt 27:52-53, which describes how, after Christ's death, the tombs opened and the bodies of many holy people rose from the dead, and these, after his Resurrection, came out of the tombs, entered the holy city and appeared to a number of people. Mary's privilege must clearly be greater than this.
[59] Ibid., 8-9.

Father from all eternity. She, the Virgin, pleased the life-giving Spirit, the enlightener of all, who fashions all the citizens of heaven."[60]

The chief patristic witnesses to the doctrine of the Assumption are to be found in the seventh and eight centuries, when theological reflection on this theme became ripe. However, it is clear that before then there was much written by figures like Gregory of Tours, whom we have cited above. The aspect of the incorruptibility of Mary's body was stressed by St. Modestus of Jerusalem (+634): "As the most glorious Mother of Christ, our Savior and our God and the giver of life and immortality, has been endowed with life by him, she has received an eternal incorruptibility of the body together with him who has raised her up from the tomb and has taken her up to himself in a way known only to him."[61]

St. Germanus of Constantinople (+733) argued, from the great dignity of the divine maternity and the holiness of her virginal body, to the fact of the Assumption of Mary: "You are she who, as it is written, appears in beauty, and your virginal body is all-holy, all-chaste, entirely the dwelling place of God, so that it is henceforth completely exempt from all dissolution into dust. Though still human, it is changed into the heavenly life of incorruptibility, truly living and glorious, undamaged and sharing in perfect life."[62] St. Andrew of Crete (+740) dedicated three beautiful homilies to the Dormition of Our Lady, which are rich in doctrine and devotion. For him the Dormition is a consequence of the redemptive Incarnation, in which the physical nature of the mystery is highlighted:

> For look, all of you who hear my words, look at what is now before our eyes: the Queen of the nations—I mean the Church of the faithful—today leads the solemn procession for the Queen of our race, who today is received royally into the Kingdom of Heaven by God, the King who rules over all. The Church brings in tribute today her most beautiful and festive possessions.

---

[60] *Ibid.*, 12.
[61] St. Modestus of Jerusalem, *Encomium in dormitionem Sanctissimae Dominae nostrae Deiparae semperque Virginis Mariae*, 14 in *PG* 86-II, 3306.
[62] St. Germanus of Constantinople, *In Sanctae Dei Genitricis dormitionem sermo I* in *PG* 98, 346.

> She who turned dust into heaven today strips the dust away, lays aside the veil of this world of change and gives back to the earth what belongs to it.[63]

St. John Damascene linked and compared the bodily Assumption of the Blessed Virgin with her other prerogatives and privileges:

> It was fitting that she, who had kept her virginity intact in childbirth, should keep her own body free from all corruption even after death. It was fitting that she, who had carried the Creator as a child at her breast, should dwell in the divine tabernacles. It was fitting that the spouse, whom the Father had taken to himself, should live in the divine mansions. It was fitting that she, who had seen her Son upon the Cross and who had thereby received into her heart the sword of sorrow which she had escaped in the act of giving birth to him, should look upon him as he sits with the Father. It was fitting that God's Mother should possess what belongs to her Son, and that she should be honored by every creature as the Mother and the Handmaid of God.[64]

During the Middle Ages, many saints and doctors further developed the doctrine concerning Mary's glorious assumption. St. Anthony of Padua reflected, like early writers, on the Ark of the Covenant as the prefiguration of the mystery of Mary, mentioned in Psalm 132: "Go up, Lord, to the place of your rest, you and the ark of your strength." He illustrated that just as Jesus Christ has risen from the death over which he triumphed, and has ascended to the right hand of the Father, so likewise the ark of his sanctification "has risen up, since on this day the Virgin Mother has been taken up to her heavenly dwelling."[65] St. Albert the Great confirmed a long-standing tradition of belief in the mystery of Mary's Assumption: "From these proofs and authorities and

---

[63] St. Andrew of Crete, *Oratio 2 in Beatae Mariae Virginis Dormitionem*, in *PG* 97, 1081.

[64] St. John Damascene, *Encomium in dormitionem Dei Genitricis semperque Virginis Mariae*, homily 2, n. 14 in *PG* 96, 741.

[65] St. Anthony of Padua, *Sermones Dominicales et in Solemnitatibus, In Assumptione S. Mariae Virginis Sermo*.

from many others, it is manifest that the most Blessed Mother of God has been assumed above the choirs of angels. And this we believe in every way to be true."[66] St. Thomas Aquinas never developed the theology of the Assumption in detail, but always held that Mary's body had been assumed into heaven along with her soul.[67] St. Bonaventure is part of the same chorus of belief. He considered it as entirely certain that, as God had preserved the most holy Virgin Mary from the violation of her virginal purity and integrity in conceiving and in childbirth, he would never have permitted her body to have dissolved into dust and ashes.[68] Further he argued, in a modern key, that Mary's blessedness would not have been complete unless she had been assumed as a person: "The soul is not a person, but the soul, joined to the body, is a person. It is manifest that she is there in soul and in body. Otherwise she would not possess her complete beatitude."[69]

By the end of the Middle Ages, belief in Mary's Assumption into heaven was well-established theologically, and expressed in the devotional life and culture of Christendom. Even among figures of the Reformation, the Assumption remained in some cases an object of devotion. For Martin Luther, Mary's Assumption was an understood fact, as his homily of 1522 indicates, in spite of the fact that Mary's Assumption is not expressly reported in Sacred Scripture: "There can be no doubt that the Virgin Mary is in heaven. How it happened we do not know. And since the Holy Spirit has told us nothing about it, we can make of it no article of faith. … It is enough to know that she lives in Christ."[70] For the Protestant reformer, M. Butzer (1545), there was no reason to doubt about the Assumption of the Virgin into heavenly glory. "Indeed, no Christian doubts that the most worthy Mother of the Lord lives with her beloved Son in heavenly joy."[71] H. Bullinger (1590), also a Protestant reformer,

---

[66] St. Albert the Great, *Mariale*, q. 132.
[67] St. Thomas Aquinas, *Summa Theologiae*, I-II, q. 27, a. 1; q. 83, a. 5; *Expositio Salutationis Angelicae*; *In Symbolum Apostolorum Expositio*, a.5; *In IV Sententiarum*, d. 12, q. 1, a. 3; d. 43, q. 1, a. 3.
[68] See St. Bonaventure, *De Nativitate B. Mariae Virginis*, Sermo V.
[69] St. Bonaventure, *De Assumptione B. Mariae Virginis*, Sermo I.
[70] See citation from M. Luther, Sermon of August 15, 1522, in R. Bäumer and L. Scheffczyk, (eds.), *Marienlexikon*, vol. 3 (St. Ottilien: EOS Verlag: 1991), p. 200.
[71] See citation from M. Butzer in R. Bäumer and L. Scheffczyk, (eds.), *Marienlexikon*, vol. 3 (St. Ottilien: EOS Verlag: 1991), p. 200.

sought a theological foundation for the Assumption in Scripture. He showed that the Old Testament tells of Elijah, taken to heaven bodily, to teach us about our immortality, and—because of our immortal soul—to respectfully honour the bodies of the saints. Against this backdrop he stated, "Because of this, we believe that the pure immaculate chamber of the God-bearer, the Virgin Mary, is a temple of the Holy Spirit, that is her holy body, borne by angels into heaven."[72]

Later, in the Catholic Reformation period, St. Robert Bellarmine once again adopted the Ark imagery and stated: "Who, I ask, could believe that the ark of holiness, the dwelling place of the Word of God, the temple of the Holy Spirit, could be reduced to ruin? My soul is filled with horror at the thought that this virginal flesh which had begotten God, had brought him into the world, had nourished and carried him, could have been turned into ashes or given over to be food for worms."[73] Some later authors proposed an argument from appropriateness for the Assumption. Since a basic commandment of both Old and New Testaments is for children to honor their parents, Jesus Christ must himself have observed this, in the most perfect way possible. St. Francis of Sales therefore asks: "What son would not bring his mother back to life and would not bring her into paradise after her death if he could?"[74] St. Alphonsus Liguori set the same idea in a more Christological light by affirming that Jesus did not wish to have the body of Mary corrupted after death, since it would have redounded to his own dishonor to have her virginal flesh, from which he himself had assumed flesh, reduced to dust.[75]

The development of the doctrine of the Assumption of Mary involved various elements, which can be summarized in this way. A common patristic theme is that the doctrine of the Second Eve implies assumption as the final and complete victory of the woman. Next, Mary in her predestination is always associated with her Son. Further, Mary's Immaculate Conception and sinlessness imply exemption from corruption in the grave, and so lead to her immediate resurrection and

---

[72] See citation from H. Bullinger in R. Bäumer and L. Scheffczyk, (eds.), *Marienlexikon*, vol. 3 (St. Ottilien: EOS Verlag: 1991), p. 200.
[73] St. Robert Bellarmine, *De Assumption B. Mariae Virginis* in *Conciones Habitae Lovanii* (Coloniae Agrippinae: apud Ioannem Crithium, 1615), n. 40.
[74] *Oeuvres de St. Francois De Sales*, sermon for the Feast of the Assumption.
[75] See St. Alphonsus Liguori, "Discourse I. On Mary's Immaculate Conception" in *The Glories of Mary*, p. 266.

glory. Another theme is that the perpetual virginity of Our Lady, as fleshly incorruption, involved exemption from physical corruption after death. A further argument is that the filial piety of the divine Son implied that he would grant her the favor of the Assumption, if it were otherwise possible and fitting. Mary at her death was more exalted in dignity than other creatures will ever be. If, then, other Christians are destined to be bodily with Christ in heaven, this must have applied to Mary straightway after her death. Finally, the woman of the Apocalypse is already seen in her glory, after being taken by eagle's wings.[76]

One of the aspects of Divine Revelation which impressed itself on Newman's mind was its consistency, the fact that all of its truths hang together. By means of the principle of the analogy of faith, what is taught now fits into what has already been received, a principle which, he affirms, is exemplified in many different ways in the structure and the history of doctrine. This principle he applies particularly to Marian doctrines, especially to the Assumption of Our Lady into heaven.[77] This doctrine is in harmony with the substance of the doctrine of the Incarnation, and without it, Newman points out, Catholic doctrine would be incomplete. It is a truth which he says is received on the belief of ages, but even from a rational point of view the very fittingness of it recommends it strongly. Mary's Assumption into heaven is, for Newman, in perfect harmony with the other truths of Revelation. His starting point is the doctrine of the divine maternity:

> As soon as we apprehend by faith the great fundamental truth that Mary is the Mother of God, other wonderful truths follow in its train; and one of these is that she was exempt from the ordinary lot of mortals, which is not only to die, but to become earth to earth, ashes to ashes, dust to dust. Die she must, and die she did, as her divine Son died, for he was man; but various reasons have approved themselves to holy

---

[76] See Rev 12:14 and also P. Haffner, *The Mystery of Mary* (Leominster: Gracewing; Chicago: Hillenbrand Books, 2004), p. 66, where it was stated that the figure of the woman in the book of Revelation "is symbolic, but in a polyvalent sense, referring to both Mariological and ecclesiological realities."

[77] J.H. Newman, *Discourses addressed to Mixed Congregations* (London: 1886), pp. 360-376.

writers, why, although her body was for a while separated from her soul, and consigned to the tomb, yet it did not remain there, but was speedily united to her soul again, and raised by our Lord to a new and eternal life of heavenly glory. ... And the most obvious reason for so concluding is this—that other servants of God have been raised from the grave by the power of God, and it is not to be supposed that our Lord would have granted any such privilege to anyone else without also granting it to his own Mother. ... Therefore we confidently say that our Lord, having preserved her from sin and the consequences of sin by his Passion, lost no time in pouring out the full merits of that Passion upon her body as well as her soul.[78]

The definition of the dogma of the Assumption was prepared for and preceded by a period of discussion which included a consideration of how the dogma was founded in the Scriptures and in Tradition. In May 1946, with the Encyclical *Deiparae Virginis Mariae*, Pius XII called for a broad consultation, inquiring among the bishops and, through them, among the clergy and the People of God, as to the possibility and opportuneness of defining the bodily Assumption of Mary as a dogma of faith. The result was extremely positive: only six answers out of 1,181 showed any reservations about the revealed character of this truth. The Church propounded that this truth was based in Scripture, and was visibly expressed in Tradition.[79] After many requests, Pope Pius XII solemnly defined the dogma in 1950:

> After we have poured forth prayers of supplication again and again to God, and have invoked the light of the Spirit of Truth, for the glory of Almighty God who has lavished his special affection upon the Virgin Mary, for the honor of her Son, the immortal King of the ages and the Victor over sin and death, for the increase of the glory of that same august Mother, and for the joy

---

[78] J.H. Newman, *Meditations and Devotions of the late Cardinal Newman* (Longman, Green and Co., 1893), pp. 89-91.

[79] Pope Pius XII, Apostolic Constitution *Munificentissimus Deus*, 41.

> and exultation of the entire Church; by the authority of our Lord Jesus Christ, of the blessed apostles Peter and Paul, and by our own authority, we pronounce, declare, and define it to be a divinely revealed dogma: that the Immaculate Mother of God, the ever-Virgin Mary, having completed the course of her earthly life, was assumed body and soul into heavenly glory.[80]

Pope Pius XII defined a dogma which had been believed by the Church for well over a thousand years. The definition took place in 1950, and this was of great historical significance. In took place in the middle of a century when the sacredness of the human body was denied theoretically and practically at many levels. In the first half of the twentieth century it was denied politically in the totalitarian systems of Marxism and Nazism, which denied the sacredness of the body in theory and in the slaughter of millions in the gulags and concentration camps. In the second half of the twentieth century, the assault on the sacredness of the human body was taken a step further through the massacre of untold millions through abortion and euthanasia, and also through sacrilegious experiments carried out on embryos, to say nothing of genetic engineering and attempts to clone the human being. All of this is counterbalanced by the Church's affirmation that Our Lady was assumed *body* and soul to the glory of heaven. The Church, which believes in the resurrection of the body, believes that this same body has been created in the image and likeness of God, and is called to a supernatural destiny in Christ.

The Assumption can also be understood in light of the mystery of the Church, as the Second Vatican Council elucidated. In the most Blessed Virgin Mary, the Church has already reached that perfection whereby she exists without spot or wrinkle (cf. Ep 5:27), however, the faithful still strive to conquer sin and increase in holiness. "In the meantime the Mother of Jesus in the glory which she possesses in body and soul in heaven is the image and beginning of the Church as it is to be perfected in the world to come. Likewise she shines forth on earth, until the day of the Lord shall come (cf. 2 Pet. 3:10), a sign of certain

---

[80] *Ibid.*, 44.

hope and comfort to the pilgrim People of God."[81] For Our Blessed Lady, there is no "intermediate eschatology," namely there is no "period" of waiting between death and the general judgment for the body and soul to be reunited, and this sets her apart from us: "In teaching her doctrine about man's destiny after death, the Church excludes any explanation that would deprive the assumption of the Virgin Mary of its unique meaning, namely the fact that the bodily glorification of the Virgin is an anticipation of the glorification that is the destiny of all the other elect."[82]

Recent theology has outlined further consequences of the Assumption. One line of enquiry stresses that Adam and Eve lay at the natural origin of humanity, and at the origins of sin and its transmission. On the other hand, Christ and his Mother Mary stand at the origin of the regeneration of humanity. Therefore the eschatological destiny of humanity is revealed in the association of Christ and his Mother Mary. Thus, the Assumption of Mary shows that God's plan is now realized not only in Christ the bridegroom, but also in the bride, signified by the Church, recapitulated in Mary.[83] Thus the Assumption is an exaltation of woman, in contrast to all ancient and modern paganism. If the power of sin has served to oppress women, the Assumption shows how God has empowered a woman for the spread of holiness. The Assumption is a triumph for the nobility of maternity and also of virginity. The Assumption is also an indication of the glory which awaits the body of the Christian, who in this life has been the home of the Body of Christ in the Eucharist. Finally, the Assumption indicates the glorification of the poor and their liberation from oppression, in the fulfillment of the words of the Magnificat: "The Almighty has done great things for me: Holy is his Name." The Assumption of Mary is "the glorious culmination of the mystery of God's preference for what is poor, small, and unprotected in this world, so as to make God's presence and glory shine there." It offers "hope and promise for the poor of all times and for those who stand in solidarity with them; it is hope and promise that they will share in the

---

[81] Vatican II, *Lumen Gentium*, 68.
[82] Congregation for the Doctrine of the Faith, letter on certain questions regarding eschatology *Recentiores episcoporum Synodi* (May 17, 1979), 6.
[83] See G. Gozzelino, *Vocazione e destino dell'uomo in Cristo* (Leumann: Elle Di Ci, 1985), pp. 151-152.

final victory of the incarnate God."[84] Mary assumed into heaven is also connected with the unity of the Church. Far from being an ecumenical problem, the definition of Mary's Assumption marked a great period of growth for efforts favoring Christian unity. Mary assumed into heaven indicates that only by lifting up one's gaze and one's heart heavenward can one retrieve the lost brotherhood in Christ.[85]

The Assumption and the Queenship

The mystery of the Assumption of the noble Daughter of Zion is closely linked with the mystery of her eternal glory. The Mother of God is glorified as "Queen of the Universe." She who at the Annunciation called herself the "handmaid of the Lord," remained throughout her earthly life faithful to what this name expresses. In this she confirmed that she was a true "disciple" of Christ, who strongly emphasized that his mission was one of service: "the Son of Man came not to be served but to serve, and to give his life as a ransom for many" (Mt 20:28). Mary became the first of those who, serving Christ also in others, with humility and patience lead their brothers and sisters to that King, to serve whom is to reign, and she fully obtained that "state of royal freedom" proper to Christ's disciples.[86]

The doctrine of Our Lady's queenship is by no means new. In the Annunciation episode, the Angel Gabriel's greeting ran "He shall be great, and shall be called the Son of the Most High: and the Lord God shall give unto him the throne of his father David: And he shall reign over the house of Jacob for ever; and of his kingdom there shall be no end" (Lk 1:32-33). Our Lady's queenship is thus seen as an association with Christ's Kingship.[87] Then, at the Visitation, Elizabeth used the words "Mother of my Lord" (Lk 1:43). The word Lord (*Dominus* in Latin and *Kyrios* in Greek) in this passage, as in the New Testament generally, connotes divinity and royalty, according to many modern

---

[84] I. Gebara and M.C. Bingemer, *Mary, Mother of God, Mother of the Poor*, vol. 7 of *Liberation and Theology* (Tunbridge Wells: Burns and Oates, 1989), pp. 120-121.

[85] See R. Spiazzi, "Nell'Assunzione di Maria la primizia della reintegrazione universale" in *Sacra Dottrina* 39 (1994), pp. 99-101.

[86] See Pope John Paul II, *Redemptoris Mater*, 41. See also Vatican II, *Lumen Gentium*, 36, 55, 59.

[87] See E.J. Smith, "The Scriptural Basis for Mary's Queenship" in *Marian Studies* 4 (1953), pp. 109-115.

scholars, and so Elizabeth greets Mary as Mother of God, Mother of the King.[88] Already a fragment of a homily, attributed to Origen, contains this comment on the words Elizabeth spoke at the Visitation: "It is I who should have come to visit you, because you are blessed above all women, you are the Mother of my Lord, you are my Lady."[89] The text passes spontaneously from the expression "the Mother of my Lord" to the title, "my Lady."

Another line of understanding was also developed, stemming from the Annunciation account and other scriptural testimonies to the Kingship of Christ. This idea is in continuity with the Old Testament figure of the Queen Mother.[90] Mary is described as Mother of the King, by St. Ephraem for example (+373), and by his contemporary St. Gregory Nazianzen, who speaks of the "Mother of the King of the entire universe."[91] Then an easy transition occurs from the expression "Mother of the King" to "Queen," and it appears for the first time, as far as surviving evidence goes, in the fourth century, again in the writings of St. Ephraem: "Imperial maiden and mistress, Queen, sovereign lady, take me under thy protection, guard me lest Satan, the author of destruction, rise up against me, lest the accursed enemy triumph over me."[92] Starting from the fifth century, almost in the same period in which the Council of Ephesus proclaims her "Mother of God," the title of Queen begins to be attributed to Mary. In this way, Mary is raised above all other creatures, exalting her role and importance in the life of every person and of the whole world. The expression "Lady," meaning sovereign, was later to become Queen, for example in St. John Damascene: "When she became Mother of the Creator, she truly became Queen of all creatures."[93]

---

[88] See L. Cerfaux, "Le Titre *Kyrios* et la dignite royale de Jesus" in *Revue des Sciences Philosophiques et Théologiques* 11 (1922), pp. 40-71; 12 (1923), pp. 125-153.

[89] Origen, *Fragmenta Originis ex Macarii Chrysocephali Orationibus in Lucam* in *EM* 149: "Oportebat me ad te venire: to enim super omnes mulieres benedicta: tu Mater Domini mei: tu mea Domina."

[90] See P. Haffner, *The Mystery of Mary*, pp. 32-33.

[91] St. Gregory Nazianzen, *Poemata Dogmatica*, 18, 58 in *PG* 37, 485.

[92] St. Ephraem, *Oratio ad Santissimam Dei Matrem* in *EM* 346. He also refers to Mary as the universal Queen. See Idem, *Sermo de sanctissimae Dei Genetricis Virginis Mariae laudibus* in *EM* 350. The expression is "Regina omnium."

[93] St. John Damascene, *De fide orthodoxa*, 4, 14 in *PG* 94, 1157.

With the dogma of the divine maternity of Mary, her perfect sanctity also emerged in clearer light, resulting in a fuller understanding within the Church of Mary's pre-eminence and dignity. In the sixth and seventh centuries, explicit belief in the Assumption was universal, and Mary, in body and in soul, was envisaged as resplendent with the glory of the risen Savior. By the end of the patristic period the doctrine of the queenship is clearly established: a queenship especially of excellence and grace, but also a queenship of power, of intercession, protection, and patronage. This queenship was later to find artistic expression all over Europe in paintings and sculpture depicting the crowning of Mary by her Son. These ideas are greatly developed in the Middle Ages. One of the greatest proponents was Eadmer, the disciple of St. Anselm: "just as … God, by making all through his power, is Father and Lord of all, so the blessed Mary, by repairing all through her merits, is Mother and Queen of all; for God is the Lord of all things, because by his command he establishes each of them in its own nature, and Mary is the Queen of all things, because she restores each to its original dignity through the grace which she merited."[94]

Gradually, the concept of the mediation of graces assumed great prominence. Mary is Queen principally through her influence over her Son and the guidance of her children towards salvation. The *Salve Regina* and other antiphons expressed these ideas, and Mary is invoked as Queen of Mercy, whose prayers are all-powerful. Pope Pius XII, in his Encyclical *Ad Caeli Reginam*, indicated as the basis for Mary's queenship in addition to her motherhood, her co-operation in the work of the redemption. The Pope recalls that Mary, Queen of heaven and Sovereign of the world, was first the sorrowing Mother near the Cross of our Lord Jesus Christ.[95] He then established an analogy between Mary and Christ, which helps us understand the significance of the Blessed Virgin's royal status. Christ is King not only because he is Son of God, but also because he is the Redeemer; Mary is Queen not only because she is Mother of God, but also because, associated as the New Eve with the New Adam, she co-operated in the work of the redemption of the human race.[96]

---

[94] Eadmer, *De excellentia Virginis Mariae*, c. 11 in *PL* 159, 508.
[95] See Pope Pius XII, Encyclical *Ad Caeli Reginam*, 36.
[96] *Ibid.*, p.38.

Mary, the handmaid of the Lord, has a share in the Kingdom of her Son. This arises from the fact that she co-operated in Christ's obedience even at the cost of death. He was therefore raised up by the Father (cf. Phil 2:8-9) and entered into the glory of his kingdom. To him all things are made subject until he subjects himself and all created things to the Father, that God may be all in all (cf. 1 Cor 15:27-28). The glory of Mary's royal service does not cease with her exaltation: assumed into heaven, she continues her saving service, expressed in her maternal mediation "until the eternal fulfillment of all the elect."[97] Thus, she who here on earth loyally preserved her union with her Son unto the Cross, continues to remain united with him, while all things are subjected to him, until he subjects himself to the Father who put all things in subjection under him (cf. 1 Cor 15:28). In her Assumption into heaven, Mary is, as it were, clothed by the whole reality of the Communion of Saints, and her very union with the Son in glory is wholly oriented towards the definitive fullness of the Kingdom, when "God will be all in all" (1 Cor 15:28).

Abbreviations

CCC = *Catechism of the Catholic Church*. Dublin: Veritas, 1994

CCL = *Corpus Christianorum series latina*. Tournai: Brepols, 1954–

CSEL = *Corpus Scriptorum Ecclesiasticorum Latinorum*. Wien: 1866–

DS = H. Denzinger. *Enchiridion Symbolorum, Definitionum et Declarationum de rebus fidei et morum*. Bilingual edition edited by P. Hünermann. Bologna: EDB, 1995

EM = *Enchiridion Marianum Biblicum Patristicum* (ed.D. Casagrande). Rome: «Cor Unum», 1974

EV = *Enchiridion Vaticanum*. Documenti ufficiali della Chiesa. Bologna: Edizioni Dehoniane

IG = *Insegnamenti di Giovanni Paolo II*. Vatican City: Vatican Polyglot Press, 1978–

IP = *Insegnamenti di Paolo VI*. Vatican City: Vatican Polyglot Press, 1963-1978

Mansi = J.D. Mansi, *Sacrorum Conciliorum nova et amplissima collectio*. Graz: 1960-1962

---

[97] Vatican II, *Lumen Gentium*, 62.

ND = J Neuner and J. Dupuis, *The Christian Faith in the Doctrinal Documents of the Catholic Church.* Sixth edition. New York: Alba House, 1996

OR = *L'Osservatore Romano,* daily Italian edition

ORE = *L'Osservatore Romano,* weekly English edition

PG = J.P. Migne. *Patrologiae cursus completus, series graeca.* 161 vols. Paris: 1857–1866

PL = J.P. Migne. *Patrologiae cursus completus, series latina.* 221 vols. Paris: 1844–1864

SC = *Sources Chrétiennes.* Paris: Cerf, 1942–

TN = N.P. Tanner (ed.), *Decrees of the Ecumenical Councils.* 2 vols. London: Sheed and Ward, 1990

III.
Marian Doctrine

MARY CO-REDEMPTRIX: THE BELOVED ASSOCIATE OF CHRIST

Msgr. Arthur Burton Calkins

Even though the explicit treatment of Mary's collaboration in the work of redemption has appeared in ever-sharper relief in the Papal Magisterium only within the past two centuries, there is well-founded reason to say that it is part and parcel of the Tradition that has come down to us from the apostles and makes progress in the Church under the guidance of the Holy Spirit (cf. *Dei Verbum* 8). The indissoluble link between the "woman" and "her seed," the Messiah, is already presented to us in the *Protoevangelium* (Gen 3:15),[1] where the first adumbrations of God's saving plan pierce through the darkness caused by man's sin. The identification of the "woman" with Mary is already implicit in the second and nineteenth chapters of the Gospel of St. John where Jesus addresses his mother as "woman"[2] and in the twelfth chapter of the book of Revelation.[3]

Mary, the New Eve

The Apostle Paul had already explicitly identified Jesus as the "New Adam" (cf. Rom 5:12-21; 1 Cor 15:21-22, 45-49) and it was a natural and logical development for the sub-Apostolic Fathers, Justin Martyr (+c.165),

---

[1] Cf. Michael O'Carroll, C.S.Sp., *Theotokos: A Theological Encyclopedia of the Blessed Virgin Mary* (Wilmington: Michael Glazier, Inc.; Dublin: Dominican Publications, 1982) [= *Theotokos*] 370-373; Stefano M. Manelli, F.I., *All Generations Shall Call Me Blessed: Biblical Mariology* trans. Peter Damian Fehlner, F.I. (New Bedford, MA: Academy of the Immaculate, revised and enlarged second edition, 2005) [= Manelli] 20-37.
[2] Cf. *Theotokos* 373-375; Manelli 364-383.
[3] Cf. *Theotokos* 375-377; Manelli 394-414.

Irenaeus of Lyons (+c.202) and Tertullian (+c.220), to see Mary as the "New Eve,"[4] the God-given helpmate of the "New Adam." Virtually all of the experts are agreed that the classic presentation of Mary as the "New Eve" achieves full maturity in the writings of St. Irenaeus of Lyons. Of Irenaeus' Eve-Mary comparison René Laurentin says:

> Irenaeus gives bold relief to a theme only outlined by Justin [Martyr]. *With Irenaeus the Eve-Mary parallel is not simply a literary effect nor a gratuitous improvisation, but an integral part of his theology of salvation.* One idea is the key to this theology: God's saving plan is not a mending or a "patch-up job" done on his first product; it is a resumption of the work from the beginning, a regeneration from head downwards, a *recapitulation* in Christ. In this radical restoration each one of the elements marred by the fall is renewed in its very root. In terms of the symbol developed by Irenaeus, the knot badly tied at the beginning is unknotted, untied in reverse (*recirculatio*): Christ takes up anew the role of Adam, the Cross that of the Tree of Life. *In this ensemble Mary, who corresponds to Eve, holds a place of first importance. According to Irenaeus her role is necessary to the logic of the divine plan.* ...
>
> With Irenaeus this line of thought attains a force of expression that has never been surpassed. Later writers will broaden the bases of the comparison but to our day no one has expressed it in a way more compact or more profound.[5]

Let us pause here a moment to consider why St. Irenaeus is such an important figure for our consideration. Not only is he invoked implicitly—by being included among the Fathers—in the Marian

---

[4] Cf. *Theotokos* 139-141; Luigi Gambero, S.M., *Mary and the Fathers of the Church: The Blessed Virgin Mary in Patristic Thought* trans. Thomas Buffer (San Francisco: Ignatius Press, 1999) [= Gambero I] 46-48, 53-58, 66-67; Paul Haffner, *The Mystery of Mary* (Leominster, Herefordshire: Gracewing; Chicago: Liturgy Training Publications, 2004) [= Haffner] 75-76.

[5] René Laurentin, *A Short Treatise of the Virgin Mary* trans. by Charles Neumann, S.M. (Washington, N.J.: AMI Press, 1991) 54, 57. Emphasis my own (except for "recapitulation" and "recirculatio").

magisterium of Bl. Pius IX, but he is also referred to explicitly in that of Pius XII, Paul VI, the Second Vatican Council and most notably in that of John Paul II. The Lutheran scholar Jaroslav Pelikan provides us with a fascinating hint about the importance of the Bishop of Lyons:

> When it is suggested that for the development of the doctrine of Mary, such Christian writers as Irenaeus in a passage like this [in *Proof of the Apostolic Preaching*] "are important witnesses for the state of the tradition in the late second century, *if not earlier*" that raises the interesting question of whether Irenaeus had invented the concept of Mary as the Second Eve here or was drawing on a deposit of tradition that had come to him from "earlier." It is difficult, in reading his *Against Heresies* and especially his *Proof of the Apostolic Preaching*, to avoid the impression that he cited the parallelism of Eve and Mary so matter-of-factly without arguing or having to defend the point because he could assume that his readers would willingly go along with it, or even that they were already familiar with it. One reason that this could be so might have been that, on this issue as on so many others, Irenaeus regarded himself as the guardian and the transmitter of a body of belief that had come to him from earlier generations, from the very apostles. A modern reader does need to consider the possibility, perhaps even to concede the possibility, that in so regarding himself Irenaeus may just have been right and that therefore it may already have become natural in the second half of the second century to look at Eve, the "mother of all living," and Mary, the Mother of Christ, together, understanding and interpreting each of the two most important women in human history on the basis of the other.[6]

Put simply, Irenaeus was a disciple of Polycarp who was a disciple of the Apostle John. There is every reason, then, to believe that what he

---

[6] Jaroslav Pelikan, *Mary Through the Centuries: Her Place in the History of Culture* (New Haven and London: Yale University Press, 1996) 43-44.

transmits to us about Mary as the "New Eve" is an integral part of "the Tradition that comes to us from the apostles."[7]

This datum of the tradition has come into ever-clearer focus through the teaching of the popes in the course of the past 150 years, most notably in Bl. Pope Pius IX's Bull of 1854, *Ineffabilis Deus*,[8] Pius XII's Apostolic Constitution of 1950, *Munificentissimus Deus*,[9] and his encyclicals *Mystici Corporis* of 1943[10] and *Ad Cæli Reginam* of 1954. In the last-mentioned document the Holy Father spoke in these explicit terms:

> From these considerations we can conclude as follows: Mary in the work of redemption was by God's will joined with Jesus Christ, the cause of salvation, in much the same way as Eve was joined with Adam, the cause of death. Hence it can be said that the work of our salvation was brought about by a "restoration" (St. Irenaeus) in which the human race, just as it was doomed to death by a virgin, was saved by a virgin.
>
> Moreover, she was chosen to be the Mother of Christ "in order to have part with him in the redemption of the human race" [Pius XI, *Auspicatus profecto*].
>
> "She it was who, immune from all sin, personal or inherited, and ever most closely united with her Son, offered him on Golgotha to the eternal Father together with the holocaust of her maternal rights and motherly love, like a New Eve, for all the children of

---

[7] Cf. Arthur Burton Calkins "Maria Reparatrix: Tradition, Magisterium, Liturgy" in *Mary at the Foot of the Cross*, III: *Maria, Mater Unitatis – Acts of the Third International Symposium on Marian Coredemption* (New Bedford, MA: Academy of the Immaculate, 2003) [= *MFC* III] 223-232.

[8] Cf. Arthur Burton Calkins, "The Immaculate Coredemptrix in the Life and Teaching of Bl. Pius IX" in *Mary at the Foot of the Cross*, V: *Redemption and Coredemption under the Sign of the Immaculate Conception – Acts of the Fifth International Symposium on Marian Coredemption* (New Bedford, MA: Academy of the Immaculate, 2005) [= *MFC* V] 508-541.

[9] *Acta Apostolicae Sedis* [= *AAS*] 42 (1950) 768; Amleto Tondini, *Le Encicliche Mariane* (Rome: Belardetti, Editore) [= Tondini] 626; *Our Lady: Papal Teachings* trans. Daughters of St. Paul (Boston: St. Paul Editions, 1961) [= *OL*] 519.

[10] *AAS* 35 (1943) 247-248 [*OL* 383].

Adam contaminated through this unhappy fall" [*Mystici Corporis*]...

From this we conclude that just as Christ, the New Adam, is our King not only because he is the Son of God, but also because he is our Redeemer, so also in a somewhat similar manner the Blessed Virgin is Queen not only as Mother of God, but also because she was associated as the Second Eve with the New Adam.[11]

We may note that with the clarity which characterized all of his dogmatic statements the great Pontiff insists on Mary's active, but subordinate role in the work of our salvation and in doing so invokes the authority of St. Irenaeus, the "father of Catholic dogmatic theology."[12]

The theme of Mary as the "New Eve," with explicit references to St. Irenaeus, was duly cited in chapter eight of the Second Vatican Council's Dogmatic Constitution on the Church, *Lumen Gentium* 56 thusly:

Rightly, therefore, the Fathers see Mary not merely as passively engaged by God, but as freely cooperating in the work of man's salvation through faith and obedience. For, as St. Irenaeus says, she "being obedient, became the cause of salvation for herself and for the whole human race." Hence not a few of the early Fathers gladly assert with him in their preaching: "the knot of Eve's disobedience was untied by Mary's obedience: what the virgin Eve bound through her disbelief, Mary loosened by her faith." Comparing Mary with Eve, they call her "Mother of the living," and frequently claim: "death through Eve, life through Mary."

In his *Professio Fidei* of June 30, 1968, Paul VI, expressly citing *Lumen Gentium* 56 as a source, called Mary the "New Eve,"[13] and Pope John Paul II without a doubt made more references to Mary as the "New Eve" and examined the implications of this title more than all of his

---

[11] *AAS* 46 (1954) 634-635 [*OL* 705].
[12] Gambero I:51.
[13] *AAS* 60 (1968) 438-439.

predecessors combined.[14] Here is one of his last such references, which occurs in his Letter to the Men and Women Religious of the Montfort Families for the 160th Anniversary of the Publication of *True Devotion to Mary*:

> St. Louis Marie contemplates all the mysteries, starting from the *Incarnation* which was brought about at the moment of the Annunciation. Thus, in the *Treatise on True Devotion to the Blessed Virgin*, Mary appears as "the true terrestrial paradise of the New Adam," the "virginal and immaculate earth" of which he was formed (n. 261). She is also the *New Eve*, associated with the *New Adam* in the obedience that atones for the original disobedience of the man and the woman (cf. *ibid.*, n. 53; St. Irenaeus, *Adversus Haereses*, III, 21, 10-22, 4). Through this obedience, the Son of God enters the world. The Cross itself is already mysteriously present at the instant of the Incarnation, at the very moment of Jesus' conception in Mary's womb. Indeed, the *ecce venio* in the Letter to the Hebrews (cf. 10:5-9) is the primordial act of the Son's obedience to the Father, an acceptance of his redeeming sacrifice already at the time "when Christ came into the world."[15]

In this case there is a graceful reference which links St. Louis-Marie Grignion de Montfort to St. Irenaeus of Lyons, while at the same time linking the reparation accomplished by the "New Adam" for the world's salvation to that of the "New Eve."

Let us allow Father Lino Cignelli, O.F.M., an expert who has studied the Mary-Eve parallel in Irenaeus and the early Greek Fathers at length,

---

[14] Cf. the Apostolic Letter *Mulieris Dignitatem* of August 15, 1988, #11 in *Insegnamenti di Giovanni Paolo II* (Rome: Libreria Editrice Vaticana) [= *Inseg*] XI/3 (1988) 337-340, the general audience address of January, 24, 1996, in *Inseg* XIX/1 (1996) 115-117, the general audience address of May 29, 1996, #3-5 in *Inseg* XIX/1 (1996) 1390-1392, the general audience address of September 18, 1996, in *Inseg* XIX/2 (1996) 372-374. These are just a few of the more important citations.

[15] *Inseg* XXVI/2 (2003) 919 [L'*Osservatore Romano*, weekly edition in English (= *ORE*). First number = cumulative edition number; second number = page] 1829:3.

to offer us this penetrating analysis which may also serve as a summary of what we have found thus far in the Papal Magisterium:

> From the human side, both the sexes contribute actively in determining the lot of the human race, but not however to the same extent. Ruin and salvation rest with the two Adams. With regard to Christ the New Adam, he can redeem because he is the God-man. As God, he guarantees the victory over the Devil and communicates life, incorruptibility and immortality, which are essentially divine goods; as man, he is the primary ministerial cause of salvation and the antithesis of Adam, cause of universal ruin.
>
> The two virgins, Eve and Mary, beyond depending on Satan and God respectively, are ordained in their actions to the two Adams, with whom they share ministerial causality. They thus carry out an intermediate and subordinate task. Subordination, however, does not mean being simple accessories. Irenaeus clearly points back to the feminine causality of the ruin and the salvation of the human race. Eve is the "cause of death" and Mary the "cause of salvation" for all mankind.[16]

Father Cignelli further comments that Mary's "contribution, made in free and meritorious obedience, constitutes with that of Christ the man a single total principle of salvation. At the side of the New Adam, she is thus a ministerial and formal co-cause of the restoration of the human race."[17] Although we have not been able to review all of the texts here, this conclusion is fully justified by its use in the Papal Magisterium.[18]

---

[16] Lino Cignelli, O.F.M., *Maria Nuova Eva nella Patristica greca* (Assisi: Studio Teologico "Porziuncola" Collectio Assisiensis #3, 1966) 36-37 [my trans.].

[17] Cignelli 235-236 [my trans.].

[18] Cf. Arthur Burton Calkins, "They Mystery of Mary Coredemptrix in the Papal Magisterium" in Mark Miravalle, S.T.D. (ed.), *Mary Co-redemptrix: Doctrinal Issues Today* (Goleta, CA: Queenship Publishing Company, 2002) [= *MMC*] 51-64.

The *Protoevangelium* (Gen 3:15)

Intimately related to the concept of Mary as the "New Eve" are the words spoken by the Lord after the fall of our first parents. God metes out punishment first to the serpent (Gen 3:14-15), then to the woman (Gen 3:16) and finally to the man (Gen 3:17-19). What is particularly striking, however, is that the sentence passed upon the serpent already heralds the reversal of the fall. The Lord says: "I will put enmity between you and the woman, and between your seed and her seed; she shall crush your head, while you lie in wait for her heel" (Gen 3:15).[19] This text has become famous as the *Protoevangelium* ("first gospel") and the *Catechism of the Catholic Church* explains why:

> The Christian tradition sees in this passage an announcement of the "New Adam" who because he "became obedient unto death, even death on a cross," makes amends superabundantly for the disobedience of Adam. Furthermore many Fathers and Doctors of the Church have seen the woman announced in the "Protoevangelium" as Mary, the Mother of Christ, the "New Eve."[20]

Scholarly discussions as to whether the text of the *Protoevangelium* should be translated "he [the seed of the woman] shall crush your head" (*ipse conteret caput tuum* as in the *Neo-Vulgata*) or "she [the woman] shall crush your head" (*ipsa conteret caput tuum* as in the *Vulgata* of St. Jerome) continue to be advanced.[21] One wonders whether the *Neo-Vulgata*, which

---

[19] I have followed here the Douay-Rheims version which is a translation of St. Jerome's Vulgate. For a discussion on whether the pronoun in the second part of the verse should be translated as he or she (favored in the Catholic tradition for well over a millennium) cf. Thomas Mary Sennott, *The Woman of Genesis* (Cambridge, MA: The Ravengate Press, 1984) 37-60. For a discussion of whether the verb should be translated as "bruise" or "crush," cf. Sennott 61-80. For an in-depth treatment of the text, cf. Settimio M. Manelli, F.I., "Genesis 3:15 and the Immaculate Co-redemptrix" *MFC* V:263-322.

[20] *Catechism of the Catholic Church* [= *CCC*] 411.

[21] Cf. H.-L. Barth, *Ipsa conteret. Maria die Schlangenzertreterin. Philologische und theologische Überlegungen zum Protoevangelium (Gen 3,15)* (Kirchliche Umschau 2000). This work was reviewed by Brunero Gherardini in *Divinitas* XLV:2 (2002) 224-225. Cf. also Thomas Mary Sennott, *The Woman of Genesis* (Cambridge, MA:

has chosen in favor of the neuter pronoun, really accords best with the way the text has been read and understood in the course of over 1,500 years. In any case Father Stefano M. Manelli's treatment of the matter provides an excellent overview of this issue[22] and draws conclusions fully in harmony with the consistent use made of this text in the Papal Magisterium:

> As Pope Pius IX summarizes it, both according to tradition (the Fathers and ecclesiastical writers) and according to the express declarations of the Papal Magisterium, the *Protoevangelium* "clearly and plainly" foretold the Redeemer, indicated the Virgin Mary as the Mother of the Redeemer, and described the common enmity of Mother and Son against the Devil and their complete triumph over the poisonous serpent. One can, therefore, without hesitation affirm that the content of the *Protoevangelium* is "Marian" as well as messianic. Not only this, but the Mariological dimension in reference to the "woman" must be also understood literally to be exclusive to that "woman," to Mary, that is, to the Mother of the Redeemer, and not to Eve.[23]

Pope John Paul II, while even conceding full weight to the *Neo-Vulgata* rendition, puts it this way:

> Since the biblical concept establishes a profound solidarity between the parent and the offspring, the depiction of the Immaculata crushing the serpent, not by her own power but through the grace of her Son, is consistent with the original meaning of the passage.
>
> The same biblical text also proclaims the enmity between the woman and her offspring on the one hand the serpent and his offspring on the other. This is a hostility expressly established by God, which has a unique

---

The Ravengate Press, 1984) 37-60; *Ibid.*, "Mary Co-redemptrix," in *Mary at the Foot of the Cross*, II (New Bedford, MA: Academy of the Immaculate, 2002) [= *MFC* II] 49-63.

[22] Manelli 20-37.
[23] Manelli 23-24.

importance, if we consider the problem of the Virgin's personal holiness. In order to be the irreconcilable enemy of the serpent and his offspring, Mary had to be free from all power of sin, and to be so from the first moment of her existence.[24]

It should also be noted that already in drafting the Bull *Ineffabilis Deus* it was confirmed that, for Catholic faithful, it is always necessary to read the biblical texts in the light of the patristic interpretation.[25] This latter point has been further corroborated and validated in the Second Vatican Council's Dogmatic Constitution on Divine Revelation, *Dei Verbum*.[26]

Let us now proceed to the elaboration of this theme in *Ineffabilis Deus* of Bl. Pius IX.

> The Fathers and writers of the Church ... in quoting the words by which at the beginning of the world God announced his merciful remedies prepared for the regeneration of mankind—words by which he crushed the audacity of the deceitful serpent and wondrously raised up the hope of our race, saying, "I will put enmities between thee and the woman, between thy seed and her seed"—taught that by this divine prophecy the merciful Redeemer of mankind, Jesus Christ, the only-begotten Son of God, was clearly foretold; that his most blessed Mother, the Virgin Mary, was prophetically indicated; and at the same time the very enmity of both against the Evil One was significantly expressed. Hence, just as Christ, the Mediator between God and man, assumed human nature, blotted the handwriting of the decree that stood against us, and fastened it triumphantly to the Cross, so the most holy Virgin, united with him by a

---

[24] Inseg XIX/1 (1996) 1389-1390 [ORE 1444:11; John Paul II, *Theotókos—Woman, Mother, Disciple: A Catechesis on Mary, Mother of God* with a foreword by Eamon R. Carroll, O.Carm, S.T.D. (Boston: Pauline Books and Media, 2000) (= *MCat*) 93-94].

[25] Cf. Stefano M. Cecchin, O.F.M., *L'Immacolata Concezione. Breve storia del dogma* (Vatican City: Pontificia Academia Mariana Internationalis "Studi Mariologici," No. 5, 2003) 191.

[26] Cf. *Dei Verbum*, especially 8, 10, 23.

most intimate and indissoluble bond, was, with him and through him, eternally at enmity with the evil serpent, and most completely triumphed over him, and thus crushed his head with her immaculate foot.[27]

Here we may note that the Pontiff gives an admirable summary of the Church's understanding of the *Protoevangelium* and in so doing illuminates the teaching about Mary as the woman who was united with the Redeemer "by a most intimate and indissoluble bond, was, with him and through him, eternally at enmity with the evil serpent, and most completely triumphed over him, and thus crushed his head with her immaculate foot." We should not be ignorant, however, of what Father Settimio Manelli points out in his recently published study i.e., that in recent decades there has been an unfortunate change of course in the interpretation of this text in that some modern exegetes are no longer willing to admit a Marian interpretation.[28] By the same token the painstaking work of Father Tiburtius Gallus shows a consistent Marian interpretation of this text over the course of the centuries *in medio Ecclesiæ*,[29] and the numerous commentaries on the *Protoevangelium* by the late Pope John Paul II continue to sustain the Marian interpretation on the part of the Magisterium. Let us conclude this part of our discussion with an excerpt from his Marian catechesis of January 24, 1996:

> The protogospel's words also reveal the unique destiny of the woman who, although yielding to the serpent's temptation before the man did, in virtue of the divine plan later becomes God's first ally. Eve was the serpent's accomplice in enticing man to sin. Overturning

---

[27] Tondini 46 [*OL* 46].
[28] Settimio M. Manelli, F.I., "Genesis 3:15 and the Immaculate Co-redemptrix" in *MFC* V:263; Cf. Edward Sri, *Queen Mother: A Biblical Theology of Mary's Queenship* (Steubenville, Emmaus Road Publishing, 2005) 58-66, 146-154.
[29] Cf. Tiburtius Gallus, S.J., *Interpretatio Mariologica Protoevangelii*, Vol. I: *Tempore post-patristico ad Concilium Tridentinum* (Romae: Libreria Orbis Catholicus, 1949); Vol. II: *Ætas Aurea Exegesis Catholicæ a Concilio Tridentino usque ad Annum 1660* (Roma: Edizioni di Storia e Letteratura, 1953); Vol. III: *Ab Anno 1661 usque ad Definitionem Dogmaticam Immaculatae Conceptionis (1854)* (Roma: Edizioni di Storia e Letteratura, 1954).

this situation, God declares that he will make the woman the serpent's enemy.

Exegetes now agree in recognizing that the text of Genesis, according to the original Hebrew, does not attribute action against the serpent directly to the woman, but to her offspring. Nevertheless, the text gives great prominence to the role she will play in the struggle against the tempter: in fact the one who defeats the serpent will be her offspring.

Who is this woman? The biblical text does not mention her personal name but allows us to glimpse a new woman, desired by God to atone for Eve's fall; in fact, she is called to restore woman's role and dignity, and to contribute to changing humanity's destiny, cooperating through her maternal mission in God's victory over Satan.

In the light of the New Testament and the Church's Tradition, we know that the new woman announced by the protogospel is Mary, and in "her seed" we recognize her Son, Jesus, who triumphed over Satan's power in the Paschal Mystery.

We also observe that in Mary the enmity God put between the serpent and the woman is fulfilled in two ways. God's perfect ally and the Devil's enemy, she was completely removed from Satan's domination in the Immaculate Conception, when she was fashioned in grace by the Holy Spirit and preserved from every stain of sin. In addition, associated with her Son's saving work, Mary was fully involved in the fight against the spirit of evil.

Thus the titles "Immaculate Conception" and "Cooperator of the Redeemer," attributed by the Church's faith to Mary, in order to proclaim her spiritual beauty and her intimate participation in the wonderful work of redemption, show the lasting antagonism between the serpent and the New Eve.[30]

---

[30] *Inseg* XIX/1 (1996) 116-117 [*ORE* 1426:11; *MCat* 62-63].

There are a number of points to be emphasized in this important catechesis. First, the Pope refers to the new woman, the antithesis of Eve, as "God's first ally" [*la prima alleata di Dio*] and "the serpent's enemy" [*la nemica del serpente*], and subsequently "God's perfect ally and the Devil's enemy" [*Alleata perfetta di Dio e nemica del diavolo*]. Secondly, he points out that "the text gives great prominence to the role she will play in the struggle against the tempter" and that this new woman is called "to contribute to changing humanity's destiny, cooperating through her maternal mission in God's victory over Satan." Thirdly, without hesitation he identifies the new woman as Mary "in the light of the New Testament and the Church's tradition." This is an assertion of capital importance in the light of the resistance to a Marian interpretation even in certain contemporary Catholic exegetical circles. Fourthly, he points out that the enmity between the serpent and Mary is fulfilled in two ways: (1) she was removed from Satan's dominion through her Immaculate Conception, which thus enabled her (2) to be "fully involved in the fight against the spirit of evil." Fifthly, because of "her intimate participation in the wonderful work of redemption," Mary is described as "Cooperator of the Redeemer" [*Cooperatrice del Redentore*], and thus there is a state of "lasting antagonism between the serpent and the New Eve." Hence this catechesis serves as an excellent summary of the great lines of Catholic exegesis, the Catholic Tradition and the Papal Magisterium on the *Protoevangelium*.

Development of Doctrine

In his catechesis of October 25, 1995, Pope John Paul II traces the history of doctrinal development regarding Our Lady's cooperation in the work of redemption in broad strokes, beginning, not surprisingly, with the Bishop of Lyons:

> At the end of the second century, St. Irenaeus, a disciple of Polycarp, already pointed out Mary's contribution to the work of salvation. He understood the value of Mary's consent at the time of the Annunciation, recognizing in the Virgin of Nazareth's obedience to and faith in the angel's message the perfect antithesis of Eve's disobedience and disbelief, with a beneficial effect

on humanity's destiny. In fact, just as Eve caused death, so Mary, with her "yes," became "a cause of salvation" for herself and for all mankind (cf. *Adv. Haer.*, III, 22, 4; *SC* 211, 441). But this affirmation was not developed in a consistent and systematic way by the other Fathers of the Church.

Instead, this doctrine was systematically worked out for the first time at the end of the tenth century in the *Life of Mary* by a Byzantine monk, John the Geometer. Here Mary is united to Christ in the whole work of redemption, sharing, according to God's plan, in the Cross and suffering for our salvation. She remained united to the Son "in every deed, attitude and wish" (cf. *Life of Mary*, Bol. 196, f. 123 v.).

Mary's association with Jesus' saving work came about through her Mother's love, a love inspired by grace, which conferred a higher power on it. Love freed of passion proves to be the most compassionate (cf. *ibid.*, Bol. 196, f. 123 v.).

In the West, St. Bernard, who died in 1153, turns to Mary and comments on the Presentation of Jesus in the Temple: "Offer your Son, sacrosanct Virgin, and present the fruit of your womb to the Lord. For our reconciliation with all, offer the heavenly Victim pleasing to God" (*Serm. 3 in Purif.*, 2: *PL* 183, 370).

A disciple and friend of St. Bernard, Arnold of Chartres, shed light particularly on Mary's offering in the sacrifice of Calvary. He distinguished in the Cross "two altars: one in Mary's heart, the other in Christ's body. Christ sacrificed his flesh, Mary her soul." Mary sacrificed herself spiritually in deep communion with Christ, and implored the world's salvation: "What the Mother asks, the Son approves and the Father grants" (cf. *De septem verbis Domini in cruce*, 3: *PL* 189, 1694).

From this age on, other authors explain the doctrine of Mary's special cooperation in the redemptive sacrifice.

At the same time, in Christian worship and piety contemplative reflection on Mary's "compassion" developed, poignantly depicted in images of the *Pièta*. Mary's sharing in the drama of the Cross makes this event more deeply human and helps the faithful to enter into the mystery: The Mother's compassion more clearly reveals the Passion of the Son.[31]

In time the seed of the doctrine expounded with such clarity by St. Irenaeus would continue to bear fruit through the meditations of Fathers, Doctors, saints and theologians on Mary's presentation of the infant Jesus in the Temple, with special reference to Simeon's prophecy (Lk 2:22-35) and her presence at the foot of the Cross (Jn 19:25-27). Here we can only hope to highlight a few of the important moments in this fascinating history of the development of the doctrine of Mary's collaboration in the work of redemption.[32] One can find an excellent historical overview in the treatment of Marian Coredemption through two millennia by Mother Maria Francesca Perillo, F.I., and Sister Maria

---

[31] *Inseg* XVIII/2 (1995) 934-936 [*ORE* 1414:11; *MCat* 25-27].

[32] To date there are four volumes edited by Mark Miravalle: *Mary Co-redemptrix, Mediatrix, Advocate, Theological Foundations: Towards a Papal Definition?* (Santa Barbara, CA: Queenship Publishing Company, 1995) [= *CMA* I], *Mary Co-redemptrix, Mediatrix, Advocate, Theological Foundations II: Papal, Pneumatological, Ecumenical* (Santa Barbara, CA: Queenship Publishing Company, 1997) [= *CMA* II], *Contemporary Insights on a Fifth Marian Dogma; Mary Co-redemptrix, Mediatrix, Advocate: Theological Foundations III* (Santa Barbara, CA: Queenship Publishing Company, 2000) [= *CMA* III], *Mary Co-redemptrix: Doctrinal Issues Today* (Goleta, CA: Queenship Publishing Company, 2002) [= *CMA* IV]. To date there are also six volumes of *Mary at the Foot of the Cross* published by the Franciscan Friars of the Immaculate (New Bedford, MA: Academy of the Immaculate, 2001-2006) and there are seven volumes of *Studi e Ricerche* published by the Franciscan Friars of the Immaculate in their *Bibliotheca Corredemptionis B. V. Mariae* (Frigento: Casa Mariana Editrice, 1998-2005). There is a further volume entitled *Maria "Unica Cooperatrice alla Redenzione." Atti del Simposio sul Mistero della Corredenzione Mariana, Fatima, Portogallo 3-7 Maggio 2005* (New Bedford, MA: Academy of the Immaculate, 2005). All of these volumes contain numerous detailed historical studies of our argument.

Rosa Pia Somerton, F.I.,[33] and in Mark Miravalle's *"With Jesus": The Story of Mary Co-Redemptrix.*[34]

As always, in the history of doctrine, the patristic era is one of special importance because of the foundation laid by the Fathers. The late Father Bertrand de Margerie, S.J., in his essay, "Mary Co-redemptrix in the Light of Patristics,"[35] analyzes the patrimony of St. Irenaeus at length and insists that "with him, the mystery of the Cross is already included in that of the Incarnation."[36] Indeed, he demonstrates that this is very largely the case with St. Ambrose, St. Augustine and many of the Fathers of the East and West.[37] Mother Abbess Elizabeth Marie Keeler, O.S.B., performed a great service in marshalling the testimony of the Benedictine monastic tradition from the sixth to the twelfth centuries regarding Our Lady's collaboration in the work of redemption,[38] unearthing data heretofore not taken into consideration which developed from the patristic foundation. Here is a particularly significant text from Paschasius Radbertus (865):

> Consider the love that was crucifying (*cruciabatur*) the Virgin in thinking of all she had heard and seen and known ... filled as she was with the Holy Spirit ... she was both Virgin and martyr ... the sword piercing her soul set her above the martyrs (*plusquam martyr fuit*)... she loved more than all, and so suffered more than all... she was more than a martyr because she suffered with her soul, her love was so much stronger than her own, because the Virgin made her own the death of Christ.[39]

---

[33] Mother Maria Francesca Perillo, F.I., and Sister Maria Rosa Pia Somerton, F.I., "The Marian Coredemption Through Two Millennia," in *MFC* II:79-111.

[34] Mark Miravalle, *"With Jesus": The Story of Mary Co-Redemptrix* (Goleta, CA: Queenship Publishing, 2003) [= *With Jesus*], chapters five through ten, 63-148.

[35] Bertrand de Margerie, S.J., "Mary Co-redemptrix in the Light of Patristics" trans. Salwa Hamati in *CMA* I:3-44].

[36] *CMA* I:7.

[37] Cf. *With Jesus* 63-75.

[38] Mother Abbess Elizabeth Marie Keeler, O.S.B., "The Mystery of Our Lady's Cooperation in our Redemption as Seen in the Fathers of Benedictine Monasticism from the VI to the XII Century" in *MFC* III:259-294.

[39] *MFC* III:281. Cf. *With Jesus* 87-88.

Foremost among the development of Marian Coredemption at this time are the contributions of St. Bernard (+1153) and his disciple, Arnold of Chartres (+1156). St. Bernard, who has sometimes been called "the last of the Church Fathers," is the first to teach of Mary's "offering" of Jesus as the divine Victim to the heavenly Father for the reconciliation of the world. St. Bernard's teachings are in the context of Mary's offering of Jesus at the Presentation of the Temple (and not yet at Calvary):

> O hallowed Virgin, offer thy Son; and present anew to the Lord this fruit of thy womb. Offer for our reconciliation this Victim, holy and pleasing to God. With joy, God the Father will receive this oblation, this Victim of infinite value.[40]

The Abbot of Clairvaux is also the first to refer to the "compassion"[41] of Our Lady, a term which etymologically comes from the Latin "cum" (with) and "passio" (suffering or receiving), and therefore refers to her "co-suffering" or "suffering with" Jesus. According to Bernard, the Virgin Mother welcomes the "price of redemption";[42] stands at "redemption's starting point";[43] and "liberates prisoners of war from their captivity."[44]

In addition, St. Bernard is the first theologian and Doctor of the Church to preach that Mary provided "satisfaction" for the disgrace and ruin brought about by Eve:

> Run, Eve, to Mary; run, mother to daughter. The daughter answers for the mother; she takes away the opprobrium of the mother; she makes satisfaction to thee, Father, for the mother... O woman singularly to be venerated ... Reparatrix of parents.[45]

---

[40] St. Bernard of Clairvaux, *Sermo 3 de Purificatione Beatae Mariae*; *PL* 183, 370.
[41] St. Bernard; *PL* 183, 438 A.
[42] St. Bernard, *Homil. 4 sup. Missus est*; *PL* 183, 83 C.
[43] St. Bernard, *Sermon des 12 étoiles*; *PL* 183, 430 C.
[44] *Ibid.*; *PL* 183, 430 D; *Homil. 4 sup. Missus est*; cf. Laurentin, *Le Titre de Corédemptrice, Etude Historique*, Paris, Nouvelles Editions Latines, 1951, p. 14 ff.
[45] St. Bernard, *Homilia 2 super Missus est*; *PL* 183, 62.

The pivotal Mariologist, Arnold of Chartres, St. Bernard's renowned disciple, can rightly be considered the first author who formally expounds the explicit doctrine of Mary Co-redemptrix at Calvary. While two centuries earlier, John the Geometer had referred to the suffering of Mary with the crucified Jesus, Arnold specifies *that it is Jesus and Mary who together accomplish the redemption through their mutual offering of the one and the same sacrifice to the Father.* The French abbot tells us:

> Together they [Christ and Mary] accomplished the task of man's redemption ... both offered up one and the same sacrifice to God: she in the blood of her heart, he in the blood of the flesh ... so that, together with Christ, she obtained a common effect in the salvation of the world.[46]

In a theological and terminological breakthrough, Arnold states that Mary is "co-crucified" with her Son[47] at Calvary, and that the Mother "co-dies" with him.[48] In response to objections first raised by Ambrose that Mary did not suffer the Passion, was not crucified like Christ, and did not die as Christ died at Calvary, Arnold responds that Mary experienced "com-passion" or "co-suffering" (using the term of his master, Bernard) with the Passion of Christ: "what they did in the flesh of Christ with nail and lance, this is a co-suffering in her soul."[49] Further, Arnold explains that Mary is in fact "co-crucified" in her heart with Jesus crucified,[50] and that the Mother "co-dies" with the death of her Son. Mary "co-died with the pain of a parent."[51]

Arnold concludes that the Mother of the Redeemer does not "operate" redemption at Calvary, but rather "co-operates" in redemption, and to the highest degree.[52] It is the love of the Mother that co-operates in a unique way at Calvary, in a way most favorable to God: "[On

---

[46] Arnold of Chartres, *De Laudibus B. Mariae Virginis*; PL 189, 1726-1727.
[47] Arnold of Chartres; PL 189, 1693 B.
[48] Ibid.
[49] Cf. Laurentin, *Le Titre de Corédemptrice*, p. 15, note 51; "quod in carne Christi agebant clavi et lancea, hoc in ejus mente compassio naturalis"; PL 189, 1731 B.
[50] Ibid., p. 15, note 52; "concrucifigebatur affectu"; PL 189, 1693 B.
[51] Ibid., p. 15, note 53; "parentis affectu commoritur"; PL 189, 1693B
[52] Ibid., p. 15, note 54; "co-operabatur ... plurimum"; *Tractatus de septem verbis Domini in cruce*, tr. 3; PL 189, 1695 A.

Calvary] the Mother's love co-operated exceedingly, in its own way, to render God propitious to us."[53]

How truly extraordinary was the contribution of Bernard and Arnold. The Mother's role in redemption is affirmed by Bernard in the terms, *offering*, *satisfying*, and *compassion*. Her role at Calvary is proclaimed by Arnold in the terms *co-crucified*, *co-dying*, *co-operating*. These testimonies can be likened, in their theological insight and maturity, to contemporary testimonies to Mary Co-redemptrix by popes of the twentieth and twenty-first centuries. The doctrine and title development of the Co-redemptrix story, exemplified in an extraordinary way during this late patristic and early medieval period, will soon bear even greater fruit in bringing forth the singular title which most clearly expresses the Mother's unique collaboration with and under Jesus in the redemption.

Mother Elizabeth also cites these beautiful texts from Arnold of Chartres:

> The affection of his Mother touches him [Jesus crucified], since in that moment there is only one will in Christ and Mary and it is the same holocaust that the two offer together, she in the blood of her heart, he in the blood of his flesh.[54]
>
> The apostles having fled, the Mother stood beside her Son and, pierced by the sword of sorrow, was wounded in her spirit and *concrucified* (*concrucifigebatur*) by love.[55]

The High Middle Ages ushers in a period in which references to "Mary's special cooperation in the redemptive sacrifice" become ever more abundant both on the part of the great scholastic Doctors[56] and the mystics.[57] Here I must limit myself to choosing a representation from each category. In his *De donis Spiritus Sancti* the Seraphic Doctor, St. Bonaventure (+1274), states:

---

[53] Arnold of Chartres, *Tractatus de septem verbis Domini in cruce*; tr. 3; *PL* 189, 1694.

[54] *MFC* III:290. On Arnold, cf. Luigi Gambero, *Mary in the Middle Ages: The Blessed Virgin Mary in the Thought of Medieval Latin Theologians* trans. Thomas Buffer (San Francisco: Ignatius Press, 2005) [= Gambero II] 148-154, esp. 150.

[55] *MFC* III:291.

[56] Cf. Mother Maria Francesca Perillo, F.I., and Sr. Maria Rosa Pia Somerton, F.I., "The Marian Coredemption Through Two Millennia" *MFC* II:90-94.

[57] Cf. *With Jesus* 93-100.

Eve expels us from paradise and sells us [into the slavery of sin], but Mary brings us back and buys our freedom.

Mary, the strong and faithful woman, paid this price, since when Christ suffered on the Cross to pay this price to redeem us, the Blessed Virgin was present, accepting God's will and consenting to it.[58]

At this historical point enters the mystical contribution of St. Bridget of Sweden (+1373). The *Revelations*, the written record of a series of visions and prophecies granted to St. Bridget by Jesus and Mary, are highly regarded and revered by the Church during the Middle Ages, including a large number of popes, bishops, and theologians.[59] The revealed words spoken by both Jesus and his Mother regarding Our Lady's coredemptive role are truly significant in the development of the Co-redemptrix doctrine, as they will influence numerous theologians during the seventeenth century "Golden Age of Coredemption," some 300 years later.

The Mother of Sorrows reveals in these prophetic visions through St. Bridget that "My Son and I redeemed the world as with one heart."[60] Jesus confirms the same truth in his own words: "My Mother and I saved man as with one heart only, I by suffering in my heart and my flesh, she by the sorrow and love of her heart."[61] It is difficult to argue with the supernatural testimony from such a Church-sanctioned and revered prophecy regarding the role of Mary Co-redemptrix—a testimony from the lips of the Redeemer and the Co-redemptrix themselves. The medievals, as a whole, did not.

The Rhineland Mystic, John Tauler (+1361) offers his own theological and mystical contribution to Mary Co-redemptrix. Like no

---

[58] Gambero II:211. On the foundation of the Franciscan doctrine of Marian coredemption in Sts. Francis and Bonaventure and Bl. John Duns Scotus, cf. Peter Damian Fehlner, F.I., "The Sense of Marian Coredemption in St. Bonaventure and Bl. John Duns Scotus" in *Mary at the Foot of the Cross – Acts of the International Symposium on Marian Coredemption* (New Bedford: Academy of the Immaculate, 2001) [=*MFC* I] 103-118.

[59] Cf. St. Bridget, *Revelationes*, ed. Rome, ap. S. Paulinum, 1606.

[60] St. Bridget, *Revelationes*, L. I, c. 35.

[61] St. Bridget, *Revelationes*, IX, c. 3.

other author before him, this Dominican theologian articulates with precision the *sacrificial offering* of the Mother at Calvary.

In the teachings of Tauler, the Mother of Jesus offers herself with Jesus as a living victim for the salvation of all,[62] and the eternal Father accepted this oblation of Mary for the salvation of the entire human race: "God accepted her oblation as a pleasing sacrifice, for the utility and salvation of the whole human race ... so that, through the merits of her sorrows, she might change God's anger into mercy."[63] In the natural progression of the New Eve patristic recapitulation brought to its fullness at Calvary, John speaks of the sorrow the Mother plucked from the tree of the Cross in order to redeem humanity with her Son:

> Just as Eve, boldly plucking from the tree of the knowledge of good and evil, destroyed men in Adam, so thou hast taken sorrow upon thyself from the tree of the Cross, and with thy suffering sated, thou has redeemed men together with thy Son.[64]

Addressing Our Lady, Tauler tells us of Mary's foreknowledge of her co-suffering with Jesus, in which she would share in all his redemptive merits and afflictions:

> He foretold to thee [Mary] all thy passion whereby he would make thee a sharer of all his merits and afflictions, and thou would co-operate with him in the restoration of men to salvation....[65]

St. Catherine of Siena (+1380), the great Church Doctor and Co-patroness of Europe, calls the Blessed Mother the "Redemptrix of the human race" both in virtue of giving birth to the Word and for the sorrow of "body and mind" that our Mother suffers with Jesus:

> O Mary ... bearer of the light ... Mary, Germinatrix of the fruit, Mary, Redemptrix of the human race because,

---

[62] John Tauler, *Sermo pro festo Purificat. B. M. Virginis*; *Oeuvres complètes*, ed. E. P. Noël, Paris, vol. 5, 1911, p. 61.
[63] *Ibid.*, vol. 6, pp. 253-255.
[64] *Ibid.*, p. 256.
[65] *Ibid.*, p. 259.

by providing your flesh in the Word, you redeemed the world. Christ redeemed with his Passion and you with your sorrow of body and mind.[66]

When one of the foremost theologians of the Council of Trent becomes the champion of Mary Co-redemptrix, the theological and doctrinal credibility of the Co-redemption title becomes promulgated throughout Catholic theological circles. Jesuit Father Alphonsus Salmerón (+1585), renowned theologian, exegete, and one of the original followers of St. Ignatius, repeatedly explains and defends the title of Co-redemptrix in an unprecedented systematic treatment of the doctrine.

In a remarkable passage, Salmerón defends the Marian titles of Co-redemptrix, Mediatrix, Advocate, and others as legitimate titles that rightly bespeak of the goodness and glory of Mary, full of grace:

> Truly Mary, very near and uniquely joined to him, is called full of grace ... how much he prepared that she as mother would pour out the fullest graces among us all as her sons as one who had been assumed by Christ, not out of any necessity, or out of weakness, but on account of the necessity to share and make clear, certainly, the goodness and glory in the mother that she would be (if it is permitted thus to speak) Co-redemptrix, Mediatrix, Cooperatrix of the salvation of mankind and to whom, as to an individual advocate, all the faithful ought to approach and fly for help.[67]

Salmerón goes on to note that the participation of Mary Co-redemptrix does not distract, but rather adds glory to Christ himself, for all her excellence and her capacity to share in redeeming is derived from the redeeming capacity of Jesus:

> The Mother stood near the Cross for this: that the restoration of mankind would correspond with the collapse of the world. As the fall of the world was

---

[66] St. Catherine of Siena, *Oratio* XI, delivered in Rome on the day of the Annunciation, 1379, in *Opere*, ed. Gigli, t. IV, p. 352.

[67] Alphonsus Salmerón, *Commentarii in Evangel.*, Tr. 5, Opera, Cologne, ed., Hiérat, 1604, t. III, pp. 37b- 38a.

accomplished by two, but especially by a man, so the salvation and redemption came about from two, but especially from Christ; for whatever excellence Mary has, she received from Christ, not only on account of a certain proper harmony, but also on account of the eminent capacity of Christ in redeeming, a capacity which with his Mother (whose works he needed least of all) he wished to share as Co-redemptrix, not only without her dishonor, but with the great glory of Christ himself.[68]

According to Salmerón, the simple motive of the Co-redemptrix in the exercise of her many functions on behalf of humanity, which are identified in her titles, is Christian maternal love: "For love of us ... she is all ours who is called Mother of Mercy, Queen of heaven, Mistress of the world, Star of the sea, Advocate, Co-redemptrix, Preserver, Mother of God."[69]

Throughout Salmerón's extraordinary treatment on Marian Coredemption we find the repeated use of the prefix, "co," in emphasizing the Mother's rightful subordination and dependency on the Lord of redemption. He refers to the Mother's "co-suffering,"[70] "co-misery,"[71] "co-sorrowing";[72] that she was "co-crucified,"[73] that she "co-died,"[74] "co-suffered," "cooperated,"[75] and was "co-united"[76] with Jesus in the redemption. This clear and generous theology of Mary Co-redemptrix provides solid dogmatic foundation for the following century's explosion of theological literature on Coredemption.

St. Veronica Giuliani (+1727), a Capuchin Poor Clare and outstanding mystic, writes in her diary about Mary's suffering on Calvary:

---

[68] Salmerón, *Commentarii*, vol. 10, tr. 41, p. 359b.
[69] *Ibid.*, vol. 11, tr. 38, p. 312a.
[70] *Ibid.*, vol. 3, tr. 43, 495a; cf. X, 51, 425 a; cf. Laurentin, *Le Titre de Corédemptrice*, pp. 15-16.
[71] *Ibid.*, vol. 3, 51, 426a, 424a, 429 b; vol. 11, 38, 311b; vol. 10, 51, 426a; cf. Laurentin, *Le Titre de Corédemptrice*, pp. 15-16.
[72] *Ibid.*, vol. 3, 43, 495a.
[73] *Ibid.*, vol. 3, 43, 399 b; vol. 11, 2, 188a.
[74] *Ibid.*, vol. 10, 51, 426b.
[75] *Ibid.*, vol. 6, 6, 39a.
[76] *Ibid.*, 36b.

> She participated in the same torments, not by way of the executioners, like Jesus, but she, by way of love and sorrow, participated in all the torments, one by one. The heart of Jesus and the heart of Mary both stood united in suffering and in love, and this they offered to God the Father for all of us mortals.[77]

It is fascinating to note in St. Veronica Giuliani a common thread that can be found in the writings of saints and theologians, especially from the seventeenth century onwards: The hearts of Jesus and Mary become the symbols of redemption and coredemption respectively. In terms of the world of both academic and mystical theology one can speak of the seventeenth century as "the Golden Age of Marian Coredemption," which largely coincides with the sunset of "the golden age of Spanish mysticism" and the "the golden age of French mysticism."[78] During this period consensus on Mary's role in the work of redemption continued to grow and major clarifications became the common property of Catholic theology. Here is an example of that clarity in a book by Giovanni Agostino Nasi, *Le Grandezze di Maria Vergine*, published in Venice in 1717:

> The pains of our Lord Jesus Christ, as pains of a God made man, were all of an infinite worth, so that the least of these would have been a superabundant price for the redemption of a thousand worlds. It is true, then, that the pains of the Virgin were not of such weight as to possess infinite worth and that *per se* they alone would not have sufficed for the redemption of the world. ... But granting all this, as the pains of the Mother of God they indeed still had an exceptional worth beyond the human mind to conceive; and if they could not in truth be said to be infinite, one could however say that they were a

---

[77] Mother Maria Francesca Perillo, F.I., "Marian Coredemption in St. Veronica Giuliani," in *MFC* I:246. Cf. the entire article *MFC* I:237-265 and also Mother Maria Francesca's doctoral thesis, *Maria nella Mistica: La mediazione mariana in santa Veronica Giuliani* (Pregassono: Europress; Piano della Croce: Casa Mariana Editrice, Collana di Mariologia curata da Manfred Hauke, #5, 2004).

[78] Mother Maria Francesca Perillo, F.I., and Sr. Maria Rosa Pia Somerton, F.I., "The Marian Coredemption Through Two Millennia" *MFC* II:94-95; *With Jesus* 113-129.

quasi-participation in the infinite worth of the Savior's merits. Our Lord Jesus Christ, by means of his pains, redeemed the world *condignly*. His most holy Mother, who was made his companion (*socia*) in this truly grand work, in contributing to it as well the most precious riches of her sorrows, in union with the pains of the Son, *merited congruently to obtain in such a way the redemption of the world*. So the human race is indebted to both the Son and the Mother for the incomparable blessing which by their mutual consent has been apportioned to it.[79]

Now it cannot be said that there was never any opposition to the doctrine briefly outlined above, but neither did such opposition cause a major disruption or discontinuity in its development. One very notable voice of opposition came from the Jansenist Adam Widenfeld (+1678) in his anonymously published pamphlet of 1673 entitled *Salutary Admonitions of the Blessed Virgin Mary to her Indiscreet Devotees* [*Monita salutaria B.V. Mariae ad cultores suas indiscretos*], in which Our Lady is quoted as saying: "Do not call me *Salvatrix* and *Co-redemptrix*." Widenfeld's little work effectively launched a "pamphlet war" and was eventually put on the Roman Index.[80] Worthy of note in the popularization of the teaching on Mary's role in the work of our redemption and the term Co-redemptrix in the nineteenth century was *The Foot of the Cross*, a very popular book, written by Frederick William Faber (+1863), a convert from Anglicanism and the founder of the Brompton Oratory in London.[81] Another significant stage in the divulgation of the teaching was the publication of the little book, *L'Immacolata, Corredentrice Mediatrice*, in 1928 by the distinguished Servite Mariologist and theologian, Cardinal Alexis Lépicier.[82] In fact, by the time of this publication, the word Co-redemptrix had already passed into the Papal Magisterium.

---

[79] Mother Maria Francesca Perillo, F.I., and Sr. Maria Rosa Pia Somerton, F.I., "The Marian Coredemption Through Two Millennia" *MFC* II:98. The original Italian text is found in Juniper B. Carol, O.F.M., *De Corredemptione Beatae Virginis Mariae: Disquisitio Positiva* (Vatican City: Typis Polyglottis Vaticanis, 1950) 373.

[80] Cf. *Theotokos* 66-67; *With Jesus* 121-123.

[81] Cf. Arthur Burton Calkins, "Mary the Coredemptrix in the Writings of Frederick William Faber (1814-1863)" in *MFC* I:317-343.

[82] Cf. Angelo M. Tentori, O.S.M., "Mary Co-redemptress in the Writings of Cardinal Alexis Henry Mary Lépicier, O.S.M." in *MFC* II:361-379.

Papal Teaching on Marian Coredemption before the Second Vatican Council

In his Rosary Encyclical *Jucunda Semper* of September 8, 1894, Pope Leo XIII drew out explicitly Mary's sufferings on Calvary:

> When she professed herself the handmaid of the Lord for the mother's office, and when, at the foot of the altar, she offered up her whole self with her child Jesus—then and thereafter she took her part in the painful expiation offered by her Son for the sins of the world. It is certain, therefore, that she suffered in the very depths of her soul with his most bitter sufferings and with his torments. Finally, it was before the eyes of Mary that the divine sacrifice for which she had borne and nurtured the Victim was to be finished. As we contemplate him in the last and most piteous of these mysteries, we see that "there stood by the cross of Jesus Mary his Mother" (Jn 19:25), who, in a miracle of love, so that she might receive us as her sons, offered generously to divine justice her own Son, and in her heart died with him, stabbed by the sword of sorrow.[83]

In this passage Leo touched upon themes that his successors would continue to develop in an ever-swelling crescendo in the course of the twentieth century: Mary's offering of herself in union with Jesus in expiation for the sins of the world, her "mystical death" described in terms of "dying with him in her heart" [*cum eo commoriens corde*] and the spiritual maternity which flows from her participation in the sacrifice.

The word "Co-redemptrix" makes its preliminary appearance on the magisterial level by means of official pronouncements of Roman Congregations during the reign of Pope St. Pius X (1903-1914) and then enters into the papal vocabulary.

The term first occurs in the *Acta Apostolicæ Sedis* in a response to a request made by Father Giuseppe M. Lucchesi, Prior General of the Servites (1907-1913), requesting the elevation of the rank of the feast of the Seven Sorrows of Our Lady to a double of the second class for the entire Church. The Sacred Congregation of Rites, in acceding to

---

[83] Tondini 204-206 [*OL* 151].

the request, expressed the desire that thus "the cultus of the Sorrowful Mother may increase and the piety of the faithful and their gratitude toward *the merciful Co-redemptrix* of the human race may intensify."[84]

Five years later the Sacred Congregation of the Holy Office in a decree signed by Cardinal Mariano Rampolla expressed its satisfaction with the practice of adding to the name of Jesus that of Mary in the greeting "Praised be Jesus and Mary" to which one responds "Now and forever":

> There are Christians who have such a tender devotion toward her who is the most blessed among virgins as to be unable to recall the name of Jesus without accompanying it with the glorious name of the Mother, *our Co-redemptrix*, the Blessed Virgin Mary.[85]

Barely six months after this declaration, on January 22, 1914, the same congregation granted a partial indulgence of 100 days for the recitation of a prayer of reparation to Our Lady beginning with the Italian words *Vergine benedetta*. Here is the portion of that prayer which bears on our argument:

> O blessed Virgin, Mother of God, look down in mercy from heaven, where thou art enthroned as Queen, upon me, a miserable sinner, thine unworthy servant. Although I know full well my own unworthiness, yet in order to atone for the offenses that are done to thee by impious and blasphemous tongues, from the depths of my heart I praise and extol thee as the purest, the fairest, the holiest creature of all God's handiwork. I bless thy holy name, I praise thine exalted privilege of being truly Mother of God, ever-Virgin, conceived without stain of sin, *Co-redemptrix of the human race*.[86]

---

[84] *AAS* 1 (1908) 409; my trans. (emphasis my own); cf. Laurentin 23; *Prob* 21.
[85] *AAS* 5 (1913) 364; my trans. (emphasis my own); cf. Laurentin 24; *Prob* 21.
[86] *AAS* 6 (1914) 108; Joseph P. Christopher, Charles E. Spence and John F. Rowan (eds.), *The Raccolta* (Boston: Benziger Brothers, Inc., 1957) #329, pp. 228-229 (it should be noted that the English translation is rendered in the first person plural whereas the Italian is in the first person singular; emphasis my own); cf. Laurentin 24-25; *Prob* 21.

On the basis of these last two instances Monsignor Brunero Gherardini comments that

> The authority of that dicastery [the Sacred Congregation of the Holy Office], now designated as "for the Doctrine of the Faith," is such as to confer on its interventions a certain definitive character for Catholic thought.[87]

Surely one of the most famous passages on this theme is that which we find in Benedict XV's letter *Inter Sodalicia* of May 22, 1918:

> The choosing and invoking of Our Lady of Sorrows as patroness of a happy death is in full conformity with Catholic doctrine and with the pious sentiment of the Church. It is also based on a wise and well-founded hope. In fact, according to the common teaching of the Doctors it was God's design that the Blessed Virgin Mary, apparently absent from the public life of Jesus, should assist him when he was dying nailed to the Cross. Mary suffered and, as it were, nearly died with her suffering Son; for the salvation of mankind she renounced her mother's rights and, as far as it depended on her, offered her Son to placate divine justice; so we may well say that she with Christ redeemed mankind.[88]

It should be noted here that Benedict indicates that Mary's presence beneath the Cross of Christ was "not without divine design" [*non sine divino consilio*], the very same phrase reproduced verbatim in *Lumen Gentium* 58, although with no reference to this text. Evidently deriving from the principle that "God, by one and the same decree, had established the origin of Mary and the Incarnation of divine Wisdom,"[89] Benedict XV held that God had also predestined Mary's union with her Son in his sacrifice, to the extent of offering him in sacrifice insofar as she was able to do so [*quantum ad se pertinebat*]. It should also be pointed out here

---

[87] Brunero Gherardini, *La Madre: Maria in una sintesi storico-teologica* (Frigento [AV]: Casa Mariana Editrice, 1989) 271 (my trans.).
[88] *AAS* 10 (1918) 181-182 [*OL* 267].
[89] Tondini 32 [*OL* 34].

that Benedict was certainly not stating that the sacrifice of Jesus was not sufficient to redeem the world, but rather that, on the basis of the understanding of the "recapitulation" already articulated by St. Irenaeus, God wished the sacrifice of the New Eve to be joined to that of the New Adam, that he wished the active participation of a human creature joined with the sacrifice of the God-man.

The first papal usage of the term occurs in an allocution by Pope Pius XI (1922-1939) to pilgrims from Vicenza on November 30, 1933:

> From the nature of his work the Redeemer ought to have associated his Mother with his work. For this reason *we invoke her under the title of Co-redemptrix*. She gave us the Savior, she accompanied him in the work of redemption as far as the Cross itself, sharing with him the sorrows of the agony and of the death in which Jesus consummated the redemption of mankind.[90]

On March 23, 1934, the Lenten commemoration of Our Lady of Sorrows, Pius XI received two groups of Spanish pilgrims, one of which was composed of members of Marian Congregations of Catalonia. *L'Osservatore Romano* did not publish the text of the Pope's address, but rather reported his principal remarks to these groups. Noting with pleasure the Marian banners carried by these pilgrims, he commented that they had come to Rome to celebrate with the Vicar of Christ

> not only the nineteenth centenary of the divine redemption, but also *the nineteenth centenary of Mary, the centenary of her Coredemption, of her universal maternity*.[91]

---

[90] *Il Redentore non poteva, per necessità di cose, non associare la Madre Sua alla Sua opera, e per questo noi la invochiamo col titolo di Corredentrice. Essa ci ha dato il Salvatore, l'ha allevato all'opera di redenzione fino sotto la croce, dividendo con Lui i dolori dell'agonia e della morte, in cui Gesù consumava la redenzione di tutti gli uomini.* Domenico Bertetto, S.D.B., ed., *Discorsi di Pio XI* 2:1013; OL 326 (emphasis my own); cf. Laurentin 26; Carol, "Our Lady's Coredemption," *Mariology* 2:384.

[91] *Il Papa diceva che essi venivano a celebrare presso il Vicaro di Cristo non solo il XIX centenario della Divina Redenzione, ma anche il XIX centenario di Maria, il centenario della Sua Corredenzione, della Sua universale Maternità.* OR 25 marzo 1934, p. 1 (my trans.; emphasis my own).

He continued, addressing himself especially to the young people, saying that they must

> follow the way of thinking and the desire of Mary most holy, who is our Mother and our Co-redemptrix: they, too, must make a great effort to be coredeemers and apostles, according to the spirit of Catholic Action, which is precisely the cooperation of the laity in the hierarchical apostolate of the Church.[92]

Finally Pope Pius XI referred to Our Lady as Co-redemptrix on April 28, 1935, in a radio message for the closing of the holy year at Lourdes:

> Mother most faithful and most merciful, who as *Co-redemptrix and partaker of thy dear Son's sorrows* didst assist him as he offered the sacrifice of our redemption on the altar of the Cross ... preserve in us and increase each day, we beseech thee, the precious fruits of our redemption and thy compassion.[93]

Let us consider now how this theme is treated in two encyclicals of the Servant of God Pope Pius XII. Our first passage comes from the Encyclical *Mystici Corporis* of June 29, 1943, promulgated during the height of World War II:

> She [Mary] it was who, immune from all sin, personal or inherited, and ever most closely united with her Son, offered him on Golgotha to the eternal Father together

---

[92] *Quei giovani dovevano seguire il pensiero ed il desiderio di Maria Santissima, che è nostra Madre e Corredentrice nostra: dovevano sforzarsi ad essere, anch'essi, corredentori ed apostoli, secondo lo spirito dell'Azione Cattolica, ch'è appunto la cooperazione del laicato all'apostolato gerarchico della Chiesa.* OR 25 marzo 1934, p. 1 (my trans.; emphasis my own); cf. *Prob* 21; Laurentin 26-27. Laurentin comments that coredeemer here is simply a synonym for apostle in the larger sense of the word!

[93] *O Mater pietatis et misericordiæ, quæ dulcissimo Filio tuo humani generis Redemptionem in ara crucis consummanti compatiens et Coredemptrix adstitisti ... conserva nobis, quæsumus, atque adauge in dies pretiosos Redemptionis et tuæ compassionis fructus.* OR 29-30 aprile 1935, p. 1; *OL* 334 (emphasis my own); cf. Laurentin 27; Carol, "Our Lady's Coredemption," *Mariology* 2:384.

with the holocaust of her maternal rights and motherly love, like a New Eve, for all the children of Adam contaminated through this unhappy fall, and thus she, who was the mother of our Head according to the flesh, became by a new title of sorrow and glory the spiritual Mother of all his members.[94]

Let us underscore here the emphasis on Mary's offering of Christ to the eternal Father as a "New Eve," effectively drawing out the implications of the teaching of St. Irenaeus. Pius XII would offer yet another beautiful perspective on this joint offering of the Son and the Mother in his great Sacred Heart Encyclical, *Haurietis Aquas*, of May 15, 1956:

> That graces for the Christian family and for the whole human race may flow more abundantly from devotion to the Sacred Heart, let the faithful strive to join it closely with devotion to the Immaculate Heart of the Mother of God. By the will of God, the most Blessed Virgin Mary was inseparably joined with Christ in accomplishing the work of man's redemption, so that our salvation flows from the love of Jesus Christ and his sufferings intimately united with the love and sorrows of his Mother.[95]

In this classic passage every word is carefully weighed and measured in order to make a declaration on the redemption and Mary's role in it, which remains unparalleled for its clarity and precision. No doubt for this reason it is included in Denzinger-Hünermann's *Enchiridion Symbolorum*.[96] Pius professes that "our salvation flows from the love of Jesus Christ and his sufferings" [*ex Iesu Christi caritate eiusque cruciatibus*] which are "intimately united with the love and sorrows of his Mother" [*cum amore doloribusque ipsius Matris intime consociatis*]. The Latin preposition *ex* indicates Jesus as the source of our redemption while three other Latin words, *cum* and *intime consociatis*, indicate Mary's inseparability from the source. Finally, let us note Pius' insistence on the fact that this union

---

[94] *AAS* 35 (1943) 247-248 [*OL* 383].
[95] *AAS* 48 (1956) 352 [*OL* 778].
[96] *D-H* 3926.

of Jesus with Mary for our salvation has been ordained "by the will of God" [*ex Dei voluntate*].[97]

The Situation on the Eve of the Second Vatican Council

First, it must be remembered that the Second Vatican Council was convoked just at a time when Marian doctrine and piety had reached an apex,[98] which had been building on a popular level since the apparition of Our Lady to St. Catherine Labouré in 1830[99] and on the magisterial level since the time of the dogmatic definition of the Immaculate Conception on December 8, 1854.[100] This Marian orientation had accelerated notably during the 19-year reign of the Servant of God Pope Pius XII (1939-1958) with the consecration of the world to the Immaculate Heart of Mary on October 31, 1942,[101] the dogmatic definition of the Assumption of Our Lady on November 1, 1950,[102] the establishment of the Feast of the Immaculate Heart of Mary in 1944[103] and of the Queenship of Mary in the Marian Year of 1954.[104]

Secondly, and as a consequence of this comprehensive "Marian movement," much study, discussion and debate had been devoted to Mary's role in salvation history, specifically to the topics of coredemption and mediation. These scholarly deliberations were largely occasioned by the initiatives undertaken by Cardinal Désiré Joseph Mercier (1851-1926)

---

[97] On this topic I have only been able to highlight some of the most important texts from among the numerous passages which could have been cited. For further references, cf. *MMC* 64-79.

[98] Cf. Michael O'Carroll, C.S.Sp., "Still Mediatress of All Graces?", *Miles Immaculatæ* 24 (1988) 121-122; *Theotokos* 351-352.

[99] This apparition of Our Lady would be succeeded by a number of others in the nineteenth and twentieth centuries which would eventually be recognized by the Church as worthy of credence. Cf. Donal Foley, *Marian Apparitions, the Bible, and the Modern World* (Herefordshire: Gracewing, 2002) 113-346.

[100] Cf. *Theotokos* 179-180. Interestingly, Father O'Carroll acknowledges an impetus for the definition in the apparition of 1830, cf. *Theotokos* 182.

[101] Cf. Arthur Burton Calkins, *Totus Tuus: John Paul II's Program of Marian Consecration and Entrustment* (New Bedford, MA: Academy of the Immaculate "Studies and Texts," No. 1, 1992) [= *Totus Tuus*] 98-101.

[102] Cf. *Theotokos* 555-56.

[103] Cf. *Totus Tuus* 100.

[104] Cf. *Totus Tuus* 104-105.

in favor of the proclamation of Our Lady as Mediatrix of all graces,[105] and continued until the International Mariological Congress held at Lourdes in 1958. These disputes are carefully chronicled and analyzed in Juniper Carol's masterful study on "Our Lady's Coredemption" which appears in the three-volume *Mariology*.[106] Major adversaries were Professors Werner Goosens and Heinrich Lennerz, S.J. Goosens argued against the incompatibility of secondary mediators and redeemers with Christ as the "One Mediator" according to 1 Timothy 2:5-6,[107] a matter which had already been addressed and clarified by St. Thomas Aquinas[108] and Pope Leo XIII in his Encyclical *Fidentem Piumque* of September 20, 1896.[109]

Lennerz, on the other hand, presented what Carol considered to be "the gravest speculative difficulty" to the doctrine of Marian coredemption. If Mary was herself redeemed by the Precious Blood of Christ, how could she at one and the same time cooperate in the redemption of others?[110] Carol had already carefully summarized a response on the basis of the competent scholarship at the time that he wrote,[111] which is in full harmony with what I now present in ways that may be less technical for the modern reader. Let us begin with these observations by the biblical and patristic scholar, Father Lino Cignelli, O.F.M.:

> Insofar as *redeemed* by God through the merits of Christ, Mary is revealed as the receptive, graced, object

---

[105] Cf. Manfred Hauke, "Mary, 'Mediatress of Grace': Mary's Universal Mediation of Grace in the Theological and Pastoral Works of Cardinal Mercier." Supplement to *Mary at the Foot of the Cross* – IV [Part B] (New Bedford, MA: Academy of the Immaculate, 2004).

[106] Juniper B. Carol, O.F.M., S.T.D., "Our Lady's Coredemption" in Carol, *Mariology* Vol. 2 (Milwaukee: The Bruce Publishing Company, 1957) 377-425, esp. 416-424.

[107] Cf. W. Goosens, *De cooperatione immediata Matris Redemptoris ad redemptionem objectivam* (Parisiis, 1939) 30-31; Carol, "Coredemption" 416.

[108] St. Thomas says "There is no reason why certain others should not be called in a certain way mediators between God and man, that is to say in so far as they cooperate by predisposing and ministering in the union of man with God" in *Summa Theologica* III, q. 26, a. 1.

[109] *Acta Sanctae Sedis* [= *ASS*] 29 (1896-1897) 206 [*OL* 194].

[110] Cf. Heinrich Lennerz, S.J., "Considerationes de doctrina B. Virginis Mediatricis" in *Gregorianum* 19 (1938) 424-425; George D. Smith, *Mary's Part in Our Redemption* (P. J. Kenedy & Sons, 1954) 92-99.

[111] Cf. Carol, "Coredemption" 418-422.

of redemption, both with respect to the One and Triune God, the principal Savior, and with respect to the man Christ, ministerial Savior. Insofar as *Co-redemptrix*, she is instead the complement of the man Christ and his "helper" in the work of universal salvation. She represents the feminine component of the dimension or the human causality of the objective redemption, and is thus the associate of the historical Christ or the Second Adam and Savior.

Mary, therefore, is soteriologically active only in relation to other men, not already in relation to herself. In the work of redemption it is necessary to distinguish two logical moments: Christ alone redeems Mary and, together with her, redeems the rest of humanity.[112]

Thus Father Cignelli presents the mystery of the Immaculate Conception and the coredemption in terms of the classical teaching of Irenaeus and the Fathers: in order to function as the New Eve, Mary had to be redeemed in advance; only then could she collaborate in the redemption of others. While she could not be actively involved in her own initial grace of redemption, which is always a pure gift, she could be in the case of others.

Now let us consider these further clarifications about the "two logical moments of the redemption" offered to us by the late Father Gabriele M. Roschini, O.S.M. (+1977),[113] founder and first President of the Theological Faculty "Marianum" and a master in the field of Mariology:

> The objective redemption of Christ therefore is constituted by two elements: 1) by the Passion and death of Christ and 2) by the *intention* with which Christ offered his life to the Father. The first of these two elements is common to both Mary and to all the other redeemed; the second, on the contrary (which is the principal element in

---

[112] Lino Cignelli, O.F.M., *Maria Nuova Eva nella Patristica greca* (Assisi: Studio Teologico "Porziuncola" Collectio Assisiensis #3, 1966) 241 (my trans.). Emphasis in second paragraph my own.

[113] Cf. *Theotokos* 314-315; Pietro Parrotta, *La Cooperazione di Maria alla Redenzione in Gabriele Maria Roschini* (Pregassona, Switzerland: Europress, 2002).

the objective redemption), is different. The first intention of Christ was that of redeeming Mary with preservative redemption; the second intention of Christ, instead, was to redeem, along with Mary (the New Adam with the New Eve) all the others with liberative redemption.

This *double intention is implicit* in the *double mode* of redemption: preservative for the Virgin and liberative for all the rest. Otherwise (or without this double intention) these two undeniable modes of redemption would be inexplicable. The *end* then for which the Redeemer intended first to redeem the Virgin (with preservative redemption) is precisely so that the Virgin would be in a position to be able to cooperate with him in the (liberative) redemption of all the others. *In short: Immaculate because Co-redemptrix.*[114]

Father Roschini's clarifications are of the greatest importance to what we are considering. What Father Cignelli presented in terms of the logical, but not chronological, difference between the "two moments of redemption" Father Roschini further differentiates in terms of "preservative" and "liberative" redemption. Mary's redemption was "preservative," i.e., she was preserved from original sin and its effects from the first moment of her existence.[115]

In his Marian catechesis of January 24, 1996, Pope John Paul II verified these insights and effectively responds to the arguments put forth by Heinrich Lennerz:

> In the light of the New Testament and the Church's tradition, we know that the new woman announced by the *Protoevangelium* is Mary, and in "her seed" we recognize her son Jesus who triumphed over Satan's power in the Paschal Mystery.

---

[114] Gabriele M. Roschini, O.S.M., *Maria Santissima nella Storia della Salvezza*, II (Isola del Liri: Tipografia Editrice M. Pisani, 1969) 193-194 (my trans.) Last emphasis my own.

[115] This argument is also taken up in a less technical way by Galot in "Mary Co-redemptrix: Controversies and Doctrinal Questions" in *CMA* IV:14-17 and in *Marie, Mère et Coréremptrice* 177-178.

> We also observe that in Mary the enmity God put between the serpent and the woman is fulfilled in two ways. God's perfect ally and the Devil's enemy, she was completely removed from Satan's domination in the Immaculate Conception, when she was fashioned in grace by the Holy Spirit and preserved from every stain of sin. In addition, associated with her Son's saving work, Mary was fully involved in the fight against the spirit of evil.
>
> Thus the titles "Immaculate Conception" and "Cooperator of the Redeemer" show the lasting antagonism between the serpent and the New Eve. The Church's faith attributes these titles to Mary in order to proclaim her spiritual beauty and her intimate participation in the wonderful work of redemption.[116]

In other words the enmity between the woman and the serpent point both to the mystery of Mary's Immaculate Conception, a totally gratuitous gift from God, and to the mystery of Mary's active collaboration in the work of the redemption. The gratuitous gift was necessary in order for Mary to play the role which God intended for her in our redemption. Here is the way the Pope draws this truth out for our benefit in his catechesis of May 29, 1996:

> The same biblical text [Gen 3:15] also proclaims the enmity between the woman and her offspring on the one hand and the serpent and his offspring on the other. *This is a hostility expressly established by God, which has a unique importance, if we consider the problem of the Virgin's personal holiness. In order to be the irreconcilable enemy of the serpent and his offspring Mary had to be free from all power of sin, and to be so from the first moment of her existence.*
>
> In this regard, the Encyclical *Fulgens Corona*, published by Pope Pius XII in 1953 to commemorate the centenary of the definition of the dogma of the Immaculate Conception, reasons thus: "If at a given moment the Blessed Virgin Mary had been left without divine grace, because she was defiled at her conception by the

---

[116] *Inseg* XIX/1 (1996) 116-117 [*MCat* 62-63].

hereditary stain of sin, between her and the serpent there would no longer have been—at least during this period of time, however brief—that eternal enmity spoken of in the earliest tradition up to the definition of the Immaculate Conception, but rather a certain enslavement" (*AAS* 45 [1953] 579).[117]

Hence it is clear according to the Papal Magisterium, that Mary was conceived without original sin and filled with grace precisely so that she could fulfill her role as Mother of God and Co-redemptrix. The enmity between the woman and the serpent, according to God's plan, must have begun at the first moment of her existence so that she would have no "Achilles' heel" whereby she could be attacked and so that she could be "God's perfect ally" in the supreme battle fought on Calvary. In fact, the use of Genesis 3:15 in the modern Papal Magisterium almost always comprises these two points of reference: Mary's Immaculate Conception and her role as Co-redemptrix. This is readily verifiable in *Ineffabilis Deus*,[118] as it is in the entire tradition.[119] Hence the response to Father Lennerz' objection is even more clearly affirmed in the Magisterium now than it was when he raised it.

Hence while there had been vigorous disputation regarding Mary's active collaboration in the work of our redemption during the reign of Pope Pius XII, by the time of the International Mariological Congress in Lourdes in 1958 at the end of his reign, there was a fairly unanimous consensus regarding Our Lady's true cooperation in acquiring the universal grace of redemption.[120]

---

[117] *Inseg* XIX/1 (1996) 1389-11390 [*MCat* 93-94]. Emphasis my own.

[118] Cf. my study "The Immaculate Coredemptrix in the Life and Teaching of Blessed Pius IX" in *Mary at the Foot of the Cross – V: Redemption and Coredemption under the Sign of the Immaculate Conception* (New Bedford, MA: Academy of the Immaculate, 2005) 508-541.

[119] Many other studies in Volume V of *Mary at the Foot of the Cross* also treat of the relationship between Mary's Immaculate Conception and her role as Co-redemptrix, but the one which has the most direct bearing on responding to Lennerz's objection is Msgr. Brunero Gherardini's "The Immaculate Co-redemptress" 47-73.

[120] Cf. Alessandro M. Apollonio, F.I., *Il "calvario teologico" della Coredenzione mariana* (Castelpetroso, IS: Casa Mariana Editrice, 1999) [= *Calvario*] 7-8. This conclusion is summarily and categorically denied by Stefano De Fiores, S.M.M., in his *Maria:*

Not surprisingly, then, a good number of bishops entered the Council with the desire to see a comprehensive treatment of these questions. Father Michael O'Carroll, C.S.Sp., notes that of the 54 bishops at the Council who wanted a conciliar pronouncement on Mary as Co-redemptrix, 36 sought a definition and 11 a dogma of faith on this matter.[121] On the related question of Mary's mediation, he tells us that 362 bishops desired a conciliar statement on Mary's mediation while 266 of them asked for a dogmatic definition.[122] Father Besutti, on the other hand, holds that over 500 bishops were asking for such a definition.[123] A fundamental reason why no such definition emanated from the Council was the expressed will of Bl. Pope John XXIII that the Council was to be primarily pastoral in its orientation, specifically excluding any new dogmatic definitions.[124]

Finally, at the very same time another current was entering into the mainstream of Catholic life, that of a newly emphasized ecumenical sensitivity. While Father Besutti confirms that the word "Co-redemptrix" did appear in the original *schema* of the Marian document prepared in advance for the Council,[125] the *Prænotanda* to the first conciliar draft document or *schema* on Our Lady contained these words:

> Certain expressions and words used by supreme pontiffs have been omitted, which, in themselves are absolutely true, but which may only be understood with difficulty by separated brethren (in this case Protestants).

Nuovissimo Dizionario I (Bologna: Edizioni Dehoniane, 2006) [=*Nuovissimo*] 325 who speaks of an "unhealable division between two currents."

[121] Cf. *Theotokos* 308.

[122] Cf. Michael O'Carroll, C.S.Sp., "Mary's Mediation: Vatican II and John Paul II" in *Virgo Liber Verbi: Miscellanea di studi in onore di P. Giuseppe M. Besutti, O.S.M.* (Rome: Edizioni «Marianum», 1991) 543; *Theotokos* 352. In the latter article Father O'Carroll gave the number of Fathers asking for a statement on Mary's mediation as 382. Toniolo gives the number as 381, cf. Ermanno M. Toniolo, O.S.M., *La Beata Vergine Maria nel Concilio Vaticano II* (Rome: Centro di Cultura Mariana «Madre della Chiesa», 2004) [= Toniolo] 34.

[123] G. Besutti, O.S.M., *Lo schema mariano al Concilio Vaticano II* (Rome: Edizione Marianum-Desclée, 1966) [= Besutti] 17.

[124] Cf. *Calvario* 14.

[125] Besutti 28-29; cf. Toniolo 36.

Among such words may be numbered the following: "Co-redemptrix of the human race" [Pius X, Pius XI].[126]

This original prohibition was rigorously respected and hence the term "Co-redemptrix" was not used in any of the official documents promulgated by the Council and, undeniably, ecumenical sensitivity was a prime factor in its avoidance,[127] along with a hesitancy for the general language of mediation on the part of certain theologians.[128] We remain free to debate about the wisdom and effectiveness of such a strategy.[129]

The Second Vatican Council

The above discussion already gives some idea about the various currents that came to the fore at the time of the Second Vatican Council (which have been dealt with as well in other places).[130] Here I will limit our examination to the positive presentation on Our Lady's active participation in the work of the redemption which emerged in the Council's great Marian synthesis, chapter 8 of the Dogmatic Constitution on the Church, *Lumen Gentium*. *Lumen Gentium* 56 speaks forthrightly of Mary's collaboration in the work of redemption:

> Committing herself whole-heartedly to God's saving will and impeded by no sin, she devoted herself totally, as a handmaid of the Lord, to the person and work of her Son, under and with him, serving the mystery of redemption, by the grace of Almighty God.[131]

In the same paragraph there is further specification about the active nature of Mary's service, which I have already cited in the discussion of

---

[126] *Acta Synodalia Sacrosancti Concilii Oecumenici Vaticani Secundi*, Vol. I, Pt. VI (Typis Polyglottis Vaticanis, 1971) 99 (my trans.). Cf. Toniolo 98-99; Gabriele M. Roschini, O.S.M., *Maria Santissima nella Storia della Salvezza* II:111-112.

[127] Cf. Thomas Mary Sennott, O.S.B., "Mary Mediatrix of All Graces, Vatican II and Ecumenism," *Miles Immaculatæ* 24 (1988) 151-167; *Theotokos* 242-245.

[128] Cf. Ralph M. Wiltgen, S.V.D., *The Rhine Flows into the Tiber; A History of Vatican II* (Rockford, IL: Tan Books and Publishers, Inc., 1985, c. 1967) 90-95, 153-159.

[129] Cf. my article "'Towards Another Marian Dogma?' A Response to Father Angelo Amato," *Marianum* LIX (1997) 163-165.

[130] Cf. *MMC* 35-41.

[131] Flannery 416 (I have altered the word order of the translation).

Mary as the "New Eve." Quite clearly, then, the Council Fathers speak of an active collaboration of Mary in the work of the redemption and they illustrate this with the Eve-Mary antithesis as found in St. Irenaeus.

Further, the Council Fathers did not content themselves with a general statement on Mary's collaboration in the work of the redemption, but went on to underscore the personal nature of the "union of the Mother with the Son in the work of salvation" [*Matris cum Filio in opere salutari coniunctio*] throughout Jesus' hidden life (57) and public life (58). Finally, in 58 they stress how she

> faithfully persevered in her union with her Son unto the Cross, where she stood, in keeping with the divine plan, enduring with her only-begotten Son the intensity of his suffering, associated herself with his sacrifice in her mother's heart, and lovingly consenting to the immolation of this Victim which was born of her.[132]

Not only, then, does the Council teach that Mary was generally associated with Jesus in the work of redemption throughout his life, but that she associated herself with his sacrifice and consented to it. Furthermore, the Council Fathers state in 61 that Mary

> shared her Son's sufferings as he died on the Cross. Thus, in a wholly singular way she cooperated by her obedience, faith, hope and burning charity in the work of the Savior in restoring supernatural life to souls.[133]

Not only did Mary consent to the sacrifice, but she also united herself to it. In these final two statements we find a synthesis of the previous papal teaching on the Our Lady's active collaboration in the work of the redemption, as well as a stable point of reference for the teaching of the post-conciliar popes.

While it may well be argued, as Pope John Paul II has done, that "the Council's entire discussion of Mary remains vigorous and balanced,

---

[132] Flannery 417. Galot's reflections on this text and its hesitation to speak more directly of Mary's offering of her Son and herself to the Father for our salvation are illlluminating. Cf. his article "Mary Co-redemptrix: Controversies and Doctrinal Questions" in *CMA* IV:17-19.

[133] Flannery 418.

and the topics themselves, though not fully defined, received significant attention in the overall treatment,"[134] it is also true that the battles on Our Lady's mediatorial role which took place on the council floor and behind the scenes continue to have their effects.[135]

---

[134] *Inseg* XVIII/2 (1995) 1369 [*MCat* 51].

[135] Cf. *Theotokos* 351-356. Effectively, the interpretation of the Second Vatican Council's Marian treatise found most frequently in both learned and popular publications after the Council is well represented by this relatively recent statement by Cardinal Avery Dulles, S.J.:

> The achievements of Vatican II have been called a watershed. The chapter on Mary in the Constitution on the Church seemed to mark the end of an isolated, maximizing Mariology, and the inclusion of Mary in the theology of the Church (Avery Cardinal Dulles, S.J., "Mary Since Vatican II: Decline and Recovery," *Marian Studies* LIII (2002) 12. This position is delineated at much greater length in Stefano De Fiores' article "Concilio Vaticano II" in *Nuovissimo* I:323-358).

This departs notably from all of the commentaries on the Mariology of Vatican II offered by Pope John Paul II in the course of his long pontificate and constitutes what I refer to as "Vatican II triumphalism."

"Vatican II triumphalism" is virtually always a partial and one-sided interpretation of the council documents which favors a position espoused by one party at the time of the Council and studiously avoids mention of any conciliar statements which would counterbalance the "favored" position. In the case of chapter eight of *Lumen Gentium* on "The Blessed Virgin Mary, Mother of God, in the Mystery of Christ and of the Church," the "favored" position heavily emphasizes Mary's role as model of the Church. This reflects the rediscovered insights of ecclesiotypical Mariology (which sees an analogy between Mary and the Church) which were emerging again at the time of the Council, while very largely ignoring Christotypical Mariology (which sees an analogy between Christ and Mary) and dismissing it as deductive and "privilege-centered" (cf. the comments by Fathers George F. Kirwin, O.M.I., and Thomas Thompson, S.M., in Donald W. Buggert, O.Carm., Louis P. Rogge, O.Carm., Michael J. Wastag, O.Carm. (eds.), *Mother, Behold Your Son: Essays in Honor of Eamon R. Carroll, O.Carm.* (Washington, DC: The Carmelite Institute, 2001), 17 and 202.) In an essay significantly entitled "Revolution in Mariology 1949-1989," Father Eamon R. Carroll, O.Carm., consistently presents the ecclesiotypical Mariology as the great triumph of the Council, even as he discloses his discomfort at the Christotypical elements which remained in the eighth chapter of *Lumen Gentium*:

> The Council did indeed favor the notion that Mary is model to the Church, even archetype, without using that word, but its chapter on Our Lady is in

The Contribution of John Paul II

I believe that the Marian magisterium of the late Pope John Paul II may well constitute his greatest single legacy to the Catholic Church. While certain prominent modern Mariologists have settled for presenting us with an interpretation of the Second Vatican Council's Marian teaching in an almost exclusively ecclesiotypical key, Pope John Paul II managed to keep a remarkable balance in his presentation of Marian doctrine, emphasizing both the Christotypical and ecclesiotypical dimensions and clearly illustrating the continuity in the Church's teaching on Our Lady. He quoted extensively from chapter 8 of *Lumen Gentium* both in his Marian Encyclical *Redemptoris Mater* as well as in the extensive corpus of his Marian teaching, opening the conciliar texts up to their maximum potentiality. In terms of the number and depth

---

fact a complicated compromise that sought to keep a balance between Mary's association with her son's mediation and the obedient faithful Virgin as ideal of the Church's own response to the Lord (Eamon R. Carroll, O.Carm, "Revolution in Mariology 1949-1989," in *The Land of Carmel: Essays in Honor of Joachim Smet, O.Carm.* (Rome: Institutum Carmelitanum, 1991) 457-458. On the former page one also finds his evaluation of Fathers Cyril Vollert, S.J., Juniper B. Carol, O.F.M., and Charles Balić, O.F.M., all of whom represent the Christotypical approach to Mariology).

There were obviously many theological insights which were coming to the fore at the time of the Council, largely due to the historical researches begun in the previous century in the areas of biblical, liturgical, patristic and ecclesiological studies. Many of these found expression in the council documents, and specifically in chapter eight of *Lumen Gentium*. All too often, however, an overemphasis on certain of these insights on the part of the majority of commentators to the exclusion of the other insights has, in fact, led to a "low Mariology" which focuses on Mary much more as "woman of faith," "disciple" and "model" than as "spiritual mother" or "mediatrix," and tends to depreciate the importance of the antecedent Papal Magisterium. All too often this virtually exclusive emphasis on ecclesiotypical Mariology is coupled with the whole-hearted embracing of the historical-critical method of biblical exegesis and "lowest common denominator" ecumenism (cf. Carroll, "Revolution in Mariology" 455). In a real sense the practitioners of this methodology can be identified as sustainers of the thesis that the teaching of the Second Vatican Council represents a "break" or "rupture" with the pre-conciliar Catholic tradition, (this thesis was clearly declared unacceptable by Pope Benedict XVI in his memorable speech to the Roman Curia on December 22, 2005. Cf. *Insegnamenti di Benedetto XVI* I (2005) 1023-1031 [*ORE* 1925:5-6]), and are almost always notably devoid of that awe before the mystery of Mary which comes instinctively to "little ones."

of his Marian discourses, homilies, Angelus addresses and references in major documents, there is no doubt that his output exceeds that of all of his predecessors combined. His Marian magisterium alone would fill several large volumes and in assessing it, one should not forget the clear indications given in *Lumen Gentium* 25 for recognizing the authentic Ordinary Magisterium of the Roman pontiff:

> This loyal submission of the will and intellect must be given, in a special way, to the authentic teaching authority of the Roman pontiff, even when he does not speak *ex cathedra* in such wise, indeed, that his supreme teaching authority be acknowledged with respect, and sincere assent be given to decisions made by him, conformably with his manifest mind and intention, which is made known principally either by the character of the documents in question, or by the frequency with which a certain doctrine is proposed, or by the manner in which the doctrine is formulated.

What is true in general about his Marian magisterium is true in particular about his teaching on Our Lady's active cooperation in the work of the redemption, or coredemption. His teaching in this area has been extraordinary.[136]

---

[136] I have already published two lengthy essays on it, and some shorter ones, as well as treating it in the course of other studies of the Papal Magisterium on Marian coredemption, without in any way having analyzed it exhaustively. Cf. Arthur Burton Calkins, "Pope John Paul II's Teaching on Marian Coredemption" in *CMA* II:113-147; also published in *Miles Immaculatæ* XXXII (Luglio/Dicembre 1996) 474-508 and "Pope John Paul II's Ordinary Magisterium on Marian Coredemption: Consistent Teaching and More Recent Perspectives" in *MFC* II:1-36; also published in *Divinitas* XLV «Nova Series» (2002) 153-185. Cf. also "The Heart of Mary as Coredemptrix in the Magisterium of Pope John Paul II" in *S. Tommaso Teologo: Ricerche in occasione dei due centenari accademici* (Vatican City: Libreria Editrice Vaticana "Studi Tomistici #59," 1995) 320-335; "Il Cuore di Maria Corredentrice nel Magistero di papa Giovanni Paolo II" in *Corredemptrix: Annali Mariani 1996 del Santuario dell'Addolorata* (Castelpetroso, Isernia, 1997) 97-114; "Amorosamente consenziente al sacrificio del Figlio: Maria Corredentrice nei discorsi di Giovanni Paolo II," *Madre di Dio* 67, N° 11 (Novembre 1999) 28-29. Cf. also "Il Mistero di Maria Corredentrice nel Magistero Pontificio" in Autori Vari, *Maria Corredentrice: Storia e Teologia I* (Frigento [AV]: Casa Mariana

Perhaps occupying pride of place among these is his treatment of Our Lady's suffering in his Apostolic Letter *Salvifici Doloris*. In that letter he had already stated in 24 that "The sufferings of Christ created the good of the world's redemption. This good in itself is inexhaustible and infinite. No man can add anything to it."[137] That is a premise from which no Christian can depart, but the mystery is even deeper, as he tells us in 25 of that same letter:

> It is especially consoling to note—and also accurate in accordance with the Gospel and history—that at the side of Christ, in the first and most exalted place, there is always his Mother through the exemplary testimony that she bears *by her whole life* to this particular Gospel of suffering. In her, the many and intense sufferings were amassed in such an interconnected way that they were not only a proof of her unshakable faith but also a contribution to the redemption of all. In reality, from the time of her secret conversation with the angel, she began to see in her mission as a mother her "destiny" to share, in a singular and unrepeatable way, in the very mission of her Son. ...
>
> It was on Calvary that Mary's suffering, beside the suffering of Jesus, reached an intensity which can hardly be imagined from a human point of view but which was mysteriously and supernaturally fruitful for the redemption of the world. Her ascent of Calvary and her standing at the foot of the Cross together with the beloved disciple were a special sort of sharing in the redeeming death of her Son. And the words which she heard from his lips were a kind of solemn handing-over of this Gospel

---

Editrice «Bibliotheca Corredemptionis B. V. Mariae» Studi e Richerche 1, 1998) 141-220 and "The Mystery of Mary the Co-redemptrix in the Papal Magisterium," in *CMA* IV:25-92.

To my knowledge, Monsignor Brunero Gherardini (Cf. Brunero Gherardini, *La Corredentrice nel mistero di Cristo e della Chiesa* (Rome: Edizioni Vivere In, 1998) 135-139) and I are the only students of Mariology to have done so *in extenso*; *Inseg* I (2005) 1023-1031; *OR* 23 dicembre 2005, pp. 5-6; *ORE* 1925:5-6. Besides the passages which I have already presented in the course of this paper, I can only hope to share a small sampling of what I consider to be the most outstanding texts.

[137] *Inseg* VII/1 (1984) 307 [St. Paul Editions 37].

of suffering so that it could be proclaimed to the whole community of believers.

As a witness to her Son's Passion by her *presence*, and as a sharer in it by her *compassion*, Mary offered a unique contribution to the Gospel of suffering, by embodying in anticipation the expression of St. Paul which was quoted at the beginning. She truly has a special title to be able to claim that she "completes in her flesh"—as already in her heart—"what is lacking in Christ's afflictions."

In the light of the unmatched example of Christ, reflected with singular clarity in the life of his Mother, the Gospel of suffering, through the experience and words of the apostles, becomes *an inexhaustible source for the ever new generations* that succeed one another in the history of the Church.[138]

These two citations from *Salvifici Doloris* help us to hold in tension the dynamic truths which underlie Marian coredemption. On the one hand, "The sufferings of Christ created the good of the world's redemption. This good in itself is inexhaustible and infinite. No man can add anything to it." On the other hand, "Mary's suffering [on Calvary], beside the suffering of Jesus, reached an intensity which can hardly be imagined from a human point of view but which was mysteriously and supernaturally fruitful for the redemption of the world." Thus the Pope strikes that careful balance which is always a hallmark of Catholic truth: he upholds the principle that the sufferings of Christ were all-sufficient for the salvation of the world, while maintaining that Mary's suffering "was mysteriously and supernaturally fruitful for the redemption of the world." Is this a contradiction? No. It is a mystery. The sacrifice of Jesus is all-sufficient, but God wished the suffering of the "New Eve," the only perfect human creature, to be united to the suffering of the "New Adam." Does that mean that Mary could redeem us by herself? By no means. But it does mean that she could make her own unique contribution to the sacrifice of Jesus as the "New Eve," the "Mother of the living."

---

[138] *Inseg* VII/1 (1984) 308-309 [St. Paul Editions 40-41].

Let us see how skillfully the Holy Father states this in his truly extraordinary Angelus address on Corpus Christi, June 5, 1983:

> "Ave, verum Corpus natum de Maria Virgine!"
> Hail, true Body born of the Virgin Mary! ...
>
> That divine Body and Blood, which after the consecration is present on the altar, is offered to the Father, and becomes Communion of love for everyone, by consolidating us in the unity of the Spirit in order to found the Church, preserves its maternal origin from Mary. She prepared that Body and Blood before offering them to the Word as a gift from the whole human family that he might be clothed in them in becoming our Redeemer, High Priest and Victim.
>
> At the root of the Eucharist, therefore, there is the virginal and maternal life of Mary, her overflowing experience of God, her journey of faith and love, which through the work of the Holy Spirit made her flesh a temple and her heart an altar: because she conceived not according to nature, but through faith, with a free and conscious act: an act of obedience. And if the Body that we eat and the Blood that we drink is the inestimable gift of the Risen Lord, to us travelers, it still has in itself, as fragrant Bread, the taste and aroma of the Virgin Mother.
>
> "Vere passum, immolatum in Cruce pro homine." That Body truly suffered and was immolated on the Cross for man.
>
> Born of the Virgin to be a pure, holy and immaculate oblation, Christ offered on the Cross the one perfect sacrifice which every Mass, in an unbloody manner, renews and makes present. In that one sacrifice, Mary, the first redeemed, the Mother of the Church, had an active part. She stood near the Crucified, suffering deeply with her firstborn; with a motherly heart she associated herself with his sacrifice; with love she consented to his immolation (cf. *Lumen Gentium*, 58; *Marialis Cultus*, 20): she offered him and she offered herself to the Father.

> Every Eucharist is a memorial of that sacrifice and that Passover that restored life to the world; every Mass puts us in intimate communion with her, the Mother, whose sacrifice "becomes present" just as the sacrifice of her Son "becomes present" at the words of consecration of the bread and wine pronounced by the priest (cf. Discourse at the Celebration of the Word, June 2, 1983, n. 2 [*ORE* 788:1]).[139]

The Eucharist, according to the Holy Father, bears "the taste and aroma of the Virgin Mother" not only because Jesus was born of Mary, but also because in the Mass her sacrifice, her offering of Jesus and herself to the Father, becomes present along with his.

This final text is from a homily given at the Shrine of Our Lady of the Dawn in Guayaquil, Ecuador, on January 31, 1985:

> Mary goes before us and accompanies us. The silent journey that begins with her Immaculate Conception and passes through the "yes" of Nazareth, which makes her the Mother of God, finds on Calvary a particularly important moment. There also, accepting and assisting at the sacrifice of her Son, Mary is the dawn of redemption; and there her Son entrusts her to us as our Mother: "The Mother looked with eyes of pity on the wounds of her Son, from whom she knew the redemption of the world had to come" (St. Ambrose, *De Institutione Virginis*, 49). Crucified spiritually with her crucified Son (cf. Gal 2:20), she contemplated with heroic love the death of her God, she "lovingly consented to the immolation of this Victim which she herself had brought forth" (*Lumen Gentium*, 58). She fulfills the will of the Father on our behalf and accepts all of us as her children, in virtue of the testament of Christ: "Woman, there is your son" (Jn 19:26). ...
>
> At Calvary she united herself with the sacrifice of her Son that led to the foundation of the Church; her maternal heart shared to the very depths the will of Christ "to gather into one all the dispersed children of God" (Jn

---

[139] *Inseg* VI/1 (1983) 1446-1447 [*ORE* 788:2].

> 11:52). Having suffered for the Church, Mary deserved to become the Mother of all the disciples of her Son, the Mother of their unity. ...
>
> The gospels do not tell us of an appearance of the risen Christ to Mary. Nevertheless, as she was in a special way close to the Cross of her Son, she also had to have a privileged experience of his Resurrection. In fact, *Mary's role as Co-redemptrix did not cease with the glorification of her Son.*[140]

The late Holy Father used the adjectival form of Co-redemptrix in Spanish [*corredentor*], just as he used the Italian term Corredentrice in speaking of Mary on six other occasions.[141] In effect, he used the word more than twice as much as his last predecessor to do so, Pius XI.[142]

Where does all of the above discussion leave us? According to Monsignor Brunero Gherardini

> The conditions by which a doctrine is and must be considered Church doctrine are totally and amply verifiable in Marian Coredemption: its foundation is indirect and implicit, yet solid, in the Scriptures; extensive in the Fathers and theologians; unequivocal in the Magisterium. It follows, therefore, that the Coredemption belongs to the Church's doctrinal patrimony.

---

[140] *Inseg* VIII/1 (1985) 318-321 [*ORE* 876:7]. I refer those interested to my commentary on this text elsewhere, cf. Arthur Burton Calkins, "Pope John Paul II's Ordinary Magisterium on Marian Coredemption: Consistent Teaching and More Recent Perspectives" in *MFC* II:32-34.

[141] *Inseg* III/2 (1980) 1646; [*ORE* 662:20]; *Inseg* V/3 (1982) 404; *Inseg* VII/2 (1984) 1151 [*ORE* 860:1]; *Inseg* VIII/1 (1985) 889-890 [*ORE* 880:12]; *Inseg* XIII/1 (1990) 743; *Inseg* XIV/2 (1991) 756 [*ORE* 1211:4]. Cf. my presentation of all but the first of these texts in *MMC* 41-46. John Paul II's first use of the title Co-redemptrix thus far documented, that of December 10, 1980, occurred in a greeting to the sick after the general audience and was identified by Fr. Paolo M. Siano, F.I., and is cited in his article, "Uno Studio su Maria Santissima «Mediatrice di Tutte le Grazie» nel Magistero pontificio fino al pontificato di Giovanni Paolo II" *Immaculata Mediatrix* VI:3 (2006) 348.

[142] Cf. *MMC* 32-34.

The nature of this present relation, in virtue of a theological conclusion drawn from premises in the Old and New Testaments, is expressed by the note *proxima fidei*.[143]

We can safely say that the teaching on Mary's collaboration in the work of redemption is part of the Ordinary Magisterium, and our late Holy Father, Pope John Paul II, especially by the frequency with which he returned to this theme, brought it to a new peak of explicitness and prominence in the Church.[144]

Conclusion

It has been noted that there are already four dogmas about Mary. They are that she is (1) the Mother of God (*Theotókos*);[145] (2) ever-Virgin;[146] that she was (3) immaculately conceived[147] and (4) assumed body and soul into heaven.[148] All of these truths of the faith pertain to the person of Mary, but thus far the Church has not yet proposed to the faithful in the most solemn manner the truth about Mary's role in their lives. In his brilliant essay, "*Mariæ Advocatæ Causæ*: The Marian Issue in the Church Today," Father Peter Damian Fehlner, F.I., has argued cogently that the theological question about Mary Co-redemptrix is **the** theological issue of our era and that until it is clarified the fruits hoped for from the Second Vatican Council will not be brought forth:

> Nonetheless, there is a hesitation on what I maintain has been for nearly a century the theological issue of our time: the doctrine of coredemption, in view of which

---

[143] Brunero Gherardini, "The Coredemption of Mary: Doctrine of the Church," in *MFC* II:48.

[144] Unfortunately, despite the clarity of the Holy Father's teaching many have not embraced this important truth. For a more in-depth exploration of this resistance, see the special note at the end of this chapter.

[145] Defined by the Council of Ephesus in 431. Cf. *D-H* 252.

[146] By the time of the Council of Ephesus belief in Mary's virginity before, during and after the birth of Christ was in possession and was explicitly defined at the Lateran Council of 649, convoked by Pope St. Martin I. Cf. *D-H* 503.

[147] Defined by Bl. Pope Pius IX on December 8, 1854. Cf. *D-H* 2303.

[148] Defined by the Servant of God Pope Pius XII on November 1, 1950. Cf. *D-H* 3903.

> on the eve of Vatican II theologians were divided into maximalists (those in favor, a majority) and minimalists (those who insisted that the doctrine was inopportune). Vatican II left the question open, like Trent with the Immaculate Conception, teaching the mystery of coredemption, but not dotting the "i's" and crossing the "t's." Is this why the crisis continues, and why the hoped-for fruits of the Council have not been realized, above all the resolution of the ecumenical question (division among the baptized) and the problem of a genuine, and radical renewal of theology (confusion, even in the Roman schools)?[149]

One really needs to follow his entire exposition in order to grasp the full force of his argumentation, but I remain convinced that his evaluation is absolutely correct. What, then, is to be done?

In his essay "Verso un Altro dogma Mariano?", which was actually a kind of book review of the first book of essays edited by Dr. Mark Miravalle, Father Angelo Amato, S.D.B., indicated that to arrive at a dogmatic definition, one needs three elements: (1) a widespread movement of favorable opinion on the part of the faithful, (2) impetus on the part of the Papal Magisterium and (3) the contribution of theologians.[150] We can say that the conviction of the faithful continues to grow because the teaching about Marian coredemption is deeply implanted in the *sensus fidelium*. It will grow much stronger to the extent that it is preached, celebrated and taught. If this is not the case at present, it is because for almost two generations it has not been taught in seminaries. The doctrine is clearly taught by the Magisterium; about that there is no doubt and even Father Amato had to admit it. The biggest single problem is the theologians, but this, too, can and must change. More and more convincing studies are being published. The theological establishment cannot ignore solid theological research and

---

[149] Peter Damian M. Fehlner, F.I., "*Mariæ Advocatæ Causæ*: The Marian Issue in the Church Today" in *Maria "Unica Cooperatrice alla Redenzione." Atti del Simposio sul Mistero della Corredenzione Mariana, Fatima, Portogallo 3-7 Maggio 2005* (New Bedford, MA: Academy of the Immaculate, 2005) 559.

[150] Angelo Amato, S.D.B., "Verso Un Altro Dogma Mariano?" in *Marianum* LVIII (1996) 231.

block indefinitely. I believe that the more bishops, priests and deacons preach and teach the doctrine, the more the faithful will be fired up. The Holy Spirit will not tolerate indefinite obstacles.

The more that the Church consciously and deliberately recognizes Mary's role in our salvation, proclaims it and celebrates it, the more Satan will be vanquished and the more Jesus will reign. The Fathers of the Second Vatican Council already gave voice to this intuition when they stated in *Lumen Gentium* 65 that

> Having entered deeply into the history of salvation, Mary, in a way unites in her person and re-echoes the most important doctrines of the faith: and when she is the subject of preaching and worship she prompts the faithful to come to her Son, and to his sacrifice and to the love of the Father. Seeking after the glory of Christ, the Church becomes more like her lofty type, and continually progresses in faith, hope and charity, seeking and doing the will of God in all things.

★ ★ ★

Special Note:

Status Quaestionis: It appears as if most of those who hold prominent positions in academic Mariology and other high places have taken little note of the clear papal teaching and all of the positive scholarship that has been produced in this regard during the past 15 years. The most positive statement to come from one of their representatives thus far was an admission in a footnote by the late Father Ignazio M. Calabuig, O.S.M., on behalf of his colleagues, that my study of the use of the term Co-redemptrix published in *Maria Corredentrice: Storia e Teologia I* was done with praiseworthy precision and clearly indicates that the title Co-redemptrix is not proscribed and is susceptible of a correct reading, even though they seem to maintain that the word only occurs in documents of a non-magisterial character (Ignazio Calabuig, O.S.M., e il Comitato di redazione della rivista Marianum, "Riflessione sulla richiesta della definizione dogmatica di «Maria corredentrice, mediatrice, avvocata»," *Marianum* LXI, nn. 155-156 (1999) 157, n. 50).

In addition, an *ad hoc* committee was convened at the Mariological Congress held in Częstochowa, Poland, in August 1996, to deal with petitions which the Holy See had been receiving for a dogmatic definition of Mary's role in the work of our redemption as Co-redemptrix, Mediatrix and Advocate. Unfortunately, none of those who had done any studies in support of such a definition were consulted, and of the 23 theologians who rendered the negative decision against considering a definition, one was Anglican, one was Lutheran and three were Orthodox. The reasoning proffered was the following:

"The titles, as proposed, are ambiguous, as they can be understood in very different ways. Furthermore, the theological direction taken by the Second Vatican Council, which did not wish to define any of these titles, should not be abandoned" (*OR* 4 giugno 1997, p. 10 [*ORE* 1494:12]).

What is difficult to understand about this statement is that the prologue to the Marian chapter of *Lumen Gentium* 54 explicitly states that

> This sacred synod ... does not, however, intend to give a complete doctrine on Mary, nor does it wish to decide those questions which the work of theologians has not yet fully clarified. Those opinions therefore may be lawfully retained which are propounded in Catholic schools concerning her, who occupies a place in the Church which is the highest after Christ and also closest to us.

The same edition of *L'Osservatore Romano* which carried their declaration also carried an unsigned article stating that

> With respect to the title of *Co-redemptrix*, the Declaration of Częstochowa notes that "from the time of Pope Pus XII, the term *Co-redemptrix* has not been used by the Papal Magisterium *in its significant documents*" and there is evidence that he himself intentionally avoided using it. An important qualification, because here and there, in papal writings which are marginal and therefore devoid of doctrinal weight, one can find such a title, be it very rarely (*OR* 4 giugno 1997, p. 10 [*ORE* 1497:10]).

It seems that the primary reason why Pius XII did not use the title, even though he clearly taught the doctrine as we have seen, was because of the discussion of theologians which had only reached a definite theological consensus at the Mariological Congress of Lourdes in 1958, a few months before his death (Cf. *Calvario* 7-8). The fact that Pope John Paul II used the term "Co-redemptrix" five times and "coredemptive" once in speaking about Our Lady is apparently set aside as "marginal and therefore devoid of doctrinal weight," with no reference to *Lumen Gentium* 25. I would simply add that the Częstochowa Declaration itself is hardly above criticism for the way it attempts to deal with facts, and may be far more appropriately described as "marginal and therefore devoid of doctrinal weight." Although it was published in *L'Osservatore Romano*, a semi-official organ of the Holy See, its various editorials and articles do not form part of the Church's official Magisterium.

Subsequently, the Pontifical International Marian Academy issued a publication entitled *La Madre del Signore* on the occasion of the Great Jubilee of 2000 which stated that

> In our opinion such study [of Our Lady's role in the work of redemption] should not be conducted by re-proposing the presuppositions, the terminology and the metaphors used by

many theologians before the Second Vatican Council, but rather according to the lines traced by the Constitution *Lumen Gentium*. Within this ambit John Paul II has amply considered the cooperation of the Virgin in the Trinitarian work of salvation under the categories of "mediation in Christ" and of "maternal mediation," that is as a particular function of the universal motherhood of Mary in the order of grace; to many theologians this way of presenting the question of the mediation of Mary appears more rich, based on a good biblical foundation (cf. Jn 19:25-27), more in conformity with the *sensus fidelium*, less subject to controversy (*La Madre del Signore. Memoria, Presenza, Speranza. Alcune questioni attuali sulla figura e la missione della b. Vergine Maria* (Vatican City: Pontificia Accademia Mariana Internationalis, 2000) hereafter cited as *La Madre del Signore* 80 (my trans.).

Here it is necessary to comment. (1) To the uninitiated, at first glance this statement might seem unexceptionable, but, in fact it suggests sidestepping the entire millennial Catholic tradition of understanding and elucidating Our Lady's unique mediatorial role by saints, mystics and theologians, along with the Papal Magisterium of Bl. Pius IX, Leo XIII, St. Pius X, Benedict XV, Pius XI and Pius XII which has put this matter in ever-sharper relief, (Cf. *Theotokos* 238-242; Gabriele M. Roschini, O.S.M., *Maria Santissima nella Storia della Salvezza*, Vol. II (Isola del Liri: Tipografia Editrice M. Pisani, 1969) 198-235; Brunero Gherardini, *La Madre: Maria in una sintesi sotrico-teologica* (Frigento: Casa Mariana Editrice, 1989) 287-324; Arthur Burton Calkins, "Mary as Co-redemptrix, Mediatrix and Advocate in the Contemporary Roman Liturgy," in *CMA* I:68-82). (2) This statement infers that the preconciliar methodology employed in exploring this topic is "less rich" than the conciliar treatment found in *Lumen Gentium*, and is based on less-solid biblical foundations. Such a vague statement, of course, implies and effectively promotes the thesis that the teaching of the Second Vatican Council represents a "break" or "rupture" with pre-conciliar teaching. (3) Without any supporting evidence, the authors of this communication state that their approach is in greater conformity to the *sensus fidelium* (Cf. *Lumen Gentium* 12, 34; *Dei Verbum* 10; *Catechism of the Catholic Church* 889; *Theotokos* 322-323). (4) They also state that their proposed methodology is less subject to controversy, but that is only because by prescribing the methodology to be used, they have effectively eliminated any opposition. (5) Without stating it in so many words here, the authors appear to be concerned about avoiding controversy on the ecumenical level as they clearly indicate elsewhere (Cf. *La Madre del Signore* 112-116). Specifically, they state that students of Mariology

> – should abstain from the will to impose on brethren not in communion with the Catholic Church "other obligations beyond those which are indispensable (cf. Acts 15:28)," that is doctrinal questions about the Mother of the Lord which are *quæstiones disputatæ* among Catholic theologians;
> – should proceed to a supervised and correct use of terms and formulae (purification of language); the use of formulae and terms which, on the one hand, are not ancient nor accepted by many Catholic theologians and on the other hand provoke grave discomfort in brothers and sisters who are not in full communion with the Catholic Church is certainly not useful for reciprocal understanding; rather it is wise to use a terminology which expresses doctrine with exactness and efficacy, but which does not provide grounds for false interpretations (*La Madre del Signore* 115, my trans.).

This kind of language is concerning. In the name of what could appear as less-than straightforward ecumenical correctness camouflaged as "purification of language," the authors seem to seek to impose silence on Catholics about matters which were not fundamentally "*quæstiones disputatæ* among Catholic theologians" until after the Council. It could be interpreted that they are concerned about not "provoking grave discomfort in brothers and sisters who are not in full communion with the Catholic Church," but not among their own Catholic brothers and sisters.

The dossier published in *Marianum* regarding the request for the dogmatic definition of Mary Co-redemptrix, Mediatrix and Advocate takes the very same approach as what has just been quoted above, with even more specific indications about terminology which it says the Second Vatican Council wished to avoid. This is perhaps because the same persons were involved in the redaction of these documents. In that dossier, the late Father Ignazio Calabuig, O.S.M., the principal redactor, goes on to state that the Council consciously and deliberately renounced

> – using the title *Co-redemptrix* and the term *coredemptio* with reference to the Blessed Virgin; to the latter the Council preferred *cooperatio* and this because since it has an ecclesial point of reference with a biblical foundation (cf. 1 Cor 3:9), it could effectively designate the collaboration given by Mary, in faith, obedience and love, to the formation both of the body of Christ in the mystery of the incarnate

Word and of his mystical body, the Church, which is indissolubly linked to Christ the Head and from whose life she herself lives;

– making use of a terminology of Western scholastic coinage: objective and subjective, mediate and immediate redemption, merit *de congruo* and *de condigno*, terms alien to the theological tradition of the East; such terminology could certainly have continued to be used in theological research, but it was unthinkable that an ecumenical council would make its own these terms which of themselves recall the disputes of the schools;

– defining in conceptual terms the association of Mary in the redemptive work of Christ, preferring to have recourse to the category of salvation history: thus describing the *acts* which, from the Incarnation all the way to the death on the Cross, show the Mother intimately united to the redemptive work of the Son (cf. *LG* 61);

– using the term *mediatio* with reference to the Virgin, employing in its place expressions like "maternal function" (*munus maternum*) and "saving influence" (*salutaris influxus*) or words like "cooperation" (*cooperatio*), in passages in which it was legitimate to expect the word "mediation" to be used with regard to the requirements of parallelism (cf. *LG* 61, 63).

– configuring the "mediatorial action" of Mary in geometric or spatial terms or in symbolic terms like *ladder* or *neck*, as if between Christ and the faithful there were a rampart which they could only surmount by means of the mediatorial intervention of the Virgin.

– the use of any expressions like that of "Mediatrix of all graces" which, although recurring in papal documents previous to the Council, were the object of dispute among theologians; and the use of expressions such as "Mediatrix with the Mediator," "Christ *and* Mary" in contexts which could produce the impression that the grace of the redemption is attributable, almost at the same level, to Christ and to the Virgin of Nazareth (Ignazio M. Calabuig, O.S.M., "Riflessione sulla richiesta della definizione dogmatica di 'Maria corredentrice, mediatrice, avvocata'" in *Marianum* LXI (1999) hereafter cited as Calabuig 154-155, my trans.).

The impression is given that the underlying principle in all of this discussion about what is to be avoided is precisely the idea that a general council of the Church can simply renounce the Church's patrimony and banish the use of any terminology which was not used in the council documents and thus come to be regarded as "ecumenically" incorrect. Indeed, it is the doctrine taught by the Council which is of ultimate importance. The study of the background from which the document emerged is also of value precisely insofar as it indicates how and why matters were treated in a particular way. Thus a study like Ermanno Toniolo's (Ermanno M. Toniolo, O.S.M., *La Beata Maria Vergine nel Concilio Vaticano II: Cronistoria del capitolo VIII della Constituzione Dogmatica "Lumen Gentium" e sinossi di tutte le redazioni* (Rome:

Centro di Cultura Mariana «Madre della Chiesa», 2004)), which furnishes a great deal of background information on how chapter 8 of *Lumen Gentium* arrived at its final form is of great value, but the methodology followed in establishing the final form of chapter 8 need not become *ipso facto* the methodology which must be followed by all who work in the field of Mariology. This will to impose a particular approach and methodology, and to effectively rule out the employment of terminology and systems of thought that have developed in the Church in the course of centuries and even millennia, is a fundamental component of what I refer to as "Vatican II triumphalism" (Cf. *TTMM* 15-22).

On the one hand it is not difficult to perceive that there has been a consistent development and clarification of doctrine on the active collaboration of the Mother of God in the work of our redemption in the course of two millennia of the Church's history and that it clearly constitutes a non-negotiable element of the Church's teaching (Cf. Brunero Gherardini, "The Coredemption of Mary: Doctrine of the Church" in *Mary at the Foot of the Cross* II (New Bedford, MA: Academy of the Immaculate, 2002) 37-48). On the other, there can be no doubt that in the present situation there is very formidable resistance to a solemn recognition of this truth of faith on the part of many who are considered major and authoritative proponents of post-conciliar Mariology. Often the reasons adduced for such resistance are "ecumenical." The then Father Angelo Amato, S.D.B., stated that such a solemn proclamation "from the ecumenical perspective would constitute a wound that would be hard to heal," (Angelo Amato, S.D.B., "Verso Un Altro Dogma Mariano?" in *Marianum* LVIII (1996) 232. Cf. my response, "'Towards Another Marian Dogma?': A Response to Father Angelo Amato" in *Marianum* LIX (1997) 159-167), but this begs the entire question of what the principles of Catholic ecumenism are (Cf. Brunero Gherardini, *Una sola Fede – una sola Chiesa. La Chiesa Cattolica dinanzi all'ecumenismo* (Castelpetroso: Casa Marian Editrice, 2000). Can the Catholic teaching on Mary's active collaboration in the work of our salvation—which is a paradigm for the collaboration of all Christians in the work of salvation—be reconciled with the Lutheran dogma that there can be no human collaboration in the work of salvation? It would seem that that is only possible by contradicting the "principle of non-contradiction," i.e., that a thing cannot be and not be at the same time in the same way (Cf. Brunero Gherardini, "Unity and Coredemption" in *Mary at the Foot of the Cross* III (New Bedford, MA: Academy of the Immaculate, 2003) 54-69; Ibid., "Ecumenismo e Corredenzione" in *Maria "Unica Cooperatrice alla Redenzione." Atti del Simposio sul Mistero della Corredenzione Mariana, Fatima, Portogallo 3-7 Maggio 2005* (New Bedford, MA: Academy of the Immaculate, 2005) 463-475). However, some present-day ecumenists, such as those Protestant and Catholic theologians known as "the Dombes Group," (Cf. Alain Blaincy and Maurice Jourjon and the Dombes Group, *Mary in the Plan of God and in the Communion of Saints* trans. by Matthew J. O'Connell with Foreword by Joseph A. Fitzmyer, S.J. (NY: Paulist Press, 2002) [= Dombes] 2-5) believe that they have found a way through the impasse:

> Since the term "cooperation" is there and is alive in the mentalities of both sides, we cannot act as if it did not exist. Our effort

will therefore be to both purify and "convert" it, to "reconstruct" it, as it were. Some day, perhaps, a different term will emerge from our dialogue, one that is more satisfactory to all concerned, because it will be free of all equivocations. ...

Mary was also present at the Cross. She did not cooperate in the unparalleled sacrifice which Christ alone offered. ... She responded with all the freedom her faith gave her by accepting the loss of her son Jesus and welcoming the beloved disciple as son.

Mary is an example of the lot of all the saved. Salvation consists in a relationship: there is no salvation if this relationship is not accepted, if it does not meet with a response of thanksgiving. Passivity in the presence of grace, faith's "letting itself be moved" by grace—there are the source of a new activity; receptivity turns into obedience. Docility to the Holy Spirit becomes an active force. The passivity is never total; in a second moment receptivity itself becomes active. But every response is at one and the same time the work of God's grace and the work of human freedom stirred into action by grace. The only thing that belongs exclusively to human beings is the rejection of grace....

But here a distinction is needed: acceptance is not a work. One who accepts a gift plays no part in the initiative that produces the gift. On the other hand, a gift is not fully a gift unless it is received (Dombes 89-91).

There appear to be few Catholic elements remaining in this statement. The Catholic participants had already professed that "The very term 'coredemption' is objectively flawed, because it suggests that Mary's role is of the same order as that of Christ. Vatican II consciously abandoned the term; it has not reappeared since then in official texts and ought to be deliberately dropped" (Dombes 88). While the work of the Dombes Group has been hailed in many Catholic circles, and even Jean Galot sees it as "a great step forward in the direction of the doctrine held by Catholics," (Galot, *Marie, Mère et Corémptrice* 142), I confess to finding this statement lacking from a Catholic perspective.

Another objection to the doctrine of Marian coredemption from the Catholic side comes from Archbishop Angelo Amato, S.D.B., who stated in an interview:

The title of Co-redeemer is neither biblical nor patristic nor theological and has been used rarely by any pontiff and only in minor addresses. Vatican Council II avoided it deliberately. It's well to remember that in theology the principle of analogy can be used, but not that of equivocality. And in this case, there is no analogy, but only equivocality. In reality Mary is the "redeemed in the most perfect way," she is the first fruit of the redemption by her Son, the sole Redeemer of mankind. Wanting to go further seems hardly prudent to me (Gianni Cardinale, "A life as a halfback" in *30 Days* Year 22 (2004:4) 59).

To Monsignor Gherardini goes the credit for a carefully balanced response (Cf. Brunero Gherardini, "A proposito di un intervista" in *Immaculata Mediatrix* IV:3 (2004) 437-443). The denial that there could be any analogy between Jesus and Mary is contradicted by the Church's theological Tradition from the time of St. Irenaeus, and indeed from the doctrinal development stemming from the *Protoevangelium* which we have outlined above. Analogy does not mean equality, but rather that there is a likeness in difference (Cf. *Totus Tuus* 162-168). A recent publication by a Dutch student of theology rehearses a wide variety of attacks on the theology of Marian coredemption which are rather superficial (Hendro Munsterman, *Marie corédemptrice? Débat sur un titre marial controversé*, Paris: Cerf, 2006); it has been more than adequately answered by Father Peter Damian Fehlner (Peter M. Fehlner, F.I., "Marian Minimalism on Coredemption: *Marie corédemptrice? Débat sur un titre marial controversé*" in *Immaculata Mediatrix* VI:3 (2006) 397-420). While it is not possible to respond in detail here to all of the objections to the doctrine of Marian coredemption, the interested reader is referred to an excellent resumé which considers the principal ones (Cf. Mark Miravalle, "Mary Co-redemptrix: A Response to 7 Common Objections" in *CMA* IV: 93-138).

A rather unique and irenic position has been taken by Jean Galot, S.J., who is basically a supporter of the doctrine of Marian coredemption and its eventual definition (Jean Galot, S.J., "Maria: Mediatrice o Madre Universale?" in *La Civiltà Cattolica* 1996 (quaderno 3495) I:236-237). In various publications, however, he takes the position that it would be easier and therefore more immediately possible to define Our Lady's spiritual maternity as a dogma of faith, but even this will require time and further in-depth study ("Maria: Mediatrice o Madre Universale?" 241-244; "La Mediazione di Maria: Natura e Limiti" in *La Civiltà Cattolica* 1997 (quaderno 3535) IV:25; *Marie, Mère et Coréremptrice* 140). According to scholars like Brunero Gherardini, however, the coredemption along with the divine maternity are the two doctrinal bases of the spiritual maternity (Brunero Gherardini, "The Coredemption and Mary's Universal Maternity" in *Mary at the Foot of the Cross* IV (New Bedford, MA: Academy of the Immaculate, 2004) 28). This also seems quite clearly to be the position of the Papal Magisterium. I will limit myself to just a few citations. We have already noted above that the Servant of God Pope Pius XII, in his encyclical of June 29, 1943, declared that

> She [Mary] it was who, immune from all sin, personal or inherited, and ever most closely united with her Son, offered him on Golgotha to the eternal Father together with the holocaust of her maternal rights and motherly love, like a New Eve, for all the children of Adam contaminated through this unhappy fall, and thus she, who was the Mother of our Head according to the flesh, became by a new title of sorrow and glory the spiritual Mother of all his members (*AAS* 35 (1943) 247-248 [*OL* 383]).

In his general audience of May 11, 1983, the Servant of God Pope John Paul II said:

> This universal motherhood in the spiritual order was the final consequence of Mary's cooperation in the work of her divine Son, a cooperation begun in the fearful joy of the Annunciation and carried through right to the boundless sorrow of Calvary. ...
>
> On Calvary she was indeed united with the sacrifice of her Son who was looking to the formation of the Church; her motherly heart shared completely Christ's will "to gather into one all the dispersed children of God" (Jn 11:52). Having suffered for the Church, Mary deserved to become the Mother of all her Son's disciples, the Mother of their unity. For this reason the Council states that "the Catholic Church, taught by the Holy Spirit, honors her with filial affection and piety as a most beloved Mother" (*Lumen Gentium*, 53). (*Inseg* VI/1 (1983) 1201, 1202 [*ORE* 784:1])

In his homily at the Marian Shrine of Guayaquil, Ecuador, on January 31, 1985, John Paul II preached this same message:

> In fact, at Calvary she united herself with the sacrifice of her Son that led to the foundation of the Church; her maternal heart shared to the very depths the will of Christ "to gather into one all the dispersed children of God" (Jn 11:52). Having suffered for the Church, Mary deserved to become the Mother of all the disciples of her Son, the Mother of their unity. For this reason, the Council affirms that "Taught by the Holy Spirit, the Catholic Church honors her with filial affection and piety as a most beloved Mother" (*Lumen Gentium*, 53). Mother of the Church! Mother of us all! (*Inseg* VIII/1 (1985) 319 [*ORE* 876:7]).

Likewise, Pope Benedict XVI has reinforced this teaching. In his homily at the Marian Shrine of Altötting, Germany, on September 11, 2006, he offered this reflection:

> We can understand, I think, very well the attitude and words of Mary [at Cana], yet we still find it very hard to understand Jesus' answer. In the first place, we don't like the way he addresses her: "Woman." Why doesn't he say: "Mother"? But this title really expresses Mary's place in salvation history. It points to the future, to the hour of the Crucifixion, when Jesus will say to her: "Woman, behold your son—Son, behold your mother" (cf. Jn 19:26–27). It anticipates the hour when he will make the woman, his Mother, the Mother of all his disciples.
>
> On the other hand, the title "woman" recalls the account of the creation of Eve: Adam, surrounded by creation in all its magnificence, experiences loneliness as a human being. Then Eve is created, and in

her Adam finds the companion whom he longed for; and he gives her the name "woman."

In the *Gospel of John*, then, Mary represents the new, the definitive woman, the companion of the Redeemer, our Mother: the name, which seemed so lacking in affection, actually expresses the grandeur of Mary's enduring mission (*OR* 27 settembre 2006, p. VII; [*ORE* 1961:3]).

Again at the Marian Shrine of Meryem Ana Evì, Ephesus, Turkey, on November 29, 2006, he reiterated:

We have listened to a passage from St. John's Gospel which invites us to contemplate the moment of the redemption when Mary, united to her Son in the offering of his sacrifice, extended her motherhood to all men and women, and in particular to the disciples of Jesus (*OR* 13 dicembre 2006, p. V [*ORE* 1972:5]).

Why is there such resistance to recognizing the development of doctrine which has taken place, especially in the course of the last pontificate, and in celebrating and proclaiming the role that the "New Eve" had in the working out of our redemption and the role which she continues to carry out in dispensing the graces of the redemption and interceding on our behalf? There are many partial answers, but ultimately, I believe the opposition can only be explained in terms of the eternal enmity between the serpent and the "woman" of the *Protoevangelium*.

Mary Mediatrix
of All Graces

Fr. Alessandro M. Apollonio, F.I.

Marian mediation and its foundations have been the subject of extensive study, easily available in the published acts of congresses,[1] anthologies,[2]

---

[1] Aa. Vv., *Mary at the Foot of the Cross. Acts of the International Symposium on Marian Coredemption*, 6 vv., Academy of the Immaculate, New Bedford, MA, 2001-2007. The six volumes (together, over 3,000 pages) report the acts of the symposia held in England annually from 2000 to 2005, thereafter in Fatima. A seventh volume is in the course of publication. The symposia and the publication of their acts are under the direction of the Franciscan Friars of the Immaculate (Academy of the Immaculate, New Bedford, MA). The unique role of Mary as maternal Mediatrix in the Church rests proximately on her position as Immaculate Co-redemptrix on Calvary; hence the importance of these studies for our theme.

There are, in addition, two other events of great importance regarding studies on Marian coredemption:

1) *Il Simposio internazionale sul mistero di Maria Corredentrice*, Shrine of Castelpetroso (Italy), September 8-12, 1996, promoted by his excellency Msgr. Ettore Di Filippo (+2006), archbishop of Campobasso-Boiano (Italy) and president of the Bishop's Conference of Abruzzo-Molise.

2) *Il Simposio sul Mistero della Corredenzione Mariana*, held at Fatima May 3-7, 2005, promoted and directed by the following cardinals: Telesphore Toppo, Luis Aponte Martínez, Varkey Vithayathil, Edouard Gagnon, Ricardo Vidal, Ernesto Corripio Ahumada. Acts: *Maria: "Unica Cooperatrice alla Redenzione"* – *Mary: "Unique Cooperator in the Redemption,"* Academy of the Immaculate, New Bedford, MA, 2005, 583 pp.

[2] M. Miravalle:

1) *Mary Co-redemptrix, Mediatrix, Advocate*, Queenship Publishing, Santa Barbara (CA) 1993, pp. 80;

2) *Mary Co-redemptrix, Mediatrix, Advocate: Theological foundations. Towards a Papal Definition?*, Queenship Publishing, Santa Barbara 1995, 325 pp.

3) *Mary Co-redemptrix, Mediatrix, Advocate: Theological foundations II. Papal, Pneumatological, Ecumenical*, Queenship Publishing, Santa Barbara 1997, 329 pp.

collections,[3] monographs,[4] and articles.[5] The theme has been analyzed along biblical, patristic, liturgical, magisterial and dogmatic lines. If every published study on Marian mediation over the past one hundred years were to be cited, the mere listing of titles would probably fill a large book. An adequate, clear grasp of the *status quaestionis*, however, can be had by consulting the references just listed. With a few important exceptions, post-conciliar studies generally give greater attention to the sources, while those prior to the Council, though not neglecting the sources, place greater emphasis on the speculative aspects of this question.

---

4) *Mary Co-redemptrix, Mediatrix, Advocate: Theological foundations III. Contemporary Insights on a Fifth Marian Dogma*, Queenship Publishing, Santa Barbara 2000, 272 pp.

Mark Miravalle, Professor of Mariology at the University of Steubenville (Ohio), has also edited the volume Aa. Vv., *Mary Co-redemptrix. Doctrinal Issues Today*, Queenship Publishing, Santa Barbara 2002, 274 pp. In addition, he is the author of two excellent monographs on this subject: *The Dogma and the Triumph*, Queenship Publishing, Santa Barbara 1998, 152 pp.; *"With Jesus": The Story of Mary Co-redemptrix*, Queenship Publishing, Goleta, CA, 2003, 252 pp.

[3] Aa. Vv., *Maria Corredentrice. Storia e Teologia*, CME, Frigento 1998-2005, 7 vv. Of particular interest is the study on our specific theme in M. Hauke, *La mediazione materna di Maria secondo papa Giovanni Paolo II*, in *op. cit.*, vol. VII, 2005, pp. 35-158.

[4] For example, A. Escudero Cabello, S.D.B., *La cuestión de la mediación en la preparación del Vaticano II*, LAS, Rome 1997, 422 pp.; B. Gherardini, *La Corredentrice*, ed. Vivere, Rome 1998, 408 pp.; M. Hauke, *Maria "Mediatrice di tutte le grazie." La mediazione universale di Maria nell'opera teologica e pastorale del Cardinale Mercier*, Eupress FTL [Faculty of Theology of Lugano]—Reggiani SpA [Varese], Lugano, Switzerland—Varese, Italy 2005, 212 pp.; D. Lacourture, *Marie Médiatrice de toutes les grâces*, ed. des Béatitudes, Saint-Amand (France) 1997, 324 pp.; J. Ferrer Arellano, *La Mediación Materna de la Inmaculada. Esperanza Ecuménica de la Iglesia*, ed. Arca de la Alianza, Madrid 2006, 318 pp.; J.D. Miller, *Marian Mediation: Is it True to Say that Mary is Coredemptrix, Mediatrix of All Graces and Advocate?*, Academy of the Immaculate, New Bedford, MA, 2004, 168 pp; J. Schug, O.F.M. Cap., *Mary, Mother*, St. Francis Chapel Press, Springfield, MA, 1992.

[5] For example, J. Galot, S.J., *Maria: mediatrice o madre universale?*, in *La Civiltà Cattolica*, 147/1 (1996) 213-225; J. Galot, *La mediazione di Maria: natura e limiti*, ibid., 148 (1997) 13-25; P. Siano, F.I., *Uno studio su Maria Santissima 'Mediatrice di tutte le Grazie' nel magistero pontificio fino al pontificato di Giovanni Paolo II*, *Immaculata Mediatrix*, 6 (2006) 299-356. See also the articles of Fr. Peter Damian Fehlner in the periodical *Immaculata Mediatrix* for the years 2001-2003; J. Schug, O.F.M. Cap. and M. Miravalle, *Mary Coredemptrix: The Significance of Her Title in the Magisterium of the Church*, in M. Miravalle, ed., *Coredemptrix, Mediatrix, Advocate: Foundations. Towards a Papal Definition?*, *op. cit.*, pp. 215-246.

The goal of this study is to strike a happy balance between sources and reflection on the sources so as to arrive at a concise and correct understanding of Catholic doctrine on Marian mediation here and now in the economy of salvation. Our point of departure will be an elaboration of the problematic in the formularies whereby it has been handed on in the Church. Thereafter, via a reflection on the sources of this doctrine, both remote and proximate, we will point out in a brief, summary conclusion how the traditional speculative questions arise and what is their significance for theology and for the life of the Church.[6]

Although, as Cardinal Giacomo Biffi, archbishop emeritus of Bologna, Italy, often shrewdly repeats, a good theologian should strive

---

[6] Historically, the mystery of Mary, in one way or another, is at the very heart of many theological controversies since the foundation of the Church. That this is so is no reason to question the certainty of that mystery as an article of faith, for we believe, as do the apostles and their successors, in the Christ, the Son of the living God, born of the Virgin Mary. Rather, division over this mystery arises from the centrality of Mary with Jesus in the mystery of salvation, and the ongoing struggle between the Woman and the serpent-dragon (cf. Gen 3:15 and Rev 12:1ff.) which accounts for the violence of the controversy at times. Today the controversy continues about the question of the Woman's active role in the work of redemption, viz., the maternal role of Mary *qua* Mediatrix. A good introduction to these controversies can be found in Miravalle, *"With Jesus": The Story of Mary Coredemptrix*, cit.; and to the type of atmosphere leading to denial of Marian mediation and the title Mediatrix cf. G. Morrissey, *For the Love of Mary. Defending the Church from Anti-Marianism*, Brooklyn NY 1999. On the historical background cf. M. Hauke, Mary, *"Mediatress of Grace." Mary's Universal Mediation of Grace in the Theological and Pastoral Works of Cardinal Mercier*: Supplement to *Mary at the Foot of the Cross IV*, New Bedford, MA, 2004. For the bearing of the Encyclical *Redemptoris Mater* on the problematic cf. J.F. Bifet, *La mediación maternal de Maria. Aspectos específicos de la enciclica "Redemptoris Mater,"* in *Ephemerides Mariologicae* 39 (1989) 237-254; E. Llamas, *La mediación maternal de Maria en la enciclica "Redemptoris Mater,"* in *Estudios Marianos* 61 (1995) 149-180.

We can be quite sure of her triumph, precisely because as maternal mediatrix Christ entrusted, consecrated, the entire Church and each member to his Mother, the Woman foretold in Genesis 3:15 and revealed in glory in Revelation 12:1ff. But we cannot be sure of our share in that victory, unless we understand clearly and accept in practice the universal mediation of Mary in the Church and in the lives of each and every member, actual and potential. In practice, this means we must engage in true devotion to the Virgin, as St. Louis-Marie Grignion de Montfort calls our basic response to the mystery of Marian mediation here and now, or live total consecration to the Immaculate, as St. Maximilian M. Kolbe defines the same basic response.

to say new things, demonstrating that they are old. For us, however, who do not believe ourselves able to say new things, it is enough to explain the old things with order and clarity, so demonstrating them to be forever new. For the truth never grows old and never passes out of style. This is especially the case with such venerable terms as maternal and mediation, especially at a time when so many of the feminist persuasion (not all women, nor always women) want to erase them from the human vocabulary. Such a project, were it ever to be successful, would bear consequences of immeasurably tragic proportions for everyone. Between the human family and such success of the serpent-dragon there stands only one secure bulwark: the Woman, the maternal Mediatrix.

The Problematic of Marian Mediation

In theology, the term mediation is employed in a variety of senses to designate basic dimensions of the economy of salvation. These various senses, though clearly denoting distinct aspects of the work of salvation, are all interrelated, whether we are speaking of the mediation of Christ, and therefore of Christ as Mediator, or of the mediation of his Virgin Mother and therefore of Mary as Mediatrix, or of the mediation of the Church and therefore of that found in the sacramental-hierarchical order (ministerial graces linked to a stable office in the Church), or of the mediation of members of the Church and therefore of their active cooperation in the work of salvation via the ministerial charisms or graces of all kinds bestowed on them (*gratiae gratis datae*).

The reason for this is very simple: in the eternal counsels of the Father (cf. Eph 1:3ff.) all these various dimensions of a single economy of salvation were willed in correlation to one another within the unity of the predestination of Christ to be Head of the new creation, a creation to be realized concretely or in the execution of the divine counsels in history via what from the days of St. Justin Martyr and St. Irenaeus of Lyons has been called "recapitulation." The absolute predestination of Christ as incarnate Son of God, to be Head and Savior of his body, the Church and of all his members, constitutes what is commonly known as "the order of the hypostatic union." To that order, in a special way, belongs one of the saved, the Immaculate Virgin, Mother of the Savior-Word incarnate, "pre-eminent member" of the Church according to Vatican II. This unique and non-repeatable relation to Christ as Head in the order of the hypostatic union arises from what is called by Bl. Pius IX and Pius XII "the joint predestination of the incarnate Word and Mother of God in one and the same decree."[7]

To understand Catholic doctrine on Marian mediation, it is necessary from the start to grasp this essential point: Mary, because Mother of God, belongs as no other creature to the order of the hypostatic union, foundation of all saving mediation, perfect or subordinate. Therefore, by the merits of Christ she is incomparably holy. Therefore, in a way unique to her (cf. *Lumen Gentium*, 56-58, 60-62) she is able to cooperate actively with Jesus, the one Mediator of God and man: as his Mother, as our Co-redemptrix, and as our Mediatrix and Advocate. Mary's mediation is the divinely appointed means by which the whole of creation and in particular the human family is recapitulated in Christ the Head, and so enjoys the blessings willed by the Father and gained for us by Christ in his stupendous work consummated on Calvary. Or in the words of St. Maximilian M. Kolbe, the mediation of Mary crystallized in her *fiat* is the high point where all the love of the Blessed Trinity appropriated to the Holy Spirit meets all the love of creation, a juncture which brings to pass the Incarnation and economy of salvation.[8]

Evidently all these themes cannot be treated in a single chapter of a single volume devoted to the whole of Mariology. Nonetheless, to understand the specific theme of this chapter, one dealing with the maternal mediation of Mary here and now, a few general considerations are necessary. These bear on 1) Mary's active role of intercession with Jesus (ascending mediation), and 2) her direct, active role in the distribution of all the graces of salvation (descending mediation). Both roles are extensions of her unique participation as Co-redemptrix in the sacrifice of Calvary in which she participated as Co-redemptrix, a sacrifice perpetuated in the mystery of the Eucharist (descending mediation). The first role is more properly called advocacy, and the second mediation in the restricted sense.

---

[7] Pius IX, Apostolic Constitution *Ineffabilis Deus*, December 8, 1854; Pius XII, Apostolic Constitution *Munificentissimus Deus*, November 1, 1950, in AAS 42 (1950).

[8] St. Maximilian M. Kolbe, *Scritti d Massimiliano Kolbe*, Rome 1997, n. 1318. This profound essay, an example of contemplative theology of the highest order, was dictated by the saint only hours before his final arrest by Gestapo, Feb. 17, 1941. Unfortunately, there exists no satisfactory English translation to date.

Sacred, Revealed Use of the Term

As a term with a very specific theological sense (and not merely ethical-political), mediator, or intermediary, is found five times in the New Testament, always in the Pauline corpus. These are the passages in question:

> Why then the law? It was added because of transgressions, till the offspring should come to whom the promise had been made; and it was ordained by angels through an intermediary. Now an intermediary implies more than one; but God is one (Gal 3:19-20).
>
> For there is one God, and one mediator between God and men, the man Jesus Christ, who gave himself up as a ransom for all (1 Tim 2:5-6).
>
> But as it is, Christ has obtained a ministry which is as much more excellent than the old as the covenant he mediates is better, since it is enacted on better promises (Heb 8:6).
>
> Therefore he is the mediator of a new covenant, so that those who are called may receive the promised eternal inheritance, since a death has occurred which redeems them from the transgressions under the first covenant (Heb 9:15).
>
> ... and to Jesus, the mediator of a new covenant ... (Heb 12:24).

We may summarize the thought of St. Paul in these passages on the theological meaning of Mediator thus: It designates both 1) an office or responsibility rooted in and made possible by the Incarnation of the Son of God, not only in virtue of his divinity, but of his humanity as well (cf. 1 Tim 2:5), and 2) the major act of that office or ministry, viz., the redemptive sacrifice together with its fruit, the Church, the reconciliation of the saved with God in the one Body of Christ, the Head.

In all but one of these texts (Gal 3:19-20) the term mediator is ascribed expressly only to Christ. But in view of its ascription to Moses and to angels under the Old Covenant one can hardly affirm *a priori* that the presence of mediators other than Christ is excluded in affirming the unicity and sufficiency and excellence of the mediation of Christ, at least on biblical grounds. This is an observation crucial to any understanding of the traditional teaching of the Church on the mediation of Mary and of the Church itself. Deny the title Mediatrix to Mary as did Luther and the Protestant Reformation and nothing is left of the other mediations in the Church, that is, our active cooperation as "collaborators" in the distribution of the fruits of Christ's sacrifice. Biblical grounds for the denial are claimed, but none are apparent, except on the assumption of extra-biblical premises of a theological or philosophical kind (individualism, combined with nominalism and voluntarism), not shared by the Tradition of the Church.

The texts just cited make clear that the title is that of an office, how the office is defined and what is the basis for the exercise of such an office in making one two who are not only separated, but in a condition of hostility (cf. Eph 2:11ff.). The creature alone, in particular man after the fall into original sin, cannot successfully resolve the problem of division between Creator and creation. But if the role of Mediator belongs radically to one all-sufficient person, this in itself is no necessary bar to the inclusion of others in a subordinate role, anymore than the existence of God excludes the possibility of a creation which does not compromise the all-sufficiency and transcendence of God.

At the level of theory the observation is perfectly valid. Unfortunately, it is not immediately effective in dealing with popular objections to the very concept of Marian mediation in theology, viz., that by definition participation in the one work of mediation compromises the uniqueness of Christ as one Mediator. Why this is so, but also what can be done to get beyond the impasse at the pastoral level, can be illustrated from a reflection on an analogy frequently used to justify the classic Protestant position: only Christ is Mediator in the proper sense. Mediation, in particular sacerdotal mediation, it is claimed, must be likened to bridge-building between earth and heaven. Indeed, the Latin version of Hebrews translates the Greek word for high priest (*archiereus*) as *pontifex*, or bridge builder. Perhaps a kindred Greek word, *architect*, or head builder, in addition to the title of the head priest: *Pontifex*, and also head-builder of bridges over the Tiber River in Rome, may have suggested the choice. In any case the objection to the Catholic doctrine about Mary goes like this: if two bridges are necessary to cross a stream, then neither by itself is sufficient. And if one is all-sufficient, then the second can hardly be described as functionally necessary to mediate the gap between the two sides of a single stream or abyss.

The answer very simply is to distinguish between two kinds of sharing in a single role or perfection: spiritual and material, qualitative and quantitative. It is perfectly true that sharing in a single patrimony by way of inheritance by several heirs requires a division of the patrimony with no one single heir being master of all. So, too, in the case of physical mediation represented by the example of the two bridges, neither bridge can be described as fully adequate, as Christ is described in the passage from 1 Timothy 2:5, if the work must be equally divided. Bridge building, political mediation, etc., because quantitative realities, cannot be absolutely perfect, shared or not shared.

Christ, on the other hand, is said to be perfect as one Mediator. This kind of unity is spiritual, and only spiritual mediation can reconcile God and man. The perfection of spiritual mediation, not being subject to division as in the case of sharing in a material good, is not affected by the number of other persons who participate in that perfection dependently on, or in subordination to, the one who possesses this absolutely. By way of example, neither the perfection of my thought nor that of my love is diminished by the fact that others share my thoughts and my love. And again, not every inheritance is material. The heavenly patrimony of those redeemed by Christ, is real, but spiritual, hence shared by many, yet not divided. Our Lord himself made this point in the parable of the laborers in the vineyard: the same denarius, God himself, undivided, is the wages of all. Failure to make this distinction is a sure sign of pride (cf. Mt 20:1-16). Why can there not be a "spiritual bridge," viz., a mediation in which many are involved according to a certain order, yet leaving the mediation undivided?

There is a still more important observation crucial in the teaching of St. Paul: viz., that mediation involves not merely God, but someone who is also man, a creature. As St. Bonaventure so clearly saw,[9] human nature by definition is mediatory, and hence that nature in its most perfect state, viz., in the God-man, is enhanced by the participation of others in this mediation, above all by Mary Immaculate. All this is foreshadowed by the formation of man as male and female. Human nature is first fully

---

[9] St. Bonaventure, *Breviloquium*, p. II, in particular chapters 2 and 9.

mediatory in Adam, and for that reason is also mediatory in Eve, who does not detract from, but underscores the nobility of God's image.[10]

Simply put, the reply to the objection drawn from the analogy of two bridges is simply to say that it is only a metaphor, and does not clarify the essential difference between Christ as one Mediator and those associated with him in the work of mediation. Each bridge is an insufficient means of mediating a distance before they are united as one. With Christ his mediation *qua* man is perfectly one before shared by others. With the participation of others there remains but one mediation, as the thought and love of Christ remain perfect, no matter how many share his thoughts and affection; but there are many persons active in that mediation according to a certain order in relation to Christ, the one Mediator. This is true of Mary in a unique and non-repeatable way because of her fullness of grace in view of the divine and spiritual

---

[10] More technical discussion of this issue is carried out via use of the terms "transcendental" and "predicamental" participation, the first denoting sharing in a spiritual perfection, the second sharing in material goods. Mediation *par excellence* is a form of metaphysical analogy, in the first instance the reconciliation of like and unlike. Cf. J. Ferrer Arellano, *Marian Coredemption in the Light of Christian Philosophy*, in *Mary at the Foot of the Cross II*, New Bedford, MA, 2002, pp. 113-150. The effective recognition of the real difference between these two forms of predication requires a discussion of the relation between analogy and univocity in metaphysics, a point clearly recognized by Bl. John Duns Scotus, especially in regard to matters touching the will and the person, such as mediation. Analogy in order to mediate requires a mean or the "univocal." Here are two key texts from his commentaries on Book I of the *Sentences*: "Teachers who speak of God and of God's knowable attributes employ univocity in their manner of reasoning, even if they reject the word" (*Rep. Par.* I, d 3, q 1, n 7); and "Analogy would be useless if those truths that are evident in creatures were not attainable by the same reasoning as those which are attributed to God in an eminent degree" (*Ord.*, d 8, p 1, q 3). Mediation is precisely one of these perfections classed by Scotus as "pure perfections" only accessible via "metaphysical univocity," and therefore permitting participation without diminution of unity. On the difference between simple perfections and simply simple, or pure perfections cf. W. Hoeres, *Die Wille als reine Vollkommenheit nach Duns Scotus*, Munich 1962. Unfortunately there is nothing comparable in English. The classic Protestant position on Christ alone as Mediator rests on a wrongheaded denial of these basics of sound metaphysics, and leads straight to the monophysite theory of salvation excluding human cooperation in any form at any level, even of subordinate good works. Marian minimalism among Catholics in regard to the title universal Mediatrix heads in the same direction.

maternity. And this is what Scotus means in calling Mary Immaculate *qua* Immaculate the most perfect fruit of the most perfect redemption by a most perfect Redeemer. Christ's one mediation would not be perfect unless he could so save one of his members so as to cooperate actively in the work of salvation of all others, viz., as maternal Mediatrix.[11]

Profane Usage

The term mediator, like its cognate pontifex (Latin translation for Christ as high priest in Hebrews), is not exclusive to the Bible. In ancient times both terms enjoyed a distinctive meaning in a profane or secular context, in the case of mediator one still familiar to most Western societies. This usage was hardly unknown to St. Paul and without doubt had some influence in his choice of terms to describe systematically the distinctive, perfect, all sufficient and absolutely necessary role of Christ in our salvation.

The classic Latin *Lexicon*, edited by Forcellini, defines the term *mediator* in the following words: "One who interposes himself, as a *mean* or point of convergence (intermediary) between dissidents in order to settle disputes." A similar definition is found in the *Lexicon* of Grimm: "One who *intervenes* between two [others] in order to procure peace, establish or re-establish friendship, form a pact (covenant, or federation) or sanction an alliance." In common language, a mediator is a person who performs the distinctively moral action of pacification with regard to two parties in opposition to or apart from one another by providing a common focus (univocal) for the unity of two entities once simply different, but not joined or analogous to one another within a single pact.

It is not hard to see why such a term should be employed by the Apostle Paul to explain the work of salvation and redemption. Christ's work as priest and victim of the New Covenant is like that of a mediator who, as the old Roman pontifex threw up bridges across the Tiber River to unite or make one the two separated shores, bridges the gap between creature and Creator, between sinner and the heavenly Father, effectively making it possible for the distant creature, for the alienated sinner, to

---

[11] For an introduction to the thought of Scotus on Marian mediation and its relation to the absolute predestination of Christ, cf. Maximilian M. Dean, F.I, *A Primer on the Absolute Primacy of Christ. Blessed John Duns Scotus and the Franciscan Thesis*, New Bedford, MA, 2006.

find himself not only reconciled with God or on God's side of the great abyss (cf. Lk 16:26), but become himself active in the process of salvation as a subordinate cooperator. This is because as a genuine mediator Christ shares something with both parties: the godhead with the Father and manhood with the family of Adam. Hence, he is the mean or common ground where the parties to be reconciled can meet as friends rather than enemies or mere servants (cf. Jn 15:15).

There are, however, evident differences between the sacred and profane uses of this term and the concept standing behind it. As noted above, mediation involves an office and its exercise, the *ethical-social* dimension, and *ontological* or non-ethical basis of this office, the so-called mean.

First, the office of mediator and its exercise. In the profane order of the ancient world, as in modern secularized societies, mediation was and is a highly sophisticated and relatively successful activity when only temporal discord is involved. But wherever profound ethical and religious issues are at stake, e.g., in marriage-family discord, or in discord over religious activities or basic principles of right and social-political-economic philosophy, mediation can often be a dismal failure, if permanent resolution of discord and establishment of harmony is any criterion.[12] Whereas, the mediation of Christ Jesus, according to Hebrews, is a raging and permanent success, not only in relation to the pagan religions, but to that of the mediators of the Old Testament dispensation.

Second, the mean or ontological platform for the exercise of a mediatory office. In the case of mere human mediation in the profane order, there is nothing particularly unique about the mediator in relation to each of the parties in dispute. He is a man, and so are they. What the human mediator shares with one party rather than another pertains to personal character and ability to persuade both parties within an already existing social polity. Where such a pre-existing polity, wherein the contending parties are already united at least in principle, if not in

---

[12] Witness the quasi-universal practice of divorce today, a moral-religious plague if ever there was one. Modern forms of mediation, e.g., psychological therapy-counseling in many cases, are about as successful as the ancient Roman *pontifices* as religious mediators. Their bridges over the Tiber were masterpieces of engineering; but neither ancient nor modern technique suffices to resolve the problem of sin, social discord, and death.

practice, does not exist, and must therefore be established, as especially is the case of man in the state of fallen nature, then no mere man can succeed in mediating between an offended Creator and a sinful creation.

With this we can readily see what the Incarnation introduces into our fallen world: a new and adequate platform or "ontological mean" where the offended and offenders can be fully reconciled, a solid rock on which to establish an order of peace (cf. Mt 7:24-27, conclusion of the Sermon on the Mount). In a sense specifically theological, that of a foundation for the economy of salvation, this rock is the order of the hypostatic union.

St. Thomas, therefore, in his classic definition of theological or religious mediation, clearly indicates two elements: the office (in the ethical-social order) and the mean (or foundation in the ontological order): "Properly speaking, the office of Mediator is to join together and unite those between whom he mediates; for extremes are united in the mean."[13] The "mean" in this case is the hypostatic union of man with the divine person of the Son: because incarnate, therefore Mediator. Because Mary uniquely belongs to the order of the hypostatic union because she is Mother of this divine Person, she therefore shares the one office of redemptive Mediator with her Son. Because Mother, therefore Mediatrix. Like her Mediator Son, their one work of mediation is consummate in redemptive sacrifice. And through her the Church and her members in varying ways can also exercise a genuine part in the mediation of grace won by the merits of the one Mediator of all, the man Christ Jesus (cf. 1 Tim 2:5-6).

Mary Mediatrix in the Proper, Theological Sense of Mediation

In addition to the commonly cited profane examples, which only foreshadow the perfection or essence of mediation in Christ Jesus, there is another example of mediation in the natural order, all but forgotten in modern times, but expressly cited by such a great of theology as is the Seraphic Doctor, St. Bonaventure.[14] This example is drawn more from a

---

[13] *Summa theologiae*, III, q 26, a 1.
[14] *Breviloquium*, p. II, chapter 9. On the contributions of St. Bonaventure to an understanding of the concept of Marian mediation cf. P.D. Fehlner, *Immaculata Mediatrix—Toward a Dogmatic Definition of the Coredemption*, in *Mary Corredemptrix, Mediatrix, Advocate. Theological Foundations II*, Santa Barbara, CA, 1997, pp. 259-

metaphysical consideration of human nature as uniquely formed by the Creator on the sixth day; hence, it is not an example bearing primarily on the social order, but on the very character of any mediation as such within the order of creation.

Among all the various creatures, and grades of perfection among them, there are two basic categories of creatures: those purely material and hence *prope nihil* (near nothing), and those purely spiritual like the angels, hence *prope Deum* (near God). That both dimensions of creation be not distant and in opposition, but united to form a single universe, ultimately to be recapitulated by the incarnate Word, the Creator personally formed (hence not by an evolutionary process) a creature, part spiritual and so near God and part corporal and so near the material creation, or near nothing. The saint expressly says that there is such a created being, by nature *mediatory*. This creature, by nature mediatory, is man, or human nature. Thus at the ontological level, prior to any activity, man or Adam (formed from the virgin earth) is a mediator: indeed within the universe, but nonetheless in a religious as well as merely juridical sense as in all the previous examples drawn from the social-political-economic spheres.

But this is not all the Seraphic Doctor tells us. The Creator made man male and female. Each shares in a distinct way, yet *fully*, in a single mediatory nature: first Adam and then under, but also with Adam, Eve. The mediation of Adam, not as private person but head, is in the public order, drawing all dimensions of the universe, but in particular the human, to the love and service of the Creator. Further, Adam mediates between the private realm of the family and person and the public context wherein the human family is situated, thus being true center of the universe. In this sense Adam is a type of Christ, like Noah, Melchizedek, Moses, and so many others after him, the family of Adam being intended by the Creator to foreshadow the Holy Family.

But Eve is also a mediatrix, a type of Mary as mother of the new humanity, for no being can call itself human unless descended from Adam and incorporated into the human family through the maternal mediation of a woman, a mediation unique to her, in no wise detracting from the primary mediation in Adam, even though absolutely necessary

---

329; Idem, *Il Mistero della Corredenzione secondo il Dottore Serafico San Bonaventura*, in *Maria Corredentrice. Storia e Teologia*, vol. II, Frigento 1999, 11-91.

for Adam to realize his headship over the human family. Not only St. Bonaventure, but St. Thomas as well insist that the formation of Adam and Eve in view of the divine institution of the "mystery-sacrament" of marriage was for the sake of Christ and the Church, Christ and Mary, even before sin, a point quite explicit in St. Paul, Ephesians 5:32.[15] Christ mediates between the Creator-Father and his creation, whereas Mary, in subordination to him, mediates between the new Head of the human family and the members incorporated into him. With that it becomes clear why the one mediation of the one Mediator, the (new) man Christ Jesus (cf. 1 Tim 2:5) does not exclude, but according to the divine counsels of salvation must include in an altogether unique way that of the (new) Eve who is also the (new) virgin earth, from whom and by whom is also formed the new Adam-Mediator of the new and everlasting Covenant. Mary is our Mediatrix with Christ, because wonder of wonders she is Mother of God.[16]

St. Bonaventure provides us one other observation helpful in understanding why the mediation involved in the new and everlasting Covenant involves a Mediator, and under him a Mediatrix. The divine nature, being perfectly one, is not mediatory (cf. Gal 3:19-20). But one divine person of the three stands in relation to the other two as a "middle person": i.e., one of the personal characteristics of the Son is to be "mediatory."[17] Hence, it is altogether appropriate that if the Incarnation of a divine person is for the sake of mediation, the second person should

---

[15] St. Bonaventure, *III Sent.*, d 1, a 2, q 2; *II Sent.*, d 23, dub 4; for a parallel text in St. Thomas, *Summa Th.*, II, II, q 2, a 7. Cf. P.D. Fehlner, *Redemption, Metaphysics and the Immaculate Conception*, in *Mary at the Foot of the Cross V*, New Bedford, MA, 2005, pp. 186-262, here p. 234.

[16] St. Bonaventure writes: "Whether we speak of the [Word] becoming man, or of the Woman becoming Mother of God, we are speaking of realities beyond what is due to or comprehensible by a mere creature" (*III Sent.*, d 4, a 2, q 2). The same mysterious character belongs to the titles Mediator and Mediatrix.

[17] St. Bonaventure, *Collationes in Hexaemeron*, col. 1, nn. 12-17. The middle position of the Word in the Trinity is the basis for his role in creation, and for the appropriateness of his Incarnation for the work of recreation and recapitulation, viz., a work of sacerdotal and sacrificial mediation. Inseparable from this at its every moment is the Virgin Mother Mediatrix. Cf. P.D. Fehlner, F.I., *Immaculata Mediatrix—Toward a Dogmatic Definition of the Coredemption*, in *Mary Coredemptrix, Mediatrix, Advocate. Theological Foundations II*, Santa Barbara, CA, 1997, pp. 259-329.

become incarnate. St. Paul (Gal 3:20) also seems to allude to the non-mediatory character of the divine nature. Hence, if the Word is to mediate between God (the Father) and the masterpiece of his creation, man, and so with the rest of creation (cf. St. Paul, Rom 8:18-25), the hypostatic assumption of a human nature becomes imperative—so that a divine person can mediate in a human way. But the way of assuming such a nature hypostatically is through the mediation of a mother, the only way of being a man like us, because such is only possible via descent from Adam in being born of a Virgin Mother (cf. Lk 3:23-38). The virginal conception and birth of Jesus from the Virgin Mother, the "new virgin earth," assures both the divinity and humanity of the Child, hence his office of Mediator in our history. In virtue of her holiness and of this contribution to effecting the economy of salvation, Mary also belongs to the order of the hypostatic union and *ipso facto* shares the mediation of Jesus, distinctly, subordinately, but also properly, as no other of the saved. Here lies the importance of the Eve-Mary typology for the doctrine of Marian mediation.

With this it also becomes clear why in the Franciscan school the maternal mediation of Mary is first considered in the broad sense: neither vague nor metaphorical, but truly proper, in the same sense as it is understood first in the God-man. As he is unique Mediator, first because the mediatory or middle person of the Trinity, and second because he is the new man or Adam, fully capable of doing what the first Adam alone could only indistinctly foreshadow, so Mary is the unique Mediatrix, because she can do what the first Eve could also only indistinctly foreshadow: truly unite, incorporate into the New Adam all the dispersed children of Israel. The particular or more specialized aspects of Mary's mediation in the economy of salvation, either in the types foreshadowing her, or in herself historically, all depend on this primordial fact, her fullness of grace in Christ as the Immaculate Virgin Mother, as Christ's mediation rests uniquely on the grace of the Incarnation. The mediation of Mary is not apart from, outside of or independent of Christ, because she is also saved by him, redeemed preservatively to be Immaculate from conception. That unique sanctity permits her, under him, but also with him, to participate as no other person can, in the work of mediation proper to Christ. Thereby a new platform or basis for the exercise of diverse salutary activities by the redeemed (all in one way or another collaboration in the work of mediation) within the New Covenant is secured. Mary's precise position and role is to provide the basis for our link with the New Adam, or New Head, and so our cooperation with him in the communion of saints. Therefore she is called "our Mediatrix with Christ, as he is our Mediator with the Father" (St. Bonaventure, *III Sent.*, d 3, p 1, a 1, q 2).

The Difference between Mediator and Mediatrix in the One Work of Mediation

In this integral, moral and theological sense cited above, Mary is the Mediatrix of all creatures, angels and men, because God, in Christ, has assigned this function to her in order to reunite all creatures, above all the rational and free creatures, to Christ. In and through Christ the saved, *qua* members of his body formed by Mary, are recapitulated and so united to the Father (cf. 1 Cor 15:28). The saved are members of Christ's body in being born spiritually of the Woman, just as all men naturally have Adam as their head and the origin of their humanity through a woman, and not otherwise. In herself Mary, without sin, possesses the human nature of Adam that unites her to sinful humanity, the spirit that unites her to the angels, and the fullness of grace that brings her into union with the God-man and so brings him into union, not with a generic humanity, but with that precisely first headed by Adam. Through Mary, Christ descends from Adam as well as Abraham (cf. Christ's genealogy recorded by Luke 3:23-38). Therefore, through Mary, he is our Savior and Mediator. We go to him in the same way he comes to us, viz., through Mary. By reason of the integrity of her human nature and the fullness of grace she is superior to all men. She is superior also to the angels by the sole reason of her fullness of grace. She is inferior to God because of the finite manner in which she possesses both this grace and this nature. This Mediatrix brings the grace of God, viz., that of the redemptive Incarnation, to men and angels, and she brings the redeemed natures of angel and man to the incarnate Mediator, who brings them to the Father.

As for man, he is not only separated from God, but is also inimical toward him by reason of original and actual sin, which is an affront to God. The mediation that reconstructs the unity between God and man must, therefore, also *merit* in order to obtain the remission of fault and *satisfy* in order to remit the *punishment*. The angel must also consider himself redeemed, though in a more sublime manner in a certain sense, because the good angels have been granted perseverance in grace and the grace of being preserved from sin in view of the merits of Christ and Mary.

Now, while the merit of Christ in the order of mediation is absolute, that of Mary is relative, because it originates in Christ and is exercised in conjunction with his.

In this broad, all-inclusive sense, the title of Mary Mediatrix includes the coredemption, the distribution of all graces, and her infallible intercession. This is the sense intended by those cardinals, bishops and theologians who, when they were assembled in Fatima in 2005, signed a petition to the Pope asking for the dogmatic definition of Mary Mediatrix, Co-redemptrix, Dispensatrix of all graces, and Advocate.[18]

That Mary's mediation is said to be derived by participation and by analogy from the mediation of Christ is a doctrine clearly taught by St. Paul in his epistles.[19] Based on this conclusion it is evident that Christ's mediation, when consummated on Calvary, involves two aspects, the first ascending and the second descending: 1) redemption, continued in his intercession during the time of the Church, above all in the Eucharistic mystery as sacrifice (cf. Heb 9:23ff.; 1 Jn 2:1); and 2) the acquisition of grace, succeeded by its distribution in the time of the Church, especially in the Eucharist as communion (cf. Heb 12:18ff.; 13:9-15). The two moments are strictly tied to each other, because redemption is the basis for intercession and the acquisition of grace for its distribution. The same is true, *servatis servandis*, for Mary's mediation.

Also from St. Paul's doctrine is derived the Christocentric vision of the universe, which becomes, as a logical consequence, also Mariocentric. "All things were created through him and for him" (Col 1:16), but also through her and for her, as exemplary cause, because she is willed with Christ *"uno eodemque decreto"* by God (Bl. Pius IX, *Ineffabilis Deus*). If Christ and Mary are the center of creation, they are even more so in the order of grace that they have acquired through the

---

[18] Cf. Aa.Vv., *Maria: "Unica Cooperatrice alla Redenzione"* – *Mary: "Unique Cooperator in the Redemption,"* New Bedford, MA, 2005.

[19] Cf. I. Bover, *Pauli doctrina de Christi Mediatione Mariae mediationi applicata*, in *Marianum*, 4 (1942) 81-90.

work of the redemptive sacrifice. Therefore all creatures, both earthly and heavenly, have their *raison d'être* in Christ and Mary, and they receive their sanctifying grace and beatific glory from Christ through Mary.

Mediatrix in the Restricted Sense of Distributrix of Graces after Calvary

St. Bonaventure identifies three moments in the maternal mediation of Mary, taken in the broad sense: the moment of begetting the price of our salvation, the moment of paying that price on Calvary, and the moment of distributing the price of salvation which she possesses in the time of the Church.[20] It is to this last phase of her mediation that the title "Mary, Mediatrix of all graces," is commonly referred. When recent popes (like Benedict XVI in his homily for the Annunciation, March 25, 2006)[21] refer to the Marian principle at the heart of the Church, they refer precisely to this third aspect of Mary's work as Mediatrix in the economy of salvation, one realizing the final phase of her maternal vocation, that of spiritual Mother of the redeemed and of the Church.

As immediately consequent on the coredemption, as it were its continuation, this mediation has two aspects. The first is one of intercession whose high point is the Holy Sacrifice of the Mass. One need only reflect on the *Communicantes* prayer of the Roman canon to grasp that the intercession of all the saints united to that of Christ passes through and depends upon the unique intercession and presence of Mary in the sacrifice of Christ, as John Paul II makes so clear in his Encyclical *Ecclesia de Eucharistia*, under the heading "Woman of the Eucharist."[22] Mary, as Immaculate Spouse of the Holy Spirit, is invoked *in primis* in every Eucharist, that is before and above all other saints, including the apostles. Because she is the Immaculate and so Spouse of the Holy Spirit, invoking her in this way is an aspect of the *epiclesis* of the Holy Spirit. Without Mary and the Holy Spirit, no Incarnation, and hence no Real Presence.

---

[20] St. Bonaventure, *Collationes de septem Donis Spiritus Sancti*, col. 6. Cf. P.D. Fehlner, *Il mistero della Corredenzione secondo il Dottore Serafico San Bonaventura*, in *Maria Corredentrice. Storia e Teologia II* , Frigento 1999, pp. 11-92.

[21] Cf. Pope Benedict XVI, homily at the ordinary public consistory for the creation of new cardinals, March 25, 2006.

[22] Pope John Paul II, Encyclical *Ecclessia de Eucharistia*, April 17, 2003, Chapter Six.

The other aspect is that of distribution of the graces acquired in the sacrifice of Calvary. This, too, has its highpoint in the Eucharist at Communion. In the worthy communicant is him who first dwelt in the immaculate womb of the Virgin Mother, so that like the Word incarnate the Christian might fully become a child of Mary and so child of the Father, on both counts perfectly conformed to Christ, perfectly incorporated into him. There is no grace, no charism, no aspect of sanctification which does not involve the maternal mediation of Mary here and now. This is perfectly logical when we recall that Mary is Spouse of the Holy Spirit at the Incarnation and at Pentecost, at the birth of the Savior and at the birth of the Church, that is, she is Spouse of him by whose working the whole Christ, Head and Body, comes to be. In other words she is Mediatrix *par excellence*.

Theological Meaning of the Title of Mediatrix: Sources of the Doctrine

The title of Mediatrix means that Mary possesses a dignity intermediate between that of all other creatures and that of the incarnate Son by reason of her fullness of grace. This intermediate dignity fits her to carry out the role of maternal intermediary entrusted to her by God the Father to reunite man to his Son, our Mediator with the Father, by means of the coredemption, the dispensation of all graces and intercession.[23] Such mediation is carried out, not apart from, but in Christ, in dependence upon him. It is a necessary aspect of the economy of salvation, said to be hypothetical, not absolute necessity: necessary not because God could not have done otherwise, but because God has so willed, and has so willed because this is the most perfect, orderly or rational way to accomplish our salvation. It is this aspect of the saving counsels of God, implicitly present in such classic passages as Ephesians 1:3-14; Galatians 4:4-7; Philippians 2:5-10, and Hebrews 10:5-10, which is witnessed in Scripture without the title *Mediatrix*, and in Tradition

---

[23] It is in this all-inclusive sense that the title of Mediatrix is taken in the petition that the cardinals and bishops united at Fatima in 2005 addressed to the Pope. Cf. Aa.Vv., *Maria: "Unica Cooperatrice alla Redenzione"* – *Mary: "Unique Cooperator in the Redemption,"* op. cit. This delineation of the all-inclusive sense is essentially that of St. Bonaventure, *Collationes in Hexaemeron*, col. 6.

with the title, and in modern times expressly incorporated into the ordinary magisterial teaching of the Church.

Sacred Scripture

As has been already noted, Scripture never explicitly attributes the title of Mediatrix to Mary.[24] That is not surprising, because neither does it ascribe to her the titles of Mother of God, Immaculate Conception, or ever-Virgin, nor does it attribute the Assumption to her, all of which titles are defined dogmas. Nor, moreover, does the word *Trinity*, the most important dogma of our faith, appear in Scripture; the term *consubstantial*, which forms part of the dogmatic definition of Nicaea, is absent; the same is true of *hypostatic union, real presence, transubstantiation, pontifical infallibility*, etc. If we had to delete all of the words and their related concepts that do not explicitly appear in Sacred Scripture from Catholic dogma, we would first have to annul 2,000 years of Church history. Why, therefore, has God not revealed everything in an explicit manner in Scripture? Bl. Duns Scotus responds:

> I say that it is more pleasing to understand something if it is hidden under some literal sense rather than if it were stated expressly. ... Moreover, Origen, in his *Homily on Noah's Ark*, affirmed: "It seems that Sacred Scripture has maintained an appropriate silence regarding those things whose discovery reason would show as consequences of those truths [directly revealed in Scripture]. Therefore many necessary truths are not explicitly related in Scripture, although they are contained there virtually, as conclusions within the principles; the work of the Doctors and commentators was useful for defining these conclusions" (*Ordinatio. Prologus*, n. 122-123).

The very clear, although implicit, biblical basis for the mediation of Mary beside her Son is found in the association of Mary with Christ,

---

[24] For the biblical foundation of all of dogmatic Mariology, including the doctrine on Marian mediation, see S.M. Manelli, F.I., *All Generations Shall Call Me Blessed: Biblical Mariology*, Academy of the Immaculate, New Bedford, MA, 2005, 442 pp.; I. De La Potterie, S.J., *Mary in the Mystery of the Covenant*, New York, 1992; P.C. Landucci, *Maria Santissima nel Vangelo*, Ed. San Paolo, Rome 2000, 537 pp.

central theme of the history spanning both Old and New Testaments, from the *Protoevangelium* (Gen 3:15) to the book of Revelation (Rev 12).

Regarding mediation in the restricted sense of dispensation of all graces, the biblical passages in which theologians have discovered the basis for the doctrine are the following:

> a) Genesis 3:15: I will put enmity between you and the woman, and between your seed and her seed; she shall crush your head, and you shall lie in wait for her heel.

The woman is Mary, by exclusion and by identification. By exclusion, because it cannot be Eve, as she could never appear as a victorious enemy of the serpent, but instead as his victim, first in the fault and then in the punishment. By identification, because Mary is the only woman who fully realizes enmity and victory over the serpent. Enmity and victory over Satan always signifies the work of the redemption, accomplished by Mary and by Christ, the firstborn of her offspring. Associated with Christ in the redemption in the first phase, Mary is associated also in the redemption in the second phase, that is, in the distribution of the acquired graces.

> b) 1 Kings 18:44: And at the seventh time he said, "Behold, a little cloud like a man's hand is rising out of the sea." And he said, "Go up, say to Ahab, 'Prepare your chariot and go down, lest the rain stop you.'"

This is the cloud that Elijah caught sight of on Mount Carmel which brought rain after a long drought. Here the cloud has been viewed as a symbol of Mary and the rain as a symbol of the graces Mary brings.

> c) Luke 1:28: Hail, full of grace, the Lord is with you.

If it is true that *from his [Christ's] fullness have we all received, grace upon grace* (Jn 1:16), it is also true that we have received it by means of Mary's fullness of grace. The passive participle *kecharitomene* (full of grace) is used to indicate a permanent fullness *par excellence*. This is what St. Francis had an intuition of when, in his *Salute to the Virgin*, he gave this description of her: "On you descended and in you still remains all the fullness of grace and every good." Why has God filled the Virgin Mary with his grace if not in order for her to communicate this grace to others who, by their nature, are devoid of them?

> d) Luke 1:38: And Mary said, "Behold, I am the handmaid of the Lord; let it be done to me according to your word."

Mary's *fiat* is her free and personal assent to the redemptive Incarnation, of which she is defined as the "handmaid," and the fulfillment of which is realized in the regeneration of men into the life of grace. It matches the *fiat* of her Son: I come to do your will (cf. Heb 10:5-10). Both are efficacious as acts of mediation, because each, though distinctively, is contained within the order of the hypostatic union as willed by the Father as the radical foundation for saving mediation. Through her *fiat*, Mary mediates to the world Jesus Christ, the Mediator, and the Author of all grace. The title, "Mediatrix of all graces," is rightly and uniquely ascribed to Mary in virtue of her mediation of the Savior alone.

> e) Luke 1:43-44: And why is this granted me, that the mother of my Lord should come to me? For behold, when the voice of your greeting came to my ears, the babe in my womb leaped for joy.

Here Mary's physical presence brings the grace of Christ's presence to Elizabeth, who prophesies, and to the Baptist, who exults with joy in his mother's womb. The joy consequent on Mary's mediation, a joy which is a foretaste of that of heaven, contrasts sharply with the sadness consequent on the mediation of the first Eve and the expulsion from paradise. As Eve in fact mediated tragedy for the human family, Mary mediates the presence of the Savior and salvation, even to those such as John enclosed in his mother's womb. It is she who mediates the working of the Holy Spirit, and therefore it is she who at the most intimate reaches of the human heart guarantees faith, as it is she who is the prime evangelist and sign of the presence of the invisible Savior-God, she who is Mother of "the Lord" or Yahweh, who spoke to Moses from the burning bush as Christ speaks to us from Mary, the Ark of the New Covenant. The importance of Mary's Visitation to Elizabeth in the revelation of the mystery of Marian mediation, specifically the distribution of all the blessings of salvation, cannot be underestimated.

Further, the mediation of Jesus and Mary, inseparable and related to one another according to a typology established by the Creator in the formation of the first man and woman, is also shown here in its antitypes. It is the mediation of Mary which brings the Mediator to us and enables us to be united to him and so enabled by him to return to the Father's house. The basis for a Mediator and Mediatrix within a single work of mediation is also clear: what the theologians have come to call the order of the hypostatic union embracing the incarnate Word and the divine maternity. It is this order which defines concretely the basis of the work of mediation or salvation.

> f) Luke 2:35: And a sword will pierce through your own soul also, that thoughts out of many hearts may be revealed.

The Presentation of Jesus in the Temple (cf. Lk 2:22-40) further clarifies the bases of this mediation: not only Mary's vocation as Mother of God, but her role as Co-redemptrix in the realization of the redemptive sacrifice which secures the "salvation of his people." Mary's role as Advocate (intercessor) and Mediatrix (distributrix of the blessings won on Calvary) is a continuation of her role as Co-redemptrix outlined in the Presentation of Jesus in the Temple: to the Father and to the Church (represented by Simeon and Anna).

> g) John 2:3-5: When the wine failed, the mother of Jesus said to him, "They have no wine." And Jesus said to her, "O woman, what have you to do with me? My hour has not yet come." His mother said to the servants, "Do whatever he tells you."

Again Mary's physical presence carries with it the physical presence of Christ with his divine power. The Lord's words, which express a certain distance between him—who was about to perform an act as God—and his Mother (who always remained simply a creature), make us understand that, if it had not been for her, he would not have worked the miracle. Curiously, those who reject the concept of Marian mediation as revealed will affirm the difference between the Creator Son and created Mother. But they seemingly fail to realize that the difference and distance between the Word incarnate and the rest of us is even greater if Mary is not Mediatrix. From this comes the need of a Mediatrix between ourselves and our Savior, as well as a Mediator between ourselves and the Father. Mary by her physical presence as Mother of God enables us also to be present to him who is our Mediator with the Father. This is what is so clearly communicated by this event at the beginning of our Lord's public ministry. He, the bridegroom, is Savior-Mediator of the Church, the bride represented by the newly wed couple. The role of his Mother at this marriage feast for the groom is that of one who arranges this great marriage covenant, that is to say, she is the Mediatrix. Cana reveals the Mother of Jesus as physical and moral (willed) mediatrix between Jesus and humanity, in the midst of its wants and needs. As John Paul II explains, she acts as a "mediatrix not as an outsider, but in her position as mother."[25]

> h) John 19:26-27: When Jesus saw his mother, and the disciple whom he loved standing near, he said to his mother, "Woman, behold, your son!" Then he said to the disciple, "Behold, your mother!" And from that hour the disciple took her to his own home.

John's presence at the feet of the crucified Redeemer engages the mediation of the Mother, from whom John receives the fruit of the redemption. In the Encyclical *Ecclesia de Eucaristia*, John Paul II teaches that in every Mass the reality of Marian mediation is re-presented for the benefit of believers, of beloved disciples who, like John, assist at the sacrifice of the Redeemer and Co-redemptrix.

The radical structure of Marian mediation observed in all the foregoing texts is here proclaimed by our Savior himself, revealing precisely its immediate grounds in the unique part Mary played as Mother and Co-redemptrix in the redemptive sacrifice of Calvary. In effect, Jesus reveals and proclaims his Mother as maternal Mediatrix between himself and us: both the entire Church and each disciple personified here in John, and in a special way those who are successors of the apostles and their immediate associates, the priests. And he insists that we make use of her mediation, because by his will it is a necessary aspect of Christian life. Hence, our first obligation as disciples is to take Mary into our homes. Mary is our Mother in the order of grace; her spiritual maternity

---

[25] Pope John Paul II, Encyclical *Redemptoris Mater*, March 25, 1987, 21.

is the fruit of her love and suffering on Calvary. What is said here in principle, is shown in the next text from Acts to be operative from day one of the Church, and in Revelation 12:1ff. to be a raging success, for as Co-redemptrix Mary merited to be assumed and gloriously crowned as Queen of heaven and earth, precisely to act efficaciously on earth as maternal Mediatrix. The Woman of Revelation 12:1ff., who is first of all the Mother of the victorious Savior Jesus, swept up to heaven, must be pondered in conjunction with Revelation 21:1-4, where the woman is the heavenly Jerusalem descending from heaven on earth. The Church is the new and glorious Jerusalem or Daughter Zion descending from heaven, because in some unique way Mary Immaculate is the Church as its "pre-eminent" member. Through the dynamic presence of the Immaculate Mediatrix, the Church becomes the Immaculate Bride of her Savior and Head (cf. Eph 5:21-32).[26]

> i) Acts 1:14: All these with one accord devoted themselves to prayer, together with the women and Mary the mother of Jesus, and with his brethren.

Here Mary is Mother of the infant Church. In the Apostolic Church she was the Mother of Jesus, almost a living sacrament of his presence. The intercession of the Church rises to God through Mary's prayer, and the grace of the Holy Spirit descends upon men because of this prayer and this intercession. The ancient Church Tradition clearly confirms this understanding of the central role of Mary in the Church: that of intercession (ascending mediation) and that of distribution of graces (descending mediation), particularly that of sustaining and quietly guiding all Christians in the understanding and living of their faith. "And they continued steadfastly in the teaching of the apostles and in

---

[26] On the patristic development of this point cf. H. Rahner, *Our Lady and the Church*, New York 1961. Within the context of a contemplative Mariology see Ven. Mary of Agreda, *Mystical City of God*, in particular *The Coronation* (part III, in the complete English version, vol. 4: a good introduction is available in E. Llamas, *The Ven. Mary of Agreda and the Mariology of Vatican II*, New Bedford, MA, 2006). The pattern of Marian mediation embedded in the Bible continues from the earliest days of the Church as a fixed context, within which from the sixth century the title *Mediatrix* will commonly be ascribed to the Virgin Mother. Further, the ecclesio-typical aspects of active Marian mediation are clearly shown to depend on the Christo-typical, in a proximate fashion on Mary's role as Co-redemptrix.

the communion of the breaking of the bread and in the prayers" (Acts 2:42), all this in the presence of Mary Mediatrix. For this is what above all the Pentecost scene illustrates: the permanent, "pre-eminent" place of Mary in the midst of the apostles and faithful as maternal Mediatrix.

From all these passages of Scripture there surfaces repeatedly a Marian mode according to which God works our redemption. St. Bonaventure tells us (*Breviloquium*, p. IV, ch. 3) that the mode of the Incarnation is Marian, viz., through the virginal maternity. The one whom Mary begets is our Mediator, the price of our ransom; hence the mode of our redemption is Marian. It is Mary, says the same Seraphic Doctor who begets that price in Nazareth, pays that price on Calvary, and now possesses that price as Mediatrix of all graces (cf. *Collationes in septem donis Spiritus Sancti*, c. 6). The two major features of this last, intercession or ascending mediation, and distribution of graces or descending mediation, are clearly indicated as fact, even if not expressly explained. Meditating on these passages, Bossuet rightly concludes that "Mary's charity is the general instrument of the operations of grace."[27]

Teaching of the Church Fathers

The Eve-Mary parallelism, already put in evidence by St. Justin (+165), is the *leitmotiv* of patristic Mariology, as it developed during the course of the first eight centuries of the Christian era.[28] Its foundation is in the economy of salvation established by God and implicitly revealed by him in Sacred Scripture. The first to single out the Marian characteristic of this salvific economy was St. Ignatius of Antioch (+110): "Our God, Jesus Christ, was conceived by Mary in accord with God's plan."[29] It is the first Marian fruit of patristic reflection on the biblical datum.

---

[27] Bossuet, *Homily III on the Conception of the Virgin*.
[28] Cf. St. Justin, *Dialogus cum Tryphone*, n. 100, in PG 6, 709-711a. For the patristic foundation of Marian mediation, see L. Gambero, S.M., *Maria nel pensiero dei Padri della Chiesa*, Ed. Paoline, Alba (Cn) 1991 [English version: *Mary and the Fathers of the Church: The Blessed Virgin Mary in Patristic Thought*, San Francisco: Ignatius Press, 1999]; G. Roschini, O.S.M., *Maria Santissima nella Storia della Salvezza*, vol. II, Ed. Pisani, Isola del Liri (Fr), pp. 171-179, 209-222; L. Cignelli, O.F.M., *Maria Nuova Eva nella patristica greca*, Assisi 1966; *Testi mariani deli primo millennio*, ed. G. Gharib, E. Toniolo, L. Gambero, G. Di Nola, Roma 1988-1993, 4 vv.
[29] St. Ignatius of Antioch, *Letter to the Ephesians*, 18, 2, cit. by W.A. Jurgens, *The Faith of the Early Fathers*, vol. 1, The Liturgical Press, Collegeville (Minn.) 1970,

The Mariology of St. Irenaeus of Lyons (+202) is the wonderful result of the fruitful encounter between the Eastern tradition, from which he came, and that of the West, in which he exercised his episcopal ministry. He developed the antithetical Eve-Mary parallelism and was the first to attribute the title of "Eve's advocate" to the Virgin.[30] The concept of mediation is contained in the term Advocate because, according to St. Irenaeus, as Advocate, Mary performs the role of Mediatrix of reconciliation between the just divine Judge and the guilty Eve. The Devil, on the other hand, is the one who accuses Eve before God and requests her condemnation.[31]

Origen (+254) interprets the episode of the Visitation as an example of the Virgin's mediation. Her journey took place so "that she might communicate some of the power she derived from him [whom] she had conceived, to John, yet in his mother's womb."[32] In a text attributed to Origen but not recognized as authentic by the critics, the title of Mediatrix appears for the first time: "All human creatures have been renewed through Mary ... Mediatrix of life."[33]

The prayer *Sub Tuum Praesidium*, written in Egypt in the third century: "Under your mercy we take refuge, Mother of God, do not reject our supplications in necessity. But deliver us from danger. [You] alone chaste, alone blessed."[34] This ancient prayer, with minor variations,

---

p. 18 (n. 42).

[30] St. Irenaeus of Lyons, *Adversus haereses*, V, 19, 1; *Demonstratio praedicationis apostolicae*, 31, 33, cit. by B. de Margerie, *Mary Coredemptrix in the Light of Patristics*, in *Mary Coredemptrix, Mediatrix, Advocate: Theological Foundations*, op. cit., p. 9.

[31] Cf. G. Jouassard, *Le rôle des chrétiennes comme intercesseurs auprès de Dieu dans la chrétienté lyonnaise au second siècle*, in *Revue des sciences religieuses*, 30 (1956) 217-229; M. Jourion, *Aux origines de la prière d'intercession de Marie*, in *Etudes Mariales*, 23 (1966) 37-42.

[32] Origen, *Commentary on the Gospel of John*, 6, 49, in GCS, IV-57, p. 27. [English cit. in A. Menzies, ed., *Ante-Nicene Fathers*, vol. 9, 4th ed., 1897, p. 375.]

[33] Pseudo-Origen, in *Florilegium casinense*, 2, p. 154, 2c.

[34] Translation from the original Greek. The papyrus that relates this prayer is property of the John Rylands Library of Manchester (England). Published in the critical edition of M.C.H. Roberts, *Catalogue of the Greek and Latin Papyri in the John Rylands Library Manchester*, vol. III, Manchester 1938, p. 46. See also *La mariologia dei Padri. Età pre nicena*, LAS, Roma; G. Giamberardini, O.F.M., *La mediazione di Maria nella Chiesa Egiziana*, Cairo 1952, 124 pp.; G. Giamberardini, *Il culto mariano in Egitto*, 3 vv., Franciscan Printing Press, Jerusalem 1974-1978. English translation cit. by J.D. Miller, *Marian Mediation: Is It True to say that Mary*

is found from time immemorial in the antiphonary of the Roman, Ambrosian, Byzantine and Coptic liturgies.[35] The intercession ascending toward God ("do not reject our supplications") and the descending mediation that brings God's help to men ("deliver us from danger") is clearly seen.

In the ancient *Cimitero Maggiore* (Main Cemetery) on the Via Nomantana in Rome, there is the depiction of the Virgin Mary in a position of prayer, of intercession, which dates back to the fourth century.

The doctrine of mediation recurs often in the authentic scripts of St. Ephraem (+373), the great Doctor of the Syriac Church, or in scripts simply attributed to him by tradition. He does not use the term itself, but equivalent expressions: "The human race ... depends upon your patronage and has you alone as its refuge and defense. ... Your prayer, in fact, is powerful with your Son."[36] She has received an unlimited power from God: "You are true Mother of God, and therefore you are powerful."[37]

In the celebrated hymn *Akathistos*, attributed to St. Romanos the Melodist (+560), Mary's help is invoked in various ways: "By your invincible power, deliver me from every kind of danger";[38] "Deliver all from every evil, and save from future suffering all who cry to thee. Alleluia."[39]

Theoteknos, bishop of Livias (sixth century) is the first in the West to use the title Mediatrix: "She has departed for heaven as our Mediatrix ... and because she is certainly accepted by God, she obtains spiritual graces for us. During her time on earth she watched over us; she was like a universal providence for all her subjects. Now in heaven, she remains an impregnable defense, interceding for us with her Son and God."[40]

---

is *Coredemptrix, Mediatrix of all Graces and Advocate?*, op. cit., p. 58; Maria Francesca Perilla, F.I., *Sub Tuum Praesidium. Incomparable Marian Praeconium*, in *Mary at the Foot of the Cross IV*, New Bedford, MA, 2004, pp. 138-169.

[35] Cf. P.F. Mercernier, *L'antienne mariale la plus ancienne*, in *Le Museon*, 53 (1939) 229-233; Mercernier, *La plus ancienne prière à la Sainte Vierge*, in *Les Questions Liturgiques et Paroissales*, 25 (1940) 33-36.

[36] St. Ephraem, *Opera*, Ed. Assemani, vol. III, p. 532-533.

[37] *Ibid*, p. 526.

[38] Hymn *Akathistos*. Cf. *The Catholic Encyclopedia*, vol. I, Robert Appleton Co., 1907.

[39] *Ibid*.

[40] Theoteknos, *Homily on the Assumption*, n. 9, in A. Wenger, *L'Assomption de la Très Sainte Vierge dans la Tradition Byzantine du VI au X siècle*, Paris 1955, pp. 289, 291.

Except for the literature ascribed to pseudo-Ephraem, this is the first time that the title of Mediatrix is explicitly attributed to Mary in a text the author of which is known with certainty.

Patristic Mariology reached its zenith with the three great Eastern homilists of the eighth century. They are St. Germanus of Constantinople (+733), St. Andrew of Crete (+740), and St. John Damascene (+749). Besides using the term Mediatrix explicitly, they study the doctrine of her universal dispensation of graces in depth.

For St. Germanus the Most Blessed Virgin Mary is the "manifest Mediatrix of all goods";[41] "no one obtains a grace by mercy except through you, who were worthy to harbor God himself in your womb."[42] "You cannot not be answered from the time that it pleased God to dwell with you, like a son with his true and irreproachable Mother. ... And because of this the Christian people, recognizing its miserable state, entrusts its prayers to you so that you may present them to God."[43]

St. Andrew of Crete appeals to Mary "Mediatrix of law and grace."[44] St. John Damascene illustrates the doctrine of Mary's mediation with a splendid biblical image: "As Jacob saw the ladder uniting heaven to earth ... so you also, fulfilling the role of Mediatrix become a stairway for God who descends to us so that he might assume our weak nature and join and unite it to himself";[45] "You are the perennial source of the true light ... the cause of all our goods ... [from heaven] you bless the world, you sanctify the universe."[46]

Theological Development: Medieval, Post-Tridentine and Neo-Scholastic Epochs

St. Bernard of Clairvaux (+1153) stands out among the large group of writers who in the twelfth century affirm Mary's mediation. His

---

[41] St. Germanus of Constantinople, *Homily 2 on the Dormition,* in PG 98, 357.
[42] *Idem, Homily on the Dedication of the Virgin to the Temple,* in PG 98, 380-381.
[43] *Idem, Homily 2 on the Dormition,* in PG 98, 352b.
[44] St. Andrew of Crete, *Sermon 4 On the Birth of Mary,* PG 97, 865A. English cit. in "Appendix IV: English Translation of Chapter VIII of Lumen Gentium," *Marian Studies,* Vol. XXXVII (1986), p. 248, note 15.
[45] St. John Damascene, *Homily 1 On the Dormition of the B.V. Mary,* 8, PG 96, 712bc–713a. Cf. "Appendix IV: English Translation of Chapter VIII of Lumen Gentium," *art. cit.*
[46] *Ibid.,* 716c. 717a.

doctrine is clear and precise: "God has willed that we should have nothing that would not pass through the hands of Mary. ... Do you also desire someone to intercede for you with him? Run to Mary."[47] Mary is defined by the Mellifluous Doctor as the "aqueduct" through which all graces flow from God to men. The works of St. Bernard influenced the entire subsequent Mariology during the Middle Ages.

Pseudo-Albertus Magnus asserts that the Blessed Virgin Mary "is numerically full of all graces, which, numerically, pass through her hands."[48]

St. Bonaventure of Bagnoregio (O.Min., +1274) writes explicitly that "every grace comes to us through Mary's intervention."[49]

St. Bernardine of Siena (O.Min., +1444) affirms that "all gifts, virtues and graces of the same Holy Spirit are administered by her hands to whomever she desires, when, in what manner, and to what degree she wishes."[50]

The universal mediation of all graces is common doctrine among the post-tridentine theologians: Francisco Suárez (S.J., +1617), St. Robert Bellarmine (S.J., +1621), Ven. James Olier (+1657), St. John Eudes

---

[47] St. Bernard, *In Vigilia Navitatis Domini Sermo* 3, in PL 183, 100. Cf. P. Haffner, *The Mystery of Mary* (Wiltshire, England: Anthony Rowe Ltd. 2004), p. 258.

[48] Pseudo Albertus Magnus, *Mariale*, p. 164.

[49] St. Bonaventure, *Opera omnia*, vol. IX, p. 641a. On Marian mediation in St. Bonaventure cf. L. Di Fonzo, *Doctrina Sancti Bonaventurae de Universali Mediatione B. Virginia Mariae*, Rome 1938; P.D. Fehlner, *Il mistero della Corredenzione...*, cit. St. Bonaventure is rightly considered the "Doctor of Marian Mediation," so profound and so many are his insights, so systematically thought out. Alone among the great Doctors of the thirteenth century, his teaching is at once a witness to the riches of the preceding tradition and a key to the subsequent development of Mariology in the West, particularly with Scotus. For the clinching argument for the Immaculate Conception in Scotus (and in the Bull of definition, *Ineffabilis Deus*, of Bl. Pius IX) rests on the concept of a most perfect redemption by a most perfect Redeemer. What makes that redemption most perfect is clearly expounded by St. Bonaventure in terms of Marian mediation, whence the need of a unique sanctity or fullness of grace in Mary as the ontological "mean" of her office between Christ and us.

[50] St. Bernardine of Siena, *Homily on the Nativity of the B.V. Mary*, chapter 8, cit. by M.J. Scheeben, *Mariology*, vol. II (New York: B. Herder Book Co., 1947), p. 271. St. Bernardine is another great "Doctor of Marian Mediation," particularly as a foundation of Catholic spirituality. The substance of his teaching is doubtless what Scotus might have written, had he not died so young.

(+1680), Henry Boudon (+1702), Jacques-Benigne Bossuet (+1704), Pierre de Berulle (+1629), to mention only a few. It is one of the major themes of the golden age of Spanish Mariology, the seventeenth century, notable not only for works of theological erudition, but also for one of the greatest and most influential works of Mariology in a contemplative key, *The Mystical City of God*, by the Ven. Mary of Jesus of Agreda (+1665).[51] St. Louis-Marie Grignion de Montfort (+1716), with his timeless work, *True Devotion to Mary*, is another outstanding figure in the history of this doctrine. In the seventeenth century the Jansenistic influences gave rise to a certain diffidence toward the Marian cult and everything in Mariology which seems to, in their opinion, overly exalt the Virgin's excellence. The first major representative of this minimizing current was the Rhinelander Adam Widenfeld, with his *Monita salutaria* (1673), whose publication gave rise to violent polemics. In Italy the authoritative spokesman of this critical current was the famous historian Ludovico Antonio Muratori. St. Alphonsus Maria de' Liguori (+1787) responded to his anti-Marian theses so effectively, above all with his superb book *The Glories of Mary*, that they were not given credence again until our days.

In the twentieth century the doctrine of Mary's universal mediation gained the universal consent of theologians. First-rate monographic studies demonstrate the inclusion of the doctrine on Mary's mediation into the patrimony of Catholic faith and illustrate its wonderful *conexio dogmatum*. Among these the studies of Godts,[52] Bittremieux[53] and Lepicier[54] stand out.

By initiative of Cardinal Desiré Mercier (+1926),[55] archbishop of Malines-Brussels, the international movement for the proclamation of the dogma of Mary Mediatrix of all graces was born. On January 12, 1922, in response to the Belgian Cardinal's request, Benedict XV (+1922) granted to all dioceses of Belgium the Mass in honor of Mary Mediatrix

---

[51] By way of introduction to the theological value of this work and the significance of the golden age of Spanish Mariology in particular cf. E. Llamas, *The Ven. Mary of Agreda and the Mariology of Vatican II*, New Bedford, MA, 2006.

[52] F.X. Godts, C.Ss.R., *De definibilitate Mediationis universalis Deiprarae*, Brussels 1904, 451 pp.

[53] J. Bittremieux J., *De mediatione universali B.M. Virginis quoad gratis*, Brugis 1926.

[54] A. Lépicier, O.S.M. (Card.), *L'Immacolata Corredentrice Mediatrice*, Rome 1928.

[55] Cf. M. Hauke, *Maria "Mediatrice di tutte le grazie." La mediazione universale di Maria nell'opera teologica e pastorale di cardinale Mercier*, op. cit.

of all graces, to be celebrated on May 31. In November 1922, Pius XI (+1939) instituted three commissions—one Roman, one Spanish and one Belgian—to study the definability of Marian mediation. The documents of the Spanish and Belgian commissions have been recently published in the periodical *Marianum*, both with a positive conclusion in support of the doctrine's definability.[56]

Mary Mediatrix of all Graces in the Pontifical Magisterium: From Benedict XIV to Benedict XVI

Mary's universal mediation has been the object of the unchanging Ordinary Papal Magisterium for at least the past three centuries and therefore must be considered Catholic doctrine, *definitive tenenda*, not dogmatically defined, but certainly definable.[57] Despite this fact, a certain debate exists among some Mariologists today concerning the legitimacy and significance of the title *Mediatrix of all graces*. Those who deny its legitimacy generally also deny Mary's coredemption, thus witnessing the logical nexus linking these two truths.[58]

Pope Benedict XIV (+1758) describes Our Blessed Lady as the "heavenly stream which brings to the hearts of wretched mortals all God's gifts and graces."[59]

---

[56] G. Besutti, O.S.M., *La mediazione di Maria secondo gli studi di due Commissioni istituite da Pio XI*, with introduction by I.M. Calabuig, O.S.M., *Marianum*, 47 (1985) 37-174. Dr. Manfred Hauke is presently conducting detailed archival research seeking to locate the mysterious, elusive report of the Roman Commission.

[57] We will follow the outline of the positive historical study of Fr. Paolo M. Siano, F.I., which may be consulted upon further inquiries. P. Siano, F.I., *Uno studio su Maria Santissima "Mediatrice di tutte le Grazie" nel magistero pontificio fino al pontificato di Giovanni Paolo II, op. cit.*

[58] Cf. A. Apollonio, F.I., *Il "calvario teologico" della Corredenzione mariana*, Presentation of Fr. Paolo M. Siano (pp. 3-6), Casa Mariana Editrice, Castelpetroso 1999, pp. 43. Standing out, unfortunately, among the voices contrary to the Marian title of "Co-redemptrix" and "Mediatrix of all Graces" is that of Salvatore Perella, O.S.M., *Virgo Ecclesia facta. La Madre di Dio tra due millenni. Summa storico-teologica*, *Miles Immaculatae*, Anno XXXVII, fasc. II, 2001, pp. 357-434. See in particular pp. 408-410.

[59] Benedict XIV, Bull *Gloriosae Dominae*, 1748, Op. Omnia, v. 16, ed. Prati, 1846, p. 428, cit. in *Our Lady: Papal Teachings*, trans. Daughters of St. Paul (Boston: St. Paul Editions, 1961), p. 26, n. 4.

Pope Pius VII (+1823) calls Mary the "Dispensatrix of all graces [*gratiarum omnium dispensatricem*]."[60]

Bl. Pius IX (+1878) places his hopes in the Most Blessed Virgin Mary, she who "with her only-begotten Son, is the most powerful Mediatrix and Conciliatrix in the whole world. ... [She] who has destroyed all heresies and snatched the faithful people and nations from all kinds of direst calamities; in her do we hope who has delivered us from so many threatening dangers."[61]

Leo XIII (+1903) writes that "with equal truth may it be also affirmed that, by the will of God, Mary is the intermediary through whom is distributed unto us this immense treasure of mercies gathered by God, for mercy and truth were created by Jesus Christ. Thus as no man goes to the Father but by the Son, so no man goes to Christ but by his Mother."[62]

In another encyclical, Leo XIII explains that in the vocal recitation of the Rosary we address first the *Father who is in heaven* and then the Virgin Mary. "Thus is confirmed that law of merciful meditation of which we have spoken, and which St. Bernardine of Siena thus expresses: 'Every grace granted to man has three degrees in order; for by God it is communicated to Christ, from Christ it passes to the Virgin, and from the Virgin it descends to us.'"[63] At the end of the encyclical the Holy Father, citing the authority of St. Bernard of Clairvaux, reaffirms that God has given us a "Mediatrix" in Mary, willing "that all good should come to us by the hands of Mary."[64]

---

[60] Pius VII, *Ampliatio privilegiorum ecclesiae B.M. Virginis ab angelo salutatae in cenobio Fratrum Ordinis Servorum B.M.V.* Florentiae, A.D., 1806, § 1, in J.J. Bourassé, *Summa Aurea de laudibus Beatissimae Virginis Mariae, Dei Genitricis sine labe conceptae...*, Tomus VII, Paris 1862, col. 546.

[61] Pius IX, Apostolic Constitution *Ineffabilis Deus*, December 8, 1854, in R. Spiazzi, O.P., ed., *Maria Santissima nel Magistero della Chiesa. I documenti pontifici da Pio IX a Giovanni Paolo II*, Massimo, Milano 1987, p. 38.

[62] Leo XIII, Encyclical on the Rosary *Octobri mense*, September 21, 1891, in H. Denzinger, *Enchiridion symbolorum definitionum et declarationum de rebus fidei et morum*, bilingual edizione, ed. Peter Hünermann, EDB, Bologna 1996, n. 3274. Abbreviation: Denz. The entire text of the encyclical is in *Acta Sanctae Sedis* [ASS], 24 (1891-1892) 193-203.

[63] Leo XIII, Encyclical on the Rosary *Iucunda semper*, September 8, 1894, in ASS 27 (1894-1895) 179.

[64] Cf. *ibid.*, pp. 183-184.

In Leo's Encyclical *Adiutricem populi*, we read that the Blessed Virgin Mary, "who was so intimately associated with the mystery of human salvation is just as closely associated with the distribution of the graces which for all time will flow from the redemption. ... Among her many other titles we find her hailed as 'Our Lady, our Mediatrix,' 'the Reparatrix of the whole world,' 'the Dispenser of all heavenly gifts.'"[65]

And in his Encyclical *Fidentem piumque* we read:

> Undoubtedly the name and attributes of the absolute Mediator belong to no other than to Christ, for being one person, and yet both man and God, he restored the human race to the favor of the heavenly Father: *One Mediator of God and men, the man Christ Jesus, who gave himself a redemption for all* (1 Tim 2:5-6). And yet, as the Angelic Doctor teaches, *there is no reason why certain others should not be called in a certain way mediators between God and man, that is to say, in so far as they co-operate by predisposing and ministering in the union of man with God* (Summa, p. 3, q. 26., a. 1, 2). Such are the angels and saints, the prophets and priests of both Testaments; but especially has the Blessed Virgin a claim to the glory of this title. For no single individual can even be imagined who has ever contributed or ever will contribute so much towards reconciling man with God. She offered to mankind, hastening to eternal ruin, a Savior, at that moment when she received the announcement of the mystery of peace brought to this earth by the angel, with that admirable act of consent *in the name of the whole human race* (Summa. p. 3, q. 30., a. 1). She it is *from whom is born Jesus*; she is therefore truly his mother, and for this reason a worthy and acceptable "Mediatrix to the Mediator."[66]

---

[65] Leo XIII, Encyclical *Adiutricem populi*, September 5, 1895, in ASS 28 (1895-1896) 130-131. in R. Spiazzi, ed., *Maria Santissima nel Magistero della Chiesa. I documenti pontifici da Pio IX a Giovanni Paolo II*, Massimo, Milano 1987, p. 60 (ASS 28 (1895-1896) 130-131).

[66] Leo XIII, Encyclical *Fidentem piumque*, September 20, 1896, in ASS 29 (1896-1897) 206 (Denz. 3320-3321).

St. Pius X (+1914), in the Encyclical *Ad diem illum*, writes:

> It cannot, of course, be denied that the dispensation of these treasures is the particular and peculiar right of Jesus Christ, for they are the exclusive fruit of his death, who by his nature is the mediator between God and man. Nevertheless, by this companionship in sorrow and suffering already mentioned between the Mother and the Son, it has been allowed to the august Virgin to be the most powerful Mediatrix and Advocate of the whole world with her divine Son [*totius terrarium orbis potentissima apud unigenitum Filium suum mediatrix et conciliatrix*]. The source, then, is Jesus Christ. ... But Mary ... is the channel, or, if you will, the connecting portion the function of which is to join the body to the head and to transmit to the body the influences and volitions of the head—we mean the neck. ... We are then, it will be seen, very far from attributing to the Mother of God a productive power of grace—a power which belongs to God alone. Yet, since Mary carries it over all in holiness and union with Jesus Christ, and has been associated by Jesus Christ in the work of redemption ... she is the supreme minister of the distribution of graces [*princeps largiendarum gratiarum ministra*].[67]

Pope Benedict XV (+1922), in the Apostolic Letter *Inter sodalicia* (March 22, 1918), affirms the role of Mary Co-redemptrix and Mediatrix at the foot of the Cross of her Son:

> Mary suffered and, as it were, nearly died with her suffering Son; for the salvation of mankind she renounced her mother's rights and, as far as it depended on her, offered her Son to placate divine justice; so we may well say that she with Christ redeemed mankind. Consequently ... the graces which we receive from the

---

[67] Pius X, Encyclical *Ad diem illum*, February 2, 1904, in ASS 36 (1903-1904) 449-462.

treasury of the redemption are distributed, so to speak, by the hands of this sorrowful Virgin.[68]

In the context of the canonization of St. Joan of Arc, Benedict XV observed that "every grace and blessing comes to us" by means of Our Blessed Lady. Therefore, besides the intercession of the saints, "one must include the influence of her whom the Holy Fathers greeted with the title, *Mediatrix omnium gratiam*."[69]

On January 12, 1921, the Holy See received the requests of Cardinal Mercier (archbishop primate of Belgium) and of the Belgian bishops, approving the Mass and Office of the Feast of the *Blessed Virgin Mary Mediatrix of all graces*, established on the date of May 31. The liturgical celebration of this feast was granted to the dioceses of Belgium and to all dioceses and religious orders requesting it.[70]

With the Apostolic Letter *Sodalitatem Nostrae Dominae*, Benedict XV granted plenary and partial indulgences to the *Sodalizio di Nostra Signora della buona morte* (Association of Our Lady of a Happy Death); he also granted indulgences for the day of May 31, Feast of the Blessed Virgin Mary "Mediatrix of all graces."[71]

Pius XI (+1939) calls the Virgin Mary the "Mediatrix of all graces with God";[72] he writes that Christ has associated Mary with himself as "minister and mediatress of grace";[73] he makes reference to the most efficacious patronage of the Blessed Virgin Mary "Mediatrix of all graces";[74] he establishes the Blessed Virgin Mary of graces of Mount Philerimos as the principal patroness of the Archdiocese of Rhodes;

---

[68] Benedict XV, Apostolic Letter *Inter sodalicia*, March 22, 1918, in R. Spiazzi, *op. cit.*, p. 87 (Denz. 3370). English translation cit. in *Papal Teachings: Our Lady*, *op. cit.*, p. 194, nn. 267-268.

[69] Benedict XV, Decree of April 6, 1919, cited by Hauke M., *Maria "Mediatrice di tutte le grazie." La mediazione universale di Maria nell'opera teologica e pastorale di cardinale Mercier*, art. cit., p. 64. English translation cit. by M. Hauke, *Mary, Mediatress of Grace: Mary's Mediation of Grace in the Theological and Pastoral Works of Cardinal Mercier*, Supplement to *Mary at the Foot of the Cross IV*, *op. cit.*, p. 52.

[70] Cf. *ibid.*, pp. 67-72.

[71] Benedict XV, Apostolic Letter *Sodalitatem Nostrae Dominae*, May 31, 1921, *Acta Apostolicae Sedis* [AAS] 13 (1921) 345.

[72] Pius XI, Apostolic Letter *Galliam, Ecclesiae filiam*, March 2, 1922, AAS 14 (1922) 186.

[73] Pius XI, Encyclical *Miserentissimus Redemptor*, May 8, 1928, AAS 20 (1928) 178.

[74] Pius XI, Encyclical *Caritate Christi compulsi*, May 3, 1932, in AAS 24 (1932) 192.

and, in the related document, the Blessed Virgin is called "Mediatrix of all graces."[75]

Pius XII (+1958) very often makes use of the titles *Mediatrix omnium gratiarum, gratiarum omnium apud Deum sequestra,* and other similar expressions.[76] **In the Encyclical** ***Ad Caeli Reginam*****, Pius XII wonderfully illustrates the doctrine of the Blessed Virgin Mary's universal mediation:**

> Certainly, in the full and strict meaning of the term, only Jesus Christ, the God-man, is King; but Mary, too, as Mother of the divine Christ, as his associate in the redemption, in his struggle with his enemies and his final victory over them, has a share, though in a limited and analogous way, in his royal dignity. For from her union with Christ she attains a radiant eminence transcending that of any other creature; from her union with Christ she receives the royal right to dispose of the treasures of the divine Redeemer's kingdom; from her union with Christ finally comes the inexhaustible efficacy of her maternal intercession before the Son and his Father.

---

[75] Pius XI, Apostolic Letter *Rhodiensis archidioecesis*, October 4, 1934, in AAS 26 (1934) 545-546.

[76] Pius XII, Apostolic Letter *Claverenses dioecesis*, August 5, 1942, in AAS 34 (1942) 364; *idem*, Apostolic Letter *Beatissimae Virgini*, August 15, 1942, in AAS 34 (1942) 365; *idem*, radio message *Benedicite Deum caeli*, October 31, 1942, AAS 34 (1942) 317; *idem*, radio message *Bendito seja o Senor*, May 13, 1946, AAS 38 (1946) 264; *idem*, Apostolic Letter *Hungaricae gentis*, March 25, 1948, AAS 40 (1948) 499; *Id.*, Apostolic Letter *Maximo Nos*, October 10, 1949, AAS 44 (1952) 808; *idem*, Apostolic Letter *Imaginem Beatae*, July 31, 1950, AAS 43 (1951) 111; *idem*, Apostolic Letter *Caelorum Reginae*, July 31, 1950, AAS 43 (1951) 79; *idem*, Apostolic Letter *Mirum sane*, July 31, 1950, AAS 43 (1951) 156; *idem*, radio message *Quando lasciate*, December 8, 1953, AAS 45 (1953) 849-850; *idem*, Apostolic Letter *Eadem ratione*, June 30, 1954, AAS 47 (1955) 710; *idem*, radio message *On the occasion of the fourth centenary of the foundation of the city of Sao Paolo, Brazil*, September 7, 1954, AAS 46 (1954) 546; *idem*, Apostolic Constitution *Sedes sapientiae*, May 31, 1956, AAS 48 (1956) 354, in D. Bertetto, ed., *Il Magistero mariano di Pio XII. Edizione italiana di tutti i documenti mariani di Pio XII*, (Rome: Edizioni Paoline, 1960), p. 641; *idem*, Apostolic Letter *In vitae huius*, January 4, 1958, in AAS *51 (1959)* 159.

The Latin feminine noun, *sequestra, -ae,* is equivalent to *mediatrix*. Cf. L. Castiglioni – S. Mariotti, *Vocabolario della lingua latina. Latino-Italiano, Italiano-Latino*, (Rome: Loescher Editore, 1990), p. 1040.

Hence it cannot be doubted that Mary most holy is far above all other creatures in dignity, and after her Son possesses primacy over all. ...

For if through his humanity the divine Word performs miracles and gives graces, if he uses his sacraments and saints as instruments for the salvation of men, why should he not make use of the role and work of his most holy Mother in imparting to us the fruits of redemption? "With a heart that is truly a mother's," to quote again our predecessor of immortal memory, Pius IX, "does she approach the problem of our salvation, and is solicitous for the whole human race; made Queen of heaven and earth by the Lord, exalted above all choirs of angels and saints, and standing at the right hand of her only Son, Jesus Christ our Lord, she intercedes powerfully for us with a mother's prayers, obtains what she seeks, and cannot be refused." On this point another of our predecessors of happy memory, Leo XIII, has said that an "almost immeasurable" power has been given Mary in the distribution of graces; St. Pius X adds that she fills this office "as by the right of a mother."[77]

Bl. John XXIII (+1962) granted the title and privilege of minor basilica to the church dedicated to the Blessed Virgin Mary Mediatrix of All Graces, Sultana of Africa, located in the locality of Lodonga, in Uganda. In the text of the related apostolic letter there are three references to the "Mediatrix of all graces."[78]

The Mediation of the Blessed Virgin Mary at the Second Vatican Council

On November 21, 1964, after an editorial work of about four years (if we include the preparatory work before the Council), Paul VI promulgated the Dogmatic Constitution *Lumen Gentium*, the eighth

---

[77] Pius XII, Encyclical *Ad Caeli Reginam*, October 11, 1954, in AAS 46 (1954) 635-637.
[78] Cf. John XXIII, Apostolic Letter *Beatissimam Virginem Mariam*, May 26, 1961, in AAS 65 (1961) 150-151.

chapter of which is entirely dedicated to the Mother of God and of men.[79] Before arriving at this definitive text, there was no shortage of lively discussions on the title of Mediatrix. Many bishops asked for its dogmatic definition, but others were opposed to it for various reasons, not the least of which were those of an ecumenical nature.[80]

Among the Fathers of the Central Preparatory Commission of the Second Vatican Council, 16 expressed reservation with the Marian title of *Mediatrix*.[81] The use of the title would damage the ecumenical dialogue with the Protestants.[82] Archbishop Alter (Cincinnati, Ohio), with cardinals Koenig (Vienna, Austria) and Godfrey (Westminster), echoed these sentiments.[83] Instead of *mediation*, Cardinal Montini preferred to speak of the Blessed Virgin's spiritual maternity, her regality and her intercession.[84]

Fr. Paolo Siano rightly observes in his above-cited article that there was, in this attitude, a kind of opposition to the pontifical thought, because, almost on the morrow of the conclusion of these discussions, July 23, 1962, Bl. John XXIII approved the new Missal which contained

---

[79] Cf. G. Besutti, O.S.M., *Lo schema mariano al Concilio Vaticano II. Documentazione e note di cronaca*, (Rome: Edition Marianum—Libreria Desclée, 1966), pp. 183-185.

[80] For the story of Chapter 8 of *Lumen Gentium*, see E. Toniolo, O.S.M., *La beata Vergine nel Concilio Vaticano II*, Centro di Cultura Mariana "Madre della Chiesa," Rome 2004, 453 pp.

[81] Cf. G. Besutti, *Lo schema mariano del Concilio Vaticano II, op. cit.*, p. 22. Among this group was the Archbishop of Milan, Cardinal John Baptist Montini, who declared "inopportune, indeed, harmful" the presentation of the title of *Mediatrix*, since— as the illustrious cardinal explained—in the first place, "the term Mediator must be attributed solely and exclusively to Christ" according to St. Paul's teaching (cf. 1 Tim 2:5).

[82] Cf. Acta et Documenta Concilio Oecumenico Vaticano II apparando, Series II (Preparatoria), Volumen II: Acta pontificiae Commissionis Centralis praeparatoriae Concilii Oecumenici Vaticani, Pars IV: Sessio septima, 12-19 Iunii 1962, Vatican City 1968, p. 777, cited by A. Escudero Cabello, *La cuestión de la mediación mariana en la preparación del Vaticano II*, Libreria Ateneo Salesiano, Rome 1997, pp. 251-253.

[83] Cf. A. Escudero Cabello, *op. cit.*, p. 251.

[84] Acta et Documenta Concilio Oecumenico Vaticano II apparando, Series II (Preparatoria), Volumen II: Acta pontificiae Commissionis Centralis praeparatoriae Concilii Oecumenici Vaticani, Pars IV: Sessio septima, 12-19 Iunii 1962, Vatican City 1968, p. 777, cited by A. Escudero Cabello, *op. cit.*, p. 260.

the Holy Mass to the *Beata Maria Virgo omnium gratiarum Mediatrix* (Blessed Virgin Mary, Mediatrix of all graces).[85]

During the Second Vatican Council, particularly in the third session held in 1964, there was a lively discussion on various Mariological themes, and there was also a discussion on the title of Mediatrix.[86] Such a title was commonly accepted by everyone, but a few, including cardinals Alfrink, Léger and Bea, who preferred it to be omitted from the official documents of the Council in order to promote ecumenism toward Protestant Christians (the great majority of whom rejected the title then and continue to reject it presently).[87] There were, in fact, rumors that the Protestants were threatening to break off all ecumenical dialogue if the title of Mediatrix were to be inserted into the conciliar dogmatic constitution. Meanwhile, 310 Council Fathers desired an authoritative, extraordinary and dogmatic pronouncement by the Council in favor of Mary's mediation-coredemption.[88] To reconcile the two parties it

---

[85] Proprium Sanctorum pro aliquibus locis, 8 maii Beatae Mariae Virginis omnium gratiarum Mediatricis, in Missale Romanum ex decreto SS. Concilii Tridentini restitutum Summorum Pontificum cura recognitum, editio typica, Typis Plyglottis Vaticanis 1962, pp. [159]-[160].

[86] Cf. G. Besutti, *Lo schema mariano del Concilio Vaticano II. Documentazione e note di cronaca*, Rome: Marianum-Desclée, 1966; G. Roschini, O.S.M., *Maria santissima nella storia della salvezza*, vol. II, (Isola del Liri: Pisani, 1969), pp. 111-116; idem, *La Mediazione mariana oggi*, (Rome: Pontificia Facoltà Teologica "Marianum" – Istituto di Mariologia, Edizioni "Marianum," 1971), pp. 47-49; A. Escudero Cabello, S.D.B., *La cuestión de la mediación en la preparación del Vaticano II*, LAS, Rome, 1997; E. Toniolo, O.S.M., *La beata Maria Vergine nel Concilio Vaticano II*, Centro di cultura mariana "Madre della Chiesa," Rome, 2004, 453 pp.

[87] For a Protestant defense of Mediatrix, cf. J. Macquarrie, "Mary Co-redemptrix and Disputes over Justification and Grace: An Anglican View," *Mary Co-redemptrix. Doctrinal Issues Today*, pp. 139-150, and C. Dickson, "Mary Mediatrix: A Protestant Response," *Mary Coredemptrix, Mediatrix, Advocate: Theological foundations III. Contemporary Insights on a Fifth Marian Dogma*, pp. 181-184.

[88] This is the number that results from the examination of the written requests preserved in the Council archive. Obviously an even greater number must be presumed, because, while everyone who submitted the written requests were in favor, not everyone who was in favor submitted a written request, as is always the case with contingent matters. Cf. A. Escudero Cabello, *La cuestion de la mediación mariana...*, op. cit., p. 88. According to Fr. Roschini, the written requests numbered about 400 (cf. Roschini G., *La Mediazione mariana oggi*, Pontificia Facoltà Teologica "Marianum" – Istituto di Mariologia, Edizioni "Marianum," Rome 1971, p. 47).

was decided to insert the title of Mediatrix into the Marian document of the Council, but also to include adequate explanations to respond to Protestant objections and to omit all examination regarding the nature of this mediation.

The Protestant "observers" invited to the Council were not satisfied, but they did not break off the dialogue.[89] The omission of the title, in fact, would have cast a shadow upon the preceding Ordinary Magisterium and could have perhaps diverted the ecumenical dialogue from the level of truth to the level of political ambiguity. It could have contributed to "maintaining rather than dissipating the ambiguous" at the service of a "mistaken ecumenism."[90]

Fr. Carlo Balić (O.F.M., +1977), one of the original drafters of chapter 8 of *Lumen Gentium*, provides a suitable response to those who wish to interpret the Council as the moment of departure from the preceding Mariological tradition: "The Council has not mitigated or deprived the concept of the mediation of the Virgin of its content in the sense in which in which it has been propagated by the theologians of our [twentieth] century."[91]

In examining the conciliar text of No. 62 of *Lumen Gentium*, we read the following:

> Taken up to heaven she did not lay aside this salvific duty, but by her constant intercession continued to bring us the gifts of eternal salvation. By her maternal charity, she cares for the brethren of her Son, who still journey on earth surrounded by dangers and difficulties, until they are led into the happiness of their true home. Therefore the Blessed Virgin is invoked by the Church under the titles of Advocate, Auxiliatrix, Adjutrix, and Mediatrix. This, however, is to be so understood that it neither

---

[89] They could not reasonably justify the imposition of their Protestant beliefs upon an essentially Catholic ecumenical council.
[90] C. Journet, *De la Vierge Marie et la Collegialité*, in *Nova et vetera*, 2 (1965) 109.
[91] C. Balić, O.F.M., *El Capitulo VIII de la Constitución "Lumen Gentium" Comparado con el Primer Esquema de la Beata Virgen Madre de la Iglesia*, Estudios Marianos, 27 (1966) 169.

takes away from nor adds anything to the dignity and efficaciousness of Christ the one Mediator.[92]

That is why, in the Church, the Blessed Virgin Mary is also invoked under the title of "Mediatrix." The Council document cites other magisterial documents as proof of the complete catholicity of the title: Leo XIII, *Adiutricem populi*; St. Pius X, *Ad diem illum*; Pius XI, *Miserentissimus Redemptor*; Pius XII, *Nuntius Radiophonicus* (in AAS 38 (1946) 266).

In order to prevent an interpretation of Marian mediation as "mere" intercession, many Council Fathers proposed the Marian title of "Dispensatrix of all graces," already fully accepted by the Magisterium and perfectly in conformity to common Catholic doctrine. The Doctrinal Commission replied that the Council text did not intend to deny this doctrine.[93] Therefore, the Second Vatican Council does not at all repudiate the doctrine of *Mary Mediatrix of all graces*,[94] a doctrine also clearly taught in the papal documents expressly cited by the Council text.

Paul VI (+1978): He preferred to speak of Mary as our intercessor[95] with Christ rather than as Dispensatrix of graces,[96] but this is a question of a different emphasis, not of a denial. Still, Pope Paul VI was certainly

---

[92] Vatican II Council, Costituzione dogmatica *Lumen gentium,* November 21, 1964, n. 62.

[93] Cf. Roschini G., *Maria Santissima nella storia della salvezza*, vol. II, *op. cit.*, p. 202.

[94] Besides the Protestants and Jansenists, included among those who deny this doctrine are a few modern ecumenists and all modernist ecumenists. Critical opposition is widespread: even some of the writings of Abbot Laurentin are infected by this criticism (cf. R. Laurentin, *La Vergine Maria. Mariologia postconciliare*, Rome: Edizione Paoline, 1973, pp. 302-304).

[95] Cf. Paul VI, Letter for the 750th Anniversary of the Indulgence of the Portiuncula, July 14, 1966, in *Encicliche e discorsi di S.S. Paolo VI*, vol. X, May-August 1966, (Rome: Edizioni Paoline, 1967), p. 256; *idem,* address to a group of Hungarian pilgrims, in *Encicliche e discorsi di S.S. Paolo VI,* vol. XXIII, January-December 1972, (Rome: Edizioni Paoline, 1973), p. 299; *idem,* Apostolic Letter *Le Memorie apostoliche,* May 2, 1974, in *Insegnamenti di Paolo VI,* vol. XII, 1974, p. 500; *idem,* general audience, May 14, 1975, in *Insegnamenti di Paolo VI,* vol. XIII, 1975, p. 502; *idem* allocution to the participants of the International Marian-Mariological Congress, May 16, 1975, in *Insegnamenti di Paolo VI,* vol. XIII, 1975, p. 522; *idem,* address to German-speaking pilgrims, August 15, 1975, in *Insegnamenti di Paolo VI,* vol. XIII, 1975, p. 854.

[96] Cf. Paul VI, Encyclical *Christi Matri,* September 15, 1966, in *Enchiridion Vaticanum. Omissa 1962-1987, Supplementum I,* EDB, Bologna 2000, n. 94, p. 87; *idem,* General

less inclined to speak on these subjects than his predecessors, from Leo XIII to Pius XII.

By a faculty granted by Paul VI, Cardinal James Lercaro, assisted by the Secretary Msgr. Annibale Bugnini, approved and confirmed the "Proper" of the Masses of the Order of Friars Minor Capuchin, for use in the Italian provinces,[97] in which is found the Mass of "Mary Most Holy Mediatrix of All Grace," a feast of third class, on the date of May 8.[98]

In the Apostolic Exhortation *Signum Magnum*, Paul VI recalls that Mary, assumed into heaven, assists her still-pilgrim children:

> She makes herself their Advocate, Auxiliatrix, Adjutrix and Mediatrix. Of this intercession of hers for the People of God with the Son, the Church has been persuaded, ever since the first centuries, as testified to by this most ancient antiphon which, with some slight difference, forms part of the liturgical prayer in the East as well as in the West: "We seek refuge under the protection of your mercies, Oh Mother of God; do not reject our supplication in need but save us from perdition, O you who alone are blessed." ... Therefore, as each one of us can repeat with St. Paul: "The Son of God loved me and gave himself up for me," (Gal 2:29) so in all trust he can believe that the divine Savior has left to him also, in spiritual heritage, his Mother, with all the treasures of grace and virtues with which he had endowed her, that she may pour them over us through the influence of her powerful intercession and our willing imitation. This is why St. Bernard rightly affirms: "Coming to her the Holy Spirit filled her with grace for herself;

---

audience, May 30, 1974, in *Insegnamenti di Paolo VI*, vol. XI, 1973, (Vatican City: Tipografia Poliglotta Vaticana, 1974), p. 475.

[97] Consilium ad Exsequendam Constitutione de Sacra Liturgia, Prot. N. 3577/65, in *Proprio dei Santi dell'Ordine dei Frati Minori Cappuccini*, (Turin-Rome: Casa Editrice Marietti—Centro Nazionale T.O.F. Cappuccini, 1966), p. [2].

[98] *Proprio dei Santi dell'Ordine dei Frati Minori Cappuccini* May 8th [Mass of] "Maria SS. Mediatrice di ogni grazia," in *Messale Romano quotidiano*, 1966, pp. [50]-[52].

when the same Spirit pervaded her again she became superabundant and redounding in grace for us also."[99]

At the end of the apostolic exhortation the Pope remembers the 25th anniversary of the "consecration" of the Church and of the human race to the Immaculate Heart of Mary and exhorts "all the sons of the Church to renew personally their consecration to the Immaculate Heart of the Mother of the Church."[100]

In his letter to Cardinal Suenens, archbishop of Malines-Brussels, on the occasion of the Marian International Congress of May 13, 1975, Paul VI writes:

> In confirmation of these reflections, we are happy to recall the testimony that also the Fathers and Doctors of the Eastern church, exemplary as they are in the faith and in worship of the Holy Spirit, have borne to ecclesial faith and the cult of the Mother of Christ, as the mediator of divine favors. Their affirmations, however surprising, should not disturb anyone, since it is understood and sometimes clearly mentioned in them that the source of the Virgin's mediating action is dependent on the action of the Spirit of God. So, for example, St. Ephraem exalts Mary in these superlative tones: "Blessed is she who has been made the source for the whole world, emanating all goods" (S. Ephraem Syri hymni et serm., ed. Th. Lamy Malines, 1882-1902, II, p. 548); and again: "Most holy Lady the only one that has been made the dwelling of all the graces of the Holy Spirit" (Assem. græc. III, 542). St. John Chrysostom sums up Mary's salvific work in the following stupendous eulogy: "A virgin chased us out of paradise; thanks to the intervention of another virgin, we have found eternal life again. As we were condemned by the fault of a virgin, so we have been crowned by the merit of a virgin" (Expos. in ps. 44, 7: PG 55, 193). They are echoed, in the eighth century, by St. Germanus

---

[99] Paul VI, Apostolic Exhortation *Signum magnum*, May 13, 1967, 2.5, in *Enchiridion Vaticanum,* vol. II. 1963-1967, (Bologna, Italy: EDB, 1992), pp. 987, 999.
[100] *Ibid.*, 8, in *Enchiridion Vaticanum,* vol. II, p. 1003.

of Constantinople, who addresses the following moving invocations to Mary: "You, oh pure, excellent and most merciful Lady, comfort of Christians, protect us with the wings of your kindness; guard us with your intercession, giving us eternal life; you who are the hope of Christians that does not deceive. Your gifts are innumerable. For no one, unless through you, oh holy one, obtains salvation. No one, unless through you, is delivered from evil. Who like you, in agreement with your only Son, looks after mankind?" (Concio in sanctam Mariam: PG 98, 327).

This traditional faith, which is common both to the Eastern and to the Western Church, found authoritative confirmation in the teaching of our great predecessor Leo XIII, who, while he published numerous Encyclicals to promote the cult of the Mother of God, invoked especially under the title of Queen of the Holy Rosary, also dedicated a long document encyclical to the exaltation, even more excellent, of the Holy Spirit and promotion of his worship (Enc. *Divinum illud munus*, May 9, 1897; *Acta Leonis*, Vol. XVII, pp. 126-128).[101]

John Paul II (+2005) brought the title of *Mary Mediatrix of all graces* back into favor, despite the reticence of a few theologians who appealed to a restrictive interpretation of conciliar Mariology.[102] Pope John Paul II used the title "Mediatrix of all graces" literally at least seven times in his addresses (homilies, discourses, angelus, etc.),[103] according to the research

---

[101] Paul VI, *Lettera al Card. Leo Jozef Suenens in occasione del Congresso Mariano Internazionale – La Vergine Maria nell'opera dell'umana Redenzione*, May 13, 1975, in *Insegnamenti di Paolo VI*, vol. XIII, 1975 (Vatican City: Tipografia Poliglotta Vaticana, 1976), pp. 495-496. English cit. by P. Siano, *Mary 'Mediatrix of All Graces' in the Papal Magisterium up to the Pontificate of Paul VI*, to be published in *Mary at the Foot of the Cross VII: Coredemptrix, Therefore Mediatrix of all Graces*. See note 1.

[102] Cf. S. Perrella, *Maria Serva del Signore e della Redenzione. Tra richieste e approfondimenti*, in *Miles Immaculatae*, fasc. 2, July-December 1998, pp. 262-263; T. Sennott, "Mary Mediatrix of All Graces, Vatican Council II and Ecumenism," *Miles Immaculatae*, fasc. 1-2, 1988, pp. 151-167.

[103] John Paul II, *Allocution*, in *L'Osservatore Romano*, Monday-Tuesday, January 18-19, 1988, p. 1; *idem*, *L'Osservatore Romano*, Monday-Tuesday, April 11-12, 1988, Supplement n. 84, p. IV; *idem*, in *L'Osservatore Romano*, Monday-Tuesday, July

conducted by Msgr. Arthur Burton Calkins, Dr. Mark Miravalle, Don Manfred Hauke,[104] and Fr. Paolo Siano, F.I.[105]

On other occasions John Paul II used the expressions "Universal Mediatrix of all grace,"[106] "Mother of all graces,"[107] "Dispensatrix of all grace,"[108] giver of "all grace,"[109] "Mediatrix of all grace,"[110] and "Mediatrix of graces."[111]

In the Marian Encyclical *Redemptoris Mater* (March 25, 1989), the Pontiff of *Totus Tuus* illustrates in an in-depth manner the theology of Mary's *maternal mediation*.

In the "Parish Priest's Prayer to Mary Most Holy" contained in the appendix to the Instruction of the Congregation for the Clergy, *The*

2-3, 1990, p. 5; *idem*, in *L'Osservatore Romano*, Saturday, June 29, 1996, p. 5; *idem*, Apostolic Letter *Amor Noster*, April 30, 1980, in AAS 72 (1980) 384-385; *idem*, Apostolic Letter *Frequentissimae dioeceses*, in AAS 79 (1987) 437.

[104] Cf. M. Hauke, *La Mediazione materna di Maria secondo Papa Giovanni Paolo II*, in Aa. Vv., *Maria Corredentrice. Storia e Teologia. VII*, Bibliotheca Corredemptionis B.V. Mariae, Casa Mariana Editrice, Frigento 2005, pp. 86-88. Concerning these passages of Pope John Paul II (in which he makes reference to the *Mediatrix of all graces* or other similar expressions), Don Hauke makes reference to Msgr. Calkins (cf. Hauke, *op. cit.*, p. 86, note 107). On Mary "Co-redemptrix" and "Mediatrix" in the Marian Magisterium of John Paul II, see also Msgr. Calkins' recent study, A.B. Calkins, ed., *Totus Tuus. Il magistero mariano di Giovanni Paolo II*, preface by Msgr. Carlo Caffana, archbishop of Bologna, (Siena, Italy: Edizioni Cantagalli, 2006), pp. 242-245, 306-319. [Msgr. Calkins has also recently presented the results of his study in English at the 7th Annual Symposium on Marian Coredemption: *Mary, Mediatrix of All Graces in the Papal Magisterium of Pope John Paul II*, to be published in *Mary at the Foot of the Cross VII: Coredemptrix, Therefore Mediatrix of all Graces*. See note 1.] In other pronouncements, Pope John Paul II has emphasized Mary's *singular cooperation in the Redemption* (cf. *ibid.*, pp. 217-227).

[105] *Art. cit.*

[106] John Paul II, *Allocution*, in *Insegnamenti di Giovanni Paolo II*, vol. 1, 1978, (Rome: Libreria Editrice Vaticana 1979), p. 250.

[107] John Paul II, *Allocution*, in *L'Osservatore Romano*, Monday-Tuesday, September 19-20, 1994, pp. 6-7.

[108] John Paul II, *Allocution*, September 26, 1982.

[109] Cf. M. Hauke, *La Mediazione materna di Maria secondo Papa Giovanni Paolo II*, p. 86.

[110] John Paul II, *Allocution*, Wroclaw, Poland, June 21, 1983.

[111] John Paul II, *Homily*, in *L'Osservatore Romano*, Sunday, August 26, 2001, p. 5.

Priest, Pastor and Leader of the Parish Community (August 4, 2002), Our Blessed Lady is also invoked with the title "Mediatrix of all graces."[112]

Contained in the *Collectio missarum de beata Virgine*, approved and promulgated by John Paul II on the occasion of the Marian Year[113] is a Mass of the *Virgin Mary Mother and Mediatrix of grace*; in the preface of this Mass, we read that the Most Blessed Virgin Mary carries out "a maternal role in the Church: of intercession, of pardon, of prayer and grace, of reconciliation and peace."[114] The Virgin Mary is "Mother of mercy and handmaid of grace."[115] The title of *Dispensatrix of grace* reappears in other eucological texts of the same *Collectio Missarum*.[116]

As proof that the title of *Mediatrix*, in the broadest sense, includes that of *Co-redemptrix*, John Paul II did not hesitate to use the former as well as the latter term. In his article cited above, Fr. Siano has identified a seventh Woytylian text in which the title of *Co-redemptrix* appears,[117] complementing the other six references previously "discovered" by Msgr. Calkins.

Pope Benedict XVI has recently continued the overall succession of papal writers on Our Lady's role as Mediatrix of all graces. In his May 11, 2007, homily in which he canonized the Brazilian Franciscan, Fr. Antônio de Sant'ana Galvão, O.F.M., Benedict XVI uses the extraordinary foundation of the Marian mediation of every grace of the

---

[112] Congregation for the Clergy, *Il presbitero, pastore e guida della comunità parrocchiale*, Istruzione del 4 agosto 2002, Figlie di San Paolo, Milano 2002, p. 82. [English: "Parish Priest's Prayer to Mary Most Holy," in (an appendix to) Congregation for the Clergy, *The Priest, Pastor and Leader of the Parish Community*, Instruction of August 4, 2002 (Vatican City: Libreria Editrice Vaticana, 2002), pp. 53-55.]

[113] Cf. Congregation for Divine Worship, *Decree*, prot. N. 309/86, August 15, 1986, in Conferenza Episcopale Italiana, *Messe della Beata Vergine Maria*, Libreria Editrice Vaticana, Città del Vaticano 1989 (3rd reprint), pp. X-XI.

[114] *Messe della beata Vergine Maria*, op. cit. p. 101. [English cit. by A.B. Calkins, "Mary as Coredemptrix, Mediatrix and Advocate in the Liturgy," in *Mary Coredemptrix Mediatrix Advocate: Theological Foundations. Towards a Papal Definition?* ed. M. Miravalle (Santa Barbara, CA, Queenship, 1995), p. 89.]

[115] *Ibid.*

[116] *Messa di Santa Maria Madre del Signore. Prefazio*, in *Messe della Beata Vergine Maria*, op. cit., p. 66; *Messa di Maria Vergine regina e madre della misericordia. Prefazio*, in op. cit., p. 128; *Messa di Maria Vergine Madre della Divina Provvidenza. Prefazio*, in op. cit., p. 131.

[117] John Paul II, general audience, *Saluto agli ammalati*, December 10, 1980, in *L'Osservatore Romano*, Thursday, December 11, 1980, p. 2.

redemption in a generous manner somewhat reminiscent of St. Bernard, St. Louis-Marie and St. Maximilian: "There is no fruit of grace in the history of salvation that does not have as its necessary instrument the mediation of Our Lady."[118]

Benedict reiterates the essence of Marian mediation as he continues: "Let us give thanks to God the Father, to God the Son, to God the Holy Spirit from whom, through the intercession of the Virgin Mary, we receive all the blessings of heaven."[119]

The Nature of the Blessed Virgin Mary's Influence in the Application of the Redemption

The fact of this mystery of the maternal mediation of Mary here and now, both as intercession and as spiritual begetting of Christ within the minds and hearts of all believers, since the golden age of scholastic theology (thirteenth century), has led to a great deal of speculation on the nature of this mediation and the type of causal influence exercised directly and immediately by a human person on the souls of other men, such as in fact is ascribed to the Virgin Mother as Mediatrix of all graces. Neither the terminology employed by the representatives of various schools of theology, such as the Thomistic and Scotistic, even within the same school is uniform, nor are the concepts behind the terminology uniformly defined. Hence for those not fully informed about these discussions the significance of the speculation is hard to grasp. Nor is it necessary for all to grasp it in order to appreciate the meaning and importance of the maternal mediation of Mary here and now.

Briefly, those who follow a Thomistic orientation tend to stress the importance of what is called "physical-instrumental" causality to appreciate in some way the mystery of this mediation and its relevance to many practical, spiritual, pastoral, missionary dimensions of Christian life. Those of the Scotistic persuasion tend to stress more the moral, exemplary, meritorious aspects of causal activity to illustrate not merely the intercession (advocacy) of Mary at the throne of grace in heaven where she is gloriously assumed, but also the unique personal, or voluntary, features of her direct action in the Church and on souls for the

---

[118] Benedict XVI, homily at canonization Mass of Fr. Antônio de Sant'ana Galvão, O.F.M., May 11, 2007, n. 5.
[119] Ibid., n. 6.

distribution of all graces. Without doubt valid points are made by both approaches, and neither exhausts the subject, nor can pretend to do so.[120]

With Pope John Paul II, however, a certain impulse was given to reopening these speculative discussions, not only on the very nature of mediation in Christ and Mary as a unique form of causality (on which rests that of the sacramental order), but also of others, not much discussed in the speculative realm since the middle ages. I refer here to the role of Mary as Mediatrix in the sacramental order and the manner in which she directly and immediately touches the heart of every one of her spiritual children.[121] Both Pope John Paul II and his successor, Benedict XVI, have spoken of the Marian principle of the Church and the unique place of Mary at the very heart of the Church.[122] This is simply another way of talking about Marian mediation, but it is also a way of setting study of grace and free will, and still more the indwelling of the Holy Spirit

---

[120] For general historical information on this question see J. Schug, *Mary Mother*, cit.; I. Gomá y Thomás, *Estudios y escritos pastoralos sobre la Virgen*, Barcelona 1947. For a classic exposition of the neo-Thomistic pre-conciliar Mariology cf. G. Roschini, *De natura B.M. Virginis in applicatione redemptionis*, in *Maria et Ecclesia*, vol. II, Rome 1959, pp. 223-295; also P. Parrotta, *La Mariologia di Gabriele Roschini*, Lugano 2002. For a recent approach from a Scotistic point of view, see P.D. Fehlner, F.I., *Mater et Magistra Apostolorum*, in *Immaculata Mediatrix* 1 (1/2001) 15-95; Idem, *De Metaphysica Mariana Quaedam*, in *Immaculata Mediatrix* 1 (2/2002) 13-42; Idem, *Scientia et Pietas*, in *Immaculata Mediatrix* 1 (3/2001) 11-48; Idem, *Io sono L'Immacolata Concezione. Adhuc quaedam de Metaphysica Mariana*, in *Immaculata Mediatrix* 2 (2002) 15-41. Significant contributions to a renewed Thomistic approach have been made by the Spanish metaphysical Mariologist, J. Ferrer Arellano, *La Mediación Materna de la Immacolada. Esperienza Ecumenica de la Iglesia*, Madrid 2006. See also his *Marian Coredemption and Sacramental Mediation*, in *Mary at the Foot of the Cross III*, New Bedford, MA, 2003, pp. 70-126; Idem, *The Immaculate Conception as the Condition for the Possibility of the Coredemption*, in *Mary at the Foot of the Cross V* New Bedford, MA, 2005, pp. 74-185.

[121] Cf. especially the Spanish Dominican, A. Bandera, *La Virgen María y los Sacramentos* (Madrid 1978), and above all the recent study of Serafino M. Lanzetta, F.I., *Il sacerdozio di Maria nella teologia cattolica del XX seculo. Analizi storico-teologica*, Rome 2006. In English, cf. J. Samaha, *The Sacerdotal Quality of Mary's Mission. Mother and Associate of Christ the Priest*, in *Immaculata Mediatrix* 2 (2002) 197-207.

[122] Benedict XVI, *Homily for the Solemnity of the Annunciation*, 2006, insists on the central importance of the Marian principle of the Church, viz., the maternal mediation of Mary at the heart of the Church, and in particular its pastors, and affirms that this mystery was repeatedly underscored by his predecessor, John Paul II, in accord with his motto, *Totus tuus*.

in the Church and in every believer in the state of grace, in a radically Marian context. St. Maximilian M. Kolbe does more than hint at all this in speaking of transubstantiation into the Immaculate, as she is transubstantiated into the Holy Spirit, in order to "mediate" in the order of conversion and sanctification.[123]

That these discussions should continue is not something otiose. Not only do the metaphysical insights of Christian philosophers help us to enter more profoundly into the understanding of an extremely important feature of our faith, one in the thirteenth century described as the very foundation and primary character of the spirituality of St. Francis of Assisi,[124] and repeated again in our times by St. Maximilian M. Kolbe, this time however in reference to the spiritual and intellectual life of the Church: Mary, mother and teacher,[125] but the very effort to undertake such speculations bears fruit in the form of a deepened appreciation of the basic themes of Christian philosophy. A medieval English Benedictine Abbot, Odo of Canterbury, an older contemporary of St. Francis, in a homily preached around the year 1200, called not Aristotle, but Mary our philosopher and added also our philosophy.[126] For the love of wisdom cannot merely be an abstraction, but of that person who is Wisdom incarnate, the Way, the Truth and the Life, loved as only the Virgin Mother can know and love the Wisdom who became her Child.

Conclusion

With the Encyclical *Redemptoris Mater* (March 25, 1987) of John Paul II, a step forward has been taken in the theological comprehension of Mary's mediation in the light of her maternity. The excellent theological intuition of the Pope is completely summarized in the simple and

---

[123] For texts of St. Maximilian on this subject, see P.D. Fehlner, F.I., *St. Maximilian M. Kolbe, Martyr of Charity, Pneumatologist. His Theology of the Holy Spirit*, New Bedford, MA, 2004.

[124] St. Bonaventure, *III Sent.*, d 3, p 1, a 1, q 2 : "The Virgin Mother is our Mediatrix with Christ as Christ is our Mediator with the Father."; Henry d'Avranches, *Legenda versificata S. Francisci*, in almost the same words describes the spirituality of St. Francis of Assisi.: *Analecta Franciscana*, vol. X, Quaracchi 1941, pp. 405-491, here p. 445.

[125] See Fehlner, *Mater et Magistra Apostolorum*, op cit.

[126] Odo of Canterbury, *Maria Christianorum Philosophia*, ed. by J. Leclercq, in *Mèlanges de science religieuse* 13 (1956) 103-106.

effective title of Mary as *maternal Mediatrix*. What is maternity if not an excellent form of mediation from every point of view, in particular the personal and spiritual? We could define it as the feminine mode of collaborating with God in the generation of the natural and supernatural life of persons. Since it puts the woman in an intermediary position between God, source of life, and the child, who receives it, in which she unites the two extremes (God and the child) to each other, this maternal collaboration is true mediation. Evidently, understanding of the maternal mediation of Mary which touches both heaven and earth is crucial not only in the spiritual order, but wherever fundamental questions of human existence arise, whether personal or social, familial or political. Without some essential reference to the mystery of Mary, attempted resolutions of such problems can only end in human tragedy, and betrayal of our dear Savior.

But while the mother is always a mediatrix, not every mediation is maternal. Christ, in fact, is Mediator but not mother; Mary, instead, was maternal Mediatrix before being physically mother, because her mediation was completely oriented and preordained, from the moment of conception, to the divine-human maternity. When the woman collaborates with God in procreation, she is always a mother. She is a natural mother if mother of a natural life, a supernatural mother if mother of a supernatural life, divine Mother if mother of the divine Life. And supernatural maternity is true maternity not only and not so much by analogy to natural maternity, but above all by its reference to the exemplar (or *analogatum princeps*—major analogue), or to Mary's divine-human maternity, in which every maternity, natural and supernatural, finds its own incomparable perfection.

Reflection on the theological concept of mediation found in the Pauline corpus and serving as a kind of profound synthesis of all aspects of the mystery of salvation as this is grounded in the order of the hypostatic union, viz., of the joint predestination of Jesus and Mary, illumines the profound insights of the late Holy Father. In turn these enable us to see that there is nothing inherently contradictory in insisting on the unicity and sufficiency of Christ's mediation and at the same time affirming his Mother as our maternal Mediatrix. And that seen, the mystery of Marian mediation appears everywhere in Scripture and Tradition, in the liturgy and in sacred art, sometimes with, sometimes without the title. Nor will we be inclined to underestimate the importance of this mystery, practically as well as speculatively. This is but another way of saying that the presence of Mary here and now is crucial to our understanding and love of Christ, to our sharing in the fruits of redemption. Mary is our Mediatrix with Christ as Christ is our Mediator with the Father. Put in the more humble language of the street: know Mary, know Jesus; no Mary, no Jesus. That is the bottom line making the difference between heaven and hell. That is why true devotion to Jesus means total consecration to the Immaculate Mediatrix, why we can never say enough about Mary, why we can never be too devoted to Mary.[127] For she is our Mother, the Immaculate Mediatrix, ever sustaining us as disciples of her Son.

---

[127] Cf. St. Bonaventure, *III Sent.*, d 3, p 1, a 1, q 1, ad 4: *Mariae nullus nimis potest esse devotus.*

Advocate and Queen

Edward Sri, S.T.D.

Introduction

Belief in Mary's loving intercession was expressed in early Christian art, prayer and teaching. Whether it be in the many frescoes of the Roman catacombs depicting Mary in a prayerful position, or through early Church Fathers who portray Mary in heaven as praying for those on earth, or through other Fathers who address Mary and prayerfully seek her supplication, Mary's intercessory role is clearly attested to in the first four centuries of the Church.[1] As an example of how highly developed the understanding of Mary's intercessory power could become in the early church, consider the prayer *Sub Tuum Praesidium*, which can be dated approximately to the mid-third century: "We fly to thy protection, O holy Mother of God, despise not our petitions in our necessities, but deliver us from all danger, O ever glorious and blessed Virgin." From this we see evidence of early Christians confidently turning to Mary for protection in the face of the trials and dangers in life and asking her to intercede for them. It is not surprising that the Church throughout the centuries would refer to Mary as our "Advocate," indicating her unique power of intercession, taking petitions from God's people on earth and presenting them before her Son in heaven.

Closely related to Mary's advocacy is her role as Queen—another Marian title found in the early Church and developed in the Tradition throughout the centuries. In fact, many magisterial teachings will note how Mary exercises her royal office through her role as Advocate, interceding on our behalf. This article will examine Mary's role as Advocate and Queen, first by exploring an important Biblical foundation

---

[1] See J. Murphy, "Origin and Nature of Marian Cult" in *Mariology*, vol. 3, ed. J. Carol (Milwaukee: Bruce Publishing, 1961).

for these two titles: the queen mother, who held a royal office in the kingdom of David, and exercised her office especially through her role as advocate, interceding for the people of the kingdom. Next, we will outline how the Church's Tradition and magisterial teaching has developed the understanding of Mary's advocacy and queenship throughout the centuries. And finally, some theological issues regarding Mary's role as Advocate and Queen will be addressed.

Biblical Foundations

The Queen Mother and Advocate in the Davidic Kingdom

The mother of a ruling monarch held an important position in many Ancient Near Eastern kingdoms. She is known to have influenced political, military, economic and cultic affairs in the royal court and played a key part in the process of dynastic succession. In fact, it was generally the king's mother who ruled as queen, not the king's wife. We see this in Hittite, Ugaritic, Egyptian and Assyrian kingdoms, as well as in ancient Israel.[2]

The importance of the king's mother may seem odd until we recall that most Ancient Near Eastern kings practiced polygamy and had large harems. While kings may have had many wives, they each had only one mother, and the queenship was given to her. This, in fact, is what one finds in ancient Israel, where the king's mother was given preeminence over all the women in the kingdom of Judah, even over the king's wives. She was given the title Gebirah—or "Great Lady"—and reigned as queen in her son's kingdom.

We can see the importance of the queen mother expressed in many texts of the Old Testament. First, the succession narratives of 1 and 2 Kings present the mother of the king as having such importance that almost every time a new Davidic king is introduced in the Kingdom of Judah, the *mother's* name also is mentioned—but the wife's name is not.

---

[2] See my *Queen Mother: A Biblical Theology of Mary's Queenship* (Steubenville, Ohio: Emmaus Road Publishing, 2005), pp. 45-53. See also: N. Andreasen, "The Role of the Queen Mother in Israelite Society" *CBQ* 45 (1983), pp. 179-194; L. Schearing, "Queen" in D. Freedman, ed., *The Anchor Bible Dictionary*, vol. 5 (New York: Doubleday, 1992), pp. 583-588; R. De Vaux, *Ancient Israel* (New York: McGraw-Hill, 1961), pp. 115-119; G. Kirwin, *The Nature of the Queenship of Mary* (Ann Arbor, Michigan: UMI Dissertation Services, 1973), pp. 297-312.

Thus, at the crucial transition points of dynastic succession, the narrative consistently highlights the queen mother's important place alongside the new king. As one commentator has explained, "On the throne the queen mother represented the king's continuity with the past, the visible affirmation of God's ongoing plan for his people, the channel through which the Lord's dynastic promise to David was fulfilled."[3]

The queen mother held an official position in the kingdom of Judah. She is described as having a crown (Jer 13:18) and a throne (1 Kings 2:19; cf., Jer 13:18). It is also significant that 2 Kings 24 mentions the queen mother among the members of the royal court whom King Jehoiachin surrenders to the king of Babylon. In this passage, the queen mother is the first of the king's royal court listed as being given over to Babylon to go into exile (2 Kings 24:12-15). Miguens notes how this highlights the queen mother's preeminence in the royal court:

> She is mentioned *before* the "wives of the king" (2 Kings 24:15) and before the ministers, dignitaries and officers (2 Kings 24:12, 15; Jer 29:2). Significantly these biblical passages say that the *gebirah* is the second, only to the king, in the list of prominent official persons brought into captivity. This detail speaks very highly of the political significance of "the mother of the king."[4]

The queen mother was not simply a "figurehead" position. She had real royal authority, participating in her son's reign. For example, consider the following prophecy, which the prophet Jeremiah addresses both to the king and the queen mother:

> Say to the king and the queen mother: "Take a lowly seat, for your beautiful crown has come down from your head. ... Lift up your eyes and see those who come from the north. Where is the flock that was given you, your beautiful flock?" (Jer 13:18, 20).

By addressing both the king and the queen mother, this passage recognized the queen mother's important royal office. In ominous

---

[3] G. Montague, *Our Father, Our Mother* (Steubenville: Franciscan University Press, 1990), p. 92.

[4] M. Miguens, *Mary: 'Servant of the Lord'* (Boston: St. Paul Editions, 1978), p. 65.

imagery, the king and queen mother are told to "take a lowly seat"—symbolizing how both had thrones, but would lose them soon. Moreover, both are told they will lose their crowns—also foreshadowing their political downfall. Most of all, both king and queen are described as having the responsibility to shepherd the flock of the people of Judah, a flock that is about to be taken away from them: "Where is the flock that was given you, your beautiful flock?" The important point for our purposes is to note how this prophecy portrays the queen mother as participating in the king's reign: she has a throne and a crown with the king, and she shares in the king's mission of shepherding the people.

The queen mother's royal authority can best be seen if we compare Bathsheba's role in the kingdom when she was the wife of the king, to her role when she became the mother of the king. In 1 Kings 1, her husband David, the king, is still alive, so she is just the king's wife. When she wants to enter the royal chamber to meet him, she bows before her husband and pays him homage (1 Kings 1:16). As she leaves she honors the king, saying, "May David live forever!" (1 Kings 1:31).

In the next chapter, David has died and Bathsheba's son Solomon has assumed the throne, making her queen mother. When she enters the royal chamber this time as mother of the king, she is treated much differently than when she was just the wife of the king. The narrative tells not of Bathsheba bowing before the king, but of King Solomon rising and bowing down before *her*. Then Solomon has a throne brought in for her, symbolizing her royal status. Even more striking is the place where Solomon places Bathsheba's royal seat: at his right hand. The queen mother being seated at the king's right hand has the greatest significance, for in the Bible the right is a position of authority and supreme honor. As Gray observes, "Nowhere else in the Bible does the king honor someone as Solomon does the Gebirah."[5]

The queen mother also served as a counselor to the king.[6] We have some evidence of this in the Old Testament. For example, in Proverbs 31, a queen mother gives wise counsel to her son about how to serve the poor, rule the people with justice, avoid too much alcohol and choose a

---

[5] T. Gray, "God's Word and Mary's Royal Office," *Miles Immaculatae* 13 (1995), p. 377.

[6] P. De Boer, "The Counselor," *VTSup* 3 (Leiden: Brill, 1955), p. 54; N. Andreasen, "The Role of the Queen Mother in Israelite Society," pp. 190-191.

good wife. Although not always this positive, the queen mother's counsel seems to have had the ability to greatly influence affairs in the kingdom. 2 Chronicles 22:3, for example, tells how King Ahaziah "walked in the ways of the house of Ahab [an evil king], for his mother was his counselor in doing wickedly." This shows how at least this particular queen mother's counsel was so influential it led the king into wickedness.

The influence of the queen mother is seen in the intercessory role she played in ancient Israel.[7] She served as an advocate, taking petitions from the people and presenting them to the king. Her intercessory function can be seen in the passage from 1 Kings 2 when Bathsheba went to meet her royal son, Solomon. In the context, Solomon has been crowned king, and Bathsheba has thus become queen mother. Her new intercessory power is immediately recognized when a man named Adonijah asks Bathsheba to bring a petition of his to the king. Adonijah expresses great confidence in her intercessory role, saying "Pray ask King Solomon—he will not refuse you" (1 Kings 2:17). Bathsheba agrees and then goes to the king.

After she is welcomed by the king, who bows before her and gives her a throne at his right hand, Bathsheba tells Solomon she has a small request to bring to him. Solomon responds by saying "Make your request my mother, for I will not refuse you." Indeed, Solomon's words reveal the king's ordinary commitment to the queen mother's petitions.[8]

---

[7] P. De Boer, "The Counselor," pp. 60-61; N. Andreasen, "The Role of the Queen Mother in Israelite Society," pp. 194.

[8] See F. Rossier, *L'intercession Entre les Hommes dans la Bible Hébraique Orbis Biblicus et Orientalis 152* (Gottingen: Vandenhoeck & Ruprecht, 1996), p. 189. Also, see Gray's note on this passage: "The fact that Solomon denies the request in no way discredits the influence of the Gebirah. Adonijah wanted Abishag the Shunammite for the treacherous purpose of taking over the kingdom from Solomon." T. Gray, "God's Word and Mary's Royal Office," p. 381, n. 16. Taking the king's concubine was a sign of usurping the throne in the Ancient Near East. For example, see how Absalom (Adonijah's older brother), in his attempt to take the throne from David, took his concubines (2 Sam 16:20-23). Gray continues, "Thus *the wickedness of Adonijah's intention is the reason for denial, which in no way reflects negatively upon the Gebirah's power to intercede. The narrative bears out the fact that the king normally accepted the Gebirah's request,* thus Solomon says, 'Ask, I will not refuse you.' To say then that this illustrates the weakness of the Gebirah's ability to intercede would be to miss the whole point of the narrative, which tells how Adonijah uses the queen mother's position in an attempt to become king." T. Gray, "God's Word and Mary's Royal Office," p. 381, n. 16, emphasis added. For more on the political

In sum, we have seen that the queen mother held an official position in the royal court, sharing in the shepherding responsibilities of the king, and serving as a counselor for the king and as an advocate for the people.

The Queen Mother in Prophecy: Isaiah 7:14

We also see the importance of the queen mother in Israel's prophetic tradition, particularly in the Emmanuel prophecy of Isaiah 7:14. This passage, filled with strong Davidic overtones, is important for our study because it is associated with Israel's messianic hopes and was explicitly related to Mary and Jesus in the New Testament (Mt 1:23).

The prophecy comes during a period of dynastic crisis. Syria and the Northern Kingdom of Israel threaten to invade the Kingdom of Judah. Ahaz, the king of Judah, fears that the dynasty may be coming to an end with him (Is 7:1-6). Isaiah is sent by God to assure a doubting Ahaz that the kingdom will survive this foreign threat and challenge him to entrust his throne to the Lord. Isaiah then gives a sign to the house of David that will serve as a confirmation of Yahweh's protection of the Davidic dynasty:

> Here then O house of David! Is it too little for you to weary men, that you weary my God also? Therefore the Lord himself will give you a sign. Behold, a virgin [*almah*] shall conceive and bear a son and shall call his name Emmanuel (Is 7:13-14).

At a most basic level, the child represents an heir to the Davidic throne. Such a view best demonstrates how this sign for the house of David relates to the immediate context of the dynastic crisis at hand. Not only is the Davidic line in danger of expiring (Is 7:6), but as a result, God's faithfulness to the Davidic dynasty (2 Sam 7:11-14) is called into question. It is within this setting that Isaiah specifically addressed "the house of David" with this oracle announcing the Immanuel child in 7:14. Given this context, the child seems to represent some type of dynastic sign guaranteeing the succession of the endangered Davidic line.

---

symbolism of usurping a member of a king's harem, see R. De Vaux, *Ancient Israel*, p. 116.

This view finds further support in the fact that the child's name ("God with us") is itself bound up with the idea of the preservation of the Davidic dynasty. Since God promised to be "with" the sons of David in a special way (2 Sam 7:9; 1 Kings 1:37; Ps 89:22, 25; 1 Kings 11:38), the sign of a child named "Immanuel" gives assurance that God will remain faithful to his promise to the Davidic dynasty: God will still be with his people even through this crisis in which the house of David appears to be crumbling. All this strongly supports an understanding of the child as a successor to the Davidic throne—someone in whom the dynasty would continue. And in light of the fact that this child in Isaiah 7 is also associated with the great prophecies of Isaiah 9 (a child who would bring about a never-ending kingdom) and Isaiah 11 (a royal son who would unify all people and whom all nations would seek), we can see even more clearly that this prophecy ultimately will be fulfilled in the great messiah king to come, Jesus Christ (cf., Mt 1:23).

Once we see the Immanuel child as a Davidic king, the young woman (*almah*) conceiving this child would have been understood as the mother of the king. Furthermore, in this oracle addressed specifically to the Davidic household (Is 7:13), the young woman bearing the royal son, an heir to the throne, would have been understood as a *queen mother*. With Isaiah's overriding concern for dynastic succession in the house of David, it is fitting that this prophecy links the royal son with his queen mother—the very woman who played an important role in dynastic succession and in the royal court. Indeed, Matthew's Gospel will employ this queen mother and son prophecy in relation to Mary and her royal Davidic son, Jesus, in the New Testament (Mt 1:22-23).

Mary as Queen Mother and Advocate in the New Testament

Up to this point, we have seen the important role of the queen mother in the Davidic kingdom and in the prophetic tradition about the future of the kingdom. We now can turn our attention to the New Testament. Here we will consider how Luke, Matthew and the Johannine writings portray Mary in ways that bring to mind the queen mother of the Old Testament.

Luke 1:26-38

Luke evokes many Davidic kingdom themes in his infancy narrative. In the Annunciation scene, Luke presents Mary's vocation as Mother of the Messiah within a Davidic kingdom framework. She is introduced in the narrative as being betrothed to a man who is "of the house of David" (Lk 1:26). Luke mentions this detail of Joseph's heritage in order to prepare the reader for understanding Jesus as a Davidic heir.

The angel's announcement to Mary in Luke 1:32-33 highlights that her child will be the son of David, fulfilling the promises God made to David in 2 Samuel 7. First, she is told by Gabriel that her Son will be called "Son of the Most High" (1:32). Since "Most High" was a title for God in the Old Testament, and a common divine title in Luke as well,[9] the description of Jesus as "Son of the Most High" would indicate that he has a filial relationship with God. This expression also could be understood in light of the Old Testament designation of the Davidic king as God's son. Thus, Jesus as "Son of the Most High" likely recalls Nathan's oracle (2 Sam 7:14) and the royal Psalms (Ps 2:7; 89:26-27; cf. Ps 110:1)—both of which describe the Davidic king as having a special filial relationship with Yahweh.

That this is the primary meaning of the child's divine sonship in 1:32 is made clearer in the following verses, which include even more direct allusions to the Davidic covenant and thus bring Jesus' kingship into sharper focus. The angel goes on to tell Mary that her child will be given "the throne of his father David" (Lk 1:32), showing that Jesus fulfills Nathan's promise for the Davidic dynasty in which God would establish "the throne of his kingdom forever" (2 Sam 7:13). When the angel describes how the child will "reign over the house of Jacob forever" and says "of his kingdom there will be no end" (Lk 1:33), these words further explicate Jesus' kingship in terms of the hopes surrounding the Davidic dynasty (2 Sam 7:13; Ps 89:36ff; Is 9:6ff).

Furthermore, there are several direct parallels between Luke 1:32-33 and the promises God made to David in 2 Samuel 7:9-16 (great name, throne, divine sonship, house and kingdom). Indeed, Gabriel's words clearly echo Nathan's oracle, which became the foundation for Jewish

---

[9] See Luke 1:35, 76; 6:35; 8:28; Acts 7:48; 16:17. J. Fitzmyer, *The Gospel According to Luke* (Garden City, New York: Doubleday, 1981) p. 348.

messianic hopes. The parallels can be demonstrated in the following chart:

Luke 1:
32a: He will be great and will be called Son of the Most High.
32b: And the Lord God will give to him the throne of his father David
33a: and he will reign over the house of Jacob forever,
33b: and of his kingdom there will be no end.

2 Sam 7:
9: I will make for you a *great* name . . .
13: I will establish *the throne of his kingdom forever*.
14: I will be his father, and he shall be *my* son . . .
16: And your *house* and your *kingdom* shall be made sure forever.[10]

With these words, Gabriel is clearly identifying the child as the Davidic messiah, fulfilling the hopes of 2 Samuel 7. Therefore, the narrative shows that Mary is given the vocation to be the mother of the king.

This is why some have suggested that the queen-mother tradition may be in the background of the Annunciation scene.[11] Indeed, this passage portrays Mary as a mother linked with the house of David and giving birth to a Davidic son. Especially since Luke places this scene in the context of the Davidic kingdom, it seems that Mary's role should be understood in light of that Davidic tradition as well. In that context, Mary, as mother of the Davidic king, would be seen as queen mother of her royal son. As Cazelles has pointed out, while the angel's words speak

---

[10] R. Brown, *Birth of the Messiah* (New York: Doubleday, 1993), p. 310.
[11] S. De Fiores, "Regina: Approfondimento Teologico Attualizzato," in S. De Fiores and S. Meo, eds., *Nuovo Dizionario di Mariologia* (Milan: Edizioni San Paolo, 1996), pp. 1080-1081; A. Serra, "Regina," pp. 1073-1074; J. Ibánez and F. Mendoza, *La Madre del Redentor* (Madrid: Ediciones Palabra, 1988), p. 290; G. Del Moral, "Santa María, La Guebiráh Messiánica," p. 44; T. Gray, "God's Word and Mary's Royal Office," p. 384; H. Cazelles, "La Mère du Roi-Messie" in *Mater et Ecclesia*, Congressus Mariologicus, vol. 5 (Lourdes, 1958), pp. 55-56; A. Valentini, "Lc 1, 39-45: Primi Inizi di Venerazione delle Madre del Signore," *Marianum* 58 (1996), p. 348.

of Jesus as the Messiah-King, they also provide a basis for Mary's royal maternity. "One could not more explicitly announce the birth of the Messiah who was waited for and announced by the prophets. However, by speaking directly to the Mother of the Messiah, the angel implicitly evoked the woman who was the mother of the king, linked to her son. It is thus that these words contain a theology of the queenship of Mary."[12]

Luke 1:39-45

In Luke's account of the visitation, we will see how Elizabeth's greeting Mary with the title "the mother of my Lord" (Lk 1:43) is charged with great royal significance that is helpful for our topic.

This is the first time Jesus is called "Lord" in Luke-Acts. While *kurios* was used often in the Old Testament as a circumlocution for avoiding the Tetragrammaton (*Yahweh*), it also referred to the Davidic king (2 Sam 24:21; 1 Kings 1:13-47) and the royal messiah (Ps 110:1). Within the Lucan narrative, the title "Lord" later came to refer to Jesus' total authority and placed him on par with Yahweh (Acts 2 and 10).[13] However, at this point in the narrative, its use by Elizabeth could be "a prophetic foreshadowing" of Jesus' full identity to be revealed later in the narrative. But in this first use of the title "Lord," "it could also be seen to signify simply the Lordship of the Messiah (Lk 20:41-44)."[14]

Furthermore, Elizabeth's words to Mary, "And why is this granted me, that the mother of my Lord should come to me?" (Lk 1:43), echo 2 Samuel 24:21 where the phrase "my Lord" is used as a royal title honoring the king. In that text, Araunah greets King David, saying: "Why has my lord the king come to his servant?" (2 Sam 24:21). With this in the background, Elizabeth's words here in 1:43 would have regal connotations that further present Jesus as a Davidic king.

It is also significant that the title in 1:43 is not used in an absolute sense, but stands alongside the first person possessive, "*my* Lord." This may further signify its royal messianic meaning, since this expression was

---

[12] H. Cazelles, "La Mère du Roi-Messie," p. 56.

[13] D. Bock, *Proclamation from Prophecy and Pattern* (*JSNTSup* 12) (Sheffield: Sheffield Academic Press, 1987) pp. 69-70.

[14] Bock continues: "...but in view of Luke's later development of this term, clearly something more is in mind here, though this deeper intention is *not clear by this text alone*. It only emerges from later Lucan usage." D. Bock, *Proclamation from Prophecy and Pattern*, p. 70.

used in the Old Testament to denote the king and the future messiah. As Brown has observed, "Both in the gospel (20:41-44) and in Acts (2:34) Luke uses Psalm 110:1, 'the Lord said to *my Lord*,' to show that Jesus is the Messiah and Son of God; and Elizabeth is recognizing Mary as the mother of 'my Lord' i.e., of the Messiah."[15]

Thus, when Elizabeth calls Mary "the mother of my Lord," these words not only point to Jesus as the Messiah, but they also tell us something important about Mary. While recognizing the messianic lordship of Mary's child, Elizabeth, at the same time, acknowledges Mary as the mother of her king. Here it should be pointed out that in the New Testament, Mary often is referred to as the "mother of Jesus" or "his mother," but nowhere is she called the "mother of my Lord" except here in 1:43.[16] Thus, this unique title for Mary seems to draw attention to her position not just as mother of Jesus in general, but as mother of Jesus specifically in his role as messianic Lord. In other words, Elizabeth, in greeting Mary as "the mother of my Lord," refers to her as *mother of the Messiah-King*.

This is why the words "the mother of my Lord" point to Mary as a queen-mother figure. It has been noted that in royal court language of the Ancient Near East, the title "Mother of my Lord" would have been used to address the queen mother of the reigning king (who himself was addressed as "my Lord"; cf., 2 Sam 24:21).[17] Thus, within the strong Davidic context of Luke's infancy narrative, Elizabeth addressing Mary with this royal title provides a basis for viewing her in light of the queen-mother tradition of the Old Testament.

Matthew 1-2

The infancy narrative in Matthew's Gospel is framed largely around the hopes surrounding the Davidic kingdom. For example, in the very first verse, Jesus is called "*christos*," which translated the Hebrew word *masiah* (1:1). This title was used often in the Old Testament to describe

---

[15] R. Brown, *Birth of the Messiah*, p. 344.
[16] M. Miguens, *Mary: Servant of the Lord*, p. 61.
[17] B. Ahern, "The Mother of the Messiah" in *Marian Studies* 12 (1961), p. 28; G. Kirwin, *The Nature of the Queenship of Mary*, p. 29, n. 72; G. Del Moral, "La Realeza de María segun la Sagrada Escritura," p. 176; M. Miguens, *Mary: Servant of the Lord*, pp. 60-62.

Israel's king, and in post-exilic times to designate the future Davidic king whom God would use to restore the kingdom and establish a perfect, everlasting reign. By using *"christos"* five times in the first two chapters, Matthew draws attention to Jesus' Davidic heritage, identifying him as the long-awaited king who would restore the kingdom (Mt 1:1, 16, 17, 18; 2:4).

This messianic portrait is filled in more by another title used in the first verse: "the Son of David" (1:1). By the first century, this title designated the messianic king who would fulfill the promises God made to David. Thus, Matthew's Gospel shows that Jesus is not just any descendant of David, but is *the* son of David who would inaugurate the perfect kingdom that would never end.

After tracing Jesus' royal lineage all the way back to King David in Matthew 1:6-17, Matthew's Gospel goes on to show how Jesus' birth itself fulfills hopes surrounding the Messiah-King and the restoration of the Davidic dynasty. Matthew notes that Jesus is born in Bethlehem (2:1), the same place where David was born. The magi call him "the king of the Jews" (2:2) and want to give royal homage to this newborn king (2:2). The scene of the magi paying royal homage to the child also reveals Jesus' kingship. This is especially seen in the gifts which the magi bring, for they are gifts fit for a king, as seen in this passage's allusions to Isaiah 60:1ff.; Psalm 72:10-11 and 1 Kings 10:2, 10. Matthew also highlights how Jesus' birth fulfills prophecies about Davidic kings, including the Immanuel prophecy of Isaiah 7:14 (see Mt 1:22-23) and the prophecy about the future ruler being born in Bethlehem in Micah 5:2 (see Mt 2:5-6).

Within this resounding chorus of Davidic kingdom allusions, Matthew also associates the royal Son with his Mother in several ways that may recall the queen mother.

First, Matthew associates Mary and Jesus with the queen mother and royal son prophecy of Isaiah 7:14. In 1:23, Matthew identifies Mary as the *parthenos*, whom Isaiah prophesied would give birth to the Immanuel child in Isaiah 7:14 (LXX). As we saw earlier, in the Isaian oracle, the queen mother of Immanuel brings forth a child who would ensure the perseverance of the Davidic dynasty. Here in Matthew 1, Mary does the same, bringing forth the Davidic heir who would secure the true Davidic kingdom forever. As Serra explains, "Just as she [the queen mother in

Isaiah 7:14] gave birth to a son who guaranteed the continuation of the House of David, so Mary gives birth to a son who will reign forever on the throne of David, in the house of Jacob, in the 'Israel of God' (cf., Mt 28:20; 16:18; Gal 6:16; 2 Sam 7:16). One notes the royalty of the two women."[18]

Second, Matthew frequently records the newborn king alongside his mother. In fact, some have pointed out how Matthew constantly mentioning the child and his mother together—five times in chapter two alone—could draw attention to Mary's association with her royal Son in a way that recalls the Old Testament queen-mother tradition.[19] Matthew's recurring phrase "the child and his mother" has "a Davidic resonance,"[20] which might bring to mind the way the books of Kings repeatedly introduced each new Davidic king alongside the queen mother.

Third, she holds an important narrative position alongside her royal Son when the magi pay him homage (Mt 2:11). This scene involves a number of Davidic kingdom themes. Jesus is called the "king of the Jews" (2:2). The star guiding the magi recalls the star in Balaam's oracle about the royal scepter rising out of Israel (Num 24:17). The narrative centers on the city of Bethlehem, where David was born (1 Sam 17:12) and out of which the future Davidic king would come (Mic 5:2). And the magi bringing gifts and paying the child Jesus homage recall the royal Psalm 72:10-11 (cf., Is. 60:6).

Within this Davidic kingdom context, Matthew records Mary with the child when the three magi come to honor the newborn king. Notice how mention of Joseph is conspicuously absent: "...going into the house, [the magi] saw *the child with Mary his mother*, and they fell down and worshipped him" (Mt 2:11). Why does Matthew focus on Jesus and Mary and leave Joseph out of the picture at this point? All throughout the narrative in Matthew 1-2, Joseph is much more prominent than Mary. Matthew traces Jesus' genealogy through Joseph. The angel appears to Joseph three times. It is Joseph who leads the Holy Family to Bethlehem, to Egypt and back to Nazareth. However, as Aragon notes, in this particular scene of the magi coming to honor the newborn king,

---

[18] A. Serra, "Bibbia," p. 219.
[19] Matthew 2:11, 13, 14, 20, 21. See, for example, B. Nolan, *The Royal Son of God* (Gottingen: Vandenhoeck & Rupprecht, 1979), p. 43.
[20] B. Nolan, *The Royal Son of God*, p. 43.

Mary takes center stage, and surprisingly, Joseph is not mentioned at all in the entire pericope. "Her mention in this moment, along with the omission of Joseph, underlines that Mary is a person especially important for the narrator, and that is why he puts her in this very high position."[21] This link between royal child and mother in such a regal context again may bring to mind the queen-mother tradition. Indeed, if Jesus is the newborn "king of the Jews" in this scene (2:2), then Mary, as the mother of this king (cf., 2:11), could be understood as a queen mother.[22] Brown draws a similar conclusion: "[S]ince the magi story puts so much emphasis on homage paid to a Davidic king in Bethlehem of Judah, 'the child with his mother' might evoke the peculiar importance given to the queen mother (*gebirah,* 'the Great Lady') of a newborn or newly installed king in the Davidic dynasty."[23]

Revelation 12

When interpreting the "woman clothed with the sun" in Revelation 12, some identify the "woman" merely in a collective way—as a symbol for the Old Testament people of God, as a symbol for the New Testament church, or as a symbol of God's people in general, spanning both the old and the new. However, as discussed in the chapter on New Testament foundations, while Revelation 12 portrays the woman in ways that might recall Israel or the Church, the "woman clothed with the sun" is also meant to be understood as Mary. Since Revelation 12 presents the woman as the Mother of the Messiah, a Marian interpretation makes most sense. As Andre Feuillette once put it: "Is it conceivable that a Christian author of the late first century could speak about the Mother of Christ while prescinding entirely from the Virgin Mary?"[24] Once a Marian interpretation of the woman in Revelation 12 is held, the ways in which this book presents Our Lady's queenship become quite apparent.

---

[21] R. Aragon, "La Madre con el Niño en la Casa" *EphMar* 43 (1993), pp. 54-55. See also: G. Segalla, "Il Bambino con Maria Sua Madre" *Theotokos* 4 (1996), p. 19.

[22] "Matthew makes it very clear that the infant is king, Israel's messiah, son of David (1:1, 20; 2:2, 6, 11). Clearly, Mary is the Gebirah, the queen-mother." G. Montague, *Our Father, Our Mother*, p. 97. See also: G. Segalla, "Il Bambino Con Maria Sua Madre in Matteo 2," p. 18; A. Serra, "Regina," p. 1073; G. Del Moral, "Santa María, La Guebiráh Mesiánica," p. 42.

[23] R. Brown, *Birth of the Messiah*, p. 192, n. 32.

[24] A. Feuillet, *Jesus and His Mother* (Still River: St. Bede's Publications, 1984), p. 23.

Like the other Marian passages we have studied, Revelation 12 is filled with royal themes. On one level, this is seen in the woman's son, who is described as the messianic king exercising his universal dominion. The book of Revelation uses the messianic Psalm 2 to describe how this child will "rule all the nations with a rod of iron" (12:5). He is taken up to heaven to sit on a throne (12:5). This son ushers in the kingdom of God as the enemy is defeated: "Now ... the kingdom of our God [has] come, for the accuser ... has been thrown down" (12:10).

On another level, royal images are also associated with the woman herself, who as the mother of this king, is portrayed as a majestic queenly figure: "And a great sign appeared in heaven, a woman clothed with the sun, with the moon under her feet and on her head a crown of twelve stars" (Rev 12:1). First, the woman's crown is a symbol of royal authority and victory. In the book of Revelation, the symbol of the crown is never a superfluous decoration, but connotes a real reign.[25] It often refers to the share the saints have in Christ's kingship and the reward they receive for victorious perseverance during times of persecutions and temptations (Rev 2:10; 3:11; 4:4, 10; 6:2; 14:14). Thus, the woman having a crown of her own shows that she too has a royal status. The twelve stars point to her relationship with the twelve tribes of Israel (Rev 21:12) or the Church, founded on the twelve apostles (Rev 21:14).

Second, the woman described as having the moon *under her feet* also may point to her royal authority. In the Scriptures, under-the-feet imagery was often used to denote royal dominion and subjugation of enemies, especially within a Davidic kingdom context.[26] Hence, Vanni concludes: "To have someone or something under the feet signifies having power."[27] Thus, the woman depicted as subjugating the moon under her feet suggests that she too has some type of royal position.[28]

---

[25] See G. Stevenson, "Conceptual Background to Golden Crown Imagery in the Apocalypse of John (4:4, 10; 14:14)," *JBL* 114 (1995), p. 260; U. Vanni, "La Decodificazione 'Del Grande Segno' in Apocalisse 12,1-6," *Marianum* 40 (1978), p. 131;

[26] Ps 89:23; 110:1; 2 Sam 22:37-43; cf. Gen 3:15; Ps 8:6. See W. Witfall, "Gen 3:15—A Protoevangelium?" *CBQ* 36 (1974), p. 363.

[27] U. Vanni, "La Decodificazione 'Del Grande Segno,' " p. 129.

[28] "The moon beneath her feet (perhaps a footstool) speaks of dominion." R. Mounce, *The Book of Revelation* (Grand Rapids: Eerdmans, 1998), p. 232. Since the moon was important for time (Gen 1:14-19 and the Jewish lunar calendar),

Further, the images of the sun, moon and twelve stars portray the woman in light of an Old Testament passage that may highlight the woman's royal authority. It is sometimes proposed that Isaiah's depiction of the new Jerusalem's splendor in 60:19-20 (illumined by God's glory, no longer in need of the sun or moon) and Song of Songs 6:10 (the bride described as beautiful as the moon and resplendent as the sun) have foreshadowed the woman's radiant description in Revelation 12:1. While these texts may be in the background, Joseph's dream in Genesis 37:9-11 seems to be even more related, because it has even stronger parallels with Revelation 12:1-2. In this famous dream, the sun, moon and stars bow down before Joseph, symbolizing the royal authority he would have over his father, mother and brothers when he would rise to a pre-eminent position in Egypt as the most powerful person in Pharaoh's royal court. Thus, in light of the royal significance of the sun, moon and stars in Genesis 37:9-11, the woman in Revelation 12:1 being depicted with these celestial images may add further color to her royalty.

Therefore, the woman in Revelation 12, portrayed alongside her kingly son and depicted with all these royal images clearly would be seen as some type of queenly figure. And once again, the Old Testament tradition of the *gebirah* could shed light on this queenly woman of Revelation 12. Indeed, she is the mother of the Davidic king (Rev 12:5; Ps 2:7), and she wears a crown as did the queen mothers in the Davidic kingdom (Jer 13:18). Revelation 12 presents a *royal* woman (12:1) giving birth to the messiah-king (12:5). Although corporate interpretations often view the woman as a symbol for God's people, no Old Testament or Jewish text speaks of a *queenly* figure personifying the collective people of God *and giving birth to the messiah*. However, a close fit can indeed be found in the Old Testament tradition of the queen mother. The queen mother was a royal woman well-known in the Scriptures for having given birth to the Davidic king and for being closely associated with his reign.[29] This is similar to the queenly figure in Revelation 12. As such, the queen mother may be in the background for understanding the royal woman who gave birth to the Davidic messiah in Revelation

---

this image may symbolize dominion over the temporal realm. See also: A. Serra, "Bibbia," p. 265; *idem*., "Regina," pp. 1079-1080.

[29] P. Farkas, *La Donna di Apocalisse 12* (Rome: Editrice Pontificia Universita Gregoriana, 1997), pp. 210-211.

12. Kirwin draws a similar conclusion: "The woman of Apocalypse 12 is the Mother of the Messiah-King who on the day of his birth, 'caught up to the throne of God' is ruler of the universe... Here too, she is the Queen Mother, Mother of Christ – Head and members, Mother of the Church."[30]

These insights would be strengthened by considering how Revelation 12 portrays the woman in light of the Emmanuel prophecy of Isaiah 7:14, which as we saw involves a queen mother who will give birth to a Davidic son. The woman in Revelation 12:1 is introduced as *"a sign"* (σημειον), recalling the sign (σημειον) given to the house of David in this prophecy (Is 7:10 LXX). This sign in Revelation is located in the heavens, like the sign as high as heaven that was offered to King Ahaz (Is 7:10). The sign in Revelation involves a royal woman giving birth to a kingly son (12:1-2, 5) like the queen mother who would conceive and bear a Davidic heir in the Immanuel prophecy (Is 7:14).

Since the woman is portrayed with a number of royal images, she is presented to the reader as some type of queenly figure. And since she is presented as the Mother of the Davidic Messiah (12:5), the queen-mother tradition of the Old Testament can shed light on the woman's queenly position in this passage. It is thus, as we have seen, that Revelation 12 lends strong biblical support for an understanding of Mary as Queen Mother.

The Queen-Advocate at Cana

In summary, we have examined the portrayal of Mary in Luke 1:26-38, Luke 1:39-45, Matthew 1-2 and Revelation 12. By considering Mary in light of the Davidic kingdom themes that these passages evoke, we have seen how the queen mother can serve as an important background for understanding Mary in the New Testament. As the mother of the Messiah-King, she appears as the new *Gebirah*. And as the Queen Mother of Christ's Kingdom, Mary would serve as Advocate, interceding for God's people. By way of conclusion, let us briefly consider one New Testament passage which illustrates how effective Mary can be as an Advocate in the Kingdom: the Wedding Feast at Cana (Jn 2:1-11).

First, this scene expresses Mary's compassion and attentiveness to others' needs. Vatican II described Mary at Cana being "moved with

---

[30] G. Kirwin, *The Nature of the Queenship of Mary*, p. 297.

pity" when she noticed the wine ran short at the wedding.[31] John Paul II said Mary was "prompted by her merciful heart" to help this family by bringing her concern for them to Jesus. "Having sensed the eventual disappointment of the newly married couple and guests because of the lack of wine, the Blessed Virgin compassionately suggested to Jesus that he intervene with his messianic power."[32]

Second, this scene serves as a pattern for Marian intercession. Just as Mary at Cana noticed the family's needs first and brought those needs to Christ, so does she continue to bring our needs to her Son through her intercession for us. John Paul II noted how this scene at Cana exemplifies how she intercedes for *all* mankind. It demonstrates, he says, "*Mary's solicitude for human beings*, her coming to them in the wide variety of their wants and needs" and presenting those needs to Jesus. He continues:

> At Cana in Galilee there is shown only one concrete aspect of human need, apparently a small one of little importance ("They have no wine"). But it has a symbolic value: this coming to the aid of human needs means, at the same time, bringing those needs within the radius of Christ's messianic mission and salvific power. Thus there is a mediation: Mary places herself between her Son and mankind in the reality of their wants, needs and sufferings.[33]

Finally, the Wedding at Cana illustrates Mary's *effectiveness* as an advocate. Mary notices the problem the family is facing, and in her unique position as the Mother of the King, she confidently turns to her royal Son for help in a way that no one else could. As John Paul II explained, as Christ's Mother, Mary knows that "she can point out to her Son the needs of mankind, and in fact, she 'has the right' to do so" (RM, 21). And when she presents those needs to her Son, Jesus responds to his Mother's intercession quite powerfully. As the passage bears out, Mary's request is fulfilled. Jesus performs the miracle and provides the wine that was lacking. And even more, Jesus supplies for them in an abundant way

---

[31] Vatican II, *Lumen Gentium*, 58.
[32] John Paul II, general audience of March 5, 1997, in *Theotokos* (Boston: Pauline Books and Media, 2000), p. 177.
[33] John Paul II, *Redemptoris Mater*, 21 (Boston: Pauline Books and Media, 1987).

that goes well beyond one's expectations—at least 120 gallons worth (cf. Jn. 2:6). Thus, Mary is portrayed as a powerful advocate for the family of the bride and groom at Cana, bringing their needs to the King and effectively receiving from her royal Son what the people need.

Advocate: Foundations in Tradition and Magisterium

Let us turn our attention to Mary's advocacy role as it unfolds in Catholic Tradition. The early Church quickly perceived the important role Mary played in God's redemptive plan. The role of Mary as New Eve beside her Son in the economy of salvation is found already in the writings of St. Justin Martyr, St. Irenaeus of Lyons and Tertullian (and possibly other earlier sources[34]). In Justin's *Dialogue with Trypho*, Eve is the virgin who "conceived the word of the serpent" and "brought forth disobedience and death"; whereas Mary is the virgin filled with faith, who through her obedience to the angel's annunciation conceived the child who destroys the serpent and delivers from death those who believe in him.[35] In Irenaeus' *Against the Heresies*, Mary is described as the cause of salvation (*causa salutis*) whose obedience untied "the knot of Eve's disobedience."[36] And in Tertullian's *De Carne Christi*, he describes how Eve believed the serpent and conceived the Devil's word; whereas Mary believed the angel and conceived in her womb the Word of God.[37] However, it is St. Irenaeus who is the first to bestow upon Mary the title "advocate" with this Eve-Mary parallel, calling Mary the "advocate of the virgin Eve":

> And if the former [Eve] did disobey God, yet the latter [Mary] was persuaded to be obedient to God, in

---

[34] For a discussion of possible Eve-Mary parallels in the middle second century, *Epistle to Diognetus*, and in a possible allusion to Papias in Victorinus of Pettau's treatise *De Fabrica Mundi*, see L. Gambero, "Patristic Intuitions of Mary's Role as Mediatrix and Advocate: The Invocation of the Faithful for Her Help" *Marian Studies* 52 (2001), pp. 79-83.

[35] St. Justin Martyr, *Dialogue with Trypho* 100, *PG* 6, 711-12; L. Gambero, "Patristic Intuitions," pp. 83-84.

[36] St. Irenaeus, *Adversus Haereses* 3:22 *PG* 7, 958-960; L. Gambero, *Mary and the Fathers of the Church* (San Francisco: Ignatius Press, 1999), p. 58; *idem*, "Patristic Intuitions," p. 88.

[37] Tertullian, *De Carne Christi*, 17, *PL* 2, 827; L. Gambero, "Patristic Intuitions," pp. 95-96.

order that the Virgin Mary might become the advocate [Latin: *advocata*] of the virgin Eve. And thus, as the human race fell into bondage to death by means of a virgin, so it is rescued by a Virgin; virginal disobedience having been balanced in the opposite scale by virginal obedience."[38]

In another text of St. Irenaeus called *Proof of the Apostolic Teaching*s, Mary again is called "advocate" of the virgin Eve:

> And just as it was through a virgin who disobeyed that man was stricken and fell and died, so too it was through the Virgin who obeyed the word of God that man, resuscitated by life, received life. For the Lord came to seek back the lost sheep, and it was man who was lost; and therefore he did not become some other formation, but likewise of her that was descended from Adam, preserved the likeness of formation; for, Adam had necessarily to be restored in Christ; that mortality be absorbed by immortality and Eve in Mary; that a Virgin became the advocate of a virgin should undo and destroy virginal disobedience by virginal obedience."[39]

According to Luigi Gambero, this text, preserved in Armenian, "seems to indicate the word might have been *parakletos,* whose meaning is 'defender, comforter, advocate.' In fact, in another passage the author applies the title *parakletos* to the Holy Spirit with a meaning that seems to be in opposition to the term 'prosecutor.'"[40]

That early Christians already were invoking Mary as a powerful intercessor is seen clearly by about the third century. A prayer preserved in a papyrus that was discovered in the John Rylands library of Manchester in 1917, gives the first instance of a prayer addressed to Mary that bears witness to belief in Mary's intercessory power and her being a source of protection in the face of life's trials and temptations. The prayer, known as the *Sub Tuum Praesidium,* refers to Mary as the Mother of God in

---

[38] St. Irenaeus, *Adversus Haereses* 5, 19, 1, *PG* 7, 1175-1176; The Ante-Nicene Fathers, 1:547.
[39] Cf. L. Gambero, *Mary and the Fathers of the Church,* p. 55.
[40] L. Gambero, "Patristic Intuitions," p. 93.

whom we find protection ("Under your mercy we fly for refuge"). The prayer then asks Mary to hear our prayers ("despise not our petitions in our necessities") and asks Mary to "deliver us always from all dangers"—echoing the petition from the "Our Father" and in fact using the same word for deliver (*rysai*) from that prayer (cf. Mt 6:13).[41]

The testimony of Mary's role as Advocate continued to unfold with greater clarity and elaboration throughout the centuries. St. Ephraim described Mary as "the friendly advocate of sinners."[42] St. Germanus of Constantinople describes Mary's advocacy role: "For, just as in your Son's presence you have a mother's boldness and strength, do you wish your prayers and intercessions save and rescue us from eternal punishment, for we have been condemned by our sins and do not dare even to lift our eyes to heaven above."[43] St. Romanus the Singer envisioned Mary addressing Adam and Eve, saying "Cease your lamentations, I shall be your advocate with my Son."[44]

The twelfth-century liturgical antiphon *Salve Regina* portrays Mary as the Advocate interceding on our behalf: "…To thee we cry out, poor banished children of Eve; to thee we send up our sighs, mourning and weeping in this valley of tears. Turn then, O most gracious Advocate, thine eyes of mercy toward us, and after this our exile, show unto us the blessed fruit of thy womb, Jesus. O clement, O loving, O sweet Virgin Mary." Around this period, St. Bernard of Clairvaux refers to Mary's role as Advocate in his *De Aqueductu*: "You wish to have an advocate with him [Christ]? … Have recourse to Mary." He beautifully pleads for Mary to be our Advocate before Jesus in his second sermon for Advent "Our Lady, our Mediatrix, our Advocate, reconcile us to your Son, commend us to your Son, represent us before your Son."[45]

---

[41] See M. O'Carroll, *Theotokos*, p. 326.
[42] St. Ephraim, *S. Ephraiem Syri testim. De B.V.M. meditatione, Ephemeredes Theologicae Lovanienses*, IV, fasc. 2, 1927. As cited in M. Miravalle, *Mary: Coredemptrix, Mediatrix, Advocate* (Santa Barbara: Queenship Publishing, 1993) p. 63.
[43] St. Germanus of Constantinople, *Homily on the Cincture* PG 98, 380 D-381 A. As translated in L. Gambero, *Mary and the Fathers of the Church*, p. 388.
[44] St. Romanus the Singer, *Homily on the Nativity*, II, SC 110, 100. As translated by M. O'Carroll, "Advocate" in *Theotokos*, p. 6.
[45] *De Aqueduc*, 7 ed. J. Leclercq. V, 279. As translated by M. O'Carroll, in *Theotokos*, p. 6; PL 183, 43C.

Papal teaching from the sixteenth century onward has often used the title "Advocate" to describe Our Lady. Popes Leo X (in 1520), Sixtus V (in 1587), Clement IX (in 1667) and Clement XI (in 1708) all referred to Mary as Advocate.[46] In his 1805 Apostolic Constitution *Tanto Studio,* Pius VII explained how Mary's role as Advocate is more powerful than that of the saints by virtue of her being the Mother of Christ. "For, while the prayers of those in heaven have, it is true, some claim on God's watchful eye, Mary's prayers place their assurance in a mother's right. For that reason, when she approaches her divine Son's throne, as advocate she begs, as handmaid she prays, but as Mother she commands."[47] Pope St. Pius X, in his 1903 prayer "Virgine Sanctissima," links Mary's advocacy with her queenship and asks Mary to present our petitions before God to be protected from the snares of the Devil: "Ah! Do thou, our Blessed Mother, our Queen and Advocate ... do thou gather together our prayers and we beseech thee (our hearts one with thine) present them before God's throne."[48]

Pius XI also affirmed Mary's title as Advocate. In his 1928 Encyclical *Miserentissimus Redemptor,* he mentioned that Christ wished to make Mary "the advocate of sinners and dispenser and mediatrix of his grace."[49] Later, in a 1933 papal allocution, he showed how Mary's advocacy role is animated by the love between a mother and her son: "...though the grace comes from God, it is given through Mary, our advocate and mediatrix, since motherly affection on the one hand finds response in filial devotion on the other."[50]

Pius XII underscored the universal scope of Mary's role as Advocate. In a 1947 radio message to the National Marian Congress of Argentina, he notes that while the saints can intercede for our particular needs, Mary's intercession as Advocate can address more effectively *all* our

---

[46] Leo X, Bull *Pastoris Aeterni* (October 6, 1520); Sixtus V, Bull *Gloriosae* (June 8, 1587); Clement IX, Brief *Sincera Nostra* (October 21, 1667); Clement XI, Bull, *Commissi Nobis* (December 8, 1708). As Cited in M. O'Carroll, *Theotokos,* p. 6.

[47] Pius VII, Apostolic Constitution *Tanto Studio* (Feb. 19, 1805) in *Our Lady* (Boston: St. Paul Editions, 1961), p. 42.

[48] St. Pius X, prayer for the 50th anniversary of the definition of the Immaculate Conception, "O Most Holy Virgin" (Sept. 8, 1903) in *Our Lady,* p. 165.

[49] Pius XI, Encyclical *Miserentissimus Redemptor* (May 8, 1928) in *Our Lady,* p. 209.

[50] Pius XI, Papal Allocution to pilgrims present at the reading of the decree *de tuto* for the canonization of Bl. Antida Thouret (August 15, 1933) in *Our Lady,* p. 223.

needs. He quotes Francisco Suárez, S.J.: "We have the Virgin as universal advocate in all things, for she is more powerful in whatever necessity than are the other saints in particular needs."[51]

Vatican II affirmed the title Advocate in its Dogmatic Constitution on the Church, *Lumen Gentium*. First, the constitution relates Mary's intercession as flowing from her "maternal charity," by which she "cares for the brethren of her Son." *Lumen Gentium* then mentions the title Advocate: "Therefore, the Blessed Virgin is invoked in the Church under the titles of Advocate, Helper, Benefactress, and Mediatrix" (LG, 62).[52] The constitution goes on to explain that this title Advocate (and the other related titles) do not take away from or add to "the dignity and efficacy of Christ the one Mediator" (LG, 62). Finally, *Lumen Gentium* itself concludes with a call to Mary to intercede for the unity of the entire human family in Christ's Church:

> The entire body of the faithful pours forth urgent supplications to the Mother of God and of men that she, who aided the beginnings of the Church by her prayers, may now, exalted as she is above the angels and saints, intercede before her Son in the fellowship of all the saints, until all families of people … may be happily gathered together in peace and harmony into the one People of God (LG, 68).

We can see how Pope John Paul II reaffirmed Mary's role as Advocate at different points in his pontificate. For example, in his 1987 Encyclical, *Redemptoris Mater*, John Paul II notes how Mary intercedes for us, and quotes *Lumen Gentium's* teaching about the Church invoking Mary as Advocate (RM, 40, cf. LG, 62). And like *Lumen Gentium*, this encyclical also calls on Mary to pray for unity (RM, 30). Ten years later, as part of a series of general audience addresses on Mary, John Paul II taught that the Church, following Mary's example of intercession at Cana and at Pentecost, "learns to be bold in her asking, to persevere in her

---

[51] Pius XII, radio message to the National Marian Congress of Argentina (Oct. 12, 1947) in *Our Lady*, p. 280.
[52] *Vatican Council II: The Conciliar and Post-Conciliar Documents*, ed. A. Flannery (Collegeville: Liturgical Press, 1992).

intercession."[53] In a later address in 1997, he goes on to explicitly discuss the title "Advocate." He first quotes *Lumen Gentium's* affirmation of the title (in LG, 65). Second, he notes how the title goes back to St. Irenaeus, who described Mary's yes at the Annunciation as the moment she "became the Advocate" of Eve, freeing her "from the consequences of her disobedience, becoming the cause of salvation for herself and the whole human race." Third, he explains how Mary, as Advocate, works in union with her Son and the Holy Spirit to protect her spiritual children on earth:

> Mary exercises her role as "Advocate" by cooperating both with the Spirit (the Paraclete) and with the one who interceded on the Cross for his persecutors (cf. Lk 23:34), whom John calls our "advocate with the Father" (1 Jn 2:1). As a mother, Mary defends her children and protects them from the harm caused by their own sins.[54]

Queenship: Foundations in Tradition and Magisterium

Although the earliest Fathers of the Church did not explicitly give Mary the title "Queen," they did express the reality of her queenship in two ways.[55] First, some saw royal significance in Mary's name. For example, St. Jerome noted that Mary in Syriac can be translated as "*domina*,"[56] meaning Lady, or sovereign, indicating her dignity. Similarly, Peter Chrysologus held that Mary should be translated from the Hebrew as "*domina*."[57] Subsequent Western authors such as Eucher of Lyons, Isidore of Seville and Venerable Bede followed this approach when discussing Mary's royal position.[58]

---

[53] John Paul II, "Mary is a Model of Faith, Hope and Charity" general audience of September 10, 1997, in *Theotokos* (Boston: Pauline Books & Media, 2000).

[54] John Paul II, "Mary Has a Universal Spiritual Motherhood," general audience of September 24, 1997, in *Theotokos*.

[55] L. Gambero, "La Regalità di Maria nel Pensiero dei Padri," p. 435

[56] "Sciendumque quod Maria sermone Syro domina nuncupetur." Jerome, *Liber de Nominibus Hebraicis*, PL 23, 842. See also M. Donnelly, "The Queenship of Mary During the Patristic Period," p. 90.

[57] Peter Chrysologus, *Sermon 142*, PL 52, 579c.

[58] L. Gambero, "La Regalitá nel Pensiero dei Padri," pp. 441-442; M. Donnelly, "The Queenship of Mary During the Patristic Period," pp. 99-100.

On a more exegetical level, initial attention was given to Mary being called "the mother of my Lord" in the Visitation scene (Lk 1:43). For example, Clement of Alexandria, Jerome, Ambrose and Augustine all emphasized Mary being the *mater domini*.[59] With deeper reflection on what it meant for Mary to be the Mother of the Lord, there arose a deeper understanding of Mary being associated with Christ's kingship. Origen was one of the first to make this move, by referring to Mary as *kuria* in his commentary on this passage. Origen viewed Elizabeth's greeting of Mary with the words "Mother of my Lord" as honoring her with a royal dignity.[60] Similarly, St. Ephrem referred to Mary as "the Most Holy Sovereign Lady (*Domina*), Mother of God."[61] Jerome[62] and Augustine[63] also spoke of Mary's sovereignty.[64]

Another line of development can be seen in patristic references to Mary as the mother of the king.[65] With the New Testament bestowing on Jesus the title of king, it was easy for some Fathers to describe the Mother of Jesus as the mother of the king, thus linking her closely with Christ's royal status.[66] This set the stage for the title "queen" being used explicitly by later Church Fathers. Chrysippus of Jerusalem, for example,

---

[59] M. Donnelly, "The Queenship of Mary During the Patristic Period," p. 87.

[60] *Fragmenta Origenis, Ex Macarii Chrysocephali Orationibus in Lucam*, PG 13, 1902. "Cur me igitur prior salutas? Nunquid ego sum quae Salvatorem pario? Oportebat me ad te venire: tu enim super omnes mulieres benedicta: tu Mater Domini mei: tu mea Domina."

[61] Ephrem, *Ed. Assemani*, III, 524 as cited in M. Donnelly, "The Queenship of Mary During the Patristic Period," p. 87.

[62] Jerome, *Homilia in die Dom. Paschae*, ed. D. Morin, *Anecdota Maredsolan*, t. III, pars. II, p. 414 as cited by M. Donnelly, "The Queenship of Mary," p. 88.

[63] Augustine, *In Joannis Evangelium VIII*, PL 35, 1456.

[64] M. Donnelly, "The Queenship of Mary During the Patristic Period," p. 88. On the significance of this title "Domina," see G. Kirwin, *The Nature of the Queenship of Mary*, p. 39: "The name, 'Domina' indicates a great dignity and the fact that it is applied to Mary who is the Mother of the 'Dominus' leads us easily to the conclusion that she too is a sovereign."

[65] For example: Gregory of Nanzianzus, *Poemata Dogmatica*, PG 37, 485a; Hesychius, *de Sancta Maria Deipara Homilia*, PG 93, 1465-1468; Sedulius, *Opus Paschale*, PL 19, 599; cf., John Chrysostom, *In Annuntiationem Deiparae*, PG 62, 765.

[66] M. Donnelly, "The Queenship of Mary During the Patristic Period," pp. 88-89; L. Gambero, "La Regalità di Maria nel Pensiero dei Padri," pp. 438-441.

in his homily on Psalm 44, describes Mary as the *mother of the king*, who herself will be changed into a heavenly *queen*.[67]

As the early Church developed its understanding of basic Marian truths (especially after the Council of Ephesus), there arose greater reflection on the meaning and extent of Mary's queenship.[68] For example, Idelfonse of Toledo not only viewed Mary as a royal figure, but even placed himself as a servant of the queenly Mother of Jesus: "I am your servant, for your Son is my Lord. You are my Queen because you have become the handmaid of my King."[69] Andrew of Crete elaborated on Mary's royal office, describing her as being crowned in heaven and being the "*Regina universorum hominum*."[70] St. Germain of Constantinople referred to Mary as "Queen of the Universe,"[71] while John Damascene taught that she is queen because she is the Mother of the Creator,[72] and even went on to ask Mary to rule over his entire life.[73]

Moving into the medieval period, there was frequent mention of Mary's queenship by writers such as Peter Damian, Anselm, Eadmerus and Bernard of Clairvaux[74]—the latter two laying deeper theological foundations for the queenship in Mary's divine maternity and her unique cooperation in Christ's redemptive work.[75] This two-fold foundation was discussed more in subsequent centuries. For example, a famous medieval work, the *Mariale super missus est*, explained how Mary's queenship is based on her being the Mother of God and her being uniquely associated with Christ's triumph and royal reign in the kingdom.[76]

In this period, the nature and function of Our Lady's queenship were treated in more detail. Bernardine of Siena taught that Mary reigned over all creatures, including souls on earth, in purgatory and in heaven,

---

[67] Chrysippus of Jerusalem, *In S. Mariam Deiparam*, PO 93, 339.
[68] Cf. L. Gambero, "La regalità di Maria nel Pensiero dei Padri," p. 433.
[69] Idelfonse of Toledo, *Liber de Virginitate Perpetua S. Mariae*, PL 96, 106.
[70] Andrew of Crete, *In Dormitionem S. Mariae*, PG 97, 1107.
[71] Germain of Constantinople, *In Praesentationem SS. Deiparae I*, PG 98, 304.
[72] John Damascene, *De Fide Orthodoxa Lib. IV*, PG 96, 1157, 1162.
[73] John Damascene, *Homilia II in Dormitionem B.V. Mariae*, PG 96, 721.
[74] W. Hill, "Our Lady's Queenship in the Middle Ages and Modern Times," pp. 135-143.
[75] W. Hill, "Our Lady's Queenship," pp. 139, 143; F. Schmidt, "The Universal Queenship of Mary," p. 530.
[76] W. Hill, "Our Lady's Queenship," p. 148.

and even all devils.⁷⁷ The function of her royal office is to direct, protect and intercede—thus showing Mary's advocacy in relationship to her queenship.⁷⁸ A popular title for Mary in this period was "Queen of Mercy," which described her royal position in terms of her intercessory role.⁷⁹ At the same time, there were some suggestions that Mary is queen not only because of her intercessory influence at her Son's throne, but also in a formal and proper sense. This can be seen, for example, in the writings of Peter Canisius and the *Mariale*.⁸⁰

In the seventeenth century, there was increased emphasis on Mary's queenship in the strict, formal sense. Ferdinand de Salazar and Christopher de Vega treated Mary's queenship as having real power, with Mary having real reign over her subjects. Although subordinate to her Son, Mary truly rules with Christ the king. If a king receives his reign by natural right or by right of conquest, the parents participate in that reign. They concluded that since Mary was mother of the king and shared in her Son's victorious work of redemption, she was queen by natural right and right of conquest and therefore gained a share in her Son's royalty.⁸¹

Bartholomew de los Rios is another theologian of the period who stressed Mary's queenship as a real dominion. In scholastic fashion, he outlined the different kinds of royal authority and showed how all apply to Mary.⁸² These notions find themselves worked out in the eighteenth-century reflections on the spiritual dimension of Mary's queenship, as seen in St. Alphonsus Ligouri's *The Glories of Mary*, and St. Louis-Marie Grignion de Montfort's *True Devotion to Mary*.⁸³

Liturgical worship in both East and West attest to the queenship of Mary. For example, the non-Byzantine liturgies of the East mention Mary's queenship implicitly, in texts referring to her as "Lady" or "Our

---

[77] G. Kirwin, *The Nature of the Queenship of Mary*, p. 53. Conrad of Saxony drew a similar conclusion. F. Schmidt, "Universal Queenship of Mary," p. 531.

[78] G. Kirwin, *The Nature of the Queenship of Mary*, p. 53.

[79] W. Hill notes Bonaventure, the *Mariale*, Richard of St. Lawrence, Bernardine of Siena, and Denis the Carthusian as examples. W. Hill, "Our Lady's Queenship," pp. 146, 149-152.

[80] W. Hill, "Our Lady's Queenship," p. 153.

[81] G. Kirwin, *The Nature of the Queenship of Mary*, p. 55. W. Hill, "Our Lady's Queenship," pp. 159, 161.

[82] G. Kirwin, *The Nature of the Queenship of Mary*, p. 55. W. Hill, "Our Lady's Queenship," pp. 164-167.

[83] W. Hill, "Our Lady's Queenship," p. 168.

Lady." The Ethiopian Rite expresses the universal nature of Mary's reign, calling her "The Lady of us all."[84] The Byzantine liturgy often calls Mary "Queen." For the feast of the Dormition, Mary is honored as being set upon a throne and reigning with her Son.[85] Since the eleventh century, the West has honored Mary as queen quite explicitly in sacred songs. The great Marian hymns *Salve Regina* and *Ave, Regina Caelorum* (eleventh century) as well as the *Regina Caeli* (twelfth-thirteenth century) all express her queenly status and came to be part of the Church's liturgical worship.[86] Further witness to Mary's queenship is found in popular devotions such as the Rosary (the fifth Glorious Mystery), the Litany of Our Lady, which invokes Mary as "Queen" (Litany of Loreto),[87] and in sacred art, which has commonly depicted Mary with queenly imagery (seated on a throne, crowned, wearing royal clothes, surrounded by angels and saints venerating her, and even being crowned by her Son).[88] Such evidence from popular piety and sacred art reflects an understanding of Mary's royal status in the believing Church.

★ ★ ★

Although Mary's queenship was not an explicit topic of discussion in early magisterial teachings of the first millennium, a number of popes and councils referred to Mary as a queenly figure in passing. For example, the Third Council of Constantinople described Mary as Lady—"*despoina*"—a queenly title. In a letter to St. Germain, the patriarch of Constantinople, Pope Gregory II expressed the universality of Mary's queenship, calling her the ruler of all Christians who will triumph over enemies of the faith.[89] While defending the legitimacy of

---

[84] G. Kirwin, *The Nature of the Queenship of Mary*, pp. 62-63.
[85] G. Kirwin, *The Nature of the Queenship of Mary*, p. 63.
[86] E. Lodi, "Preghiera Mariana" in *Nuovo Dizionario di Mariologia*, eds. S. De Fiores & S. Meo (Milan: Edizioni San Paolo, 1996), p. 1029. C. O'Donnel, *At Worship with Mary: A Pastoral and Theological Study* (Wilmington, Delaware: Michael Glazier, 1988), p. 153.
[87] G. Besutti, "Litanie," in *Nuovo Dizionario di Mariologia*, eds., S. De Fiores & S. Meo (Milan: Edizioni San Paolo, 1996), p. 684.
[88] G. Kirwin, *The Nature of the Queenship of Mary*, pp. 40-41, 68-79. Pius XII, *Ad Caeli Reginam*, *AAS* 46 (1954) 632-633.
[89] E. Carroll, "Our Lady's Queenship in the Magisterium of the Church," pp. 38-39.

sacred images, the Second Council of Nicea referred to images of "our undefiled Lady (*dominae*), or holy Mother of God."[90]

In his constitution on the Immaculate Conception, *Cum Praecelsa* (1477), Pope Sixtus IV referred to Mary as "the Queen of Heaven, the glorious Virgin Mother of God, raised upon her heavenly throne."[91] Pope Benedict XIV's (1740-1758) papal bull *Gloriosae Dominae* (1748)[92] not only spoke of Mary as "Queen of heaven and earth," but also discussed how Christ grants to her "nearly all his empire and power."[93]

Turning to the nineteenth century, Pius IX's 1854 definition of Mary's Immaculate Conception (*Ineffabilis Deus*) described the universal extent of her queenship ("Queen of heaven and earth") and directly linked Mary's royal office with her intercessory power.[94]

Popes from the time of Leo XIII to John Paul II have continued to teach of Mary's queenship with increased frequency and precision. Leo XIII (1878-1903) referred to Mary as queen in several encyclicals and other teachings.[95] Pope St. Pius X (1903-14), in his Encyclical *Ad Diem Illum* (1904), based Mary's queenship on her unique participation in Christ's redemptive work.[96] Writing during World War I, Pope Benedict XV (1914-22) often entrusted the world to the protection of Mary "Queen of Peace."[97] Pope Pius XI (1922-39) entrusted the Church's missionary efforts to Mary "Queen of Apostles,"[98] and the unity of the Church was entrusted to Mary "the heavenly Queen."[99]

This brings us to Pope Pius XII (1939-58), who was described by one theologian as making Our Lady's queenship the Marian doctrine

---

[90] *Council of Nicea II* in *The Sources of Catholic Dogma*, ed. H. Denzinger (St. Louis: Herder, 1957), p. 121.
[91] E. Carroll, "Our Lady's Queenship," p. 41.
[92] Benedict XIV, *Gloriosae Dominae* (September 27, 1748) in *Our Lady*, pp. 25-29.
[93] Benedict XIV, *Gloriosae Dominae*, in *Our Lady*, p. 26.
[94] Pius IX, *Ineffabilis Deus* in *Our Lady*, p. 82.
[95] For example: *Supremi Apostolatus*, *ASS* 16 (1883) 116; *Octobri mense*, *ASS* 24 (1891-1892) 202; *Magnae Dei Matris*, *ASS* 25 (1892-1893) 140; *Laetitiae sanctae*, *ASS* 26 (1893-1894) 193; *Iucunda semper*, *ASS* 27 (1894-1895) 177; *Adiutricem populi*, *ASS* 28 (1895-1896) 129; *Fidentem piumque*, *ASS* 29 (1896-1897) 204. See E. Carroll, "Our Lady's Queenship," pp. 47-53.
[96] Pius X, *Ad Diem Illum*, *AAS* 36 (1903-1904) 454. See *Our Lady*, pp. 165-182.
[97] See E. Carroll, "Our Lady's Queenship," pp. 55-56.
[98] Pius XI, *Rerum Ecclesiae*, *AAS* 18 (1926) 83. Trans. from *Our Lady*, p. 207.
[99] Pius XI, *Lux Veritatis*, *AAS* 23 (1931) 515. Trans. from *Our Lady*, p. 218.

most illumined throughout his papal teachings.[100] His Encyclical *Mystici Corporis* refers to Mary as the "true Queen of Martyrs,"[101] and as reigning with her Son in heaven.[102] In the Apostolic Constitution *Munificentissimus Deus*, defining the Assumption, Pius XII mentions the queenship in his explanation of the Assumption: As the New Eve sharing in the suffering and victory of the New Adam, Mary "finally obtained, as the supreme culmination of her privileges that she should be preserved free from the corruption of the tomb and that, like her own Son, having overcome death, she might be taken up body and soul to the glory of heaven where, as Queen, she sits in splendor at the right hand of her Son, the immortal King of Ages."[103]

Pius XII offered the Magisterium's most extensive treatment on Mary's royal office in 1954, when he instituted the feast of the Queenship of Mary in the Encyclical *Ad Caeli Reginam*. Near the beginning of this document, the Pope explains that he does not intend to propose Mary's royal status as a *new* doctrine, but that he is reaffirming a truth held by the faithful for centuries and instituting a liturgical feast to promote that truth.[104] The encyclical discusses two theological foundations for Mary's royal office: her divine motherhood and her unique cooperation in her Son's work of salvation. The divine maternity is "the main principle" on which Mary's queenship rests.[105] Pius XII says "it is easily concluded that she is a queen, since she bore a son who, at the very moment of his

---

[100] "If we should wish to determine from the documents we have what truth Pius XII has above all illuminated in Our Lady, it seems no mistake to say: the queenship ... On this point the teaching of Pius XII far surpasses in richness and development that of his predecessors." D. Bertetto, "La Dottrina Mariana di Pio XII," *Salesianum* 11 (1949), pp. 22-23 as cited in E. Carroll, "Our Lady's Queenship," pp. 61-62. Note how this statement was made about Pius XII even before the definition of the Assumption and his encyclical on Mary's queenship, *Ad Caeli Reginam*!

[101] Pius XII, *Mystici Corporis*, AAS 35 (1943) 248.

[102] *AAS* 35 (1943) 248.

[103] *AAS* 42 (1950) 768-769. Trans. from *Papal Teachings*, p. 318.

[104] Pius XII, *Ad Caeli Reginam*, AAS 46 (1954) 626-627. For more extensive treatments on this encyclical, see: N. Peña, "La Encíclica 'Ad Caeli Reginam,'" *EphMar* 46 (1996), pp. 485-501; M. Peinador, "Propedeutica a la Encyclica 'Ad Caeli Reginam,'" *EphMar* 5 (1955), pp. 291-316; G. Roschini, "Breve commento all'Enciclica 'Ad Caeli Reginam,'" *Marianum* 16 (1954), pp. 409-432.

[105] *AAS* 46 (1954) 633. Trans. from *Ad Caeli Reginam*, 34 in *The Papal Encyclicals*.

conception, because of the hypostatic union of the human nature with the Word, was also as man King and Lord of all things."[106] However, since Christ is king not only by natural right, but also by his salvific work, Mary in a similar way is queen not only by her divine motherhood, but also by her unique cooperation in Christ's work of redemption. Describing her cooperation in redemption as a second basis for Mary's queenship, Pius XII, quoting Suárez, teaches

> For "just as Christ, because he redeemed us, is our Lord and king by a special title, so the Blessed Virgin also (is our Queen), on account of the unique manner in which she assisted in our redemption, by giving of her own substance, by freely offering him for us, by her singular desire and petition for, and active interest in, our salvation."[107]

The encyclical then expounds on the two-fold meaning of Mary's queenship. First, Pius XII says it is a "queenship of excellence." "Hence, it cannot be doubted that Mary Most Holy is far above all other creatures in dignity, and after her Son possesses primacy over all."[108] This unique dignity flows from Mary's Immaculate Conception. Citing Pope Pius IX's *Ineffabilis Deus*, Pius XII notes how Mary, from the first moment of her conception, was filled with every heavenly grace and thus possessed a fullness of innocence and holiness to be found nowhere outside of God.[109]

Second, her queenship is one of "efficacy." This refers to Mary's real share in Christ's influence over humanity. As queen, Mary has "a share in that influence by which he, her Son and our Redeemer, is rightly said to reign over the minds and wills of men."[110] The encyclical explains this royal power of Mary in the context of her role in the "distribution of graces"[111] through her motherly intercession—again linking Mary's queenship with her advocacy.

---

[106] *Ibid.*
[107] *AAS* 46 (1954) 634. Trans. from *Ad Caeli Reginam*, 36 in *The Papal Encyclicals*.
[108] *AAS* 46 (1954) 635. Trans. from *Ad Caeli Reginam*, 40 in *The Papal Encyclicals*.
[109] *AAS* 46 (1954) 636.
[110] *AAS* 46 (1954) 636. Trans. from *Ad Caeli Reginam*, 42 in *The Papal Encyclicals*.
[111] *AAS* 46 (1954) 637. Trans. from *Ad Caeli Reginam*, 42 in *The Papal Encyclicals*.

> With a heart that is truly a mother's ... does she approach the problem of our salvation, and is solicitous for the whole human race; made *Queen* of heaven and earth by the Lord, exalted above all choirs of angels and saints, and standing at the right hand of her only Son, Jesus Christ, our Lord, she *intercedes* powerfully for us with a mother's prayers, obtains what she seeks, and cannot be refused.[112]

Vatican II, in the Dogmatic Constitution *Lumen Gentium*, explicitly refers to Mary as "Queen over all things," linking it to her Immaculate Conception and Assumption (LG, 59). Later, the document alludes to Mary's royal status by speaking of her being "exalted above all angels and men to a place second only to her Son, as the most holy Mother of God who was involved in the mysteries of Christ: she is rightly honored by a special cult in the Church" (LG, 66).

In Pope Paul VI's Apostolic Exhortation *Marialis Cultus*, he explicitly treats the feast of Mary's queenship, showing its link with the solemnity of the Assumption of Mary. Here, he explains how in the revised liturgical calendar the Solemnity of the Assumption is prolonged in the celebration of Mary's queenship, which occurs seven days later. And he does so in a way that links Mary's queenship with her advocacy role of interceding before her Son on our behalf: "On this occasion we contemplate her who, seated beside the King of ages, shines forth as *Queen* and *intercedes* as Mother" (MC, 6).[113]

A significant development on Mary's queenship can be seen in Pope John Paul II's *Redemptoris Mater*. While re-affirming the teaching of Pius XII and Vatican II, and associating Mary's queenly position with her Assumption, the Pope then expounds upon a new emphasis: he places Mary's exalted queenship in the context of her humble service in the kingdom. Peña notes three principal ideas set forth by John Paul II along these lines. The Pope first illustrates how Mary's exalted royal office must be understood in relation to Christ's *kenosis* and royal exaltation. Christ himself humbly served even to the point of death

---

[112] Emphasis added. *AAS* 46 (1954) 636-637. Trans. from *Ad Caeli Reginam*, 42 in *The Papal Encyclicals*.

[113] Emphasis added. *AAS* 66 (1974) 121. Trans. from *Marialis Cultus*, 6 (Boston: St. Paul's Editions, 1974).

and was therefore raised and entered into the glory of his kingdom, exalted as Lord over all (cf. Phil 2:8-9). The Pope discusses the gospels' portrayal of the true disciple who will reign in the kingdom as the one who follows Christ's example through service: "to serve means to reign!" (RM, 41).[114] In this regard, the Pope notes how Mary is the model disciple. At the Annunciation, she called herself the "handmaid of the Lord" and lived out this title throughout her life. She is the first disciple who served Christ in others and led them to him. This is the basis of her queenship: "Mary, the handmaid of the Lord, has a share in this Kingdom of the Son" (RM, 41).[115]

Secondly, the Pope shows how Mary's queenship continues to be based on her servanthood, even in heaven. "The *glory of serving* does not cease to be her royal exaltation: assumed into heaven, she does not cease her saving service, which expresses her maternal mediation 'until the eternal fulfillment of all the elect'" (RM, 41).[116]

Thirdly, John Paul II also shows the ecclesial dimension of Mary's unique royal privilege, placing it in the context of the Communion of Saints who all participate in Christ's reign. "Thus in her Assumption into heaven, Mary is as it were clothed by the whole reality of the Communion of Saints, and her very union with the Son in glory is wholly oriented towards the definitive fullness of the Kingdom, *when 'God will be all in all'*" (RM, 41).[117]

Theological Conclusions and Applications

In summary, our exploration of the Biblical foundations for Mary as Queen and Advocate has demonstrated the important role of the queen mother in the Old Testament Davidic kingdom: she had a real participation in the reign of her son, served as a counselor to her son and most especially, served as an advocate for the people, bringing their petitions to the king. Then we have seen how the New Testament

---

[114] *AAS* 79 (1987) 417. Trans. from *Redemptoris Mater*, 41 (Boston: Pauline Books, 1987).

[115] *AAS* 79 (1987) 417. Trans. from *Redemptoris Mater*, 41 (Boston: Pauline Books, 1987). See N. Peña, "La Encíclica 'Ad Caeli Reginam,'" p. 499.

[116] *AAS* 79 (1987) 417. John Paul II *Redemptoris Mater*, 41 (Boston: Pauline Books, 1987).

[117] *AAS* 79 (1987) 418. Trans. from *Redemptoris Mater*, 41 (Boston: Pauline Books, 1987). See N. Peña, "La Encíclica 'Ad Caeli Reginam,'" p. 499.

portrays Mary in ways that recall this queen-mother tradition, thus presenting Mary as the new Queen Mother and Advocate in Christ's kingdom. Next, we have seen how the Church's understanding of Mary as Queen and Advocate emerged in the early Church, and has deepened and developed throughout the centuries in her Tradition and magisterial teachings. Now, we will briefly consider some ways the biblical queen-mother theme can shed light on certain aspects of Mary's position as Advocate and Queen.

The queen-mother background offers strong Biblical support for Mary's intercessory role as Advocate. Since the queen mother served as an Advocate, bringing petitions from the people to the king, the fact that the New Testament presents Mary as the new Queen Mother in Christ's kingdom indicates that, from a scriptural perspective, Mary should be understood as our Advocate, interceding for us citizens in the Kingdom of her Son.

The queen-mother background also underscores the Christological basis of Mary's titles as Queen and Advocate. As Vatican II taught, Mary's queenly and intercessory role should be seen in their relationship with Christ—as dependent upon him and subordinate to him (cf. LG, 62), and as a participation in his reign (cf. LG, 59). The queen-mother theme highlights exactly this point. Just as the queen mother's royal office and advocacy role in the Davidic kingdom was completely dependent on her son's reign as king, so too Mary's position as Queen Mother and her ability to exercise that office through intercession as our Advocate is completely dependent on Christ and his kingship.

Mary's queenship and advocacy being thus seen as a participation in Christ' kingship will further highlight how it is not merely an honorific title, but a real queenship, with real power, rooted in humility, service, and sacrifice. The kingdom in which Mary reigns—the kingdom of Christ—is presented in the Scriptures as very different from the kingdoms of this earth. Christ's kingship "is not of this world" (Jn 18:36), and it is not based on political, militaristic or economic power. While rulers of worldly kingdoms "lord it over" their subjects, Christ exercises his reign through humility and becoming a servant, even to the point of giving his life as a ransom for many (Mt 20:25-28; Phil 2:5-11). Furthermore, the New Testament describes how because of his humble service Christ is exalted by the Father and enthroned over all things (Heb

1:9, 13), victorious over the enemies of sin (Heb 1:3), the Devil (Heb 2:14) and death (1 Cor 15:24).[118] This abasement-exaltation of Christ is seen especially in Philippians 2:5-11, which describes how every knee shall bend to Christ and every tongue shall confess him as Lord, but also emphasizes that his supreme exaltation flows from his abasement, becoming a slave, being obedient unto death, death on a cross.

All this is important because Mary is portrayed in the New Testament as a person who exemplifies this Christ-like abasement-exaltation pattern. She is described as a humble servant of the Lord (Lk 1:38, 48); she is the first who obediently hears God's word and accepts it (Lk 1:38, 45; Lk 11:27-28), and she perseveres even unto the greatest human suffering, second only to her divine Son (Lk 2:34-35; Jn 19:25-27).[119] And it is precisely in her lowliness as the Lord's servant that God has exalted her (Lk 1:46-55). In this light, one can conclude that the life of Mary is a testimony to the kingdom of God, and it is through her humble, obedient service that she has a share in Christ's reign, reigning with him over the powers of sin and death.[120]

This is the proper context for understanding the meaning of Mary's queenship. Mary's royal position, when viewed through the Biblical view of the kingdom, will be seen in light of the way she imitates Christ's reign through humble service, obedience to God and persevering faith. As Pope John Paul II has taught in *Redemptoris Mater*, this perseverance of Mary as "the handmaid of the Lord" is an important basis for understanding her queenship in the kingdom of Christ.

> In this she confirmed that she was a true "disciple" of Christ, who strongly emphasized that his mission was one of service: the Son of Man "came not to be served but to serve, and to give his life as a ransom for many" (Mt 20:28). In this way Mary became the first of those who, "serving Christ also in others, with humility and patience lead their brothers and sisters to that King whom to serve is to reign," and she fully obtained that "state

---

[118] A. Serra, "Regina," p. 1076.
[119] See C. O'Donnell, *Life in the Spirit and Mary* (Wilmington, Delaware: Michael Glazier, 1981), p. 45. Cf., *idem.*, *At Worship with Mary*, pp. 153-154.
[120] S. De Fiores, *Maria nel Mistero di Cristo*, p. 89.

of royal freedom" proper to Christ's disciples: to serve means to reign! (RM, 41)[121]

This also sheds light on the ecclesial dimension of Mary's queenship. The Scriptures attest that Christ promised *all* his faithful disciples a share in his reign. The New Testament describes how those disciples who have been willing to give up everything and follow Christ will "sit on thrones judging the twelve tribes of Israel" (Mt 19:28-30). Anyone who hears Christ's voice and "opens the door" will sit with him on his throne (Rev 3:20-21). His disciples who have continued with him through trials will rule over the new Israel (Lk 22:28-30), and those who will die with him will reign with him (2 Tim 2:11-12).

Mary certainly meets the Biblical criteria for reigning with Christ.[122] From the Annunciation to Pentecost, Mary is portrayed as a model disciple who heard God's word and accepted it (Lk 1:38, 45; 8:21; 11:27-28), and persevered throughout her life (Acts 1:14), following Christ even through the torment of her Son's death (Lk 2:34-35; Jn 19:25-27). Thus, having been a true disciple of Christ, it is fitting that she would share in the reign Christ promised all of his disciples.

One Mariologist has noted how this Biblical understanding of Christ's kingdom also places Mary's queenship more clearly in the context of the royalty of the whole people of God, highlighting the ecclesial dimension of her royal office:

> The insertion of the queenship of the Virgin in the context of the royal office of the people of God (1 Pet 2:9; Rev 1:6; 5:9; 20:4-6), while not detaching the person of Mary from the ecclesial community, helps to understand better the significance of Mary's queenship and its meaning for Christians today.[123]

Mary's queenship is not something far removed from the Christian life, an exalted position in heaven that we are to honor only from a distance. "She is not an isolated and extraneous figure, but one who,

---

[121] *AAS* 79 (1987) 417. John Paul II, *Redemptoris Mater*, 41 (Boston: Pauline Books & Media, 1987).
[122] A. Serra, "Regina," pp. 1074-1075.
[123] See S. De Fiores, *Maria Presenza Viva nel Popolo di Dio* (Rome: Edizioni Monfortane, 1980), p. 58.

in communion with all Christians, participates in the same reign of Christ."[124] As such, Mary becomes "an example from within the people of God" of the destiny to which we are all called.[125] We can see in Mary a model of what all faithful disciples will become. Through imitating Mary's humble service as a faithful disciple of the Lord, we can hope to have a share in the same Kingdom of Christ that she does. In this light, we can see that Mary's queenship has great practical significance for Christians of all ages, of all cultures and in all states of life. As Pope John Paul II taught in an Angelus exhortation in 1981:

> Therefore, fixing our gaze on the mystery of Mary's Assumption, of her "crowning" in glory, we daily learn to serve—to serve God in our brothers and sisters, to express in our attitude of service the "royalty" of our Christian vocation in every state or profession, in every time and in every place. To carry over into the reality of our daily life through such an attitude the petition, "thy kingdom come," which we make every day in the Lord's Prayer to the Father.[126]

---

[124] S. De Fiores, *Maria Presenza Viva nel Popolo di Dio*, p. 59.

[125] M. Masciarelli, "Laici," in S. De Fiores and S. Meo, eds., *Nuovo Dizionario di Mariologia*, (Milan: Edizioni San Paolo, 1986), p. 659.

[126] Pope John Paul II, "To Serve is to Reign," Angelus Message at Castel Gandolfo (August 23, 1981) in *L'Osservatore Romano*, English edition, 35 (699) August 31, 1981, p. 3.

MARY, MOTHER AND MODEL OF THE CHURCH

Fr. Enrique Llamas, O.C.D.

Two titles, two parts: Mary, mother and model, are two titles and two distinct concepts, although related to each other. One characteristic of a mother, even in the natural order, is to be a model and example for her children. Because these two concepts are formally distinct, I have divided this study into two parts:

I. Mary, Mother of the Church—Mary's Spiritual Maternity.
II. Mary as Model of the Church—Her Exemplarity vis-a-vis the Church.

The relationship between these two titles or concepts is radically based in nature itself. The essential character of a mother makes her ever an example, and for her own children potentially the most perfect example. If she has given them their very being, it is only normal her example should exert a profound influence on everything which pertains to their perfection. If *filii matrizant*—as the old maxim goes [children resemble their mothers]—it is only logical that their mother be their example and model, obviously in the physical order, but especially in the moral order.

This observation is perfectly applicable to spiritual and supernatural realities. Mary as Mother of Grace, is also model and paradigm for all the children of God as they strive for the highest levels of perfection. Hence, it is quite reasonable to hold that in the supernatural order there exists a positive, dynamic influence of this Mother over her children, and in them an attraction towards their Mother. In a rightly ordered world, this is the natural, mutual relationship which should be found among those who participate in the same life, the same nature. All the more so should this be the case in the realm of grace and supernatural life.

Part One: Mary, Mother of the Church

Introduction

Mary is essentially a Mother. She was predestined from all eternity, included in the very decree of the Incarnation, to be the Mother of the Son of God made man. In that predestination is included not only her physical or biological maternity in relation to her Son, but also her spiritual maternity in regard to all the redeemed children of God, the disciples of her Son. We shall return to this point further on.

All of God's children, redeemed by Jesus' blood, death and Resurrection, constitute the family of God which is the Church. Mary is thus, at the same time, Mother of the Church, of the people of God, of the pastors and the faithful.

This title, Mary, Mother of the Church, was solemnly proclaimed by Pope Paul VI on November 21, 1964, at the closing ceremony of the third session of Vatican II.

> For the glory of the Blessed Virgin Mary and our own consolation, we declare most Holy Mary Mother of the Church, that is of the whole Christian people, both faithful and pastors, who call her a most loving Mother; and we decree that henceforth the whole Christian people should, by this most sweet name, give still greater honor to the Mother of God and address prayers to her.[1]

With this proclamation Paul VI did not create out of nothing the fact of Mary's maternity in relation to the Church. This title sums up and synthesizes a well-known doctrine, acknowledged by the Church since the Middle Ages, and for many centuries expressly taught by the living Magisterium.[2]

---

[1] Paul VI, discourse at closing ceremony of the third session of Vatican II, Nov. 21, 1964: *Acta Synodalia Sacrosancti Concilii Vaticani II*, vol. III, pars VIII, p. 916.

[2] I refer here to the antiquity and origin of the title: *Mother of the Church*, and not to the antiquity of the doctrine, as old as the Church itself. Cf. the research of: Domenico Bertetto, *Maria, Mater Ecclesiae*, in *Salesianum*, 27 (1965), 3-64; Idem, *Maria, Madre della Chiesa*, Catania 1965; D. Fernández, *Orígenes históricos de la expresión "Mater Ecclesiae,"* in *Ephemerides Mariologicae*, 32 (1982), 189-200.

Paul VI, by the authority of his Ordinary, Supreme Magisterium, solemnly proclaimed a truth universally known and accepted in the Church. Although this proclamation was carried out within a conciliar context, it was not the equivalent of a dogmatic definition as such. Nevertheless, it retains the full doctrinal value of a solemn action of the Ordinary Magisterium of the Church. Pope Paul implicitly recognized and accepted a teaching transmitted to us by the Tradition of the Church. Further, he interpreted and, as it were, complemented a document of Vatican II: the Dogmatic Constitution *Lumen Gentium*, and by his papal authority reaffirmed a conciliar act binding on all, even though not a solemn dogmatic definition.[3]

Spiritual Maternity

The title, *Mary, Mother of the Church*, is itself a solemn recognition of Mary's spiritual maternity, as such and in its universality, viz., as Mother of all those redeemed through her Son's love and obedience in fulfilling the will of his Father by his Passion and Resurrection. She is the Mother of God's people, Mother of the Mystical Body of Christ, including all generations. The Council's reticence regarding the use of this title does not as such in the least affect its doctrinal contents. That reticence rather was motivated by other factors, only incidentally related to this mystery.

Nor could it be otherwise, since the doctrine of Mary's spiritual maternity is something very old in the Tradition of the Church and most intimate to her life. "Nothing," José Antonio de Aldama says, "is more ancient in Catholic doctrine than addressing the Blessed Virgin Mary as Mother of men."[4]

---

[3] Here we must take into account and distinguish the formulation of the title as such, *Mary, Mother of the Church*, and its contents. Although the Council did not in fact include the formulation of this title in its documents, it does teach the doctrine as a universal teaching of the Church. The posture adopted by the Council in this instance does not seem entirely logical or consistent; hence, it does not seem permissible to deduce from this a degree of hesitation in the Council about affirming the doctrine. The doctrinal aspect should not be confused with a posture which may be the fruit of external prudence. See D. Bertetto, *Maria, la Serva del Signore. Trattato di Mariologia*, Naples 1988, pp. 552-553.

[4] "Nihil antiquius est in doctrina catholica, quam B(eatam) Mariam Virginem appellare Matrem hominum." (J.A. de Aldama, *Mariología, seu de Matre Redemptoris*, in *Sacrae Theologiae Summa*, Madrid 1961, vol. III, p. 409, n. 132). This affirmation is to be understood in the sense according to which supernatural spiritual life is

From the time of St. Irenaeus, and even before, precisely within the context of the doctrine about Mary as co-worker with her Son in the redemption, and thereafter in perfect harmony with the progressive elaboration of ecclesiology, Mary has been called *Mother of the Church*. Before the 1950s, this custom never created any difficulties of a doctrinal kind. After the mid-twentieth century, however, the relations between Mary and the Church were explained by way of a *parallelism* between the two, one involving both maternity and exemplarity on a par.

Eventually it was realized that spiritual maternity did not fully fit this approach, or did not fully correspond to the canons of a strict *parallelism* between Mary and the Church. Mary's spiritual maternity far surpasses, and in Mary evidently indicates, a certain superiority which in some way or under some aspect is beyond question. Thus, as ecumenism gathered momentum, especially during the time of Vatican II (1962-1965), some participants in that Council, in favor of an ecclesio-typical approach in Mariology, objected to introducing the title *Mary, Mother of the Church*, into the documents of the Council. They claimed that title would constitute an obstacle or be a source of difficulties for the Council in achieving one of its primary goals, the promotion of ecumenism. Monsignor Philips, Professor at Louvain University, with a bit of graphic overkill, describes the advent of ecclesio-typology in the Mariological world as "being hit by a comet's tail."[5]

Leaving aside considerations bearing on many other aspects and questions touching the relationship of Mary and the Church, we now turn our attention to the theological-Mariological analysis of Mary's spiritual maternity as expressed in the title *Mother of the Church*.

---

communicated through grace to souls by an action called maternal. At root, his is the action of Mary, associated with her son in the work of redemption, where she acted as mother Co-redemptrix.

[5] Msgr. G. Philips, who lived the movements, atmosphere and controversies of those years and who also together with the Franciscan, Fr. Carlo Balic, President of the International Pontifical Marian Academy of Rome, redacted the text of *Lumen Gentium*, ch. 8, gave his opinion about *Mary, Mother of the Church* before Vatican II: "The issue of a parallelism between Mary and the Church arose in contemporary theology before 1964 like an unexpected lightning bolt. Al. Müller has compared its appearance in the world of Mariology to a comet" (G. Philips, *Marie et l'Eglise*, in H. de Manoir, *Maria. Etudes sur la Sainte Vierge*, t. VII, Paris 1964, p. 365).

Methodology and Execution

Spiritual maternity is not to be conceived as a substantive reality like sanctifying grace. It is rather a quality, a role, a responsibility, in Latin *munus*, that Mary, Mother of God, fulfilled according to the designs of God—and still fulfills—in the history of salvation in relation to men. It is in itself a general function enveloping and including other activities with a more specialized and restricted significance. Yet, because Mary's presence in the Church is primarily a *maternal presence*, as Pope John Paul II declared,[6] all of these subordinate roles possess a basic maternal tint or character.

Just as the divine motherhood is an essential factor determining what moves the Virgin Mary to act always and in all matters as Mother of God, so her spiritual maternity also moves her to act always and in all matters as Mother of the redeemed because she is Mother of the Church. Her presence in the mystery of Christ and of the Church is at every moment a *maternal presence*.

Now, this spiritual maternity, when exercised and in its concrete realization, takes on diverse modalities. Considered as maternal collaboration with her Son in the redemption of the human race, it appears as coredemptive maternity. Considered as "salvific influence over men" in the Church, as did Pope John Paul II, it appears as *mediatory* maternity or maternal *mediation*.[7] Finally, considered in reference to the graces granted, the exercise of her maternity is equivalent to *intercession* for and *distribution* of graces.

Mariologists and authors of Mariological manuals employ various methodologies in the treatment of this theme. Some authors study it in a *relative* form. If they consider this relation as a union with, or connection to other mysteries, they treat the question in terms of these fundamental

---

[6] John Paul II, *Redemptoris Mater*, March 25, 1987. The Pope entitles the third part *Marian Mediation*, but in other important writings he calls it maternal presence. Thus, in his homily for the inauguration of the Marian Year at St. Peter's Basilica, Pentecost, June 6, 1987, he says: "The Bishop of Rome joins the rest of his brothers in the episcopate, in order to deepen in the whole Church, within the perspective of the Marian Year, awareness of the *maternal presence* of the Mother of God" (*Insegnamenti di Giovanni Paolo II*, X/2, Vatican City 1988, pp. 2005-06, n. 6). Cf. my study: Enrique Llamas, La *"mediación materna" de María en la Encíclica "Redemptoris Mater,"* in *Estudios Marianos*, 61 (1995), pp. 149-180.

[7] John Paul II, *Redemptoris Mater*, third part, nos. 38 ff.

themes: *coredemption, mediation, distribution of graces*, etc. This is how, after a preliminary explanation, José Antonio de Aldama approaches the theme.[8]

Spiritual maternity can also be considered directly as such, by treating it as a particular question with theological meaning and content in its own right, one embracing and including the aforementioned aspects as relative to itself. It is to *spiritual maternity* as a theological question in its own right that Vatican II refers when it states:

> This motherhood of Mary in the economy of grace continues uninterruptedly from the consent in faith, which she loyally gave at the Annunciation and which she sustained without wavering beneath the Cross, until the eternal fulfillment of all the elect.[9]

To what kind of spiritual maternity was the Council referring in this passage? Was it not to spiritual maternity as a specific, singular quality unfolding from the Annunciation unto Calvary, one still continuing in the Church until the end of time? Certainly, spiritual maternity here is that maternity as such, even if from a didactic and conceptual point of view we may consider it in relation to different stages in the history of salvation with which the various aspects of that maternity correspond. As I understand this text, these aspects correspond to specific, concrete exercises of spiritual maternity, which at this stage of the history of salvation Vatican II equates with the *multiple intercession* of Mary whereby we obtain *the gifts of eternal salvation*.[10]

Fr. Domenico Bertetto, S.D.B., in his book *Mary, Handmaid of the Lord*, takes a more personal approach. He frames the broad and complex mystery of spiritual maternity within the general theme of *Mary in the mystery of the Church*. He explains Mary's spiritual maternity in terms

---

[8] "Cum hac spirituali maternitate intime connectuntur, uno vel alio modo, corredemptio, dispensatio gratiarum, et universalis mediatio. Disputatur vero inter theologos quo ordine haec munera logice inter se connectuntur.": J.A. de Aldama, *Mariología…*, cit., p. 408, n. 131. He goes on to explain various theories regarding the relative priority of these privileges: coredemption, mediation, etc.

[9] *Lumen Gentium*, 62 [hereafter abbreviated: LG].

[10] LG 62: "[Mary] taken up into heaven, did not lay aside this saving office but by her manifold intercession continues to bring us the gifts of eternal salvation." "Saving office" in this text is termed "motherhood of Mary" earlier in LG.

of a *relationship* to four points of reference: 1) efficacy; 2) relevance; 3) exemplarity; 4) finality.[11] Each of these terms corresponds to one of the fundamental aspects of Mary's spiritual maternity.[12]

But before any further consideration is undertaken, it seems to me that a preliminary, general question concerning methodology in the study of Mary's spiritual maternity as a theological question in its own right must be raised. Prior to any of the foregoing remarks, we must take as central to this methodology the analogy between spiritual and divine maternity, and the role which spiritual maternity plays in the general outline of Mariology. Just as the divine maternity is the starting point for considering Mary in relation to Christ, so spiritual maternity in itself is the starting point for considering Mary in relation to Christ and to the Church.

My Approach

From a theological and methodological viewpoint the spiritual maternity should be considered as a quality, prerogative or permanent condition of the Virgin Mary as a person, as a supernatural gift, a grace bestowed by the Father of mercies so that Mary might become Mother of all the redeemed. Thus, Mary as spiritual Mother of all her Son's disciples, frames every other aspect of this grace: its origin, important moments, forms and aspects. This maternity is a permanent, well-determined modality of her existence, and confers on her a singular dignity and special role within the life of the Church: to be Mother of the Church.

This prerogative finds its basis in several events of salvation history, *historia salutis*. First, by her participation in the mystery of the Incarnation as Mother of the Redeemer and the redeemed; and second, by her effective collaboration with her Son in the redemption of the human

---

[11] D. Bertetto, *Maria, la Serva* ..., cit., pp. 471 ff.
[12] Authoritative theologians do not agree about the logical arrangement or determination of priorities among these various privileges. In my opinion, priority belongs to the collaboration of Mary with her son in the work of redemption, viz., coredemptive maternity; it seems to me to be the basis of all the rest. I think that Vatican II favors this opinion in saying that Mary during different stages of her life "in a wholly singular way cooperated by her obedience, faith, hope and ardent charity in the work of the Savior to restore supernatural life in souls. For this reason she is our Mother in the order of grace" (LG 61).

race from his birth until his death on the Cross. Nor should we overlook what Vatican II teaches in this regard:

> The Blessed Virgin ... in the designs of divine providence was the gracious Mother of the divine Redeemer here on earth, and above all others and in a singular way generous associate and humble handmaid of the Lord. She conceived, brought forth, and nourished Christ, she presented him to the Father in the Temple, shared her Son's sufferings as he died on the Cross. Thus, in a wholly singular way she cooperated by her obedience, faith, hope and burning charity in the work of the Savior in restoring supernatural life to souls. For this reason she is a Mother to us in the order of grace.[13]

This prerogative or permanent quality of Mary, her spiritual maternity, serves as point of reference for all other questions which might be raised. It is a general reality, whether understood functionally or as a *mission* to accomplish. It is the point of departure and a general presupposition for all specific aspects and questions to be proposed. This spiritual maternity is the maternity Jesus proclaimed from the Cross: "*Woman, behold, your son*" (cf. Jn 19:25-27). It is a maternity, on which converge, and from which are to be contemplated, all other aspects and particular questions: forms and modalities of spiritual maternity, mother of the Church, mother and mediator, mother who intercedes, spiritual maternity as a "maternal presence" in the Church, in the terminology of John Paul II.[14]

Elsewhere[15] I have expounded in considerable detail these general aspects just summarized, which for the rest have been the subject of countless studies over the past half-century.[16]

---

[13] LG 61.
[14] Cf. my study: E. Llamas, *La mediación mariana de María en la Encíclica "Redemptoris Mater,"* cit., pp. 149-180.
[15] Cf. *ibid*.
[16] Bibliography on this subject during the past 50 years is very abundant. Because of its singular interest, I cite only the study of Jean Marie Salgado, *La Maternité Spirituelle de la trés Sainte Vierge Marie*, Vatican City 1990. The author has published many other historical and doctrinal studies.

The specific objective of this study is an analysis of three very important and singular moments in the exercise and unfolding of Mary's spiritual maternity. These are: 1) the mystery of the Incarnation; 2) Calvary, 3) the wedding feast of Cana.

These three moments constitute the principal foundation for the title, *Mary, Mother of the Church*, when the Mother is not only acting as the *potior pars* [preeminent part] of the Church—after Christ, Head of the Mystical Body—but is the most perfect and eminent personalization and representation of the Church. She is the New Eve who represents with her Son, the New Adam, the entire human family reborn, the Church of God.

Mary, Mother of the Church: Theological-Spiritual Development

General Consideration

The title, Mary, *Mother of the Church*, so gladly accepted by the people of God, does not appear as a positive recognition of the spiritual maternity of the Mother of God, of the Mother of Jesus the Redeemer, in the documents of Vatican II: this notwithstanding Pope Paul's manifest concern that the Council expressly accept and solemnly approve that title to the glory of the Blessed Mother and for the good of the Church. Still more, on December 4, 1963, the Pope made public his desire and hope, pleading as it were, that in its next session, the Council would expressly acknowledge the unique place occupied by the Mother of the Redeemer in the history of salvation and in the life of the Church: "The highest after that of Christ, and at the same time the closest to us, so that we might honor her with the title of 'Mother of the Church.' This would honor her and contribute to our consolation."[17]

The hope of Paul VI was frustrated by the negative attitude of a large number of Council Fathers. Paul VI at this time did not receive his hoped-for consolation. But surely from heaven the Virgin Mother would not deny him this, considering how strenuously he had labored to make known her dignity, her greatness, her sanctity, her spiritual beauty, and her divine and spiritual maternity.

---

[17] Paul VI, allocution during the second session of Vatican II, Dec. 4, 1963: AAS., 56 (1964), p. 37.

On this occasion, the Council's negative attitude did not reflect doctrinal considerations. Quite the contrary. The Council itself, in its Dogmatic Constitution on the Church, chapter 8, and in other related documents, very clearly teaches Mary's spiritual maternity in harmony with the content and meaning of the title, Mother of God.[18]

Despite the reticence of so many Council Fathers and the fact that the title, *Mary, Mother of the Church*, was not officially recognized in documents of the Council, its solemn proclamation by Pope Paul VI in St. Mary Major on November 21, 1964, at the conclusion of the third session of Vatican II, was roundly applauded:

> For the glory of the Blessed Virgin Mary and our own consolation, we declare most Holy Mary Mother of the Church, that is of the whole Christian people, both faithful and pastors, who call her a most loving Mother; and we decree that henceforth the whole Christian people should, by this most sweet name, give still greater honor to the Mother of God and address prayers to her.[19]

In its formulation the title is in part new, but in regard to its content and significance it is neither new nor unknown. Paul VI himself stated this. The title expresses an old doctrine of the Church based on Divine Revelation: in texts, allusions and references of the New and Old Testaments, especially when the New Testament refers to the exercise of a spiritual maternity by the Mother of the Redeemer, as we shall see below, and in chapter 12 of the book of Revelation.

The mysteries of the life of the Virgin Mary, after Jesus proclaimed her spiritual maternity on Calvary, and after the death and Resurrection of her Son, are an unveiling of her presence and maternal role at the

---

[18] In those years some authors, using the terminology father, mother, etc., as basis for an explanation of personal relations among Christians, but without making due allowance for differences in meaning when such terms are transferred to indicate realities of the supernatural, spiritual order, drew absurd conclusions, at times irreverent, such as claiming the Virgin would be "grandmother" of Christians, if the Church were their mother and Mary the mother of the Church. This was a great error in terms of an even minimally correct understanding of spiritual maternity, an error assigning unilateral importance to biological maternity and other like factors on that level. Cf. D. Bertetto, *Maria, la Serva...*, cit., pp. 553-554.

[19] *Acta Synodalia...Concilli Vaticani II.*, vol. III, part VIII, p. 916.

dawn of the Church, and of the protection and care which she bestows on her children. This is the spirit of her presence at Pentecost, of her glorious Assumption into heaven and of the maternal protection she exercises over the Church.[20]

The life and Tradition of the Church are an inexhaustible treasury of documentation and testimony, recognizing and proclaiming the Blessed Virgin Mary "Mother of the Church." During recent centuries this unbroken Tradition has been confirmed by the living Magisterium. The popes, from Blessed Pius IX (1854) to John Paul II, have entrusted the life and activities of the Church to the Virgin Mary as her Mother, pleading for and asking as well her protection and help in the most difficult and adverse circumstances of the Church's history. Mary as a diligent and powerful Mother has always protected the Church and Christians, sometimes in extraordinary ways.[21]

As facts of our time, we can recall actions of Pope Paul VI, who solemnly proclaimed the title *Mary, Mother of the Church* during the closing of the third session of Vatican II and who previously had entrusted this cause and other problems of the Church to the Blessed Virgin. After the solemn and touching proclamation of the title, the Pope stated:

> This is the reason why we ... ardently raise our eyes to her with the confidence and love of children. She who gave us Jesus, font of supernatural grace, will not fail to offer the Church her maternal love, especially at this time when the Bride of Christ is ceaselessly working to fulfill her saving mission.[22]

---

[20] Cf. LG 62.
[21] A very striking and significant instance was the situation of the Church at the time of Bl Pius IX, who defined the Immaculate Conception as dogma (1854), imploring Mary's maternal help. And he received it!
[22] Paul VI, discourse at the closing ceremony of the third session of Vatican II, Nov. 21, 1964: *Acta Synodalia...*, vol. III, pars VIII, p. 916. The Council itself referred to the Virgin Mary's help and maternal protection over the Church, that it is something which the Church "constantly experiences and recommends to the heartfelt attention of the faithful" (LG 62).

More Important Moments of Mary, Mother of the Church

Presentation

Some authors ask *when and how* the Blessed Virgin became our Mother in the order of grace; when and how she began and continues to exercise her spiritual maternity over her children to this very day. The greater number of authors treating the spiritual maternity in general had no intention of determining such details. But in explaining the more important aspects of Mary's spiritual maternity, affirmations and insinuations are met in the majority of cases touching its origins and the various ways and aspects involved in communicating, or in collaborating with, the communication of supernatural grace to souls. With this in mind, the proposed theme can in part be illustrated.

In some important documents dealing with Mary's spiritual maternity, recent popes occasionally make more or less direct reference to those matters. Neither circumstances of time, nor external modalities of this spiritual maternity, are anywhere near so important as the doctrinal explanations which these popes offer for its theological content, specifically in relation to moments and mysteries in the life of Jesus where the Virgin Mary collaborated as Mother of grace and associate of her Son in the salvation of the human race.

In general, most authors insist on Vatican II's affirmation that the life of the Virgin Mary, the life Pope Paul VI describes as that *"of the humble handmaid of the Lord, who from the moment she was greeted by the angel until her Assumption into heaven's glory, body and soul, lived as a life of love and service,"*[23] was a life spent in the exercise of her spiritual maternity, in the exercise of maternal solicitude.

Pope John Paul—in a document to be quoted more than once—states firmly that: *"Mary's spiritual maternity regarding the spirit (quoad spiritum) rightly began with her physical maternity regarding the body (quoad corpus)."* And referring to the mystery of the Annunciation and the conversation between Mary and the angel, he concludes: *"At the very moment her physical maternity (quoad corpus) began, so also did her spiritual maternity (quoad spiritum)."*[24]

---

[23] The idea is expounded in LG 57, a text on which I have already commented.
[24] John Paul II, allocution, Jan. 10, 1979.

According to the living Magisterium of the Church, spiritual maternity began at the time of the Annunciation, as John Paul states, with the Virgin Mary's consent (*consensus*) to the angel's request. In virtue of this "consent," the Word of God was made flesh in Mary's virginal womb as universal Redeemer and Savior. Thus, her biological maternity was at the same time her spiritual maternity of salvation. The Mother of the Redeemer was at the same moment also Mother of all redeemed. For this reason, according to the teaching of the Second Vatican Council, she began her maternity "*freely cooperating in the work of man's salvation through faith and obedience.*"[25]

During the progress and unfolding of the history of salvation, Mary's spiritual maternity enjoyed some singular, characteristic moments during which various details and aspects defining the nature and intensity of Mary's collaboration in the work of redemption become clear.

Here attention will be focused only on the most important of these in the life of Mary. The principles and norms of interpretation followed here are equally applicable to other mysteries in her life. These moments are:

1. Mary's spiritual maternity and the mystery of the Incarnation.
2. Mary's maternal presence at Calvary.[26]
3. Ecclesial maternity at the wedding feast of Cana.

Mary, Mother of the Church, in the Mystery of the Incarnation

The Blessed Virgin Mary is properly and formally Mother of the Church by her collaboration in or consent to the mystery of the Incarnation.

1. Explanation

Here spiritual maternity is understood in its most proper sense: as a spiritual action by which the Mother, the Virgin Mary, the Mother of the Son of God, at the same time collaborates efficaciously in the communication of grace and supernatural life to souls and to the world. The term mother is not a metaphor or a mere symbol; rather it connotes

---

[25] LG 56.
[26] Cf. A. Luis Iglesias, CSSR., *Dos Momentos culminantes de la maternidad espiritual: la anunciación y el calvario*, in *Estudios Marianos*, 20 (1959), 109-156.

a reality of the supernatural order: the world's restoration from sin by the coming of the Son of God, the Savior, and rebirth of souls by supernatural grace gushing forth from Christ, the fountain of salvation.

This rebirth by divine disposition is realized in the mystery of the Incarnation of the Son of God, Redeemer and universal Savior. In this rebirth the Virgin Mary collaborated spiritually and formally in two ways: 1) by her loving, faithful and obedient consent[27] to the will of the Father: *Behold, I am the handmaid of the Lord, be it unto me according to thy word* (Lk 1:38); and 2) through the work of the Holy Spirit providing of her own nature the matter to be assumed by the Word of God, the God made man so as to become the Redeemer of the human race by means of the mysteries of his flesh.[28]

As Vatican II states, echoing the teachings of the Fathers of the Church, it is certain that Mary was not "merely passively engaged by God": "*Rightly therefore, the Fathers see Mary not merely as passively engaged by God, but as freely cooperating in the work of man's salvation through faith and obedience.*"[29]

Mariologists and commentators on the mystery of the Annunciation underscore the importance and significance of Mary's *consensus*. No doubt it has a definitive importance. Mary's *yes* to the will of the Father was an act of love, faith and obedience; an act that manifested her collaboration in the redemption of the human race. It was an act of her spiritual maternity[30] because as a mother, she consecrated herself to the person and work of her Son, with him and under him serving the mystery of redemption.

---

[27] Vatican II stresses the importance of this *consensus*: consent of the Mother, expressly willed and decreed by the Father of mercies before the Incarnation took place, so as to make clear that *just as a woman had a share in bringing about death, so also a woman should contribute to life*: cf. LG 56.

[28] Cf. Heb 10:1-10. LG 55 translates "mysteries of *his flesh*," rather than "mysteries of *his humanity*."

[29] LG 56.

[30] Cf. John Paul II, *Redemptoris Mater* 13-14; Paul VI, *Signum Magnum*, May 13, 1967, Part II, n. 5; J.M. Bover, *Deiparae Virginis consensus corredentionis ac Mediationis fundamentum*, Madrid 1942; José A. de Aldama, S.J., "*Mariología…*" cit., n. 133, p. 410.

2. Ecclesial Testimony

All of the above is explicitly taught, in a kind of Marian synthesis by Vatican II in such wise as to affirm the real meaning and significance of this question. It has also been taught by the Church's Magisterium, whose authority here is decisive, precisely because a truth pertaining to the deposit of faith is under consideration.

Vatican II expresses itself as follows:

> The Virgin of Nazareth is hailed by the heralding angel, by divine command, as "full of grace" (cf. Lk 1:28); and to the heavenly messenger she replies: *Behold, I am the handmaid of the Lord, be it done unto me according to thy word* (Lk 1:38). Thus, the daughter of Adam, Mary, consenting to the word of God, became the Mother of Jesus. Committing herself wholeheartedly and impeded by no sin to God's salvific will, she devoted herself totally, as a handmaid of the Lord, to the person and work of her Son, under and with him, serving diligently the mystery of redemption.[31]

Pope Paul VI, in his interpretation of the doctrine of the Council, adds other aspects in the gloss which he made in his Apostolic Exhortation *Signum Magnum*:

> Mary, as soon as she was reassured by the voice of the Angel Gabriel that God had chosen her as the unblemished Mother of his only-begotten Son, unhesitatingly gave her consent to a work which would have engaged all the energies of her fragile nature and declared: "Behold, I am the handmaid of the Lord; be it done to me according to thy word" (Lk 1:38). From that moment, she consecrated all of herself to the service not only of the heavenly Father and of the Word incarnate,

---

[31] LG 56. In this text the Council expressly associates the spiritual maternity of Mary with her intervention as Co-redemptrix with her son: *under him and with him serving the mystery of redemption* ...and *cooperating in the work of man's salvation*... It is important to keep this key intuition in mind since it offers us an authentic concept of spiritual maternity as coredemptive collaboration.

who had become her Son, but also to all mankind, having clearly understood that Jesus, in addition to saving his people from the slavery of sin, would become the King of a messianic Kingdom, universal and eternal (cf. Mt. 1:21; Lk. 1:33).[32]

Paul VI's thought regarding Mary's spiritual maternity in the Incarnation of the Son of God could not be clearer. Becoming Mother of the Word of God, she devoted herself totally to his service as a mother to the service of her Son, and also to the service of the whole human race. Why? Because she was to become spiritual Mother of all redeemed.

On this point Pope John Paul II's teaching is equally important. In his Encyclical *Redemptoris Mater* (*Mother of the Redeemer*), he refers several times to the relation between Mary's divine motherhood and her spiritual maternity. Aside from other testimonies, special note should be taken of the text of his allocution, January 10, 1979, where he directly reflects on this theme. The strength of his thought culminates in this affirmation in the form of a conclusion to his reasoning, and which I have previously quoted: "*At the very moment her physical maternity (quoad corpus) began, so also did her spiritual maternity in regard to the spirit (quoad spiritum).*"

Note should be taken that this teaching of the present Magisterium of the Church regarding Mary's spiritual maternity and its mutual relationship with the mystery of the Incarnation has remained uniform throughout the centuries. The text of St. Leo the Great expressing the convictions of the Church in his day remains a classic: "Christ's generation is the origin of the Christian people; and Christ's birth as Head is also the birth of his [Mystical] Body."[33]

St. Leo the Great's belief is clearly evident in this text. If Christ's birth is our own, then this great Doctor is implicitly affirming that Christ's Mother is also ours in the economy of salvation. Therefore, in the mystery of the Incarnation Mary is Mother of Christ the Savior and Redeemer, Head of the Church, and Mother of its redeemed members. This is the concept which the living Magisterium has always upheld.

---

[32] Paul VI, *Signum Magnum*, Part I, par. 5.
[33] St. Leo the Great, *Sermon 6 on the Nativity of the Lord*, PL 54, 213.

Later there proceeds Pope St. Pius X's exposition of this same doctrine in his important Encyclical *Ad diem illum* (Feb. 2, 1904). There he says:

> For is not Mary the Mother of Christ? Then she is our Mother also. And we must in truth hold that Christ, the Word made Flesh, is also the Savior of mankind. ... Now the Blessed Virgin did not conceive the eternal Son of God merely in order that he might be made man taking his human nature from her, but also in order that by means of the nature assumed from her he might be the Redeemer of men. ... Hence Mary, carrying the Savior within her, may be said to have also carried all those whose life was contained in the life of the Savior. Therefore all we who are united to Christ, and as the apostle says are members of his Body. ... Hence, though in a spiritual and mystical fashion, we are all children of Mary, and she is Mother of us all.[34]

Other texts of the Magisterium of the Church similar to those already quoted could be cited, but this is hardly necessary. The high point of the Magisterium on this theme came at Vatican II and in the teachings of two recent popes: Paul VI, authorized interpreter of the Council, and John Paul II.

And the link with popes of former times is Pope Pius XII, who in his Encyclical *Mystici Corporis* (June 29, 1943) concludes his reflection on Mary thus:

> Within her virginal womb Christ our Lord already bore the exalted title of Head of the Church; in a marvelous birth [Mary] brought him forth as the source of all supernatural life. ... Thus she who, according to the flesh, was the Mother of our Head ... became ... the Mother of all his members.[35]

---

[34] St. Pius X, Enc. *Ad diem Illum* (Feb. 2, 1904), 10; AAS., 36, 452-53.
[35] Pius XII, Enc. *Mystici Corporis* (June 29, 1943), 110: AAS., 35 (1943) 247.

3. Theological Tradition

The ancient Tradition of the Fathers of the Church and of the theologians down through the Middle Ages was not oblivious of the doctrine of Mary's spiritual maternity, although direct expositions of its meaning and explanations of its content and key moments in the history of salvation may be wanting. This notwithstanding, some Fathers and ecclesiastical writers do affirm the factual truth of this mystery, either directly or as a deduction from other theological premises, from an antithetical comparison Eve-Mary, an argumentation already current in the days of St. Irenaeus, or from considerations bearing on Mary's mission in the history of salvation.

In particular, Mary's spiritual maternity in the New Testament also possesses a *bridal* meaning. In the account of the Annunciation (Lk 1:26-38), in the mystery at Calvary (Jn 19:25-27) and in Mary's presence at wedding feast of Cana (Jn 2:1-11), exegetes, not restricting themselves to the merely proper, historical and literal sense of the text, also discover in the New Covenant phenomena and events of salvation history which reveal the Son of God to have been betrothed with human nature in Mary's virginal womb.

By careful analysis of reciprocal concepts and through the study of events endowed with a wide-ranging symbolism, Mary is shown to be acting as spiritual Mother and Bride. Thus, in the mystery of the Annunciation Mary pronounces her *fiat* (Lk 1:38) as mystical bride of the Word, giving birth to the Church as distinct from Christ. Of this Church Christ becomes Head, after assuming in personal union the human nature he intended to redeem.[36] It is helpful to keep this blending of types in mind, so as to recognize the various interrelated titles under which the Tradition of the Church has proclaimed Mary's spiritual maternity.

We can outline the teaching of Tradition, as some writers have done, via a series of general formulations, as it were *capita maiora* [major headings], each of which is equivalently an affirmation of the spiritual maternity of Mary, Mother of the redeemed, viz., of the disciples of Jesus.

---

[36] Cf. D. Bertetto, *Maria, la Serva...*, cit., p. 496. Likewise in the scene on Calvary, Mary as the New Eve, mystically betrothed to the New Adam, communicates the fruits of redemption to mankind.

a) The spiritual maternity of Mary is affirmed in propounding and explaining the antithetical parallelism Eve-Mary as grounded in Sacred Scripture. So true is this that Vatican II summarized this argument, saying that *"not a few of the early Fathers, comparing Mary with Eve, call her Mother of the living"*;[37] and frequently claim: *"death through Eve, life through Mary."*[38]

b) The doctrine of the Mystical Body is another reason for claiming that Mary's spiritual maternity was recognized during the patristic era. St. Augustine, in building on this insight, stated that if Mary is Mother of Christ, Head of the Church, then she is also Mother of its members.

A similar application is possible by taking Christ's conception and birth as universal Redeemer and Savior as a point of reference. Reflections along such lines are developed especially by St. Leo the Great.[39]

c) Another similar argument can be formulated, this one converging on Mary's presence on Calvary and on Jesus' proclamation of her maternity by extending it to include John, the beloved disciple, when he said to his Mother: *"'Woman, behold, your son!' Then he said to the disciple, 'Behold, your mother!'"* (Jn 19:26-27).

The proof for this argument supposes that John, Jesus' disciple, represented either the Church or mankind. According to the Church's Tradition, and in view of the content and significance of the scene on Calvary, St. John acted here not as a merely private person, but in accord with the divine counsels as representative of the human race. But in what sense?

Some commentators think that this can be affirmed only in an improper sense, or by way of a biblical accommodation. But in

---

[37] LG 56.
[38] Cf. LG 56. The Council text refers to and comments on several texts from the Tradition of the Church.
[39] Cf. José Antonio de Aldama, *Mariología*...cit., n. 139, p. 415, quoting the more outstanding sources or authors on these subjects.

view of the nature and significance of the mystery taking place on Calvary, understanding John here as representative of all mankind has unquestionable validity, as both the historical and symbolic sense of this passage. So, indeed, has the Tradition of the Church understood and proclaimed the meaning of this passage from earliest times.

Above all, the Church's Magisterium itself seems to interpret Tradition in this sense. The mind of Tradition here is not that of a mere accommodation, but of a genuine, inspired sense. This understanding Pope Benedict XIV states "the Church received under the promptings and teaching of the Holy Spirit."[40] Likewise, Pope Leo XIII affirms that the Church "has always understood that in the person of John, Jesus Christ designated the entire human race."[41]

Mary, Mother of the Church, on Calvary

Introduction

The most important moment of Mary's spiritual maternity is her presence on Calvary during her Son's crucifixion and death. Because of the importance of biblical texts, of their content and of the significance of this redemptive mystery, and because of the attention the Church has given to this supernatural event, we are face to face with the mystery that most awakens a sensitive interest in scholars to explore and elucidate all its hidden truths.

Hence, this is the most studied event of Christ's life and it is the one that has produced the most stimulating and extensive literature. Its content and significance has been plumbed by exegesis and theology, spirituality and anthropology, and it has been profusely depicted, in a variety of styles, by the arts, iconography and literature alike. Sculptured calvaries have sought to lend its presence a certain nearness, so as to make its contemplation by the faithful easier. The renaissance opened a golden era for the mystery of Calvary. Books of theology and devotion, like the anonymous *Passio duorum* (*The Passion of two...*) in Spanish at the

---

[40] Benedict XIV, Bull *Gloriosae Dominae* (Sept. 27, 1748): *Bullarium*, 2, 428. This pope states that Mary on Calvary is "*in the proper sense Mother of the Church, a gift to the Church received from the lips of her dying Bridegroom.*"

[41] Leo XIII, Enc. *Adiutricem populi* (Sept. 5, 1895): AAS 28, 130: "*In Joanne autem, quod perpetuo sensit Ecclesia, designavit Christus personam humani generis.*"

turn of fifteenth and sixteenth centuries, create just this kind of style in contemplating and living the mystery.[42]

The mystery on Calvary is naturally incomprehensible, not only because of its nature and supernatural significance, but even from a merely human standpoint, because that mystery unfolds and without explanation reaches, humanly speaking, a tragic finale. It is useless to rationalize it by adducing ancient custom or past events lost in the mists of history. Nor is it enough, in order to find a satisfactory explanation, to cite legal norms or spin hypotheses revolving about the hate for Jesus and intrigues against him indulged in by members of Jerusalem's high-ranking elite. Some other reason, beyond reason itself, has to be discovered. The mystery is contained in the heart of the Father: God will reign from a tree (*Regnabit a ligno Deus*). The triumph of the Cross explains the life of the Church to be established on the law of love.

That is why the mystery of Calvary will always awaken interest and a desire to penetrate its shadowy light; a yearning to discover the reasons for suffering so as to be healed; for dying in order to live.

From the Cross, setting his hope on God and on his merciful power alone, Jesus, a few moments before dying, uttered most tender and consoling words to his Mother and disciple. Son and Mother; the world and the Church were here represented. The Mother, a widow for some years, and a beloved disciple, virgin of love. When Jesus saw his Mother, he said to her: "'*Woman, behold, your son!*' *Then he said to the disciple,* '*Behold, your mother!*'"

Proclamation of Mary's Spiritual Maternity

"But standing by the Cross of Jesus were his mother, and his mother's sister, Mary the wife of Clopas, and Mary Magdalene. When Jesus saw his mother, and the disciple whom he loved standing near, he said to his mother, 'Woman, behold, your son!' Then he said to the disciple,

---

[42] "*Passio duorum*"; *Tractado de devotísimas y muy íntimas contemplaciones de la Pasión del Hijo de Dios, y compasión de la Virgen su Madre, por esta razón llamado Passio duorum*, Valladolid, 1526. This work had several editions. Regarding this work, cf. J. Meseguer, "*Passio Duorum.*" *Autores, ediciones, la obra*, in *Archivio Ibero-Americano*, Barcelona, 29 (1929) 73 ff. J. Antonio de Aldama, S.J., *La piedad mariana en el tratado "Passio duorum,"* in *Estudios Marianos*, 44 (1979), 53-72; E. Llamas, *El dolor salvífico de María: La "compassio Mariae" en los mariólogos españoles de los siglos XVI-XVII*, in *Estudios Marianos*, LXXII (2006), pp. 156-57 (with bibliographical note).

'Behold, your mother!' And from that hour the disciple took her to his own home" (Jn 19:25-27).

A) In regard to Mary's spiritual maternity, the scene at Calvary possesses a double content. Jesus' life on earth, in relation to the redemption of mankind, is to be considered the *constitutional* period of that redemption. From the first moment of the Incarnation until his death on the Cross, Jesus carried out and consummated his mission as Savior and Redeemer of the human race, accumulating an infinity of merit with the works accomplished in the mysteries of his flesh. Viewed from this angle, the redemption finds its culmination on the Cross, there sealed by his glorious death and victorious Resurrection.

By way of analogy, we can say the same of Mary's coredemptive collaboration with her Son and of her spiritual maternity. From the mystery of the Incarnation until her Son's death, she was continually exercising her spiritual maternity in a series of acts which, via the mysteries of her life, manifest precisely her coredemptive collaboration. Vatican II, once again, partially describes this series of events in the exercise of coredemptive collaboration:

> She conceived, brought forth, and nourished Christ, she presented him to the Father in the Temple, shared her Son's sufferings as he died on the Cross. Thus, in a wholly singular way she cooperated ... in the work of the Savior in restoring supernatural life to souls. For this reason she is a Mother to us in the order of grace.[43]

According to the Council, on Calvary Mary carried out and exercised her role of Co-redemptrix by way of her spiritual composure during those confusing moments of sorrow. By her compassion for her Son, by her union with him by virtue of the most intimate possible bond of maternal love; through her faith in and obedience to the Father's saving will; by her unshakeable hope and ardent charity, she cooperated, as the Council itself recalls, in a wholly singular, objective, immediate and supernatural way in the redemption of the human race.

This thesis is basic to assessing spiritually and supernaturally the Virgin Mother's life as Mother of the Son of God and associate in the work of redemption. Throughout her life, as the Council states, she lived

---

[43] LG 61.

spiritually and supernaturally in union with *"the Son in the work of salvation ... from the time of Christ's virginal conception up to his death."*[44] Her entire life was an exercise in spiritual maternity, an efficacious cooperation in the work of redemption.

That coredemptive collaboration, the equivalent of her spiritual maternity, found its high point on Calvary. There, the spiritual strength and living expression of her love for God and for her Son attained their *summum* [summit], because there is no greater love than to lay down one's life for others. At this point, Mary accepted her Son's death in dying with him spiritually and affectively. Mariologists during the sixteenth and seventeenth centuries strove to clarify this *union* of Christ and Mary on Calvary in relation to their pain, suffering and sacrificial oblation, all that is meant and expressed by the term *compassio*.

Mary's coredemptive collaboration with her Son was consummated on Calvary. Her spiritual maternity had attained its highest efficacy and expression. What remained to be done? The subsequent, final moment of this spiritual maternity on Calvary, its **proclamation** from the Cross, represents the culmination of what it means.

B) *The concepts*: The terms and concepts of the text just cited are sufficiently known; so also the meaning of the noun *woman*, and why Jesus used it at this moment instead of the proper name, *Mary*, or the familiar term, *mother*.

A comparison of the scene on Calvary with the Annunciation readily makes plain some notable differences in the circumstances of each event. But certain, more basic resemblances also come to light. These have their root in the presence of an identical goal in the unfolding and realization of salvation history. Although Calvary and the Annunciation are two distinct events, they are in fact one by virtue of an identical cause. Both events entail a basic nucleus in view of the fulfillment of a single objective. The content of two terms, *consensus* = *consent,* and *compassio* = *compassion*, explains the link which makes both events radically one before they are considered separately.

What Mary's *consensus* (her *fiat*) was to the mystery of Incarnation, her *compassio* was by analogy to the mystery of redemption on Calvary. This parallel is the central point of reference on which any explanation of these two salvific events turns.

---

[44] LG 57.

The *consensus* was, as it were, the door giving the Word of God access to the world of redemptive salvation: *Janua coeli* ("Gate of heaven"). In virtue of her divine motherhood Mary was the door through which the Word of the Father made himself present in the world to renew and restore it by means of the mysteries of his flesh and by means of the sacrifice of himself offered in an infinite act of love.

The *compassion* was the Mother's contribution to the sacrifice of her beloved Son, a collaboration representing also that of redeemed mankind so as to recover the beauty and loveliness of spirit disfigured by original sin and by all the sins of the world. The scene on Calvary replicates the scene in the first paradise where the woman Eve appears as active collaborator of the sin of Adam. As the New Adam, Jesus during the final episode of his life on earth, so laden with symbolism, associates the New Eve, his immaculate Mother, with his work, with his supreme act of love and obedience to the Father, and with his redemptive sacrifice, thus purifying the Church by his blood and by surrendering himself to corporal death for her.[45]

The *compassio* includes and synthesizes Mary's total collaboration in the mystery of Calvary as spiritual Mother of the new mankind; a collaboration with many facets, but above all as spiritual association and participation in her Son's pains and sufferings, in his death and in his act of acceptance: His *fiat* (cf. Mt 26:39; Lk 22:42; Heb 10:7). In this Mary conforms herself to his will perfectly united to the Father's; spiritually she becomes herself a sacrificial victim acceptable to God, in spirit nailed to the Cross with her Son.[46]

Compassio-compatiens is the terminology commonly used since the Middle Ages to describe Mary's interior composure on Calvary, her participation in her Son's sacrifice and the exercise of her

---

[45] Cf. the texts of Acts 20:28 and Eph 5:25-32. St. Paul refers to the great mystery of the Church freed from sin by the death of Christ and purified in his blood.

[46] The relation existing between the scene on Calvary and that in paradise appears to be affirmed and explained in modern Mariology and in authorized documents of Church's Magisterium. Vatican II itself, in two important texts substantially refers to these events: LG 56 on the Virgin Mary's *consensus* to the Incarnation: "*so that just as a woman had a share in bringing about death, so also a woman should contribute to life*"; and again in LG 56: "and comparing Mary with Eve, the 'Holy Fathers' call her 'Mother of the living' and frequently claim: 'death through Eve, life through Mary.'"

spiritual maternity. It may well be also the best terminology for our times. Significantly, it was used by the Second Vatican Council.[47] This terminology holds great importance for the interpretation of Mariological teaching between the fifteenth and seventeenth centuries on the coredemptive participation of the Virgin Mary in the work of her Son's redemption.[48]

Doctrine of the Church's Magisterium

The witness of the Church's Magisterium to Mary's spiritual maternity reflected in her presence and actions on Calvary is very abundant, and is distinguished by a broad and profound theological-spiritual content. By means of this doctrine we come to know the various aspects and the value of Mary's cooperation in the work of salvation, ever dependant in its every phase on the efficacious mediation and redemptive action of the Son of God.

It is not necessary to cite here all the testimonies or to make particular comments on each. The texts of themselves make clear their distinctive features and the doctrinal-spiritual value of their content.

On March 16, 1748, Pope Benedict XIV published his "Bulla aurea" entitled *Gloriosae Dominae*—quoted already above—in which he assesses Church's devotion to the Virgin of Calvary:

> The Catholic Church, prompted by the teaching of the Holy Spirit, has sought the utmost to honor her [the Virgin Mary] with countless gifts as the Mother of its Lord and Redeemer and as the Queen of heaven and earth. With great care and attention the Church strives to love her with filial piety. From the lips of her divine Bridegroom, as he was dying, the Church received her [Mary] as her very own most beloved Mother.[49]

Pope Pius VIII (1829-1830), during his short pontificate, wished to strengthen among the faithful trust in the Virgin Mary's protection:

---

[47] LG 61: "...Filioque suo in cruce morienti *compatiens*."
[48] Cf. J. Luis Bastero, *La compassion mariana hasta el siglo XIII*, and Enrique Llamas, OCD, "El dolor salvífico de María. La "*compassio Mariae*" en los mariólogos españoles de los siglos XVI-XVII, in *Estudios Marianos*, 72 (2006), pp. 109-132; and 145-173.
[49] Benedict XIV, Bull *Gloriosae Dominae*: Bullarium, 2, 428.

"because she is our Mother, Mother of piety and grace, Mother of mercy, to whom Christ, as he was dying on the Cross, entrusted us, so that she might intercede for us before her Son."[50]

Pope Leo XIII makes this crystal-clear affirmation in his Encyclical *Quamquam pluries* (1889): "From the same fact that the most holy Virgin is the Mother of Jesus Christ is she the Mother of all Christians whom she bore on Mount Calvary amid the supreme throes of the redemption."[51] The Pope explains this same doctrine in many other testimonies, one which is particularly expressive I quote here:

> Moreover, it was before the eyes of Mary that was to be finished the divine sacrifice for which she had borne and brought up the Victim. As we contemplate him in the last and most piteous of those mysteries, there stood by the Cross of Jesus his Mother, who, in a miracle of charity, so that she might receive us as her sons, offered generously to divine justice her own Son, and died in her heart with him, stabbed with the sword of sorrow.[52]

From the many testimonies bequeathed us by Pope Pius XI (1922-1939), I quote only two very important ones. During the first years of his pontificate he customarily instructed the Church about the Virgin Mary thus:

> The sorrowful Virgin took part with Jesus Christ in the work of the redemption. She was constituted Mother of men, who were confided to her as a testimony of divine love. She took them to herself as sons and she lovingly protects them.[53]

In a letter to the Order of Servants of Mary (Servites) on the celebration of the seventh centenary of their foundation, the Pope included a clear statement about Mary's spiritual maternity:

---

[50] Pope Pius VIII, *Praesentissimus* (March 30, 1830): *Bullarium Romanum*, 9, 106.
[51] Pope Leo XIII, *Quamquam pluries* (Aug. 15, 1889), 3: ASS 22, 67.
[52] Pope Leo XIII, *Iucunda semper* (Sept. 8, 1894): ASS 27, 178.
[53] Pope Pius XI, Apostolic Letter, *Explorata res est* (Feb. 2, 1923): AAS 15 (1923), 104.

Shortly, the seventh centenary of the Order's foundation will be observed, while we are celebrating the Jubilee Year of the redemption of mankind and the constitution of Virgin Mary at the foot of her Son's Cross as Mother of all men.[54]

The countless, profound testimonies regarding Mary, our spiritual Mother on Calvary, to be found in the living Magisterium of the Church, inspired later popes to publish numerous documents in which they recognize and explain that very mystery. D. Bertetto has thoroughly analyzed the important contribution of Pope Pius XII. His luminous documentation above all witnesses to the fact of Mary's spiritual motherhood, relating it especially to persons and to families,[55] and linking this title with that of Mary, Mediatrix and Distributrix of graces.[56]

Pius XII explains the general doctrine of spiritual maternity and its relation to other aspects of the mystery of Mary. Realistically, it finds its source in the divine maternity,[57] but when proclaiming it from the Cross Jesus linked the spiritual maternity to a new title, Mary's collaboration in the work of redemption. These are the essential constitutive elements of spiritual maternity.

To be added to this is the permanent, actual exercise of the spiritual maternity by the Virgin Mary from her heavenly throne, an activity commonly related to the universal distribution of graces. In his great encyclicals *Mystici Corporis* and *Mediator Dei*, Pius XII explains the reasons for Mary's spiritual maternity, and sketches other suggestive considerations which manifest both the love of Jesus Christ for mankind and the solicitude and grandeur of the Mother who collaborated in the work of redemption.[58]

---

[54] Pope Pius XI, Letter *Septimo abeunte* (July 16, 1933): AAS 25 (1933) p. 435.

[55] Pius XII, allocution, May 3, 1939, and July 10, 1945. See *Discorsi e Radiomessaggi*, I, 92; and II, 76.

[56] Pius XII, radio message, Dec. 8, 1953; See Tondini, *Le Encicliche mariane*, Rome 1954, 776.

[57] Pius XII, radio message, June 19, 1947, in AAS, 39 (1947), pp. 271-72.

[58] Pius XII, *Mystici Corporis*, (June 29, 1943), AAS 35 (1943), 247; *Mediator Dei* (Nov. 20, 1947), AAS 39 (1947), 582.

Pius XII repeatedly refers to the scene on Calvary in order to highlight the figure of the Virgin Mother; her love for her crucified Son and for her adopted children whom she loves far more than all earthly mothers; her strength of soul in bearing the atrocities and torments of the Passion; her exemplarity both for all her devotees and for the Church. His is a rich and highly documented Magisterium, which efficaciously contributed to the increase of Marian devotion, and in a very remarkable way to the development and progress of Mariology.[59]

The Marian Magisterium of Pius XII found its culmination during Vatican II, as can be verified from those particular texts where the Council affirms and describes Mary's spiritual motherhood, and while doing so cites precisely texts from this pontiff's teaching.[60] On this point, Vatican II represents both a point of arrival and a point of departure. For the Council assumed, reaffirmed and propounded in its Marian text (*Lumen Gentium*, ch. 8) the fundamental theses, up to the time of the Council sponsored by a Christo-typologically orientated Mariology, regarding the immediate, objective and singular collaboration of Mary in the work of redemption, viz., Marian coredemption (even if the term was not incorporated into the text), and those regarding Mary's mediation, spiritual maternity, intercession and distribution of graces. At the Council, Marian coredemption, as far as its content and theological significance are concerned (leaving the question of terminology aside for the time being), were both supported and guaranteed because the common teaching on coredemption passed to the level of Church doctrine—even though many prefer to ignore the fact.

In the section of this chapter where I treat the fact and nature of Mary's spiritual maternity, I quoted these texts from the Dogmatic Constitution *Lumen Gentium*: 56-58, and 60-64, and from *Apostolicam actuositatem*: 4. The importance, significance and ecclesial dimension of these texts can be verified via the commentaries on, and references

---

[59] For additional data on the spiritual maternity of Mary, see D. Bertetto, *Maria, la Serva...* cit., pp. 535-539.

[60] LG 58. In this text the Council explains Mary's presence at Calvary associated with her son as he died on the Cross. It concludes thus: "...and finally, she was given by the same Christ Jesus dying on the Cross as a Mother to his disciple, with these words: 'Woman, behold, your son!' (cf. Jn 19:26-27)." And in the note reference is made to Pius XII, Enc. *Mystici Corporis*, June 29, 1943: AAS 35 (1943) 247-248.

made to them subsequently, by Popes Paul VI and John Paul II. Many are the testimonies of these two popes which can be cited in support of this theme, so relevant to contemporary Mariology. But for our purposes here, it is enough to cite a few texts and references illustrating the unity of thought of these popes with the entire living Magisterium of the Church.

Paul VI's Magisterium is not as abundant in testimonies to Mary's spiritual maternity at the foot of the Cross on Calvary, as his references to the Immaculate Mother of God, to the Assumption of the Virgin into heaven and to her relations with the Church. But there are some documents and references which enable us to learn about that aspect of Mary's life involving her active association with her Son on Calvary.[61]

Probably the most important one is that of the Apostolic Exhortation *Signum Magnum* (1967) which we have already quoted more than once:

> The first truth is this: Mary is the Mother of the Church not only because she is the Mother of Christ and his most intimate associate in "the new economy when the Son of God took a human nature from her, that he might in the mysteries of his flesh free man from sin," but also because "she shines forth to the whole community of the elect as a model of the virtues" ... the Blessed Virgin Mary, after participating in the redeeming sacrifice of the Son, and in such an intimate way as to deserve to be proclaimed by him the Mother not only of his disciple John but—may we be allowed to affirm it—of mankind which he in some way represents.[62]

Pope John Paul II's Magisterium is far richer, abounding in texts regarding the sorrowful Mother and her spiritual maternity on Calvary. He classes the Mother's pain associated with that of her Son, as efficacious collaboration with him in the work of redemption, a model and example for the Church.

Jesus' apostolic work and preaching of the Gospel culminated

---

[61] Cf. D. Bertetto, *La Madonna nella parola di Paolo VI*, Rome 1980, *passim*.
[62] Paul VI, *Signum Magnum*, Part I, par. 1.

in the events on Calvary and on the Cross. There, as it were, "spiritual" maternity was provided a key to its significance. *"When Jesus saw his mother, and the disciple whom he loved standing near, he said to his mother, "Woman, behold, your son!"* (Jn 19:26). Thus, under a new form, Jesus has joined his own Mother to mankind; the same mankind to whom he had proclaimed the Good News.[63]

In his Encyclical *Mother of the Redeemer* (1987), he makes many theological-spiritual, ecclesial and salvific observations regarding the scene on Calvary. The Pope understands this as a confirmation of Mary's "motherhood in the salvific economy of grace at its crowning moment, namely when Christ's sacrifice on the Cross, his Paschal Mystery, is accomplished."[64] Mary's *participation in the redemptive love of her Son*, the universal significance of the scene with John's representation of the entire human family, and the ecclesial focus of Jesus' words as his testament for the economy of salvation, are set in relief.

After citing the text of St. John the Holy Father proposes a number of reflections premised on the Son's evident attention to his Mother:

> And yet the "testament of Christ's Cross" says more. Jesus highlights a new relationship between Mother and Son, the whole truth and reality of which he solemnly confirms. One can say that if Mary's motherhood of the human race had already been outlined, now it is clearly stated and established.[65]

Next, the Holy Father sets in relief and explains how Mary's universal motherhood is coredemptive collaboration in her Son's redemptive work:

> Indeed she is "clearly the mother of the members of Christ ... since she cooperated out of love so that there might be born in the Church the faithful."[66]
>
> And so this "new motherhood of Mary," generated by faith, is the fruit of the "new" love which came

---

[63] John Paul II, allocution, Jan. 10, 1979.
[64] John Paul II, *Redemptoris Mater* 23.
[65] John Paul II, *Redemptoris Mater* 23.
[66] These expressions are taken from LG 54, cited in note.

to definitive maturity in her at the foot of the Cross, through her sharing in the redemptive love of her Son.[67]

Finally, leaving aside other important considerations—and all of John Paul II's considerations in these pages are important—I want to underscore the persuasive force of the Pope's reflections on Mary's maternity over the Church: *Mary, Mother of the Church.*

On Calvary, by the Cross of her dying Son, Mary lives and experiences in her Mother's heart *a new love*: it is the "love of coredemptive pain" which she shares with her Son. Of this novel love the "*new* spiritual motherhood" is born, one which *continues in the Church and through the Church*. John, Jesus' beloved disciple, symbolizes the Church. Mary, the Mother, with John constitutes the Church.[68]

In another important document, John Paul II reiterates ideas found in the Encyclical *Redemptoris Mater*, in particular her participation in her Son's salvific pain. It was precisely on Calvary where she shared his suffering, that

> Mary's suffering, beside the suffering of Jesus, reached an intensity which can hardly be imagined from a human point of view but which was mysterious and supernaturally fruitful for the redemption of the world.[69]

In what does this fruitfulness consist? In the fact that united with her Son, Redeemer of the universe, she was *Co-redemptrix* on Calvary. The Pope explains the meaning of the scene on Calvary accenting her *"unique contribution"* via her *compassion in the redemptive death of her Son* (n. 25). All of these with aforementioned details are assembled in this important text:

> As a witness *to* her Son's Passion by her *presence,* and as a sharer in it by her *compassion,* Mary offered a unique contribution to the Gospel of Suffering, by embodying

---

[67] John Paul II, *Redemptoris Mater* 23.

[68] John Paul II, *ibid.*, 24. Basing himself here on the harmony and consistency with one another of dogmas, the Pope has recourse to Apocalypse 12:1, to the symbolic meaning of the wedding feast of Cana, already explained in the encyclical, and to patristic tradition (St. Leo the Great), which relates the Incarnation to the birth of the Church, where Mary continuously supplies "a maternal presence."

[69] John Paul II, *Salvifici Doloris*, (Feb. 2, 1984), 25.

in anticipation the expression of Saint Paul, which was quoted at the beginning. She truly has a special title to be able to claim that she "completes in her flesh"—as already in her heart—"what is lacking in Christ's afflictions."[70]

We may say by way of summary of the Church's teaching concerning Mary's maternity on Calvary, that all the essential and fundamental elements have been assembled in it. Mary's maternity is a spiritual and supernatural motherhood pertaining to the salvific economy of grace. On Calvary, that motherhood is clearly established. It is a universal motherhood; at the same time it is a participation in the redemptive death of Christ and a coredemptive collaboration: efficacious, objective and immediate in the work of Christ, universal Redeemer. It is also a motherly presence and mediation.

Theological Assessment

Many authors abstain from theologically assessing propositions relative to the Virgin Mary's spiritual motherhood. In the elaboration of this problem some theologians adopt procedures, which from a methodological and expositive point of view, hardly correspond with the formulation of these propositions in documents of the Magisterium of the Church.

In these pages I have cited many documents of the Church's living Magisterium regarding spiritual maternity, its content and various facets. The Magisterium of the Church is the norm according to which a *theological and dogmatic assessment* of a doctrine or a proposition is made.

Mary's spiritual maternity, founded on the mystery of the Incarnation and of Calvary, is a true maternity in the order of grace: this is a proposition *de fide divina et catholica* (object of divine and catholic faith) in virtue of the teaching of the Word of God and the unanimous Magisterium of the Church.

Mary's spiritual motherhood specifically entails an efficacious collaboration in every aspect of the redemption: this is a proposition *de fide divina et catholica*, with its basis in Scripture and because it is taught by the Church's Magisterium (Pius XII, Second Vatican Council, John Paul II in *Redemptoris Mater*).

---

[70] John Paul II, *ibid.*

The proposition, that in this maternal collaboration Mary immediately acted as Co-redemptrix in objective redemption, is according to some theologians a proposition *more in harmony with the ecclesial Magisterium* (José Antonio de Aldama, S.J.).

I, however, think that in light of Vatican II's clear teaching synthesizing that of Pius XII, and in the light of that of Pope John Paul II in *Redemptoris Mater*, and that because it is inspired by and explained in Scripture, this third proposition can now be qualified as *de fide catholica*.

Mary's Ecclesial Motherhood at the Wedding Feast of Cana (cf. Jn 2:1-12)

State of the Question

Some authors of contemporary Mariology and Johannine exegesis claim that Mary's presence and intervention at the wedding feast of Cana—as St. John describes it—is in the symbolic sense a description of a maternal action on her part in the spiritual order. This description of Mary at Cana is similar to that of her presence on Calvary. The author of both accounts is the same evangelist. Crucial here to a correct interpretation, whether establishing the claim or not, is the reference linking Mary to Jesus as symbolic point of convergence. The fact that Jesus, in speaking to his Mother on both occasions, addressed her with the substantive, *woman*, constitutes a strong point of reference.

Since the Middle Ages many authors have interpreted the scene described by John in a mystical-ecclesiological sense, one opening on many perspectives. Jesus worked his first *sign* there and the apostles believed. The account describes faith contextualized as the foundation of the first community or primitive Church: Jesus, Mary the Mother, and the apostles, a foundation brought to pass precisely the intervention of the Mother.

Living, symbolic exegesis, capable of far more than simple philology, has discovered other aspects and shades of meaning in the content and historical editing of John's narrative. These accent and set in relief the central importance of Mary's presence as spiritual Mother of the beginning of the Church, a presence linked to the apostles' faith.[71] St. Thomas Aquinas contemplates the heart of this scene, explaining it in

---

[71] Cf. D. Bertetto, *María, la Serva...*, cit., p. 557.

an ecclesial sense, because there the union of Christ with the fledgling Church is revealed.[72]

Analysis and Explanations

Contemporary Mariologists and biblical scholars discover other dimensions in the mystery of the wedding at Cana, which as mystery entails a profound theological symbolism yet to be fully understood.

Fr. Ignatius de la Potterie, S.J., is one of the best commentators on this subject. He has made a long philological analysis of this pericope, critiqued ideas and claims, hypothetical reconstructions and inductions, and given careful attention to grammatical rhythms in the phraseology and to the meaning of the term *woman* in John's account, one, according to J.P. Charlier, exactly parallel with that in the scene on Calvary. De la Potterie concludes as follows:

> In their actions and conversation the Virgin Mary and Christ far transcend the human and material context of that "marriage" feast at Cana; they supplant the newlyweds as the spiritual Groom and Bride of the messianic banquet.[73]

Basis of this interpretation is the symbolic sense of messianic *nuptials*, and within that messianic context the interpretation raises the wedding at Cana to a soteriological level where the Virgin Mary—as on Calvary—is revealed in her dignity as Co-redemptrix and spiritual Mother of the redeemed. Along these same lines, those emphasized by J.P. Charlier, the symbolic Bride at the wedding "collaborates" with Christ, the Groom, in preparing the "new wine," and as Bride, Mary is Christ's prime collaborator who truly becomes a helpmate similar to him (cf. Gn 2:19). And *at the hour when the first sign is wrought, John presents us to the Virgin-Bride fully and profoundly integrated within the redemptive plan*,[74] therefore Co-redemptrix.

---

[72] St. Thomas Aquinas, *In Joannem*, II, lectio 1.
[73] I. de la Potterie, S.J., "*María en el misterio de la alianza*," Madrid 1993, p. 248 [English translation: *Mary in the Mystery of the Covenant*, New York 1992]. Cf. J.P. Charlier, *Le signe de Caná. Essai de Théologie Johannique* (Brussels 1959), ch. 6, p. 77.
[74] J.P. Charlier, *Le Signe...*, cit., p. 80.

At this first study level of the nuptials we discover Mary as "collaborator" with her Son in the redemptive plan of God. Continuing the study at a second level of reflection we discover a "new theme," as de la Potterie calls it:

> In the account of Cana there is a discreet suggestion of Mary's "spiritual motherhood" in relation to the new people of God. In biblical tradition "Daughter Zion" is frequently represented in a maternal role, one very nicely articulated in Psalm 86 (87) verse 5—"And of Zion it shall be said, 'This one and that one were born in her.'"[75]

De la Potterie broadens his reflection to include still other, complementary themes. We might conclude this very suggestive approach briefly setting the wedding scene, as does our author, in relation to that of Calvary:

> In adopting such comportment and also in inviting the "servants," viz., the disciples, to a perfect obedience, Mary is the first to induce others to become the new people of God. This idea, implicit in Jn 2:1-12, only came to be recognized expressly later on ... then (cf. Jn 19:25-27) Mary's spiritual maternity would be explicitly proclaimed for Jesus' disciples.[76]

From a theological and more spiritual point of view, Hugo Rahner adopts a nuptial symbolism for his interpretation of the scene at Cana. This symbolism includes an ecclesial meaning and significance, relevant to many moments in the establishment of the New Covenant in Christ's blood. This is because the *"interpretation of the Wedding at Cana envisions the entire course of salvation history, from the first moment of the Incarnation to the*

---

[75] De la Potterie, *María en ...*, cit., p. 249. A. Serra takes the same approach in commenting on the words Mary said to the servants during the wedding feast: "*Do whatever he tells you*" (Jn 2:5). He thinks that they constitute a kind of testament similar to that on Calvary, indicating an obligation to be docile to Jesus' words: to believe, to exercise the obedience of faith, and to do his will. Therefore, citing Serra in support, de la Potterie concludes that at the wedding feast of Cana *Mary's spiritual maternity is being implicitly indicated.* Cf. A. Serra, *Maria a Cana e sotto la Croce: saggio di Mariologia Giovannea (Gv 2: 1-12 e Gv 19: 25-27)*, Rome 1991, p. 30.

[76] De la Potterie, *María en ...*, cit., pp. 249-250.

glorious return of the Lord at the end of time,"[77] symbolized by the victorious conversion of water into wine. One moves here in a mystical-symbolic context where in the Covenant Mary is *"the Mother of all those sanctified by their faith in Jesus Christ."*[78]

Rahner thinks that at Cana, when referring to the arrival of his *hour*, Jesus was alluding to the scene on Calvary, to the central point in the work of redemption, that is, to his Passion and death. Christ's blood poured out was the "new wine" of the New and eternal Covenant. His Mother, the Virgin Mary, *the grand woman of world history, whom her Son would proclaim "Mother" of the faithful and model of Mother Church,* is present at both moments.[79]

Here Rahner reaches the high point of his theological-biblical reflection linking the meaning of the wedding to the central moment in the work of redemption: his "hour." From that summit he contemplates the Lord's death on the Cross and the blood prepared by Mary and poured out for the salvation of all men. In that decisive moment, Jesus proclaims Mary, his Mother, the Mother of all peoples, of all those who will believe in him, because she is Mother, figure and model of the Church.[80]

Other authors propose quite similar interpretations to the one I have just explained. Bertetto, after critiquing several theories and interpretations, favors the thesis of Mary's spiritual-ecclesial motherhood at the "wedding of Cana," set in relation to the mystique of Calvary and the arrival of Jesus' *hour*. He acknowledges that St. Thomas and other medieval authors, in the footsteps of the holy fathers, have offered considerable data, of great help to modern theologians and biblical scholars in penetrating more deeply Mary's maternal role at the wedding feast of Cana.

A further reflection of this author is quite important. John, beloved disciple of Jesus, and author of the Cana narrative, is not simply acting as an ordinary writer, who merely contributes one or another piece of information to the history of Jesus. It seems far more likely that at this

---

[77] Hugo Rahner, *María y la Iglesia*, Madrid 2002, p. 81. [English translation: *Our Lady and the Church*, New York 1960, reprinted by Ignatius Press, San Francisco 2005. Page numbers here refer to the Spanish edition of the original German.]

[78] Rahner, *ibid.*, p. 82.

[79] Rahner, *ibid.*, pp. 83-84.

[80] Cf. Rahner, *ibid.*, pp. 83-84.

point John is acting as a "divinely inspired author," who claims to explain a mystery of salvation in relating the first miracle of Jesus.

Clearly, in this teaching the Virgin Mary reveals how great a power of intercession she wields before her Son. Thus does she appear when Jesus converts water into wine, his first miracle, and so affirms and increases the faith of his disciples. As a result of that faith, they are more spiritually united to him and vitally engrafted as branches into the vine: into Jesus Christ, Head of the Mystical Body, as first members of the Church, the family of the faithful.[81]

Mary, the Mother of Jesus, who was personally invited to the wedding at which her Son and his disciples also assisted, is already acting here as the Mother of that spiritual family which is the Church in the course of being born.

Mary's Spiritual Maternity and Patristic Doctrine

The doctrine we have explained concerning Mary's spiritual maternity, particularly stressing the teaching of the Church's Magisterium, accords with and is largely inspired by patristic tradition. On many occasions the popes in their documents have quoted from and referred to the teachings of the holy Fathers. Vatican II expressly cites the authority of the holy Fathers when referring to Mary's spiritual maternity.[82]

Mariologists and authors of handbooks on Mariology do the same but far more extensively. Textual documentation is particularly abundant in the treatment of certain aspects of spiritual maternity, e.g.: spiritual maternity as mediation, coredemption and distribution of graces. On the other hand, particular aspects of spiritual maternity have also been studied in the context of the writings of the holy Fathers. The bibliography on such studies over the past forty years has been meticulously prepared in perfect form by Fr. Giuseppe M. Besutti in his *Bibliografia Mariana*.[83]

---

[81] Cf. D. Bertetto, *Maria la Serva...*, cit., p. 500.

[82] LG 56: "Hence not a few of the early Fathers gladly assert..."

[83] For reference works on the doctrine of the Fathers, I list some authors by way of example: A. Rivera, CMF, *María, Madre de los miembros del Cuerpo Místico en la tradición Patrística*, in *Estudios Marianos*, 18 (1959) 42-73; Francesco Spedalieri, S.J., *La Maternitá spirituale di Maria. La credenza comune della Chiesa alla fine del s. IV*, and *La Maternitá spirituale di María dal Conc. di Efeso alla fine dell'età patrística*, in *Maria nella Scrittura e nella Tradizione della Chiesa*, Roma, 1965, pp. 52-118, 227-288;

Mary's Spiritual Maternity in Ecumenical Dialogue

Various authors have referred to this theme of Mary's collaboration in the work of redemption—spiritual motherhood in particular—apart from general studies. Generally speaking, however, we can say that this theme has seen little progress within the ecumenical movement. There have been no significant advances and, on occasions, there is met only silence and utter indifference to this theme.

Lutheran Churches, in contrast with the Catholic Church, have very different theories of redemption, grace and church. In general, Lutherans do not discuss the spiritual maternity of Mary. Hans Asmussen, one of their theologians closest to Catholic Mariology, states that Mary enjoys a certain relation to salvation, that we could not think of Christ without thinking of Mary, and that we have a new birth of the Virgin. But he offers no doctrinal elaboration of these points.[84]

Among authors coming from a Calvinist background, Max Thurian, a Reformed Church theologian, stands out as an exception when he talks in a soteriological sense about Mary's presence on Calvary, of her participating in her Son's sufferings, of being closely united to the mission of the Church and to the redemptive work of Christ, the only Savior. This type of affirmation is very generic, and is a commonplace of Catholic Mariology. But what specific role does the Virgin Mary play in redemption? Thurian gives no systematic form to his generic comments, nor does he offer a comprehensive explanation of this theme. That notwithstanding, he does affirm that Mary is indispensable to the

---

J.A. de Aldama, S.J., *Mariología* …, cit., pp. 408-454; Bertetto, Domenico, *Maria, la Serva* …, cit., pp. 81-110: *Mariologia Patrística*; Miguel Ponce Cuellar, *María, Madre del Redentor y Madre de la Iglesia*, Barcelona 2001, pp. 201-284, Segunda Parte: *Desarrollo en los Padres*; Carlos Ignacio González, *María, evangelizada y evangelizadora*, Bogotá 1989; pp. 181-286, II Parte: *María en la Tradición de la Iglesia*; Jean Galot, S.J., *Maria, la Donna nell'Opera della salvezza*, Rome, 1991, pp. 239-378; G.M. Besutti, O.S.M., *Bibliografía Mariana*, Rome, Marianum, 1950…: nine volumes have appeared to date.

[84] Cf. Hans Asmussen, *Maria die Mutter Gottes*, Stuttgart 1951, pp. 110-121. This book enjoyed a discrete popularity for nearly a quarter century, going through four editions between 1950 and 1973, the second edition being cited here.

work of salvation. In what sense? Probably because she is the Mother of Jesus of Nazareth, the only Savior.[85]

Closer to the Catholic position is that of the Anglican Church. Generally speaking, Anglicanism includes in its liturgical calendar the celebration of five Marian feasts. And at the level of doctrine, it admits the fundamental truths professed by the Church before Anglicans separated from Rome (1534), i.e., divine motherhood, virginity, etc. Some contemporary Anglican bishops and theologians admit a kind of Marian mediation and even intercession in the Communion of Saints.

But within Anglicanism there exists unity neither of thought nor of Marian doctrine. There does not really exist any "Anglican" Mariology as such, and the theme of Mary's spiritual maternity plays no role in Anglican theology.[86] Nonetheless, there are some Anglican theologians today who acknowledge a maternal role for Mary on Calvary vis-a-vis the Church. It would seem that Pope John Paul II refers to such theologians in his Encyclical *Redemptoris Mater*, in the section entitled "The Path of the Church and the Unity of All Christians." He says it augurs well that some non-Catholic Churches and ecclesial communities in the West agree with the Catholic Church on fundamental questions of faith and doctrine, especially one in reference to the Virgin Mary whom they recognize as Mother of God and whom they see at the foot of the Cross accepting the beloved disciple as her own son, who in turn accepts her as his Mother.[87]

This is a true recognition of Mary's spiritual maternity. Some authors even go so far as to support Marian mediation and intercession on behalf

---

[85] Cf. Max Thurian, *Marie, Mère du Seigneur, Figure de l'Eglise*, Taizé 1962, pp. 142 ff. [English translation: *Mary, Mother of the Lord, Figure of the Church*, London 1963].

[86] Cf. *Doctrine in the Church of England*: The Report of the Commission on Christian Doctrine, ... (1922), London, 1938, pp. 214-215. Cf. my work: Enrique Llamas Martínez, O.C.D., *El Anglicanismo, Origen-Historia-Mensaje*, Salamanca, Universidad Pontificia ... Centro de Estudios Orientales y Ecuménicos, 2003, p. 271: *La Virgen María* (with bibliography).

[87] John Paul II, *Redemptoris Mater*, 30: "It is good omen that these 'Western Christian' churches and ecclesial communities agree with the Catholic Church on a number of fundamental points in Christian doctrine, including points relating to the Virgin Mary. Effectively, they recognize her as Mother of the Lord and consider this title a part of our faith in Christ. ... They look to Mary who, at the foot of the Cross, receives Christ's beloved disciple as her own son, who in turn receives Mary as his Mother."

of mankind in the "Communio Sanctorum." Anglican representatives participating in international Mariological and Marian congresses have favored just such a thesis.[88]

Part Two: Mary, Model of the Church

Problematic

1) This theme, "Mary, model of the Church" together with that of "spiritual motherhood," certainly forms a unit properly covered by the title: *Mary, Mother of the Church*. They constitute two broad questions or themes mutually complementing each other.

We may also affirm, in my opinion, that it is impossible to attain a perfect, complete and adequate theological understanding of spiritual maternity, or of *Mary, model of the Church* in the history of salvation, as we are now considering her, if we do not include in that motherhood, or in the title *Mary, Mother of the Church*, some reference to the prerogative of her *exemplarity*, to the consideration of Mary as model and paradigm of the Church and souls.

Mother and *model* are two different concepts, although they enjoy an affinity and certain *similarity* from the maternal point of view. The reason is because the action of the model bears on the creation or design of a new being, or the reproduction of a copy more or less perfect. Does this not resemble a maternal action?

An exemplar transmits being and life to its copy analogically. In the configuration of the copy or reproduction, being and life are fully unique, yet also profoundly similar to the original. Thus, the being and life of the child are truly unique, truly the child's being and life, yet the child resembles its mother, with due allowances for the different modes of reproduction in the examples.

It is not possible to deny that a model exercises a truly positive influence on production or configuration of a new being, which for this reason is similar to the model. Exemplary causality, considered analogically, bears a certain likeness with maternal action, one which is

---

[88] See my studies: E. Llamas, *Declaración ecuménica del Congreso Mariológico de Malta*, in *Pastoral Ecuménica* (1984), pp. 76-77; Idem, *Declaraciones mariológicas ecuménicas (1979-1987)*, in *Renovación Ecuménica*, n. 94 (1988), pp. 7-10.

particularly stressed in the field of spiritual and supernatural realities, of which we know relatively little.

This reflection may be applied analogically, therefore, in the order of spiritual realities and within the history of salvation. It may be said that in this order perfection of being and resemblance is greater than in the natural order, where at times persons and individuals lack experience of the influence and meaning of exemplarity.[89]

This general consideration applies perfectly to the context of Mary's spiritual maternity, and to that of the life of the Church and to the exercises of the spiritual life in souls. Being a model and example are concepts certainly different from those of mother and maternity, yet even though different—as is education—they fall within the comprehensive and more perfect role of being a mother.

It is obvious that maternal action does not consist only in the act of bearing or bringing a new life into the world. Maternal duty also consists in, even if merely as a consequence, nursing and educating the child, developing its powers, and fostering the child's potential for life, as well as perfecting all its good qualities by their exercise.

These reflections are based on important statements of Pope Paul VI regarding Mary as model of the Church, which in fact serve to formulate the problematic correctly and adequately. We proceed from the human and natural toward the supernatural and spiritual, the more perfect. Echoing Vatican II the Pope says:

> Indeed, just as no human mother can limit her task to the generation of a new man but must extend it to the function of nourishing and educating her offspring, thus the Blessed Virgin Mary, after participating in the redeeming sacrifice of the Son ... now continues to fulfill from heaven her maternal function as the cooperator in the birth and development of divine life in the individual

---

[89] Pope Paul VI stresses the meaning of *influence* which a model exercises for the creation of a new image, in responding to those who insist on minimizing the positive influence of the *example*. He does this by referring to the Virgin as *Mary, model of the Church*. He discusses the "*influence*" of her powerful intercession and of still *another influence* exercised over men: *that of example*, a very real and very important influence (Paul VI, *Signum Magnum* Part II, n. 5, and Part I, par. 3). See LG 65.

souls of redeemed men. This is a most consoling truth which, by the free consent of God the All-Wise, is an integrating part of the mystery of human salvation; therefore it must be held as faith by all Christians.[90]

Pope Paul VI was keenly aware of the approach to and explanation of these problems in the wake of a Mariology enriched by the concepts and perspectives opened by Vatican II on the spiritual maternity both of Mary and of the Church. Here he has provided a very significant text which can serve as a theme of reflection and as starting point for our considerations on this part of our theme.

2) Recognition and veneration of Mary's exemplarity: Her characteristic prerogative as *model* of the Church and of souls, is the foundation for, and form of veneration by which, Mary is honored by the Church, one also known as *imitation of Mary*. This veneration has been recognized officially, and practiced by the Church in many different ways from the earliest times. It has its basis in the Bible, e.g., where Elizabeth praised Mary's faith and filled with the Holy Spirit spoke out with a loud voice saying: *Blessed are you ... and blessed is she that believed ...* (cf. Lk 1:41-45). St. Ambrose fostered this veneration in a singular form and highly recommended it to his disciples, as Pope Paul VI reminds us.[91]

The *imitation* of Mary and her role of model, a genuine dignity, is grounded in her perfection and her singularly eminent sanctity, recognized as such by the Church. But Mary becomes truly and effectively model when, by her influence and exemplarity, she actively forms her spiritual image in souls. This influence is considered a form of causality, or the positive action of a cause, which produces in souls the effect of holiness. According to some modern Mariologists, this causality is implicitly contained in the salvific designs of God who from all eternity chose Mary to be mother and collaborator with her Son,

---

[90] Paul VI, *Signum Magnum*, Part I, par. 1.

[91] Paul VI, *Marialis Cultus* (Feb. 2, 1974), 21. From St. Ambrose comes this classic phrase referring to the life of Mary: *Vita eius omnium est disciplina* ("Her life is the model of virtue for everyone") (*Expositio in Lucam*, II, 26; CSEL, 32, IV p. 45). As regards St. Ambrose on this point, cf. Martino Bertagna, O.F.M., *Elementa cultus mariani apud S. Ambrosium Mediolanensem*, in *De primordiis cultus mariani. Acta Congressus Mariologici-Mariani in Lusitania anno 1967 celebrati*, vol. III, Rome, 1979, pp. 1-16; D. Bertetto, S.D.B., *De cultu imitationis B.M. Virginis apud Patres latinos*, in *De primordiis cultus...*, cit., pp. 99-118 (on St. Ambrose, pp. 101-110).

the Redeemer, in the work of redemption. This reflection seems very plausible since the concept of spiritual maternity includes spiritual action in favor of souls. From this perspective, imitation of Mary is dignified in the highest degree, because apart from other considerations, Mary becomes the ineffable personification of the Church.[92]

From this we can infer the important value this theme has for Mariology in general, and in particular for contemporary Mariology. A profound study of Mary's relations as model of the Church leads us to a broader and profounder knowledge of the mystery of her predestination in the history of salvation.

It would be possible to clarify still further the intimate relation between Mary's exemplarity, her role as *model* of the Church, and her spiritual maternity. Such a clarification would constitute a positive contribution to Mariology and a solid advance in knowledge of the Church. This *very consoling truth*, as Pope Paul VI describes it, must not be lacking in outlines of Mariology, as so often is the case today. Few manuals of Mariology give any attention to this eminently theological and spiritual question.

Some Mariologists provide a brief explanation of this theme, tucked away in a final chapter, expounded in a vague and imprecise manner as one among secondary questions touching popular piety, Marian spirituality, etc. But this is not to give it the importance such a mystery deserves. On this point, the treatise on Mariology by Fr. Bertetto, whom I have quoted several times, is an honorable exception. He devotes an ample part of the chapter entitled, *Mary in the Mystery of the Church*, to the study of *Mary, model and Example of the Church*.[93] Methodologically, this is an exceptionally good exposition.

---

[92] About these and other introductory questions, cf. D. Bertetto, *Maria, la Serva...*, cit., pp. 268-270.

[93] D. Bertetto, *Maria, la Serva* ..., cit. In this section, taking into account the teachings of Vatican II, he studies a series of important questions: "Most Holy Mary, example and model of the Church, as Mother and Virgin" (pp. 571-579); "Most Holy Mary, model and example of the Church in sanctity and virtue" (pp. 579-584); "Most Holy Mary, model and example of the Church in the spousal association with Christ" (pp. 484-586); "Mary, model of youth" (pp. 588-593); "Conclusions" (pp. 594-595). He also makes reference to Mary and priesthood in the Church (pp. 586-588).

3) The theme *Mary, model of the Church* is divided in two sections, because it can be considered from two different points of reference. The first one is the Virgin Mary herself, the Mother of God, who efficaciously collaborates with her Son in the work of redemption. Under this aspect, we consider and contemplate the image of Mary adorned and enriched with all the graces, virtues and gifts of the Holy Spirit, and the particular charisms which constitute the basic features of her exemplarity. These features are a radiation of that perfection which the faithful must imitate.

On the other hand we can contemplate Mary as *model*, i.e., as the sum total of her supernatural gifts and perfections, as object or final goal of the spiritual, supernatural activity of those souls who exercise or practice *imitation* of Mary. The objects of this imitation are concrete realities: the Virgin Mary's virtues or interior composure. This *imitation* is, as it were, the echo of the exemplarity and perfection of the model casting rays of light into the heart of souls and moving them to imitate her; that echo is the soul's response to that influence or to the powerful attraction exerted by the model's spiritual radiation on the soul.

At first glance these two aspects might seem different, but in truth they are complementary to each other. The *model's* function is to influence those who contemplate it and by its radiation make them feel the strength of its perfections, so as to arouse in them actual *imitation*. What is the point of a model which does not influence those who know it? It can only serve as a museum piece.

We can say the same about *imitation*, or the person who must practice it. Without a model to imitate, it is not easy to realize a work of perfect form in a purely spontaneous manner. This holds special truth and relevance in the spiritual and supernatural order, in the perfecting of souls. It is a truism that by following an interior inspiration a person can achieve great, wonderful and very perfect works, but with a major proviso: such a person must be a genius and a highly, very highly gifted individual. The vast majority of persons, above all in the spiritual life, enjoy no such status, and have need of the guidance and the inspiration of a model: Jesus Christ, the Virgin Mary, St. Joseph, the saints.

In this chapter we are speaking of *Mary, model of the Church*, whereas her *imitation* is to be treated as part of another chapter. Thus, I will now discuss only questions regarding the Virgin Mary as singular *model and exemplar* for the Church and her members, over whom she exercises a beneficial and permanent maternal influence.

Mary, Model and Example of the Church—The Fact

Is Mary truly *model and example* of the Church? Is this *exemplarity* to be understood in the proper, objective sense of the term, or is it to be taken merely as a simple *metaphor*? The Virgin Mary is a real, individual person who, gloriously assumed into heaven body and soul, participates in eternal bliss. The Church, on the other hand, is a supernatural entity, a juridically constituted community with very singular characteristics. Everything relative to spiritual maternity and exemplarity, on the basis of a common denominator, may be applied both to Mary and the Church, provided their specific differences and particular characteristics are respected.[94]

This does not represent an obstacle to the reality of Mary's true spiritual *exemplarity* for the Church, an exemplarity Mary exerts over and realizes in the members of the Church. The questions we have formulated include two problems. First, the existence or the fact in itself of Mary's *exemplarity*; and second—supposing the answer to that question is affirmative and to mention just a few concrete points bearing on this—what would be the nature, the forms, the extension, the universality and the applications of such *exemplarity*?

Mary is Exemplar, Model and Figure or Icon of the Church

1) State of the question: The goal of this section is to offer theological proofs, arguments and reasons which guarantee the existence of this prerogative of the Virgin Mother of God: *model* of the Church. After acknowledging this fact, we proceed to give a theological explanation of its main significance. To attain an objective and reasoned understanding of this question, we must examine it as it is found in the supernatural order and within the history of salvation.

---

[94] See my study: Enrique del Sdo. Corazón (Llamas), O.C.D., *Comparación entre la maternidad espiritual de la Virgen María y la maternidad de la Iglesia*, in *Estudios Marianos*, 20 (1959), pp. 207-262. See also: M.M. Philipon, O.P., *Maternité spirituelle de Marie et de l'Eglise*, en *Etudes Mariales* (1952) pp. 64 ff.; Sixto González, O.P., *Maternidad de María y Maternidad de la Iglesia*, in *Estudios Marianos*, 18 (1957), pp. 301-349.

Mary's exemplarity for the Church, or her being the perfect *model of the Church*, stands in intimate relation with divine and spiritual motherhood, and depends on both by disposition of divine will. In his eternal design of salvation, God determined the reasons for the Virgin Mary's exemplarity in relation to the Church.

On this supposition, our effort to establish the existence or fact of this prerogative of *Mary, model of the Church*, should not be limited to purely human considerations. This fact is intimately linked, as mentioned above, with the spiritual motherhood and so pertains to the order of salvation, wisely and harmoniously established by God. In regard to Mary's exemplary role, I quote again an especially important passage from Pope Paul VI's Apostolic Exhortation *Signum Magnum*, referring to the spiritual maternity, but for the Pope also including her exemplarity. The Holy Father says that: "*This is a most consoling truth which, by the free consent of God the All-Wise, is an integrating part of the mystery of human salvation.*"[95]

From this perspective, in order to know the reasons for Mary's exemplarity, we must consult Divine Revelation and the teachings of Church's living Magisterium, which on so many occasions when recommending and inviting the faithful to imitate the Virgin Mary's spiritual perfections, propose her as universal *model and example*. In all of these cases the Magisterium acknowledges Mary's exemplarity and her sublime perfection as a singular *model* for the Church.

2) Mary is model and example of the Church because she is spiritual Mother. Pope Paul VI expounded this idea, stating that it was Christ himself who related the exemplarity and dignity of model to the spiritual maternity and to a point included these in it. Thus reads a very significant document:

> What must stimulate the faithful even more to follow the examples of the most holy Virgin is the fact that Jesus himself, by giving her to us as our Mother, has tacitly indicated her as the model to be followed. It is, in fact, a natural thing that the children should have the same sentiments of their mothers and should reflect their merits and virtues. Therefore, as each one of us can

---

[95] Paul VI, *Signum Magnum*, Part I, par. 1.

repeat with St. Paul: "The Son of God loved me and gave himself up for me" (cf. Gal 2:20; Eph 5:2), so in all trust he can believe that the divine Savior has left to him also, in spiritual heritage, his Mother, with all the treasures of grace and virtues with which he had endowed her, that she may pour them over us through the influence of her powerful intercession and our willing imitation.[96]

We could also add Vatican II's testimony, which affirms and sets in relief Mary's exemplarity for the Church as a matter of fact, and determining in some instances the object of this exemplarity.

3) Mary, model of the Church, by reason of her perfection: Among the reasons for Mary's exemplarity for the Church, this is one of the more important. A *model* must integrate in itself all the perfections which are possible to those who must imitate it.

The popes chiefly comment on and set in relief the importance of the Virgin Mary's moral and spiritual perfection when they exhort the faithful to imitate her. Further, one of the necessary conditions required by the category of *"model"* is highest perfection.

Religious literature is very abundant on this topic. I would like to quote the very significant text of Pope Paul VI for the proclamation of the title, *Mary, Mother of the Church,* and for this reason, *example and model.* Speaking at the closing ceremony of the third session of Vatican II, he stated, in a passage immediately following the proclamation of this title in honor of the Blessed Virgin as its justification:

> During her mortal life [Mary] achieved the perfect figure of a disciple of Christ, was a mirror of all the virtues and plainly lived the beatitudes preached by Christ. This is why the Church, in the conduct of the various features of her life and activities, takes the example of the Virgin Mother of God as the absolute norm for perfect imitation of Christ.[97]

A few paragraphs beyond he insists on the Virgin Mary's perfection as *model of the Church.* He recommends that among the Christian people

---

[96] Paul VI, *ibid.*, Part II, n. 5.
[97] Paul VI, discourse at closing ceremony, third session of Vatican II; cit., pp. 916-17.

the Council Fathers raise the level of piety and devotion toward the Mother of God,

> proposing her as an example to follow because of her fidelity, her prompt obedience to every inspiration of heavenly grace, and finally because of a life completely shaped according to Christ's precepts and nourished on love, in such wise that the faithful united among themselves by the common name of the Mother, might grow ever stronger in the confession of their faith.[98]

4) Mary, model of the Church: concrete aspects: These have been specified by Vatican II, implicitly teaching Mary's exemplarity as *model of the Church*, as *mother* and as *virgin*, and in the order of *faith, charity and perfect union with Christ*.[99]

Here the Council takes as its basis the authority and testimony of patristic tradition, particularly that of St. Ambrose, one of the most important authors on this theme:

> By reason of the gift and role of her divine motherhood, by which she is united with her Son, the Redeemer, and with her unique graces and functions, the Blessed Virgin is also intimately united to the Church. As St. Ambrose taught, the Mother of God is a type of the Church in the order of faith. … For in the mystery of the Church, which is also rightly called Mother and Virgin, the Blessed Virgin stands out in eminent and singular fashion as exemplar both of Virgin and of Mother.[100]

This text has two parts corresponding to two important ideas. The first belongs to the Council's formal statement: Mary is *type-exemplar of the Church*. This affirmation includes the exact points of reference by which her *exemplarity* is verified: Mother and Virgin. In this affirmation Mary's maternal, exemplarity for the Church is likewise clearly indicated to be in relation to her maternity, at the beginning of the text mentioned

---

[98] Paul VI, *ibid*.
[99] LG 63.
[100] LG 63.

as divine maternity, although including spiritual or soteriological maternity implicitly.

The second part of this text clarifies Mary's maternal influence on the Church by way of faith and obedience. The Council underlines—as one of the basics of its teaching—the communion of the faithful with Christ, the only-begotten Son of the Father and elder brother in God's family. The maternal influence on the Church is exercised through the cooperation of the Mother in the begetting and education of adopted children through her love.[101]

At this point we can certainly speak of a parallelism between Mary and the Church, although not perfect. The Church has a certain dependency on Christ, the Head of the Mystical Body and also on Mary, a true spiritual mother. According to St. Ambrose's thought, this parallelism is verified in the order of faith, charity and perfect union with Christ. I believe a certain *excellence* in Mary in relation to the Church must also be admitted here, for she is spiritual Mother of the faithful who make up the Church. This can also be understood of the multifaceted intercession by which from heaven the Virgin, there assumed, guides with maternal love her Son's brethren.[102]

5) Mary, model of the Church, in holiness: The Marian document of Vatican II draws special attention to the sanctity of Mary and of the Church. The role of the Mother consists in radiating and increasing holiness in the Church. The Church on her part joyfully contemplates the sanctity of the Mother of grace, and imitates her charity.[103] She

---

[101] LG 63: "Through her faith and obedience she gave birth to the Son of the Father, not through knowledge of man, but by the overshadowing of the Holy Spirit, in the manner of a New Eve who placed her faith ... in God's messenger without wavering in doubt. ... The Son whom she brought forth is he whom God placed as the firstborn among many brethren (cf. Rom 8:29), that is, the faithful in whose generation and formation she cooperates with a mother's love." In LG 64 the Council explains the spiritual-virginal maternity of the Church contemplating [Mary's] sublime sanctity so as to imitate her charity. The Church is virgin, because by the grace of the Holy Spirit and imitation of the Mother of the Lord "she herself is a virgin, who keeps in its entirety and purity the faith she pledged to her spouse ... she keeps intact faith, firm hope and sincere charity." Pope Paul VI directly treats this theme in *Signum Magnum* with the same terminology.

[102] Cf. D. Bertetto, *Maria, la Serva...*, cit., pp. 571-572.

[103] LG 64.

contemplates it in the light of the Word of God made flesh, because the Virgin Mother is her *example* and *model*.[104]

From this perspective, once we have placed ourselves at the heart of this subject, we can say something more still. Mary is not only a *model* of sanctity of the Church and for the Church. In contemplating the Virgin gloriously assumed into heaven, represented by the Woman of the Apocalypse (12:1-14), victorious over the seven-headed dragon and wearing a crown of twelve stars, we can state further that Mary is the *personification* of the Church's *sanctity*; she is much more than a simple *model*, as perfect as this might be.

Vatican II recognizes and teaches this singularity of the Immaculate Virgin, all beautiful, *beauty* itself, as being *not merely aesthetical, but essential and ontological*, as Paul VI has defined her,[105] the very *personification* of the Church in her holiness. Such is the meaning of this very important Council text:

> But while the Church in the Most Holy Virgin has already reached that perfection whereby she exists without spot or wrinkle (cf. Eph 5:27), the faithful still strive to conquer sin and increase in holiness. ... And so they turn their eyes to Mary who shines forth as model for the whole community of the elect as model of virtues.[106]

Mary has already attained full sanctity. She is the personification of the highest, most perfect, radiant and luminous sanctity, the Immaculate. She is the icon of holiness, and as a singular, most unique person, she is the most faithful, representative expression of the sanctity of the infinite God in his perfections. The Church, as she exists in her other members, is still walking the path of progress and growth in holiness.

For the greater part this progress is realized by the faithful in the practice of the virtues and the life of contemplative prayer. On this journey the faithful come to resemble the Redeemer more and more each day. And by their exercise of faith, hope and ardent charity, and by their obedience to the word and to the will of the Father of mercies, they

---

[104] LG 65.
[105] Cf. Paul VI, allocution, Sept. 9, 1973 (*L'Osservatore Romano*, Oct. 9, 1973). Cf. my study: E. Llamas, O.C.D., *Pablo VI, Promotor y Animador de la devoción mariana*, in *Revista de Espiritualidad*, n. 143 (1977) 328.
[106] LG 65.

come to unite themselves more intimately, and to configure themselves as perfectly as possible to, the image of the Risen Christ.[107]

6) Mary, model of the Church: other aspects: The considerations I have made up to this point do not exhaust the subject of Mary's exemplarity for the Church. There are many other facets of this exemplarity which derive from very important characteristics of Mary, from applications of papal teachings, and from the examination of significant moments in the life of the Church and of souls.

Those radiant features of the very imitable figure of Mary, reflected in the Marian document of Vatican II, are, as it were, concepts and ideas contributing to a more objective and deeper understanding of Mary's image. Today, such knowledge is all the more necessary, if the teaching of Vatican II regarding true Marian devotion is to be put into practice. This consists in knowledge of and filial love for our Mother, the Mother of God, and in *the imitation of her virtues*.[108]

Among those other features of Mary's exemplarity we can propose the following as among the more important:

• Mary, model of the Church in devotion consisting of making one's own life a sacrifice to God.[109]
  • Mary, model of the Church in the exercise of liturgical worship.[110]
  • Mary, model of the Church in the basic attitudes of Christian life.[111]
  • Mary, model of the Church in apostolic love.[112]
  • Mary, model of the Church, as the most perfect person after Christ.
  • Mary, model of the Church in its universality.

Mary, Model of the Church, Taken in the Proper and Objective Sense

The elements making up this section are realities with a proper and objective sense. They are neither metaphors nor mere symbols. Of course, we are dealing here with the meaning and significance of spiritual and supernatural realities, having far greater power and value than natural ones.

---

[107] Cf. LG 65.
[108] Cf. LG 67.
[109] Cf. Pope Paul VI, *Marialis Cultus*, nn. 21-22.
[110] Cf. Paul VI, *ibid.*, 34-36.
[111] Cf. Paul VI, *ibid.*, 34-36.
[112] Cf. LG 65.

Mary, as the Church's *personification*, contains in herself the total perfection and sanctity of the Church. That is why after Christ, in her own personal reality, she is the most perfect *model* of the mystery of the Church and of all her members. Nor may it be said that Mary is a mere symbol, or that this title is to be taken as pure metaphor. The meaning is real and objective, with the same objectivity that the Most Blessed Virgin Mother of God, the mystery of the Church, and grace and sanctity have.

We may not always know very well or with much precision the mechanics of that spiritual influence which the Virgin Mary, as spiritual Mother, exercises over her children. She is endowed with all perfections and in some way *unites in her person and re-echoes the most important doctrines of the faith*,[113] and radiates over souls the most sublime gifts of salvation, drawing them to Christ with the strength of her personal influence as Mediatrix between God and man.

None of this can be interpreted away as mere metaphor. The Virgin Mary is the eminent model of the Church. By her maternal influence, Mary models the Church according to her image and likeness and perfectly shapes it according to Jesus' image, absolute model of all the elect in the history of salvation. All must reflect his face to be part of the Heavenly Jerusalem (cf. Eph 1:3-12).

In this way, within the Church, her members can be configured according to the image of the Virgin Mother, model of sanctity, and thus by the shortest and most direct route, be conformed to the glorious and radiant image of the Son of God unto his praise and glory (cf. Eph 1:6).

---

[113] LG 65.

IV.
Marian Liturgy and Devotion

Mary and the Liturgical Year

Fr. Neil J. Roy

Introduction: First Principles and Goals

Mary's dignity as the *Theotókos* ("God-bearer" or "Mother of God") is the source of all her other privileges and titles. It is precisely her exalted role in the mystery of the Incarnation which accounts likewise for Mary's unique, ongoing role in the history of salvation. Having cooperated with God's grace from the very beginning of her life, and sharing intimately in Christ's suffering and redemptive death, Mary now enjoys in heaven the fullness of all that the children of the Church can hope to enjoy in eternity. Indeed, in view of Mary's relationship to the three divine Persons of the Blessed Trinity,[1] she possesses a state of glory far exceeding the rest of the human race. Any Catholic treatment of Mary in reference to the liturgy of the Church must necessarily take into account Mary's unique, complementary mediation in relation to her Son, Jesus Christ. Far from posing an obstacle to ecumenical dialogue, a clear articulation of Mary's status in the Church and her role in the lives of individual Christians is indispensable for that movement towards unity in truth which Christ himself made the central petition of his priestly prayer.[2]

---

[1] "Redeemed, in a more exalted fashion, by reason of the merits of her Son and united to him by a close and indissoluble tie, she is endowed with the high office and dignity of the Mother of the Son of God, and therefore she is also the beloved daughter of the Father and the temple of the Holy Spirit." Second Vatican Council, Dogmatic Constitution on the Church *Lumen Gentium* [LG], 53. Conciliar documents are cited from *Vatican Council II. The Conciliar and Post Conciliar Documents*, ed. Austin Flannery, new revised study ed. (Dublin: Dominican Publications and Newtown AU: E.J. Dwyer, 1992).

[2] "I do not pray for these only, but also for those who believe in me through their word, that they may all be one; even as thou, Father, art in me and I in thee, that

This chapter explores the theological foundations of the Church's liturgical cult of the Blessed Virgin Mary and her prominent place on the general Roman calendar. It first summarizes Mary's role in the life of the Church, not only in her cooperation with the divine economy in the mystery of the Incarnation, but also in the ongoing history of salvation. It also considers Mary's identity with the Church. The next section examines the relationship between liturgy and doctrine, clarifying the dependence of the Church's public worship on her *depositum fidei*, or body of teaching. What the Church in her official prayer says about Mary and to Mary reflects her belief not only in Mary's privileges and the nature of her mediation, but also in various other mysteries of the faith. Finally, the chapter presents feasts and observances of the Blessed Virgin Mary as they gradually appeared on the Roman calendar. The approach taken here is diachronic, beginning with the importation of Marian feasts from the East and continuing through to the third typical edition of the Roman Missal issued in 2002 by the authority of Pope John Paul II.[3] As the liturgical and political influence of the Roman See spread throughout the West, a distinction eventually emerged between the local calendar of the Diocese of Rome and the general calendar of what became the Roman Rite. The chapter concludes with a consideration of Mary in the two dominant seasonal cycles of the Proper of Time, namely, Advent-Christmas-Epiphany, and Lent-Easter-Pentecost. The

---

they also may be in us, so that the world may believe that thou hast sent me. The glory which thou hast given me I have given to them, that they may be one even as we are one, I in them and thou in me, that they may become perfectly one, so that the world may know that thou hast sent me and hast loved them as thou hast loved me" (Jn 17:20-23). Biblical citations and references are drawn from *The Holy Bible* Revised Standard Version Catholic Edition (London: Catholic Truth Society, 1966). For an ecumenical dialogue on the Blessed Virgin, see *Mary: Grace and Hope in Christ. The Seattle Statement of the Anglican-Roman Catholic International Commission. The Text with Commentaries and Study Guide*, eds. Donald Bolen and Gregory Cameron (London and New York: Continuum, 2006). Other studies of Mary from an ecumenical, interfaith, or broadly cultural perspective include Jaroslav Pelikan and Davide Flusser and Justin Lang, *Mary: Images of the Mother of Jesus in Jewish and Christian Perspective* (Minneapolis MN: Fortress Press, 2005) and Pelikan, *Mary through the Centuries: Her Place in the History of Culture* (New Haven and London: Yale University Press, 1996).

[3] *Missale romanum ex decreto sacrosancti oecumenici concilii Vaticani II instauratum auctoritate Pauli pp. VI promulgatum Ioannis Pauli II cura recognitum, editio typica tertia* (Vatican City: Libreria Editrice Vaticana, 2002) [MR 2002].

final Marian anthems customarily assigned to various liturgical periods set the tone of the particular season, and afford a lens through which to glimpse the Church's understanding of Mary's place in the rotation of liturgical seasons.

Mary in the Life of the Church

Mariologists mention three dimensions or "moments" of mediation: Mary's own cooperation in the redemption of the human race, her distribution of the graces won by the redemption, and her complementary intercession on behalf of the Church.[4] It is beyond the scope of this essay to rehearse in minute detail the threefold mode of Marian mediation which others have presented to full advantage elsewhere. This piece seeks rather to demonstrate how the Church's authentic devotion to the Mother of God finds expression in the sacred liturgy. It therefore treats Mary's place in the liturgical year, both in the temporal and sanctoral cycles. First, however, it briefly summarizes Mary's collaboration in the redemption of the human race, in order the better to show how the Church regards Mary as model, intercessor, and image of the heavenly communion to which all Christians are called. Taking into account the development of the Church's veneration of Mary over two millennia, this chapter examines Mary's presence in the Mass and then on the calendar.

Mary and the Incarnation

In considering the figure and role of Mary in the sacred liturgy, it is necessary first to take into account the place which she occupies in the history of salvation. Various branches of theology which, since the Reformation, have come into more distinct relief, such as Christology, soteriology, ecclesiology, and eschatology, all reflect, and in turn

---

[4] For studies on Marian mediation and the sacred liturgy, see Arthur Burton Calkins, "Mary as Coredemptrix, Mediatrix and Advocate in the Contemporary Roman Liturgy" in *Mary Coredemptrix, Mediatrix and Advocate, Theological Foundations: Towards a Papal Definition?* ed. Mark I. Miravalle (Santa Barbara CA: Queenship Publishing, 1995); Miravalle, *Mary Coredemptrix, Mediatrix, Advocate* (Santa Barbara CA: Queenship Publishing, 1993) passim; Juniper B. Carol, "Our Lady's Coredemption," *Mariology* (Milwaukee: Bruce, 1955) 2: 386-392; Armand J. Robichaud, "Mary, Dispensatrix of All Graces," in Carol, *Mariology* 2: 426-460.

contribute to, a profound understanding of Mary's figure and role in the Church's liturgy.

To begin with, Mary played a pivotal role in the mystery of the Incarnation. As mentioned earlier, all the privileges granted to Mary by God, and the titles which the Church uses in reference to Mary, are hers in view of her role in the Incarnation. It was Mary, after all, who gave to the immortal Word of the Father his human nature. This fact alone gives rise to several important implications for the sacraments, all of which are rooted in the Incarnation, but especially for the Eucharist. Since, in the Eucharist, bread and wine are converted substantially into Christ's body and blood, soul, and divinity, the faithful who approach Holy Communion receive Christ himself, whole and entire, under the sacred species.[5] The Church's faith in the reality of Christ's presence is neatly summed up in two brief phrases: the eucharistic salutation *Ave verum corpus natum ex Maria Virgine!* and the axiom *caro Christi, caro Mariae.* The Bread of Life, then, to borrow a phrase from Pope John Paul II, exudes "the taste and aroma of the Virgin Mother."[6] Communion with the eucharistic Christ, consequently, entails also communion with Mary, "the Woman of the Eucharist."[7] In the reception of the Eucharist,

---

[5] Note the precise terminology of the oath imposed on Berengarius of Tours by the Council of Rome, February 11, 1079: "Ego Berengarius corde credo et ore confiteor, panem et vinum, quae ponuntur in altari, per mysterium sacrae ordinationis et verba nostri Redemptoris substantialiter converti in veram et propriam ac vivificatricem carnem et sanguinem Iesu Christi Domini nostri et post consecrationem esse verum Christi corpus, quod natum est de Virgine et quod pro salute mundi oblatum in cruce pependit, et quod sedet ad dexteram Patris, et verum sanguinem Christi, qui de latere eius effusus est, non tantum per signum et virtutem sacramenti, sed in proprietate naturae et veritate substantiae...." *Enchiridion symbolorum definitionum et declarationum de rebus fidei et morum,* eds Heinrich Denzinger et Adolf Schönmetzer, 36th ed. emended (Barcelona and Freiburg and Rome: Herder, 1976) [DS] 700, p. 230.

[6] "... il sapore e il profumo della Vergine Madre," John Paul II, Angelus address, solemnity of Corpus Christi, June 5, 1983 in *Insegnamenti di Giovanni Paolo II,* VI.1 (Vatican City: Libreria Editrice Vaticana, 1983), 1447, trans. *L'Osservatore Romano,* 788:2, cited by Arthur Burton Calkins, "Mary's Presence in the Mass: The Teaching of Pope John Paul II," *Antiphon: A Journal for Liturgical Renewal* 10.2 (2006) 132-158, at 141.

[7] John Paul II, encyclical on the Eucharist in its Relationship to the Church *Ecclesia de Eucharistia* (April 17, 2003) 53-58. The Pope devotes an entire chapter, the sixth, titled "At the School of Mary 'Woman of the Eucharist,'" to the relationship

the faithful participate in both sacramental and ecclesial communion with Mary. Indeed, as theologian James T. O'Connor points out, "No Eucharist is ever celebrated except in union with the Blessed ever-Virgin Mary and all the saints."[8]

Mary and the History of Salvation

Mary's role in the history of salvation is by no means limited to the Incarnation. In the infancy narratives of Matthew[9] and Luke,[10] Mary conceives and bears Christ without loss of her virginity. She likewise nurtures and cares for Jesus throughout his childhood, sharing his home until he embarks on his public ministry. Luke depicts Mary as a woman of prayer and contemplative reflection. After the visit of the shepherds to the newborn Christ in the crib, for example, "Mary kept all these things, pondering them in her heart."[11] Again, after the finding of the child Jesus in the Temple, "his mother kept all these things in her heart."[12] Pope Benedict XVI remarks on Our Lady's prayerful penetration of these mysteries as they unfolded and as she later contemplated them:

> Mary's memory is first of all a retention of the events in remembrance, but it is more than that: It is an interior conversation with all that has happened. Thanks to this

---

[8] between Mary and the Eucharist, and Mary's consequent relationship to the Church. In the same encyclical, John Paul II explains how Mary leads Christians to the Eucharist and provides the correct example of contemplating this mystery. Pope Benedict XVI uses the same title of Our Lady in his post-synodal Apostolic Exhortation on the Eucharist as the Source and Summit of the Church's Life and Mission *Sacramentum caritatis* (February 22, 2007), 96, where he likewise calls Mary the Church's "finest icon" and "a singular model of the Eucharistic life."

[8] James T. O'Connor, *The Hidden Manna: A Theology of the Eucharist*, 2nd ed. (San Francisco: Ignatius Press, 2005) 83. Cf. LG 50: "when ... we celebrate the eucharistic sacrifice we are most closely united to the worship of the heavenly Church; when in the fellowship of communion we honor and remember the glorious Mary ever-Virgin, St. Joseph, the holy apostles and martyrs and all the saints."

[9] Mt 1:18-23; 2:10-23.

[10] Lk 1:26-56; 2:1-52. For the virginal conception and birth of Christ in John, see Ignace de la Potterie, *Mary in the Mystery of the Covenant*, trans. Bertrand Buby (New York: Alba House, 1993) 67-122, especially 96-122.

[11] Lk 2:19.

[12] Lk 2:51.

conversation, she penetrates into the interior dimension, she sees the events in their inter-connectedness, and she learns to understand them.[13]

Mary's prayerfulness emerges likewise in the Acts of the Apostles, where she is mentioned among the earliest members of the nascent Church, committed to prayer in the cenacle between the Ascension of the Lord and the descent of the Paraclete: "All these with one accord devoted themselves to prayer, together with the women and Mary the mother of Jesus, and with his brethren."[14]

Not only does Mary provide for the material needs of Christ in his infancy. She also presents him in the Temple to his heavenly Father in a ritual act of oblation. Luke records the prophetic words addressed to Mary on this occasion by the holy man Simeon:

> Behold, this child is set for the fall and rising
>   of many in Israel
> (and a sword will pierce through your own soul
>   also)
> that thoughts out of many hearts may be
>   revealed.[15]

In the Temple, Mary is associated liturgically with Christ's oblation to the Father. At Calvary, Christ will associate Mary with his offering on the Cross. The infancy narratives anticipate various dimensions of the Paschal Mystery. The three days which Christ spent in the Temple in Luke 3:41, for example, parallel the three days he would spend in the tomb after his Passion and death. Similarly, Mary's offering of the Infant Jesus to God in the Temple, as recounted in Luke 2:22-38, foreshadows ritually the offering she later would make as she stood at the foot of the Cross in John 19:25-27.

In the Fourth Gospel, Mary interacts with Christ at key moments of his messianic mission. At the inauguration of his public life, on the occasion of the marriage feast at Cana in John 2:1-12, Mary, the New

---

[13] Pope Benedict XVI, *Jesus of Nazareth: from the Baptism in the Jordan to the Transfiguration*, trans. Adrian J. Walker (London: Bloomsbury, 2007) 234.
[14] Acts 1:14.
[15] Lk 2:34-35.

Eve, tells Christ, the New Adam, that the wine for the wedding has failed. She thereby prompts Jesus to give the first of his "signs" of the new messianic age. Inaugurating a new creation in grace, Christ changes the six jars of water, symbol of the days of creation (nature), into wine (grace). Far from playing a peripheral role, Mary at Cana stands as the image of the Church, the new People of God, the Bride of Christ who himself is both Lamb and High Priest of the New Covenant. Mary pleads with Christ for those gathered at the wedding, observing that "They have no wine."[16] The result is a new wine surpassing in excellence the former supply that had failed.

Mary's presence at the inauguration of the New Covenant is far from passive. As St. Irenaeus of Lyons (+202) points out, "the Virgin Mary untied the knot of sin bound up by the virgin Eve."[17] Just as the first woman, Eve, tempted the first man, Adam, to disobey the Lord and grasp at equality with God,[18] so the second Eve and new Woman, Mary, urges the second Adam, Christ the new Man, to provide the new wine of divine grace upon a situation in need of divine mercy. Without in any way detracting from Christ's role as the Messiah and Mediator of the New Covenant, Mary is closely associated with his mission. Mary's message to the servants, "Do whatever he tells you,"[19] are the last words of Mary recorded in Scripture. They complement and advance his authoritative role as the Messiah.

Just as she was present and active at the inauguration of Christ's mission as Messiah, so Mary participated in the climax of Christ's redemptive suffering and death on the Cross. Mary accompanied Christ to Calvary, where she shared his sufferings. John records that, as Christ was hanging in crucifixion, Mary stood at the foot of the Cross. Mary's position, which she shared with the wife of Clopas, the Magdalene,

---

[16] Jn 2:3.

[17] "The knot of Eve's disobedience was untied through the obedience of Mary. For what the virgin Eve tied through unbelief, the Virgin Mary set free through faith." *The Scandal of the Incarnation: Irenaeus, Against the Heresies*, selected and with an introduction by Hans Urs von Balthasar, trans. John Saward (San Francisco: Ignatius Press, 1990) III, 22, 4, p. 61. For the critical edition, see *Irénée de Lyon. Contre les hérésies, livre III, tome II, édition critique, texte et traduction*, rev. ed., Adelin Rousseau and Louis Doutreleau, 2002 in *Sources chrétiennes* 211-II: 442-445.

[18] See Phil 2:7.

[19] Jn 2:5.

and the beloved disciple, again reflects her solidarity with Jesus and his redemptive mission. This solidarity stands in glaring contrast to the behavior of those followers who had denied or disowned Jesus, and who had abandoned him to his Passion and death. On Calvary, Mary shares in the sufferings of her Son. She stands in union with his self-offering to the Father.

From the Cross, Christ entrusts the beloved disciple to the maternal care of Mary: "Woman, behold, your son!" and in turn entrusts his Mother to the beloved disciple: "Behold, your mother!" In the act of entrusting the beloved disciple to Mary, Christ gives her to every faithful and beloved disciple. Hence the Church's recognition of Mary's maternal relationship to Christ's faithful followers.

As one of the Twelve, John represents not only the disciples of Christ in general, but also in particular those entrusted with the task of coordinating and celebrating the Paschal Mystery in the sacred liturgy. In the *Directory on the Life and Ministry of Priests*, The Congregation for the Clergy draws out for each priest the implications of his identity with John and his rapport with the Blessed Virgin:

> Like John at the foot of the Cross, every priest has been entrusted, in a special way, with Mary as Mother (cf. Jn 19:26-27).
>
> Priests, who are among the favored disciples of Jesus, crucified and risen, should welcome Mary as their own Mother in their own life, bestowing her with constant attention and prayer. The Blessed Virgin then becomes the Mother who leads them to Christ, who makes them sincerely love the Church, who intercedes for them and who guides them toward the Kingdom of heaven.
>
> Every priest knows that Mary, as Mother, is the most distinguished modeler of his priesthood, since it is she who moulds the priestly soul, protects it from dangers, from routine and discouragement, and maternally safeguards it, so he may grow in wisdom, age and grace, before God and men (cf. Lk 2:40).[20]

---

[20] Congregation for the Clergy, *Directory on the Life and Ministry of Priests* (Vatican City: Libreria Editrice Vaticana, 1994) 73-74.

In the celebration of the sacred liturgy, the work of our salvation continues to be accomplished.[21] Mary therefore exercises her role as Mother of Christ's beloved disciples even within the liturgy, as the Church invokes her aid and aspires to join Mary in the glory of heaven singing the everlasting praises of God.

Mary and the Church

Among the earliest Christian insights into the figure of Mary is her identity with the People of God. More recently, Jesuit theologian and Scripture scholar Ignace de la Potterie has demonstrated in remarkably clear detail how Mary stands both as a figure of Israel or Sion, and as the archetype of the Church.[22] Mary bridges the Old and the New Covenants.[23] Her canticle of praise, known in the West by its Latin incipit *Magnificat* and chanted every evening at Vespers, resonates the exaltation of Israel/the Church by divine grace. Likewise, the Woman of Revelation 12, although understood originally as a personification of Ecclesia or the Church, came to be identified with Mary. Consequently, the figure of this Woman would be incorporated into readings and antiphons for various Marian feasts and occasions.

As a sign of the Church, persecuted yet innocent, driven into exile yet protected and raised on high by God, Mary enjoys a singular position among the daughters of Eve. Her earthly life, marked not only by the joy springing from her intimacy with Christ, but also by her share in the sorrow and pain of his Passion and death, now has given way to the glory of heavenly queenship. This queenship does not suggest, even remotely,

---

[21] "quoties huius hostiae commemoratio celebratur, opus nostrae redemptionis exercetur." Super oblata, Missa in cena Domini, 15, MR 2002, p. 303 (Prayer over the offerings, Mass of the Lord's Supper on Maundy Thursday).

[22] De la Potterie, *Mary in the Mystery of the Covenant*, especially xxiii-xl, 157-208, 229-235, 239-266.

[23] See Joseph Ratzinger with Vittorio Messori, *The Ratzinger Report: An Exclusive Interview on the State of the Church*, trans. Salvator Attanasio and Graham Harrison (San Francisco: Ignatius Press) 107: "In her very person as a Jewish girl become the mother of the Messiah, Mary binds together, in a living and indissoluble way, the old and the new People of God, Israel and Christianity, synagogue and church. She is, as it were, the connecting link without which the Faith (as is happening today) runs the risk of losing its balance by either forsaking the New Testament for the Old or dispensing with the Old. Instead, we can live the unity of sacred Scripture in its entirety."

any parity with God, but depends utterly on the divine pleasure and indeed proclaims in eternity the supreme majesty of the Godhead. Both as model and Mother of the Church, Mary offers her Son and herself to the eternal Father. Inasmuch as Mary personifies the Church at prayer, she necessarily participates in the heavenly liturgy of which the earthly parallel constitutes but a pale reflection.[24]

This identification of the Church with Mary, like Mary's role in salvation history, sets before the priest an image to inspire him in the faithful celebration of the sacred mysteries, so that all who participate may grow in holiness and enjoy even on earth some foretaste of heavenly glory:

> Masterpiece of the priestly Sacrifice of Christ, the Blessed Virgin represents the Church in the purest way, "with neither stain nor blemish," completely "holy and immaculate" (Eph 5:27). This contemplation of the Blessed Virgin places before the priest the ideal to which the ministry in his community should lead, so that this be a "wholly glorious Church" (*ibid.*) through the priestly gift of his very life.[25]

The Relationship between Liturgy and Doctrine

At this point, let us consider briefly the nature of liturgy, so that we may more fully grasp Mary's place within this "source and summit"[26] of the Church's life and mission. In the prayers, readings, and chants of sacred liturgy, the Church expresses her belief in Mary's privileges and prerogatives, as well as her response to the gifts of grace. Mary's divine maternity, her freedom from all stain of sin, her perpetual

---

[24] See Vatican II, Constitution on the Liturgy *Sacrosanctum Concilium* [SC] 8: "In the earthly liturgy we take part in a foretaste of that heavenly liturgy which is celebrated in the Holy City of Jerusalem toward which we journey as pilgrims, where Christ is sitting at the right hand of God, Minister of the holies and of the true tabernacle."

[25] *Directory on the Life and Ministry of Priests*, p. 74.

[26] See SC 10; Vatican II, Decree on the Ministry and Life of Priests *Presbyterorum ordinis* (December 7, 1965) 5; "Institutio generalis" 16, MR 2002, p. 24; English translation: International Commission on English in the Liturgy [ICEL], *General Instruction of the Roman Missal*, Liturgy Documentary Series 2 (Washington DC: United States Conference of Catholic Bishops, 2003) [GIRM] 16, p. 15.

virginity before, during, and after the birth of Christ, her complete union with God's will, her participation in the sufferings of her Son, and her mediation on behalf of the human race all find expression in the Church's official prayer. The liturgy not only reflects and affirms faith in these mysteries; it integrates them into the annual, weekly, and even daily rounds of the Church's worship.

The Nature of the Sacred Liturgy: the Prayer of Christ and of the Church

The sacred liturgy is the exercise of the priestly office of Jesus Christ the High Priest and sole Mediator of the New Covenant.[27] This priestly office is carried out by the whole Christ, that is, by the entire Mystical Body of Christ, Head and members together:

> The priestly life begun with the supplication and sacrifice of his mortal Body should continue without intermission down the ages in his Mystical Body which is the Church. ... In obedience, therefore, to her Founder's behest, the Church prolongs the priestly mission of Jesus Christ, mainly by means of the sacred liturgy.[28]

This definition of the sacred liturgy resonates in the teaching of the Second Vatican Council. The Constitution on the Sacred Liturgy *Sacrosanctum Concilium* in fact echoes the very words of Pius XII:

> The liturgy, then, is rightly seen as an exercise of the priestly office of Jesus Christ. It involves the presentation of man's sanctification under the guise of signs perceptible by the senses and its accomplishment in ways appropriate to each of these signs. In it full public worship is performed by the Mystical Body of Jesus Christ, that is, by the Head and his members.[29]

---

[27] See the Letter to the Hebrews, especially 4:14 and 9:14. Christ's unique high-priestly mediation constitutes the theme of the first papal encyclical on the sacred liturgy: Pius XII, *Mediator Dei* (November 20, 1947), *Acta Apostolicae Sedis*, 39 (1947) [MD] 521-595.

[28] MD, 2 and 3.

[29] SC, 7.

Jesus Christ wills that his Church participate intimately in the exercise of his high-priestly office. According to *Sacrosanctum Concilium*, "Christ, indeed, always associates the Church with himself in this great work in which God is perfectly glorified and men are sanctified. The Church is his beloved Bride who calls to her Lord, and through him offers worship to the eternal Father."[30] When the Church prays, therefore, it is Christ praying in unison with his Body and Bride the Church. "From this it follows that every liturgical celebration, because it is an action of Christ the Priest and of his Body, which is the Church, is a sacred action surpassing all others. No other action of the Church can equal its efficacy by the same title and to the same degree."[31]

It is Christ who associates with himself all the members of his Mystical Body, his pilgrim people, his Church in this privileged public prayer, which constitutes "the summit toward which the activity of the Church is directed; it is also the fount from which all her power flows."[32] Foremost among the members of Christ's Mystical Body ranks the Blessed Virgin Mary. At each stage of his saving mission, Christ associated Mary with himself and with the work of redemption. Without in any way diminishing Christ's role as Redeemer, Mary played, and continues to play, a unique role in the economy of salvation. Hence her place is of high honor in the Church's liturgical prayer.

The Role of Liturgy in the Development of Doctrine

At this point it is useful to recall the connection between the Church's deposit of faith and her liturgical worship. In the first papal encyclical on the sacred liturgy, *Mediator Dei*, Pius XII clarified this relationship by correcting a popular misreading of Prosper of Aquitaine (c. 390-post 455). Prosper's dictum *Legem credendi lex statuat supplicandi* (let the rule for prayer determine the rule of belief)[33] had been exposed to potential misinterpretation by the more pithy axiom *lex orandi, lex credendi* (the rule of prayer, the rule of belief), which in some circles had been taken to suggest that the prayer of the Church determines the Church's faith. Pius XII confronts this fallacy in unambiguous terms:

---

[30] SC, 7.
[31] SC, 7.
[32] SC, 10.
[33] Prosper of Aquitaine, *De gratia Dei seu 'Indiculus'*, 8, DS 238, p. 88.

> We refer to the error and fallacious reasoning of those who have claimed that the sacred liturgy is a kind of proving-ground for the truths to be held of faith, meaning by this that the Church is obliged to declare such a doctrine sound when it is found to have produced fruits of piety and sanctity through the sacred rites of liturgy, and to reject it otherwise. Hence the epigram: *"Lex orandi, lex credendi"*—the law for prayer is the law for faith.
>
> But this is not what the Church teaches and enjoins. ... The entire liturgy ... has the Catholic faith for its content, inasmuch as it bears witness to the faith of the Church. ...
>
> Hence the well-known and venerable maxim: *"Legem credendi lex statuat supplicandi"*—let the rule for prayer determine the rule of belief. The sacred liturgy, consequently, does not decide or determine independently and of itself what is of Catholic faith. More properly, since the liturgy is also a profession of eternal truths, and subject, as such, to the Supreme Teaching Authority of the Church, it can supply proofs and testimony, quite clearly of no little value, towards the determination of a particular point of Christian doctrine. But if one desires to differentiate and describe the relationship between faith and the sacred liturgy in absolute terms, it is perfectly correct to say: *"Lex credendi legem statuat supplicandi"*—*let the rule of belief determine the rule of prayer.*[34]

Liturgical celebration, then, must cohere with, and bear authentic witness to, the Church's faith.

It is true, nonetheless, that the sacred liturgy has exercised considerable influence on the clarification of points of doctrine. This is particularly evident in the case of the Church's teachings about Mary. The feasts of the Immaculate Conception and of the Assumption, for example, were celebrated in the liturgy long before they were solemnly

---

[34] MD, 46-48.

defined and decreed, respectively, in 1854 and 1950. Both Pius IX, in the Bull *Ineffabilis Deus* (December 8, 1854), and Pius XII, in the Apostolic Constitution *Munificentissimus Deus* (November 1, 1950), appealed to the liturgical tradition in framing their declarations.[35] Because the sacred liturgy in this way stands as a privileged witness to the *depositum fidei*, it serves as a reliable touchstone of orthodoxy.

Pope Pius XI, in establishing the feast of Christ the King by means of the Encyclical *Quas primas* (December 11, 1925), stressed the power of the liturgy to impress upon the awareness of the faithful the truths of faith and to elicit from Christians signs of intense devotion to the divine mysteries:

> The Church's teaching affects the mind primarily; her feasts affect both mind and heart, and have a salutary effect upon the whole of man's nature. Man is composed of body and soul, and he needs these external festivities so that the sacred rites, in all their beauty and variety, may stimulate him to drink more deeply of the fountain of God's teaching, that he may make it a part of himself, and use it with profit for his spiritual life.[36]

The Pope then makes specific reference to the role played by the feasts of the saints and especially of the Mother of God in the building up of the Church:

> History in fact tells us that in the course of ages these festivals have been instituted one after another according as the needs or the advantage of the people of Christ seemed to demand: as when they needed strength to face a common danger, when they were attacked by insidious heresies, when they needed to be urged to the pious consideration of some mystery of faith or of some divine blessing. Thus in the earliest days of the Christian era, when the people of Christ were suffering cruel

---

[35] See Pius IX, Bull *Ineffabilis Deus*, December 8, 1854, and Pius XII, Apostolic Constitution on the Assumption of the Blessed Virgin Mary *Munificentissimus Deus*, November 1, 1950, AAS 42 (1950), 760.

[36] Pius XI, Encyclical on the Feast of Christ the King *Quas primas*, December 11, 1925 (Vatican translation, Boston: St. Paul) 21. AAS, 17 (1925) 603.

persecution, the cult of the martyrs was begun in order, says St. Augustine, "that the feasts of the martyrs might incite men to martyrdom." The liturgical honors paid to confessors, virgins and widows produced wonderful results in an increased zest for virtue, necessary even in times of peace. But more fruitful still were the feasts instituted in honor of the Blessed Virgin. As a result of these men grew not only in their devotion to the Mother of God as an ever-present advocate, but also in their love of her as a mother bequeathed to them by their Redeemer. Not least among the blessings which have resulted from the public and legitimate honor paid to the Blessed Virgin and the saints is the perfect and perpetual immunity of the Church from error and heresy. We may well admire in this the admirable wisdom of the Providence of God, who, ever bringing good out of evil, has from time to time suffered the faith and piety of men to grow weak, and allowed Catholic truth to be attacked by false doctrines, but always with the result that truth has afterwards shone out with greater splendor, and that men's faith, aroused from its lethargy, has shown itself more vigorous than before.[37]

The Marian solemnities, feasts, and memorials examined below demonstrate the profound relationship between the rule of faith and the Church's liturgical prayer. They reflect the Church's recognition of both Scripture and Tradition as the twofold channels of Divine Revelation.[38] Since we have examined earlier the figure of Mary in the New Testament, we now turn to that figure as it emerged in the Church's Tradition.

a. Mary in Tradition

---

[37] *Quas primas*, 22, AAS 17 (1925) 603-04.

[38] See Vatican II, Dogmatic Constitution on Divine Revelation *Dei Verbum* (November 18, 1965), 7-9, especially this sentence from section 8: "What was handed on by the apostles comprises everything that serves to make the People of God live their lives in holiness and increase their faith. In this way the Church, in her doctrine, life and worship, perpetuates and transmits to every generation all that she herself is, all that she believes."

Details of the conception and birth of Mary, of her girlhood and espousal to St. Joseph, and of her final years all appear in non-canonical sources that seek to satisfy the curiosity of believers and to heighten regard for the Blessed Virgin. Foremost among these sources, the *Protoevangelium of James*, compiled in the middle of the second century of the Christian era, has left its mark on the portrayal of Mary in art and iconography, as well as the celebration of certain feasts, such as the Presentation of Mary in the Temple (November 21), Sts. Joachim and Anne, parents of Our Lady (July 26), and the Espousals of the Blessed Virgin and St. Joseph (formerly January 23).[39] Over the course of the centuries, ongoing theological consideration of Mary's privileges and prerogatives has led to the observance of these honors in the sacred liturgy. This tradition of liturgical observance in turn has played a role in formalizing the Church's teaching about Mary's Immaculate Conception in the womb of her mother, the perpetual virginity of Mary, the virginal birth of Jesus Christ the Son of God, the Assumption of Mary, her queenship in heaven, and her continuing mediation with Christ on behalf of the Church.[40]

Never has the Church claimed Mary's motherhood of the Church or her mediation to be exercised independently of her Son. On the contrary, the Second Vatican Council, in fidelity to the Church's constant tradition, insisted that Mary's maternal mediation rests entirely upon the disposition of the divine economy, or plan of salvation:

> In the words of the apostle there is but one mediator: "for there is but one God and one mediator of God and men, the man Christ Jesus, who gave himself as

---

[39] For an English translation of the *Protoevangelium of James* and other non-canonical sources, see *New Testament Apocrypha*, vol. 7: *Gospels and Related Writings*, ed. Wilhelm Schneemelcher, trans. R.M. Wilson, revised ed. (Louisville KY: Westminster John Knox Press, 1991) 421-439. For a more recent translation of the *Protoevangelium of James* with introduction and notes, see Frederica Mathewes-Green, *The Lost Gospel of Mary. The Mother of Jesus in Three Ancient Texts* (Brewster MA: Paraclete Press, 2007) especially pp. ix-81.

[40] For an excellent treatment of Mary in the tradition of the Church, see Luigi Gambero, *Mary and the Fathers of the Church. The Blessed Virgin Mary in Patristic Thought*, trans. Thomas Buffer (San Francisco CA: Ignatius Press) and idem, *Mary in the Middle Ages. The Blessed Virgin Mary in the Thought of Medieval Latin Theologians*, trans. Thomas Buffer (San Francisco CA: Ignatius Press, 2005).

redemption for all" (1 Tim 2:5-6). But Mary's function as mother of men in no way obscures or diminishes this unique mediation of Christ, but rather shows its power. But the Blessed Virgin's salutary influence on men originates not in any inner necessity but in the disposition of God. It flows forth from the superabundance of the merits of Christ, rests on his mediation, depends entirely on it and draws all its power from it, It does not hinder in any way the immediate union of the faithful with Christ but on the contrary fosters it.[41]

Over the past two millennia, interest in and devotion to the Mother of God have waxed and waned. A brief mention of the high points of Marian devotion is worthwhile. By confirming the orthodoxy of the title *Theotókos*, a title, it should be noted, that was used in prayer formulae at least since the early third century, the Council of Ephesus (431) gave rise to an increased awareness of the importance of Mary in the Church's life and liturgy. In Rome, Pope Sixtus III (reigned 432-440) reconstructed the older Liberian basilica on the Esquiline Hill, and dedicated it to Mary under the title Mother of God. After the iconoclast controversy (730-843) and the vindication of the veneration of sacred images, the Mother of God again rose to prominence in Christian art and devotion. Under the influence of such zealous pastors and teachers as St. Anselm (+1109) and St. Bernard of Clairvaux (+1153), no less than through the charismatic efforts of St. Dominic (+1221) and St. Francis of Assisi (+1226), Marian piety flourished throughout the twelfth and thirteenth centuries, resulting in what has been called the "age of Mary." At that time, numerous churches throughout Western Christendom were dedicated under the title of Our Lady. Religious orders, often placed under the principal patronage of Mary, vied with one another in promoting their various devotions to the Mother of God (the Rosary, scapular, Stations of the Cross, little office of the Blessed Virgin Mary).

The exuberance of the Catholic reform inspired by the Council of Trent brought Marian devotion to the ends of the known world, planting it firmly in mission lands. The preservation of the Christian religion despite divisions between Catholicism and Protestantism on the

---

[41] LG 60.

one hand and the constant threat of invasion by Turkish forces on the other, exercised a dominant claim of the attention of the popes in the emerging modern era. Various Marian feasts appeared on the calendar in thanksgiving for deliverance from imminent disaster.

The period between 1850 and 1954 witnessed another "age of Mary." The papal definition and promulgation of the dogma of the Immaculate Conception in 1854 reinforced the identity of the glorious Virgin with the Church, even under siege from the hostile forces of the "Enlightenment." Marian devotion became a vivid hallmark of Catholic piety and culture in the nineteenth century and throughout the first half of the twentieth.

Just under a century after the declaration of the Immaculate Conception, Pope Pius XII confirmed the dogma of the Assumption of the Blessed Virgin Mary, leaving unresolved, however, the debate whether Mary actually died or was spared this consequence of sin by virtue of the redemption won by Christ and in view of Mary's providential role in the history of salvation.[42] Marian apparitions reported in Paris (1830), Lourdes (1858), and Fatima (1917) won ecclesiastical recognition, and each in due course was accorded a commemoration on the liturgical calendar.

After the definition and declaration of Our Lady's Assumption in 1950, some expectation was raised that the Holy See would solemnize the Marian titles of Mediatrix of all Graces, Advocate, and Helper. The Second Vatican Council (1962-1965), however, did not dedicate a separate document to the Blessed Virgin Mary. Instead, the Council Fathers chose to treat Mary within its Dogmatic Constitution on the Church, *Lumen Gentium*, dedicating the eighth chapter entirely to her. *Lumen Gentium* specifically acknowledges Mary's mediation:

---

[42] Note the neutral language regarding the end of the Blessed Virgin's life in the actual definition: Pius XII, Apostolic Constitution on the Assumption of the Blessed Virgin Mary *Munificentissimus Deus*, November 1, 1950 (Boston MA: St. Paul Editions, 1950), 44: "We pronounce, declare, and define it to be a divinely revealed dogma: that the Immaculate Mother of God, the ever-Virgin Mary, having completed the course of her earthly life, was assumed body and soul into heavenly glory." "… pronuntiamus, declaramus et definimus divinitus revelatum dogma esse: Immaculatam Deiparam semper Virginem Mariam, expleto terrestris vitae cursu, fuisse corpore et anima ad caelestem gloriam assumptam." AAS 42 (1950) 780.

> By her maternal charity, she cares for the brethren of her Son, who still journey on earth surrounded by dangers and difficulties, until they are led into their blessed home. Therefore the Blessed Virgin is invoked in the Church under the titles of Advocate, Helper, Benefactress, and Mediatrix. This, however, is so understood that it neither takes away anything from nor adds anything to the dignity of Christ and efficacy of Christ the one Mediator. ...
>
> The Church does not hesitate to profess this subordinate role of Mary, which it constantly experiences and recommends to the heartfelt attention of the faithful, so that encouraged by this maternal help they may the more closely adhere to the Mediator and Redeemer.[43]

The Council reoriented Marian scholarship and piety, encouraging new research into and contemplation of the Blessed Virgin as she figures in Scripture, the Fathers of the Church, and early medieval theology. Nevertheless, the years immediately following Vatican II witnessed a decline in Mariological studies and Marian piety. Pope Paul VI (reigned 1963-1978) sought to revive devotion to Mary, particularly by the encyclical on the month of May, *Mense Maio* (April 30, 1965),[44] and by the apostolic exhortation for the right ordering and development of devotion to the Blessed Virgin Mary, *Marialis cultus* (February 2, 1974),[45] but with limited success.[46]

During a well-known interview given in as the newly appointed prefect of the Congregation of the Doctrine of the Faith, Cardinal Joseph Ratzinger acknowledged the decline in interest in Mary:

> By inserting the mystery of Mary into the mystery of the Church, Vatican II made an important decision which should have given a new impetus to theological

---

[43] LG 62.
[44] Paul VI, Encyclical *Mense Maio*, April 30, 1965, AAS 57 (1965) 353-358.
[45] Paul VI, Apostolic Exhortation *Marialis cultus*, February 2, 1974, AAS 76 (1974) 113-168.
[46] For a somewhat trenchant analysis of the decline in Marian piety since Vatican II, see Eamon Duffy, "May Thoughts on Mary," *Faith of Our Fathers: Reflections on Catholic Tradition* (London UK: Continuum, 2004) 29-38.

research. Instead, in the early post-conciliar period, there has been a sudden decline in this respect—almost a collapse, even though there are now signs of a new vitality.[47]

The pontificate of John Paul II (1978-2005), on the other hand, did much to reawaken popular devotion to Mary and to restore the figure of Mary in theological studies and higher scholarship. By fostering interest in the treasury of patristic and medieval texts, by presenting fresh theological insights, and by vigorously promoting of devotions like the Rosary and the scapular, John Paul II imbued Marian theology and piety with a new élan.[48]

Historian Eamon Duffy attributes the recovery of Mary's identity with the Church as one of the finest instincts of Vatican II:

> Where post-medieval Mariology often emphasized Mary's difference from every other Christian, her purity contrasting with our filth, her powerful intercession contrasting with our helplessness, the Council, following the mainstream of patristic and early medieval exegisis, emphasized her role as type and model for the Church, and each of its members. Thus her excellences and

---

[47] Ratzinger with Messori, *Ratzinger Report*, 104. Note Ratzinger's appreciation of the role of Marian doctrines in maintaining the Christological content of the *depositum fidei*: "It is, moreover in direct service to faith in Christ—not, therefore, primarily out of devotion to the Mother—that the Church has proclaimed her Marian dogmas: first that of her perpetual virginity and divine motherhood and then, after a long period of maturation and reflection, those of her Immaculate Conception and bodily Assumption into heavenly glory. These dogmas protect the original faith in Christ as true God and true man: two natures in a single Person. They also secure the indispensable eschatological tension by pointing to Mary's Assumption as the immortal destiny that awaits us all. And they also protect the faith—threatened today—in God the Creator, who (and this, among other things, is the meaning of the truth of the perpetual virginity of Mary, more than ever not understood today) can freely intervene also in matter. Finally, Mary, as the Council recalls: 'having entered deeply into the history of salvation, … in a way unites in her person and reechoes the most important mysteries of the Faith' (*Lumen Gentium*, no. 65)." *Ratzinger Report*, 106-107.

[48] See *Mother of Christ, Mother of the Church: Documents on the Blessed Virgin Mary*, introductions by M. Jean Frisk, ed. Marianne Lorraine Trouve (Boston MA: Pauline Books and Media, 2001) 186-488.

privileges, like her Assumption into heaven, were not alienating measures of her distance from us, but pledges of the dignity which awaits us all, and which, in grace, is already taking shape within us.[49]

Duffy contrasts the way in which the Fourth Gospel casts Mary in such sharp relief that she emerges, at Cana and at Calvary, in utter distinction from all others around her, with Luke's treatment of Our Lady as one with whom the ordinary Christian can more readily identify:

> The Mary of Luke is less easy to misunderstand, and Catholic exegesis had constantly seen her *'fiat'* at the Annunciation, for all its momentous uniqueness, as the model of every believer's response to the call of God. In this perspective Mary is still a light to guide, but her light is a measure not of our darkness, but of the glory promised to all the saints.[50]

b. Mary and the Church at Prayer

The Dogmatic Constitution on the Church *Lumen Gentium* echoes the ancient Christian insight that the Blessed Virgin Mary is identified in a unique and mysterious way with the Church:

> By reason of the gift and role of her divine motherhood, by which she is united with her Son, the Redeemer, and with her unique graces and functions, the Blessed Virgin is also intimately united to the Church. As St. Ambrose taught, the Mother of God is a type of the Church in the order of faith, charity, and perfect union with Christ (*Expositio in Lucam*, 2.7, *PL* 15, 1555). For in the mystery of the Church, which is itself rightly called Mother and Virgin, the Blessed Virgin stands out in eminent and singular fashion as exemplar both of Virgin and Mother. Through her faith and obedience she gave birth on earth to the very Son of the Father, not through the knowledge of man but by the overshadowing of the

---

[49] Duffy, 35.
[50] Duffy, 35.

Holy Spirit, in the manner of a New Eve who placed her faith, not in the serpent of old but in God's messenger without wavering in doubt. The Son whom she brought forth is he whom God placed as the firstborn among many brethren (Rom 8:29), that is, the faithful, in whose generation and formation she cooperates with a mother's love.[51]

Citing the Doctor of Grace, St. Augustine of Hippo (+430), the eighth chapter of *Lumen Gentium* explicitly recognizes Mary's motherhood of the Church:

> ... being of the race of Adam, she is at the same time also united to all those who are to be saved; indeed, "she is clearly the mother of the members of Christ ... since she has by her charity joined in bringing about the birth of believers in the Church, who are members of its head" [St. Augustine, *De s. virginitate*, 6, PL 40:399]. Wherefore she is hailed as preeminent and as a wholly unique member of the Church, and as its type and outstanding model in faith and charity. ... The Catholic Church taught by the Holy Spirit, honors her with filial affection and devotion as a most beloved Mother.[52]

The sacred liturgy itself reflects Mary's motherhood of the Mystical Body. A collect suggested for the votive Mass of the Most Holy Name of Mary, for example, refers directly to Christ's will that his Mother exercise the same role for his Church:

> *Deus, cuius Filius in ara crucis exspirans beatissimam Virginem Mariam Matrem voluit esse nostram, quam suam elegerat, concede propitius, ut, qui sub eius praesidium secure confugimus, materno invocato nomine confortemur. Per Dominum.*[53]

---

[51] LG 63.
[52] LG 53.
[53] Collecta altera, Missa votiva C: De sanctissimo nomine Mariae, MR 2002, p. 1175 (Alternative Collect, Votive Mass of the Most Holy Name of Mary). Translation mine.

> O God, whose Son, as he was dying on the altar of the Cross, willed that the most Blessed Virgin Mary, whom he had chosen as his own Mother, be also our Mother, graciously grant that we who take refuge with confidence under her protection may be comforted by having invoked her by the name of Mother.

In terms of the kind of cult which the Church accords Mary, Vatican II reaffirmed the immemorial distinction between the adoration offered to God alone (*latria*) and the veneration owed to the saints (*dulia*). As a creature, Mary is not entitled to *latria*; yet in view of her divine maternity and that unstained holiness, which alone of all humans is hers, Mary is paid a kind of super-veneration (*hyperdulia*).[54] Cautioning against false exaggerations in the presentation of Our Lady, the Council nevertheless encouraged the age-old tradition of venerating Mary above the angels and saints:

> The sacred synod ... admonishes all the sons of the Church that the cult, especially the liturgical cult, of the Blessed Virgin, be generously fostered, and that the practices and exercises of devotion towards her, recommended by the teaching authority of the Church in the course of centuries be highly esteemed, and that those decrees, which were given in the early days regarding the cult images of Christ, the Blessed Virgin, and the saints, be religiously observed. ... Let the faithful remember moreover that true devotion consists neither in sterile nor transitory affection, nor in a certain vain credulity, but proceeds from true faith, by which we are led to recognize the excellence of the Mother of God, and we are moved to a filial love towards our Mother and to the imitation of her virtues.[55]

Finally, alluding to the rich liturgical and devotional cult of Mary in East, *Lumen Gentium* summarizes the whole Church's attitude of filial reverence for the Mother of God:

---

[54] See LG 66.
[55] LG 67.

The entire body of the faithful pours forth urgent supplications to the Mother of God and of men that she, who aided the beginnings of the Church by her prayers, may now, exalted as she is above all the angels and saints, intercede before her Son in the fellowship of all the saints, until all families of people, whether they still do not know the Savior, may be happily gathered together in peace and harmony into one People of God, for the glory of the Most Holy and Undivided Trinity.[56]

Upon the approval and promulgation of the Dogmatic Constitution *Lumen Gentium*, Paul VI officially accorded Mary the title Mother of the Church (*Mater Ecclesiae*).[57]

Mary and the Liturgy

This section explores how Mary figures in the liturgy of the Roman Rite. The calendar, developed organically over the centuries under a wide variety of influences, indicates the many ways in which the Blessed Virgin accompanies the faithful through the liturgical year. The ordinary of the Mass mentions Mary in key places: at the beginning of Mass when the Confiteor asks Mary and the saints to pray for those who have confessed their unworthiness and who prepare to enter the Liturgy of the Word; during the Creed, which serves as the response of the faithful to the Word of God just proclaimed in the readings and elaborated in the homily; and, most dramatically, in the Eucharistic Prayer, where the celebrant calls upon the intercession of the Blessed Virgin Mary as he offers the most august sacrifice of the Lord's body and blood.

Of all the eucharistic prayers currently available in the Roman Rite, none approaches the Roman Canon in its reverential treatment of Mary. Here Mary appears in counterpoint with St. John the Baptist. Each heads a list of saints: Mary before the Narrative of Institution, John after the conversion of the elements into the Lord's body and blood. As in the well-known icons of the *Deesis* (Christ in Majesty), the Blessed Virgin and St. John the Baptist flank the eucharistic Lord. Reading through the Roman Canon, the celebrant gives utterance to

---

[56] LG 69.
[57] AAS 56 (1965), p. 1015.

a verbal icon, as it were. In the *Communicantes,* Mary leads a throng of twenty-four saints, plus St. Joseph.⁵⁸ The list comprises mainly saints who exercised some hierarchical rank in the Church: twelve apostles (including Paul), six bishops (five of whom were bishops of Rome), a deacon, and five laymen associated with generous donations to the Church. In the *Nobis quoque,* the Baptist, for his part, leads a throng of fourteen saints predominantly associated with the Holy Spirit (Stephen, Matthias, Barnabas) and prophetic witness (especially the virgin martyrs). The Roman Canon, though, sets the Blessed Virgin apart from all the other saints by introducing her name with the phrase *in primis.* This indicates priority not simply in sequential order, but in actual rank, for "the glorious ever-Virgin Mary, Mother of God and Lord Jesus Christ"⁵⁹ enjoys a status unrivalled by the angels and saints. This clear example of *hyperdulia* made its way into the Roman Canon sometime in the fifth century, likely in response to the controversy resolved at Ephesus in 431.⁶⁰

The proper, common, and votive Masses of the Blessed Virgin Mary all focus on distinct privileges, specific virtues, or dimensions of Our Lady's intercession reflected in the many titles conferred on her by the Church.⁶¹ This is particularly true of the generous selection of Marian

---

[58] In the 1962 edition of the Roman Missal, Bl. John XXIII inserted the name of St. Joseph into the Roman Canon.

[59] Ordo missae 86, MR 2002, p. 572: "Communicantes et memoriam venerantes, *in primis gloriosae semper Virginis Mariae, Genetricis Dei et Domini nostri Iesu Christi* ...." Emphasis added.

[60] See Vincent Lorne Kennedy, *The Saints of the Canon of the Mass,* 2nd revised ed., Studi di Antichità Cristiana 14 (Vatican City: Pontificio Istituto di Archeologia Cristiana, 1963), 98-100, especially 100.

[61] For a study of the common of the Blessed Virgin Mary in MR 2002, see Maurizio Barba, "Il commune della beata Vergine Maria nel nuovo Messale Romano," *Notitiae* 38 (2002) 588-601. Note that the General Instruction of the Roman Missal [GIRM] encourages the use of the common and votive Masses of the Blessed Virgin, especially on Saturday: GIRM 378: "It is especially recommended to celebrate the commemoration of the Blessed Virgin Mary on Saturday, because it is to the Mother of the Redeemer in the Liturgy of the Church that in the first place and before all the saints veneration is given [n. 145: Second Vatican Ecumenical Council, Dogmatic Constitution on the Church *Lumen Gentium,* no. 54; Paul VI, Apostolic Exhortation *Marialis cultus,* February 2, 1974, no. 9; AAS 66 (1974), pp. 122-123;]" 355: "Where ... the optional memorials of the Blessed Virgin Mary or of the saints are dear to the faithful, the priest should satisfy their legitimate devotion;" 375: "Votive Masses of the mysteries of the Lord or in honor

Mass formularies provided by the *Collection of Masses of the Blessed Virgin Mary* and its accompanying lectionary issued in 1987 by the Congregation for Divine Worship at the behest of John Paul II.[62] The final blessings before the dismissal include one to be used on Marian occasions.[63] Even the prayers before and after Mass include separate prayers addressed to Our Lady.[64]

The General Instruction of the Roman Missal directs the performance of gestures and signs to reflect the hyperdulia offered to Mary by the People of God.[65] The readings of the lectionary reveal to the faithful the image of Mary in the types or foreshadowings of the old covenant and Mary's fulfillment of them as their antitype in the new. The Church joins Mary in proclaiming the greatness of the Lord in psalms and canticles, and in the Gospel follows with close attention Mary's participation in the life and mission of her Son, Jesus Christ. The faithful invoke Mary's intercession during the celebration of the sacraments and such ritual Masses as religious profession and Christian funerals. Finally, in the Liturgy of the Hours, the Church daily echoes Mary's own canticle of praise, the Magnificat, and salutes her in a final anthem before retiring from the day's activities.

---

of the Blessed Virgin Mary or of the angels or of any given saint or of all the saints may be said for the sake of the faithful's devotion on weekdays in Ordinary Time, even if an optional memorial occurs. It is not, however, allowed to celebrate as Votive Masses, those that refer to mysteries related to events in the life of the Lord or of the Blessed Virgin Mary, with the exception of the Immaculate Conception, since their celebration is an integral part of the unfolding of the liturgical year."

[62] *Collectio missarum de beata Maria Virgine, editio typica* (Vatican City: Libreria Editrice Vaticana, 1987) and *Lectionarium pro missis de beata Maria Virgine* (Libreria Editrice Vaticana, 1987).

[63] Benedictiones sollemnes 15: De beata Maria Virgine, MR 2002, pp. 612-613.

[64] See Preparatio ad missam: oratio ad B. Mariam Virginem "O Mater pietatis et misericordiae" MR 2002, p. 1291; Gratiarum actio post missam: orationes ad B. Mariam Virginem "O Maria, Virgo et Mater sanctissima," "Ave Maria," MR 2002, p. 1295. The Ave Maria is an addition to the prayers after Mass.

[65] Note GIRM 275a: "A bow of the head is made when the three divine Persons are named together and at the names of Jesus, of the Blessed Virgin Mary, and of the saint in whose honor Mass is being celebrated;" and 275b: "A bow of the body, that is to say a profound bow, is made ... in the Creed at the words *Et incarnatus est* (*by the power of the Holy Spirit ... and became man*).

Mary and the Liturgical Year

Over the course of the liturgical year, from the first Sunday of Advent to the solemnity of Christ the King, the Church celebrates the mysteries of Jesus Christ. The liturgical year follows the rotation of two cycles: the proper of time, or the temporal cycle, and the proper of the saints, known as the sanctoral cycle. Mary figures conspicuously in both cycles. In the temporal cycle, the liturgy presents the life and mission of Christ: his coming in the Incarnation, his Passion, death, and Resurrection, his Ascension into heaven and the descent of the Holy Spirit at Pentecost, and, finally, the anticipation of his second coming as Judge and King of all nations. The liturgy invites the Church to consider Mary's involvement in each of these mysteries celebrated during the temporal cycle. In the sanctoral cycle, the liturgy presents the Paschal Mystery of Christ as lived out in the lives and deaths of the saints.

As mentioned earlier, Mary surpasses in holiness all the saints, hence she is rightly invoked as Queen of All Saints. The solemnities, feasts, and commemorations of Mary on the calendar constantly remind us of Mary's faithful imitation of her Son and her union with him now in heaven, where she prays to him for the Church and for all humanity. For the sake of convenience, this section employs the generic term "feast" to refer to any public observance of a Mass or office dedicated in honor of Our Lady. This avoids the technical distinctions used in specifying the rank or grade of a given observance in the hierarchy of feasts. Only occasionally shall reference be made to a particular grade of feast, and this occurs only in treating the elevation or demotion of a given feast.

Origins

The earliest commemoration of Mary in the liturgy occurred in connection with celebration of such mysteries of the Lord mentioned in Scripture as Christmas (late fourth century), Epiphany, and the Presentation of Christ in the Temple. Mary's intimate participation in these mysteries assured her a prominent place in their liturgical commemorations. No separate feast dedicated exclusively to Our Lady emerged until the fifth century, after the Council of Ephesus (431). Nevertheless, devotion to the Mother of God had found expression as early as the second and third centuries. At least a century before the establishment of the feast of Christmas in the 380s, there circulated in Alexandria a Greek prayer now familiar to Westerners in its Latin version:

> *Sub tuum praesidium confugimus, sancta Dei Genetrix; nostras deprecationes ne despicias in necessitatibus; sed a periculis cunctis libera nos semper Virgo gloriosa et benedicta.*
>
> We fly to thy patronage, O holy Mother of God; despise not our petitions in our necessities, but deliver us from all dangers, O ever-Virgin glorious and blessed.[66]

Three important features of this brief invocation bear comment. The prayer addresses Mary by the title Mother of God (*Theotókos*) more than a century before this title will have been confirmed by the Council of Ephesus.[67] It likewise acknowledges Mary's perpetual virginity. Finally, it invokes Mary to deliver us from all dangers. The verb reflects great confidence in Our Lady's power, since Christians use the same imperative, "deliver," in addressing God the Father in the final petition of the Lord's Prayer. The prayer continues to be used in the Greek Orthodox office or Book of Hours and, since the revision of the Roman-Rite Liturgy of the Hours in the 1970s, may serve as one of the Marian antiphons concluding the daily office of either Vespers or Compline.

---

[66] Manchester UK: John Rylands Library, Papyrus 370, commonly known as Rylands Papyrus 370; dated by papyrologist Edward Lobel, and later historian James Shiel, to the mid-third century. See M.C.H. Roberts and E.G. Turner, eds, *Catalogue of the Greek and Latin Papyri in the John Rylands Library, Manchester* (Manchester: Manchester University Press, 1938) 3:46; F. Mercenier, "L'Antienne mariale grecque la plus ancienne," *Muséon* 52 (1939) 229-33; O. Stegmüller, "Sub tuum praesidium: Bemerkungen zur ältesten Ueberlieferung," *Zeitschrift für katholische Theologie* 74 (1952) 76-82; Gambero, *Mary and the Fathers of the Church*, 69-70; Mathewes-Green, 85-88. The dating refers only to the papyrus on which the prayer is written. It is likely that the prayer itself predates the written record. This translation differs from the traditional English version of the prayer as handed down for generations, inasmuch as it corrects the final invocation of Mary from "ever glorious and blessed Virgin" to "ever-Virgin glorious and blessed." The version of the prayer in the 1975 edition of the *Liturgia horarum* places a comma after *semper*, thereby having it modify the verb *libera*, hence: "deliver us always, O Virgin glorious and blessed."

[67] Origen uses the term *Theotókos* around 250, as does St. Athanasius (ca. 295-373) in the next century.

Feasts and Seasons[68]

Marian Feasts: Eastern Roots

The liturgical cult of Mary began in Jerusalem, where August 15 marked the particular feast day of the *Theotókos*. According to a legend in circulation as early as the mid-second century, the Blessed Virgin *en route* to Bethlehem, where she would be delivered of the infant Christ, had paused for a rest. In the early fifth century, a woman named Ikelia built an oratory to identify this resting place. This chapel saw the first liturgical celebration of the Mother of God. The name of the feast, *Kathisma*, means the sitting- or resting-place. Around 450, the venue of the celebration shifted to Jerusalem, specifically Gethsemane, a spot then supposed to be Mary's final resting place on earth. Here, in a basilica which enshrined her reputed tomb, the feast became known as the *Anapausis* ("falling asleep") or Dormition of the Mother of God. At the end of the sixth century, Emperor Maurice (reigned 582-602) extended this feast throughout the empire.[69] By the seventh century, it had reached Rome, where it was known first as the Dormition or *Pausatio*. In the eighth century, the Sacramentary of Pope Hadrian referred to it as the

---

[68] This section treats the development of the various feasts of Mary as they made their way onto the general Roman calendar. For convenience, it adopts the basic structure of Pierre Jounel, "The Veneration of Mary," section II, chapter 5 in Martimort, ed., *The Church at Prayer: An Introduction to the Liturgy*, new edition (Collegeville MN: Liturgical Press, 1986) 4:130-156, especially 138-147. I am indebted for much of its content to Jounel, as well as to Simeon Daly, "Mary in the Western Liturgy," Juniper B. Carol, ed., *Mariology*, 1:248-276, Michael O'Carroll, "Liturgy," *Theotókos*, 220-224, and James Dunlop Crichton, *Our Lady in the Liturgy* (Collegeville: The Liturgical Press, 1997). I have corrected slight errors and updated the information presented in these sources.

[69] The information on the first Marian feasts derives from Bernard Capelle, "La fête de la Vierge à Jérusalem au Ve siécle," in *Travaux liturgiques de doctrine et d'histoire* (Louvain: Abbaye Mont-César, 1967) 3:276-455, especially 281-301 for the Assumption; Irenée Henri Dalmais, "Les Apocryphes de la Dormition et l'ancienne liturgie de Jérusalem," *Bible et Terre Sainte*, 179 (1976), 13-14; Jounel, "The Veneration of Mary," Martimort (ed.), *The Church at Prayer* 4:130-131; Crichton, *Our Lady in the Liturgy*, 23-26. Crichton attributes the imperial propagation of the feast to Justinian (p. 24) but does not support his claim. Stephen J. Shoemaker, *Ancient Traditions of the Virgin Mary's Dormition and Assumption* (Oxford: Oxford University Press, 2002) p. 73, n.157 cites the standard source: Nicephorus Callistus, *Historia ecclesiastica* 1. 17, 28 (PG 147:292).

Assumption of the Blessed Virgin Mary (*Adsumptio sanctae Mariae*).[70] The earliest Jerusalem feast of Our Lady, then, comprised elements of Mary's motherhood and her dormition, with a resting-place as the common denominator.

At the beginning of the sixth century, a church north of the ruined Temple of Jerusalem became associated with Mary's nativity. This is likely the source of the feast of her birth observed on September 8.

A third church dedicated to Mary arose in the middle of the sixth century. Built on what had once been the Temple square, the Nea or New St. Mary's afforded the faithful the opportunity to commemorate the presentation of the child Mary in the Temple mentioned in the fourth chapter of the *Protoevangelium of James*. The anniversary of its dedication on November 21, 543, gave rise to the feast of the Presentation of the Blessed Virgin in the Temple.

The Marian feasts established in Jerusalem spread throughout the East. In connection with Christmas, a separate commemoration of Mary's divine motherhood served to pay due reverence to the Mother shortly after the birth of the Son. In East Syria, such a feast, called the Congratulation of the Mother of God, fell on the day after Christmas (December 26). Again in direct, even literal, reference to the birth of Christ, two further feasts emerged. The Annunciation, on March 25 (nine months before Christmas), commemorated the message of the Archangel Gabriel to the Virgin Mary and Our Lady's consent to become the Mother of the Word incarnate. On February 2, forty days after the Lord's nativity, the liturgy marked his presentation in the Temple. The feast originally was called *Hypapante* or the "Meeting" between Christ and Simeon.[71]

---

[70] Jean Deshusses, ed., *Le Sacramentaire grégorien. Ses principales formes d'après les plus anciens manuscrits*, 3rd ed. Spicilegium Friburgense 16 (Fribourg, Switzerland: Éditions universitaires, 1992), vol. 1: Hadrianum ex authentico (ad fidem codicis Cameracensis 164) 147 and 148, p. 262.

[71] For more on Mary in the Byzantine liturgy, see Robert Taft, "'What shall we call you?' Marian Liturgical Veneration in the Byzantine Tradition," *Úcta ku preservätej Bohorodicke na krest'anskom Východe. Medzinárodná vedecká konferencia 25.-26. novembra 2005* (Kosice: Centrum spirituality Východ Západ Michala Lacka, Teologická fakulta Trnavskej university, 2005) 121-140; idem, "Maria SS. Madre di Dio," in G. Marani, ed., *Omelie di Natale* (Betel—brevi saggi spirituali 4, Rome: Lipa, 1997) 43-57; idem, "Marian Liturgical Veneration: Origins, Meaning, and Contemporary Catholic Renewal," in *Proceedings, Orientale Lumen III Conference*

Mary and the Roman Calendar

a. *Natale s. Mariae*: January 1

The first Marian feast of the Roman liturgy, observed on January 1, first came in the seventh century.[72] Originally called *Natale S. Mariae*,[73] it served as the Roman counterpart of the Eastern feasts extending congratulations to the Blessed Virgin on the occasion of Christ's birth. Owing, however, to the feast's occurrence on the octave day of Christmas, the Marian character of that day eventually gave way to a focus rather on the circumcision of the Lord. As the feasts of the Annunciation (March 25) and the *Hypapante* (February 2) gradually made their way onto the Roman calendar by the seventh century, they retained a distinctly and indeed increasingly Marian character, even in nomenclature, until the liturgical reform of Paul VI in 1970.[74] Exclusively Marian feasts, like the Nativity of Mary (September 8) and the Assumption (August 15), grew in prominence and overshadowed the original Roman feast of Mary on January 1. By the mid-seventh century, however, a pre-Christmas commemoration found its way onto the Roman calendar, as it had done likewise on other Western calendars, thereby compensating for the diminution of the Marian character of January 1.[75] Moreover, two readings on the Ember days following the third Sunday of Advent refer to Mary's participation in the events leading to the Lord's birth. The

---

June 15-18, 1999, at *The Catholic University of America, Washington, DC* (Fairfax VA, Eastern Churches Publications, 1999) 91-112.

[72] See Bernard Botte, "La première fête mariale de la liturgie romaine," *Ephemerides liturgicae* 47 (1933) 425-430.

[73] In the case of the saints, except for St. John the Baptist and the Blessed Virgin Mary, the *dies natalis* refers to their heavenly birthday or entry into heaven. On the controversy surrounding the correct title of this feast, see Simeon Daly, "Mary in the Western Liturgy," pp. 252-253, n. 23. In addition to the human Nativity of Jesus Christ (December 25), the Church observes the earthly birthdays also of St. John the Baptist (June 24) and of Our Lady (September 8).

[74] With the revision of the Roman calendar in 1970, the Annunciation of the Blessed Virgin Mary became the Annunciation of the Lord, while the Purification of the Blessed Virgin Mary became the Presentation of the Lord. Without excluding the Marian dimensions of these feasts, Paul VI restored their more ancient titles and consequently increased the general awareness of their dominical character.

[75] See Jounel, "The Veneration of Mary," Martimort, ed., *The Church at Prayer*, 4:133-34.

Lucan account of the Annunciation was read on that Wednesday, and the account of Mary's Visitation to Elizabeth occurred on that Friday.[76]

b. Mary and Christmas

Mary's role in the celebration of Christmas in Rome was given sharper focus upon the erection near or in St. Mary Major of an oratory dedicated specifically to the Nativity of the Lord sometime between the pontificate of St. Leo I (440-461) and that of St. Gregory I (590-604). Of the three Masses celebrated by the pope at Christmas, this oratory became the venue for the first, that at midnight. By the twelfth century, the daytime Mass, too, had been transferred to St. Mary Major, again underscoring in topographical terms Our Lady's part in the birth of Christ.

The earliest extant Roman euchological texts of Christmas present Mary in close association with the Savior's birth.[77] Collects found in both the "Old" Gelasian[78] and Gregorian[79] sacramentaries attest to Mary's presence in the liturgy of Christmas:

---

[76] See below, B.3.a: Advent-Christmas-Epiphany.

[77] It is to be regretted that the earliest extant collection of Roman Mass formularies, the Veronese collection or so-called Leonine Sacramentary" (Verona: Biblioteca Capitolare 85 [80]) lacks the formularies from January to March. The standard edition is *Sacramentum Veronense (Cod. Bibl. Capit. Veron. LXXXV [80])*, ed. Leo Cunibert Mohlberg with Leo Eizenhöfer and Pierre Siffrin, Rerum Ecclesiasticarum Documenta, series maior: Fontes I (Rome: Herder, 1966). Hence it is impossible to know how Mary figured in the euchology of Christmas or of January 1 in the sixth century or earlier.

[78] The "Old" or "Vatican" Gelasian sacramentary (Vatican City: Biblioteca Apostolica Vaticana: Vat. Reg. lat. 316) contains a fundamentally Roman liturgical book compiled around 650, but copied with Gallican influences, around 750, near Paris. For a description and history of this sacramentary, see Eric Palazzo, *A History of Liturgical Books from the Beginning to the Thirteenth Century*, trans. Madeleine Beaumont (Collegeville MN: Pueblo/Liturgical Press, 1998) 42-46. The edition of this sacramentary is *Liber sacramentorum Romanae aecclesiae ordinis anni circuli (Cod. Vat. Reg. lat. 316/Paris Bibl. Nat. 7193, 41/56) (Sacramentarium Gelasianum)*, ed. Leo Cunibert Mohlberg (Rome: Herder, 1968) [Va=Vatican Gelasian].

[79] The sacramentary of the papal court sent in the 770s by Pope Hadrian I to Charlemagne. Later supplemented and adapted for presbyteral use in the Frankish realms, it eventually became the chief source of the Roman liturgical books until 1970. For a description and history of the Gregorian sacramentary, see Palazzo,

> *Deus, qui per beatae Mariae sacrae uirginis partum, sine humana concupiscentia procreatum, in filii tui membra uenientis paternis fecisti praeiudiciis non teneri: praesta, quaesumus, ut huius creaturae nouitate suscepta uetustatis antiquae contagiis exuamur: per eundem Dominum.*[80]

O God, who through the offspring of the holy Virgin St. Mary, begotten without human concupiscence, didst cause the members of thy coming Son not to be bound by the condemnation of their fathers, grant, we implore, that we who have been taken up by the newness of this creation, may put off the harmful influences of our former state. Through the same Lord.

> *Omnipotens sempiterne Deus, qui hunc diem per incarnationem uerbi tui et partum beatae Mariae uirginis consecrasti, da populis tuis in hac caelebritate consortium, ut qui tua gratia sunt redempti, tua sint adoptione securi. Per.*[81]

Almighty, everlasting God, who didst consecrate this day through the Incarnation of thy Word and the childbirth of the Blessed Virgin Mary, grant to thy peoples a share in this festival, that those redeemed by thy grace may be saved by thine adoption. Through.

c. The "Four Feasts" of Mary

In the late seventh century, Pope Sergius I (reigned 687-701), a native of Syria, decreed that a procession from the church of St. Hadrian (formerly the senate) in the Roman forum to St. Mary Major should mark each of what came to be known for centuries as the four Marian feasts of the Roman calendar: the Annunciation (March 25), the Dormition or, as it was later known, the Assumption (August 15), the Nativity of Mary (September 8), and *Hypapante* (February 2).[82] Litanies accompanied these

---

A History of Liturgical Books, 51-56. The edition consulted is Deshusses, ed., *Le Sacramentaire grégorien*. 3rd ed. [Ha=Hadrianum].

[80] Va 10, p. 8 assigns it as the collect of the Christmas Mass at dawn; Ha 56, p. 105 offers it as an alternate prayer. Translation mine.

[81] Va 17, p. 9 assigns it as the collect of the Christmas Mass in the day; Ha 58, p. 105 presents it as an optional prayer. Translation mine.

[82] See Louis Duchesne, ed., *Le Liber pontificalis. Text, introduction, et commentaire*, 2nd ed. by Cyrille Vogel (Paris: Boccard, 1955-57) 1: 376: "Constituit autem ut

processions to Rome's most impressive Marian basilica. Divided roughly among the four seasons of the year, they served, until the fourteenth century, as the Roman feasts in honor of the Virgin Mary. By then, the papacy, often in response to the devotion of religious orders or as a votive commemoration of either petition or thanksgiving, began to embellish the Roman calendar with new Marian observances.

d. Medieval Marian Feasts

Visitation

The next Marian feasts introduced to Rome came, like the first great four, from the East. In 1389, Pope Urban VI (reigned 1378-1389) placed the feast of the Visitation on the general Roman calendar. It is essentially a votive feast recalling the protection of the Mother of God. Originally observed in Constantinople on July 2 as the Deposition at the Blachernae of the Holy Mantle (or Veil) of the *Theotókos*, the feast commemorated the miraculous intervention of the Mother of God at her principal church (named the Blachernae) in the Byzantine capital. The Gospel of the day, drawn from St. Luke's account of the visit of Mary to her kinswoman Elizabeth,[83] reflects the loving concern of Mary for those close to her. It likewise suggests the joy that derives from peace and harmony.

In 1263, the Franciscans, who served as preachers and missionaries in the Holy Land and elsewhere in the East, adopted it under the title of the Visitation of the Blessed Virgin Mary. More than a century later, Urban VI extended it to the rest of the Church with a view toward achieving, through Our Lady's intercession, ecclesial unity in the wake of the Western Schism. Over the course of the fifteenth century, local churches and religious orders eventually adopted it. In 1441, the Council of Basel, convoked to put an end to the Western Schism, commissioned a Mass formulary for the feast and encouraged its adoption. Toward the end of the fifteenth century, Sixtus IV (reigned 1471-1484) arranged for the feast to be given a new formulary. The votive character of the feast came into renewed focus in the nineteenth century. In thanksgiving for

---

diebus Adnuntiationis Domini, Dormitionis et Nativitatis sanctae Dei genetricis semperque virginis Mariae ac sancti Symeonis, quod Ypapanti Greci appellant, letania exeat a sancto Hadriano et ad sanctam Mariam populus occurrat." See also p. 381, nn. 43-44.

[83] Lk 1:39-56.

the victory of the papal troops over the forces of the Italian Risorgimento on July 2, 1849, Pius IX raised the feast to a higher dignity (double-of-the-second-class in the reckoning of the period).

Conception of the Blessed Virgin Mary

The Immaculate Conception of the Blessed Virgin began as the Byzantine feast of the Conception of St. Anne, observed on December 9. By the mid-eleventh century, the feast came to England where it was celebrated on December 8. By the early twelfth century, it received a new title: the Conception of Mary. From England it spread to Normandy and, over the course of the twelfth century, to other parts of Europe. Upon its advent at the University of Paris, through the agency of students from Normandy, the feast met opposition from some theological circles. St. Bernard, for example, opposed it as a novelty of dubious doctrinal quality and urged the canons of Lyons against its adoption.[84]

Promoted first by English Benedictines, particularly under the influence of Eadmer of Canterbury (+1124),[85] precentor, historian, and biographer of St. Anselm, the doctrine of the Immaculate Conception of Our Lady gained much ground with the later support of the Franciscans. Adopting the feast in 1263, the Friars Minor championed its cause. In reply to objections raised against the doctrine, Franciscan theologian Bl. John Duns Scotus (+1308), for example, taught that the merits of Christ's Paschal Mystery had been applied in anticipation to the Blessed Virgin from the first moment of her conception. The feast came with the Minors to the papal court in Avignon. Finally in 1477, Sixtus IV, himself a Franciscan, placed it on the Roman calendar by the constitution *Cum praeexcelsa*. In honor of Mary's Immaculate Conception, Sixtus likewise built within the Vatican complex the famous chapel that bears his name. The decoration of the ceiling, commissioned by Sixtus' nephew Julius II and executed by Michelangelo, illustrates the preparation of the world for the Immaculate Conception of Mary. In 1708, Clement XI made the feast of Our Lady's Conception obligatory for the Roman Rite.

---

[84] St. Bernard of Clairvaux, *Epistula* 174, in *Opera omnia*, ed. Jean Leclercq and H. Rochais, 7 (Rome: Editiones Cistercienses, 1974) 388-392.

[85] Eadmer of Canterbury, *Tractatus de conceptione s. Mariae*, ed. Herbert Thurston and T. Slater (Freiburg: Herder, 1904).

Zealously advocated by the Franciscans, both the doctrine and the feast of Mary's Immaculate Conception faced opposition from various quarters, most notably from the Order of Preachers (Dominicans), whose most illustrious theologian, St. Thomas Aquinas (+1274), had argued against the doctrine. In view of this longstanding dispute, the name of the feast was simply the Conception of the Virgin Mary. After Pius IX had defined the dogma of the Immaculate Conception in 1854, however, the typically Franciscan phrase 'immaculate conception' reasserted itself in the title and euchology (prayer formulae) of the feast. By the Brief *Quod iampridem* (September 25, 1863), Pius IX solemnly promulgated a Mass formulary (known by the incipit of its Introit *Gaudens gaudebo*) drawn chiefly from one composed 400 years earlier by a papal chamberlain, Leonardo Nogaroli, at the behest of Pope Sixtus IV.[86] The language, particularly that of the collect, refers unambiguously to the Immaculate Conception of Our Lady:

> *Deus qui per immaculatam Virginis Conceptionem dignum Filio tuo habitaculum praeparasti: quaesumus; ut, qui ex morte eiusdem Filii tui praevisa, eam ab omni labe praeservasti, nos quoque mundos eius intercessione ad te pervenire concedas. Per eundem Dominum.*[87]

O God who by the Immaculate Conception of the Virgin didst make her a worthy dwelling place for thy Son, grant, we implore, that as thou didst, by his foreseen death, preserve her from all stain of sin, so by her intercession, we too may come to thee cleansed [of sin]. Through the same Lord.

e. Later Medieval Feasts of Our Lady

The Presentation of Mary in the Temple

---

[86] R. Lippe, *Missale Romanum Mediolani 1474* II. *A Collation with Other Editions Printed before 1570* Henry Bradshaw Society Publications 33 (London: Henry Bradshaw Society, 1907) 165-166. For the Mass of the Visitation of the Virgin Mary (*Gaudeamus omnes*) commissioned in 1441 by the Council of Basel, see p. 208.

[87] Collecta in Conceptione immaculate beatae Mariae Virginis, MR 2002, p. 878. Translation mine.

The church in Jerusalem, as noted earlier, had conflated the Presentation of Mary in the Temple, recorded in the apocryphal *Protoevangelium of James*, with the more historically reliable Dedication of the Basilica of St. Mary the New, near the entrance of the Temple (543). Both events, in any case, highlight Mary's dedication to God. From Jerusalem, the combined feast soon spread throughout the East. In 1372, Pope Gregory XI introduced the feast to the papal court at Avignon in response to a petition from an enterprising French knight, Philippe de Mézières, who sued for cooperation between England and France, and sought union with the Greeks, in order to launch a new crusade.[88]

Dedication of Our Lady of the Snows

A thirteenth-century legend surrounding the foundation of the Roman basilica of St. Mary Major gave rise in the fourteenth century to the extension of its anniversary of dedication (August 5) to other churches in Rome. According to this legend, a miraculous snowfall in the heat of the Roman August indicated to the patrons and the pope of the day the precise dimensions of the basilica. In 1568, a Dominican pope, St. Pius V, extended the feast of the Dedication of St. Mary Major to the rest of the Church. In so doing, he displaced the feast of no less a figure than St. Dominic, the very founder of the pope's order! Pius V further displayed his devotion to this renowned church of the Mother of God by choosing it as the site of his own tomb. A "snowfall" of flower petals is released each year in the Borghese chapel of the basilica during the intonation of the Gloria. In addition to a relief in marble depicting the original snowfall of the legend, this chapel contains an image of Mary holding the Christ child. Titled *Salus populi Romani* (Health and salvation of the people of Rome), this highly venerated image of Mary enjoyed pride of place in Roman processions in antiquity and the Middle Ages.

f. Marian Feasts of the Modern Era

Holy Name of Mary

---

[88] See W.E. Coleman, *Philippe de Mézières' Campaign for the Feast of Mary's Presentation*, Medieval Latin Texts (Toronto: Pontifical Institute of Mediaeval Studies, 1981), 1-10; Mary Jerome Kishpaugh, The Feast of the Presentation of the Virgin Mary in the Temple: An Historical and Literary Study (Washington DC: The Catholic University of America Press, 1941).

The seventeenth and eighteenth centuries witnessed a further increase in Marian feasts on the general Roman calendar. This multiplication of feasts in honor of Our Lady reflects a vivid faith in Mary's intercession on behalf of Christ's Mystical Body, the Church, in the world. These feasts underscore Mary's ongoing role in the life of the Church as evidenced in the preservation of the Church from various catastrophes and perils. In 1683, Bl. Innocent XI adopted an earlier Spanish feast of the Holy Name of Mary to commemorate the liberation of Vienna on September 12, 1683, by the Polish king, John Sobieski. Although dropped from the Roman calendar by Paul VI in 1970 and relegated to the status of a votive Mass, the Holy Name of Mary reappeared as a memorial in the third typical edition of the Roman Missal in 2002 under John Paul II.

Our Lady of Ransom

The Mercedarians, founded in the thirteenth century to liberate Christians enslaved by the Moors, inaugurated the feast of Our Lady of Ransom (September 24) in the early 1600s. By 1696, Pope Innocent XII placed it on the calendar of the Roman Rite. Expunged from the general Roman calendar in 1970, the feast still occurs on local calendars. In England, for example, the Guild of Our Lady of Ransom conducts an annual pilgrimage to the National Shrine of Our Lady of Walsingham on or near the feast, which at Walsingham is observed as a solemnity.[89]

Rosary of the Blessed Virgin Mary

In thanksgiving for the victory of the Christian forces over the Turks at the Battle of Lepanto, St. Pius V inaugurated a votive feast in honor of Our Lady of Victory to be observed on the first Sunday of October. His successor, Gregory XIII, conflated it with an earlier Dominican observance of the Rosary, giving it the title of the Rosary of Our Lady and assigning it for celebration in the City of Rome. In 1716, Clement XI extended it to the general Roman calendar in gratitude for another military victory over the Turks at Peterwardein. In his reform of the calendar, St. Pius X fixed the feast permanently on October 7, the date

---

[89] See Anne Vail, *Shrines of Our Lady in England* (Leominster: Gracewing, 2004) 190.

of the battle of Lepanto. The Roman Missal of 1970 rendered the title of the feast as Our Lady of the Most Holy Rosary.

Our Lady of Mount Carmel

In 1726, Pope Benedict XIII assigned the fourteenth-century Carmelite feast of Our Lady of Mount Carmel (July 16) to the Roman calendar. Closely associated with the sacramental popularly known as the "brown scapular," bequeathed by the Blessed Virgin herself to St. Simon Stock, general of the order of Carmelites, this feast has remained on the general Roman calendar since the eighteenth. The Roman Missal 1970 assigned it the rank of an optional memorial.

Sorrows of the Blessed Virgin Mary

The Servites (Servants of Mary) obtained permission to observe a feast of the Seven Dolors or Sorrows of the Virgin Mary on the Sunday following the more solemn feast of the Triumph of the Holy Cross (September 14). In gratitude for his safe return from captivity in France to Rome in 1814, and for the preservation of the Church during both the French Revolution and the reign of Napoleon Bonaparte, Pope Pius VII extended the feast to the general Roman calendar. In 1913, Pius X assigned September 15 as the feast, thereby juxtaposing it more dramatically with the feast of the Triumph of the Holy Cross.

With the approval of Benedict XIII in 1724, Friday of the fifth week of Lent, that is, the Friday before Good Friday, likewise had served as another feast of the Seven Sorrows of the Blessed Virgin Mary, particularly in those places which observed Passiontide with outdoor processions featuring the Blessed Virgin's perspective of the Passion of Christ. On both feasts of Our Lady's sorrows, namely that on September 14 and the other on the Friday after the fifth Sunday of Lent, the medieval poem *Stabat Mater* served as a sequence, highlighting the emotional reaction of participants in these liturgies. Both the feast of the Holy Cross and the liturgy of the Lord's Passion on Good Friday underscore the objective, theological dimensions of Christ's accomplishment of the Paschal Mystery. This is particularly evident in the Passion account of John read each year on Good Friday. The comments of pastoral liturgist Pius Parsch on the contrast of the feast of the Seven Sorrows with the older, more sober Lenten ferial which it had displaced, applies equally to its contrast with both the Triumph of the Cross and Good Friday itself:

> Very different is the spirit characterizing the feast of the Seven Sorrows. Here sentiment and emotion is [sic] strong. We see Christ's agony through the heart of his mother. She is our guide, she teaches us how to suffer and sympathize with her Son. Where the ancient liturgy stops, the newer form begins; the old gives theology and history, the new stimulates our hearts and feelings. Thus one complements the other.[90]

Addressing the September feast of Our Lady's Seven Sorrows in reference to the Triumph of the Cross, Parsch elaborates in even greater detail:

> In contrast to yesterday's feast with its emphasis on Christ's kingship, today's concentrates on the human side of his sufferings. Its liturgy stems from an entirely different spiritual mentality; the feast of the Exaltation showed and praised the Cross as the sign of objective redemption; it unfurled, as it were, the *crux gemmata* [bejewelled cross]. Today's feast sees the human, the suffering Christ, it emphasizes Mary's role as a co-sufferer. These two feasts in honor of Christ's Cross, following so closely upon one another, clearly show two trends of Catholic spirituality, that of ancient times and that of the Middle Ages, trends which are often designated as objective and subjective spirituality. The former sees the Passion as the *beata passio* (blessed suffering), the latter as the *passio amara* (bitter suffering and co-suffering).[91]

It must be granted, in general, that the modern Marian feasts introduced to the calendar of the Roman Rite express a rather demonstratively emotional devotion, and reflect a concern for the needs of personal piety. As this trend continues into the twenty-first century, it

---

[90] Pius Parsch, *The Church's Year of Grace*, 2nd ed., trans. William G. Heidt (Collegeville MN: Liturgical Press, 1964) 2:285-286.
[91] Parsch, 5:206-207.

may be useful to consider it as a means of harmonizing, if not altogether integrating, both devotional and liturgical piety.

g. Twentieth-Century Feasts of Mary

Our Lady of Lourdes

In 1858, just four years after the papal definition of the dogma of the Immaculate Conception, Bernadette Soubirous, a native of Lourdes, France, reported a series of apparitions of a woman who identified herself as the Immaculate Conception. After decades of careful investigation into the reliability of Bernadette and into the accounts of healings unexplained by science, ecclesiastical authorities recognized the authenticity of the apparitions. In 1890, Leo XIII granted the Diocese of Tarbes permission to observe February 11, the date of the first of the visions, as the feast of the Apparition of the Immaculate Virgin at Lourdes. In response both to the widespread fame of the shrine at Lourdes and to the demands of popular Marian piety directed in particular toward the Immaculate Conception, St. Pius X extended the feast to the general Roman calendar in 1907. The Missal of 1970 records the title of the feast simply as Our Lady of Lourdes. Although it functions as a reminder of the truth of the Immaculate Conception, the feast also recalls the intercession of Mary and, since the pontificate of John Paul II, serves as the World Day of Prayer for the Sick.

Since 1751, with the permission of Benedict XIV, Portugal had observed a feast of Our Lady's Maternity on regional calendars. In 1931, in order to mark the fifteen-hundredth anniversary of the Council of Ephesus, Pius XI placed the Maternity of Mary on the general Roman calendar. Pius assigned the feast to October 11, in honor of what then was presumed to have been the conclusion of the Council of Ephesus.

Devotion to the Sacred Heart of Jesus, which from the seventeenth century flourished particularly in opposition to Jansenism, inspired a parallel devotion to the Heart of Mary. St. John Eudes (+1680) effectively promoted devotion to both Holy Hearts. By 1646, he had secured approval for a Mass of the Immaculate Heart of Mary. By 1807, the Augustinians were celebrating the Most Pure Heart of Mary on the Sunday within the Octave of Our Lady's Assumption. In 1855, Bl. Pius IX granted it a proper Mass formulary (*Omnis gloria*). Some local churches, though, observed it on July 9, while others kept it on the Sunday, or, after 1920, the Saturday, after the Sacred Heart. In 1880, Pope Leo XIII placed the feast on the local Roman calendar. Pope Pius XII, in view of the coincidence of his episcopal ordination with the first apparition of the Blessed Virgin at Fatima (May 13, 1917), exercised a personal devotion to the Immaculate Heart. To commemorate his consecration of the world to the Immaculate Heart in 1942, he extended the feast to the general Roman calendar in 1944, giving it a new formulary (*Adeamus cum fiducia*) and assigning it to August 22, the octave day of the Assumption. The 1970 Roman Missal assigns it, instead, to the Saturday after the Sacred Heart of Jesus. In 2002, John Paul II raised it to the rank of an obligatory memorial.

The medieval church developed the concept of kingship rooted in Scripture and common to many peoples. In order to be a queen, a woman must be the daughter, the mother, or the consort of a king. The Psalms and other inspired texts refer to God as King of heaven and earth: Hence the title "The Lord," or "Our Lord." Mary's queenship is utterly dependent upon the kingship of the Triune God, for she is the daughter of God the Father, the Mother of God the Son, and the Bride of the Holy Spirit. Since the early Middle Ages, the Church has hailed Mary in both devotional and liturgical texts as the Queen of heaven and earth, the Queen of all the angels and saints, Our Lady, and so forth. Andrew of Crete (+c.740) is among the earliest theologians to comment on Mary as both queen and mediatrix.[92] Images of the Blessed Virgin crowned as queen proliferated during the Middle Ages and continue to enjoy popularity even today. The apsidal mosaic of St. Mary Major, Rome, for example, depicts Christ crowning Mary queen of heaven. Countless popular prayers and hymns, as well as three of the Marian anthems chanted after Compline (*Ave Regina caelorum, Regina caeli, Salve Regina*) all address Mary as Queen. In 1954, on the occasion of the centenary of the dogma of the Immaculate Conception, Pius XII inaugurated the feast of the Blessed Virgin Mary, Queen, assigning it to the last day of May, the month which popular piety dedicates to Mary. Since 1970, the Roman Rite celebrates Mary's queenship on August 22,

---

[92] See Gambero, *Mary and the Fathers of the Church*, 397-398. The homilies of Andrew of Crete are available in Jacques-Paul Migne, *Patrologiae cursus completus, series graeca* (Paris: Montrouge, 1857-1866), 97: 805-882 [homilies 1-4 on the Nativity of the Bessed Virgin Mary], 882-914 homily 5 on the Annunciation of Our Lady]; 1046-1110 [homilies 12-14 on the Dormition].

the octave day, as it were, of the Assumption, and marks the Immaculate Heart, as mentioned earlier, on the Saturday following the solemnity of the Sacred Heart of Jesus.

Religious orders and local churches continued to celebrate a variety of Marian Masses and offices, as well as to observe Marian feasts inaugurated in some cases as early as the Middle Ages. The *Graduale Romanum* of 1908 supplies chants for the following feasts: Translation of the Holy House of Loreto (December 10); the Expectation of the Childbirth of the Blessed Virgin Mary (December 18); the Espousals of Our Lady and St. Joseph (January 23); Our Lady of Good Counsel (April 26); Our Lady Help of Christians (May 24); Most Pure Heart of Mary (third Sunday after Pentecost); Our Lady of Perpetual Help (Sunday before June 24); Motherhood of Mary (second Sunday of October); Purity of Mary (third Sunday of October); Patronage of Mary (second Sunday of November); and Manifestation of the Miraculous Medal (November 27).[93]

The primary goal of Pope St. Pius X's pontificate (1903-1914), summarized in his motto *Instaurare omnia in Christo* "to restore all things in Christ" led him to give liturgical renewal pride of place in his legislation. As popes of the twentieth century sought to reform the calendar of the Roman Rite, they underscored the prominence of Sunday as the Day of the Lord. Hence, in 1913, Pius X began to displace Marian observances that occurred on Sundays. Despite these efforts at reform, followed in turn by those of Pius XII and John XXIII,[94] several Marian feasts still remained as moveable feasts, if only on local calendars, in the Missal of 1962 issued by John XXIII.

The Johannine Missal of 1962 provided sixteen proper formularies for the following feasts of the Blessed Virgin Mary to be celebrated in various places, that is, to be celebrated on local calendars and those of religious orders and societies (in order of occurrence over the liturgical year): Our Lady of Good Counsel (April 26); Mother of Fair Love (May 8); Our Lady of the Sacred Heart of Jesus (likewise May 8); Our Lady Mediatrix of All Graces (also May 8); Our Lady Help of Christians (May

---

[93] *Graduale romanum sacrosanctae romanae ecclesiae de tempore et de sanctis ... restitutum et editum cui addita sunt festa novissima. Editio ratisbonensis juxta Vaticanam* (Ratisbonne and Rome and New York and Cincinnati: Pustet, 1908).

[94] John XXIII, *Instructio de calendariis particularibus ... ad normam et mentem Codicis rubricorum revisendis* 33, in AAS 53 (1961) 168-180.

24); Queen of Apostles (Saturday after the Ascension); Our Mother of Grace (June 9); Our Lady of Perpetual Help (June 27); Mother of Mercy (Saturday before the fourth Sunday of July); Refuge of Sinners (August 12); Our Lady of Consolation (Saturday after the feast of St. Augustine, August 28); Mother of the Divine Pastor (September 4); Mother of Divine Providence (Saturday before the third Sunday of November); and Our Lady of the Miraculous Medal (November 27).

h. Roman Missal 1970

By means of his revision of the Roman Missal in 1970, Pope Paul VI reduced to thirteen the number of Marian feasts on the general Roman calendar. This new, simplified calendar of the Roman Rite arranged liturgical observances according to the following scheme, in descending order of importance: solemnities, feasts, and memorials (either obligatory or optional). Naturally the Blessed Virgin figures prominently in such solemnities of the Lord as Annunciation of the Lord, Christmas, Epiphany, Holy Family (now the Sunday within the octave of Christmas) and feasts of the Lord such as the Presentation of the Lord in the Temple. The 1970 Missal provides three Marian solemnities (Mother of God on January 1;[95] Assumption on August 15; Immaculate Conception on December 8), two feasts (Visitation on May 31, Nativity of the Blessed Virgin Mary on September 8), four obligatory memorials (Queenship on August 22, Our Lady of Sorrows on September 15 complete with sequence *Stabat Mater*, Our Lady of the Rosary on October 7, Presentation of the Blessed Virgin Mary on November 21), and four optional memorials (Our Lady of Lourdes on February 11, Immaculate Heart [Saturday after the Most Sacred Heart of Jesus], Our Lady of Mount Carmel on July 16, Dedication of the Basilica of St. Mary Major on August 5).

i. Roman Missal 2002

---

[95] The restored solemnity of Mary Mother of God renders obsolete the October 11 feast of the Maternity of Mary, which recalled the confirmation of this title at Ephesus in 431.

The third typical edition of the Roman Missal,[96] supervised by Cardinal Jorge Arturo Medina Estévez and promulgated by John Paul II in 2002, restored one Marian feast to the general Roman calendar, namely, the optional memorial of the Most Holy Name of Mary on September 12. Having recovered from an attempt on his life in St. Peter's Square in the Vatican on May 13, 1981, the anniversary of the first of five apparitions of Our Lady at Fatima, Portugal, John Paul II added a new feast, that of Our Lady of Fatima, as an optional memorial on May 13. Since the promulgation of the third typical edition of the Roman Missal, the Immaculate Heart of Mary, a focus of the Fatima devotions, now enjoys an increase in rank as an obligatory memorial. Hence the tradition of votive feasts marking Mary's intervention in the life of the Church continues even into the twenty-first century.

Our Lady of Guadalupe

The Church in the Americas observes the feast of Our Lady of Guadalupe on December 12. The apparitions of Mary associated with the figure of St. Juan Diego on Tepeyac Hill in sixteenth-century Mexico (1531) gave rise to widespread devotion to Our Lady under this title, particularly among the peoples indigenous to the region. Countless pilgrims to the shrine in Mexico even today visit the tilma, or cloak, of Juan Diego, which displays an image of the Blessed Virgin. On May 25, 1754, Pope Benedict XIV proclaimed Our Lady of Guadalupe the patron saint of New Spain (Spanish Central and North America) and approved the Mass and office in her honor. Leo XIII approved a new formulary in 1891. The patronage of Our Lady of Guadalupe has expanded over the centuries. Pius X declared her patroness of Latin America in 1910. Pius XI pronounced her patroness of the Philippines in 1935. On January 22, 1999, John Paul II, by means of the post-synodal Apostolic Exhortation *Ecclesia in America*, decreed Our Lady of Guadalupe the patroness of the Americas;[97] hence the Church in the Americas celebrates Our Lady of

---

[96] *Missale Romanum*, 3rd typical edition (Vatican City: Libreria Editrice Vaticana, 2002) [MR 2002].
[97] See *Notitiae* 35 (1999) 227-247.

Guadalupe as a feast. In 2002, John Paul II placed Our Lady of Guadalupe on the general Roman calendar, with the rank of optional memorial.[98]

The Seasonal Cycles of the Liturgical Year

In addition to the various feasts which commemorate Mary's role in the life of Christ, the history of salvation, the earthly pilgrimage of the Church, or the communion of saints, the Blessed Virgin figures in both liturgical cycles which drive the Church's year. The minor cycle of Advent-Christmas-Epiphany reflects on a smaller scale the major, indeed central, cycle of Lent-Easter-Pentecost. Both cycles provide the model of Christian participation in the Lord's own mysteries: interior preparation—celebration—public proclamation. This cycle corresponds to the sacramental process of: catechesis and ascesis-sacraments of initiation-apostolic public witness. Those only just entering the Church experience the process in the Rites of Christian Initiation in this way. For fully initiated Catholics, however, the liturgical seasons of Christmas and Easter afford, on a semi-annual basis, the model of spiritual and sacramental renewal: a period of asceticism (prayer, fasting, almsgiving all fortified by a good confession), followed by the renewal of baptismal promises and holy Communion; this in turn leads to prophetic witness by the grace of the Holy Spirit already bestowed in confirmation. Such a model applies to the process of sacramental renewal on a weekly or even daily basis. In any case, Mary accompanies the faithful in the liturgy, guiding them to Christ in the Eucharist, and urging obedience to his command to bring his Gospel and the fruits of sacramental participation to others.

Mary enjoys unique prominence in the liturgical cycle of Advent, Christmas, and Epiphany. In Advent, Our Lady's spirit of tranquil meditation prepares us for the coming of her Son. At Christmas, Mary gives birth to Christ in the mystery of the Incarnation. She brings him to birth likewise in every individual and community who welcomes her. At Epiphany, Mary presents Christ to us and exhorts us to faith and proclamation: "Do whatever he tells you." In the history of doctrinal development, it is worth noting that the Council of Ephesus preceded

---

[98] See *Notitiae* 40 (2004) 194-206. At the same time, John Paul II placed St. Juan Diego on the general Roman calendar, likewise as an optional memorial.

Chalcedon by twenty years. Even in matters of doctrine, then, Mary plays the dawn to Christ the rising Sun of Justice.[99]

Similarly in the Lent-Easter-Pentecost cycle, Mary accompanies the Church on her pilgrimage through the desert of Lent. She offers Christ and herself to the Father on Calvary; she rejoices in the Resurrection of her Son and Lord from the dead; finally, she prays with and for the Church in anticipation of the Holy Spirit at Pentecost. In the cycle of ascetic preparation, celebration of the mysteries, and proclamation of the Good News, Mary aids the Church by both her example and her intercession.

a. Advent-Christmas-Epiphany

The Advent season draws attention to the comings of Christ. The liturgy recalls his first coming in the humility of the Incarnation, so that the Church might prepare worthily and well for his second coming in glory as Judge of the living and the dead. Hence the Church looks to Mary, who welcomed him in blessed hope. The character of the first part of Advent is distinctly eschatological. The liturgy, in its prayers, readings, and antiphons, anticipates Christ's coming as Judge at the Last Day. Both the solemnity of the Immaculate Conception on December 8, and, in the Americas, the feast of Our Lady of Guadalupe on December 12, remind us of Mary's unique role in the history of salvation and the life of the Church. Like the dawn before the sunrise, Mary prepares the world and the Church for the coming of Christ. Moreover, during the immediate preparation for the Nativity of the Lord, from December 17-24, Mary emerges in even more distinct relief through the scriptural lessons and especially in the Preface to the Eucharistic Prayer. Here, as in the Roman Canon, Mary appears in tandem with that other great figure of Advent, John the Baptist and Precursor of the Lord:

> The Virgin Mother bore him in her womb with
>   love beyond all telling.
> John the Baptist was his herald
>   and made him known when at last he came.[100]

---

[99] See Mal 4:2.
[100] Preface Advent II, ICEL, *The Roman Missal revised by decree of the Second Vatican Council and published by the authority of Pope Paul VI: The Sacramentary* (New York:

A few notes are in order regarding the structure of Advent and its dynamics over the history of its development in the Roman Rite. Although Rome adopted a six-week Advent in the second half of the sixth century, St. Gregory I reduced it to four weeks. On the Roman calendar until 1970, the Ember days, falling after the third Sunday of Advent, recalled the Blessed Virgin in a particularly striking way. On Ember Wednesday of Advent, the text of the first reading featured the prophecy of Isaiah 7:10-15 *Ecce virgo concipiet, et pariet filium, et vocabitur nomen eius Emmanuel* ("Behold a virgin shall conceive and bear a son and his name shall be called Emmanuel."[101] Then followed the Lucan account of the annunciation of Gabriel to the Blessed Virgin: *Missus est angelus* (Lk 1:26-38).[102] On Ember Friday in Advent, the first reading was drawn from Isaiah 11:1-5, *Egredietur flos de radice Iesse* (A flower shall come forth from the root of Jesse).[103] The Marian significance of this passage is obvious to all admirers of the Jesse tree, depicted in the Middle Ages often through the medium of stained-glass windows or elaborate illustrations in manuscript prayer books and bibles. The Gospel pericope of the day recounted the visitation of Mary to Elizabeth (Lk 1:39-47).[104]

The Ember days called the faithful to fast and pray in anticipation of the ordinations that would take place on that Saturday. The accounts of Mary's faithful reception of the Word incarnate (Annunciation), and her generosity in bringing that Word to others (Visitation), would have exhorted the ordinands to embrace with worthy joy their respective vocations.

The season of Advent shares the quiet and prayerful expectation of the Blessed Virgin Mary. Through the "O Antiphons," recited during Vespers in conjunction with the Canticle of Mary (Magnificat), and used as well at Mass for the Gospel acclamation of the day, the liturgy invokes Christ by various messianic and divine titles (Wisdom, Adonai, Root of

---

Catholic Book Publishing Co., 1985) 377.

[101] *Missale Romanum anno 1962 promulgatum*, eds Cuthbert Johnson and Anthony Ward, Bibliotheca "Ephemerides Liturgicae" Subsidia Instrumenta Liturgica Quarreriensia Supplementa 2 (Rome: Centro Vincenziano Liturgico—Edizioni Liturgiche, 1994) [MR 1962] 36, p. 6.

[102] MR 1962, 38, pp. 6-7.

[103] MR 1962, 45, p. 7.

[104] MR 1962, 47, p. 8. Cf. Gertrud Schoiller, *Iconography of Christian Art*, trans. Janet Seligma (Greenwich CT: New York Graphics Society, 1971) 1:14-21.

Jesse, Key of David, Rising Sun, King of Nations, Emmanuel). A custom originating in the early Middle Ages and transmitted through religious orders and congregations assigned an additional O Antiphon, *O Virgo virginum* ("O Virgin of virgins) to salute Mary.[105] This title, too, implies the eschatological coming of Christ who makes fruitful the barren and who crowns with everlasting splendor the pure of heart.

The *Alma Redemptoris mater* serves as the Marian anthem customarily chanted after Compline (or solemn Vespers) from the First Sunday of Advent until the end of the Christmas season (February 2, Candlemas Day):

> *Alma Redemptoris Mater, quae pervia caeli*
> *porta manes, et stella maris, succurre cadenti,*
> *surgere qui curat, populo; tu, quae genuisti,*
> *natura mirante, tuum sanctum Genitorem,*
> *Virgo prius ac posterius, Gabrielis ab ore*
> *sumens illud Ave, peccatorum miserere.*[106]

The anthem invokes Our Lady not only as Mother of the Redeemer, but also as *pervia caeli porta* (Open Gate of Heaven) and *stella maris* (Star of the Sea). Going "to Jesus through Mary," the Church merely follows the example of Christ himself, who chose to come to us through his Mother Mary.[107] The title Star of the Sea plays on the meaning of the Hebrew name Miriam as interpreted by Western theologians. As the star of the sea, Mary guides the faithful over the waves and through the storms of this life to the final port of heaven. The virginal birth of Christ as the fruit of Mary's obedience causes wonderment in nature itself, for the creature will give birth to the creative Word through whom all things came into being. Mary is both Virgin and Mother. Indeed the anthem stresses the perpetual virginity of Mary, *virgo prius ac posterius* ("virgin

---

[105] See Amalarius of Metz (c.775-c.850), *Liber de ordine antiphonarii*, 13.30, J.M. Hanssens, ed., *Amalarii episcopi opera liturgica omnia*, vol. 1, Studi e testi 140 (1950) 48-9.

[106] *Liturgia horarum iuxta ritum romanum, editio typica* (Vatican City: Vatican Polyglot Press, 1977) [LH] I: *tempus Adventus, tempus Nativitatis*, 540.

[107] St. Louis de Montfort drives this point home in his treatise *True Devotion to Mary*, trans. Frederick William Faber (New York: Fathers of the Company of Mary, 1941; reprinted Rockford IL: TAN, 1985) p. 3 and passim.

beforehand and afterwards), echoing St. Jerome's defense of this immemorial doctrine.

Finally, the anthem denotes the power of Mary's intercession and assistance inasmuch as it petitions Mary to have pity on sinners. In the litanies approved for use in both the sacred liturgy and personal devotions, the invocation *Miserere nobis* is reserved for the Persons of the Blessed Trinity. The anthem reflects the great confidence which the Church places in Mary's mediation for a people fallen yet striving to rise from their sinful condition.

The season of Christmas encompasses the birth of Christ, the solemnity of the Holy Family on the Sunday within the octave of Christmas, the solemnity of Mary Mother of God on January 1, and the Epiphany. It is worth mentioning that Mary figures in two stages or moments of Christ's epiphany: the manifestation of his divinity to the Gentiles, and the revelation of his divine sonship to the disciples at Cana. Matthew records that the Magi, at the end of their journey from the East, entered the house and "saw the child with Mary his Mother, and they fell down and worshipped him."[108] Early frescoes in the catacombs of St. Priscilla on the via Salaria depict Mary seated and in the act of presenting the Christ child to three figures dressed in Persian caps and offering gifts to the infant.

Mary does not appear in any of the scriptural accounts of Christ's manifestation to the House of Israel on the banks of the Jordan. Instead, John the Baptist exercises his role as the precursor and baptizer of the Lord. Mary prepared a home for Christ; John prepared the people of Israel for him. Now, on the threshold of Christ's public ministry, the Father and the Holy Spirit in a theophany present Jesus to Israel as the beloved Son sent to redeem the people from their sins.

Mary reappears at Cana, where Christ gives the first of his signs at her prompting. He thereby brings to a close the cycle of the three epiphanies: first to the Gentiles, then to the Israelites, and finally to the disciples. The appropriate response to the epiphany of divine glory is faith: "the disciples believed in him."[109] Christ then carries out his public ministry, and brings his messianic mission to its culmination in the Paschal Mystery.

---

[108] Mt 2:11.
[109] Jn 2:11.

b. Lent-Easter-Pentecost

The season of Lent prepares the Church for the celebration of the Paschal Mystery during the sacred Triduum of Maundy Thursday, Good Friday, and Holy Saturday. In Lent, members of the Church examine their conscience and engage in some form of asceticism in order to participate fruitfully in the Eucharist. The connection of the Lenten season with Mary is not always obvious. The Stations of the Cross, like the Sorrowful Mysteries of the Rosary, do offer the faithful some insight into the Passion of Christ from the perspective of the Blessed Virgin Mary. Our Lady figures in the fourth, twelfth, and thirteenth stations: Jesus meets his sorrowful Mother, Jesus dies on the Cross, Jesus is taken down from the Cross and placed in the arms of his Mother. In many places, the custom still obtains of chanting a strophe of the hymn *Stabat Mater* when moving from one station to the next. This however, pertains to the realm of popular piety, rather than to the sphere of liturgy. It is significant that MR 2002 offers no common Masses of the Blessed Virgin during Lent, whereas it does for Advent, Christmas, Easter, and throughout the year (*per annum*).

For those Catholics privileged to stay in Rome itself during Lent, Mary's role in the Lenten liturgy is only slightly more discernible in the assignment of the stational churches. During the early Middle Ages, the pope and his court would celebrate the Eucharist at specific churches designated according to their place in the seven regions or districts of the city. In the pontificate of Bl. John XXIII (1958-1963), the Diocese of Rome revived the custom of observing the stational churches during Lent and the octave of Easter.[110] On Wednesday of the first week (formerly Ember Wednesday) of Lent, and again on Wednesday of Holy Week, St. Mary Major hosts the liturgy of the day. On the second Sunday of Lent, S. Maria in Domnica serves as the stational church. S. Maria in Trastevere is the venue of the liturgy on Thursday of the second week of Lent, and S. Maria in via Lata on Wednesday of the fifth week of Lent. The original pilgrims' handbook issued for those participating in the Roman stations contains a visit to the Blessed Sacrament and another to Our Lady, preceded by this notice:

---

[110] See Placido Lugano, *Le sacre stazioni romane per la quaresima e l'ottava di Pasqua: note storiche e preci stazionali* (Vatican City: Libreria Editrice Vaticana, 1960) 7-13.

> The booklet contains the visit to the Most Blessed Sacrament and to the Blessed Virgin Mary, so that the first act of anyone visiting the church is directed to the divine Redeemer in the holy Eucharist and to his Mother. Then follow the litanies of the saints with the stational prayers.[111]

Citing the Pio-Benedictine Code of Canon Law (1917), the compiler of the booklet Placido Lugano explains the continuity of the revived stations:

> The modern discipline is but the continuation of the ancient. "It is a good and useful thing to invoke in supplication the servants of God, reigning together with Christ, and to venerate their relics and images: but before everything else let all the faithful honor with filial devotion the most Blessed Virgin Mary" (can. 1276). And the stational visit brings the tribute of honor and the incense of filial love to the Mother of God in the golden basilicas of her glorification and the aroma of veneration to the relics of the martyrs and saints who give increased and lasting value to our Roman churches.[112]

Although scarcely in evidence throughout the liturgical texts of Lent, Mary emerges in the liturgy of Good Friday in the Passion according to John. Here, as mentioned earlier, the Church marks Mary's association with the sacrifice of Christ on the Cross and her motherhood of all Christ's disciples.

From the end of the Christmas season until Holy Week, *Ave Regina caelorum* stands as the final Marian anthem of the day:

---

[111] Lugano, 14; see also 15-18.

[112] "La moderna disciplina non è che la continuazione dell'antica. "È cosa buona e utile invocare supplichevolemente i servi di Dio, regnanti insieme con Cristo, e venerarne le reliquie e le immagini: ma prima di ogni altro tutti fideli onorino con filiale devozione la beatissima Vergine Maria" (can. 1276). E la visita stazionale reca il tribute dell'onore e l'incenso dell'amore filiale all Madre di Dio nelle dorate basiliche della sua glorificazione, e il profumo della venerazione alle reliquie dei Martiri e dei Santi che impreziosiscono per l'immortalità le nostre chiese romane." Lugano, 12-13.

Ave, Regina caelorum,
ave domina angelorum,
salve, radix, salve porta,
ex qua mundo lux est orta.

Gaude, Virgo gloriosa,
super omnes speciosa;
vale, o valde decora,
et pro nobis Christum exora.

Although the Roman Missal of 1962 retains the ancient liturgical preparation for Lent known as Pre-Lent, including the Sundays of Septuagesima, Sexagesima, and Quinquagesima, the Missal of 1970 omits Pre-Lent altogether. In any case, the Church at this season invokes the Blessed Virgin under the title of Queen of the heavens, mistress of angels, root, and gate through which light arose upon the world. This could imply, as did the *Alma*, that Mary is the dawn or gate of day, through which shines Christ the Sun.[113]

Traditionally sung from February 2 to Wednesday of Holy Week, this anthem makes no allusion to the sufferings of Christ; indeed the second stanza actually bids Our Lady rejoice, and remarks on her unsurpassed beauty, comments scarcely suited to a somber occasion or season. Nevertheless, the *Ave Regina caelorum* alone of all the final Marian anthems begins with a descent of the musical scale. Perhaps this accounts for its selection as the anthem commonly sung during Lent and Passiontide.

Finally, on bidding the Virgin farewell, the anthem begs her graciously to pray for us. Perhaps not surprisingly, in the twelfth century it was assigned as the antiphon to be sung at None (the midafternoon hour, or 3 p.m.) on the feast of the Assumption.[114] The current breviary recommends it as the Marian anthem for both the Assumption and the Queenship of Mary.[115]

Although the Gospel accounts of the Lord's Resurrection do not mention the Blessed Virgin Mary, a tradition dating at least to the

---

[113] Joseph Connelly, *Hymns of the Roman Liturgy* (Westminster MD: Newman, 1957) 45.
[114] Connolly, 45.
[115] See LH 4:1067 and 1081.

fifth century maintains that the risen Christ appeared to his Mother. According to the Latin poet Sedulius, Christ appeared first to the Virgin Mary before any of the other witnesses mentioned by the evangelists or St. Paul (1 Cor 15:6). Indeed, in this account, Mary who at the Annunciation served as the gate through which Jesus entered the world, now received the good news of the Lord's Resurrection precisely in order to become the herald of his second coming.[116] More recently, Pope John Paul II recalled this tradition in several of his Easter messages.[117] After citing Sedulius, the Pope considers the value of the tradition:

> It seems reasonable to think that Mary, as the image and model of the Church which waits for the Risen One and meets him in the group of disciples during his Easter appearances, had had a personal contact with her risen Son, so that she too could delight in the fullness of paschal joy.
>
> Present at Calvary on Good Friday (cf. Jn 19:25) and in the Upper Room on Pentecost (cf. Acts 1:14), the Blessed Virgin, too, was probably a privileged witness of Christ's Resurrection, completing in this way her participation in all the essential moments of the Paschal Mystery. Welcoming the risen Jesus, Mary is also a sign and anticipation of humanity, which hopes to achieve its fulfillment through the Resurrection of the dead.[118]

The non-canonical tradition of Christ's appearance to his Mother may well be reflected in the choice of the Roman stational church for Easter Day: St. Mary Major.

From Easter until Pentecost the Church chants the *Regina caeli* as the final Marian anthem:

---

[116] Sedulius, *Paschale Carmen*, 5, 357-364, *Sedulii opera omnia*, ed Iohannes Huemer (Vienna: Gerold, 1885) *Corpus scriptorum ecclesiasticorum latinorum* 10: 140-141.

[117] John Paul II, Wednesday general audience, April 3, 1996, *L'Osservatore Romano*, English ed. April 10, 1996: Mary "alone remains to keep alive the flame of faith, preparing to receive the joyful and astonishing announcement of the Resurrection"; Wednesday general audience May 21, 1997, *L'Osservatore Romano*, English ed. May 28, 1997, 11.

[118] John Paul II, Wednesday general audience, May 21, 1997, *L'Osservatore Romano*, English ed. May 28, 1997, 11.

Regina caeli laetare, alleluia,
Quia quem meruisti portare, alleluia,
Resurrexit sicut dixit, alleluia,
Ora pro nobis Deum, alleluia.

With all the exuberance of paschal joy, the Church bids Mary rejoice in the Lord's Resurrection. The anthem connects the two moments of the birth of Christ and his glorious Resurrection, praising Our Lady for her role in bearing Christ worthily, and asking her to pray for us to God.

The Easter season concludes with Pentecost, an event which underscores Mary's relationship to the Church as model and Mother. Christian art frequently depicts Mary in the very midst of the apostles, recalling the figure of the Woman of Revelation 12, who is surrounded by twelve stars. After Pentecost, the apostles go forth to bear witness to the Paschal Mystery. Accordingly, those who have received the Holy Spirit in the sacrament of confirmation go forth to testify to the truth of the Gospel. For this apostolic task, they plead with the Blessed Virgin to help them by her prayers. From Pentecost until the end of the liturgical year, the Church customarily chants the *Salve Regina*:

Salve, Regina, mater misericordiae; vita, dulcedo et spes nostra, salve.
Ad te clamamus, exsules filii Evae.
Ad te suspiramus, gementes et flentes in hac lacrimarum valle.
Eia ergo, advocate nostra, illos tuos misericordes oculos ad nos converte.
Et Iesum, benedictum fructum ventris tui, nobis post hoc exsilium ostende.
O clemens, o pia, o dulcis Virgo Maria.

The anthem greets Mary not only as queen, mother of mercy, life, sweetness, and hope, but also as "our advocate." During the time after Pentecost, or *per annum*, the ministers of the Roman Rite are clad in green, the color of hope. At Pentecost, the Holy Spirit descended as the Paraclete, the consoler of faithful Christians and apostles. How fitting that the Church should salute Mary as advocate in this final anthem sung throughout much of the year. The anthem reminds of Mary's compassionate disposition toward the members of the Church, and begs her to turn the eyes of her mercy toward us and, after our exile through this valley of tears, to show us the blessed fruit of her womb, the Lord Jesus. Here again, as at Epiphany, Mary presents Christ to others.

As noted earlier, the Church encourages the venerable tradition of observing Our Lady's Saturday as a bridge from the week to the Lord's Day.[119]

Conclusion

The liturgical year unfolds for the Church the mysteries of Jesus Christ. Because Mary played an intimate part in these mysteries of her Son, the Church commemorates her with admiration and devotion. The liturgy extols the privileges and prerogatives that belong to Mary in view of her role as the Mother of God the Son. Mary always leads the faithful to a greater knowledge and a deeper appreciation of her Son. Of Mary there never can be enough, since she brings us to ever deeper levels of Christ. Each evening, the Church echoes Mary's canticle of praise, hoping at last to enjoy the fulfillment of God's promises to Abraham and to all his descendants. In this spirit of joyful anticipation, the Church continues on earth to celebrate the Paschal Mystery. Eucharistic communion with Jesus Christ entails communion likewise with Mary. This alone ought to prompt more research into the inexhaustible riches of the Church's public act of worship, so that, through Mary, the Church may gaze upon the face of Christ with deeper comprehension and increasing love.

---

[119] See p. 17, n. 60.

Marian Devotion, the Rosary, and the Scapular

Fr. Etienne Richer

Introduction

Veneration of the Mother of the Lord, which is an integral part of Christian worship, is manifested in an eminent manner in the celebration of the Church's liturgy, but also by means of other forms of devotion, which are valuable auxiliary practices that harmonize with the liturgy but without becoming confused with it. These are precisely the other forms of Marian devotion—most specifically those of the Rosary and the scapular—which will be dealt with in the present chapter, but not without having first carefully laid the doctrinal foundation, that is to say the profound roots of all authentic veneration of Mary, liturgical or not, in Scripture, Tradition and the Magisterium. The liturgy, which is the "summit and source of the Church's life" (*SC* 10), according to the teaching of the Constitution *Sacrosanctum Concilium*, "does not exhaust the entire activity of the Church" (*SC* 9) and consequently "the spiritual life is not limited solely to participation in the liturgy" (*SC* 12). Such truths are particularly reflected in the Marian dimension of the Christian life and in the various modes of expression of the piety of the faithful towards the Blessed Virgin Mary. That is why chapter 8 of the Constitution *Lumen Gentium* not only admonishes "all the sons of the Church that the *cultus*, especially the liturgical *cultus*, of the Blessed Virgin, be generously fostered" (*LG* 67),[1] but also "that the

---

[1] Translator's note: Throughout this chapter I have consistently rendered the Latin word *cultus*, the French word *culte* and the Italian word *culto* by the Latin word *cultus*, except where the English word "devotion" was more clearly indicated. I did this for two reasons: first, because of the negative associations of the English

practices and exercises of devotion towards her, recommended by the teaching authority of the Church in the course of the centuries be highly esteemed" (*LG* 67). By the same token, the *Directory on Popular Piety and the Liturgy* (2002) exhorts

> all the faithful—sacred ministers, religious and laity—to develop a personal and community devotion to the Blessed Virgin Mary through the use of approved and recommended pious exercises. Liturgical worship, notwithstanding its objective and irreplaceable importance, its exemplary efficacy and normative character, does not in fact exhaust all the expressive possibilities of the People of God for devotion to the Holy Mother of God.[2]

Veneration of the Mother of God is at the same time indissociably ecclesial and personal since it is both liturgical and popular, integrating the sacramental life and devotion.

Since "Popular devotion to the Blessed Virgin Mary is an important and universal ecclesial phenomenon" (*Directory* 183), it is important that pastors and future pastors of the Church should be instructed in this matter as much by study as by their own lived experience. The People of God expect that their pastors should be credible teachers of an authentic

---

word "cult" and secondly, because the range of the words *cultus*, *culte*, and *culto* in the respective languages is sufficiently broad to include the worship given only to God, as well as the special veneration given to Mary and the veneration given to the angels and saints. Thus the Latin word *cultus* and its derivatives in French and Italian can be translated as worship, veneration and devotion depending on its context. In the eighteenth and nineteenth centuries one still spoke of the "worship" of the Blessed Virgin Mary without intending by this the "adoration" which belongs exclusively to God. Modern English tends to avoid using the word "worship" in that sense and can cause stumbling blocks with our Protestant brethren.

[2] Congregation for Divine Worship and the Discipline of the Sacraments, *Directory on Popular Piety and the Liturgy: Principles and Guidelines* (Boston: Pauline Books & Media, 2002) #183. Cf. the commentary offered by J. Castellano Cervera, O.C.D., (+2006), "Maria nella liturgia e nella pietà popolare da *Sacrosanctum concilium* (1963) a *Rosarium Virginis Mariae* (2002)," in *La Vergine Maria nel cammino orante della Chiesa—Liturgia e pietà popolare*, (Rome: Centro di Cultura mariana, 2003) pp. 9-29.

Marian devotion which, as the Constitution *Lumen Gentium* says, "consists neither in sterile or transitory affection, nor in a certain vain credulity, but proceeds from true faith, by which we are led to recognize the eminent dignity of the Mother of God, and we are moved to a filial love towards our Mother and to the imitation of her virtues" (*LG* 67). The pastoral practice of true devotion to Mary, in its triple dimension of veneration, invocation and imitation, must then be rooted on solid theological foundations and offer a pedagogy which is simultaneously progressive and universal, in order to respond to the thirst of the faithful with regard to doctrine, to experience and to a mystagogy oriented to the knowledge of the love of Jesus in Mary which surpasses all knowledge. In this perspective the pages that follow would like to propose with clarity and modesty a brief testament complementary to the other chapters of this anthology which deal with the liturgy and Marian consecration.

After a synthetic exposition on the Gospel origins, then on the nature and the "necessity" of Marian devotion, we will briefly present the astonishingly rich relationship of canon law on this matter, before offering specific indications on the prayer of the Rosary and the scapular devotion. In conclusion, we will underline the importance of situating "true devotion to Mary" and the various modes of its expression in a dynamic of spiritual growth which promotes the contemplative discovery of the mystery of the Virgin Mary, Mother of God and Mother of all men.

Gospel Origin and Divine Institution

As Pope Paul VI recalled in his Apostolic Exhortation *Marialis Cultus* (1974), in presenting in a wonderful manner the plan of God for the salvation of men, the Bible is entirely "replete with the mystery of the Savior, and from the book of Genesis to the book of Revelation, also contains clear references to her who was the Mother and associate of the Savior" (Paul VI, *MC* 30). From the third chapter of the book of Genesis, the *Protoevangelium* (Gen 3:15) announces the mystery of Mary and her role. The Jesuit Mariologist J.B. Terrien asks:

> Was Mary not offered to the admiration and homage of the universe when she was divinely announced as the perpetual enemy of the Devil and the Mother of him who would crush the head of the infernal serpent; as

the Virgin who would conceive and give to the world Emmanuel; as the associate of the Savior and Redeemer? Assuredly, this was not yet the *cultus* of the New Testament in its marvelous development; but it was its germ and its beginning.[3]

"When the fullness of time had come, God sent his Son, born of a woman" (Gal 4:4). It is this verse from the Letter to the Galatians which opens Pope John Paul II's Encyclical *Redemptoris Mater* (1987), as well as his catechesis of October 15, 1997, on the foundations of Marian devotion, to indicate clearly that this "is based on the wondrous divine decision, as the Apostle Paul recalls, to link forever the Son of God's human identity with a woman, Mary of Nazareth."[4]

An attentive reading of the angel's salutation (Lk 1:28), which forms with the salutation of Elizabeth (Lk 1:42) the first part of the *Hail Mary*, shows that "Marian devotion before being practiced by men, was already practiced by heavenly spirits and by the greatest among them and on the order of God himself,"[5] so that as Terrien underscores with reference to St. Thomas Aquinas' *Exposition on the Angelic Salutation*:

> It was not fitting that an angel should pay respect to a man until one should be found in human nature who would surpass the angels ... and such was the Blessed Virgin. Wherefore in order to show that she excelled him, the angel was pleased to show reverence to her by saying *Hail*. Accordingly the Blessed Virgin surpassed the angels in these three points ... **Preeminence of the fullness of grace:** Hail, full of grace, he says ... **Preeminence in her familiarity with God:** the Lord

---

[3] J.B. Terrien, S.J., *La Mère de Dieu et la Mère des Hommes d'après les Pères et la théologie* (Paris, Lethielleux, 1902) Deuxième partie, tome II, Livre IX, chap. I, p. 177. Cf. also the catechesis of John Paul II of January 24, 1996, on the Protoevangelium in *Insegnamenti di Giovanni Paolo II* (Città del Vaticano: Libreria Editrice Vaticana) [= *Inseg*] XIX/1 (1996) 115-117. [Henceforth. *Theotókos—Woman, Mother, Disciple: A Catechesis on Mary, Mother of God* with a Foreword by Eamon R. Carroll, O.Carm, S.T.D. (Boston: Pauline Books and Media, 2000) [= *MCat*] 61-63.

[4] John Paul II, "Devotion to the Blessed Virgin Mary," Catechesis of October 15, 1997, #1, in *Inseg* XX/2 (1997) 563 [*MCat* 244].

[5] J.B. Terrien, *op.cit.*, p. 174-175, note 1.

is with you, to such an extent with you that you will be his mother, and consequently queen and sovereign ... **Preeminence in purity**: not only was the Virgin pure in herself, but she also obtains purity for others.[6]

In the Gospel account of the Visitation, the exclamation of Elizabeth, filled with the Holy Spirit in receiving the visit of Mary, is the translation of a profound veneration in which, with John Paul II, "we can discern the initial expressions of and reasons for Marian devotion":[7] *Blessed are you among women, and blessed is the fruit of your womb! And why is this granted me, that the mother of my Lord should come to me? ... And blessed is she who believed that there would be a fulfillment of what was spoken to her from the Lord* (Lk 1:42-43, 45). As Brunero Gherardini points out here, this is not a simple matter of courtesy, but a "higher illumination on that which is humanly inconceivable and unintelligible, raises Elizabeth to the knowledge of the divine maternity of Mary and brings back on her lips the same words of the angel, an echo of those formerly pronounced by Uzziah to Judith (cf. Jud 13:18) ... Mary emerges as the object of veneration for today, tomorrow and forever."[8]

As to the *Magnificat*, it contains at once, according to Terrien, "the cause and the prophetic approbation of the homage which the human race should render to Mary"[9] until the end of time: "Traces of a veneration already widespread among the first Christian community are present in the *Magnificat* canticle: 'All generations will call me blessed' (Lk 1:48). By putting these words on Mary's lips, Christians recognized her unique greatness, which would be proclaimed until the end of time."[10]

On the occasion of the Marian Year of 1987, Cardinal Joseph Ratzinger presented a remarkable commentary on this prophecy of Luke 1:28 before an audience of priests and pastoral workers gathered at the shrine of Loreto (Italy):

---

[6] J.B. Terrien, *op. cit.*, p. 174-175. [Our use of bold]. Cf. St. Thomas Aquinas, *Expositio super Salut. Angelic.*

[7] John Paul II, "Devotion to the Blessed Virgin Mary," Catechesis of October 15, 1997, #1, in *Inseg* XX/2 (1997) 564 [*MCat* 245].

[8] B. Gherardini, *La Madre*, Frigento, 1989, p. 433.

[9] J.B. Terrien, *op. cit.*, p. 175.

[10] John Paul II, "Devotion to the Blessed Virgin Mary," Catechesis of October 15, 1997, #1, in *Inseg* XX/2 (1997) 564 [*MCat* 245].

"From this day forward, all generations will call me blessed." This word of the Mother of Jesus, transmitted to us by Luke (1:48), is at once a prophecy and a mandate to the Church of all times. Therefore this verse of the Magnificat, Mary's Spirit-filled prayer in praise of the living God, is one of the essential foundations of Christian veneration of Mary. The Church has not of herself invented something new in beginning to extol Mary; nor has she plunged from the heights of worshipping the one God into glorifying a human being. She is doing what she must and what she was commanded to do from the beginning. ... The evangelist certainly would not have transmitted this prophecy of Mary's had it seemed to him either indifferent or obsolete. ... Mary's prophecy belonged to those elements which he ascertained "carefully" and considered important enough to pass on to others as part of the Gospel. A prerequisite for his decision was that the word had not remained without confirmation in reality. One recognizes in the first two chapters of Luke's Gospel a range of tradition in which Mary's memory was preserved, in which the Mother of the Lord was loved and revered. It takes for granted that the somewhat naïve cry of the unidentified woman, "happy the womb that bore you" (Lk 11:27), had not been silenced, but rather had been accorded a purer, more valid form through the Church's deepening understanding of Jesus. Obviously, also, Elizabeth's greeting, "of all women, you are the most blessed" (1:42), which Luke characterized as a word spoken in the Spirit (1:41), did not remain a once-for-all episode. The ongoing honor shown to Mary ... is the foundation of the Lucan infancy narrative. The inclusion of the word in the gospel raises this Marian veneration from a mere fact to a commission for the Church at all places and in all times. The Church fails to carry out part of that which she has been commanded to do if she does not extol Mary. She deviates from the biblical word if praise of Mary is silenced in her. For then she would not be praising God in an adequate manner. ... The verse from the Magnificat shows us that Mary is one of the persons who belongs in a very special way inside the Name of God, so much so that we will not give this Name the proper praise if we leave her out of it. We would then be forgetting something about him which may not be forgotten.[11]

Nunc et semper the Name of the Lord should be magnified because of Mary, and with her who ought to be proclaimed blessed because the "The Almighty has done great things for me" (Lk 1:49). In *Lumen Gentium* 66, the development of Marian devotion is interpreted by the Council as the realization of the prophecy of Luke 1:48:

> From the earliest times the Blessed Virgin is honored under the title of Mother of God, under whose protection the faithful take refuge together in prayer in all their perils and needs. Accordingly, following the Council of Ephesus, there was a remarkable growth in the *cultus* of the People of God towards Mary, in veneration and love, in invocation and imitation, according to her own prophetic words: "all generations shall call me blessed" (*LG* 66).

When one goes back to the origins of Marian devotion, one meets the witness of the *Magnificat*, this word attributed to the Mother of Jesus which resounds as a prophecy and a duty of loving veneration. It is in opening the fourth gospel, however, that we arrive, in the company of the Servant of God John Paul II, at the primordial source of this devotion: "By noting Mary's presence at the beginning and at the end of her Son's public life, John's Gospel suggests that the first Christians were keenly aware of Mary's role in the work of redemption, in full loving dependence on Christ."[12] It is in the words of Christ on the

---

[11] J. Ratzinger, "'You Are Full of Grace': Elements of Biblical Devotion to Mary" in *Communio* [English edition] 16 (1989) 54–56.

[12] John Paul II, catechesis of October 15, 1997, #2, in *Inseg* XX/2 (1997) 564 [*MCat* 245].

Cross reported in the fourth gospel: "Woman, behold your son. ... *Behold, your Mother*" (Jn 19:26-27), which he commented on very often, that Pope John Paul II discerned the Christological foundation of the devotion which the Church renders to the Virgin Mary. Among many other treasures of his Marian Magisterium of the venerated Pope, the catecheses of May 7 and October 15, 1997, are particularly significant:

> The Church's devotion to the Virgin is not only the fruit of a spontaneous response to the exceptional value of her person and the importance of her role in the work of salvation, but is based on Christ's will. The words, "Behold, your mother!" express Jesus' intention to inspire in his disciples an attitude of love and trust in Mary, leading them to recognize her as their mother, the mother of every believer.[13]
>
> On Calvary, with the words: "Behold, your son!" "Behold, your mother!" (Jn 19:26-27), Jesus gave Mary in advance to all who would receive the Good News of salvation, and was thus laying the foundation of their filial affection for her. Following John, the faithful would prolong Christ's love for his Mother with their own devotion, by accepting her into their own lives.[14]

Thus not only does Marian devotion have a Gospel foundation, but it is of divine institution. The consequences of this affirmation are particularly well-presented by the Jesuit Jean Galot in a perspective very harmonious of the Marian Magisterium of John Paul II:

> Marian devotion had its first manifestation when, responding to the will of the Master, John took Mary into his home. It is important to underscore this initial will of Christ. Marian devotion does not simply have as its origin the desire of Christians to honor and pray to the Mother of the Savior. It is not the result of popular sentiment. ... It is not even first of all the product of an

---

[13] John Paul II, catechesis of May 7, 1997, #2, in *Inseg* XX/1 (1997) 903 [*MCat* 192].
[14] John Paul II, catechesis of October 15, 1997, #1, in *Inseg* XX/2 (1997) 563 [*MCat* 244].

admirable reflection on the virtues possessed by Mary, on the abundance of the divine favor granted to her, on the greatness of her maternity, on the role that she played in the work of salvation. It flows from a fundamental word of Jesus, a word pronounced once for all at the supreme moment of his sacrifice. One can understand from this that Marian devotion is a requirement of the divine plan. From the fact that Marian devotion was expressly willed by Jesus, one must immediately conclude that this devotion cannot be an obstacle to that which is due to the Savior himself; it cannot be in competition with the veneration which belongs to Christ. Even more, one must recognize that the devotion which has developed toward Mary is an integral part of our attachment to the Redeemer ... the Church and Christians venerate Mary because Christ wills this by a will which embraces the entire future of the Christian community, and which remains ever present. It is Christ who has willed to be inseparable from his Mother. Further, it is important to observe that this devotion, according to the will of the Savior, aspires to honor Mary as the Mother of each of us. It does not consist only in seeing in Mary the model of virtues to imitate. ... It has to do with recognizing in her a mother, who exercises a function of solicitude and plays an active role of mediation or of intercession in the development of the life of grace.[15]

The Gospel foundations of Marian devotion, in its triple dimension of veneration, invocation and imitation, being solidly established, it is now appropriate to examine with the help of the Magisterium and of theology the nature and the necessity of such devotion.

---

[15] J. Galot, S.J., *Marie Mère et Corédemptrice* (Paris: Parole et Silence, 2005), pp. 203-205. Cf. also by the same author: Id., «Sens et valeur du culte marial», in *Seminarium* XXVII (1975) 3, pp. 507-518.

Nature and Necessity

In paragraphs 66, 67 of the Constitution *Lumen Gentium* already cited, which treats explicitly the question of Marian devotion, the Second Vatican Council affirms with clarity the legitimacy of this rightful veneration and recalls its nature and foundations:

> Mary has been exalted by grace above all angels and men to a place second only to her Son, as the most holy Mother of God who was involved in the mysteries of Christ: she is rightly honored by a *special cultus* in the Church... This *cultus*, as it has always existed in the Church, *for all its uniqueness*, differs essentially from the *cultus* of adoration which is rendered to the incarnate Word and to the Father and the Holy Spirit, and promotes it in a special way (*LG* 66).

A Special and Absolutely Unique Cultus: The Cultus of Hyperdulia

With these words the Constitution *Lumen Gentium* recalls the characteristics of Marian devotion. In willingly underscoring with precision its *special* and *absolutely unique* character, the Second Vatican Council affirms the irreducible specificity of Marian veneration which cannot and must not be confused either with the *cultus* of the adoration due to God alone (*latria*), or even with the *cultus* of the saints (*dulia*). Even though the terms *latria*, *dulia* and *hyperdulia*, classically employed in theology, were not explicitly employed either in the Constitution *Lumen Gentium* or in the post-conciliar documents, it is not useless to recall here their existence and always-valid significance. Certainly, in the depth of popular consciousness, clear conception of what distinguishes the homage rendered to God from what is rendered to Mary, to the saints or to holy things, is often missing, and this is understandable. But theologically speaking, the religious *cultus*, an expression of the moral virtue of religion, has been made the object of a triple distinction well-established by St. Thomas Aquinas and St. Bonaventure, then taken up by the majority of Catholic theologians since the thirteenth century:[16] "Since, therefore, the Blessed Virgin is a mere rational creature, the worship of *latria* is not due to her, but only that of *dulia*: but in a higher degree than to other creatures, inasmuch as she is the Mother of God. For this reason we say that not any kind of *dulia* is due to her, but *hyperdulia*."[17]

One must distinguish very carefully, then, the kinds of veneration which are indicated by the three following expressions:

> a) the *cultus* of *latria*, or the veritable worship or adoration which is due to God alone and to the holy humanity of Christ by virtue of the hypostatic union.
>
> b) the *cultus* of *hyperdulia*, or the special veneration which is due to the Virgin Mary, by virtue of her uniqueness as Mother of the incarnate Word and as cooperator absolutely without parallel in the work of the redemption.
>
> c) the *cultus* of *dulia*, or the simple veneration due to the saints, inasmuch as they are the faithful friends of God.

With the rather dry sobriety proper to juridic style, canon 1255 of the 1917 *Code of Canon Law* had the merit of clearly summarizing these distinctions: "To the Most Holy Trinity, to each of the persons who belong to it, to Christ our Lord, even under the sacramental species, is

---

[16] On this subject one can always consult with profit: J.H. Newman, *Mary: The Virgin Mary in the Life and Writings of John Henry Newman* edited with and introduction and notes by Philip Boyce (Leominster, Herefordshire: Gracewing; Grand Rapids, MI: William B. Eerdmans Publishing Company, 2001) 105-128, 271-282, 288-302; *Du culte de la Sainte Vierge dans l'Eglise catholique*, Paris, Téqui, 1908; R. Garrigou-Lagrange, O.P., *The Mother of The Saviour and Our Interior Life*, (St. Louis: B. Herder Book Company, 1949) Part II, chapter VI, art. I "The cult of hyperdulia and the benefits it confers," pp. 246-250; A. David, «La dévotion à la Sainte Vierge», in *Maria: Etudes sur la Sainte Vierge* (under the direction of Hubert de Manoir, S.J.), V, pp. 691-720; M.J. Nicolas, O.P., *Marie Mère du Sauveur*, Paris, Desclée, 1967, chap. V «Le culte marial», pp. 116-120; B. Gherardini, *La Madre - Maria in una sintesi storico-teologica*, (Frigento: Casa Mariana Editrice, 1989) Parte terza, cap. XI "La venerazione," pp. 381-400; A. Bodem, "Hyperdulie," in *Marienlexicon* 3 (1991) 277.

[17] St. Thomas Aquinas, *Summa Theologica* [= *ST*], IIIa pars, q. XXV, art. 5.

due the *cultus* of *latria*; to the Blessed Virgin Mary, the *cultus* of *hyperdulia*; to the others who reign with Christ in heaven, the *cultus* of *dulia*."[18]

In a more ample perspective the French Mariologist René-Marie de la Broise knew how to recapitulate with clarity the profound spiritual sense which these distinctions evoke:

> In the manifestation of our respect and confidence, in our acts of reverence and invocation, we conform to the various means which connect us with God, with the Holy Virgin, and with the saints. And the *special* manner in which the Church honors and prays to the Mother of God, exactly expresses her pre-eminent dignity, and corresponds to the rank which she occupies above saints and angels. To God alone belongs "latria," or adoration properly so-called, for he is the only Creator and the only Almighty. To angels and saints belongs the inferior worship or "dulia," for they are princes of the heavenly court, and we recognize ourselves as their servants and dependants. To Mary, and to her alone, belongs the worship "hyperdulia," that is to say, a superior worship to that of the other saints and of the angels, and this because of the divine motherhood which has given her a particular affinity with God. To her then must be paid the greatest honor; upon her must we place the most entire and absolute dependence; to her must ascend the most frequent prayers, most sure of being granted. ... The eyes of the Church are always raised towards her, recognizing by this her limitless power and universal mediation.
>
> From the doctrine and preaching of the pastors, from the teaching of Christian leaders, from the communities filled with the spirit of the faith, the faithful draw the true idea of Mary and the sentiments which they must entertain towards her. She is the Mother of God, the queen of the world, the all-holy, and by these titles

---

[18] *Codex Iuris Canonici* (Romae: Typis Polyglottis Vaticanis, 1917) canon 1255: "... Beatae Mariae Virgini cultus hyperduliae; aliis cum Cristo in caelo regnantibus cultus duliae."

she is worthy of all respect and of all honor. She is the pattern of all the virtues, and her example encourages more especially purity without stain, humility, and love towards God and man. She is the Mother, the Mother of Jesus whom the child learns to know by seeing him represented in her arms; the Mother of Christ's brethren by that more than earthly motherhood before which all Christian mothers bow themselves and teach their children to bow. Mother of Jesus and our Mother, she is worthy of the most filial love. Compassionate to the sorrows of her children on earth, and influencing the heart of her Son in heaven, she deserves and inspires a confidence which, as witnessed through all ages, has never been deceived.[19]

Without having employed the slightly technical term *hyperdulia* which was habitually used before the Second Vatican Council, and whose sense is so well described by de la Broise, it is certainly the same sense of the word which is expressed in *Lumen Gentium* 66. The absence of the word, actually unused in the East, but which figured, however, in one of the eight successive redactions of the conciliar text,[20] should not then be interpreted as its rejection from Catholic vocabulary for the Church of our times.[21] If the nature of Marian devotion, which differs essentially

---

[19] René-Marie de la Broise, *Saint Mary the Virgin* trans. by Harold Gidney (London: Duckworth & Co., 1906) pp. 261-263. On the use of the word "worship" here, which is not intended to put the veneration of Mary on the level of the "adoration" given only to God, cf. translator's note in the first footnote. In fact the word which Gidney renders as "worship" here is actually *culte* in the French original.

[20] *Redactio II* of November 27, 1963, from the pen of the Croatian Mariologist, Carlo Balić, contained the following sentence: *Quae autem in excellentia similem non habet sui, utpote Dei Mater et Alma Socia Redemptoris, una etiam hyperduliae cultu ab Ecclesia colitur.* Cf. Ermanno M. Toniolo, *La Beata Maria Vergine nel Concilio Vaticano II, Cronistoria del capitolo VIII della costituzione dogmatica Lumen Gentium e sinossi di tutte le redazioni* (Rome: Centro di cultura Mariana "Madre della Chiesa," 2004) p. 406.

[21] Cf. V. Macca, "Maria Santissima," in the *Dizionario enciclopedica di Spiritualità* II (Rome: Città Nuova Editrice, 1995) p. 1504: "the *cultus* to Mary must be 'special' and 'altogether singular' (*LG* 66). The Second Vatican Council avoided technically calling it *hyperdulia*, but the concept of such a typically Western name is effectively admitted by the appellatives used and by the theological principles

from the *cultus* of adoration rendered to God, is qualified as *absolutely unique* (*singularis omnino quamquam est*) this is certainly in comparison with the veneration of the other saints, as Monsignor Philips, one of the principal redactors of the text explained.[22] It is moreover possible to recognize in this expression a trace of the influence of the great Italian Mariologist G.M. Roschini on the "principal of transcendent singularity": "Mary most holy, being an altogether singular creature who transcends all others so as to constitute an order unto herself, is also the subject of privileges which are altogether singular and which have been granted to no other creature."[23]

G.M. Roschini alludes here to a fundamental truth, all too often passed over in silence in our days, namely "the belonging of the Virgin Mary to the order of the hypostatic union"[24] according to metaphysical terminology which has proven itself. There exist in effect three orders of reality which are irreducible but ordained among themselves "in view of a more and more intimate communication of the Divinity":[25] the order of nature, the order of grace and the hypostatic order. This last is most certainly distinct from the hypostatic union which designates the union of the two natures, human and divine, in the one divine person of Christ. But the hypostatic union is the principle of an *order* which includes two members, namely the human nature of Christ (which does not subsist apart from his divine person) and the Mother of God. As the French Dominican Mariologist M.J. Nicolas explains: "There are two in this order because God wished to bring about the Incarnation by means of birth and not by way of creation."[26] In the final analysis, this is to take into account the fact that the Virgin Mary is party to the divine decree, constitutive of the hypostatic order, which ordained the Incarnation of

---

undergirding the *cultus* itself, first among all of them the eminent royalty of the Theotókos."

[22] Msgr. Philips, *L'Eglise et son mystère au IIe Concile du Vatican—Histoire, texte et commentaire de la Constitution Lumen Gentium*, Vol. II (Paris-Tournai, Desclée, 1967-1968) p. 278.

[23] G.M. Roschini, *Dizionario di Mariologia* (Rome: Ed. Studium, 1961) p. 458. Cf. also Id., "Il valore teologico e pastorale del culto mariano," in *Marianum* (1977) 81-111.

[24] Cf. M.J. Nicolas, O.P., "L'appartenance de la Mère de Dieu à l'ordre hypostatique" in *Bulletin de la Société Française d'Etudes Mariales* (1937) 147-181.

[25] *Ibid.*, 160-161.

[26] *Ibid.*, 176.

the Word. It is this belonging of Mary to the hypostatic order which fully justifies the Church's practice of rendering to the Mother of God a *cultus* which is entirely special, having as its foundation a grace of another order than that venerated in the other saints, that is to say the grace of the divine maternity:

> Mary, by her divine maternity is above the entire order of common grace and comes closer to God than any other creature. That is why we owe her an exceptional veneration. It is not only the incarnate Word whom we honor in her, it is she herself in her own person, for her own greatness with which she is ever endowed from her relation to HIM.[27]

The fact that this belonging of Mary to the hypostatic order is no longer taught in our days[28] probably contributes to explaining why in numerous post-conciliar publications there is often a unilateral insistence on the specific difference between the veneration of Mary and the *cultus* of adoration reserved for God, which nevertheless causes no difficulty, but is made at the cost of a second important difference, that of recognizing and stating, although more subtly, that which exists between Marian devotion (*hyperdulia*) and the *cultus* of the saints (*dulia*).

Moreover, the Ordinary Papal Magisterium has addressed itself to this issue on several occasions. Pope Paul VI wanted to return to the teaching of Vatican II "to remove doubts and, especially, to help the development of that devotion to the Blessed Virgin which in the Church is motivated by the Word of God and practiced in the Spirit of Christ."[29] The mere reading of the introductions of the respective apostolic exhortations *Signum Magnum* (1967) and *Marialis Cultus* (1974) suffices to show the doctrinal and pastoral solicitude of this pope to reaffirm that to the altogether special place which Mary occupied in the redemptive plan of God corresponds a *special* and *totally unique cultus* towards her.

---

[27] M.J. Nicolas, *Marie Mère du Sauveur* (Paris: Desclée, 1967) p. 116.
[28] Cf. B. Sesboué, S.J., *Marie: ce que dit la foi* (Paris: Bayard) 2004, p. 26.
[29] Paul VI, Apostolic Exhortation *Marialis Cultus*, in *AAS* 66 (1974) 113-168; introduction.

More recently, Pope John Paul II, whose Marian Magisterium is of an unequalled depth and richness, devoted an entire catechesis on the nature of Marian devotion which constitutes a prolongation of that of Paul VI and a precious commentary on *Lumen Gentium* 66 and its authentic interpretation:

> Although the veneration of the faithful for Mary is superior to their devotion to the other saints, it is nevertheless inferior to the *cultus* of adoration reserved to God, from which it essentially differs. ... Nonetheless, there is a continuity between Marian devotion and the worship given to God. The honor paid to Mary is ordered and leads to adoration of the Blessed Trinity. The Council recalled that Christian veneration of the Blessed Virgin "is most favorable to" the worship of the incarnate Word, the Father and the Holy Spirit. ... Since the Church's earliest days, Marian devotion has been meant to foster faithful adherence to Christ. To venerate the Mother of God is to affirm the divinity of Christ. In proclaiming Mary *Theotókos*, "Mother of God," the Fathers of the Council of Ephesus intended to confirm belief in Christ, true God. ... Marian devotion also encourages adoration of the Father and the Holy Spirit in those who practice it according to the Church's spirit. By recognizing the value of Mary's motherhood, believers discover in it a special manifestation of God the Father's tenderness. ... The titles of Comforter, Advocate, Helper—attributed to Mary by popular Christian piety—do not overshadow but exalt the action of the Spirit, the Comforter, and dispose believers to benefit from his gifts. Lastly, the Council recalled the "uniqueness" of Marian devotion and stressed its difference with regard to the adoration of God and the veneration of the saints. This devotion is unrepeatable because it is directed to a person whose personal perfection and mission are unique.[30]

---

[30] John Paul II, "The nature of Marian Devotion," catechesis of October 22, 1997, in *Inseg* XX/2 (1997) 647-649 [*MCat* 248-250 altered].

Already in his encyclical on *The Mother of the Redeemer* (1987), Pope John Paul II formulated this affirmation: "This *cultus* is altogether special: it bears in itself and *expresses* the profound *link* which exists *between the Mother of Christ and the Church*" (*RM* 42). If the Second Vatican Council didn't hesitate to present Mary as a member of the Church, it was to specify that she is such in a way that is "supereminent and altogether singular" (*LG* 53). Moreover, as Pope Pius XII pointed out, this is not a new doctrine: "Although it is true that, like ourselves, the Blessed Virgin is a member of the Church, still it is no less true that she is a unique member of Christ's Mystical Body."[31] The divine maternity, ordained to the redemptive Incarnation, cannot be purely and simply located among the ministries and functions in the Church. As a Montfortian commentator on the Marian encyclical of John Paul II well expressed it, there is truly "her double relation to Christ and to the Church (the second rooted in fact in the first) which allows us to discover the true countenance of the Virgin. It is also from inside this double relation that our attitude toward Mary should be formulated."[32] To the Mother of the Redeemer who is also Mother of the Church, of which she is a member in a "supereminent and altogether singular" way, is due a veneration which is absolutely unique.

However, there is still a question: is the *cultus* of the Virgin Mary unique in its *degree* as well as in its *kind*? The very few theologians who have occupied themselves with this question continue to propose various responses according to whether or not they consider the divine maternity as the formal object of *hyperdulia*. According to Garrigou-Lagrange "It is the more common and more probable opinion that *hyperdulia* differs from *dulia* not in degree only but in kind, just as the divine maternity belongs by its term to the hypostatic order, which is specifically distinct."[33] The Italian ecclesiologist Gherardini also argues in this sense:

---

[31] Pius XII, radio message to the International Mariological Congress, October 24, 1954, in *AAS* 46 (1954) 679: *etsi verum est Beatissimam Virginem quoque, uti nos, Ecclesiae esse membrum, tamen non minus verum est eam esse Corporis Christi Mystici membrum plane singulare.* [English translation in *Our Lady: Papal Teachings* = *OL* (Boston: St. Paul Editions, 1961) #735].

[32] A. Bossard, S.M.M., "L'encyclique *Redemptoris Mater* et Saint Louis-Marie de Montfort," in *Marianum* 51 (1989) 263.

[33] R. Garrigou-Lagrange, *The Mother of the Saviour and Our Interior Life*, p. 249.

> Between the Most Holy Virgin and the other saints considered individually or together, there cannot be a more or less limited difference ... no saint will ever be able to be compared to Mary in holiness because no saint will ever be distinguished by the unparalleled value of the divine maternity. The difference resides here: not in the greater or lesser exercise of the virtues, but in the qualitative difference of being.[34]

Without definitively settling the question of knowing if the *cultus* of *hyperdulia* due to the Virgin Mary is unique in its degree and also in its kind, the conciliar and Papal Magisterium of the second half of the twentieth century was intent to recall in season and out of season that "among the saints of heaven, the Virgin Mary, Mother of God, is the recipient of a more exalted *cultus*" (Pius XII, *Mediator Dei*),[35] "special" and "absolutely unique" (*LG* 66), and whose specific character should not be attenuated (cf. Paul VI, *Marialis Cultus* 32). The *cultus* rendered to Mary "in East and West, identical in its motivation of faith but different in its expression, is a part of the great common patrimony of Catholics and Orthodox,"[36] as Pope John Paul II loved to underscore. The hymns to the Mother of God of the Byzantine tradition beautifully evoke the mystery to be contemplated:

> *It is fitting and right to call you blessed, O Theotókos:*
> *You are ever-blessed and all-blameless and the Mother of*
> > *our God.*
> *Higher in honor than the cherubim and incomparably more glorious than the seraphim,*
> > *In virginity you gave birth to God the Word.*
> > *You are truly Mother of God: you do we exalt.*[37]

---

[34] B. Gherardini, *La Madre* (Frigento, 1989), p. 384-385.
[35] Cf. Pius XII, Encyclical *Mediator Dei*, November 20, 1947, in *AAS* 39 (1947) 521-595 [*OL* #440 altered].
[36] John Paul II, homily at the Greek Catholic Abbey of Grottaferrata, September 7, 1987, #2 in *Inseg* X/3 (1987) 330 [*L'Osservatore Romano* English edition = ORE 1008:13 (first number is cumulative edition number; second number is page number)].
[37] Commemoration of the Theotókos in the Liturgy of St. John Chrysostom after the epiclesis.

There is no doubt that it is truly right to bless and magnify the Mother of God. But what does it mean that it is truly necessary to do this and that this veneration is still more necessary than devotion to the other saints? If God does nothing by forced necessity, how can one speak of the "necessity" of Mary to God and to men?

Necessity of Marian Devotion

In his celebrated *Treatise on True Devotion to the Blessed Virgin*, St. Louis-Marie Grignion de Montfort makes the following remarks:

> We must conclude that, being necessary to God by a necessity which is called "hypothetical," (that is, because God so willed it), the Blessed Virgin is all the more necessary for men to attain their final end. Consequently, we must not place devotion to her on the same level as devotion to the other saints as if it were merely something optional.[38]

Would this be a doctrine incompatible with that of the Second Vatican Council according to which "the Blessed Virgin's saving influence on men originates not in any inner necessity but from the divine good pleasure. It flows from the superabundance of the merits of Christ" (*LG* 60)? As he himself had enunciated it briefly (cf. *TD* 39), the notion to which de Montfort has recourse is that of *ex hypothesi*. The French Mariologist Guillaume de Menthière provides a clear and well-founded explanation of this distinction:

> A thing may be said to be necessary either absolutely or hypothetically. Absolute necessity is that whose contrary implies contradiction, such as necessity of a geometric type according to which for example the sum of the three angles of a triangle must always equal 180 degrees. *Ex hypothesi* necessity on the other hand is necessity of a moral type, whose contrary does not imply a

---

[38] St. Louis-Marie Grignion de Montfort, *Traité de la vraie dévotion à la Sainte Vierge*, #39, in *Œuvres Complètes*, Paris, Seuil, 1966, p. 508. [*True Devotion to the Blessed Virgin* in *God Alone: The Collected Writings of St. Louis Marie de Montfort* (Bay Shore, NY: Montfort Publications, 1988) = *TD*].

contradiction but unfaithfulness to the hypotheses which one is given. ... Just as the Incarnation is not necessary to the redemption absolutely speaking, so the *Fiat* of Mary is not necessary to the Incarnation. ... Nonetheless God in his mercy has willed that his creature participate to the extent possible in the redemption and that is why he deferred to the free assent of the Virgin for the execution of his saving plan for humanity. In this sense we may declare the *Fiat* of Mary necessary, by a hypothetical necessity, for the redemption. The necessity which we are describing is then very real, but as included in the divine willing of humanity's collaboration in the work of salvation. It comes under this divine "hypothesis."[39]

It is precisely in this sense that some authors like St. Anselm of Canterbury (+1109) and St. Louis-Marie Grignion de Montfort (+1716) speak of "hypothetical necessity."[40] This does not have to do, as St. Anselm well explains, with a necessity which increases or diminishes gratuitousness, in which case it would not have a place in the economy of Divine Revelation, but on the contrary of a "necessity," with regard to the end to be accomplished, which integrates and increases the gratuitousness. In his *Summa Theologica*, Thomas Aquinas does not hesitate to use and even to specify the distinction between absolute necessity of nature and necessity of fittingness, which includes gratuitousness.[41] We can then speak legitimately of the necessity (*hypothetical*, that is to say as a consequence of the divine will) of Mary to God and even still more to men, in the same way that the *Doctor Magnificus* affirmed the necessity of the Incarnation and of the Cross.[42] To speak of the necessity of Marian devotion, like Grignion de Montfort who "highlights the 'necessity of Mary' in the great perspective of the necessity of the Incarnation, of the

---

[39] G. de Menthière, *Je vous salue Marie* (Paris: Mame-Edifa, 2003), pp. 175-176.
[40] This "hypothetical necessity," dear to the speculative genius of the *Doctor Magnificus*, is very present in particular in book II of his celebrated dialogue *Cur Deus Homo*.
[41] Cf. *ST*, IIIa, q.1, a. 2; IIIa, q. 46, a. 1-3.
[42] Cf. *Meditatio redemptionis humanae*, in *L'œuvre d'Anselme de Cantorbéry*, tome V, Paris, 1988, p. 420.

redemption and of grace,"⁴³ has nothing in common then with low-level theological eccentricity, but corresponds very exactly to that which he himself in the line of Anselm qualifies as a "hypothetical necessity," an expression of the loving will of God. Thus, our observation is in profound harmony with the affirmation of the Second Vatican Council: "the Blessed Virgin's saving influence on men originates not in any inner necessity but from the divine good pleasure" (*LG* 60).

Since it is so necessary, it would be surprising that the law of the Church should be silent on this subject, especially since Leo XIII had written that "Whoever considers the height of dignity to which God has raised the most august Virgin Mary will easily perceive how important it is, both for the public and private good, that devotion to her should be assiduously practiced and daily promoted more and more."⁴⁴

Marian Devotion in the Code of Canon Law of 1983

The *Code of Canon Law* of 1983 contains exactly five canons which make explicit mention of the *cultus* or veneration of Mary. They are the following canons: 246.3; 276; 663.4; 1186 and 1246.1, which are distributed within Book II of the *Code* which treats of the "People of God" (canons 246, 276 and 663) and Book IV which concerns "The Church's Office of Sanctification" (canons 1186 and 1246). From a simple quantitative point of view, this would seem to be very little material in a *Code* which counts 1752 canons. But this would be to gravely underestimate the importance of the existence and of the qualitative content of these canons which treat of Marian devotion.

In order to take the true measure of the effective extension of the canonical data on Marian devotion in the Church's law, it is surely indispensable to make the comparison with the previous *Code*, namely that of 1917, from which we have already cited canon 1255. This comparison is particularly significant, since in the latter mention was made of Marian devotion in three canons only, namely canons 125.2,⁴⁵

---

⁴³ F.M. Léthel, *L'Amour de Jésus en Marie*, Genève, Ad Solem, 2000, tome I, p. 50.
⁴⁴ Leo XIII, Encyclical *Augustissimæ Virginis*, September 12, 1897, in *Actæ Sanctæ Sedis* [= *ASS*] 30 (1897-1898) 129 [*OL* #200].
⁴⁵ Canon 125.2: "Curent locorum Ordinarii: ... 2° Ut iidem quotidie orationi mentali per aliquod tempus incumbant, sanctissimum Sacramentum visitent, Deiparam Virginem mariano rosario colant, conscientam suam discutiant."

1255,[46] and 1276,[47] of which we indicate the Latin text at the bottom of the page.

Obviously the *Code* of 1983 has introduced new considerations as to the veneration of the Blessed Virgin Mary in the Church, in particular when it is a question of the formation of seminarians (canon 246) and of members of institutes of consecrated life (canon 663). Before proceeding to a comprehensive reading of these canons which concern particular categories of the faithful, it is fitting to begin with canon 1186 which is addressed to all the faithful without any exception. We have chosen to consider the respective canons beginning with the last, namely canon 1186, before examining the three canons of Book II (246, 276, 663), in order thus to proceed from the general to the particular.

Canon 1186 Addressed to All the Faithful:

> To foster the sanctification of the people of God the Church recommends to the particular and filial veneration of the Christian faithful the Blessed Mary ever Virgin, the Mother of God, whom Christ established as the Mother of the human race. ...

a) This canon contains elements already present in canons 1255 and 1276 of the Code of 1917 but also some altogether new elements which were not expressed previously: in particular the fact that the Virgin Mary is referred to not only as Mother of God but also as Mother of all men. It is difficult not to recognize here the "impact" of conciliar Mariology, as well as the teaching of the popes of the twentieth century and the influence of the eminent Mariologist by whom they were inspired.

Before the redaction and publication of the Code, such a Mariology had been presented and proposed by the Second Vatican Council (*SC* 103; *LG* 53, 66-67), and by the Apostolic Exhortations *Signum Magnum* (1967) and *Marialis Cultus* (1974) of Pope Paul VI, preceded by his discourse of November 21, 1964, during which the successor of Peter

---

[46] Canon 1255: "Beatae Mariae Virgini cultus hyperduliae; aliis cum Cristo in caelo regnantibus cultus duliae."

[47] Canon 1276: "Bonum atque utile est Dei Servos, una cum Cristo regnantes, suppliciter invocare eorumque reliquias atque imagines venerari; sed prae ceteris filiali devotione Beatissimam Virginem Mariam fideles universi prosequantur."

proclaimed Mary "Mother of the Church."[48] In canon 1186 of the Code an entirely preeminent place is given to Marian devotion in virtue of the very close bond of the Virgin Mary with the Son of God and his Church, and of her motherhood extended to all men.

b) If the Magisterium of the Church "recommends to the particular and filial veneration of the Christian faithful the Blessed Mary ever-Virgin, the Mother of God, whom Christ established as the Mother of the human race," this indicates that authentic Marian devotion is considered as a right which the faithful can freely and consciously exercise. Since the Code goes to the trouble of expressing such a recommendation in canonical language, it is because it is dealing with a legitimate right which deserves to be protected, knowing that the best way to indicate the value of such a right is to encourage its exercise "to foster the sanctification of the people of God."

Canon 1186 does not enunciate a juridical obligation nor a precept but a counsel, a recommendation which protects an inalienable right: that of an authentic Marian devotion as the expression of the relation of the faithful to her who is the Mother of God and Mother of the Church. Such a recommendation presupposes the existence and the recognition of this right, requires respect for it as an obligation, and fosters its expression by a spiritual counsel expressed by this canon. Here, Canon Law is at the service of the Marian dimension of the spiritual life of all the baptized. Alphonse David notes that the Code of 1917 *counseled* devotion to the saints but *prescribed* devotion to the Blessed Virgin:[49] "It is good and useful to invoke the servants of God who reign with Christ and to venerate their relics and their images. But, above all the other saints, let the faithful surround the Blessed Virgin Mary with filial devotion" (canon 1276 of the Code of 1917).

Contrary to the Code of 1917, that of 1983 does not specify that this Marian devotion constitutes the *cultus* of *hyperdulia*, but this does not indicate in any way that the traditional qualification has lost any of its value.

---

[48] Cf. Paul VI, discourse for the promulgation of the Constitution *Lumen Gentium* and of Mary Mother of the Church, November 21, 1964, in *AAS* 56 (1964) 1014; Apostolic Exhortation *Signum Magnum*, in *AAS* 59 (1967) 465-475; Apostolic Exhortation *Marialis Cultus*, in *AAS* 66 (1974) 113-168.

[49] A. David, "La dévotion à la Sainte Vierge," in *Maria—Etudes sur la Sainte Vierge* (sous la direction d'Hubert du Manoir), (Paris: Beauchesne) tome V, 1958, p. 720.

Canons 246.3 and 276.2,5° (Seminarians and Clerics):

These two canons must be treated together because the first concerns seminarians and their guides in formation and the second all clerics (deacons, priests, bishops):

> Canon 246.3: Devotion to the Blessed Virgin Mary, including the Rosary, mental prayer and other devotional exercises are to be fostered so that the students acquire a spirit of prayer and gain strength in their vocation.
>
> Canon 276.2,5°: They are to be conscientious in devoting time regularly to mental prayer, in approaching the sacrament of penance frequently, in cultivating special devotion to the Virgin Mother of God, and in using other common and particular means for their sanctification.

One ought to note first of all that canon 1367 of the *Code* of 1917 did not specifically cite Marian devotion among the means of sanctification whose practice ought to be encouraged in seminaries. This practice was certainly not absent from the teaching of the popes on the formation of seminarians, but canon law did not see a need to mention it. The *Code* of 1983 specifically names Marian devotion and the prayer of the Rosary as means to acquire the spirit of prayer and to confirm one's vocation in canon 246.3. Did the disappearance of this precious means of sanctification in numerous seminaries during the immediate period after the council perhaps motivate this useful clarification during the redaction of the new *Code*? Whatever be the case, this *Code* is the canonical interpretation of the teaching of the last popes (cf. *Menti Nostrae* of Pius XII, *Marialis Cultus* of Paul VI) and also of the conciliar decree on the formation of priests (*Optatam Totius* 8): "Let them love and venerate with filial confidence the Blessed Virgin Mary, given as a Mother to the disciples by Christ Jesus dying on the Cross."

If Marian devotion, "including the Rosary," should thus be encouraged in all the seminary formation of future priests, this indicates that the Magisterium of the Church considers it a responsibility of formation guides to encourage the candidates in this regard. Even though the Rosary, despite the wishes of numerous Council Fathers, was not explicitly mentioned in chapter 8 of the Constitution *Lumen Gentium*, its mention is not lacking in the *Code*.

With regard to canon 276, the juridical translation of that which concerns the spiritual life of clerics, it takes up in some way what was already said in the *Code* of 1917 in canon 125, in order to specify the elements which determine the way of growing in holiness for deacons, priests and bishops. Beyond the sources already indicated (*LG* 66; *MC*) this canon is to be seen in relation with the conciliar decree *Presbyterorum Ordinis*:

> They will become daily more sensitive to the mission they have undertaken in the Holy Spirit. They will always find an outstanding model of this docility in the Blessed Virgin Mary who was led by the Holy Spirit to give herself wholly to the mystery of the redemption of the human race. Priests should always venerate and love with filial devotion and *cultus*, this Mother of the eternal High Priest, Queen of apostles and protectress of their ministry (*PO* 18).

Beyond the exterior practices which give expression to Marian devotion and the filial devotion of the priest, there is the Marian attitude of total adherence to the divine plan accepted in faith and with total availability, a dimension constitutive of the ministerial priesthood in the light of God, which is here proposed for the imitation of ordained ministers.[50] It has to do with the invitation to conform oneself to the *tota tua* as it was lived by the Virgin Mary herself, the Mother of Christ, *Aeternus Sacerdos*, and Queen of the apostles. Everyone knows that this was the soul of the life, ministry and Magisterium of Pope John Paul II.[51]

---

[50] Cf. M. Caprioli, O.C.D., *Il sacerdozio, teologia e spiritualità* (Rome: Teresianum, 1992) p. 264.

[51] Cf. Giovanni Paolo II, *Totus Tuus—Il magistero mariano di Giovanni Paolo II*, Scelta antologica e introduzioni di Mons. Arthur Burton Calkins (Siena: Catangalli, 2006); F.M. Léthel, "Ecco la tua Madre! La testimonianza del Servo di Dio Giovanni Paolo II per i Sacerdoti del terzo millennio," in *Alpha Omega* IX (2006) 73-102; S.M. Perella, "La Santa Vergine nel pontificato di Giovanni Paolo II," in *Miles Immaculatae* XLII (2006/1) 53-122.

Canon 663.4 (Religious):

> They are to cultivate a special devotion to the Virgin Mother of God, model and protector of all consecrated life, including the Marian Rosary.

The Constitution *Lumen Gentium* (65) evoked the Virgin Mary as model for the Church. The decree *Perfectae Caritatis*, without using the expression "model and protector of the entire consecrated life," in citing the *De Virginitate* of St. Ambrose invited religious to have recourse to the intercession of the Virgin Mary, Mother of God "whose life is a rule of conduct for all" (*PC* 25).

The *Code* of 1917 did not contain the equivalent of canon 663.4 concerning all religious. Nonetheless, the canon addressed to all clerics was certainly also addressed to religious clerics.

It is appropriate to note that the tone of canon 663.4 is not exactly that of a simple recommendation or counsel. Certainly, one could think or suppose that the formula employed in number 2 of the same canon: "insofar as they are able," is valid also for the following numbers and that consequently the special devotion in honor of the Virgin Mother of God, like the other practices mentioned, is not presented as a strict juridical obligation of religious. But one should immediately add that this is not for all that a simple exhortation.

What is not a strict juridical obligation is nonetheless a spiritual "obligation" linked to the state of life chosen. It is not because a canon does not oblige in a strictly rigorous way according to a juridical plan that it does not oblige the spiritual conscience. Finally, it is significant that these practices should be thus "prescribed" directly by the *Code* and no longer indirectly by means of a directive given by charge of the superiors.

This rapid examination of the canons of the *Code* of 1983 which treat of Marian devotion allow us to make a double declaration:[52]

1) Marian devotion is proposed and recommended in a general way to all of the faithful on the basis of the

---

[52] Readers who wish to examine this matter more thoroughly could profitably consult: P. Etzi, *Canones mariales. Il culto alla beata Vergine Maria nel vigente Codice di Diritto Canonico*, in AA.VV., *Pax in virtute. Miscellanea di studi in onore del Cardinale Giuseppe Caprio* (Vatican City: Libreria Editrice Vaticana, 2003), pp. 711-767.

universal call to holiness (*Lumen Gentium,* chapter 5) and in a particular way to seminarians, clergy and religious.

2) To the extent that its nature and its expression are authentic, Marian devotion is a spiritual right in the universal Church, a right whose exercise is warmly recommended to all of the baptized. Consequently, one can deduce that it is the duty of each to respect the spiritual right of those who choose to exercise it. It is a particular responsibility for pastors and formation guides (especially of those who guide future clerics and male religious) that they recommend it and cultivate it among those who are confided to them. Precisely because this is a particular responsibility of pastors and formation guides, it is fitting that these, following the example of the Servant of God John Paul II (+2005), are desirous of living themselves what they propose. The post-synodal Apostolic Exhortation *Pastores Gregis* (2003) contains a significant paragraph in this regard:[53]

The bishop will also nourish his personal and communitarian Marian devotion by devotional practices approved and recommended by the Church, especially by the recitation of that compendium of the Gospel which is the holy Rosary. Being himself completely familiar with this prayer, completely centered as it is on the contemplation of the saving events of Christ's life with which his holy Mother was closely associated, every bishop is also called to promote diligently its recitation (*PG* 14).

The reader will not have missed noting the explicit mention of the Rosary in the *Code* of 1917 (c. 125.2) and in the *Code* of 1983 (c. 246.3 and 663.4): "almost considered as the elementary formula of all Marian devotion, the Rosary has thus now come to take its place even in church law,"[54] comments the Dominican historian André Duval.

---

[53] John Paul II, post-synodal Apostolic Exhortation *Pastores Gregis*, October 16, 2003, #14 in *Inseg* XXVI/2 (2003) 416 [*ORE* 1815:V].

[54] André Duval, O.P., "Rosaire," in *DSAM* (Paris: Beauchesne, 1988) t. XIII, col. 977.

Sufficiently universal to find its place in the law of the Church, the prayer of the Rosary is very specially recommended not only to families, but also to religious and clergy.[55] This declaration requires us now to present some indications about the genesis and eminent spiritual value of the Rosary, which remains, as John Paul II underscored, "at the dawn of this third millennium, a prayer of great significance, destined to bring forth a harvest of holiness" (*RVM* 1).

The Rosary of the Blessed Virgin Mary

Vatican II and the Rosary

The Constitution *Lumen Gentium* exhorts all the sons of the Church that "the practices and exercises of devotion ... recommended by the teaching authority of the Church in the course of centuries be highly esteemed" (*LG* 67), without any precise example being explicitly evoked in the conciliar text. Although a sufficiently significant number of bishops had vigorously insisted that the Rosary should at least be mentioned, the Council did not occupy itself with the enumeration of practices or exercises of piety.

On the eve of the closing of the Council and on the occasion of the Mariological Congress of Santo Domingo (1965), Pope Paul VI specified that among the exercises of piety towards the Virgin Mary recommended by the Fathers of the Council and the previous Magisterium in the course of centuries are obviously the Rosary as well as the Carmelite scapular.[56] With regard to the Rosary, Pope Paul VI considered it his duty to underscore again the following year, in his Encyclical *Christi Matri* (1966), that "The Second Vatican Council recommended the use of the Rosary to all the sons of the Church, not in express words, but in unmistakable fashion."[57] It is obviously clear, as G. Philips explained, "that the Council did not reject largely widespread practices of devotion.

---

[55] Cf. Congregation for the Clergy, *Directory for the Ministry and Life of Priests*, 1994, #39.

[56] Cf. Paul VI, Letter to the Papal Legate to the Mariological-Marian Congresses at Santo Domingo, February 2, 1965, in *AAS* 57 (1965) 376-379.

[57] Paul VI, Encyclical *Christi Matri*, September 15, 1966, in *AAS* 58 (1966) 745-749 [Paul VI, *Mary—God's Mother and Ours* (Boston: St. Paul Editions, 1979) 49].

On the contrary, it encouraged them, without entering into details."[58] These found a place later in the *Enchiridion Indulgentiarum* (1968), in the *De Benedictionibus* (1984) and especially in the fifth chapter of the *Directory on Popular Piety and the Liturgy* (2002). The Apostolic Exhortation *Marialis Cultus* (1974) contains rich indications by the same Pope Paul VI on the *Angelus* and the Rosary, two exercises of piety "widespread in the West, and with which this apostolic see has concerned itself on various occasions" (*MC* 40).

Two weeks after his election to the See of Peter, during the month of the Rosary in 1978, Pope John Paul II made this capital affirmation: "It can be said that the Rosary is, in a certain way, a prayer-commentary on the last chapter of the Constitution *Lumen Gentium* of Vatican II, a chapter which deals with the wonderful presence of the Mother of God in the mystery of Christ and the Church."[59] Thus the Rosary, already described as a "summary of the entire Gospel" (*totius Evangelii breviarium*)[60] by popes Pius XII and Paul VI, and of which Pope Leo XIII had already stated that "it epitomizes in itself the honor due to Our Lady,"[61] was elevated by Pope John Paul II to the level of being a prayer-commentary on chapter 8 of the Dogmatic Constitution *Lumen Gentium*, of which it constitutes the "summit and crown."[62] There is no doubt, as the French Mariologist Guillaume de Menthière commented, that "what the Council had wanted to do by placing the mystery of Mary in the mystery of Christ and of the Church comes about spontaneously in the meditation of the mysteries of the Rosary."[63] As privileged instruments

---

[58] G. Philips, *L'Eglise et son mystère au deuxième Concile du Vatican*, Histoire, texte et commentaire de la Constitution *Lumen Gentium* (Tournai: Desclée, 1967-1968) p. 279.

[59] John Paul II, *Angelus* of October 29, 1978, in *Inseg* I (1978) 75 [*Talks of John Paul II* (Boston: St. Paul Editions, 1979) 137-138].

[60] Pius XII, Letter *Philippinas Insulas* to the Archbishop of Manila, in *AAS* 38 (1946) 419; Paul VI, *Marialis Cultus* (February 2, 1974), #42, in *AAS* 66 (1974) 153. Cf. S.M. Perella, "*Rosarium Beatae Virginis Mariae 'totius Evangelii breviarium'. Il contributo dei Vescovi di Roma Sisto IV-Giovanni Paolo II (1478-2003): tra storia e dottrina*," in *Marianum* 66 (2004) 427-557.

[61] Leo XIII, Encyclical *Octobri Mense*, September 22, 1891, in *ASS* 24 (1891-1892) 198 [*OL*].

[62] Paul VI, discourse *Post duos menses*, November 21, 1964, in *AAS* 56 (1964) 1007.

[63] G. De Menthière, *Marie au cœur de l'œuvre de Jean-Paul II* (Paris: Mame-Edifa, 2005) p. 81.

at the service of the authentic reception of the Council, the *Catechism of the Catholic Church* as well as its *Compendium*, promulgated respectively in 1992 by Pope John Paul II and in 2005 by Pope Benedict XVI make explicit mention of the Rosary (cf. *CCC* 1674; *Compendium* 198, 353, 567).

Among all the forms of devotion to the Virgin, none of them is better known and more widespread, at least in the West, than the Rosary, a prayer loved by numerous saints[64] and warmly encouraged by the Magisterium.[65] According to Hiemer, the popes have praised the Rosary in more than 280 papal documents.[66] Leo XIII alone has been given the title of "Pope of the Rosary," for having published every year from 1883 to 1901 an encyclical on Marian devotion and in particular on the Rosary.[67] According to Louis Bouyer (+2004), the Rosary is

> probably the most generally fruitful development achieved by the inventive genius of medieval piety in the West, lending itself equally well to satisfying the elementary piety of unlettered people incapable of joining in the Divine Office (it was for this purpose that it was first

---

[64] Cf. F.M. Léthel, "Il Rosario preghiera dei santi," in Riflessioni sulla Lettera apostolica di Giovanni Paolo II Rosarium Virginis Mariae "Quaderni dell'Osservatore Romano 64" (Vatican City, 2003, p. 85-90); D. Sorrentino, Il Rosario e la nuova evangelizzazione (Milan, 2003). In particular the sub-chapter entitled: Il Rosario dei santi (Luigi-Maria di Montfort, Pio da Pietrelcina, Bartolo Longo), pp. 24-28.

[65] Cf. The Rosary: Papal Teachings, Selected and Arranged by the Monks of Solesmes, foreword by Gabriel-Marie Garrone. Texts from 1758 to 1978 with the Bull of St. Pius V on the Rosary in the appendix (Boston: St. Paul Editions, 1980); Le Rosaire dans l'enseignement des Papes, Introduction, choice and ordering of texts, index and tables by Monks of the Abbey of Solesmes, 1984.

[66] Cf. A. Hiemer, Der Rosenkranz, das wunderbare Gebet (St. Ottilien, 1979) p. 20.

[67] Cf. Leo XIII, Le Rosaire de Marie, traduction française des Lettres de Léon XIII sur le Rosaire de Marie avec notes historiques, doctrinales et pratiques par F.D. Joret, O.P., (Paris: Cerf, 1933); S.M. Perella, "Il Rosario nel Magistero dei Papi: da Leone XIII a Giovanni Paolo II," in Riflessioni sulla lettera di Giovanni Paolo II 'Rosarium Virginis Mariae' (Vatican City, 2003) pp. 15-28; D. Sorrentino, "Il Rosario nel Magistero Pontificio da Leone XIII a Giovanni Paolo II," in G. Greco (a cura di), Il pianto di Maria (Rome: Città Nuova, 2003) pp. 117-135.

conceived), and to bringing the most meditative souls to the summits of the life of prayer.[68]

Popes Paul VI and John Paul II have highlighted with care the authentically contemplative dimension of the prayer of the Rosary.[69] The Apostolic Letter *Mane nobiscum Domine*, signed by John Paul II on October 7 of the Year of the Eucharist (2004), contains this significant affirmation: "The Rosary itself, when it is profoundly understood in the biblical and Christocentric form which I recommended in the Apostolic Letter *Rosarium Virginis Mariae*, will prove a particularly fitting introduction to Eucharistic contemplation carried out with Mary as our companion and guide" (*MND* 18).

In order to gauge the exceptional value of the Rosary, one must also consider its history, "not at defining in a sort of archeological fashion the primitive form of the Rosary, but at uncovering the original inspiration and driving force behind it and its essential structure" (*Marialis Cultus* 43). This slow evolution of the prayer of the Rosary proves at times to be exciting and very complex, because all of the forms of medieval Marian piety are seen to converge here,[70] as the Dominican M.M. Gorce explains:

> Before being fixed in the fifteenth to the sixteenth centuries, in its present form, the Rosary appeared in the Middle Ages linked to a complex of popular Marian devotions. It is in these medieval antecedents that one must seek the explanation of its symbolism, its mystical spirit and—the word is not too strong—its theology.[71]

---

[68] Louis Bouyer, *Introduction to Spirituality* trans. by Mary Perkins Ryan (Collegeville, MN: Liturgical Press, 1961) pp. 87-88.

[69] Cf. Paul VI, *Marialis Cultus* (1974) nn. 42, 47, 49; and especially John Paul II, *Rosarium Virginis Mariae* (2002). Cf. the commentary by J. Castellano Cervera, "Da preghiera vocale a preghiera contemplative—Un nuova mistagogia del Rosario," in *Communio* (Italian edition.) n. 189 (2003) 8-16.

[70] Cf. Francis Rapp, "La place de Notre Dame dans la piété populaire du Moyen Age" in *Marie Mère de Dieu* (Venasque: Editions du Carmel, 1988) pp. 187-211.

[71] M.M. Gorce, O.P., "Rosaire" in *DTC* (Paris: Librairie Letouzey, 1937) t. XIII, col. 2902.

We will limit ourselves her to the exposition of some landmarks, referring our readers to numerous specialized studies[72] and above all recalling that in order to get to the heart of the sense and incomparable value of the Rosary nothing can replace the reading and study of the principal encyclicals of the popes on this subject.

The Genesis of the Rosary—Comments on Some Landmarks

The Apostolic Letter of John Paul II *Rosarium Virginis Mariae*[73] opens by recalling that the Rosary "gradually took form in the second millennium under the guidance of the Spirit of God" *(RVM* 1). In declaring himself thus on a progressive development, Pope John Paul II takes into account, following his immediate predecessors and without the least iconoclasm, the fruit of the research of historians. This research brings nuances and corrections to the centuries-old tradition which attributes the origin of the Rosary directly and principally to St. Dominic (+1221), the founder of the Order of Preachers. Numerous papal documents from the sixteenth to the beginning of the twentieth centuries, from St. Pius V to Pius XI, echo this tradition.[74] In contrast,

---

[72] Here are a few titles from an immense bibliography: M.M. Gorce, *Le Rosaire et ses antécédents historiques* (Paris, 1931); F.M. Willam, *The Rosary: Its History and Meaning* trans. by Edwin Kaiser, C.PP.S. (NY: Benziger Brothers, Inc., 1953); 1951; *Rilanciamo il Rosario* (Naples, 1973); A. Winston-Allen, *Stories of the Rose: The Making of the Rosary in the Middle Ages* (University Park, PA, 1997); E.D. Staid, "Rosario," in S. De Fiores-S. Meo (a cura di), *Nuovo Dizionario di Mariologia* (Milan: Edizioni Paoline, 1985) pp. 1207-1215; "Rosenkranz," in *Marienlexicon* (1993) 553-559; A. Lauras, "Le Rosaire—origine, histoire et sens" in *Christus* 46 (1999) 319-324; R. Barile, "Il Rosario nella storia dagli inizi al consolidamento della sua attuale struttura," in *Riflessioni sulla Lettera Apostolica di Giovanni Paolo II Rosarium Virginis Mariae* "Quaderni dell'*Osservatore Romano* 64" (Vatican City, 2003) pp. 7-12.

[73] John Paul II, Apostolic Letter *Rosarium Virginis Mariae*, in *AAS* 95 (2003) 5-36.

[74] Editor's note: For a defense of this papal tradition which does ascribe the proximate origins of the specific form of the Rosary to St. Dominic, cf. R. Garrigou-LaGrange, O.P., *Mother of Our Savior and the Interior Life*, tr. Bernard Kelly, C.S.Sp., Golden Eagle Book, Dublin, Ireland, 1948, p. 297, who writes: "Our Blessed Lady made known to St. Dominic a kind of preaching till then unknown, which she said would be one of the most powerful weapons against future errors and in future difficulties. Under her inspiration, St. Dominic went into the villages of the [Albigensians], gathered the people, and preached to them the mysteries of salvation—the Incarnation, the redemption, eternal life. As Mary had taught

as Bl. Ildefonsus Schuster, cardinal archbishop of Milan (+1954), Benedictine monk and eminent specialist in the history of the prayer of the Church appropriately indicated in 1933, it must be recognized, according to the author, that "the early biographers of St. Dominic do not attribute to him the institution of the Rosary, for this devotion was a tradition of Catholic piety long before his time."[75] This being so, it remains nonetheless true, as Pope John Paul II recalled, that "the history of the Rosary shows how this prayer was used in particular by the Dominicans at a difficult time for the Church due to the spread of heresy" (*RVM* 17).

As Cardinal Schuster had indicated, in reality the slow genesis of the Rosary takes its source upstream from the epoch of St. Dominic. A devotion does not ordinarily emerge all of a piece, but on the contrary, becomes elaborated slowly, transforms and perfects itself little by little. In the event, what characterizes the history of the formation of the Rosary, is that the majority of the great schools of spirituality brought to it their contribution: Cistercian, Carthusian, Franciscan, Dominican, the *devotio moderna*, without forgetting the French School, the Society of Jesus, etc. Let us also note that the origin of the Rosary also draws in a certain way from the *orientale lumen*, since Byzantine hymnology began to exercise its influence in the West in the ninth century with the translation into Latin of the *Akathistos* Hymn:[76] "An important beacon in the development of Marian piety which took flight from the eleventh to the twelfth centuries, this translation is seen also to be at the origin of the principal forms of expression, learned and popular, of a devotion

---

him to do, he distinguished the different kinds of mysteries, and after each short instruction, he had ten Hail Marys recited—somewhat as might happen even today at a Holy Hour. And what the word of the preacher was unable to do, the sweet prayer of the Hail Mary did for hearts. As Mary promised, it proved to be a most fruitful form of preaching."

[75] Ildefonsus Schuster, O.S.B., *The Sacramentary (Liber Sacramentorum): Historical & Liturgical Notes on the Roman Missal* Vol. V (Parts 8 and 9) trans. Arthur Levelis-Marke, M.A., and W. Fairfax-Cholmeley (London: Burns Oates & Washbourne Ltd., 1930) pp. 165-166; Cited in Albert Enard, O.P., *Assidus à la prière avec Marie Mère de Jésus – Le Rosaire régénéré à la fraîcheur de sa source*, (Paris: Parole et Silence, 2003) p. 92.

[76] This Latin version was drafted by Bishop Christopher of Venice, toward the year 800. Cf. Congregation for Divine Worship and the Discipline of the Sacraments, *Directory on Popular Piety and the Liturgy* (2002) #207 note 263.

so marked by the multiform use of the *Ave Maria*," explains Duval.[77] Cardinal Schuster discerned numerous points of resemblance between the *Akathistos* Hymn and the Rosary: "'The Hymnos Akathistos' in the East, the Rosary in the West are two admirable forms of devotion to Mary, somewhat resembling each other. ... They arose from the same faith and the same love borne by the Universal Church for her who is the Mother of God and of men."[78] This consideration deserves renewed attention today since the *Akathistos* Hymn, which insistently repeats the *chairé* (translated in Latin by *Ave* but which means "rejoice") has been happily spread in communities of the faithful of the Latin rite. Thus the prehistory of the Rosary attests that "if it is properly revitalized," according to the wishes of John Paul II, this means of sanctification "is an aid and certainly not a hindrance to ecumenism" (*RVM* 4).

To trace the Rosary devotion to its chronological source proves to be almost impossible; at the most one can attain to marking the emergence of the link between the repeated recitation of the *Ave Maria*—the most common prayer to the Virgin among Christians since the fourteenth century—and the contemplation of the mysteries of the life of Jesus.

From the end of the eleventh century a Marian devotion characterized by numerous *Aves* with rhythmic prostrations was already known and practiced in honor of the Virgin, first in honor of her joys, then in honor of her sorrows. In the twelfth century the practice of the frequent repetition of the *Ave Maria*, linked to the celebration of the joys of Mary, only included the first part of the present angelical salutation. This custom was in place in monasteries of the northwest and environs when St. Dominic began his apostolate among the Cathars. What was essential was to greet the Virgin Mary with all one's heart, either in reciting or in singing the words of the *Ave Maria*, sometimes glossed with very different strophes or refrains offered by the composers of numerous "salutations to Our Lady." As to the symbolism of the rose, dear to the Middle Ages, as the Dominican Joret summarizes,

> It came early to be joined to the joy of the Virgin and the *Ave* which was addressed to her. The words *chapelets*, or little *chapeaux*, *chapels of roses*, which would designate

---

[77] A. Duval, "Rosaire," in *DSAM* (Paris: Beauchesne, 1988) t. XIII, col. 938.
[78] I. Schuster, *The Sacramentary* Vol. V, p. 166.

these joyous devotions, are linked with the custom then in vogue of covering the head with roses as a sign of joy. The Virgin herself, contemplated in her joyful or glorious mysteries, is a rose and was greeted often with this name from the thirteenth century: *Ave Rosa!* It was also said that she is a garden of roses, *Rosarium* in medieval Latin.[79]

The gospel of the Annunciation (Lk 1:26-38) is found at the origin of this form of Marian devotion which multiplies and repeats salutations and invocations, a form by which the faith was expressed and nourished in the course of centuries. According to this popular medieval Mariology, whose beauty and fervor we have trouble imagining today, it was a matter of offering the joy of the Annunciation as a new echo to the Mother of God in repeating to Mary the words of the Angel Gabriel. It is this experience which Pope John Paul II wished to propose anew at the beginning of the third millennium:

> The first part of the *Hail Mary*, drawn from the words spoken to Mary by the Angel Gabriel and by St. Elizabeth, is a contemplation in adoration of the mystery accomplished in the Virgin of Nazareth. These words express, so to speak, the wonder of heaven and earth; they could be said to give us a glimpse of God's own wonderment as he contemplates his "masterpiece"— the Incarnation of the Son in the womb of the Virgin Mary. If we recall how, in the book of Genesis, "God saw all that he had made" (cf. Gen 1:31), we can find here an echo of that "pathos with which God, at the dawn of creation, looked upon the work of his hands." The repetition of the *Hail Mary* in the Rosary gives us a share in God's own wonder and pleasure: in jubilant amazement we acknowledge the greatest miracle of history. Mary's prophecy here finds its fulfillment: "Henceforth all generations will call me blessed" (Lk 1:48) (*RVM* 33).

---

[79] F.D. Joret, *Le Rosaire de Marie* (Paris: Cerf) p. 220.

The *Psalters of the Virgin Mary* likewise began to appear from the twelfth century in certain Cistercian communities where St. Bernard of Clairvaux (+1153) had greatly contributed to the development of Marian mysticism. This usage expanded in the monasteries where the brothers who were not priests, and unlettered monks, were bound to recite 150 *Pater Nosters* according to the number of Psalms. The lay people were not slow to imitate the prayer of these monks of the contemplative orders, in substituting for the *Psalms* the *Pater* and/or the *Ave* which they memorized more easily. The medieval contemplative religious orders, then, played a capital role in the elaboration of the Rosary, to which the mendicant orders gave the definitive and missionary form.

In the epoch of St. Dominic, and undoubtedly in harmony with the Cistercian tradition, the custom spread of uniting the repetition of the name of Jesus with the angelic salutation.[80] The author of a remarkable thesis on the sources of the Rosary, Father Mahé, is of the opinion that the original role of St. Dominic himself was less that of being at the beginning of the Rosary considered as the praying form of devotion, than of adapting this already existing form of piety as a form of preaching according to his specific charism.[81] The Dominican M.T. Poupon proposed a good synthesis of this point of view:

> Did St. Dominic have knowledge of the Rosary by an interior grace or even by an extraordinary charism? Or did he even deploy his personal genius in organizing through his preaching a devotional practice current in medieval monasteries? Without overlooking the antecedents ... the Dominican tradition, consecrated by papal encyclicals, declares in favor of heavenly inspiration. Obviously, such a grace does not exclude the play of natural faculties in terms of what concerns existing customs. ... Without any doubt, the Rosary is divinely incorporated in the personal vocation of St. Dominic. The first founder in the Church of a preaching order which is at base monastic, he had to conceive of

---

[80] The decision to insert the name of Jesus in the *Ave Maria* goes back to Pope Urban IV (1261-1264).

[81] Cf. Marcel Mahé, S.M., "Aux sources de notre Rosaire," in *Vie Spirituelle* Supplément 4 (1951) 101-120.

and practice the Rosary, especially and first as a form of preaching, the *rosaried* prayer becoming the key for opening souls to the light, to the anointing of divine grace. The theme of this preaching is Jesus-Mary, the Son of God made man who remains inseparable from his Mother. Faced with the heresy which was making a travesty of the economy of salvation, Dominic insisted on the truth of the Incarnation as well as on the earthly life of the Savior; he reestablished Mary's place in the Gospel and proclaimed with effusive enthusiasm whom the sons of St. Bernard recognized as the *Médiatrice*. He preached Jesus and Mary; he prayed to them and made the people who heard him pray to them: a prayer interspersed with the "*Ave* meditated and repeated either by the Psalter or by songs under the sign of the Rose."[82]

If it is important to go back to the flow of the history of the Rosary upstream from the epoch of St. Dominic, it is no less enriching to consider the centuries subsequent to the founder of the Order of Preachers.

According to certain historical accounts, a Carthusian monk of Cologne from the fourteenth century named Henry of Kalkar (+1408) was the first to set forth the precise number of *Paters* and *Aves*. The archives of the Charterhouse attest that the Virgin Mary manifested herself to Henry of Kalkar to reveal to him, among other things, how he could compose a more perfect "Psalter": a *Pater*, ten *Aves*, up to the total of 15 *Paters* and of 150 *Aves*. According to the accounts of the historians it was Henry of Kalkar, then, who inaugurated the subdivision into 15 decades, inserting the *Pater* between each decade. This association of the Lord's Prayer with the angelic salutation in Catholic prayer was commented on by Louis Bouyer in these terms:

> After this prayer—which can be called perfect, since it includes everything the Christian should ask for, in the unity of the perspective of the divine design in which his faith should place him—the Hail Mary causes us to enter into this mystery of the divine paternity and of our

---

[82] M.Th. Poupon, O.P., Le Saint Rosaire, sa tradition évangélique, ses mystères, ses fruits, Lyon/Paris, 1951, pp. 11-13.

adoption in Christ which dominates the "Our Father." It opens out to us, in fact, the interiorization of the Kingdom in her whom we might call the perfect prayer: She whose faith could make the "Our Father" her own as could the faith of no other creature, the Virgin Mary. Indeed, it is, under such a simple form, the whole mystery of our divine adoption through our association with the life of the Trinity that the Hail Mary salutes in the Virgin. ... The objective reality of the Kingdom, which the Our Father causes us to contemplate and invoke in faith, the Hail Mary interiorizes: to meditation on the significance of the divine maternity, it joins meditation on the significance of our adoption in the Son by the grace of the Holy Spirit. The complex ... of our relationships with the divine persons is here illuminated in the contemplation of the human person who experienced them first of all, and for the sake of all.[83]

The fifteenth century unquestionably opened a new and decisive phase in the evolution of this Marian prayer. In the heart of the Charterhouse of St. Alban, situated near Trêves, during the priorship of Adolf of Essen, Henry of Kalkar's "Psalter of Mary" flourished well along with the "Rosary." In this epoch the word "rosary" designated a series of 50 *Aves*. Adolf of Essen (+1439) prayed 50 Hail Marys each day meditating at the same time on the life of Jesus. As spiritual father he communicated his method to others and invited them to contemplate Holy Scripture with the Heart of Mary. Adolf of Essen wanted to teach this art of praying to a young student of the Charterhouse named Dominic of Prussia (+1460), but this young Carthusian proved to be incapable of concentrating on the meditation.[84] This is why he had the idea of dividing the life of Jesus into 50 phrases (*clausulae*) and of joining to each *clausula* an *Ave Maria*. These *clausulae*, composed of a few words associated with the name of Jesus, spread rapidly. And later Dominic published a series of 150 *clausulae* for the entire Marian psalter. This "Rosary" was not yet composed of "decades," but of a group of 50 *Ave*

---

[83] L. Bouyer, *Introduction to Spirituality* pp. 90-91.
[84] Yves Gourdel, "Le Rosaire de Dominique le Chartreux" in *Maria—Etudes sur la Sainte Vierge*, (Paris: Beauchesne) t. II, 1952, pp. 657-675.

Marias, where the name of Jesus received a new coloration each time while evoking a word or a different event from the Gospel. Popes Paul VI[85] and John Paul II recalled this usage, practiced since Dominic of Prussia in certain regions, to highlight the name of Christ, while adding an evocative *clausula* on the mystery which one is meditating on:[86]

> This is a praiseworthy custom, especially during public recitation. It gives forceful expression to our faith in Christ, directed to the different moments of the Redeemer's life. It is at once *a profession of faith* and an aid in concentrating our meditation, since it facilitates the process of assimilation to the mystery of Christ inherent in the petition of the *Hail Mary* (*RVM* 33).

Bl. Alan de la Roche (+1475), a Dominican of Breton origin who was associated with the Carthusians, certainly knew Henry of Kalkar's "Psalter of Mary," as well as the "rosary" of Dominic of Prussia which had begun to spread. The historians are unanimous in underscoring his determinative role not only in the evolution of the Rosary, but above all in its diffusion. It was he who presented St. Dominic as the first protagonist of the Rosary. Bl. Alan de la Roche is the author of several writings which served as a common source for numerous subsequent works on the Rosary. It was thus that the *Rosier Mystique de la Très Sainte Vierge* (1685) of the Dominican Antoninus Thomas, or yet again *The Admirable Secret of the Most Holy Rosary* of St. Louis-Marie Grignion de Montfort, not published during his life but described by Pope John Paul II as "an excellent work on the Rosary" (*RVM* 8), make numerous borrowings from Alan de la Roche. After his death, the first Confraternity of the Rosary was erected in Cologne (1475) by James Sprenger, prior of the Dominican Priory. The list of the traditional "mysteries" was established thanks to printers at the end of the fifteenth century. The appellation "Rosary" really begins to prevail from the time of Pope Leo X (1520). As to the expression "mysteries of the Rosary," this appears for the first time, it seems, under the pen of Alberto of Castello in his celebrated work *Il Rosario della gloriosa Vergine Maria* (Venice, 1521). The sixteenth century

---

[85] Cf. *Marialis Cultus* #46.
[86] This usage is recommended in the *Directory on Popular Piety and the Liturgy* (2002), #201.

will not finish without a decisive intervention on the part of the Papal Magisterium, which would define the form of the prayer of the Rosary in an epoch of troubles for the Church and for the world.

From the Magisterial Reception of the Rosary (1569) to the Introduction of the Luminous Mysteries (2002)

On September 15, 1569, with the Bull *Consueverunt Romani Pontifices* the Dominican Pope St. Pius V (+1572) officially consecrated the Rosary by imposing an imprint which it has kept up to our days. This foundational text defined the Rosary in these terms:

> This method of prayer is easy and suitable to everyone and is called the Rosary or the Psalter of the Blessed Virgin Mary. It consists of venerating this Blessed Virgin by reciting 150 angelic salutations, the same number as the Psalms of David, interrupting them at each decade by the Lord's Prayer, meanwhile meditating on the mysteries which recall the entire life of our Lord Jesus Christ.[87]

---

[87] Pius V, Consueverunt romani pontifices, September 17, 1569, in Bullarium diplomatum et privilegiorum sanctorum romanorum Pontificum Taurinensis editio..., t. VII, Augustae Taurinorum 1862, 774-775 [The Rosary: Papal Teachings p. 286 altered]. This bull is the first magisterial document to mention the meditation on the mysteries as an indispensable condition for obtaining the indulgences. At the moment of the invasion of Europe by the Turks, the same St. Pius V asked all the Rosary confraternities to pray intensely for the protection of the Church and of Europe. In remembrance of the victory of Lepanto (October 7, 1571), he instituted the commemoration of the Blessed Virgin of Victory fixed on October 7. From 1573, Gregory XIII (+1585) fixed the first Sunday of October as the Feast of the Holy Rosary of the Virgin Mary for the Dominican Order, for the churches having a confraternity or at least an altar in honor of the Virgin of the Rosary. Later, in 1716, which is also the year of the death of St. Louis-Marie de Montfort, Clement XI (+1721) extended to the universal Church this celebration in honor of the Holy Rosary of the Virgin Mary. On the occasion of the revision of the Roman calendar during the pontificate of St. Pius X, the latter judged it well to unite to the date of October 7 the feast of the Holy Rosary and the memorial of the Blessed Virgin of Victory. From 1960 the memorial of the Holy Rosary of the Blessed Virgin has become that of the Blessed Virgin of the Holy Rosary.

The preceding year, in the revision of the breviary, the same Pius V had already introduced into the official prayer of the Church the formula of the *Ave Maria*, including the second part (which dates from the fifteenth century): *Sancta Maria, Mater Dei, ora pro nobis peccatoribus, nunc et in hora mortis nostrae.* The bull of 1569 rendered this formula for the *Hail Mary* fixed and uniform which was widely spread in relation with the Rosary devotion. From the time of this bull of St. Pius V, a strong Dominican primacy was established on the creation and direction of the Rosary Confraternities,[88] for St. Dominic was then unanimously considered as the Father of the Rosary. A little more than a century later, St. Louis-Marie de Montfort himself entered the Third Order of the Dominicans on November 10, 1710, and solicited from the Master General of the Order of Preachers permission not only to preach the holy Rosary wherever he would be called, but also to found confraternities. Father de Montfort insisted much on the importance of meditating on the mysteries, and invited his hearers to ask always for one of the virtues which shine most in each mystery meditated upon.[89] The recitation of the Creed, of the Our Father followed by the three Hail Marys, along with the formula of offering and statement of the fruits of each mystery are of Montfortian origin. In the perspective of St. Louis-Marie "the holy Rosary is a sacred composition of vocal and mental prayer to honor and imitate the mysteries and the virtues of the life, of the death and Passion and of the glory of Jesus Christ and of Mary" (*SR* 9).

Grignion de Montfort can also be considered as one of the principal promoters of the "Luminous Mysteries" (*RVM* 21) which he himself proposed for meditation, as his *Methods for Saying the Rosary* (*MR* 21) testify:[90] One should read attentively the *Short Summary of the Life,*

---

[88] Pope Leo XIII solemnly conferred on the Dominicans the charge of spreading the devotion of the holy Rosary in the Apostolic Constitution *Ubi primum* of October 2, 1898 [Cf. *The Rosary: Papal Teachings* #224-227]. Cf. A. Duval, "La dévotion mariale dans l'ordre des Frères Prêcheurs," in *Maria* (Paris: Beauchesne) t. II, 1951, pp. 739-782.

[89] Cf. J. Laurenceau, "Rosary," in *Jesus Living in Mary: Handbook of the Spirituality of St. Louis Marie de Montfort* (Bay Shore, NY: Montfort Publications, 1994) 1055-1074.

[90] St. Louis-Marie Grignion de Montfort, *Method for Saying the Rosary*, in *God Alone: The Collected Writings of St. Louis Marie de Montfort* 233-262. Cf. B. Cortinovis, "Il Rosario come mezzo di santità in San Luigi Maria di Montfort," in *Spiritualità Monfortana* 6 (2005) 79-110.

Death, Passion and Glory of Jesus and Mary in the Holy Rosary, taken from his *Livre des Sermons*,[91] in order to discover that the missionary meditated principally on the mysteries of the Baptism of the Lord, the Announcement of the Kingdom, the Transfiguration and the Institution of the Eucharist. In this regard it is a duty to recall that from 1966, the founder of *Cahiers Marials* (1957-1985), namely the French Montfortian Jean Hémery, along with several Dominican heirs of an intuition of Father Marie-Joseph Lagrange (+1938),[92] had suggested the introduction of certain events from the public life of Jesus among the mysteries of the Rosary:

> If, with the Virgin Mary "present as the Most Holy Mother of God in the mysteries of Christ," [LG 66] the Rosary wishes to introduce us into the riches of salvation, it is appropriate that it should make a *place for certain mysteries of the public life*, let us say for certain key-events with which Mary was particularly associated. The Council itself, recalling "the union of the Mother with her Son in the work of salvation ... manifested from the hour of the virginal conception of Christ up to his death" [LG 57-59], enumerates the event of Cana and the proclamation of the blessedness of those who hear and practice the Word of God. But this is not meant to be limiting.[93]

We find a timid allusion to a possible evolution in this sense in an apostolic letter of Pope Paul VI, *Reccurrens mensis october*, published in 1969 on the occasion of the fourth centenary of the bull of St. Pius V:

> May the Rosary, in the form handed down by St. Pius V—as well as in other recent forms adapting it,

---

[91] Cf. *Le Livre des sermons du Père de Montfort* (Documents et Recherches IX), Rome, 1983.

[92] From 1936, in a conference given to lay Dominicans of Montpellier, Father M.J. Lagrange formulated the intuition of a renewing of the prayer of the Rosary as a meditation on the *entire* Gospel. Cf. "La lecture de la Bible et l'âme dominicaine," in *La vie dominicaine* (1936) 2.

[93] Cf. J. Hémery, "Faut-il changer le Rosaire?", in *Cahiers marials* 10 (1966) 4, 296-300.

with the consent of the lawful authority, to the needs of today—be indeed, as our beloved predecessor Pope John XXIII desired, "a great public and universal prayer for the ordinary and extraordinary needs of the holy Church, of the nations, and of the entire world.[94]

It was necessary to await the celebration of the Jubilee of the Incarnation followed by the Year of the Rosary (2002-2003), so that, thanks to the Servant of God John Paul II, a new letter on the *Rosary of the Blessed Virgin Mary* would accede to the mysteries of the public life of Christ between the Baptism and the Passion, underscoring that it is "during the years of his public ministry that *the mystery of Christ is most evidently a mystery of light*: 'While I am in the world, I am the light of the world' (Jn 9:5)" (*RVM* 19).

In order that one could say that the Rosary is a "summary of the Gospel" in a more complete manner, Pope John Paul II judged the introduction of the Luminous Mysteries appropriate:

> It is fitting to add, following reflection on the Incarnation and the hidden life of Christ (*the Joyful Mysteries*) and before focusing on the sufferings of his Passion (*the Sorrowful Mysteries*) and the triumph of his Resurrection (*the Glorious Mysteries*), a meditation on certain particularly significant moments in his public ministry (*the Mysteries of Light*). This addition of these new mysteries, without prejudice to any essential aspect of the prayer's traditional format, is meant to give it fresh life and to enkindle renewed interest in the Rosary's place within Christian spirituality as a true doorway to the depths of the Heart of Christ, ocean of joy and of light, of suffering and of glory (*RVM* 19).

The letter *Rosarium Virginis Mariae* also emphasizes the importance of an often-neglected dimension, namely the symbolic significance of the rosary beads (*corona*), the traditional instrument for reciting this prayer. The beads are not a simple instrument serving to count the Hail Marys

---

[94] Paul VI, Apostolic Exhortation *Recurrens Mensis October*, in *AAS* 61 (1969) 654 [*Mary—God's Mother and Ours* 67].

but "they can also take on a symbolism which can give added depth to contemplation": the beads converge towards the Crucified who opens and concludes the way of this Christocentric prayer; the beads, a "sweet chain" which attunes us to Mary and binds us to God according to the expression dear to Bl. Bartolo Longo (+1926),[95] the apostle of the Rosary, evoke the unceasing path of contemplation and Christian perfection; finally "a fine way to expand the symbolism of the beads is to let them remind us of our many relationships, of the bond of communion and fraternity which unites us all in Christ" (*RMV* 36). Such considerations clarify and enrich the sense and importance of the ritual of the blessing of rosary beads.

Symbolic significance is even more obvious in the case of the scapular whose pious usage is also a part of the practices and exercises of piety recommended by the Magisterium in the course of the centuries.[96]

The Scapular Devotion

In its origin, the scapular is a small version of the habit proper to a religious order. That is why it is also called a "little habit." The brown scapular of Our Lady of Mount Carmel is the best known and most widespread of these. Concretely, it is made up of two squares or rectangles of woolen fabric connected by two bands or cords; one of these pieces rests on the shoulders, between the shoulder-blades, the other on the chest of the person who wears it. For more than seven centuries, Marian piety has recognized in the scapular of Our Lady of Mount Carmel an authentic sign of belonging to Mary and a pledge of her motherly protection.

Numerous popes chose to vest themselves with the scapular of Carmel. Among the most recent, such was the case with popes Pius XII, John XXIII, and undoubtedly with the Carmelite tertiary John Paul II, who witnessed to this on several occasions.[97] During the reform

---

[95] Proclaimed Blessed by Pope John Paul II on October 26, 1980, the attorney Bartolo Longo (+1926) is the author of a well-known work entitled *I Quindici Sabati del Santo Rosario* (Pompéi) [*The Fifteen Saturdays of the Holy Rosary*].

[96] Cf. Paul VI, Letter to the Papal Legate to the Mariological Congress at Santo Domingo, February 2, 1965, in *AAS* 57 (1965) 376-379.

[97] Cf. John Paul II, *Gift and Mystery* (Nairobi: Pauline Publications Africa, 1996) chapter III. Cf. also the special dossier on "Jean-Paul II et le Carmel" in *Carmel*, Toulouse, (2001) n. 101.

of the liturgical calendar, which was made following the Second Vatican Council, numerous celebrations linked to particular devotions were suppressed, but the memorial of the Virgin of Carmel was retained and with it the devotion conveyed by the scapular. This was a happy anticipation of the judgment recently formulated by Pope John Paul II on the occasion of the 750th anniversary of the giving of the scapular:

> Over time this rich Marian heritage of Carmel has become, through the spread of the holy scapular devotion, a treasure for the whole Church. By its simplicity, its anthropological value and its relationship to Mary's role in regard to the Church and humanity, this devotion was so deeply and widely accepted by the People of God that it came to be expressed in the memorial of July 16 on the liturgical calendar of the universal Church.[98]

The Church has just given a new impetus to this devotional practice by the publication of the new ritual for the blessing and imposition of the scapular.[99] All of the baptized may receive the scapular of Our Lady of Mount Carmel by which they recognize that they are called by God to be a part of a spiritual family consecrated to the love of the Virgin Mary and her *cultus*. The *Directory on Popular Piety and the Liturgy* (2002) makes mention of the scapular in the following terms:

> The history of Marian piety also includes "devotion" to various scapulars, the most common of which is devotion to the Scapular of Our Lady of Mount Carmel. Its use is truly universal and, undoubtedly, it is one of those pious practices which the Council described as "recommended by the Magisterium throughout the centuries."
>
> The Scapular of Mount Carmel is a reduced form of the religious habit of the Order of the Friars of the

---

[98] John Paul II, Letter *Il providentiale evento di grazia*, March 25, 2001, #4 in *Inseg* XXIV/1 (2001) 601 [*ORE* 1687:5].

[99] Cf. *The Scapular of Our Lady of Mount Carmel: Catechesis and Ritual*, Prepared under the direction of the North American Provincials of the Carmelite Orders (Worcester, MA, 2000). This ritual was approved by the Congregation for Divine Worship and the Discipline of the Sacraments on April 10, 1996.

Blessed Virgin of Mount Carmel. Its use is very diffuse and often independent of the life and spirituality of the Carmelite family.

The scapular is an external sign of the filial relationship established between the Blessed Virgin Mary, Mother and Queen of Mount Carmel, and the faithful who entrust themselves totally to her protection, who have recourse to her maternal intercession, who are mindful of the primacy of the spiritual life and need for prayer.

The scapular is imposed by a special rite of the Church which describes it as "a reminder that in baptism we have been clothed in Christ, with the assistance of the Blessed Virgin Mary, solicitous for our conformation to the Word incarnate, to the praise of the Trinity, we may come to our heavenly home wearing our nuptial garb" (*Directory* 205).

The origin of this devotion of the scapular is rooted in the historical events which marked the establishment of the Order of Carmel in the Church in the thirteenth century. According to an ancient tradition, while the English Carmelite St. Simon Stock (+1265) was beseeching the Virgin Mary for his order, whose prior general he was, by devoutly reciting the hymn *Flos Carmeli*, the Mother of God appeared to him holding in her hand the scapular and saying: "Behold the privilege which I give to you and to all the children of Carmel. Whoever dies vested in this habit will be saved." A slightly longer variant presents this statement: "he who dies wearing it will not suffer eternal fire (*in hoc moriens aeternum non patietur incendium*) ... he will we saved."[100] This account belongs to the literary *genre* of *exempla* frequent in the Middle

---

[100] Cf. *Catalogo dei Santi Carmelitani*, cited in L. Saggi, "Scapulaire" in *DSAM* t. 15 (1989) col. 393. Cf. also R. Copsey, O.Carm., "Simon Stock and the Scapular Vision" in *Journal of Ecclesiastical History* 30 (1999) 652-683. This fundamental privilege of being preserved from hell was quickly extended to the secular members. According to the historians, it cannot be said that this account, which makes the scapular a privileged sacramental, is irrefutable, but it can no longer be affirmed to be certainly false. Cf. L. Saggi, "Scapulaire" in *DSAM* t.15 (1989) col. 391.

Ages, and the Marian vision which it contains is to be understood in the perspective which considers the religious life, or the simple association with a religious order, as a path toward eternal life. Beyond the particular historical circumstances which were at the origin of the reception of the scapular, a "venerable tradition of the order,"[101] according to the happy expression of Pope John Paul II, recognized in this gift a privileged sign of the motherly protection of the Virgin Mary. This sign is rooted in the benevolent provision of God for all of his children. It should be noted that the response of the Virgin Mary to Simon Stock does not consist in a miracle worked in favor of the survival of Carmel in the West, but offers a reminder of the sense of Christian death and the promise of salvation.

The Constitution *Lumen Gentium* precisely recalled the perennially active role of the Mother of the Redeemer on our behalf:

> After her Assumption into heaven she has not put aside this saving role, rather she continues by her multiform intercession to obtain for us the gift of eternal salvation. By her motherly charity she cares for the brethren of her Son who still journey on earth surrounded by dangers and difficulties until they are led into the happiness of their true home (*LG* 62).

From this conciliar text we can deduce, suggests the Italian Carmelite Antonio Sicari, that the promise made to St. Simon Stock is in some way part of the habitual activity of the Blessed Virgin: *by her repeated intercession she continues to obtain for us the gifts which assure our eternal salvation.*[102]

A second privilege, called the "Sabbatine privilege" because it contains a promise of liberation from purgatory on the first Saturday after death, is rooted in another Marian vision, quite legendary, that was received by Pope John XXII (+1334), to whom is attributed the so-called *bulla sabatina*, which is unquestionably apocryphal. It remains nonetheless true that the content of this inauthentic bull was approved by popes from the time of Clement VII (+1534) in numerous papal documents and contributed much, just as the vision of St. Simon Stock, to the diffusion

---

[101] John Paul II, Letter *Il providentiale evento di grazia*, March 25, 2001, #1, in *Inseg* XXIV/1 (2001) 599 [*ORE* 1687:5].

[102] A. Sicari, O.C.D., "L'abito della Vergine—Nel 750° anniversario dello Scapolare del Carmine," in *Rivista di Vita Spirituale* 55 (2001) 679, note 22.

of the brown scapular. Under the pontificate of Paul V, a decree of the Congregation of the Index dated February 20, 1613, (and several times confirmed), authorized the preaching of the "Sabbatine privilege" but forbade that such preaching should make reference to the apocryphal bull attributed to John XXII.[103] This precision, which has scarcely been heard, had the merit of clearly indicating that the profound meaning of the brown scapular and of the graces associated with it do not depend on visions which are historically more or less sure and of relative value, but translate, on the contrary, in practical and symbolic terms a correct understanding of the mystery of the cooperation of the Virgin Mary in our redemption and of her universal maternal mediation. The Carmelite Emanuele Boaga recently formulated a good doctrinal restatement on this matter:

> Mary's action in favor of those who wear the scapular is substantially, from the theological point of view, the concrete application of the doctrine of the spiritual maternity and of Marian mediation correctly understand in the order of dispositive causality: Mary works in us and we must be disposed to welcome her action and to respond with all of our strength, adhering to Christ offered to us by Mary. Therefore, this requires on our part the practical recognition of our dependence on Mary and on her role in the supernatural order of grace.[104]

On the occasion of the celebration of the seventh centenary, Pope Pius XII, himself a member of the confraternity of the Scapular of Carmel, explicitly recommended the scapular devotion in his letter *Neminem profecto latet*, addressed to the general of the Carmelites and dated February 11, 1950, the day which commemorates the apparition of Our Lady at Lourdes:

---

[103] The text of the decree of 1613 with the respective instruction in Irenaeus a Sancto Jacobo, *Tractatus theologicus de singulari Immaculate Virginis protectione*, Parisiis, 1650, p. 38.

[104] E. Boaga, O. Carm., "Lo Scapolare del Carmine: storia e spiritualità," in *Marianum* LXV (2003) 356. Cf. also by the same author "Carmelite Devotion toward Our Lady," in *Carmel in the World* 28 (1989/1) 29-36; Id., "La devozione dello Scapolare del Carmine: contenuti e prospettive," in *Rivista di Vita Spirituale* 55 (2001) 306-327.

As a Marian vestment, the sacred scapular is certainly a sign and guarantee of the protection of the Mother of God. However, let not those who wear it think that they can in sloth and indolence of spirit attain eternal life, for the apostle thus openly admonishes: "Work out your salvation in fear and trembling." Therefore, all Carmelites (whether in cloisters of the first or second order, in the regular or secular third order, or in the confraternities) who belong, by special particular bond of love, to the family that honors itself with the name of the most Blessed Virgin should recognize in this badge of the said Virgin a pattern of humility and chastity; in the very form of the vestment itself they should recognize an epitome of modesty and simplicity; above all they should see in the vestment itself, which they wear day and night, an eloquent expression of the prayers with which they ask for divine assistance; finally they should recognize in it an invitation to that consecration to the Immaculate Heart of the Virgin Mary which we recently recommended. On her part, the most holy Mother will not fail to intercede with God that her children who in purgatory are expiating their sins may, at the earliest possible moment, reach the eternal Fatherland in accordance with the so-called Sabbatine Privilege.[105]

An attentive reading of these words of Pius XII brings one to recognize above all the reminder of the effective role of protection and of intercession of the Mother of God. Pope Pius XII underscores in this passage that the promises linked to the pious use of the scapular may not in any case be a reward for presumption: "let not those who wear it think that they can in sloth and indolence of spirit attain eternal life." In the same sense, St. Louis-Marie Grignion de Montfort, canonized by Pius XII in 1947, reproached the "presumptuous devotees" for sleeping in peace in their bad habits while saying that they wear the scapular (cf. *TD* 97).

---

[105] Pius XII, Letter *Neminem profecto*, February 11, 1950, in *AAS* 42 (1950) 390-391 [*OL* #454].

A half century later, Pope John Paul II also took care to underscore the fact that the Marian scapular of Carmel is a sign of the "covenant" which obliges those who choose to wear it:

> The sign of the scapular points to an effective synthesis of Marian spirituality, which nourishes the devotion of believers and makes them sensitive to the Virgin Mother's loving presence in their lives. The scapular is essentially a "habit." Those who receive it are associated more or less closely with the Order of Carmel and dedicate themselves to the service of Our Lady for the good of the whole Church (cf. "Formula of Enrollment in the Scapular," in the *Rite of Blessing of and Enrollment in the Scapular*, approved by the Congregation for Divine Worship and the Discipline of the Sacraments, January 5, 1996). Those who wear the scapular are thus brought into the land of Carmel, so that they may "eat its fruits and its good things" (cf. Jer. 2:7), and experience the loving and motherly presence of Mary in their daily commitment to be clothed in Jesus Christ and to manifest him in their life for the good of the Church and the whole of humanity (cf. "Formula of Enrollment in the Scapular," cit.).
>
> Therefore, two truths are evoked by the sign of the scapular: on the one hand, the constant protection of the Blessed Virgin, not only on life's journey, but also at the moment of passing into the fullness of eternal glory; on the other, the awareness that devotion to her cannot be limited to prayers and tributes in her honor on certain occasions, but must become a "habit," that is, a permanent orientation of one's own Christian conduct, woven of prayer and interior life, through frequent reception of the sacraments and the concrete practice of the spiritual and corporal works of mercy. In this way the scapular becomes a sign of the "covenant" and reciprocal communion between Mary and the faithful: indeed it concretely translates the gift of his Mother, which Jesus gave on the Cross to John and, through him, to all of us, and the

entrustment of the beloved apostle and of us to her, who became our spiritual Mother.¹⁰⁶

The two truths indicated by the scapular are on the one hand that of a permanent protection by Mary and on the other hand that of an permanent orientation of the faithful who pledge themselves in depth and lastingly. As Guillaume De Menthière summarizes:

> The sign of the scapular evokes first of all the protection of the Virgin in the course of our days and up to the hour of our passing. It is a vestment which covers. But it is also a "habit," that is to say a habitual and permanent manner of the Christian life, woven by prayer and the interior life. For those who wear it, Marian devotion does not remain on the surface, exterior and peripheral, but becomes deep and from the heart.¹⁰⁷

Popes Pius XII and John Paul II have in common the fact that they both affirmed the explicit link between the spiritual tradition of the devotion of the scapular of Our Lady of Mount Carmel and the consecration to the Immaculate Heart of Mary. In his letter of February 11, 1950, already cited, Pius XII exhorted those who wear the scapular to make their consecration to the holy Immaculate Heart of the Virgin Mary. Pope John Paul II, in his letter addressed to the Carmelite Orders for the 750th anniversary of the giving of the scapular (2001), went still further in the same sense in affirming that the "most genuine form of devotion to the Blessed Virgin, expressed by the humble sign of the scapular, is consecration to her Immaculate Heart."¹⁰⁸ Thus the

---

¹⁰⁶ John Paul II, Letter *Il providentiale evento di grazia*, March 25, 2001, #5, in *Inseg* XXIV/1 (2001) 601-602 [*ORE* 1687:5]. For a commentary on this Letter cf. J. Castellano Cervera, "Lettera di Giovanni Paolo II per l'anno mariano carmelitano" in *Marianum* LXV (2003) 361-382.

¹⁰⁷ G. De Menthière, *Marie au cœur de l'œuvre de Jean-Paul II* (Paris: Mame-Edifa, 2005) p. 13.

¹⁰⁸ John Paul II, Letter *Il providentiale evento di grazia*, March 25, 2001, #4, in *Inseg* XXIV/1 (2001) 600 [*ORE* 1687:5]. It is interesting to recall that the apparitions of the Immaculate at Lourdes concluded on July 16, 1858, on the evening of the Feast of Our Lady of Mount Carmel (extended to the universal Church from 1726 by Benedict XIII), and also that it was in the course of the last apparition at Fatima that the Virgin Mary was seen by Lucia wearing the brown scapular of Carmel.

movement in favor of such a consecration, of which the Carmelite Sister Lucia of the Immaculate Heart of Mary was the witness and messenger before the popes,[109] is related to the Carmelite heritage and in particular with the use of the Marian scapular.

★ ★ ★

Finally let us consider in concluding that if the wearing of the scapular, as also the prayer of the Rosary, are promoted by recommendations so explicit and consistently renewed by the Papal Magisterium, it is because it is dealing here with genuine means for growth in fidelity in the "Love of Jesus which we seek through Mary" (cf. *TD* 67).

At the same time sure and popular, these practices of Marian veneration are recognized by the Church as true "secrets" of grace, comparable to those which expert artisans kept among themselves in order to function effectively in their art with promptness and skillfulness. Under like circumstances, we are dealing with some privileged means, among others, in service of the Marian dimension of the pedagogy of prayer and holiness which the Servant of God John Paul II formulated as pastoral priorities for the third millennium (cf. *Novo Millennio Ineunte* 30-32).[110]

By Way of Conclusion:

St. Louis-Marie de Montfort, the apostle of "true devotion to the Holy Virgin," would have approved without hesitation the well-known affirmation of Edith Stein with regard to "genuine prayer":

> It is not a question of placing the inner prayer ... as "subjective" piety in contrast to the liturgy as the "objective" prayer of the Church. All authentic prayer is prayer of the Church. Through every sincere prayer something happens in the Church, and it is the Church itself that is praying therein, for it is the Holy Spirit living

---

[109] Cf. Sister Lucia, *"Calls" from the Message of Fatima*, (Fatima: Secretariado dos Pastorinhos, 2002).

[110] Cf. E. Richer, *La pédagogie de sainteté de saint Louis-Marie de Montfort* (Paris: Téqui, 2003); Id. *Suivre Jésus avec Marie—un secret de sainteté de Grignion de Montfort à Jean-Paul II* (Paris: Editions des Béatitudes, 2006).

in the Church that intercedes for every individual soul "with sighs too deep for words" (Rom 8:26).[111]

If the approaches and the forms which express the *cultus* of *hyperdulia* addressed to the Virgin Mary are multiple, it is always the Holy Spirit who is the interior Master and artisan of the living Tradition of Christian Marian prayer. The *Catechism of the Catholic Church* (1992) took care to specify that if "the Church loves to pray in communion with the Virgin Mary, to magnify with her the great things the Lord has done for her and to entrust supplications and praises to her" it is "because of Mary's singular cooperation with the action of the Holy Spirit" (*CCC* 2682). St. Louis-Marie de Montfort speaks of the mystery of the Virgin Mary as of a "secret" revealed by the Holy Spirit:

> Happy, indeed sublimely happy, is the person to whom the Holy Spirit reveals the secret of Mary, thus imparting to him true knowledge of her. Happy the person to whom the Holy Spirit opens this enclosed garden for him to enter and to whom the Holy Spirit gives access to this sealed fountain where he can draw water and drink deep draughts of the living waters of grace (*SM* 20).

The pastoral guidance of Marian devotion does not have as its purpose the multiplication or accumulation of practices of piety, however good and laudable in themselves. What is essential is to promote a "contemplative discovery of the mystery of the Virgin Mary," that is to say an intimate lived and transcendent knowledge, which creates "an interior attitude and causes a filial impulse which bursts from the depths" as the Carmelite Marie-Eugène of the Child Jesus so well explained.[112] In this dynamic of growth in the love of Jesus in Mary which surpasses all knowledge, de Montfort, the author of the *Secret of Mary*, distinguishes three stages (or degrees):

---

[111] Edith Stein, "The Prayer of the Church" in *The Collected Works of Edith Stein* IV: *The Hidden Life* edited by Dr. L. Gelber and Michael Linssen, O.C.D., translated by Waltraut Stein, Ph.D. (Washington, DC: ICS Publications, 1992) 15.

[112] Marie-Eugène de l'Enfant-Jésus, O.C.D., "Les Frères de Notre Dame" in *La vie mariale au Carmel* (Ed. du Carmel, 1943) p. 29-45.

The first consists in fulfilling the duties of our Christian state, avoiding all mortal sin, performing our actions for God more through love than through fear, praying to Our Lady occasionally, and honoring her as the Mother of God, but without our devotion to her being exceptional.

The second consists in entertaining for Our Lady deeper feelings of esteem and love, of confidence and veneration. This devotion inspires us to join the confraternities of the holy Rosary and the scapular, to say the five or fifteen decades of the Rosary, to venerate Our Lady's altars and shrines, to make her known to others, and to enroll in her sodalities. This devotion, in keeping us from sin, is good, holy and praiseworthy, but it is not as perfect as the third, nor as effective in detaching us from creatures, or in practicing that self-denial necessary for union with Jesus Christ.

The third devotion to Our Lady is one which is unknown to many and practiced by very few. This is the one I am about to present to you.

Chosen soul, this devotion consists in surrendering oneself in the manner of a slave to Mary, and to Jesus through her, and then performing all our actions with Mary, in Mary, through Mary, and for Mary (SM 25-28).

In order that what has been exposed in this present chapter should be put to the service of a devotion to Mary which is not only genuine but *perfect*, because it consists in giving oneself entirely to her and to Jesus through her, it is necessary for the reader to complete the route undertaken by the attentive study of the chapter which treats specifically of *consecration* to Mary, described by John Paul II as "the most genuine form of devotion to the Blessed Virgin."[113]

---

[113] John Paul II, Letter *Il providentiale evento di grazia*, March 25, 2001, #4 in XXIV/1 (2001) 600 [*ORE* 1687:5].

Abbreviations

AAS = *Acta Apostolicae Sedis* (1909-)

ASS = *Acta Sanctae Sedis* (1865-1908)

CCC = *Catechism of the Catholic Church* (1992)

CIC = *Codex Iuris Canonici* (1983)

DSAM = *Dictionnaire de spiritualité ascétique et mystique*, Paris 1937ss.

DTC = *Dictionnaire de théologie catholique*

Inseg = *Insegnamenti di Giovanni Paolo II* (1978-2005) (Vatican City: Libreria Editrice Vaticana, 1979-2006)

LG = *Lumen Gentium* (Dogmatic Constitution of the Second Vatican Council on the Church)

MC = Apostolic Exhortation *Marialis Cultus* (Paul VI, 1974)

MND = Apostolic Letter *Mane nobiscum Domine* (John Paul II, 2005)

MR = *Methods for Saying the Rosary* by St. Louis-Marie Grignion de Montfort

OL = *Our Lady: Papal Teachings* (Boston: St. Paul Editions, 1962)

PC = *Perfectae Caritatis* (Decree of the Second Vatican Council on the Renewal of Religious Life)

PO = *Presbyterorum Ordinis* (Decree of the Second Vatican Council on the Life and Ministry of Priests)

RM = Encyclical *Redemptoris Mater* (John Paul II, 1987)

SC = *Sacrosanctum Concilium* (Constitution of the Second Vatican Council on the Liturgy)

SM = *The Secret of Mary* by St. Louis-Marie Grignion de Montfort

SR = *The Secret of the Holy Rosary* by St. Louis-Marie Grignion de Montfort

ST = *Summa Theologiae* of St. Thomas Aquinas

RVM = Apostolic Letter *Rosarium Virginis Mariae* (John Paul II, 2002)

TD = *True Devotion to the Blessed Virgin Mary* by St. Louis-Marie Grignion de Montfort

MARIAN CONSECRATION AND ENTRUSTMENT

Msgr. Arthur Burton Calkins

Some—perhaps many—Catholics, if they give any thought to it at all, may think that the practice of consecrating oneself to Our Lady or placing one's life entirely in her hands is a rather recent phenomenon in the life of the Church. Indeed, even if they are rather well informed, they may be of the conviction that this custom dates from the time of St. Louis-Marie Grignion de Montfort (+1716), the author of the famous treatises, *True Devotion to the Blessed Virgin* and *The Secret of Mary*. Surely without hesitation, St. Louis de Montfort (whom I hope will soon be named a Doctor of the Church) and St. Maximilian-Maria Kolbe (+1941) should be acknowledged as two of the principal proponents of Marian consecration in modern times. Yet the fact remains that this devotional practice dates from the earliest days of the Church and is really rooted in the Scriptures themselves, especially the words of Jesus from the Cross spoken to his Mother and to the beloved disciple (cf. Jn. 19:25-27).

Arguably the greatest proponent of Marian consecration in our own time was the Servant of God Pope John Paul II (+2005). His motto as bishop and pope was *Totus Tuus* (all yours), an abbreviated form of one of St. Louis de Montfort's formulas, *Totus tuus ego sum et omnia mea tua sunt* (I am all yours [O Mary] and everything I have is yours).[1] More than any other teacher of Marian consecration before him, this pope rooted his teaching and practice in the entrusting of John to Mary

---

[1] Cf. *True Devotion to the Blessed Virgin* [= *TD*] 179, 216, 266 in *God Alone: The Collected Writings of St. Louis Marie de Montfort* (Bay Shore, NY: Montfort Publications, 1988). In each of these passages the phrase appears with slightly different variations. The Latin formula quoted in *TD* 216 comes from a work attributed to St. Bonaventure (1221-1274), the *Psalterium Majus, Opera Omnia* (Vives Ed.), Vol. 14, 221a and 221b.

and Mary to John on Calvary. Here is a very important text from his Encyclical *Redemptoris Mater* of March 25, 1987, in which he expounded this doctrine in an authoritative manner:

> The Redeemer entrusts Mary to John because he entrusts John to Mary. At the foot of the Cross there begins that special *entrusting of humanity to the Mother of Christ*, which in the history of the Church has been practiced and expressed in different ways. The same apostle and evangelist, after reporting the words addressed by Jesus on the Cross to his Mother and to himself, adds: "And from that hour the disciple took her to his own home" (Jn. 19:27). This statement certainly means that the role of son was attributed to the disciple and that he assumed responsibility for the Mother of his beloved Master. And since Mary was given as a mother to him personally, the statement indicates, even though indirectly, everything expressed by the intimate relationship of a child with its mother. And all of this can be included in the word "entrusting." Such entrusting is *the response* to a person's love, and in particular *to the love of a mother*.
>
> The Marian dimension of the life of a disciple of Christ is expressed in a special way precisely through this filial entrusting to the Mother of Christ, which began with the testament of the Redeemer on Golgotha. Entrusting himself to Mary in a filial manner, the Christian, like the Apostle John, "welcomes" the Mother of Christ "into his own home" and brings her into everything that makes up his inner life, that is to say into his human and Christian "I": he *"took her to his own home"* (*Redemptoris Mater* 45).

Explaining the intimate relationship which Jesus wishes us to have with his Mother, the Pope pointed out that, while it is truly a personal relationship with Mary, it is ultimately oriented to Jesus himself:

> This filial relationship, this self-entrusting of a child to its mother, not only has its *beginning in Christ* but can

also be said to be *definitively directed towards him*. Mary can be said to continue to say to each individual the words which she spoke at Cana in Galilee: "Do whatever he tells you." ... Precisely with her faith as Spouse and Mother she wishes to act upon all those who entrust themselves to her as her children. And it is well known that the more her children persevere and progress in this attitude, the nearer Mary leads them to the "unsearchable riches of Christ" (Eph. 3:8) (*Redemptoris Mater* 46).

Historical Forms

The more one studies, the more one discovers Mary's maternal presence in the itinerary of the Church's life as well as the desire on the part of the faithful to entrust themselves to her. Here we can only indicate some of the major landmarks on this journey.[2]

Patristic Period

It does not seem presumptuous to see the first adumbrations of the tradition which would come to be known as Marian consecration in the Church in the most ancient recorded prayer to the Mother of God, dating from the third or fourth century, the *Sub tuum praesidium*.[3] It is the filial

---

[2] Cf. Arthur Burton Calkins, *Totus Tuus: John Paul II's Program of Marian Consecration and Entrustment* (New Bedford: Academy of the Immaculate, "Studies and Texts," No. 1, 1992) [= *Totus Tuus*] 41-74. I hope that within a year a second enlarged and revised edition of this work will appear. On the historical evolution of Marian consecration, cf. also P. Alessandro M. Apollonio, F.I., "La consacrazione a Maria," *Immaculata Mediatrix* I: 3 (2001) [Apollonio, *Cons*] 72-91.

[3] Discovered in 1917, a papyrus now kept in the John Rylands Library in Manchester, England, contains the text of this Marian prayer which makes it the oldest invocation of the Mother of God which has thus far been found. Cf. Gerard S. Sloyan, "Marian Prayers" in Juniper B. Carol, O.F.M. (ed.) *Mariology* Vol. 3 (Milwaukee: The Bruce Publishing Co., 1961) 64-68; I. Calabuig, O.S.M., "Liturgia" in Stefano De Fiores and Salvatore Meo (eds.) *Nuovo Dizionario di Mariologia* (Cinisello Balsamo: Edizioni Paoline, 1985) [= *NDM*] 778-779; Théodore Koehler, S.M., "Maternité Spirituelle, Maternité Mystique," in Hubert du Manoir (ed.), *Maria: Études sur la Sainte Vierge* Vol. VI (Paris: Beauchesne et Ses Files, 1961) [= *Maria*]; Gabriele Giamberardini, O.F.M., *Il culto mariano in Egitto*, Vol. I: *Secoli I-VI* (Jerusalem: Franciscan Printing Press, 1975) 69-97; Achille M. Triacca, "*Sub tuum praesidium*: nella *lex orandi* un'anticipata presenza della *lex*

prayer of Christians who know Mary's motherly mercy (*eusplangchnía* in the Greek text) and therefore do not hesitate to have recourse to her protection (*praesidium* in the Latin text). If it does not speak of belonging to Mary, it is surely not far removed from this concept.

The late redoubtable Marian encyclopedist, Father Michael O'Carroll, C.S.Sp., renders this third- or, at the latest, fourth-century prayer according to the reconstruction of Father Gabriele Giamberardini, O.F.M.: "Under your mercy, we take refuge, Mother of God, do not reject our supplications in necessity. But deliver us from danger. [You] alone chaste, alone blessed."[4] This Marian troparion used in almost all the rites of the Church and cited in *Lumen Gentium* 66 is ordinarily rendered into English after the Latin version: "We fly to thy patronage, O holy Mother of God, despise not our petitions in our necessities, but deliver us from all danger, O ever glorious and Blessed Virgin."[5] Mother Maria Francesca Perillo, F.I., on the basis of her recent study on the philology and doctrinal contents of the prayer, translates: "We take refuge in your womb, Holy Mother of God; do not refuse our pleas in our need, but save us from danger, O incomparable Virgin, divinely pure and blessed."[6]

This ancient Marian invocation is of capital importance from many perspectives. First, it constitutes a remarkable witness to the fact that prayer was already explicitly addressed to Mary as *Theotókos*, or "Mother of God," long before the Council of Ephesus which vindicated the use of this title in 431. Secondly, it may well reflect a tradition even older than the third century, the era from which many scholars believe the Egyptian papyrus dates, going all the way back to the apostolic period. Thirdly, while this antiphon (called a "troparion" according to Byzantine

---

credendi. La teotocologia precede la mariologia?" in *La mariologia nella catechesi dei Padri (età prenicena)*, ed. Sergio Felici (Rome: Libreria Ateneo Salesiano "Biblioteca di Scienza Religiosa" no. 88, 1989) 183-205; R. Iacoangeli, "*Sub tuum praesidium*. La più antica preghiera mariana: filologia e fede," *ibid.* 207-40; Mother M. Francesca Perillo, F.I., "*Sub Tuum Praesidium*: Incomparable Marian Praeconium" in *Mary at the Foot of the Cross – IV: Acts of the Fourth International Symposium on Marian Coredemption* (New Bedford, MA: Academy of the Immaculate, 2004) [= Perillo] 138-169.

[4] Michael O'Carroll, C.S.Sp., *Theotokos: A Theological Encyclopedia of the Blessed Virgin Mary* (Wilmington, DE: Michael Glazier; Dublin: Dominican Publications, 1982) [= *Theotokos*] 336.

[5] *Theotokos* 336.

[6] Perillo 168.

liturgical usage) does not explicitly call Mary "our Mother," it does so in equivalent and very expressive terms.

About this justly famous and most ancient of Marian prayers Father Quéméneur makes this careful observation:

> Here we do not yet have a consecration properly so called, but we already discern the fundamental elements that characterize Marian consecrations. The *Sub tuum* recognizes the patronage of the Mother of God; it is a spontaneous gesture of recourse to Mary. Originating in Egypt, the *Sub tuum*, with slight variations, will soon be taken up by the other churches; starting with the sixth century, it is inserted into the Byzantine, Ambrosian, and Roman liturgies. We can say that it is the root from which the formulas of other Marian prayers will arise.[7]

Significantly, and very conscious that he was standing in the most ancient stream of the Church's Tradition, John Paul II framed the first part of his great acts of consecration and entrustment of the world to the Immaculate Heart of Mary in 1982 and 1984 with the words of this antiphon: "We have recourse to your protection, holy Mother of God."[8] There are numerous other instances of his quotation of this most ancient Marian prayer.[9]

Father O'Carroll informs us that his confrère, the late Father Henri Barré, C.S.Sp., found evidence for the title *servus Mariae* in African sermons from the fifth and sixth centuries which indicate a personal attitude of belonging to Mary.[10] Father Stefano De Fiores, S.M.M., also points to the use of this term in St. Ephrem the Syrian (+373) and Pope John VII (+707), but indicates that these instances cannot compare with

---

[7] M. Quéméneur, S.M.M., "Towards a History of Marian Consecration," trans. Bro. William Fackovec, S.M., *Marian Library Studies* 122 (March 1966) 4. (This excellent article originally appeared as "La consécration de soi à la Vierge à travers l'histoire," *Cahiers Marials* no. 14 [1959] 119-128.

[8] *Insegnamenti di Giovanni Paolo II* [= *Inseg*] V/2 (1982) 1586, 1587 [*L'Osservatore Romano*, weekly edition in English (= *ORE*). First number = cumulative edition number; second number = page] 735:5, 12; *Inseg* VII/1 (1984) 774, 775 [*ORE* 828:9, 10].

[9] Cf. *Totus Tuus* 44-45.

[10] *Theotokos* 107.

the consistent usage and fervor of St. Ildephonsus of Toledo (+667).[11] Ildephonsus is usually considered the first major representative of the spirituality of "Marian slavery"[12] which eventually develops into what is now known as Marian consecration.[13]

Pope John Paul II himself, in his homily in Saragossa on November 6, 1982, immediately prior to the Entrustment of Spain to Our Lady, reviewed what is for us the most relevant information about this Benedictine Abbot who became the archbishop of Toledo:

> St. Ildephonsus of Toledo, the most ancient witness of that form of devotion which we call slavery to Mary, justifies our attitude of being slaves of Mary because of the singular relation she has with respect to Christ. "For this reason I am your slave, because your Son is my Lord. Therefore you are my Lady because you are the slave of my Lord. Therefore, I am the slave of the slave of my Lord, because you have been made the Mother of my Lord. Therefore I have been made a slave because you have been made the Mother of my Maker" [*De virginitate perpetua Sanctæ Mariæ*, 12: *PL* 96, 108].
>
> As is obvious, because of these real and existing relationships between Christ and Mary, Marian devotion has Christ as its ultimate object. The same St. Ildephonsus saw it with full clarity: "So in this way one refers to the Lord that which serves his slave. So, what is delivered up to the Mother redounds to the Son; thus passes to the King the honor that is rendered in the service of the Queen" [c. 12: *PL* 96, 108]. Then one understands the double employment of the desire expressed in the same blessed formula, speaking with the most Holy Virgin:

---

[11] Stefano de Fiores, "Consacrazione" in *NDM* 400. In the case of Pope John VII one might profitably consult the testimony presented by Gabriele M. Roschini, O.S.M., *Maria Santissima nella Storia della Salvezza* Vol. IV (Isola del Liri: Tipografia Editrice M. Pisani, 1969) 97-98.

[12] Cf. the excellent study by Théodore Koehler, S.M., in *Dictionnaire de Spiritualité Ascétique et Mystique* [= *DSp*] 14:730-745.

[13] Cf. Patrick J. Gaffney, S.M.M., "The Holy Slavery of Love," in Juniper B. Carol, O.F.M. (ed.), *Mariology* 3:143-146; Roschini, *Maria Santissima nella Storia della Salvezza* IV:85-86.

> "Grant that I may surrender myself to God and to you, to be the slave of your Son and of you, to serve your Lord and you" [c. 12: *PL* 96, 105].[14]

The next major witness to the development of the tradition is the great Doctor of the Church St. John of Damascus (+c.750). The last of the great Eastern Fathers of the Church interprets the name of Mary, according to Syriac etymology, to mean "lady" or "mistress." In his *Exposition of the Orthodox Faith* he says of Mary: "Truly she has become the Lady ruler of every creature since she is the Mother of the Creator."[15] In his first homily on the Dormition of the Mother of God he consequently prays:

> We are present before you, O Lady [*Despoina*], Lady I say and again Lady, binding our souls to our hope in you, and as to a most secure and firm anchor [cf. Heb. 6:9], *to you we consecrate* [*anathémenoi*] *our minds, our souls, our bodies* [cf. 1 Thess 5:23], *in a word, our very selves*, honoring you with psalms, hymns and spiritual canticles [cf. Eph. 5:19], insofar as we are able—even though it is impossible to do so worthily. If truly, as the sacred word has taught us, the honor paid to our fellow servants testifies to our good will towards our common Master, how could we neglect honoring you who have brought forth your Master? ... In this way we can better show our attachment to our Master.
>
> Turn your gaze on us, noble Lady, Mother of the good Master, rule over and direct at your discretion all that concerns us; restrain the impulses of our shameful passions; guide us to the tranquil harbor of the divine will; make us worthy of future blessedness, of the beatific vision in the presence of the Word of God who was made flesh in you.[16]

---

14 *Inseg* V/3 (1982) 1179-1180 [trans. by Debra Duncan].
15 Cited in Valentine Albert Mitchell, S.M., *The Mariology of Saint John Damascene* (Kirkwood, MO: Maryhurst Normal Press, 1930) 76; cf. also 214.
16 *Patroligia Graeca* 96, 720C-D, 721A-B; *Sources Chrétiennes* 80, 118 (my trans. made with reference to *Theotokos* 199 and Georges Gharib et al (ed.), *Testi Mariani del*

One notes how in language which is redolent with scriptural overtones St. John makes the total gift of himself and those who are joined with him, of all that they have and are, to Our Lady. He deliberately used the Greek term *anathémenoi* in order to indicate that "consecration" means "setting aside for sacred use." What is literally signified, according to the use of this word in Leviticus 27:28 and in other places in the Old Testament, is that this "giving of oneself to Mary" is so exclusive, absolute and permanent that one who would revoke the gift would be "cut off" (i.e. *anathema*) from God and his people. In analyzing this text, Father José María Canal, C.M.F., makes three major points: 1) Damascene's deliberate use of the term "consecration" which pertains to setting aside for sacred use; 2) the comprehensiveness of this act which excludes nothing; and 3) its basis in Mary's unique relationship to her divine Son by virtue of the divine maternity.[17]

Medieval Period

In the feudal setting of the early Middle Ages we find the custom of "patronage" (*patrocinium*) becoming widespread. In order to protect their lives and possessions, freemen would vow themselves to the service of their overlords; in exchange for the assurance of protection and the necessities of life, the client would place himself completely at the disposal of his protector. Here is a description of a traditional ceremony by which a vassal would put himself under the patronage and at the service of a suzerain, by the well-known liturgical scholar, Josef Jungmann, S.J.:

> He put his hands in the enfolding hands of the master, just as is done today by the newly ordained priest when he promises honor and obedience to his bishop at the end of the ordination Mass. The act is also called commendation: *se commendare, se tradere, in manus* or *manibus se commendare (tradere)*, and also *patricinio se commendare (tradere)*. From the

---

Primo Millennio Vol. 2: *Padri e altri autori bizantini* (Rome: Città Nuova Editrice, 1989) 519-520); my emphasis.

[17] P. José María Canal, C.M.F., "La Consagración a la Virgen y a Su Corazon Inmaculado," *Virgo Immaculata Acta Congressus Mariologici-Mariani Romae anno MCMLIV* (Rome: Pontificia Academia Mariana Internationalis, 1956) XII:234-235.

side of the overlord there was the corresponding *suscipere, recipere, manus suscipere* and the like.[18]

Not surprisingly, in those ages of faith this relationship of vassalage would provide a way of describing one's relationship to Mary. If Jesus is one's Lord, as we have already seen St. John of Damascus reason, then it is only logical that Mary becomes one's Lady. Fulbert of Chartres (+1028) provides us with a beautiful prayer in which he underscores that his consecration to Christ in baptism also makes of him another "beloved disciple" (cf. Jn 19:26-27) "committed" to Mary:

> Remember, O Lady, that in baptism I was consecrated to the Lord and professed the Christian name with my lips. Unfortunately I have not observed what I have promised. Nevertheless I have been handed over [*traditus*] to you and committed to your care [*commendatus*] by the Lord, the living and true God. Watch over the one who has been handed over to you [*traditum*]; keep safe the one who has been committed to your protection [*commendatum*].[19]

Likewise, a freeman who was in debt or otherwise not prospering in his affairs might present himself to an overlord "a rope around his neck, a sign that [he] was to become a serf, engaging his person, his family and his goods."[20] This, too, could be transferred into the spiritual realm and appropriated to one's relationship to Our Lady as we see in the case of St. Odilo, abbot of Cluny (+1049) who as a young man consecrated himself to Our Lady by going to a church dedicated to her and presenting himself at her altar with a rope around his neck and praying:

> O most loving Virgin and Mother of the Savior of all ages, from this day and hereafter take me into your service and in all my affairs be ever at my side as a most merciful advocate. For after God I place nothing in any way before you and I give myself over to you forever as

---

[18] J.A. Jungmann, S.J., *Pastoral Liturgy* (NY: Herder and Herder, 1962) 298.
[19] Henri Barré, C.S.Sp., *Prières Anciennes de l'Occident à la Mère du Sauveur: Des origines à saint Anselme* (Paris: Lethielleux,, 1963) 159 (my trans.).
[20] Quéméneur 6.

your own slave and bondsman [*tanquam proprium servum, tuo mancipatui trado*].[21]

Another beautiful image of the *patrocinium* of the Virgin is that of her "protective mantle," or *Schutzmantel* as it became known in German. In the Christian East the same image of the Virgin's "protective mantle" is manifested in a slightly different iconographical style in the feast and image of the *Pokrov*.[22] Here is Jungmann's description of the Marian iconography which would become classical in the medieval West:

> The emblem of Cîteaux was the image of the Mother of God with the abbots and abbesses of the order kneeling under her mantle. Caesarius of Heisterbach (+1240) also knew this motif as he shows in his description of a Cistercian monk in heaven, looking about in vain for his brothers until Mary opens out her wide mantle and discloses a countless number of brothers and nuns. In the later Middle Ages especially, the motif of the protective mantle is widespread, commonly as an expression of protection being sought or hoped for, chiefly in connection with the image of the Mother of God.[23]

Arnold Bostius (+1499), a Flemish Carmelite, wrote explicitly about Mary's patronage and protection of his order in his major Marian work, *De Patronatu et Patrocinio Beatissimae Virginis Mariae in Dicatum sibi Carmeli Ordinem*. Although he did not use the word "consecration" to describe the Carmelite's relationship to Mary because that meaning had not yet been appropriated to the word, he used all the equivalent Latin expressions such as *dicare, dedicare, devovere, sub qua vivere*, etc.,[24] and he maintained, as Pope Pius XII would in his letter, *Neminem Profecto* of

---

[21] Barré, *Prières Anciennes*, 147 (my trans).
[22] Cf. S. Salaville, A.A., "Marie dans la Liturgie Byzantine ou Gréco-Slave," in *Maria* I:280; cf. also Quéméneur 4 and *Redemptoris Mater* 33.
[23] Jungmann 300; cf. also *Theotokos* 93-94.
[24] I. Bengoechea, O.C.D., "Un precursor de la consagración a María en el siglo XV: Arnoldo Bostio (1445-1499)," *Estudios Marianos* 51 (1986) 218; cf. also Redemptus M. Valabek, O.Carm., *Mary, Mother of Carmel: Our Lady and the Saints of Carmel*, Vol. I (Rome: Institutum Carmelitanum, 1987) 74.

February 11, 1950,[25] that the wearing of the Carmelite scapular was an explicit sign of the acceptance of Mary's patronage and protection, of the Carmelite's belonging to her.[26] In continuity with his predecessor, Pope John Paul II took up the same theme in his message to the prior general of Carmelites of the Ancient Observance and the superior general of the Discalced Carmelites on the 750th anniversary of the scapular of Our Lady of Mount Carmel, stating that "the most genuine form of devotion to the Blessed Virgin, expressed by the humble sign of the scapular, is consecration to her Immaculate Heart."[27]

Modern Period

This heritage of the *patrocinium* of Mary would find expression in the Marian Congregations (sodalities) established by the Belgian Jesuit Jean Leunis in 1563 for the students of the Collegio Romano.[28] The admission to the congregation, which had as its aim the formation of militant Christians after the ideals of St. Ignatius Loyola and which was placed under the patronage of Our Lady, soon became an act of oblation to the Virgin. The text of one of these early admission ceremonies by Father Franz Coster (+1619) was published in the *Libellus sodalitatis* in 1586 and is most likely the very formula which he first used to receive students into the congregation which he had founded at Cologne, Germany, in 1576. In it the sodalist chooses Mary as "Lady, Patroness and Advocate" and begs her to receive him as her *servum perpetuum*.[29] Father Quéméneur underscores the fact that the Marian Congregations introduce yet another perspective into the question of Marian consecration which is inherited from the late Middle Ages: the corporate dimension.[30]

In 1622, the Marian Congregation admission formulae of the Italian Jesuit Pietro Antonio Spinelli as well as that of Father Coster were published in the book *Hortulus Marianus* of Father La Croix. The two formulae are described respectively as *modus consecrandi* and *modus vovendi* to the Blessed Virgin. Jungmann comments that this is the first

---

[25] *Acta Apostolicæ Sedis* [= *AAS*] 42 (1950) 390-391; *Our Lady: Papal Teachings* (Boston: St. Paul Editions, 1961) [= *OL*] 452-454.
[26] Bengoechea 224-225; Valabek 76.
[27] *Inseg* XXIV/1 (2001) 600 [*ORE* 1687:5].
[28] Cf. E. Villaret, S.J., "Marie et la Compagnie de Jésus" in *Maria* 2:962-968.
[29] Jungmann 303.
[30] Quéméneur 8.

appearance of the word *consecrare* (to consecrate) with the meaning of putting oneself under the *patrocinium* of Mary and it is taken as being synonymous with the word *devovere* which in classical Latin meant to devote oneself to a deity.[31] In effect, the understanding from the beginning of this usage has been that by the act of consecration to Our Lady the sodalist places himself at the service of Christ the King through her mediation and under her patronage.[32] The use of the term "consecration," with the meaning of giving oneself completely to Mary in order to belong more perfectly to Christ, enters into the common Catholic lexicon from this period and has continued to be used in this sense by the popes of the past hundred years.

During virtually the same period of time that the Jesuit Marian Congregations were developing, confraternities of the Holy Slavery of Mary were germinating in the soil of Spain. In fact, the earliest of these, founded under the inspiration of Sister Agnes of St. Paul at the convent of the Franciscan Conceptionists at Alcalá de Henares, dates from August 2, 1595,[33] and thus antedates the foundation of the sodality movement. The first theologian of this "Marian slavery" as it was practiced in Alcalá was the Franciscan Melchor de Cetina "who composed in 1618 what may be called the first 'Handbook of Spirituality' for the members of the confraternity."[34]

As the seventeenth century progressed, the confraternities multiplied and papal approval followed. One of the great promoters and proponents of this spirituality was the Trinitarian, St. Simon de Rojas (+1624),[35] who was canonized by Pope John Paul II on July 3, 1988. The Augustinian Bartolomé de los Rios (+1652)[36] extended the work of his friend de Rojas

---

[31] Jungmann 304.
[32] Villaret 968.
[33] Gaffney 146; Canal 250 and especially J. Ordoñez Marquez, "La Cofradía de la Esclavitud en las Concepcionistas de Alcalá," *Estudios Marianos* 51 (1986) 231-248.
[34] Gaffney 146; Canal 252-53; Gaspar Calvo Moralejo, O.F.M., "Fray Melchor de Cetina, O.F.M., el primer teólogo de la 'Esclavitud Mariana' (1618)," *Estudios Marianos* 51 (1986) 249-271; Juan de los Angeles – Melchior de Cetina, *Esortazione alla devozione della Vergine Madre di Dio: Alle origini della "schiavitù mariana"* Introduzione, traduzione e note di Stefano Cecchin, O.F.M., (Vatican City: Pontificia Academia Mariana Internationalis, 2003).
[35] Cf. Juan Pujana, "Simón de Rojas," *DSp* 14:877-884; Gaffney 147; Canal 253-254.
[36] Cf. Quirino Fernandez, "Los Rios y Alarcón (Bartolomé de)" *DSp* 9:1013-1018.

into the Low Countries and propagated it by means of his writings, which were known and cited by St. Louis de Montfort.[37]

Perhaps the single most important figure to emerge thus far in our brief consideration of the forms of Marian consecration in the spiritual journey of the Church is Cardinal Pierre de Bérulle (+1629). Founder of the Oratory of Jesus and promoter of the Teresian reform of Carmel in France, his greatest glory in terms of the history of spirituality is probably one of which he was never conscious, that of being the "founder of the French School" of spirituality. His spiritual paternity would enrich the Church through St. John Eudes and the Ven. Jean-Jacques Olier, Sts. Louis-Marie Grignion de Montfort and Jean-Baptiste de la Salle. His disciples of even the second and third generations would continue to develop his doctrine with their own refinements and emphases. The depth of thought and the ponderousness of his style rendered him somewhat inaccessible so that often his immediate followers such as Olier and Eudes presented the fruits of his contemplation in ways which were much more appealing,[38] but there can be no doubt that he was "le chef d'école."

Of specific interest to us is that while visiting Spain in 1604 Bérulle, who had been a member of the Marian Congregation in his days in the Jesuit College of Clermont, came into contact with the confraternities of the Slaves of the Virgin and in particular with that of Alcalá de Henares, where he went to see the general of the Carmelites.[39] This exposure would seem to have had a notable influence on the development of his own spirituality, for he would eventually formulate a "vow of servitude" to the Virgin Mary because of his conviction that in the divine design God wished to include in the vocation and predestination of Jesus Christ his divine filiation as well as the divine maternity.[40] Hence Mary, the

---

[37] TD 160; Gaffney 255-259.

[38] Raymond Deville, P.S.S., *L'école française de spiritualité*, n. 11 de la "Bibliothèque d'Histoire du Christianisme" (Paris: Desclée, 1987) 29.

[39] A. Molien, "Bérulle," *DSp* 1:1547.

[40] *Opuscule de piété*, 93, 1103 quoted in Paul Cochois, *Bérulle et l'École française*, n. 31 de "Maîtres Spirituels" (Paris: Editions du Seuil, 1963) 105. Cf. also William M. Thompson (ed.), *Bérulle and the French School: Selected Writings* (NY: Paulist Press, 1989) 14-16; 41-50; Théodore Koehler, S.M., "Servitude (saint esclavage)," *DSp* 14:738-741.

first to have made the vow of servitude to Jesus, "pure capacity for Jesus filled with Jesus,"[41] relates one perfectly to him. Here are his words:

> To the perpetual honor of the Mother and the Son, I wish to be in the state and quality of servitude with regard to her who has the state and quality of the Mother of my God. ... I give myself to her in the quality of a slave in honor of the gift which the eternal Word made of himself to her in the quality of Son.[42]

We have already indicated a number of Bérulle's illustrious disciples, but surely the greatest of them all was St. Louis-Marie Grignion de Montfort, described as "the last of the great Bérullians."[43] According to François-Marie Léthel, O.C.D.:

> All of his teaching is marked by the powerful Christocentrism of the French School, with the same insistence on the mystery of the Incarnation and on the place of Mary in this mystery. But in receiving this precious talent, he makes it fruitful in a way that is personal and original. Above all, he renders accessible to all, especially the poorest and the smallest, the doctrine which Bérulle had formulated in a very theological manner, but in difficult language.[44]

While Bérulle had already indicated the link between baptism and his "vow of servitude to Jesus," de Montfort would associate Mary with one's baptismal commitment as well. What he proposes in his classic

---

[41] Quoted in Cochois 105.
[42] *Theotokos* 80.
[43] Henri Brémond, *Histoire littéraire du sentiment religieux en France*, IX, (Paris: Librairie Bloud et Gay, 1932) 272. This appellation is also cited in Deville 139.
[44] Louis-Marie Grignion de Montfort, *L'Amour de Jésus en Marie: Le Traité de la vraie dévotion, Le Secret de Marie,* Nouvelle édition établie et présentée par François-Marie Léthel, O.C.D., I: *Présentation Générale* (Geneva: Ad Solem, 2000) 23-24 (my trans.). Cf. also *Ibid.*, "La Maternité de Marie dans le mystère de l'Incarnation et de notre divinisation selon saint Louis-Marie Grignion de Montfort et le Cardinal de Bérulle" in François-Marie Léthel, O.C.D, *Théologie de l'Amour de Jésus: Écrits sur la théologie des saints* (Venasque: Éditions du Carmel, 1996) 105-138.

work, *True Devotion to the Blessed Virgin*, is a renewal of one's baptismal promises "through the hands of Mary":

> In holy baptism we do not give ourselves to Jesus explicitly through Mary, nor do we give him the value of our good actions. After baptism we remain entirely free either to apply that value to anyone we wish or keep it for ourselves. But by this consecration we give ourselves explicitly to Jesus through Mary's hands and we include in our consecration the value of all our actions.[45]

If Louis-Marie had written a special formula of consecration in conjunction with his treatise, *True Devotion*, it has not thus far come to light. This is because the first and last pages of the manuscript, only discovered in 1842, have never been found. The formula which he has left us in his earlier work, *The Love of Eternal Wisdom*, clearly highlights the fact that Jesus is the goal of the act of consecration which he proposes while Mary is its intermediary:

> Eternal and incarnate Wisdom, most lovable and adorable Jesus, true God and true man, only Son of the eternal Father and of Mary always Virgin, ... I dare no longer approach the holiness of your majesty on my own. That is why I turn to the intercession and the mercy of your holy Mother, whom you yourself have given me to mediate with you. Through her I hope to obtain from you contrition and pardon for my sins, and that Wisdom whom I desire to dwell in me always. ... O admirable Mother, present me to your dear Son as his slave now and for always, so that he who redeemed me through you, will now receive me through you.[46]

Thus, while de Montfort readily and very frequently speaks of "consecrating oneself to Mary," this must always be understood as a

---

[45] *TD* 126 (in *God Alone* 329).
[46] *Love of Eternal Wisdom* 223, 226 (in *God Alone* 112, 113). Léthel points out in *L'Amour de Jésus en Marie*, II: *Textes*, pp. 198-201, that in 66-69 of the *Secret of Mary* [= *SM*] three prayers addressed to Jesus, to the Holy Spirit and to Mary effectively constitute a renewal of this consecration.

shorthand form of "consecrating oneself to Jesus through the hands of Mary."[47] It is precisely in these terms that Pope John Paul II presented him as a proponent of authentic Marian spirituality in *Redemptoris Mater*.[48]

Further, that same Pope defended the whole tradition of Marian slavery of which de Montfort is a major exponent—and, as we have seen, is deeply embedded in the whole tradition—in a discourse to his brother Polish bishops on December 17, 1987:

> On May 3 of the year of the Millennium of the Baptism of Poland [1966] we were witnesses to the participants in the *Act of Consecration* proclaimed by Cardinal Stefan Wyszyński at Jasna Góra. The title of the act stimulated reflection, and at the same time it gave rise to certain objections, even protests. Can one speak of giving oneself "as a slave," even if it is only a question of a "maternal slavery" and the act in question concerns the Mother of God and Queen of Poland?
>
> One could say that the Act of Jasna Góra *is itself rooted in the history* of that *"great paradox"* whose first setting is the Gospel itself. Here it is a question not only of verbal paradoxes, but of ontological ones as well. The most profound paradox is perhaps that of life and death, expressed, among other places, in the parable of the seed which must die in order to produce new life. This paradox is definitively confirmed by the Paschal Mystery.
>
> The tradition of a "holy slavery"—that is of a *"maternal slavery"* which is a "slavery of love"—has grown up on the same soil, and has been passed on by certain figures in the history of Christian spirituality. Suffice it to mention St. Louis de Montfort and our own St. Maximilian. Of course, the primate of the millennium inherited this tradition of Marian spirituality in part from his predecessor in the primatial see as well. It is known that

---

[47] Cf. Reginald Garrigou-Lagrange, O.P., *The Mother of the Saviour and Our Interior Life* trans. by Bernard J. Kelley, C.S.Sp., (St. Louis: B. Herder Book, Co., 1957) 256, note 19.
[48] *Redemptoris Mater* 48.

Cardinal Hlond died with these words on his lips: "*Victory, if it comes, will be victory through Mary.*"

Thus it is that "maternal slavery" must reveal itself as the path towards victory, the price of freedom. For that matter, it is difficult to imagine any being less inclined to "enslave" than a mother, than the Mother of God. And if what we are speaking of is an "enslaving" through love, then from that perspective "slavery" constitutes precisely *the revelation of the fullness of freedom*. In fact, freedom attains its true meaning, that is, its own fullness, through a true good. Love is synonymous with that attainment. ...

If we are speaking of the *act of consecration* itself "in maternal slavery" to the Mother of God, it is certainly, like every expression of her authentic cult, *profoundly Christocentric*. It introduces us into the whole mystery of Christ. Furthermore, we have a solid basis for affirming that the experiences of our country (which in a certain sense culminate in the *Act of Consecration* proclaimed at Jasna Góra) are also *very close* to the *Mariology* which found expression in *Lumen Gentium*: The Mother of God "present in the mystery of Christ and of the Church."[49]

Although there continue to be those who call into question and criticize the terminology of "maternal slavery,"[50] as John Paul II acknowledged, it remains one of those Gospel paradoxes which reflects

---

[49] *Inseg* X/3 (1987) 1435-1437 [*ORE* 1022:11].

[50] Here, for example, is the critique of E. Schillebeeckx, O.P.: "Let us take one example of antiquated terminology in this context, the phrase 'slave of Mary.' It is quite obvious, both from the cultural and from the *religious* point of view, that this term cannot hope to make a favorable impact or produce the right effect nowadays. In the past this phrase may well have concealed a deep religious reality. Today it is absolutely unacceptable, and its use can only lead to total misunderstanding. The reader should not impute pride to this condemnation—the very opposite is true. It is simply that the present-day Christian is incapable of embodying in his life the idea of total loving surrender if this is presented to him in the form of 'loving slavery.' The greatest tribute which could be paid to St. Louis Grignion de Montfort would be to free his profound vision from its now out-of-date terminology, which today hinders rather than promotes devotion to the Blessed Virgin." *Mary Mother of the Redemption* trans. by N.D. Smith (NY: Sheed and Ward, 1964) 139.

the fact that the Son of God himself took on the "form of a slave" (Phil. 2:7) and that his followers glory in being "slaves of Christ" (cf. 1 Cor. 7:22; Col. 1:7, 4:7). In recent years Fathers François-Marie Léthel, O.C.D., and Étienne Richer of the Community of the Beatitudes have offered extended reflections on its perennial validity.[51]

While it is only right to recognize de Montfort's teaching as the highpoint of the Marian consecration championed by the "French School," it would be unfair to consider the subsequent history of this phenomenon in the life of the Church simply in terms of denouement. The unfolding of this process continued even in that difficult period after the French Revolution with holy founders such as Bl. William Joseph Chaminade (+1850), who incorporated total consecration to Mary into the Society of Mary which he founded as the object of a special perpetual religious vow.[52] The specific influence of de Montfort has been experienced, deepened according to the particular gifts of each and spread directly or indirectly by many other holy persons in the nineteenth and twentieth centuries. Among these are the Ven. Mother Mary Potter (+1913), the Servant of God Frank Duff (+1980), Bl. Edouard Poppe (+1924), Bl. Dina Bélanger (+1929) and the Servant of God Marthe Robin (+1981).

I believe, however, that in terms of the extent of the influence of de Montfort on his life and teaching and his subsequent diffusion of that teaching in his own unique way no twentieth-century figure can equal the Servant of God Pope John Paul II. He testified to that influence on his formation on many occasions.[53] I am convinced that

---

[51] Cf. François-Marie Léthel, O.C.D., "La Maternité de Marie dans le mystère de l'Incarnation et de notre divinisation selon saint Louis-Marie Grignion de Montfort et le Cardinal de Bérulle" in François-Marie Léthel, O.C.D, *Théologie de l'Amour de Jésus: Écrits sur la théologie des saints* (Venasque: Éditions du Carmel, 1996) 127-133; Ibid., *L'Amour de Jésus en Marie*, I: *Présentation Générale* I:81-119; Étienne Richer, *La pédagogie de sainteté de saint Louis-Marie de Montfort* (Paris: Pierre Téqui, éditeur, 2003) 179-188; Ibid., *Suivre Jésus avec Marie: Un secret de sainteté de Grignion de Montfort à Jean-Paul II* (Nouan-le-Fuzelier: Éditions des Béatitudes, 2006) 267-281.

[52] Cf. Henri Lebon, S.M., "Chaminade (Guillaume-Joseph)," *DSp* 2:454-59; Peter A. Resch, S.M., "Filial Piety" in *Mariology* 3:162-167.

[53] Cf. Alberto Rum, S.M.M., "Montfort e Giovanni Paolo II: Due Testimoni e Maestri di Spiritualità Mariana," *Fragmenta Monfortana 3* (Rome: Edizioni Monfortane, 1999) 107-142; Ibid., "Giovanni Paolo II" in *Dizionario di Spiritualità*

his Marian Magisterium is his greatest single legacy to the Church and that he has not only consolidated the teaching of his predecessors on Marian consecration, but has raised it to a new level by making it such a fundamental feature of his Ordinary Magisterium.

It should also be noted that there are other approaches to Marian consecration which have come into existence in modern times which are not a direct result of the influence of great saint of Montfort-la-Cane. These are surely not in conflict with de Montfort's; they simply have had their genesis under different circumstances and are a beautiful example of how the Holy Spirit draws unity out of diversity. It seems that St. Maximilian Maria Kolbe discovered de Montfort's *True Devotion* only after he had been led to the necessity of Marian consecration through his immersion in the great Franciscan Marian tradition.[54] Maximilian, who was familiar with de Montfort and saw the movement which he founded as a means of fulfilling his prophecy on the latter times,[55] was also conscious of standing in the great tradition of Marian slavery. Although he did not employ the word with the frequency of de Montfort, he leaves no doubt about its implications in the following text:

> You belong to her as her own property. Let her do with you what she wishes. Do not let her feel herself bound by any restrictions following from the obligations a mother has towards her own son. Be hers, her property; let her make free use of you and dispose of you without any limits, for whatever purpose she wishes.
>
> Let her be your owner, your Lady and absolute Queen. A servant sells his labor; you, on the contrary,

---

Monfortana (Rome: Edizioni Monfortane, 2005) 798-816; André Frossard, *"Be Not Afraid!"* trans. by J.R. Foster (NY: St. Martin's Press, 1984) 125-127; Pope John Paul II, *Crossing the Threshold of Hope* edited by Vittorio Messori and trans. by Jenny and Martha McPhee (London: Jonathan Cape, 1994) 212-215; Ibid., *Gift and Mystery: On the 50th Anniversary of My Priestly Ordination* (Vatican City: Libreria Editrice Vaticana, 1996) 41-43.

[54] Cf. Alessandro Maria Apollonio, F.I., *Mariologia Francescana: Da san Francesco d'Assisi ai Francescani dell'Immacolata*. Dissertationes ad Lauream in Pontificia Facultate Theologica «Marianum» 71, Estratto (Rome, 1997) [= Apollonio, *MF*].

[55] Cf. *TD* 35, 46-59; *Scritti di Massimiliano Kolbe* (Rome: Editrice Nazionale Milizia dell'Immacolata, 1997) 1129 [Anselm W. Romb, O.F.M. Conv., *The Kolbe Reader* (Libertyville, IL: Franciscan Marytown Press, 1987) 36-39].

offer yours as a gift: your fatigue, your suffering, all that is yours. Beg her not to pay attention to your free will, but to act towards you always and in full liberty as she desires.

Be her son, her servant, her slave of love, in every way and under whatever formulation yet devised or which can be devised now or in the future. In a word, be all hers.

Be her soldier so that others may become ever more perfectly hers, like you yourself, and even more than you; so that all those who live and will live all over the world may work together with her in her struggle against the infernal serpent.

Belong to the Immaculate so that your conscience, becoming ever purer, may be purified still more, become immaculate as she is for Jesus, so that you too may become a mother and conqueror of hearts for her.[56]

Standing in the great tradition which we have been sketching, Maximilian brings a note of urgency about the battle, Mary's "struggle against the infernal serpent" (cf. Gen. 3:15) and, hence, the all-consuming goal of his life was to mobilize an army, a militia completely at her disposal. This is clearly illustrated in the official Act of Consecration for the Militia Immaculatae:

> O Immaculata, Queen of heaven and earth, refuge of sinners and our most loving Mother, God has willed to entrust the entire order of mercy to you. I, N ... a repentant sinner, cast myself at your feet humbly imploring you to take me with all that I am and have, wholly to yourself as your possession and property. Please make of me, of all my powers of soul and body, of my whole life, death and eternity, whatever most pleases you.
>
> If it pleases you, use all that I am and have without reserve, wholly to accomplish what was said of you: "She will crush your head," and, "You alone have destroyed all heresies in the whole world." Let me be a fit instrument in your immaculate and merciful hands for introducing and increasing your glory to the maximum in all the

---

[56] *Scritti* 1334 [Romb 194].

many strayed and indifferent souls, and thus help extend as far as possible the blessed kingdom of the most Sacred Heart of Jesus. For wherever you enter you obtain the grace of conversion and growth in holiness, since it is through your hands that all graces come to us from the most Sacred Heart of Jesus.[57]

Another twentieth century figure who developed an apostolic Marian movement based on total consecration to Our Lady was the Servant of God Joseph Kentenich (+1968). In the process of nurturing what eventually became the Schönstatt family, Father Kentenich formulated a beautiful approach to Marian consecration in richly biblical imagery as a "covenant of love":

> Through a solemn consecration, that is, *through a perfect mutual covenant of love*, we want to give ourselves to her [Mary] entirely and unreservedly for time and eternity, so that as a perfect covenant partner we may always stand in her presence and grow in holy two-in-oneness with her, and in her with the Triune God. ...
>
> The covenant of love not only gives us the right, but even makes it our duty to make proper use of our right to make claims of love on our covenant partner, and to use the power of petition which has been given to us. In other words, just as Our Lady makes claims on and expresses wishes to us, we in turn should do the same with her.[58]

The Papal Magisterium

If, as we have just seen, Pope John Paul II is the heir of the great ecclesial tradition of Marian consecration, manifested in various ways

---

[57] *Scritti* 37, 1331 [English version from Marytown, Libertyville, IL]. On the consecration proposed by St. Maximilian cf. Apollonio, *MF* 192-195; Peter Damian Fehlner, F.I., *St. Maximilian M. Kolbe, Martyr of Charity, Pneumatologist: His Theology of the Holy Spirit* (New Bedford, MA: Academy of the Immaculate, 2004) 143-145.

[58] Joseph Kentenich, *Schoenstatt's Covenant Spirituality* ed. and trans. Jonathan Niehaus (Waukesha, WI: Schoenstatt Fathers) 28, 57.

in the course of the Church's almost two millennia of history, he might be said to be even more explicitly the inheritor of the legacy of papal consecration to the Hearts of Jesus and Mary.[59] While space does not permit us to enter into this fascinating history here,[60] we wish to indicate the most important high points. On October 31, 1942, the Servant of God, Pope Pius XII, gave a radio broadcast to pilgrims at Fatima celebrating the Silver Jubilee of the last of the 1917 apparitions. Concluding the broadcast, he prayed:

> To you and to your Immaculate Heart, we, the common father of the vast Christian family, we, the vicar of him to whom was given "all power in heaven and on earth," and from whom we have received the care of so many souls redeemed by his blood; to you and to your Immaculate Heart in this tragic hour of human history, we commit, we entrust, we consecrate [*confiamos, entregamos, consagramos*], not only the Holy Church, the mystical body of your Jesus, which suffers and bleeds in so many places and is afflicted in so many ways, but also the entire world torn by violent discord, scorched in a fire of hate, victim of its own iniquities. ... Finally, just as the Church and the entire human race were consecrated to the Heart of your Jesus, because by placing in him every hope, it may be for them a token and pledge of victory and salvation; so, henceforth, may they be perpetually consecrated to you, to your Immaculate Heart [*assim desde hoje Vos sejam perpetuamente consagrados também a Vós e ao vosso Coração Imaculado*], O our Mother and Queen of the

---

[59] Cf. Arthur Burton Calkins, "The Cultus of the Hearts of Jesus and Mary in the Papal Magisterium from Pius IX to Pius XII" in *Acta Congressus Mariologici-Mariani Internationalis in Sanctuario Mariano Kevelaer (Germania) Anno 1987 Celebrati* II: *De Cultu Mariano Saeculis XIX et XX usque ad Concilium Vaticanum II Studia Indolis Generalioris* (Rome: Pontificia Academia Mariana Internationalis, 1991) 355-392; Ibid., "The Hearts of Jesus and Mary in the Magisterium of Pope John Paul II" *Acta Congressus Mariologici-Mariani Internationalis in Civitate Onubensi (Huelva – Hispania) Anno 1992 Celebrati* IV: *De Cultu Mariano Saeculo XX a Concilio Vaticano II usque ad Nostros Dies* (Vatican City: Pontificia Academia Mariana Internationalis, 1999) 147-167.

[60] Cf. *Totus Tuus* 75-98.

world, in order that your love and protection may hasten the triumph of the Kingdom of God.[61]

The act of consecration, originally made in Portuguese, was renewed in Italian in St. Peter's Basilica on the Feast of the Immaculate Conception, 1942. This was been referred to many times by Pope John Paul II, especially in his own major consecrations to the Immaculate Heart of Mary of May 13, 1982, and March 25, 1984.[62] Here it should be pointed out that, even though this first consecration of the world to the Immaculate Heart of Mary was carried out in conjunction with celebrations in Fatima, the fundamental impetus for this came not from Sister Lúcia (who had a particular mission calling for the consecration of Russia to the Immaculate Heart of Mary), but from Bl. Alexandrina da Costa (whose mission was to implore the consecration of the world to the Immaculate Heart of Mary).[63]

Another important pronouncement of Pius XII may be found in his address to the Jesuit Marian Congregations or Sodalities on January 21, 1945:

> Consecration to the Mother of God in the Marian Congregation is total gift of oneself, for life and for eternity; it is not just a mere matter of form nor a gift of mere sentiment, but it is an effective gift, fulfilled in an intensity of Christian and Marian life, in the apostolic life, making the member of the congregation a minister of Mary and, as it were, her hands visible on earth through the spontaneous flow of a superabundant interior

---

[61] *AAS* 34 (1942) 318-19, 324 25; *Our Lady: Papal* Teachings (Boston: St. Paul Editions, 1961] [= *OL*] 374, 380 [alt.]. Cf. *AAS* 34 (1942) 313 25 for the text of the radio message and the Act of Consecration in both Portuguese and Italian. For a commentary on this act, cf. *Totus Tuus* 99-102.

[62] December 8, 1981, *Inseg* IV/2 (1981) 869, 873 [*ORE* 714:2, 12]; May 13, 1982, *Inseg* V/2 (1982) 1574-75, 1586 [*ORE* 735:5]; May 19, 1982, *Inseg* V/2 (1982) 1759 [*Portugal: Message of Fatima* (Boston: St. Paul Editions, 1983) 200]; March 25, 1984, *Inseg* VII/1 (1984) 775 [*ORE* 828:9]; December 31, 1984, *Inseg* VII/2 (1984) 1684 [*ORE* 869:4]; September 22, 1986, *Inseg* IX/2 (1986) 699; October 16, 1988, *Inseg* XI/3 (1988) 1240 [*ORE* 161:1].

[63] Cf. *Totus Tuus* 96-98; Umberto M. Pasquale, S.D.B., *Messaggera di Gesù per la Consacrazione del Mondo al Cuore Immacolato* (Rome: Postulazione Casa Generalizia Salesiana, n.d.).

life which overflows in all the exterior works of deep devotion, of worship, of charity, of zeal.[64]

On November 21, 1964, at the end of the third session of the Second Vatican Council, when he solemnly declared Mary Mother of the Church, the Servant of God Pope Paul VI wished to commemorate the consecration of the world to the Immaculate Heart of Mary by Pius XII and prayed in these words:

> We commit [*committimus*] the human race, its difficulties and anxieties, its just aspirations and ardent hopes, to the protection of our heavenly Mother.
> O Virgin Mother of God, most august Mother of the Church, we commend [*commendamus*] the whole Church and the Ecumenical Council to you. ... We commend [*commendamus*] the whole human race to your Immaculate Heart, O Virgin Mother of God.[65]

A frequently overlooked reference to entrusting oneself to Our Lady is found in the Second Vatican Council's Decree on the Apostolate of the Laity: "Everyone should have a genuine devotion to her [Mary] and entrust his life to her motherly care" [*Hanc devotissime colant omnes suamque vitam atque apostolatum eius maternæ curæ commendent*].[66]

On May 13, 1967, Pope Paul VI issued his Apostolic Exhortation *Signum Magnum* to coincide with the fiftieth anniversary of the first apparition of Mary to the children of Fatima and his own pilgrimage to that shrine. Recalling the great act of consecration of Pius XII in 1942 and his own reaffirmation of it in 1964, he went on to make this appeal.

> So now we urge all members of the Church to consecrate [*consecrent*] themselves once again to the Immaculate Heart of Mary, to translate this pious act into concrete action in their daily lives. In this way they will comply ever more closely with God's will and as imitators

---

[64] *Discorsi e radiomessaggi di sua Santità Pio XII*, Vol. VI (Vatican City: Tipografia Poliglotta Vaticana, 1951) 281 [*OL* 389].

[65] *AAS* 56 (1964) 1017-18 [*The Pope Speaks* (= *TPS*) Vol. 10:140-141]. Cf. *Totus Tuus* 106-108.

[66] *Apostolicam Actuositatem* 4. Cf. *Totus Tuus* 73, 108.

of their heavenly Queen, they will truly be recognized as her offspring.[67]

Bringing with him to the papacy the great heritage of Polish Marian piety and the collective consecrations of Poland to Our Lady (in 1920, 1946, 1956, 1966, 1971, and 1976)[68] and his total appropriation of the spirituality of St. Louis-Marie de Montfort, the Servant of God Pope John Paul II promoted Marian consecration and entrustment as no other successor of St. Peter has ever done. Here I can only present a few highlights. His first solemn entrustment of the Church to Our Lady took place at the Basilica of St. Mary Major in Rome on December 8, 1978.[69]

The prototype of great acts of consecration/entrustment was that pronounced by previous recording for Pentecost Sunday, June 7, 1981,[70] in conjunction with the celebration of the 1600th anniversary of the First Council of Constantinople and the 1550th anniversary of the Council of Ephesus. The event itself had been planned well in advance by the Pope. The double observance had been the object of a Pontifical Letter, *A Concilio Constantinopolitano I*, addressed to the bishops of the world,[71] in which he spoke of Mary's divine maternity as establishing a "permanent link with the Church" (*perpetuum vinculum maternum cum Ecclesia*).[72] His more active participation in the festivities marking the observance of these two great councils and culminating on Pentecost Sunday, however, was precluded by an assassin's bullet. The circumstances of this act of entrustment to Mary which addresses her as "entrusted to the Holy Spirit more than any other human being" and "linked in a profound and maternal way to the Church"[73] are particularly poignant, then, and may also be reckoned as the plea of a stricken father on behalf of his family. The very same act was renewed again on the Feast of the Immaculate Conception in 1981 before the icon of the *Salus Populi Romani* in St. Mary Major's.[74]

---

[67] *AAS* 59 (1967) 475 [*TPS* 12:286].
[68] Cf. *Totus Tuus* 113 137.
[69] *Inseg* I (1978) 313-314 [*Talks of John Paul II* (Boston: St. Paul Editions, 1979) 423-424].
[70] *Inseg* IV/1 (1981) 1241-1247 [*ORE* 688:7, 10].
[71] *Inseg* IV/1 (1981) 815-828 [*ORE* 678:6-8].
[72] *Inseg* IV/1 (1981) 824 [*ORE* 678:7].
[73] *Inseg* IV/1 (1981) 1245 [*ORE* 688:10].
[74] *Inseg* IV/2 (1981) 876-879 [*ORE* 714:12].

The above cited act of entrustment became the archetype of two subsequent acts, closely modeled upon it, which gained considerably more public notice. The first of these was made on May 13, 1982, the Feast of Our Lady of Fatima, in that humble village in Portugal where Our Lady had first appeared 65 years earlier.[75] It was also the first anniversary of the near fatal attempt on his life. The second of the acts deriving from that of Pentecost Sunday, 1981, was given more advance publication and correspondingly more emphasis was placed on the collegial nature of the act. It was announced in a pontifical letter to all the bishops of the world dated from the Vatican on December 8, 1983, but only published on February 17, 1984.[76] It was intended to be one of the crowning acts of the Holy Year of the Redemption which began on March 25, 1983, and concluded on Easter Day, April 22, 1984. John Paul presented the rationale to his brother bishops in this way:

> In the context of the Holy Year of the Redemption, I desire to profess this [infinite salvific] power [of the redemption] together with you and with the whole Church. I desire to profess it through the Immaculate Heart of the Mother of God, who in a most particular degree experienced this salvific power. The words of the act of consecration and entrusting which I enclose, correspond, with a few small changes, to those which I pronounced at Fatima on May 13, 1982. I am profoundly convinced that the repetition of this act in the course of the Jubilee Year of the Redemption corresponds to the expectations of many human hearts, which wish to renew to the Virgin Mary the testimony of their devotion and to entrust to her their sorrows at the many different ills of the present time, their fears of the menaces that brood over the future, their preoccupations for peace and justice in the individual nations and in the whole world.
>
> The most fitting date for this common witness seems to be the Solemnity of the Annunciation of the Lord during Lent 1984. I would be grateful if on that day

---

[75] *Inseg* V/2 (1982) 1586-1590 [*ORE* 735:5, 12].
[76] *Inseg* VII/1 (1984) 416-418 [*ORE* 823:2].

> (March 24, on which the Marian Solemnity is liturgically anticipated, or on March 25, the Third Sunday of Lent) you would renew this act together with me, choosing the way which each of you considers most appropriate.[77]

The act itself was carried out by the Pope on Sunday March 25, 1984, in St. Peter's Square before the statue of Our Lady of Fatima which ordinarily occupies the site of Mary's appearances at the Cova da Iria in Fatima, Portugal, and which was especially flown to the Vatican for this occasion. The act of entrustment[78] was recited by the Pope after the Mass commemorating the Jubilee Day of Families. Already the Holy Father has referred to his program of entrustment in his address to the Roman Curia on the Vigil of the Feast of Sts. Peter and Paul in 1982:

> This year, in a special way, after the attempt on my life which by coincidence occurred on the anniversary of the apparition of the Virgin at Fatima, my conversation with Mary has been, I should like to say, uninterrupted. I have repeatedly entrusted to her the destiny of all peoples: beginning with the act of consecration of December 8, (1981), Feast of the Immaculate Conception, to the consecration to the Virgin of the countries visited: of Nigeria at Kaduna, of Equatorial Guinea at Bata, of Gabon at Libreville, of Argentina at the Sanctuary of Lujan. I remember the visits to the Italian sanctuaries of Our Lady of Montenero in Livorno, and of Our Lady of St. Luke in Bologna; culminating in the pilgrimage to Fatima in Portugal, "Land of St. Mary," which was a personal act of gratitude to Our Lady, almost the fulfillment of a tacit vow for the protection granted me through the Virgin,

---

[77] *Inseg* VII/1 (1984) 417-418 [*ORE* 823:2].

[78] *Inseg* VII/1 (1984) 774-77; *ORE* 828:9-10. The text is exactly the same as that earlier transmitted to all the bishops of the Church in *Inseg* VII/1 (1984) 418-21 [*ORE* 823:2, 12], with the exception that the Pope inserted between the two sentences of the last paragraph of number 2 these additional words when he recited it in St. Peter's Square: *Illumina specialmente i popoli di cui tu aspetti la nostra consacrazione e il nostro affidamento* "Enlighten especially the peoples whose consecration and entrustment by us you are awaiting." *Inseg* VII/1 (1984) 776 [*ORE* 828:10].

and a solemn act of consecration of the whole human race to the Mother of God, in union with the Church through my humble service.[79]

There was never any veering from the path of this "program of entrustment" from the beginning of the pontificate to its very conclusion.[80] Pope Benedict XVI has continued to follow in the footsteps of his venerated predecessor, most frequently using the term entrust. Here is one of his strongest exhortations to date. It occurred in his homily at the canonization of Frei Antônio de Sant'Ana Galvão at Campo de Marte, São Paulo, Brazil on May 11, 2007:

> In fact, the saint that we are celebrating gave himself irrevocably to the Mother of Jesus from his youth, desiring to belong to her forever and he chose the Virgin Mary to be the Mother and Protector of his spiritual daughters.
>
> My dearest friends, what a fine example Frei Galvão has left for us to follow! There is a phrase included in the formula of his consecration which sounds remarkably contemporary to us, who live in an age so full of hedonism: *"Take away my life before I offend your blessed Son, my Lord!"* They are strong words, the words of an impassioned soul, words that should be part of the normal life of every Christian, whether consecrated or not, and they enkindle a desire for fidelity to God in married couples as well as in the unmarried. The world needs transparent lives, clear souls, pure minds that refuse to be perceived as mere objects of pleasure. It is necessary to oppose those elements of the media that ridicule the sanctity of marriage and virginity before marriage.
>
> In our day, Our Lady has been given to us as the best defense against the evils that afflict modern life; Marian devotion is the sure guarantee of her maternal protection and safeguard in the hour of temptation. And what an

---

[79] *Inseg* V/1 (1982) 2442-2443 [*ORE* 744:6].
[80] My book *Totus Tuus* takes up the major documentation on this matter until 1991. I hope to conclude the documentation in the second enlarged edition.

unfailing support is this mysterious presence of the Virgin Most Pure, when we invoke the protection and the help of the *Senhora Aparecida*! Let us place in her most holy hands the lives of priests and consecrated laypersons, seminarians and all who are called to religious life.[81]

A Question of Terminology?

In recent years not a few Mariologists have taken the position that not only the terminology of Marian slavery—as we have seen above—but also the concept of Marian consecration itself is no longer acceptable.[82] The argument is that consecration pertains to God alone and depends on his sovereign initiative and that our part can only be one of response.[83] Further some argue that in a larger passive sense one cannot be consecrated to anyone but God.[84] These authors argue that Pope John Paul II fully accepted their perspective and so decided to use the words entrust and entrustment to describe our relationship with Mary, effectively avoiding the "defective and discredited formulas of the past."

In contrast, Father George Kosicki, C.S.B., has considered at some length the meaning of the Polish word most frequently used by John Paul II, translated into Italian as *"affidare"* and into English as "entrust." The word is *zawierzać*, the same word employed in Cardinal Wyszyński's various consecrations of Poland.[85] Let us allow Father Kosicki to share some of his discoveries about this word:

---

[81] *L'Osservatore Romano* [= OR] 24 maggio 2007, pp. VI-VII [ORE 1994:14].

[82] Thus René Laurentin wrote: "Our votive formulas of consecration to God need to recognize more clearly the place God has accorded to Mary. We need to ensure that our vocabularies and terminologies in this regard always rise above some of the ambiguous and discredited formulas of the past; these defective formulas have sometimes served to discredit the great modern spiritual movement of consecrations through Mary." René Laurentin, *The Meaning of Consecration Today: A Marian Model for a Secularized Age* trans. by Kenneth D. Whitehead (San Francisco: Ignatius Press, 1992) 165. Cf. my review of this book in *Divinitas* XXXVII (1993, fasc. III) 304-308.

[83] Cf. Stefano De Fiores, S.M.M., *Maria: Nuovissimo Dizionario*, Vol. 1 (Bologna: Centro editoriale dehoniano, 2006) 8.

[84] Cf. Laurentin, *The Meaning of Consecration Today* 98-99.

[85] George W. Kosicki, C.S.B., *Born of Mary: Testimonies, Teachings, Tensions* (Stockbridge, MA: Marian Press, 1985) 64.

I continued to wonder about the word "entrust" until I met a priest from Poland, a colleague of the present Pope while at the University of Lublin where Karol Wojtyła taught as bishop of Krakow. I asked him about the word "entrust" and its Polish meaning, mentioning that I was disappointed that he didn't use the word "consecrate" to Mary in his *Letter to All Priests* [of April 8, 1979].[86] His response was very clear and reassuring. He pointed out that the Polish word *"zawierzać"* (translated as "entrust") is a strong word and is used for what we call in English "consecration" to Mary. He went on to say that the Polish word which is the equivalent root word to the English "consecration" (viz. *"konsekracia"*) is usually reserved for the consecration at Mass. He went further to point out that the word "entrust" was a special word for John Paul II because of the way he has used it in his Polish writings. He added that the motto of John Paul, "Totus Tuus," (I am) all yours (Mary), means, "I consecrate myself to you, Mary" and is what Pope John Paul has in mind when he uses *"zawierzać"* (translated into English as "entrust"). In short the Polish "to entrust" means "to consecrate."[87]

I have studied the question of consecration to Our Lady vis-à-vis entrustment to her, both in terms of contemporary theological discussion[88] as well as John Paul II's use of the term entrustment,[89] and am convinced that he frequently used the words interchangeably along with other words such as dedicate, offer, commend, place in the hands of, etc.[90] At the same time I have chosen as the title for this chapter the binomial "consecration and entrustment" because I believe that each word can be justified and offers shades of meaning not conveyed by the other.

---

[86] *Inseg* II/1 (1979) 860-861 [*ORE* 577:9].
[87] Kosicki 66-67.
[88] Cf. *Totus Tuus* 143-151.
[89] Cf. *Totus Tuus* 171-178.
[90] Cf. *Totus Tuus* 143-144; Apollonio, *Cons* 87.

The Theological Foundations of Consecration/Entrustment

A classical presentation on personal consecration provides us an important approach to the theological questions underlying our presentation:

> Strictly speaking, one can consecrate himself only to God, for only God has the right to man's total dedication and service. Consecration to Christ, to the Sacred Heart, is legitimate because of the hypostatic union. But "consecration" to the Blessed Virgin, or even to St. Joseph or to other saints, is not unknown to Christian piety. In the case of St. Joseph or the other saints, this is to be understood as consecration in a broad sense of the term, and it signifies no more than an act of special homage to one's heavenly protector. The case of the Blessed Virgin, however, is not the same. The importance of her role in Christian spirituality is such that formulas of dedication to her appear to have more profound meaning. Her position in the economy of salvation is inseparable from that of her Son. Her desires and wants are his, and she is in a unique position to unite Christians fully, quickly, and effectively to Christ, so that dedication to her is in fact dedication to Christ. French spirituality has made much of consecration to Mary. Cardinal Bérulle encouraged the vow of servitude to Jesus and Mary. St. John Eudes propagated the devotion of consecration not only to the Sacred Heart, but to the Heart of Mary as well. But the practice achieved its strongest expression in the *Traité de la vraie dévotion à la Sainte Vierge* of St. Louis-Marie Grignion de Montfort. The act of personal consecration according to Montfort, is an act of complete and total consecration. It consists in giving oneself entirely to Mary in order to belong wholly to Jesus through her.[91]

---

[91] N. Lohkamp, "Consecration, Personal" in *New Catholic Encyclopedia 4* (NY: McGraw-Hill Book Co., 1967) 209; cf. also Joseph de Finance, S.J., "Consécration" in *DSp* 2:1579-1582.

In effect the author of this article points to a resolution of this problem along two complementary lines. First and, admittedly, only very implicitly he evokes the principle of analogy. Secondly and quite explicitly he points to the unique role of Mary in the mystery of Christ and the economy of our salvation, particularly her mediation.

The Principle of Analogy

In the perspective of the *philosophia perennis* (perennial philosophy), analogy means a "likeness in difference." Here are two excerpts from his article on consecration in the *Nuovo Dizionario di Mariologia*:

> The only way to be able to apply a term to God and to a creature is to have recourse to analogy which is based precisely on the likeness in the difference. The analogical use of consecration referred to Mary maintains a sense of "total and perpetual gift" which is required in order to bring this usage in line with the light of revelation and theology. ... The gift to her is analogous to that which is made to God since it maintains the significance of the total and perpetual gift, but on the different level proper to a creature.[92]

Consequently, when one speaks of "consecration to God" and "consecration to Mary" one is effectively speaking in the first place of what the disciples of St. Thomas call the "analogy of attribution." Gardeil says that

> In the analogy of attribution there is always a primary (or principal) analogate (or analogue), in which alone the idea, the formality, signified by the analogous term is intrinsically realized. The other (secondary) analogates have this formality predicated of them by mere extrinsic denomination.[93]

---

[92] *NDM* 409, 412 (my trans.).
[93] H.D. Gardeil, O.P., *Introduction to the Philosophy of St. Thomas Aquinas* IV: *Metaphysics* trans. by John A. Otto (St. Louis: B. Herder Book Co., 1967) 53.

Following this paradigm, then, "consecration to God" is the primary analogate whereas "consecration to Mary" is a secondary analogate. In other words, the term "consecration" signifies something which is common to both analogates, the recognition of our dependence on them, but since God is our Creator and Mary is a creature that dependence cannot be exactly the same.[94]

But it can be held as well that such usage of the term "consecration to Mary" is also an instance of the "analogy of proportionality" which Gardeil explains in this way:

> It will be remembered that in the analogy of attribution the (secondary) analogates are unified by being referred to a single term, the primary analogue. This marks a basic contrast with the analogy now under consideration, that of proportionality; for here the analogates are unified on a different basis, namely by reason of the proportion they have to each other. Example: in the order of knowledge we say there is an analogy between seeing (bodily vision) and understanding (intellectual vision) because seeing is to the eye as understanding is to the soul.[95]

Theologians have long recognized that there exists an analogy, a certain "likeness in difference," between Jesus and Mary, a certain symmetry and complementarity, though not identity, between them.[96]

Admittedly, today this classical Catholic principle is more and more being called into question, and yet it is a fundamental building block of Catholic theology. Indeed, without it the discipline of theology

---

[94] Cf. J. Bittremieux, "Consecratio Mundi Immaculato Cordi B. Mariae Virginis," *Ephemerides Theologicae Lovanienses* 20 (1943) 102.

[95] Gardeil 54.

[96] On the principle of analogy as it pertains to Mariology, cf. José M. Bover, S.J., "El Principio Mariologico de Analogia," *Alma Socia Christi: Acta Congressus Mariologici-Mariani Romæ Anno Sancto MCML Celebrati* (Rome: Pontificia Academia Mariana Internationalis, 1953) I:1-13; Gabriele M. Roschini, O.S.M., *Dizionario di Mariologia* (Roma: Editrice Studium, 1961) 30-31; Roschini, *Maria Santissima nella Storia della Salvezza* I: *Introduzione Generale* (Isola del Liri: Tipografia Editrice M. Pisani, 1969) 171-77; Brunero Gherardini, *La Madre: Maria in una sintesi storico-teologica* (Frigento: Casa Mariana Editrice, 2006) 309-10; Emile Neubert, S.M., *Mary in Doctrine* (Milwaukee: Bruce Publishing Co., 1954) 5-8.

is impossible and without it there is no understanding of Marian consecration. Even authors whom I have cited, like De Fiores, today distance themselves from it.[97] In this regard Father Joaquín Ferrer Arellano has done us a great favor in recent years exposing the weakness of so much modern theology and Mariology[98] and clearly indicating the Lutheran/Barthian animus against the principle of analogy.[99] Let us have a few examples of how the great masters employ this concept. Here are some very important instances from St. Louis-Marie Grignion de Montfort:

> As all perfection consists in our being conformed, united and consecrated to Jesus it naturally follows that the most perfect of all devotions is that which conforms, unites, and consecrates us most completely to Jesus. Now of all God's creatures Mary is the most conformed to Jesus. It therefore follows that, of all devotions, devotion to her makes for the most effective consecration and conformity to him. The more one is consecrated to Mary, the more one is consecrated to Jesus. That is why perfect consecration to Jesus is but a perfect and complete consecration of oneself to the Blessed Virgin, which is the devotion I teach; or in other words, it is the perfect renewal of the vows and promises of holy baptism.[100]
>
> This devotion consists in giving oneself entirely to Mary in order to belong entirely to Jesus through her.[101]

---

[97] *Maria: Nuovissimo Dizionario* I:383-386. A fundamental premise of Laurentin's *The Meaning of Consecration Today* is the unacceptablity of the use of the concept of analogy and thus of the term "consecration to Mary." His revision of the entire history of Marian consecration is most unfortunate and is outside the Tradition.

[98] Cf. *Totus Tuus* 162-178.

[99] Joaquín Ferrer Arellano, "Marian Coredemption in the Light of Christian Philosophy" in *Mary at the Foot of the Cross* II (New Bedford, MA: Academy of the Immaculate, 2002) 122-124, 135-139; *Ibid.*, "La mediación materna de María a la luz de la Filosofía Cristiana. Perspectivas ecuménicas" in *Maria: "Unica Cooperatrice alla Redenzione"* (New Bedford, MA: Academy of the Immaculate, 2005) 485-491.

[100] *TD* 120.

[101] *TD* 121.

It follows that we consecrate ourselves at one and the same time to Mary and to Jesus. We give ourselves to Mary because Jesus chose her as the perfect means to unite himself to us and unite us to him. We give ourselves to Jesus because he is our last end.[102]

The Principle of Marian Mediation

The astute reader will recognize that de Montfort's texts cited above are a marvelous fusion of the principle of analogy and that of Marian mediation. He was, indeed, an extraordinary teacher who knew how to present sound theology to the poor and little ones. It was one of the great achievements of the late Pope John Paul II to re-launch discussion on Mary's maternal mediation in the third part of his great Marian encyclical, *Redemptoris Mater* (38-47), at a time when such discourse had been out of favor in most theological and Mariological circles since the time of the Second Vatican Council.[103] Perhaps even less noticed are his profound statements about Our Lady in his first encyclical, which speaks about Mary's mediation without using the word. In *Redemptor Hominis* 22, he wrote:

> For if we feel a special need, in this difficult and responsible phase of the history of the Church and of mankind, to turn to Christ, who is Lord of the Church and Lord of man's history on account of the mystery of the redemption, we believe that nobody else can bring us as Mary can into the divine and human dimension of this mystery. Nobody has been brought into it by God himself as Mary has. It is in this that the exceptional character of the grace of the divine motherhood consists. Not only is the dignity of this motherhood unique and unrepeatable in the history of the human race, but Mary's participation, due to this maternity, in God's plan for man's salvation through the mystery of the redemption is also unique in profundity and range of action. ... The

---

[102] *TD* 125.
[103] Cf. *Theotokos* 242-245, 351-356; *Ibid.*, "Still Mediatress of All Graces?", *Miles Immaculatæ* 24 (1988) 122-125.

Father's eternal love, which has been manifested in the history of mankind through the Son whom the Father gave, "that whoever believes in him should not perish but have eternal life," comes close to each of us through this Mother and thus takes on tokens that are of more easy understanding and access by each person. Consequently, Mary must be on all the ways for the Church's daily life. Through her maternal presence the Church acquires certainty that she is truly living the life of her Master and Lord and that she is living the mystery of the redemption in all its life-giving profundity and fullness.[104]

In his own unique style he was already reaffirming the Church's teaching about Mary's mediation of all graces.[105]

The teaching about the analogy between Jesus and Mary, between his Heart and her Heart, and her unique role as Mediatrix, he would draw out in many different ways in the course of his pontificate of over 26 years, precisely in his presentation of Marian consecration and entrustment. Here a few examples must suffice. In his homily at Fatima on May 13, 1982, before making his solemn Act of Consecration and Entrustment to the Immaculate Heart of Mary, he stated:

> On the Cross Christ said: "Woman, behold your son!" With these words he opened in a new way his Mother's Heart. A little later, the Roman soldier's spear pierced the side of the Crucified One. That pierced Heart became a sign of the redemption achieved through the death of the Lamb of God.
>
> The Immaculate Heart of Mary opened with the words "Woman, behold, your son!" is spiritually united with the Heart of her Son opened by the soldier's spear. Mary's Heart was opened by the same love for man and for the world with which Christ loved man and the

---

[104] *Inseg* II/1 (1979) 607-608 [U.S.C.C. Edition 97, 98].

[105] Cf. Father Alessandro Apollonio's treatment of this topic in this book. Cf. also my article "Mary, Mediatrix of All Graces, in the Papal Magisterium of Pope John Paul II" to appear in *Mary at the Foot of the Cross*, VII.

world, offering himself for them on the Cross, until the soldier's spear struck that blow.

Consecrating the world to the Immaculate Heart of Mary means drawing near, through the Mother's intercession, to the very Fountain of life that sprang from Golgotha. This Fountain pours forth unceasingly redemption and grace. In it reparation is made continually for the sins of the world. It is a ceaseless source of new life and holiness.

Consecrating the world to the Immaculate Heart of the Mother means returning beneath the Cross of the Son. It means consecrating this world to the pierced Heart of the Savior, bringing it back to the very source of its redemption. Redemption is always greater than man's sin and the "sin of the world." The power of the redemption is infinitely superior to the whole range of evil in man and the world.

The Heart of the Mother is aware of this, more than any other heart in the whole universe, visible and invisible.

And so she calls us.

She not only calls us to be converted: she calls us to accept her motherly help to return to the source of redemption.

Consecrating ourselves to Mary means accepting her help to offer ourselves and the whole of mankind to him who is holy, infinitely holy; it means accepting her help—by having recourse to her motherly Heart, which beneath the Cross was opened to love for every human being, for the whole world—in order to offer the world, the individual human being, mankind as a whole, and all the nations to him who is infinitely holy. God's holiness showed itself in the redemption of man, of the world, of the whole of mankind, and of the nations: a redemption brought about through the sacrifice of the Cross. "For their sake I consecrate myself," Jesus had said (Jn 17:19).

By the power of the redemption the world and man have been consecrated. They have been consecrated to him who is infinitely holy. They have been offered and entrusted to Love itself, merciful Love.

The Mother of Christ calls us, invites us to join with the Church of the living God in the consecration of the world, in this act of confiding by which the world, mankind as a whole, the nations, and each individual person are presented to the Eternal Father with the power of the redemption won by Christ. They are offered in the Heart of the Redeemer which was pierced on the Cross.[106]

He sounded very similar notes when he spoke on the last day of 1984 in the Church of the Gesù in Rome, commenting on his Act of Consecration and Entrustment to the Immaculate Heart of Mary on March 25 of that same year:

> Closely united with the Jubilee Year was the Act of Entrustment to the Immaculate Heart of Mary which I carried out in union with all the bishops of the world.
>
> I had already made such an act of entrustment and consecration on May 13, 1982, during my pilgrimage to Fatima, thus linking myself with the two acts carried out by Pius XII in 1942 and 1952. On March 25 of this year the same act of entrustment and consecration had a collegial character, because it was made simultaneously by all the bishops of the Church: it was carried out in Rome and at the same time all over the world.
>
> *This Act of Consecration was a drawing nearer of the world, through the Mother of Christ and our Mother, to the source of life, poured out on Golgotha: It was a bringing back of the world to the same fount of redemption, and at the same time, to have the Madonna's help to offer men and peoples to him who is infinitely holy* (cf. Homily at Fatima, n. 8).
>
> Before the venerated statue of Our Lady of Fatima, brought to Rome for the occasion, I offered the hopes and anxieties of the Church and the world, invoking the aid of Mary in the struggle against evil and in

---

[106] *Inseg* V/2 (1982) 1573-1574; *Portugal: Message of Fatima* (Boston: St. Paul Editions, 1983) 79-81. Emphasis my own.

preparation for the third millennium. *Now is the hour when every person must make an effort to live faithfully this Act of Consecration to Mary.*[107]

Again on September 22, 1986, the late Holy Father offered yet another synthesis of his great acts of consecration and entrustment:

> We see symbolized in the Heart of Mary her maternal love, her singular sanctity and her central role in the redemptive mission of her Son. It is with regard to her special role in her Son's mission that devotion to Mary's Heart has prime importance, for through love of her Son and of all humanity she exercises a unique instrumentality in bringing us to him. The act of entrusting to the Immaculate Heart of Mary that I solemnly performed at Fatima on May 13, 1982, and once again on March 25, 1984, at the conclusion of the Extraordinary Holy Year of the Redemption, is based upon this truth about Mary's maternal love and particular intercessory role. If we turn to Mary's Immaculate Heart she will surely "help us to conquer the menace of evil, which so easily takes root in the hearts of the people of today, and whose immeasurable effects already weigh down upon our modern world and seem to block the paths towards the future"
>
> Our act of consecration refers ultimately to the Heart of her Son, for as the Mother of Christ she is wholly united to his redemptive mission. As at the marriage feast of Cana, when she said "Do whatever he tells you," Mary directs all things to her Son, who answers our prayers and forgives our sins. Thus *by dedicating ourselves to the Heart of Mary we discover a sure way to the Sacred Heart of Jesus, symbol of the merciful love of our Savior.*
>
> The act of entrusting ourselves to the Heart of Our Lady establishes a relationship of love with her in which we dedicate to her all that we have and are. This consecration is practiced essentially by a life of grace, of purity, of

---

[107] *Inseg* VII/2 (1984) 1683-84 [*ORE* 869:4]. Emphasis my own.

prayer, of penance that is joined to the fulfillment of all the duties of a Christian, and of reparation for our sins and the sins of the world.[108]

He would draw out the implications of consecration/entrustment to Mary for both individuals and peoples in countless ways in the course of his long pontificate. Perhaps one of his last and greatest gifts to the Church was his teaching in his last encyclical, *Ecclesia de Eucharistia*, 57:

> "Do this in remembrance of me" (Lk. 22:19). In the "memorial" of Calvary all that Christ accomplished by his Passion and his death is present. Consequently *all that Christ did with regard to his Mother for our sake* is also present. To her he gave the beloved disciple and, in him, each of us: "Behold, your son!" To each of us he also says: "Behold your mother!" (cf. Jn 19: 26-27).
>
> Experiencing the memorial of Christ's death in the Eucharist also means continually receiving this gift. It means accepting—like John—the one who is given to us anew as our Mother. It also means taking on a commitment to be conformed to Christ, putting ourselves at the school of his Mother and allowing her to accompany us. Mary is present, with the Church and as the Mother of the Church, at each of our celebrations of the Eucharist.[109]

While an enormous number of further texts could be adduced, it is my sincere hope that those already presented will be an encouragement to take up the exhortation which John Paul II made on December 31, 1984: "Now is the hour when every person must make an effort to live faithfully this act of consecration to Mary."[110]

---

[108] *Inseg* IX/2 (1986) 699-700; *ORE* 959:12-13.
[109] *Inseg* XXVI/1 (2003) 508 [*ORE* 1790:IX-X]. The teaching about accepting/welcoming Mary into our lives is another aspect of Marian entrustment which the Pope developed over the course of the years. Cf. *Totus Tuus* 240-248.
[110] *Inseg* VII/2 (1984) 1683-84 [*ORE* 869:4].

Marian Private Revelation: Nature, Evaluation, Message

Mark I. Miravalle, S.T.D.

The Church began with miracles and divine gifts, and being one she continues the same. As the ancient dispensation began with Moses, and was inaugurated with miracles, so it continues from age to age, to the pond of Probatica (cf. Jn 5:2). The dispensation of the Gospel is more glorious than that of the law (2 Cor 3:9), and is fulfilled in measure beyond the capacity of its predecessor. … If the miracles of the law ceased not at the death of Moses, and if the record of them is not confined to the Pentateuch, but is continued through the history of kings and prophets, much more are we to expect a similar result in the history of Holy Church. The Acts of the Apostles do but carry on the miraculous record of the four gospels; and is there any reason that we should suppose that marvellous gifts, graces, and miracles ceased with the apostolic age? This would be the reasoning of the Sadducees, who confined themselves to the five books of Moses, and disowned the prophets. They had closed their hearts against the perpetual evidence of their Temple, and refused to believe in the interference of God, and his dealings with that economy under which they were living.[1]

Preface, Benedict XIV,
On Heroic Virtue

---

[1] From the preface of *Heroic Virtue: A Portion of the Treatise of Benedict XIV on the Beatification and Canonization of the Servants of God*, Vol. I of the original five-volume work in Latin by Pope Benedict XIV (Cardinal Prospero Lambertini), *De Servorum Dei Beatificatione et de Beatorum Canonizatione*, translated by the English Fathers of the Oratory, London, Thomas Richardson and Son, 1850, pp. xii-xiii; New York, Edward Dunigan and Brother.

Within the last two hundred years, there have been more reported private revelations of the Mother of Jesus that have received some form of ecclesiastical approval than in any other period of the Church's history.² The examination of the nature of Marian private revelation, its purpose, its fundamental message, and the criteria used by the Church in the discernment of authenticity has become more and more relevant for today's bishop, parish priest, religious, or lay leader. This issue has merited renewed attention in an era that also has unfortunately experienced proliferating manifestations of the occult, "New Age" movements, and false prophecy.

The definitive study of private revelation and its concurring mystical phenomena is generally accepted to be the five-volume work by Pope Benedict XIV, *De Servorum Dei Beatificatione et de Beatorum Canonizatione* (1734-1738), (written while he was Cardinal Prospero Lambertini). Our synopsis will draw heavily from Pope Benedict's work and its three-volume English synthesis, *On Heroic Virtue*, as we explore the nature of Marian private revelation and the fundamental principles which should govern the discernment of reported private revelation.

Discerning Private Revelation

Public and Private Revelation

Public Revelation consists of God's self-manifestation of divine truths for the salvation of mankind, a revelation which is protected by the Holy Spirit, is given to the prophets and apostles, and ends with the death of the Apostle John. These divine revelations are transmitted through Scripture and Apostolic Tradition, which are safeguarded through the Magisterium of the Church to constitute the *depositum fidei*, the deposit of Christian faith entrusted to the Church.³ No form of revelation

---

[2] Since the approval of the Marian apparitions at Rue de Bac (1830), the following apparitions are among the reported Marian private revelations which have received some form of ecclesiastical approval: La Salette, France (1846); Lourdes, France (1858); Pontmain, France (1871); Knock, Ireland (1879); Fatima Portugal (1916-1917); Beauraing, Belgium (1932); Banneaux, Belgium (1933); Amsterdam, Netherlands (1945-1984); Syracuse, Italy (1953); Zeitun, Egypt (1968); Akita, Japan (1973-1981); Cuapa, Nicaragua (1980); Kibeho, Rwanda (1981-1989); Betania, Venezuela (1976-1990); and San Nicolás, Argentina (1983-1990).

[3] Cf. Second Vatican Council, *Dei Verbum*, nn. 9-10.

received after the death of John, the last apostle, however authentically supernatural, may be considered to be part of public Revelation. As St. Thomas Aquinas confirms: "For our faith rests on the revelation made to the apostles and prophets who wrote the canonical books, but not on a revelation, if any, made to others."[4]

Private revelation, in contrast, constitutes a manifestation of divine truth given to an individual for the spiritual benefit of the person, a particular group, or for the universal benefit of the Church and the world. In contrast to public Revelation, private revelation has as its purpose not the revealing of new doctrine, but rather the guiding of humanity in its efforts to incorporate more fully the truths of the Gospel already contained in public Revelation. Bl. Pope John XXIII conveys this distinction in his February 18, 1959, address at the close of the celebration of the hundredth anniversary of the Lourdes apparitions:

> We urge you to listen with simplicity of heart and sincerity of mind to the salutary warnings of the Mother of God. ... The Roman pontiffs ... if they are instituted the guardians and interpreters of Divine Revelation, contained in Holy Scripture and Tradition, they also take it as their duty to recommend to the attention of the faithful—when, after responsible examination, they judge it for the common good—the supernatural lights which it has pleased God to dispense freely to certain privileged souls, not for proposing new doctrines, but to guide us in our conduct.[5]

In the Old Testament revelation to the people of Israel and the full revelation in the person of Jesus Christ given to the apostles, God revealed in totality what was necessary for human salvation, and hence there would never be any intrinsic need for the revelation of any additional doctrine through the means of private revelation. The purpose of private revelation is rather to assist us in the ongoing Christian challenge to incorporate more authentically and more generously the Gospel call of

---

[4] St. Thomas, I, 1, a. 8; *Heroic Virtue*, Vol. III, pp. 369.
[5] Bl. Pope John XXIII, *Papal Radio Address at the Close of the Celebration of the 100th Anniversary of the Lourdes Apparitions*, February 18, 1959; *L'Osservatore Romano*, Daily Issue, February 18, 1959.

Jesus Christ to Christian faith, hope, and love—to guide us in the fullest possible implementation of what has already been revealed in Scripture and Tradition for the perfection of love in Christian holiness.[6]

The Church from its apostolic days has always experienced some form of authentic private revelation, in greater or lesser degrees, according to the promptings of the Holy Spirit. Regarding this fact, the Fathers of the Oratory write in their preface to the English edition of *Heroic Virtue*:

> It is not only consistent with reason, that in the Christian economy marvels and miracles should be found, but it is also a fulfilling of a type going before. Christians are the true Israelites, of whom the inhabitants of Palestine under the old law, were only a figure. What happened to them, and what is written of them, is, according to St. Paul, written for our learning and correction. If, then, the successors of Moses, such as Joshua, the judges, and the kings and prophets of Israel, led strange and unnatural lives, and were the objects of divine gifts and visitations, much more are we to expect that pontiffs, priests, and monks, who walk in the footsteps of One greater than Moses, should in like manner, but in a greater and nobler way, be favored and visited.
>
> The apostles of our Lord were endowed with the gift of miracles; and there is no hint that this gift was personal, or to be confined to a certain age. On the contrary, St. Paul speaks of these extraordinary gifts as if they were to continue in the Church forever, for he gives rules for their exercise, and a test to discern them from the counterfeit likenesses of them with which the evil spirit would endow the children of perdition.[7]

Benedict XIV explains that throughout its rich history the Church has always experienced cases of private revelation for the positive directing of human activity (quoting St. Thomas): "John also wrote a

---

[6] Cf. Second Vatican Council, Dogmatic Constitution on the Church, *Lumen Gentium*, n. 11.

[7] From the Preface of *Heroic Virtue*, Vol. I, pp. xiv-xv.

prophetic book on the end of the Church; and in every age there has not been wanting men with the spirit of prophecy, not indeed, to bring forth a new doctrine of faith, but to direct the course of human acts."[8] Benedict also refers to a patristic example of private revelation received by St. Cyprian concerning an upcoming Roman persecution, as well as citing medieval examples of valid private revelation:

> [There]... are heavenly and divine private revelations by which God sometimes illuminates and instructs a person for his own eternal salvation, or that of others. We have an instance of a heavenly revelation in an epistle of St. Cyprian, when he says that he had a revelation from God of the Decian persecution. ... The same St. Cyprian made known to his clergy that future peace had been divinely revealed to him. ...[9] We have the revelations of the Blessed Hildegarde, the Blessed Litgarde, the Blessed Angela, daughter of the king of Bohemia, St. Gertrude, St. Bridget, and St. Teresa. ...[10]

The Second Vatican Council also confirms the ongoing presence of extraordinary charisms in the Church (which includes the domain of private revelation), as well as its proper discernment by the Church:

> It is not only through the sacraments and the ministries of the Church that the Holy Spirit sanctifies and leads the people of God and enriches it with virtues, but, "allotting his gifts to everyone according as he wills" (1 Cor 12:11), he distributes special graces among the faithful of every rank. By these gifts he makes them fit and ready to undertake the various tasks and offices which contribute toward the renewal and building up of the Church, according to the words of the apostle: "The manifestation of the Spirit is given to everyone for profit" (cf. 1 Cor 12:7). These charisms, whether they be the more outstanding or the more simple and

---

[8] St. Thomas, II-II, 174, a. 6; *Heroic Virtue*, Vol. III, p. 369.
[9] St. Cyprian, *Ep* 11, p. 186; *Heroic Virtue*, Vol. III, pp. 370-371.
[10] Pope Benedict XIV, *Heroic Virtue*, Vol. III, pp. 370-371, 373.

widely diffused, are to be received with thanksgiving and consolation for they are perfectly suited to and useful for the needs of the Church. Extraordinary gifts are not to be sought after, nor are the fruits of apostolic labor to be presumptuously expected from their use; but judgment as to their genuineness and proper use belongs to those who are appointed leaders in the Church, to whose special competence it belongs, not indeed to extinguish the Spirit, but to test all things and hold fast to that which is good (cf. 1 Thess 5:12; 19-21).[11]

Authentic private revelation serves the People of God by contributing to the Church's ongoing development of doctrine. Private revelation can accentuate certain doctrinal elements already contained in Scripture and Tradition, which leads to a greater emphasis on that particular doctrinal truth to the great benefit of the Church in a given historical age. A recent example of this function of private revelation is evident in the institution by Pope John Paul II in 2000 of the Feast of Divine Mercy, a public liturgical feast which is to be celebrated each year on the Sunday following Easter Sunday.[12] Clearly the Christian revelation of God's infinite mercy is already contained within the public Revelation of the Church. Nonetheless, the request for the Feast of Divine Mercy, which originated specifically from the ecclesiastically approved revelations of Jesus to St. Faustina Kowalska, along with the call for a greater emphasis on Divine Mercy in our present age, has been the source of untold spiritual good for the People of God at the beginning of the third millennium.[13]

Prophecy

Prophecy is generally understood as a gift of God whereby a person foretells some aspect of a future event by supernatural enlightenment. The gift of prophecy can also refer to a supernatural knowledge of

---

[11] Second Vatican Council, *Lumen Gentium*, 12.
[12] Cf. Pope John Paul II, Homily during the Canonization Mass of St. Mary Faustina Kowalska, April 30, 2000, n. 4; *L'Osservatore Romano*, English edition, May 2, 2000, p. 1
[13] Cf. St. Mary Faustina Kowalska, *Diary. Divine Mercy in My Soul*, Marians of the Immaculate Conception, 1996, and particularly nn. 49, 570, 699.

hidden things in the present or the past. Pope Benedict XIV explains the charism of the prophet:

> A prophet, then, is he who foretells future events, or reveals to others things past, or present things hidden; although generally, and for the most part, prophecy is confined to the foretelling of future events. St. Thomas teaches that prophetic knowledge comprises all those things mentioned above, and that these are of three kinds: one, far removed from the cognizance of one man, but not from that of all men; one man has a sensible cognizance of what is present to him, as to place but of which another has no human sensible cognizance, because they are distant: the second is, of those things which transcend universally the cognizance of all, not because in their own nature they cannot be known, but because of the deficiency of human knowledge, as, for instance, the mystery of the most Holy Trinity. The last is, of those things which are far removed from all human cognizance, because in themselves they cannot be known, as future contingencies, the truth of which is not determinate.[14]
>
> ... Prophecy is the foreknowledge of future events, but it sometimes extends to past events, of which there is no recollection nor any certain indications; and to present events distant in place and hidden, and to the inward thoughts of the heart; so that he is a prophet who divinely knows those things which are removed from sense and the natural knowledge of men, and is able to make them known.[15] ... Prophecy extends sometimes to past events of which there is no recollection nor certain indications, as appears from the Gospel of St. John, 4:18, where our Savior says to the Samaritan woman, "Thou hast had five husbands, and he whom thou now hast is not thy

---

[14] Cf. St. Thomas, II-II, 174, a. 3; *Heroic Virtue*, Vol. III, p. 137.
[15] Pope Benedict XIV, *Heroic Virtue*, Vol. III, p. 135.

husband." The woman answered, "Sir, I perceive that thou art a prophet."[16]

The gift of prophecy did not cease with the coming of Jesus Christ into the world. Christian prophecy continues in the life of the Church after the Incarnation and redemption. Although it has been objected that prophecy should end with John the Baptist and the coming of Christ, Benedict XIV responds that only prophecy specific to the Messiah would end with the Baptist and the coming of Jesus Christ, while the Spirit's gift of prophecy would continue to be exercised in the ongoing life of the Church:

> The order of the law and prophets ceased in John [the Baptist], because [it was] fulfilled, not destroyed. From this it is concluded that there have been, are, and will be, true prophets in the Church, although in the way mentioned, the order of the prophets had ceased in John, as is observed by Cornelius à Lapide on that text, and Noel Alexander, by Thomas à Jesu, and Torreblanca. It is also the doctrine of St. Thomas, who, after making an objection from the words of St. Matthew: "The law and the prophets prophesied until John," thus replies to it: "The prophets, who foretold the coming of Christ, could continue only until John, who pointed out Christ present before him, and yet, as St. Jerome says on this point, this is not to exclude prophets that come after John."[17]

Benedict XIV identifies certain fundamental characteristics of authentic Christian prophecy: 1) the supernatural knowledge itself is revealed by God alone; 2) the recipient of the prophecy clearly understands that it is God who has revealed this supernatural knowledge; 3) that there is no natural predisposition required by the individual; 4) there is no supernatural requirement of grace or charity in the individual; and 5) the prophetic gift was never permanently possessed by the individual:

---

[16] Pope Benedict XIV, *Heroic Virtue*, Vol. III, p. 136.
[17] Thomas à Jesu, *Opp. Tom.* 2, part. 1, q. 24; Torreblanca, *De Magia*, lib. 1, c. 1, n. 59; St. Thomas, II-II, 174, a. 6; *Heroic Virtue*, Vol. III, pp. 189-190.

> It is of the essence of true prophecy, that the prophet should not only know what are revealed to him, but also that it is God who reveals them; that no natural disposition is required for prophecy; that union with God by charity is not requisite in order to have the gift of prophecy, and thus it was at times bestowed even upon sinners; that prophecy was never habitually possessed by any mere man.[18] ... "For prophecy came not by the will of man at any time, but the holy men of God spoke, inspired by the Holy Spirit" (2 Pet 1:21).[19]

In the New Testament, we see the apostolic teaching and exercise of the gift of prophecy. For example, St. Paul instructs, "Do not quench the Spirit, do not despise prophesying" (1 Thess 5:19-20; cf. also 1 Cor 12:10, 28; Rom 12:6; 1 Cor 14:1-5, 29-33). St. Paul personally received prophecy and visions (cf. 2 Cor 12:4). St. Peter likewise received prophetic dreams and visions (cf. Acts 2:17; 10:10-16). St. John received the prophetic visions which comprise the book of Revelation (*Apocalypsis* or "unveiling").[20] Benedict XIV confirms the existence of New Testament and early Church prophecy: "It appears from Acts 11 and 21, that Agabus and the four daughters of Philip prophesied, and from 1 Corinthians 14, and Ephesians 4, that there were many prophets in the primitive Church."[21]

Theologically, the gift of prophecy is classified under the category of grace, *gratia gratis data*, a supernatural gift freely given by God, which is not in itself supernaturally meritorious, but is principally given to an individual for the benefit of others.[22] The fundamental distinction between grace *gratum faciens* (the sanctifying grace or actual grace that sanctify the recipient) and grace *gratis data* ("freely given" grace which includes private revelation and prophecy), is that the latter does not require the individual to be in the state of grace when the gift is operative:

---

[18] Pope Benedict XIV, *Heroic Virtue*, Vol. III, p. 160.
[19] Pope Benedict XIV, *Heroic Virtue*, Vol. III, pp. 136-137.
[20] Cf. Revelation 1:1.
[21] Pope Benedict XIV, *Heroic Virtue*, Vol. III, p. 189.
[22] Cf. Pope Benedict XIV, *Heroic Virtue*, Vol. III, p. 88.

> Grace *gratis data* is also a supernatural gift, freely given by God, which does not of itself make him who receives it pleasing to God, but is chiefly directed to the profit of others. …[23] Grace *gratis data* differs from grace *gratum faciens*, primarily because it may exist with mortal sin, and in the absence of charity. …[24] Graces *gratis data* are enumerated by the apostle, [in] 1 Cor 12:4: "Now there are diversities of graces, but the same Spirit: … to another prophecy; to another, the discerning of spirits…" (1 Cor 12:4, 10).[25]

Although prophecy can become an occasion of conversion and holiness for the individual exercising the gift, the state of sanctifying grace is not in itself a necessary precondition for prophecy to be exercised. For this reason, no degree of grace *gratis data* can ever replace sanctifying grace as the foundation for the individual Christian's sanctification and salvation.

Nevertheless, Benedict XIV confirms that persons in mortal sin can still participate in valid prophecy:

> What St. Thomas says, namely, that wicked men may have the grace *gratis data* of prophecy, is confirmed out of Gratian, where we read thus: "Prophecy … is found even in wicked men." … "Saul, also a wicked king, prophesied, and even then, when he was persecuting holy David. Let them not boast, then, who perhaps have this great gift of God without charity, but let them consider what account they must give to God who do not use holy things in a holy manner."[26] … We know that Caiphas, a wicked and unjust priest, also prophesied. And according to St. Matthew 7, to those who say to our Lord, "have

---

[23] Pope Benedict XIV, *Heroic Virtue*, Vol. III, p. 88.
[24] Viguer, *Iust. Theol. tit. degratia*; *Heroic Virtue*, Vol. III, p. 92.
[25] Pope Benedict XIV, *Heroic Virtue*, Vol. III, pp. 89, 90.
[26] Gratian, *De Fide*, disp. 8. §§ 7. n. 2; I, qu. 1, *Prophetatri*; *Heroic Virtue*, Vol. III, pp. 155-156.

we not prophesied in thy name?" He clearly answers, "I never knew you."[27]

Further theological distinctions concerning the nature and exercise of prophecy are made, based upon four central elements: 1) the illumination and its level of understanding; 2) the type of prophecy according to its content; 3) the means by which the prophecy is represented to the recipient; and 4) the manner in which the knowledge is conveyed:

> Prophecy may be considered in many ways; either with reference to the illumination, or to the object or thing known, or to the means by which the representation is made known, or to the way in which knowledge is conveyed. With reference to the illumination, it is perfect or imperfect; the first is, when not only the matter revealed, but also the revelation itself is known, and that it is God who makes it: this only is called absolutely and simply prophecy. The second is that, when, although a truth is made known, it is yet not so certainly nor sufficiently perceived from whom the revelation proceeds, and whether the prophetic or the individual spirit speaks: this is called the prophetic instinct, wherein it is possible, because of the manner of it, that a man may be deceived.
>
> With reference to the object, it may be a prophecy of denunciation, or foreknowledge, or predestination. The first is, when God reveals future events, which he knows not in themselves, or in an absolute decree, but in the order of their own causes, and in conditional decrees, which may be hindered from taking effect by other decrees which are absolute: wherefore the meaning of the revelation is, not that such things will absolutely come to pass, but only from the influences of causes determinate for that end; in these is involved the condition, unless hindered from above, though the prophets do not express it, but seem to speak absolutely. The second is that when

---

[27] Fr. Niccolo Baldelli, S.J., manuscript (c. 1643) addressed to Fr. Mutio Vitelleschi; *Heroic Virtue*, Vol. III, p. 164.

God reveals future events, depending on created free-will, which he sees as things present in eternity. The third is, when he reveals what he alone will do, and sees them in eternity and in the absolute decrees. With reference to the means or the species by which the objects revealed are represented, prophecy is divided into that of the intellect, the imagination, and the body, according to the foregoing observations. Finally, with reference to the way in which the foreknowledge is conveyed, prophecy is divided into that which takes place when the senses are not suspended, and this retains the general name of prophecy, and that which takes place when they are suspended, this is called rapture, of which we shall speak hereafter.[28]

Perfect prophecy requires that the contents of the prophecy are supernaturally revealed, that the contents are known and that the recipient knows with certainty that it is God who has revealed it. Imperfect prophecy refers to cases where the recipient of the supernatural knowledge is not certain that it is from God, but nonetheless conveys a true prophecy; or when the seer provides an erroneous interpretation of a true prophecy. Benedict refers to the Thomistic use of the term "prophetic instinct" to include this form of imperfect prophecy:

> St. Thomas having said that it is not perfect prophecy, but the prophetic instinct, when a man is moved by God, and knows not that it is God who moves him, makes this golden observation: There is no contradiction in this that the revelation should be true and from God, and the human explanation of it false, for man may interpret it otherwise than God understands it.[29]

A more serious form of imperfect prophecy (which is often referred to within the same category of "prophetic instinct" or "prophetic habit") occurs when a person who consistently receives and conveys authentic prophecy misjudges, on an individual occasion, that a particular concept

---

[28] *Heroic Virtue*, Vol. III, pp. 146-147.
[29] Pope Benedict XIV, *Heroic Virtue*, Vol. III, p. 201; St. Thomas, II-II, 173, a. 4.

had been given supernaturally by God when it was in fact the product of his own natural thoughts:

> It is possible for an otherwise true prophet to foretell what shall not come to pass, that is, believe himself to be speaking by revelation from God, when in truth he was speaking by the prophetic instinct. ...[30]
>
> "And perhaps it is thus, that it has sometimes happened that different persons have published contradictory revelations, as for example, that the Blessed Virgin was, and was not, conceived without original sin; one only of these had received a true revelation, the other believed he had it, but in truth had spoken only of his own spirit, and not by inspiration of God. ...[31] At times, through the exercise of prophecy, a prophet speaks and thinks he is speaking in the prophetic light, but speaks only in his own spirit, and deceives himself. 'Sometimes the prophets, while they are consulted,' says St. Gregory, 'by reason of their frequent prophesying, speak in their own spirit, thinking that they are speaking in the spirit of prophecy. But in order to prevent delusion, the Holy Spirit quickly corrects them, and they hear from him what is true, and blame themselves who have spoken falsely.'"[32]

As the task of conveying authentic prophecy typically includes a courageous presentation of supernatural truth in the face of substantial skepticism, or even denial, on the part of the recipients of the prophetic message, the prophet can become habituated to a strong delivery of what they believe to be given by God, even on the rare occasion when the object of the revelation is not from God. Such occasional occurrences of flawed prophetic habit should not lead to the condemnation of the entire body of the supernatural knowledge communicated by the prophet, if it is properly discerned to constitute authentic prophecy. Nor, in cases of the examination of such individuals for beatification or canonization,

---

[30] Pope Benedict XIV, *Heroic Virtue*, Vol. III, p. 204.
[31] Baldelli, S.J., Vitelleschi manuscript; *Heroic Virtue*, Vol. III, p. 163.
[32] Baldelli, S.J., *ibid.*; *Heroic Virtue*, Vol. III, p. 162.

should their cases be dismissed, according to Benedict XIV, as long as the individual humbly acknowledges his error when it is brought to his attention.[33]

In certain cases, conditional prophecy can be conveyed by God through the prophet. This occurs when the fulfillment of the specific future events transmitted through authentic prophecy will take place only conditionally, if man cooperates with God's request. If the future event does not come to pass because the necessary human cooperation for the providential condition was not satisfied, this does not indicate a lack of the supernatural character of the original prophecy. Recall the scriptural example of the conditional prophecy of Jonah concerning the destruction of Nineveh (cf. Jonah 3:3-10). The fact that the destruction did not take place, due to the proper human cooperation of conversion and penance by the people of Nineveh, in no way invalidates the supernatural character of Jonah's prophecy. Benedict XIV quotes St. Thomas, Cajetan, and Valentia in his extended explanation:

> In order to pronounce a correct judgment on the subject of prophecy, it is necessary to ascertain whether that secret thing which the prophet revealed be such as it was revealed, and whether the contingent future event occurred in the way he foretold it. This rule is derived from Deuteronomy 18:21, "And if in silent thought thou answer: How shall I know the word that the Lord hath not spoken! Thou shalt have this sign: Whatsoever that same prophet foretelleth in the name of the Lord and it cometh not to pass: that thing the Lord hath not spoken, but the prophet hath forged it by the pride of his mind: and therefore thou shalt not fear him."
>
> There are some limitations to this rule, the first is this: if the prophecy was not absolute, but containing threatenings only, and tempered by conditions, namely,

---

[33] "[Regarding] those who prophesy in the prophetic instinct, and whose prophecies, therefore, are sometimes not fulfilled. In order that the servant of God whose beatification and canonization is under discussion should not only be defended with reference to these prophecies, but also be held to have truly prophesied, it is necessary that proof may be had of his correction." Pope Benedict XIV, *Heroic Virtue*, Vol. III, p. 210.

with a condition expressed or implied. This kind of prophecy is uttered according to the laws of divine justice, having respect to present circumstances and the demerits of men, which being changed, God afterwards turns aside the evil foretold by the prophet. The subject is well explained by Valentia; "God is wont to reveal by the prophets not only that which, all things considered, will take place, but that also which, regard being had to inferior causes, as the merits of men, may be truly considered as about to take place: although by the will of God, and all causes considered, it will happen otherwise."[34] ... St. Thomas treats of these prophecies which contain threatenings and are conditional, as does also Cardinal Cajetan who says that a prophet to whom a future event is revealed in its causes, evidently knows that it will take place from those causes, but it is not necessary he should know whether it must result from those causes, and in virtue of that prophetic knowledge, it may remain doubtful to his mind whether it will take place or not: it is sufficient for a true prophet to know evidently that he prophesies of that which is revealed to him, though he knows not the rest.[35]

Visions and Apparitions

Prophecy is sometimes conveyed through supernatural visions or apparitions, which "chiefly tend towards revealing to men some secret thing for their salvation and instruction."[36] Although often used interchangeably, the terms "revelation," "apparition," and "vision" have slightly different connotations. A "revelation" can refer to the illumination as intended by God, the giver and revealer of the illumination. An "apparition" is the illumination seen from the

---

[34] Pope Benedict XIV, *Heroic Virtue*, Vol. III, pp. 198-199; Valentia, *Analys. Fidei Catholic.* Lib 8, c. 5, p. 76.

[35] Pope Benedict XIV, *Heroic Virtue*, Vol. III, p. 200; St. Thomas, II-II, 171, a. 6; Cajetan, 2. 2dae, qu. 171, art. 4.

[36] Pope Benedict XIV, *Heroic Virtue*, Vol. III, p. 367; cf. Cardinal Bona, *Discret. Spirit.* c. 20, n. 1; Scacchus, *De not. et Sign. Sanct.* §§ 8, c. 4, p. 617.

perspective of the person who receives it. A "vision" includes both the illumination of the apparition and an understanding that can accompany the illumination. Benedict XIV cites the explanations of cardinal-theologians De Lauraea and Bona:

> [De Lauraea] says, that visions may be said to be revelations, and otherwise if they be of secret, future, present, or past subjects; and on the part of God, who shows these things, or the Devil deceiving, they may be called revelations, and on the part of man, who receives them, visions. Cardinal Bona says that the term vision and apparition may be used for one and the same thing; but there is this difference, that an apparition is that which presents itself to our contemplation, but without our knowing what it is; but a vision is that, the understanding of which is given also with the external apparition. The subject is thus explained by Bordoni: "Apparitions are visions in reference to those who see the marvellous thing."[37]
>
> "Vision and revelation refer to the same thing, with only this difference, that revelation presupposes vision, and contains in addition understanding of that which is seen, according to the words, Daniel 10:1, 'For there is need of understanding in a vision.'"[38]

Visions are classically categorized as a) external, sensible, or corporal (bodily); b) imaginative; or c) intellectual. An external vision is a vision perceived by the external senses of the eyes. As Poulan explains, a material being is formed, or seems to be formed outside of the individual, and is perceived like everything else in our eternal reality through our external senses.[39] Garrigou-Lagrange adds that if the apparition is visible to several people, it can be an indication that it is external.[40]

---

[37] Pope Benedict XIV, *Heroic Virtue*, Vol. III, p. 284; Cardinal Bona, *De Discret. Spirit.* c. 15, n. 2; Bordoni, *Medit.* 3, *de Miraculosa apparit.* SS. n. 20.

[38] Arauxo, *Decis. Moral.* tr. 3, qu. 23, §§ 2, n. 32; *Heroic Virtue*, Vol. III, p. 368.

[39] R.P. Augustin Poulan, *Graces of Interior Prayer*, Ch. XX, p. 301.

[40] Reginald Garrigou-Lagrange, O.P., *The Three Ages of the Interior Life*, Vol. II, p. 586.

An imaginative vision is a vision of a material object without the assistance of the eyes, and is perceived by the imaginative sense.[41] Imaginary visions are produced and presented to the internal sense of imagination by God and can be received while conscious or during sleep.[42] God can infuse a phantasm or sense image into the imagination without any use of the external senses. A supernatural imaginative vision given to an individual while conscious is almost always accompanied by at least some form of ecstasy (for example, momentarily loss of sight) so that the individual may distinguish the internal vision from external sense data.[43]

An intellectual vision is a vision perceived by the mind without any interior sense image.[44] The illumination is given to the intellect without any dependence on sense images or external senses. This can be the effect of supernaturally infused ideas or previously acquired ideas which are supernaturally modified.[45]

Benedict XIV discusses these three types of visions with examples from Scripture:

> Thus much with respect to the bodily visions and apparitions of God in the Old Testament ... we say, in the first place, that the bodily, ideal, and intellectual vision and apparition are of three kinds ... we must reckon among the imaginary apparitions of God in the Old Testament, that of which we read in 3 Kings, 3 [1 Kings 3:5 in modern scriptural referencing], when he appeared to Solomon in a dream, that he might ask of him what he desired, and also that of which we read in Esther, 11:5, when Mordecai, in a dream, saw voices, and tumults, and thunders, and earthquakes. Among the instances of intellectual visions must be reckoned all those visions and apparitions in which it is certain that God spoke and appeared, and uncertain whether he appeared under an outward form, and spoke with a human voice. Such was

---

[41] Poulan, *Graces of Interior Prayer*, Ch. XX, p. 301.
[42] Garrigou-Lagrange, *The Three Ages*, Vol. II, p. 586.
[43] *Ibid.*
[44] Poulan, *Graces of Interior Prayer*, Ch. XX, p. 301.
[45] Garrigou-Lagrange, *The Three Ages*, Vol. II, p, 587.

that described in 4 Kings 3 [2 Kings 3], when the three kings—that is, the king of Israel, the king of Judah, and the king of Edom, about to fight with the king of Moab, were in distress through want of water, in the desert of Edom—inquired of Elisha the will of God, and the hand of the Lord came upon him, and he said: "Make the channel of this torrent full of ditches." As the prophet Elisha was not then asleep, or in a reverie, neither do we read that God appeared in visible form, or spoke with an audible and external voice, we can come to no other conclusion, than that God spoke to his spirit without words. ..."[46] We read in 1 Kings 28 [1 Samuel 28], that Samuel was raised from the dead, and appeared to Saul.[47]

We now come to visions and apparitions of which mention is made in the New Testament. Among these is that celebrated one of Paul, the teacher of the Gentiles, which he speaks of in 2 Corinthians 12:2, saying, that he was "rapt even to the third heaven ... and heard secret words which it is not granted to man to utter." ... The Apocalypse of the Apostle St. John is filled with visions and apparitions.[48] ... In the New Testament we also have many apparitions of our Lord Christ; he made himself visible at three seasons, the first after his birth before his Passion, the second after his Resurrection, the third after his Ascension. ... We learn from the gospels, Matthew 26, Mark 18, John 20, that he appeared to many after his Resurrection.[49]

A consistent theme throughout Benedict XIV's treatment on visions and apparitions is their legitimate and documented presence throughout Church history. He refers to other reputable ecclesiastical testimonies of authentic apparitions, which includes St. Ambrose's testimony of the apparition of Jesus to St. Peter in the *Quo Vadis* revelation, and the vision received by St. Benedict as testified to by Pope St. Gregory:

---

[46] Pope Benedict XIV, *Heroic Virtue*, Vol. III, pp. 286-287.
[47] Pope Benedict XIV, *Heroic Virtue*, Vol. III, p. 288.
[48] Pope Benedict XIV, *Heroic Virtue*, Vol. III, p. 293.
[49] Pope Benedict XIV, *Heroic Virtue*, Vol. III, pp. 294-295.

St. Ambrose relates that Christ appeared to St. Peter, prince of the apostles: "The same afterwards, having defeated Simon, while teaching the precepts of God to the people, and inculcating chastity, roused the fury of the heathens. While they were in search of him, the Christians implored him to retire for a time. And although he was eager for martyrdom, yet he suffered himself to be moved by the prayers of his people. They entreated him to reserve himself for the instruction and confirmation of his flock. Why speak more? At night he left the city, and at the gate thereof he saw Christ enter it, and said to him, 'Lord, whither goest thou?' Christ answered, 'I come to be crucified again.' Peter understood the divine answer to mean his own crucifixion. Christ could not be crucified again, he had put off his mortal body, and had suffered the pains of death; Peter then understood that Christ was to be crucified in his servant, and so willingly returned. He gave this answer to the questions of the Christians; and being immediately seized, glorified our Lord Jesus Christ by his crucifixion."[50]

Martin del Rio speaks at length of the visions and apparitions which are recorded in ecclesiastical history, and so also does Gravina. ... We shall speak here only of some of the apparitions, which are chiefly mentioned by theologians. The first is that of St. Benedict, which Gregory speaks of in his Life. He saw the whole world before him, collected together, as it were, beneath one ray of the sun, and while he was intently beholding the splendor of that light, he saw angels carry the soul of Germanus, bishop of Capua, to heaven.[51]

The angels frequently exercise an integral role in the process of visions and apparitions. Although commentators disagree as to whether

---

[50] Pope Benedict XIV, *Heroic Virtue*, Vol. III, pp. 296-297; St. Ambrose, *In Auxent. de Basilic.* n. 13, Tom. 1, col. 866.

[51] Pope Benedict XIV, *Heroic Virtue*, Vol. III, pp. 298-299; cf. Martin del Rio, *Disquis. Magic.* qu. 20; Gravina, *Lap. Lyd.* pp. 29-65.

all or simply some apparitions and visions of God in Scripture were ministered through the angels, the common ministration of the angels with regard to visions is generally accepted:

> According to the general opinion of theologians, the apparitions of God under the old Law were not personal, but, as they say, impersonal: for God himself did not assume a body and appear, but he did that by the ministry of angels who represented him: as Durant proves ... all these visible apparitions were accomplished by the ministry and service of angels, who formed and assumed bodies, and represented God. ... Angels were also the efficient causes of those ideal apparitions of the Old Testament, and especially of those which occurred during sleep. ... And though it is said in Genesis 22:2, that God commanded Abraham to sacrifice his son, yet we learn from the same place, that it was an angel that did this: "And behold an angel of the Lord called to him saying, Abraham ... lay not thy hand upon the boy ... now I know that thou fearest God, and hast not spared thy only-begotten Son for my sake."[52]
>
> ... "No one can therefore deny there is prophecy which is angelic, and that most true. Yea, there are some who believe all prophecy to be inspired by means of the angels."[53] ... "It must be remembered that God speaks in two ways: either he speaks himself, or his words come to us through the angels."[54]

Eucharistic apparitions, whereby Jesus seeks to strengthen faith in his Eucharistic presence by means of a supernatural manifestation of the appearance of his flesh and blood, his Sacred Heart, the infant Jesus, or some other Christological appearance, constitutes another valid form of apparition treated by Benedict XIV. These apparitions take place either

---

[52] Pope Benedict XIV, *Heroic Virtue*, Vol. III, pp. 289-291; cf. Durant, *De Visionibus*, c. 4.
[53] Peter John Olivarez; *Heroic Virtue*, Vol. III, p. 143.
[54] Cardinal Torquemada; *Heroic Virtue*, Vol. III, p. 145.

in virtue of a miraculous change in the sacramental species themselves, or as perceived through supernatural means by the observer:

> Another apparition of which we must here speak, is that of Christ our Lord, in the Sacrament of the Altar, under species and forms strange and unusual. There are many instances of this apparition on record. At one is seen in the Sacred Host a man, at another, part of man, at another, an infant, at another, blood. ... St. Thomas discusses the question, and shows that such an apparition may take place in two ways; first, on the part of the beholder, in whose eyes a change may be wrought, so that they expressly see flesh, or blood, or an infant, there being no change in the sacrament; secondly, by a change in the sacramental species themselves. He says that it may happen in the first manner, when one sees the apparition, and others see it not, and the second is when, under the species, all see a body, flesh, blood, and that not for an hour, but for a long time. Moreover, he says that Christ remains in the sacrament in the first way as well as the second; in the first, there is no change in the sacrament; in the second, dimensions continuing, which are the foundations of the other accidents, the Body of Christ must be said to remain in the sacrament; no deception results either in the first or second way from the apparition, for the apparition is granted, in order to make manifest that Christ is truly in the sacrament.[55] ... [And quoting Cardinal de Vitry:] "God, therefore, to strengthen the faith of the weak in this sacrament, has shown forth the truth of it by diverse miracles. Indeed, the likeness of flesh with blood has been frequently seen in the holy sacrament, through the power of our Lord. And I, with my own eyes, have seen it, in the monastery of Premontré, at Braine, in France."[56]

---

[55] Pope Benedict XIV, *Heroic Virtue*, Vol. III, pp. 300-301; cf. St. Thomas, III, 76, a. 8.

[56] Cardinal de Vitry; *Heroic Virtue*, Vol. III, pp. 301-302.

Locutions

Locutions refer to words supernaturally revealed to an individual and, similar to visions, can be received on the external, imaginative, and intellectual levels.[57] External locutions are heard by the external sense of hearing through the ear, and are received as natural speech is received, but produced supernaturally.[58] Imaginative locutions are also composed of words, but are received directly by the imaginative sense without external use of the ear, and are often referred to as "interior locutions."[59] Intellectual locutions consist of supernatural communications of thought which are given immediately to the intellect without words, and therefore without any definitive use of language.[60]

Benedict XIV speaks of the legitimacy of locutions and visions, as forms of prophetic revelation that are proven in Scripture to be authentic supernatural modes through which God communicates with his people:

> It is certain that the invisible God appeared in a visible form at times under the Old Testament, and that eleven times. The first was when he was pleased to appear to our first parents, the second to their son Cain, the third to Noah, the fourth to the maid Hagar, the fifth to Abraham, the sixth to Lot, the seventh to Jacob, the eighth to Moses, the ninth to Joshua, the tenth to Gideon, the eleventh to the parents of Samson. We learn also from various instances in the Old Testament, that God spoke with an external voice, and was heard [for example, to Moses and Abraham].
>
> Whether, however, and wherein a voice only was heard, and nothing seen, and wherein God speaking, was not only heard but seen, it is not our present purpose to enquire. Let it be sufficient to observe, that the external voice of God has been heard, now from a cloud, now from a burning bush, now through fire, now in the whirlwind, now in the whistling of a gentle air, now

---

[57] Poulan, *Graces of Interior Prayer*, p. 299.
[58] Ibid.
[59] Ibid.
[60] Ibid.

from the propitiatory, now from heaven, and now by Urim and Thummin. The upper part of the ark was called the propitiatory, the covering, the oracle. ... From the propitiatory God promised to speak to Moses, and did speak to him.[61]

Levels of Assent to Private Revelation

Various levels of assent to private revelation have been discussed by theologians according to the two principal issues of: a) certainty of divine origin; and b) proximity of the message to the individual in question.

According to Benedict XIV, the individual who directly receives a private revelation, and who is certain that it is from God, is morally obliged to accept the private revelation as true: "Are they to whom a revelation is made, and who are certain it comes from God, bound to give a firm assent thereto? The answer is in the affirmative. ..."[62]

The only remaining issue for Benedict XIV concerning the case where a person is the direct recipient of the revelation and has certainty of its divine origin is regarding the level of faith with which it should be assented to. Should it be received by the individual on the level of divine theological faith? Without offering a conclusion himself, Benedict quotes two different opinions:

> Some, indeed, think that he to whom a revelation is made neither can believe, nor is bound to believe, such a revelation with Catholic faith, that is, that by which we are made Christians; seeing that it is not contained in the habit of the formal object of the same, but from another special light from above, either of a particular faith, or of prophecy, or of discerning of spirits. Arauxo adopts this opinion. Others says that a private revelation, even with reference to the object revealed, ought to be believed by him to whom it is made, with divine theological faith; and consequently, whatever God reveals is a material object of divine faith, for the first truth revealing is the proper and proximate ground of assenting to everything

---

[61] Pope Benedict XIV, *Heroic Virtue*, Vol. III, pp. 284-286.
[62] Pope Benedict XIV, *Heroic Virtue*, Vol. III, p. 390.

God reveals, whether to a private person or to the whole Church, and whether the revelations have regard to the general, or private good; of this opinion is Cardinal Gotti of good memory.[63]

Since the category of divine theological faith is essentially determined by the fact that God is the direct agent who reveals the "material object" [the substance of the message] of divine faith, public or private, and when this is accompanied by a certainty of its divine origin on the part of the recipient, it could rightly be held that the person receiving the vision, for example, St. Bernadette at Lourdes, or Blesseds Jacinta and Francisco at Fatima, would be expected to accept their revelations on the level of divine faith, since God is the certain source of the revelation. Other theologians hold that anyone who receives a certain private revelation should assent to it immediately, not on the level of divine faith, but in virtue of "prophetic light."[64]

Pope Benedict XIV refers to the old prophet of 1 Kings 13:11-25 who failed to assent to a private revelation given to him by God, and instead accepted another alleged private revelation from a prophet who deceived him, which in turn led to his death:

> In 3 Kings, 13, [1 Kings 13] a prophet of God was killed by a lion because he acted against a certain divine revelation which he had received, to the effect that he must not eat in Bethel. ... He gave heed to a probable revelation, which another prophet of God, although a wicked man, said he had received himself, namely that God had given him leave to eat.[65]

The probability of divine origin of a private revelation is, therefore, never sufficient for an assent of divine faith, nor appropriate for the overruling of another authentic private revelation given directly by God.[66]

---

[63] Pope Benedict XIV, *Heroic Virtue*, Vol. III, p. 390; cf. Arauxo, *Decis. Moral.*, tr. 3, q. 23, n. 35; cf. Cardinal Gotti, *Theolog. Scholastico. Dogmatic.*, Tom. 10, q. 1, dub. 3, §§ 2.

[64] Cf. Garrigou-Lagrange, *The Three Ages*, p. 581.

[65] Pope Benedict XIV, *Heroic Virtue*, Vol. III, pp. 392-393.

[66] Cf. Pope Benedict XIV, *Heroic Virtue*, Vol. III, p. 390.

What, then, is the appropriate level of assent for a person to whom an authentic private revelation is directed? The difference between this second category and the first category of the prophet himself is the issue of proximity, in that the person receiving the message does so through the mediation of another human being, the prophet, and does not receive the message directly from God. Benedict quotes Cardinal de Lugo as supporting the principle that the person to whom the revelation is directed is still morally bound to accept the revelation if it is properly evaluated as possessing sufficient evidence of authenticity:

> He to whom that private revelation is proposed and announced, ought to believe and obey the command or message of God, if it be proposed to him on sufficient evidence. ... For God speaks to him, at least by means of another, and therefore requires him to believe; hence it is, that he is bound to believe God, who requires him to do so.[67]

Regarding the proper level of assent for persons to whom the private revelation is not directed, the conclusions of theologians quoted by Benedict XIV maintain that while these people may freely accept these revelations, they are not morally bound to accept the revelation, and if they do believe, it is not on the level of divine or Catholic faith.[68] The reasons posed by these theologians for not requiring an assent of divine faith by those to whom the revelations are not directed are: a) it does not rest upon divine testimony; b) it is not a "mediate" revelation directed to them; c) it is not God speaking directly to them. They conclude that "it resolves itself only into the human testimony of him who relates to others his own private revelation; therefore as the formal object of divine faith is wanting therein, the assent can only be that of a human faith."[69]

Regarding private revelations approved by the Holy See, Benedict XIV reiterates that an assent of "human faith" and not of "Catholic faith" is appropriate:

---

[67] Pope Benedict XIV, *Heroic Virtue*, Vol. III, p. 394.
[68] Cf. Pope Benedict XIV, *Heroic Virtue*, Vol. III, p. 395.
[69] Pope Benedict XIV, *Heroic Virtue*, Vol. III, p. 395.

> What is to be said of those private revelations which the Apostolic See has approved of, those of the Blessed Hildegard, of St. Bridget, and of St. Catherine of Sienna? We have already said that those revelations, although approved of, ought not to, and cannot receive from us any assent of Catholic, but only of human faith, according to the rules of prudence, according to which the aforesaid revelations are probable, and piously to be believed.[70]

What should be clear in these categories of assent is the necessary distinction between the guarantee of the divine testimony present in the sources of Divine Revelation contained in public Revelation, in comparison with supernatural truths proposed through authentic private revelation. What is likewise certain is Benedict's teaching that divine testimony received directly by the individual through authentic private revelation should also, in virtue of its divine origin, be received with a genuine assent of faith.

There does appear to be some inconsistency in the categories of assent as discussed by the theologians cited above. In the second category concerning persons who do not directly receive the revelation, but are directed in a revelation given to someone else, the individual is encouraged under some moral obligation to accept the contents of a divine testimony, and therefore the potential "material object" for divine faith, even though the divine revelation is transmitted through another. In the third category of persons who are not specifically directed by a revelation, they are said to lose the dimension of divine testimony since they did not directly receive the revelation. And yet, this is also true for the second category of persons who are directed by a revelation, but who have not received the revelation directly from God.

Individuals in this third category who are not specifically directed in a private revelation can also hear of a revelation from a prophet that can be of divine testimony, and therefore essentially retain the material object of divine faith, or at least prophetic light, and offer their assent based on the evidence of a supernatural origin. If the criteria for divine faith rests upon divine testimony or prophetic light, as is specified for those to whom a private revelation is directed, then it appears plausible

---

[70] Pope Benedict XIV, *Heroic Virtue*, Vol. III, p. 395.

that those who likewise accept a revelation as authentic based on certain evidence can respond with a faith that exceeds mere human testimony, even though they may not be specifically directed in the revelation. This would apply to people, for example, who accept the Marian apparitions of Lourdes and Fatima, but who were not specifically directed in the apparitions. However, it should not be forgotten, in this regard, that the universal Marian messages appear to be directing *all* mankind towards acts of faith, conversion, and Christian holiness.

The term "divine faith" refers to the material object (the substance) of the revelation as consisting of divine origin and expression. How, then, should the term "human faith" be properly understood? The term in modern parlance could imply the erroneous idea that one believes a purely human testimony based solely upon an experience of human origin. This is not what "human faith" means in the context of Benedict's teaching, since some form of supernatural grace remains the foundation for any authentic private revelation. Perhaps a category designated as "prophetic faith" would be a more theologically understandable term to describe a level of assent which is not based only on human testimony but rather on a private revelation that is divinely inspired in terms of its "material object" or substance.

Benedict XIV likewise maintains that one may refuse assent to private revelation without direct injury to Catholic faith, as long as he does so, "modestly, not without reason, and without contempt."[71] Modern commentators add that while the freedom remains for a member of the Church to reject a private revelation which has received official ecclesiastical approval, it would at the same time be reprehensible to speak publicly against it.[72] Church-approved private revelations that have been incorporated into the Church's public liturgical life would appropriately call for a higher level of respect by the People of God, in so far as certain liturgical feasts and memorials have become part of the Church's public worship (for example, the February 11 liturgical memorial of Lourdes, the solemnity of the Sacred Heart of Jesus, the

---

[71] Pope Benedict XIV, *Heroic Virtue*, Vol. III, p. 397.
[72] Cf. J. Aumann, *Spiritual Theology*, Christian Classics, 1980, p. 429.

more recently instituted memorial of Our Lady of Fatima on May 13, and the Feast of Divine Mercy).[73]

In summation, Benedict XIV's extraordinary study on mystical charisms testifies to the fact that private revelation has been a consistent part of the Church's Tradition, and has made a positive spiritual contribution in the journey of the People of God to Christian holiness. While clearly acknowledging the real possibility and danger of false prophecy, Pope Benedict's balanced examination does not leave one with an exaggerated phobia of private revelation, but rather with a cautious but open mind and heart to these supernatural "interferences" through which God has willed, and continues to will, to assist humanity in its search for Christian salvation and sanctification.[74]

Contemporary Norms for Evaluation

In 1974, the Congregation for the Doctrine of the Faith began a study of the proper principles of evaluation for reported private revelation, which could in turn be utilized by the appropriate Church authorities. On February 24, 1978, the congregation, under Prefect Franjo Cardinal Šeper, made available to local ordinaries, who notified the congregation of reported private revelation found worthy of investigation within their respective dioceses, a set of norms that could guide the bishop, and any commission of investigation appointed by him, in the process of evaluation and discernment concerning the authenticity of the reported revelation.

Beginning with a preliminary note concerning the origin and character of the norms to be presented, this 1978 document offers guiding

---

[73] Cf. *L'Osservatore Romano*, English edition, May 1, 2002, p. 8; *L'Osservatore Romano*, English edition, May 2, 2000, p. 1.

[74] In the author's opinion, some of the later commentaries on Pope Benedict XIV's study do not reflect this important balance of both caution and openness regarding private revelation, but tend to convey a more dominant tenor of negativity. This would include the otherwise valuable study by the Jesuit Father Augustin Poulan, *Graces of Interior Prayer*, where much more of the attention of the study appears to be directed to the causes of error and indications of false prophecy than to what is found in Pope Benedict's study; as well as the more recent text of Fr. Benedict Groeschel, *A Still Small Voice*, also valuable in itself, but which seems to draw most of its references to Benedict XIV from Poulan rather than from the original work, and with a similar overriding tenor which likewise does not reflect the sensitive balance maintained by Benedict XIV.

principles contained under the following three categories: 1) criteria of judgment, concerning the probability at least, of the character of the apparitions and supposed revelations; 2) intervention of the competent local authority; and 3) other authorities entitled to intervene.[75] Of particular relevance to our study is the first section, which seeks to set forth the fundamental positive norms and negative norms in the proper discernment of a reported apparition.

The positive criteria for authenticity outlined by the congregation include:

a) Moral certainty, or at least great probability, as to the existence of the fact, [revelation] acquired at the end of a serious investigation.

b) Particular circumstances relating to the existence and the nature of the fact:

1. Personal qualities of the subject—in particular mental balance, honesty and rectitude of moral life, habitual sincerity and docility towards ecclesiastical authority, ability to return to the normal manner of a life of faith, etc.

2. With regard to the revelations, their conformity with theological doctrines and their spiritual veracity, their exemption from all error.

3. A healthy devotion and spiritual fruits which endure (in particular, the spirit of prayer, conversions, signs of charity, etc).[76]

As the criteria for authenticity suggest, the process of local ecclesiastical investigation, serious in nature, should lead to a moral certainty, or at least a high probability, that the reported revelation is of supernatural origin. The specific elements that must be examined to arrive at this conclusion focus on three general criteria: 1) the nature of the reported message; 2) an examination of the reported "visionary"; and 3) the perduring spiritual fruits stemming from the reported apparitions.

Although listed second in this 1978 CDF document, the first criterion of examination is traditionally an examination of the nature of the reported message contents. The reported message must be in conformity with the doctrinal teachings of the Church, particularly in the domain of faith and morals. The Holy Spirit, who guides and protects the Church's

---

[75] Congregation for the Doctrine of the Faith, *Norms for the Evaluation of Reported Apparitions*, February 24, 1978.

[76] Ibid.

Magisterium in doctrinal truth, will never contradict himself through the vehicle of private prophecy.

As we saw in the treatment of this issue by Benedict XIV, this congregation document also allows for some secondary or occasional error that could be the result of the human conveyer of the revelation altering it with some human addition or misunderstanding (as found in upcoming negative criteria b.). This secondary human factor should not, in itself, lead to a negative decision concerning the overall body of messages and its authenticity.[77]

The second criterion focuses upon the reported visionary. The individual should possess a fundamental psychological balance, free from any substantial mental abnormalities, neuroses, psychoses, or emotional instability. The subject should likewise manifest the virtues of humility, moral integrity, and a clear disposition of obedience to legitimate spiritual direction and Church authority. There should also be a certain dimension of detachment from the apparitions themselves, not in their fidelity to the message as much as in their desires to firstly fulfill the duties of their state and vocation of life as an ordinary member of the People of God. The particular examination of virtue in the life of the visionary should focus upon their life after the initiation of that apparition, and not primarily on their moral lives before the beginning of the apparition, otherwise the possibility for conversion through the apparitions is not taken into account.

Also typical in the examination of the visionary (although not specified in the 1978 norms) is the potential state of ecstasy in the subject during the reported receipt of apparitions. It is generally agreed that at least some form of ecstasy, whereby the subject is partially suspended from their own time-space reality or from full external sense operation, is a normative characteristic when receiving external or sensible apparitions. Modern medico-scientific technology (EEG and EKG readings) can be of assistance in seeking to establish verifiable forms of ecstasy.[78]

The third criterion incorporates the scriptural teachings of Jesus as the ultimate indication of supernatural activity: "Thus you will know

---

[77] Ibid.
[78] For example, the scientific-medical studies conducted on the reported visionaries of Medjugorje, cf. René Laurentin and Henri Joyeux, *Scientific and Medical Studies in the Apparitions at Medjugorje*, Dublin, Veritas Press, 1987.

them by their fruits" (Mt 7:20). The norm specifies "fruits that endure," as even false apparitions could potentially cause temporary fruits based on an alleged call for prayer and conversion. Significant increases in prayer, conversion, sacramental confession, Christian charity, and the return to the overall prayer and sacramental life of the Church should be evidenced and should perdure in abundance when the reported apparitions are of supernatural origin.

Another common component of spiritual fruits includes concurring phenomena such as miraculous healings or physical miracles, as manifested, for example, in the miraculous spring at Lourdes and its subsequent healings,[79] or the solar miracle at Fatima as witnessed by tens of thousands.[80] Miracles or healings are not required as evidence of supernaturality, as the greatest fruits are always the spiritual ones of conversion, reconciliation and peace, whereby God acts within the context of the person's free will to bring forth the fruits of grace, redemption, and peace as infallible indications of the presence of the Spirit.

The following are negative criteria against authenticity, as delineated by the congregation:

a) A glaring error as to the facts.

b) Doctrinal errors attributed to God himself, or to the Blessed Virgin Mary, or the Holy Spirit in their manifestations (taking into account, however, the possibility that the subject may add something by their own activity—even if this is done unconsciously—of some purely human elements to an authentic supernatural revelation, these having nevertheless to remain free from any error in the natural order. Cf. St Ignatius, *Spiritual Exercises*, n. 336).

c) An obvious pursuit of monetary gain in relation with the fact.

---

[79] In the ninth apparition at Lourdes (February 25, 1858), St. Bernadette was told by Our Lady to dig in the mud and uncover what was to become a miraculous spring, cf. J.B. Estrade, J.H. Girolestone, tr., *The Appearance of the Blessed Virgin Mary at the Grotto of Lourdes*, Westminster, Art and Book Co., Ltd., 1912, p. 92; Regarding ongoing healings at the Spring, cf. *67th Lourdes Miracle Officially Proclaimed*, Zenit, English edition, November 15, 2005.

[80] Cf. Sr. Lucia of Fatima, *Memoirs*, Fourth Memoir, and Fr. Robert J. Fox, Fr. Antonio Martins, S.J., *Documents on Fatima & the Memoirs of Sister Lucia*, Fatima Family Apostolate, 2002, pp. 58-59, 214.

d) Gravely immoral acts committed by the subject, or his associates, at the time of the facts, or on the occasion of these facts.

e) Psychic disorders or psychopathic tendencies concerning the subject, which would exert an unquestionable influence on the allegedly supernatural facts, or indeed psychosis, mass hysteria, or other factors of the same kind.[81]

Beyond error and duplicity regarding the reported facts of the revelation, the issue of doctrinal error is highlighted as a prominent indication of falsity, while again granting the possibility of unconscious addition of purely human elements to the general body of the supernatural contents by the human recipient.

A direct financial motive, or any other motive of personal advancement including power, influence, or egoism in relation to the apparitions, are also indications of falsity. Seriously immoral acts by the reported visionary, or anyone in essential relation to the visionary in proximity of time or occasion to the experience, casts legitimate grave doubt on the question of authenticity. It should be noted, however, that if an individual has a personal history of immorality before the beginning of the reported revelation, this does not in itself discount the possibility of a supernatural experience, any more than the pre-conversion life of the Apostle St. Matthew or of St. Mary Magdalene discount the possibility of them having a transforming encounter with Christ.

While Benedict XIV rightly articulated that authentic prophecy can happen in the state of mortal sin since it is a *gratis data* gift, a moral integrity on the part of the visionary remains a standard indication and precedence of consistent revelations which are transmitted in obedience to Christ and the Church.[82]

The last negative criterion enumerated by the congregation returns to the issue of mental and psychological instability. This would include tendencies towards hysteria, emotional neurosis or levels of psychosis which would prevent accurate perceptions of objective reality in general, let alone any form of supernatural revelation.

Specific applications of these norms indicating falsity in reported apparitions would also include:

---

[81] *Norms for Evaluation of Reported Apparitions*, p. 2.
[82] Cf. Michael Miravalle, *Commentary on Church Norms of Evaluation for Private Revelation*, Franciscan University of Steubenville, Ohio, Senior Thesis, May, 2007.

1. When the central focus of the reported message or concurring phenomena is primarily upon the reported seer, and not on God the Father, Jesus, the Holy Spirit, the Mother of Jesus, an angel or saint, either in terms of the message contents or the overall thrust of the experience.

2. When the progression to God is not in the traditional Christian form of: to Jesus through Mary in the Holy Spirit to God the Father, *i.e.*, any "New Age" or occult progression that included another deity or spirit as the means to God, or any indication of *latria* granted to Mary as a fourth person of the Trinity.[83]

3. When the message focuses primarily on the temporal concerns of the world and only secondarily focuses upon the spiritual life and eternal destiny of humanity. This would include any exaggerated and overly detailed discussion of immediate secular, political, and economic affairs as of prior importance to the fundamental spiritual calls of faith, prayer, conversion, charity, peace (albeit with a true concern for contemporary social and political situations), and the spiritual protection which comes from Christian faith. For example, any reported messages which contain meticulous instructions for material protection such as the stockpiling of goods, or the forming of armed refuges, as opposed to the perennial spiritual protection which comes only from the hearts of Jesus and Mary in times of difficulty, would be indications of the dubious prioritizing of the temporal over the spiritual.[84]

The congregation document concludes the section on normative criteria for evaluation of authenticity with the statement: "It is important to consider these criteria, whether they are positive or negative, as indicative standards and not as final arguments, and to study them in their plurality and in relation with the other criteria."[85] Indeed, the norms must be taken collectively as a foundation for a serious evaluation

---

[83] Cf. False apparitions to a Canadian woman who claimed that Mary is co-eternal with God and that she is reincarnated in herself. On June 29, 2001, the Canadian Conference of Catholic Bishops issued a doctrinal note concerning the Army of Mary which received the *recognitio* of the Congregation for the Doctrine of the Faith on August 10, 2001 (Prot. N. 216/74-13501). It was published on August 15, 2001, http://www.cccb.ca/site/Files/armyofmary.html.

[84] Cf. *Sub Tuum Praesiduum*, third-century prayer of protection to the Mother of God.

[85] *Ibid.*

of authenticity or falsity; and final conclusions should not be based solely on the fulfillment of simply one criterion.

This counsel is especially important in making a final decision of supernatural authenticity. All the fundamental norms should be considered before a declaration of supernatural origin is pronounced. This is particularly relevant in the case where some phenomena beyond the order of nature has been reported. Keeping in mind that the Devil, as a fallen angel, has the capacity to manipulate nature, reports of "miraculous" phenomena on their own can never substantiate a conclusion of authenticity regarding external apparitions, when the preternatural phenomenon is not coupled with the other quintessential criteria of soundness of message content, balance and obedience of the visionary, and perduring spiritual fruits. Moreover, Benedict XIV rightly pointed out that the human person does not have the ability to produce prophecy of future events by any natural human faculties. If it is not of God and it is preternatural, then it is of the Devil.[86]

Sequence in the Process of Evaluation

The typical sequence of events in response to a reported private revelation determined worthy of investigation generally follows this pattern: The local ordinary decides that, based on preliminary indications of potential authenticity (i.e., message contents, phenomena, spiritual fruits, integrity of reported visionaries, favorable initial response from the faithful, etc.) that the reported revelation is worthy of further examination. The bishop then contacts the Congregation for the Doctrine of the Faith, at which point he is typically sent the norms for evaluation, and the Vatican confirmation that he is to be the first ecclesiastical judge of authenticity and any potential future approval of devotion stemming from the revelation (an approval normally arrived at only as a result of a gradual process of discernment).[87]

A key element in the evaluation process conducted by the local ordinary is often the formation of a commission of investigation. This commission will normally study theological, spiritual, historical, psychological, medical, and scientific elements of the reported revelation.

---

[86] Cf. Pope Benedict XIV, *Heroic Virtue*, Vol. III, p. 173.
[87] Cf. Congregation for the Doctrine of the Faith, *Norms for the Evaluation of Reported Apparitions*, Section II.

These topics of study would thereby call for the presence of theologians, experienced spiritual directors, psychologists, and doctors to be members of an investigative commission in conducting a serious and professional evaluation.[88]

After completion of the commission's study, a final report and recommendation is presented to the local ordinary by the commission regarding the question of authenticity. The commission's conclusion remains advisory in nature, as the ultimate decision of discernment rests exclusively with the bishop. The bishop, if he decides to make a public declaration regarding the status of the reported apparition, will publicly state his conclusion using one of the following three categories. A declaration of *constat de supernaturalitate* states that the revelation essentially consists of a supernatural origin. A declaration of *non constat de supernaturalitate* states that the revelation has not been established as supernatural, nor has it been condemned as being false. While refraining to declare positively a supernatural character, this category typically allows for the continuation of private belief in the reported message and devotion, and also permits continued private, non-diocesan sponsored pilgrimages to the reported site. This middle conclusion is sometimes used as a temporary one which in turn allows for further evaluation in the future.[89] A declaration of *constat de non supernaturalitate* states that the reported revelation has been declared to not be of supernatural origin and is normally accompanied by prohibitions concerning any further

---

[88] *Ibid.*

[89] For example, the conclusion of the 1991 statement at Zadar, Croatia, by the bishops of former-Yugoslavia, concerning the Medjugorje apparitions, which was confirmed as the official Church position on Medjugorje in a May 26, 1998, letter by the Congregation for the Doctrine of the Faith issued by Archbishop Tarcisio Bertone, then Secretary of Prefect Cardinal Joseph Ratzinger. The letter of Archbishop Bertone served to correct certain positions which presented Medjugorje as being in the *constat de non supernaturalitate* category based on the personal though unofficial opposition of the local ordinary at the time. A new commission of investigation was called for by the Congregation for the Doctrine of the Faith in July 2006. Cardinal Vinko Puljic, president of the Bosnia and Herzegovina Bishops Conference and archbishop of Sarajevo, announced at the end of the bishops conference held July 12-14, 2006, in Banja Luka, that a new commission was being created to investigate Medjugorje.

distribution of messages and devotion directly related to the reported revelation.[90]

There is no existing public knowledge of a case where a positive decision of *constat de supernaturalitate* by the local ordinary concerning a nationally or internationally known private revelation was later changed to the prohibited category of *constat de non supernaturalitate* by the Holy See. Whereas, reported revelations which at one time were prohibited under a form of *constat de non supernaturalitate* have later been re-examined and eventually been found and declared to consist of a supernatural origin.[91] The Holy See also may call, when it deems necessary, for a re-examination of the decision of the local ordinary, as it always maintains the ultimate authority over the domain of private revelation.[92]

Can an obedient member of the Catholic Church make a personal assent of belief regarding a reported revelation before the Church, local or universal, has made an official statement about its authenticity? The answer, based on the Church's repeated precedent, is in the affirmative.[93] While respecting the need for prudence and appropriate caution regarding any reported apparition about which appropriate Church authorities have not yet made a determination, the faithful are nonetheless free to make their own personal discernment and decision of authenticity, based upon the same norms which the Church uses in its authoritative evaluation. Practically speaking, it is oftentimes only after the faithful begin to

---

[90] Cf. for example, the June 7, 2003, declaration of Cardinal Keeler of the Archdiocese of Baltimore, Maryland, concerning the reported revelations to Gianna Talone; cf. the official decree on the Web site of the Archdiocese of Baltimore, www.archbalt.org/news/decree.cfm; or the negative doctrinal note of the Canadian bishops on June 29, 2001, published August 15, 2001.

[91] Cf. for example, the revelations of Divine Mercy to St. Faustina Kowalska, which were first prohibited by the local ordinary and then by the Congregation for the Doctrine of the Faith (cf. notification of March 6, 1959, *A.A.S.*, April 25, 1959, p. 271), and which later received ecclesiastical approval from the same Congregation in the statement of April 15, 1978, *A.A.S.*, June 30, 1978, p. 350.

[92] Cf. Congregation for the Doctrine of the Faith, *Document on the Evaluation of Reported Apparitions*, Section III.

[93] A recent example is evidenced in the May 26, 1998, statement by Archbishop Bertone of the Congregation for the Doctrine of the Faith regarding the legitimacy of private pilgrimages to Medjugorje while the authoritative process of investigation continues.

pilgrimage privately to reported apparitions sites that the local Church initiates its authoritative evaluation.

The beatification of Fatima visionaries Jacinta and Francisco Marto in 2000 by John Paul II further illustrates the legitimacy of the faithful personally accepting a private revelation as authentic before the Church's official decision. Francisco and Jacinta died in 1919 and 1920 respectively, some ten years before the Church's official approval of the Fatima apparitions on October 13, 1930. In matter of fact, Jacinta and Francisco were beatified for the heroic living of the Fatima message, which in their lifetimes remained a reported apparition, as yet unapproved by the Church.[94]

The Marian Message to the Modern World

The universally designated "Age of Mary," which had been anticipated by the historic Marian apparitions at Guadalupe some three centuries earlier,[95] is generally accepted to have begun in 1830 with the ecclesiastically approved apparition of the Blessed Virgin Mary to St. Catherine Labouré in what have been named the "Miraculous Medal" apparitions. From these nineteenth-century apparitions until our present time, Marian apparitions have been reported and approved by the Church on every continent. The Marian message to the modern world begins in seed form in the revelations of Our Lady of Grace at Rue du Bac, and then expands in specificity and concretization throughout the twentieth century and on into our own time. It is important to remember that this Marian message maintains its fundamental unity as one message from one Mother, which then admits of diverse historical and cultural expressions, as well as different emphases and specific calls for the implementations of the general Marian message for prayer and penance in reparation to God, and for the conversion of sinners and the salvation of souls.

---

[94] Cf. the official October 13, 1930, letter approving the apparitions of Fatima from the bishop of Leiria, Bishop José Alves Correia da Silva, Fox, Martins, S.J., *Documents on Fatima*, p. 285; cf. also Sister Lucia of Fatima, *Memoirs*, First and Fourth Memoir, (cf. footnotes).

[95] For more information on the 1531 Marian Apparitions of Our Lady of Guadalupe to St. Juan Diego, cf. Franciscan Friars of the Immaculate, eds., *A Handbook on Guadalupe*, Franciscan Friars of the Immaculate, 2001.

Within the specific context of Marian apparitions and messages, we here provide a brief synthesis of three principal revelations approved by the Church which embody the heart of the Marian message to the modern world. At the same time, they provide valuable precedents for the discernment of other reported contemporary apparitions. We will focus predominantly on the primary source delivery of the messages and their historical context, including some of the concurrent phenomena revealed in these three monumental apparitions of this Marian age.

The "Miraculous Medal" Apparitions, 1830

At the age of 24, Zoé Labouré had entered the Sisters of Charity (having been directed to this particular community founded by St. Vincent by Paul by an inspired dream at the age of 18).[96] Three principal apparitions were received by Sr. Catherine in 1830, and were referred to sequentially as: 1) The "Virgin of the Chair" (July 18, 1830); 2) the "Virgin of the Globe" (November 27, 1830); and 3) "Our Lady of the Miraculous Medal" (November 27, 1830).[97]

On the night of July 18, 1830, the eve of St. Vincent de Paul's feast day, Sr. Catherine was awakened by an angel under the appearance of a child of four or five years old, who softly called her, "Sister Labouré," and subsequently guided her to the chapel with the message: "Come to the chapel. The Blessed Virgin awaits you."[98] Shortly after arriving at the chapel, the angel said, "Here is the Blessed Virgin."[99] Sr. Catherine heard what she later described as the sound of a silk dress rustling, and then saw the Blessed Virgin descend the altar steps and seat herself in

---

[96] Cf. Ordinary Process, Cause for the Beatification and Canonization, p. 126, 349, as found in the definitive English-language account of the apparitions and messages by Joseph Dirvin, C.M., *Saint Catherine Labouré of the Miraculous Medal*, 1958, reprinted 1984 by Tan Publishers, Ch. III, p. 36; cf. also R. Laurentin, *The Life of Catherine Labouré*, Collins Liturgical Publications, 1983, p. 39.

[97] For the extensive French documentation of the messages and surrounding phenomena, cf. R. Laurentin, *Catherine Labouré et la Médaille Miraculeuse*, Paris, 1976, 2 vols.; R. Laurentin, *Vie Authentique de Ste. Catherine Labouré*, Paris, 1980, 2 vols.

[98] St. Catherine, Autograph, February 7, 1856, Archives of the Daughters of Charity, Paris, France; cf. Dirvin, *Saint Catherine Labouré*, p. 81-82; cf. also R. Laurentin, *The Life of Catherine Labouré*, p. 71

[99] Ibid.; cf. Dirvin, *Saint Catherine Labouré*, p. 83; cf. also R. Laurentin, *The Life of Catherine Labouré*, p. 73.

the director's chair in the chapel. After an initial hesitation, Catherine threw herself on the Virgin's knee and rested her hands in her lap. The Virgin then said: "My child, the good God wishes to charge you with a mission."[100]

The Virgin revealed to Catherine God's plans for her; great upcoming trials for France, for the world, and for the Church; great trials that would befall Sr. Catherine personally; and instructions on how she should bear and overcome these trials by meditating upon the glory of God, which would be her motivation for suffering all sacrifices in connection with this mission. The following excerpts are from the originally documented account:

> You will be in anguish until you have told them who is charged with directing you. You will be contradicted, but do not fear, you will have grace. Tell with confidence all that passes within you. Tell it with simplicity. Have confidence. Do not be afraid.
>
> You will see certain things; give an account of what you see and hear. You will be inspired in your prayers; give an account of what I tell you and of what you will understand in your prayers.
>
> The times are very evil. Sorrows will come upon France; the throne will be overturned. The whole world will be upset by miseries of every kind.
>
> Come to the foot of the altar [the Virgin indicates a specific spot]. There graces will be shed upon all, great and small, who ask for them. Graces will be especially shed upon those who ask for them.[101]

The Virgin Mary then conveyed specific calls for the reform of laxities that had entered both the Vincentian Fathers and the Daughters of Charity, and she prophesied that when the rule was once again properly observed a new community of sisters would request to join the Community of Rue du Bac (a prophecy fulfilled by the entrance

---

[100] *Ibid.*; cf. Dirvin, *Saint Catherine Labouré*, p. 83; cf. also R. Laurentin, *The Life of Catherine Labouré*, p. 75.

[101] *Ibid.*; cf. Dirvin, *Saint Catherine Labouré*, p. 84; cf. also R. Laurentin, *The Life of Catherine Labouré*, p. 75.

of St. Elizabeth Ann Seton's Sisters of Emmitsburg into the Paris Community).[102] The Virgin then proceeded to describe in tears the great trials that would come upon France and the world:

> The moment will come when the danger will be enormous; it will seem that all is lost; at that moment, I will be with you; have confidence. You will recognize my coming; you will see the protection of God upon the community, the protection of St. Vincent upon both his communities. Have confidence. Do not be discouraged. I shall be with you.[103]
>
> It will not be the same for other communities. There will be victims. ... There will be victims among the clergy of Paris. Monsignor, the archbishop ... (she could not continue this sentence because of her weeping); my child, the Cross will be treated with contempt. They will hurl it to the ground. Blood will flow. They will open up again the side of our Lord. The streets will stream with blood. Monsignor the archbishop will be stripped of his garments ... (once again, she is unable to continue due to her tears). My child, the whole world will be in sadness.[104]

Sr. Catherine asked herself, "When will this be?" Interiorly, she was immediately granted the understanding: forty years. The experience ended with this infused knowledge.[105]

Nine days following these prophecies, on July 27, 1830, a revolution erupted in Paris. After forty years of independence for the French people, Charles X attempted to re-establish the "divine right" monarchy of the Bourbon dynasty. His quest for Bourbon absolutism led him to dissolve the French Chamber on July 26, 1830, and to silence the press. The

---

[102] Cf. R. Laurentin, *The Life of Catherine Labouré*, p. 75.
[103] St. Catherine, Autograph, February 7, 1856, Archives of the Daughters of Charity, Paris, France; cf. Dirvin, *Saint Catherine Labouré*, p. 85; cf. also R. Laurentin, *The Life of Catherine Labouré*, p. 76
[104] Ibid.; cf. Dirvin, *Saint Catherine Labouré*, p. 86; cf. also R. Laurentin, *The Life of Catherine Labouré*, p. 76.
[105] Ibid.; cf. Dirvin, *Saint Catherine Labouré*, p. 86; cf. also R. Laurentin, *The Life of Catherine Labouré*, p. 76.

"Three Glorious Days" of the July Revolution was the tragic result, with Charles being toppled by constitutional monarchists, middle-class merchants, and radical anarchists, all of whom united in a mob which committed countless murders throughout Paris. The Church, which Charles had supported, was attacked with a particular vengeance, with bishops, priests, and religious imprisoned, beaten, and murdered; churches were desecrated, crosses and statues pulled down and trampled under foot, and Archbishop de Quélen was forced to flee for his life, all in specific fulfillment of the Marian prophecy of July 18.[106]

Both the "Virgin of the Globe" and the "Our Lady of the Miraculous Medal" visions occurred on Saturday, November 27, 1830. On the eve of the first Sunday of Advent during evening prayers with the community, Sr. Catherine once again heard the "swish of a silken gown" and immediately there appeared the Virgin Mary in the sanctuary, this time standing on a white globe with her foot crushing the head of a serpent, which was green with yellow spots.[107] The Virgin held a golden ball in her hands, which she seemed to offer to God as her eyes were directed toward heaven. At the next moment, jeweled rings appeared on her fingers. The precious stones on the rings gave off a cascade of light. The light emanating from the rings was so bright that Catherine could no longer see the Virgin's feet.[108]

The Virgin Mary lowered her eyes to Catherine, who began hearing her voice, though the Virgin's mouth did not move:

> The ball which you see represents the whole world, especially France, and each person in particular. (At this point the rays coming forth from the rings began to increase in brilliance).

---

[106] Cf. Dirvin, *Saint Catherine Labouré*, p. 89.

[107] Although later written accounts of the visions in 1841, 1856, and 1876 left out the two details of the serpent and the twelve stars, they were orally conveyed to St. Catherine's director, Fr. Jean Marie Aladel, and were conveyed to the artists who designed the medal and the artist, LeCerf, who in 1836 captured the apparitions in canvas paintings.

[108] St. Catherine, Autograph, August 15, 1841, Archives of the Daughters of Charity, Paris, France; cf. Dirvin, *Saint Catherine Labouré*, p. 93.

> These rays symbolize the graces I shed upon those who ask for them. The gems from which rays do not fall are the graces for which souls forget to ask.[109]

Immediately following this vision, the golden ball from the Virgin's hands vanished, and her arms and hands swept widely open, horizontally and downward, with her palms facing forward. The rays of light streamed from the rings on her fingers, outward and down upon the white globe under her feet. At that moment, an oval outlined frame formed around the Blessed Virgin. Written in the frame encircling the Virgin in gold letters were the words: "O Mary, conceived without sin, pray for us who have recourse to thee." The Virgin then spoke:

> Have a medal struck after this model. All who wear it will receive great graces; they should wear it around the neck. Graces will abound for persons who wear it with confidence.[110]

The vision then revolved, and Catherine saw the back of the medal image. A large "M" was in the center, which was connected to a higher cross by a horizontal bar. Beneath the M image were the hearts of Jesus and Mary, with the Heart of Jesus crowned with thorns and the Heart of Mary pierced with a sword. Encircling these details were twelve stars. Immediately, the vision vanished.[111] This same vision of the medal was repeated several times on other occasions to Sr. Catherine before the medal was eventually struck.[112]

Profound Mariological significance is contained within the multiple symbols present in the visions. On the front image, the Blessed Virgin is standing on a globe while crushing the head of the serpent, which depicts her universal coredemptive role with Jesus as prophetically

---

[109] *Ibid.*

[110] St. Catherine, Autograph, August 15, 1841, Archives of the Daughters of Charity, Paris, France; cf. Dirvin, *Saint Catherine Labouré*, p. 94.

[111] *Ibid.*

[112] Fr. Jean Marie Aladel, "Quentin" Canonical Inquiry, 1836, p. 5, pp. 10-11, Archives of the Priests of the Congregation of the Mission, Paris, France; cf. Dirvin, *Saint Catherine Labouré*, p. 100.

foreshadowed in Genesis 3:15: "She will crush your head."[113] Rays of light are streaming from her outstretched hands and her jeweled rings, signifying her role as the Mediatrix of all graces. In the first Virgin of the Globe vision, Mary held the golden ball and offered it to God, which would signify her role as universal Advocate for all humanity. But the technical difficulty for the engraver at the time in superimposing the ball over the Virgin's body seemed to encourage the striking of the second "Miraculous Medal" vision of the Virgin with outstretched arms, rather than the Virgin of the Globe vision.[114] Mary's role as Advocate is also revealed in the words written in golden letters: "…Pray for us who have recourse to thee." The dogma (at that time, doctrine) of the Immaculate Conception is revealed in the first part of the phrase, "O Mary, conceived without sin …" The original name of the medal was the "Medal of the Immaculate Conception," but such an extraordinary quantity of miracles

---

[113] For an extended discussion of the parallelism of the Genesis 3:15 text, and a defense of the ipsa ("she") pronoun from historical and medieval commentaries, particularly Cornelius à Lapide, cf. Bro. Thomas Sennott, M.I.C.M., "Mary Co-redemptrix," *Mary at the Foot of the Cross II: Acts of the International Symposium on Marian Coredemption*, Academy of the Immaculate, 2002, pp. 49-63. The author offers the following initial explanation in support of ipsa and quotes Cornelius à Lapide in support:

"In Hebrew *hu* is 'he,' and *he* 'she,' . . . There is no 'it' in Hebrew, both *hu* and *he* can be translated 'it' depending on the context.

In Greek 'he' is *autos*, 'she' *aute*, and 'it' *auto*.

In Latin 'he' is *ipse*, 'she' *ipsa*, and 'it' *ipsum* . . .

Cornelius à Lapide in his great *Commentaria in Scripturam Sacram* says that the underlying mystery is even reflected in the Hebrew grammar. 'Also *hu* is often used instead of *he* especially when there is some emphasis on action and something manly is predicated of the woman, as is the case here with the crushing *of* the serpent's head. … It makes no difference that the verb is masculine *yasuph*, that is "(he) shall crush," for it often happens in Hebrew that the masculine is used instead of the feminine and vice versa, especially when there is an underlying reason or mystery, as I have just said' (C. à Lapide, *Commentaria in Scripturam Sacram*, Larousse, Paris, 1848, p. 105). The 'underlying mystery' is, of course, that Our Lady crushes the head of the serpent by the power of Our Lord."

[114] Deposition of Fr. Jules Charles Chevalier, St. Catherine's last director, Ordinary Process, Cause for the Beatification and Canonization, June 17, 1896, s. 10, p. 136; cf. Dirvin, *Saint Catherine Labouré*, p. 95.

accompanied its release and promulgation that it was quickly named the "Miraculous Medal" by the faithful.[115]

On the reverse side of the medal vision, we see the "M" connected to the base of a cross, which re-emphasizes the doctrinal role of Mary as the Co-redemptrix[116] in the united work of redemption with and subordinate to her Son (cf. Jn 19:25-27). The depiction of the united and suffering hearts of Jesus and Mary would continue to be the most central theme throughout the Marian messages to the modern world, a theme which would be more explicitly and dramatically developed in the Fatima message.[117] The twelve stars surrounding the back medal image represents the universal queenship of Our Lady as depicted in Revelation 12:1, with its depiction of the mother of the male child (Rev 12:5), who is also mother of the "rest of her offspring" (Rev 12:17); the mother of the twelve apostles who symbolically fulfills the twelve tribes of Israel—the Mother of the Church.[118]

It is difficult to imagine a richer, more densely packed Mariological dogma, doctrine, and devotion than this, specifically and artistically represented on what was to become two sides of an approximately one-inch medal.[119] The most essential elements of the Marian message conveyed through later apparitions over the course of the following two centuries were here outlined and initiated by Our Lady of the Miraculous Medal. Also evident is the historical precedent of the Virgin Mother's concern and intercession during times of moral, social, and global degeneration, war, and disaster.

---

[115] Cf. R. Laurentin, *The Life of Catherine Labouré*, p. 94; cf. also Dirvin, *Saint Catherine Labouré*, insert 80-22.

[116] For examples of papal usages of the Co-redemptrix title by the Papal Magisterium, cf. Arthur B. Calkins, "The Mystery of Mary Coredemptrix in the Papal Magisterium," *Mary Co-redemptrix: Doctrinal Issues Today*, Mark Miravalle ed., Queenship Publications, 2002. For scriptural, patristic, and mediaeval foundations for the Co-redemptrix titles, as well as usages of the Co-redemptrix titles by popes, saints, and mystics, cf. Miravalle, *"With Jesus": The Story of Mary Co-redemptrix*, Queenship Publications, 2003.

[117] Cf. Fatima messages of July 13, 1917, and December 10, 1925, to be discussed later in this chapter.

[118] Cf. Pope St. Pius X, Encyclical *Ad Diem Illum Laetissimum*, February 2, 1904, 24; Pope Paul VI, Apostolic Exhortation *Signum Magnum*, May 13, 1967; Pope Benedict XVI, Wednesday audience of August 23, 2006.

[119] Dirvin, *Saint Catherine Labouré*, insert 80-22, 80-23.

In 1832, the Archbishop of Paris, Monsignor de Quélen, granted permission for the first medals to be struck.[120] In 1836, a process of ecclesiastical investigation led to the conclusion of supernatural authenticity for the apparitions and for numerous miracles attributed to it.[121] In 1842, the Holy See's approval was granted to the Miraculous Medal devotion as a result of a positive investigation into the conversion of the famous European Jewish figure, Alphonse Ratisbonne, which took place through a vision of Our Lady of the Miraculous Medal while Ratisbonne was in Rome.[122] It is commonly held that the private revelation of the Miraculous Medal acted as a confirming influence on Bl. Pius IX in his decision to define solemnly the doctrine of the Immaculate Conception on December 8, 1854.[123]

Sr. Catherine kept her identity as the visionary recipient of the apparitions a secret for forty-six years, and only revealed her identity when she sensed death approaching in 1876.[124] In 1933, fifty-seven years after her death, St. Catherine's body was exhumed and was found to be incorrupt.[125] She was canonized by Pius XII on July 27, 1947.

During his 1980 pilgrimage to the chapel of the apparitions on the Rue du Bac, Pope John Paul II referred to Our Lady's doctrinal roles of coredemption, mediation, advocacy, and her Immaculate Conception as they are contained in the Miraculous Medal revelations, confirming them in his own papal prayer to Our Lady of the Miraculous Medal:

> O Mary, conceived without sin, pray for us who have recourse to you.
>
> O Mary, this was the prayer that you gave to Saint Catherine Labouré in the Chapel of the Apparitions,

---

[120] J.M. Aladel, "Quentin" Canonical Inquiry, p. 2, p. 8, Archives of the Priests of the Congregation of the Mission, Paris, France; cf. Dirvin, *Saint Catherine Labouré*, p. 114; cf. also R. Laurentin, *The Life of Catherine Labouré*, p. 88.

[121] *Brouillon du Rapport de M. Quentin*, Archives of the Priests of the Congregation of the Mission, Paris, France; cf. Dirvin, *Saint Catherine Labouré*, p. 120.

[122] Cf. Theodore de Bussiere, Autograph, January 30, 1942, Archives of the Vicariate of Rome; cf. Dirvin, *Saint Catherine Labouré*, pp. 166-171; cf. also R. Laurentin, *The Life of Catherine Labouré*, p. 135.

[123] For example, cf. Dirvin, *Saint Catherine Labouré*, p. 178.

[124] Cf. R. Laurentin, *The Life of Catherine Labouré*, pp. 148-150, 211-212; cf. also Dirvin, *Saint Catherine Labouré*, p. 102-112, 218.

[125] Dirvin, *Saint Catherine Labouré*, insert 224-7, p. 229.

more than one hundred and fifty years ago. This invocation, engraved on the Miraculous Medal, is now worn and repeated by the faithful throughout the world.

... Blessed are you among women! You are intimately associated with the work of our redemption, associated with the Cross of our Savior, your heart has been pierced, next to his heart. And now, in the glory of your Son, you never cease to intercede for us, poor sinners. You watch over the Church for you are its Mother. You watch over each of your children. From God, you obtain for us all graces that are symbolized by the rays of light which radiate from your open hands, and the only condition that you demand of us is that we approach with the confidence, the hardiness, and the simplicity of a child. And it is thus that you bring us before your divine Son.[126]

The Lourdes Apparitions, 1858

The 14-year-old peasant girl, Bernadette Soubirous from the Pyrenees mountain town of Lourdes, France, received eighteen apparitions from the Blessed Virgin Mary from February 11 to July 16, 1858. Four years following the solemn papal definition of the Immaculate Conception, the essential message of the "Immaculate Conception" at Lourdes was one of reparation and coredemption: reparation to God for the sins of mankind, and coredemptive prayer and sacrifices for the conversion of sinners and their eternal salvation.

First Apparition, February 11, 1858: The first apparition received by Bernadette was accompanied by no verbal message, but did contain references to the recitation of the Rosary. The following is Bernadette's account:

> I saw a Lady dressed in white, she was wearing a white dress and a blue sash and a yellow rose on each foot, the color of the chain of her rosary ... I put my hand in my pocket, I found my rosary in it, I wanted to make the Sign of the Cross, I could not get my hand up to my

---

[126] Pope John Paul II, *Discourse in the Chapel of the Miraculous Medal*, Paris, France, May 31, 1980.

forehead, it fell back, the vision made the Sign of the Cross, then my hand shook, I tried to make it and I could, I said my Rosary, the vision ran the beads of hers through her fingers but she did not move her lips, when I had finished my Rosary, the vision disappeared all of a sudden.[127]

Second Apparition, February 14, 1858: Bernadette sprinkled holy water upon the "Lady" as an act of spiritual protection, to which the Lady smiled in return. The Lady remained until Bernadette had completed praying the Rosary:

> And I did see her as I threw the water at her; she smiled at me and nodded her head; when I finished saying my beads she disappeared.[128]

Third Apparition, February 18, 1858: Bernadette had been instructed by a local townswoman, Mme. Milhet, to ask "the Lady" to write down her name with pen and paper on a portable writing desk. The following exchange occurred between Bernadette and the Virgin Mary (whom Bernadette referred to simply as "Aqueró," or literally "That one" in her local dialect):

> *Bernadette*: "Will you have the goodness to put your name in writing?"
> *The Lady*: (smiling) "That isn't necessary." ... "Will you be kind enough to come here for a fortnight?"
> *Bernadette*: "Yes."
> *The Lady*: "I don't promise to make you happy in this world, but in the next."[129]

---

[127] Cf. R. Laurentin, *Lourdes. Histoire Authentique*, 6 vols., P. Lethielleux, Paris, 1961-1964, Vol. 2, 1962, pp. 83, 166-194; Alan Neame, *The Happening at Lourdes*, London, Catholic Book Club, 1968, p. 71. Note: This English source is in large part dependent upon the French work by R. Laurentin, *Lourdes. Histoire Authentique*.

[128] Cf. R. Laurentin, *Lourdes. Histoire Authentique*, Vol. 2, pp. 207-277; Neame, *Lourdes*, p. 76.

[129] Cf. R. Laurentin, *Lourdes. Histoire Authentique*, Vol. 2, pp. 309-371; Neame, *Lourdes*, p. 78.

Fourth Apparition, February 19, 1858: The fourth apparition reported no message for the public. The only phenomenon manifested in this apparition was the deep state of ecstasy experienced by Bernadette during the apparition, which was testified to by the seven or eight townspeople who were present.[130]

Fifth Apparition, February 20, 1858: This apparition was received by Bernadette at approximately 6:00 a.m. and also provided no publicly revealed message. The apparition lasted for approximately fifteen minutes.[131]

Sixth Apparition, February 21, 1858: The report of the sixth apparition was provided by Dr. Dozous, medical doctor at Lourdes and eyewitness to the apparition. Dozous reported the following change in Bernadette's facial expressions and disposition, and the subsequent rationale given for the change by Bernadette immediately after the event:

> As soon as she had come before the grotto, Bernadette knelt down, took out of her pocket her rosary and began to pray, saying her beads. Her face underwent a perfect transformation noticed by all who were near, and showed that she was *en rapport* with the appearance. ... Soon I saw her face, which until then had expressed the most perfect joy, grow sad; two tears fell from her eyes and rolled down her cheeks. This change occurring in her face during her station surprised me. I asked her, when she had finished her prayers and the mysterious being had disappeared, what had passed within her during this long station. She answered: "The Lady, walking away from me for a moment, directed her glance afar, above my head. Then looking down upon me again, she said, 'Pray for the sinners.' I was quickly reassured by the expression of goodness and sweetness which I saw return to her face, and immediately she disappeared."[132]

---

[130] Estrade, *Appearances*, pp. 56-57.
[131] Cf. R. Laurentin, *Lourdes. Histoire Authentique*, Vol. 4, pp. 27-40; Neame, *Lourdes*, p. 80.
[132] Estrade, *Appearances*, pp. 61-62.

Seventh Apparition, February 23, 1858: Although this apparition was accompanied by a dialogue, Bernadette never revealed the contents of the conversation. There is speculation that it was during this apparition that the Lady taught Bernadette a special prayer to be said by Bernadette every day of her life, but was never to be divulged. It also may have been during this apparition that Bernadette received three secrets from the Lady that were to remain private. The secrets were revealed to Bernadette with the directive: "I forbid you to repeat this to anyone."[133]

Eighth Apparition, February 24, 1858: The full dialogue between the "Aqueró" and Bernadette during this eighth apparition has not been revealed, but portions of the dialogue were documented. During the apparition, Bernadette, in tears, turned to the on-lookers and distinctly said, "Penitence, penitence, penitence!", words Bernadette later reported she had heard from the lips of "the Lady."[134] The Lady also said: "You're to pray to God for sinners."[135] She also directed Bernadette to go up the slope of the cave on her knees and "kiss the ground in penance for the conversion of sinners," to which Bernadette immediately responded in obedience.[136]

Ninth Apparition, February 25, 1858: The ninth apparition was accompanied by a supernaturally infused penitential directive to Bernadette to eat grass, followed by the instruction that she should "drink and wash from the spring." This led Bernadette to begin digging in the ground and to discover there what is now known as the miraculous spring, from which sixty-seven documented miracles of healing have been scientifically verified.[137] The following is Bernadette's account:

> While I was in prayer, the Lady said to me in a friendly, but serious voice, "Go, drink and wash in the spring." As I did not know where this spring was, and as I did not think the matter important, I went towards the

---

[133] Cf. R. Laurentin, *Lourdes. Histoire Authentique*, Vol. 4, pp. 178-228; Neame, *Lourdes*, p. 82.
[134] Estrade, *Appearances*, p. 90.
[135] Cf. R. Laurentin, *Lourdes. Histoire Authentique*, Vol. 4, pp. 229-277, 278-315; Neame, *Lourdes*, p. 84.
[136] *Ibid.*
[137] Cf. *67th Lourdes Miracle Officially Proclaimed*, Zenit, English edition, November 15, 2005.

> river. The Lady called me back and signed to me with her finger to go under the grotto to the left; I obeyed but I did not see any water. Not knowing where to get it from, I scratched the earth and the water came. I let it get a little clear of the mud, then I drank and washed.[138]

Upon being questioned about the reason for eating the grass, Bernadette replied: "I do not know. The Lady urged me by an inner impulse." During her acts of penance, Bernadette also said in a soft voice, "Penitence, penitence."[139]

Tenth Apparition, February 27, 1858: Bernadette performed similar prayers and penitential exercises: praying the Rosary, walking on her knees, drinking the water from the new spring, and kissing the ground. The only words reported from this tenth appearance are found in the account of an eyewitness:

> Upon her arrival at the Grotto, Bernadette without any hesitation passed by the place which she usually occupied and knelt down at the top of the slope at the point where she had scratched the earth the day before. She showed no surprise at finding the new spring flowing and, having crossed herself, drank and washed there. Having dried her face with the corner of her apron, she returned to the back and knelt down upon the stone which served her for a *prie-dieu*. She entered immediately into communication with her who was the joy of her soul, reciting the Rosary with devotion and self-abandonment, when the well-loved voice in a tone of sadness spoke to her these words: "You will kiss the earth for sinners." ... Not satisfied with having responded personally to the Lady's request, she wished to associate everyone with herself in the work of reparation. She turned towards the crowd and with a gesture of her hand ordered everyone present to bow face downwards to the ground. As if the order had come directly from the mouth of the Lady herself, every knee

---

[138] Estrade, *Appearances*, p. 90.
[139] Cf. R. Laurentin, *Lourdes. Histoire Authentique*, Vol. 4, pp. 316–451; Neame, *Lourdes*, p. 85.

was bent and every head touched for a moment the soil of the grotto. Those who could not bow so low as the ground placed their kiss of penitence upon parts of the rock.[140]

Eleventh Apparition, February 28, 1858: The Lady instructed Bernadette to have a chapel built at the grotto. The message was directed to the parish priests, as recorded in this account by the eyewitness, Jean-Pierre Estrade:

> At the end of their conversation, the Lady, so the seer told us, seemed to be thinking deeply; when she emerged from her reflections she said to her little protégée, "Go and tell the priests that a chapel must be built here."[141]

Twelfth Apparition, March 1, 1858: No message accompanied the twelfth apparition and Bernadette's now standard penitential exercises, except for the incident of the "borrowed rosary." Bernadette had been lent a rosary by a local woman, and took it from her pocket to begin her usual prayers during the apparition, at which point the Lady instructed her to return that particular rosary to her pocket, and to use her own rosary.[142]

Thirteenth Apparition, March 2, 1858: Besides the regular penitential exercises, Bernadette was reported to have had a lengthy and animated conversation with the Lady, but the only words revealed from the conversation were the instructions for the parish priest to have people come to the grotto in procession: "Go and tell the priests that people are to come here in procession."[143]

Fourteenth Apparition: March 3, 1858: During Bernadette's first visit to the grotto she prayed her usual Rosary, but no apparition took place. Later that same day, Bernadette returned to the grotto and received a

---

[140] Estrade, *Appearances*, pp. 100-101.
[141] Ibid., p. 107.
[142] Cf. R. Laurentin, *Lourdes. Histoire Authentique*, Vol. 5, pp. 53-98; Neame, *Lourdes*, p. 90.
[143] Cf. R. Laurentin, *Lourdes. Histoire Authentique*, Vol. 5, pp. 99-199; Neame, *Lourdes*, p. 91.

brief apparition. The only message revealed was the repeated request to the parish priest for the construction of a chapel at the apparition site.[144]

Fifteenth Apparition, March 4, 1858: The fifteenth apparition was technically the last in the fortnight of visits originally requested by the Lady. The appearance lasted approximately forty-five minutes, during which Bernadette smiled thirty-four times and bowed twenty-four times.[145] After the apparition ended, she was immediately questioned as to whether there was any message to be conveyed, and whether this apparition would be the last. The following eye-witness account records Bernadette's response:

> Bernadette remained nearly an hour in ecstasy. ... As soon as the seer had resumed her normal attitude, the persons near her hastened to ask her how the Lady had left her. "Just as usual," replied the child. "She smiled when she departed but she did not say good-bye to me."[146] When questioned whether Bernadette would return to the grotto, she replied: "Oh yes, I shall ... I shall keep coming, but I do not know whether the Lady will appear again."[147]

Sixteenth Apparition, March 25, 1858: After almost a three-week break in the apparitions, the Lady returned. During this period, a significant number of conversions were experienced by the people of Lourdes and by pilgrims from the surrounding regions, particularly by those who were frequenting sacramental confession and Mass with a renewed vigor. On this solemnity of the Annunciation, the Lady finally answered the question of her identity (which she had previously refused to answer) in her monumental self-identification:

> "When I was on my knees before the Lady," she [Bernadette] continued, "I asked her pardon for arriving late. Always good and gracious, she made a sign to me with

---

[144] Cf. R. Laurentin, *Lourdes. Histoire Authentique*, Vol. 5, pp. 200-245; Neame, *Lourdes*, p. 92.

[145] Cf. R. Laurentin, *Lourdes. Histoire Authentique*, Vol. 5, pp. 246-358; Neame, *Lourdes*, p. 93.

[146] Estrade, *Appearances*, p. 133.

[147] Ibid., p. 134.

her head that I need not excuse myself. Then I spoke to her of all my affection, all my respect and the happiness I had in seeing her again. After having poured out my heart to her I took up my rosary. While I was praying, the thought of asking her name came before my mind with such persistence that I could think of nothing else. I feared to be presumptuous in repeating a question she had always refused to answer. And yet something compelled me to speak. At last, under an irresistible impulse, the words fell from my mouth, and I begged the Lady to tell me who she was. The Lady did as she had always done before; she bowed her head and smiled but she did not reply. I cannot say why, but I felt myself bolder and asked her again to graciously tell me her name; however she only bowed and smiled as before, still remaining silent. Then once more, for a third time, clasping my hands and confessing myself unworthy of the favor I was asking of her, I again made my request. ... The Lady was standing above the rose-bush, in a position very similar to that shown in the miraculous medal. At the third request her face became very serious and she seemed to bow down in an attitude of humility. Then she joined her hands and raised them to her breast. ... She looked up to heaven... then slowly opening her hands and leaning forward towards me, she said to me in a voice vibrating with emotion: '*I am the Immaculate Conception!*'"[148]

Seventeenth Apparition, April 7, 1858: Bernadette followed her usual routine of the Rosary and penitential practices during this apparition. Dr. Dozous documented a noteworthy phenomenon that occurred during her state of ecstasy:

> One day when Bernadette seemed to be even more absorbed than usual in the appearance upon which her gaze was riveted, I witnessed, as also did everyone else there present, the fact which I am about to narrate.

---

[148] *Ibid.*, pp. 142-143.

> She was on her knees saying with fervent devotion the prayers of her rosary which she held in her left hand while in her right was a large blessed candle alight. The child was just beginning to make the usual ascent on her knees when she suddenly stopped and, her right hand joining her left, the flame of the big candle passed between the fingers of the latter. Though fanned by a fairly strong breeze, the flame produced no effect upon the skin which it was touching. Astonished at this strange fact, I forbade anyone to interfere, and taking my watch in hand, I studied the phenomenon attentively for a quarter of an hour. At the end of this time, Bernadette, still in her ecstasy, advanced to the upper part of the grotto, separating her hands. The flame thus ceased to touch her left hand.
>
> Bernadette finished her prayer and the splendor of the transfiguration left her face. She rose and was about to leave the grotto when I asked her to show me her left hand. I examined it most closely but could not find the least trace of burn anywhere upon it. ... I record this fact just as I have seen it without attempting to explain it.[149]

Eighteenth Apparition, July 16, 1858: On the feast of Our Lady of Mount Carmel, Bernadette received her last apparition. In spite of the barricades set up by the municipal authorities around the grotto, Bernadette sensed the inner impulse to return to the surrounding grotto area. The last apparition, documented by Estrade, presented no particular message content apart from the parting "smiles" of the Blessed Virgin Mary:

> Almost as soon as the child began to look towards the rock on the other side of the river the light of ecstasy transfigured her face and in the transports of her ravished soul she cried, "Yes, yes, there she is. She welcomes us and is smiling across the barriers!" Then instantly began between the Virgin and Bernadette that wonderful spiritual communing. ... During the whole of the vision

---

[149] *Ibid.*, pp. 148-149.

she continued gracious and smiling and when she quitted her little ecstatic, she left her in the fullness of joy.[150]

After the termination of the public apparitions and the series of ecclesiastical questionings of Bernadette, the shrine of Lourdes became the property of the See of Tarbes in 1861. Bishop Laurence of Tarbes confirmed the supernatural origin of the apparitions and granted formal permission for public devotion in 1862.[151] In 1865 Bernadette entered the Sisters of Charity and Christian Instruction in Nevers under the religious name of Sr. Marie Bernard. After an extended illness, she died on April 16, 1879.[152] Her body was exhumed three times, on September 22, 1909, April 3, 1919, and April 18, 1925, and each time found to be incorrupt. Bernadette was beatified in 1925 and canonized by Pius XI on December 8, 1933.[153]

The specific act of reparation, whereby one member of the Mystical Body of Christ can offer sacrifices of prayer and penance in atonement to God for the sins of other human beings, as well as for his own, is the fruit of Christian participation in Trinitarian life and sanctifying grace as a member of Christ's Mystical Body.[154] St. Bernadette, in her heroic response to the Lourdes message, became a living example of Christian reparation and coredemption by fulfilling the scriptural call of Colossians 1:24 to "make up what is lacking in the sufferings of Christ for the sake of his body, which is the Church." Through her prayers, specifically the Rosary which she consistently recited through the apparitions, and her varied forms of penitential practices, St. Bernadette embodied Our Lady's invitation to all followers of Christ, that they embrace the path of Christian coredemption in the generous offering of sacrifices for the

---

[150] *Ibid.*, pp. 151-152.
[151] Cf. the official declaration of authenticity of January 18, 1862; R. Laurentin – Bernard Billet, O.S.B., *Lourdes. Documents Authentiques*, 7 Vols., P. Lethielleux, Paris, 1957-1966, Vol. 6, *Procès de Lourdes. 2. Le Jugement Épiscopal*, 1961, pp. 237-245.
[152] Neame, *Lourdes*, p. 103.
[153] Cf. Pope Pius XI, document of canonization of St. Bernadette Soubirous, December 8, 1933.
[154] Cf. Pius XII, Encyclical, *Mystici Corporis*, 1943; John Paul II, Apostolic Letter, *Salvifici Doloris*, 1984, n. 27.

redemption of others and in atonement to God for sinners—to become what John Paul II was to later term a "co-redeemer in Christ."[155]

The foremost Lourdes phenomenon remains the miraculous spring, which led to a water source that presently releases over 30,000 gallons a day,[156] and to sixty-seven documented miracles of healing which have been scientifically and medically certified,[157] as well as innumerable other testimonies of physical and spiritual healings over the past one hundred and fifty years.[158]

Our Lady's self-revelation during the March 25, 1858, apparition has become a cornerstone for greater reflection on, and understanding of, the dogma of the Immaculate Conception. It is precisely Our Lady's Immaculate Conception which comprises the foundation for her maternal functions of coredemption and mediation, which are further revealed and experienced throughout the Age of Mary. St. Maximilian Kolbe offers these comments upon the Lourdes revelation and the deeper Mariological significance of Mary's Immaculate Conception as an essential, rather than an accidental, part of her nature:

> Immaculate Conception: These words fell from the lips of the Immaculata herself. Hence, they must tell us in the most precise and essential manner who she really is. ...[159] In her apparition at Lourdes she does not say: "I was conceived immaculately," but "I am the Immaculate Conception." This points out not only the fact that she was conceived without original sin, but also the manner

---

[155] John Paul II underscored the need for Christians to become "co-redeemers" at least three times, for example in addressing the sick at the Hospital of the Brothers of St. John of God (Fatebenefratelli) on Rome's Tiber Island on April 5, 1981, *L'Osservatore Romano*, English edition, April 13, 1981, p. 6; while addressing the sick after a general audience given January 13, 1982, *Inseg.*, V/1, 1982, 91; and during an address to the bishops of Uruguay gathered in Montevideo concerning candidates for the priesthood, May 8, 1988, *L'Osservatore Romano*, English edition, May 30, 1988, p. 4.

[156] Cf. "Lourdes," *New Catholic Encyclopedia*, 1967, Vol. 8, p. 1031.

[157] Cf. *67th Lourdes Miracle Officially Proclaimed*, Zenit, English edition, November 15, 2005; cf. R. Laurentin, *Lourdes. Histoire Authentique*, 6 vols., P. Lethielleux, Paris, 1961-1964, Vol. 6, p. 278, note 70.

[158] Cf. R. Laurentin, *ibid*.

[159] H.M. Manteau-Bonamy, O.P., *Immaculate Conception and the Holy Spirit: The Teachings of St. Maximilian Kolbe*, Franciscan Marytown Press, 1977, pp. 1, 2, 4.

in which this privilege belongs to her. It is not something accidental; it is something that belongs to her very nature. For she is Immaculate Conception in person.[160]

Bl. John XXIII, in a radio address at the close of the centenary celebration of the apparitions on February 18, 1959, confirmed the spiritual blessing of the Lourdes apparitions for the universal Church. He exhorted the People of God to listen with open minds and hearts to the "salutary warnings of the Mother of God" and, along with reiterating the nature and purpose of private revelation, defended the legitimacy and responsibility of the Roman pontiffs to bring to the attention of the faithful certain "supernatural lights" granted by God to guide us in our conduct:

> We ardently desire that Christendom be renewed in a unanimous zeal of Marian piety, because this, understood according to the doctrine of the Church, can only bring souls more surely and more swiftly to Jesus Christ, our sole and divine Savior. Following the pontiffs who, for a century, have recommended to Catholics that they should be attentive to the message of Lourdes, we urge you to listen with simplicity of heart and sincerity of mind to the salutary warnings of the Mother of God. Let no one be surprised, moreover, to hear the Roman pontiffs insist on this great spiritual lesson transmitted by the child of Massabielle. If they are instituted as the guardians and interpreters of Divine Revelation, contained in Holy Scripture and Tradition, they also take it as their duty to recommend to the attention of the faithful—when, after responsible examination, they judge it for the common good—the supernatural lights which it has pleased God to dispense freely to certain privileged souls, not for proposing new doctrines, but to guide us in our conduct: "*non ad navam doctrinam fidei depromendam, sed ad humanorum actuum directiones*" (S. TH. IIa IIac, Q. 174,

---

[160] St. Maximilian Kolbe, *Letter from Nagasaki to the Youth of the Franciscan Order*, February 28, 1933; cf. *Immaculate Conception and the Holy Spirit*, p. 7.

n. 6, ad 3um). Such is the case with the apparitions at Lourdes.[161]

The Fatima Apparitions, 1917

The message of Fatima was received by three young shepherd children from the mountain town of Fatima, Portugal: Lucia de Jesus Santos (born March 22, 1907) and her first cousins, Jacinta de Jesus Marto (born March 11, 1910) and Francisco de Jesus Marto (born June 11, 1908).[162] In this twentieth-century development of the Marian message, much greater specificity is given by the "Lady of the Rosary" within the general call to reparation and coredemption. It includes: 1) devotion, consecration, and reparation to the Immaculate Heart of Mary; 2) the daily praying of the Rosary for world peace; 3) the offering of all daily sacrifices for the conversion and salvation of souls; 4) prophecies of war for the twentieth century, sufferings for the Holy Father and the Church, and purification of the world, along with the Marian remedy; and 5) the five First Saturday Communions of Reparation.

1916-1917 Angelic Apparitions

The message of Fatima began with three anticipatory apparitions in 1916 by an angel who identified himself as the "Angel of Peace."[163] The following is an account of the first angelic appearance taken from the memoirs of Sr. Lucia, which were written at the request of her bishop:

> We spent the day there among the rocks, in spite of the fact that the rain was over and the sun was shining bright and clear. We ate our lunch and said our Rosary. … Our prayer finished, we started to play "pebbles."

---

[161] Bl. Pope John XXIII, *Radio Message at the close of the Centenary of the Apparitions of the Immaculata at Lourdes*, February 18, 1959, *L'Osservatore Romano*, Daily Edition, p. 1, (translated from the French).

[162] Rev. Robert Fox, *Fatima Today,* Front Royal, Virginia, Christendom Publications, 1983, p. 14.

[163] Lucia is referring to the same angel that appeared to her and three other companions briefly in 1915. Cf. Louis Kondor, S.V.D., ed., *Fatima in Lucia's Own Words: Sister Lucia's Memoirs,* Postulation Center, Fatima, Portugal, 9th edition, 1995, Second Memoir, p. 60.

> We had enjoyed the game for a few moments only, when a strong wind began to shake the trees. We looked up, startled, to see what was happening, for the day was unusually calm. Then we saw coming towards us, above the olive trees, the figure I have already spoken about. Jacinta and Francisco had never seen it before, nor had I ever mentioned it to them. As it drew closer, we were able to distinguish its features. It was a young man, about 14 or 15 years old, whiter than snow, transparent as crystal when the sun shines through it, and of great beauty. On reaching us, he said,
>
> "Do not be afraid! I am the Angel of Peace. Pray with me."
>
> Kneeling on the ground, he bowed down until his forehead touched the ground, and made us repeat these words three times:
>
> "My God, I believe, I adore, I hope and I love you. I ask pardon of you for those who do not believe, do not adore, do not hope and do not love you."
>
> Then rising, he said: "Pray thus. The hearts of Jesus and Mary are attentive to the voice of your supplications."[164]

From the very outset of the Fatima message conveyed in the first angelic apparition, the Marian call for prayer, penance, and reparation to God for those without Christian faith, hope, and love continued, both in the forms of general exhortation and specific penitential practices. The central theme of the hearts of Jesus and Mary, presented in the vision of the Miraculous Medal, was reiterated in the first angelic message.

Later in the same year of 1916 (the exact dates were not recorded), Lucia and her cousins, Jacinta and Francisco, received their second apparition of the Angel of Peace:

> Some time passed, and summer came, when we had to go home for siesta. One day, we were playing on the stone slabs of the well down at the bottom of the garden

---

[164] *Memoirs*, Second Memoir, pp. 61-62.

> belonging to my parents. ... Suddenly, we saw besides us the same figure, or rather angel, as it seemed to me.
>
> "What are you doing?" he asked. "Pray, pray very much! The most holy hearts of Jesus and Mary have designs of mercy on you. Offer prayers and sacrifices constantly to the Most High."
>
> "How are we to make sacrifices," I asked.
>
> "Make of everything you can a sacrifice, and offer it to God as an act of reparation for the sins by which he is offended, and in supplication for the conversion of sinners. You will thus draw down peace upon your country. I am its Angel Guardian, the Angel of Portugal. Above all, accept and bear with submission the suffering which the Lord will send you."[165]

The second message from the angel, now identified as the Guardian Angel of Portugal, more intensely transmitted heaven's imperative for ongoing sacrifices of prayer and penance in reparation to God for human offenses, and for the conversion of sinners. This message specified the offering of any and all sacrifices ("make of everything you can a sacrifice") for the same goals of atonement to God and supplication for sinners. The angel again emphasized devotion to the hearts of Jesus and Mary, and national peace was stated as the potential fruit of an obedient and generous response to this invitation. Most spiritually fruitful, the angel stated, is the patient acceptance and endurance of the sufferings, which God's mysterious providence would bring to the three young children.

The third appearance of the Angel of Peace (probably in the first part of 1917), in preparation for the upcoming Marian apparitions, revealed the theme of Eucharistic reparation:

> A considerable time had elapsed, when one day we went to pasture our sheep on a property belonging to my parents. ...
>
> As soon as we arrived there, we knelt down, with our foreheads touching the ground, and began to repeat the prayer of the angel:

---

[165] *Memoirs*, Second Memoir, p. 62.

"My God, I believe, I adore, I hope, and I love you." I don't know how many times we had repeated this prayer, when an extraordinary light shone upon us. We sprang up to see what was happening, and beheld the angel. He was holding a chalice in his left hand, with the Host suspended above it, from which some drops of blood fell into the chalice. Leaving the chalice suspended in the air, the angel knelt down beside us and made us repeat three times:

"Most Holy Trinity, Father, Son, and Holy Spirit, I adore you profoundly, and I offer you the most precious Body, Blood, Soul, and Divinity of Jesus Christ, present in all the tabernacles of the world, in reparation for the outrages, sacrileges, and indifference with which he himself is offended. And, through the infinite merits of his most Sacred Heart, and the Immaculate Heart of Mary, I beg of you conversion of poor sinners."

Then, rising, he took the chalice and the Host in his hands. He gave the Sacred Host to me, and shared the Blood from the chalice between Jacinta and Francisco,[166] saying as he did so:

"Take and drink the Body and Blood of Jesus Christ, horribly outraged by ungrateful men! Make reparation for their crimes and console your God."

Once again, he prostrated on the ground and repeated with us, three times more, the same prayer, "Most Holy Trinity..." and then disappeared.[167]

The strong Eucharistic emphasis in this third angelic apparition revealed the power of Eucharistic reparation, attainable through the offering of Jesus in the Eucharist to the most Holy Trinity for the outrages, sacrileges, and indifferences by which he is gravely offended. This devotional practice of the laity spiritually offering the Eucharistic species indicates the great efficacy that can come from the People of God

---

[166] Jacinta and Francisco had not yet received their first Holy Communion, but evidently neither regarded this as a sacramental Communion. Cf. *Memoirs*, footnote 18, p. 99.

[167] *Ibid.*, pp. 62-63.

exercising their own "royal priesthood" of the laity (always in proper subordination to the primary offering of the Eucharistic sacrifice by the ordained priesthood). Moreover, the offering of the Eucharistic Jesus received sacramentally, as experienced by the children, is also revealed as abundantly efficacious in atonement and consolation to God for the "crimes" of man.

The "Two Hearts" theme increased in prominence throughout the Fatima messages. The Sacred Heart of Jesus, source of infinite merits, and the Immaculate Heart of Mary, the channel to those infinite merits, were again referred to in the third angelic appearance, along with the continued request to intercede for "poor sinners." Eucharistic adoration was likewise emphasized as the Eucharist was suspended in the air, before which both the angel and children offered reverential adoration.

1917 Marian Apparitions

On May 13, 1917, a series of six monthly apparitions from Our Lady of the Rosary took place in the nearby fields where the three Portuguese shepherd children grazed their sheep. The account of this first apparition is taken from Lucia's personal memoirs.[168]

First Apparition, May 13, 1917: The first appearance consisted principally in the invitation from the "Lady from heaven," who asked the children to return for five more successive months on the same day of each month. It confirmed the angelic calls to offer oneself to God and to bear his providentially permitted sufferings as reparation for sins and for the conversion of sinners. The Eucharistic theme continued in the inspired prayer to Jesus in the Blessed Sacrament, and the Lady also requested the daily praying of the Rosary as a means to world peace and an end to World War I:

High up on the slope in the Cova da Iria, I was playing with Jacinta and Francisco at building a little stone wall around a clump of furze. Suddenly we saw what seemed to be a flash of lightning.

"We'd better go home," I said to my cousins, "that's lightning; we may have a thunderstorm."

"Yes, indeed!" they answered.

---

[168] Cf. Louis Kondor, S.V.D., ed., *Fatima in Lucia's Own Words: Sister Lucia's Memoirs*, Postulation Center, Fatima, Portugal, 9th edition, 1995.

We began to go down the slope, hurrying the sheep along towards the road. We were more or less halfway down the slope, and almost level with a large holm-oak tree that stood there, when we saw another flash of lightning. We had only gone a few steps farther when, there before us on a small holm-oak, we beheld a lady all dressed in white. She was more brilliant than the sun, and radiated a light more clear and intense than a crystal glass filled with sparkling water, when the rays of the burning sun shine through it.

We stopped, astounded, before the apparition. We were so close, just a few feet from her, that we were bathed in the light which surrounded her, or rather, which radiated from her. Then Our Lady spoke to us:

"Do not be afraid. I do you no harm."

"Where are you from?"

"I am from heaven."

"What do you want of me?"

"I have come to ask you to come here for six months in succession, on the 13th day, at this same hour. Later on, I will tell you who I am and what I want. Afterwards, I will return here yet a seventh time." [169]

"Shall I go to heaven too?"

"Yes, you will."

"And Jacinta?"

"She will go also."

"And Francisco?"

"He will go there too, but he must say many Rosaries."

Then I remembered to ask about two girls who had died recently. They were friends of mine and used to come to my home to learn weaving with the eldest sister.

"Is Maria dos Neves in heaven?"

"Yes, she is."

"And Amélia?"

"She will be in purgatory until the end of the world."

The Lady continued:

"Are you willing to offer yourselves to God and bear all the suffering he wills to send you, as an act of reparation for the sins by which he is offended, and of supplication for the conversion of sinners?"

---

[169] The "seventh time" refers to the apparition to Sr. Lucia on December 10, 1925, which revealed the First Saturdays of Reparation, as will be subsequently treated.

"Yes, we are willing."

"Then you are going to have much to suffer, but the grace of God will be your comfort."

As she pronounced these last words, "...the grace of God will be your comfort," Our Lady opened her hands for the first time, communicating to us a light so intense that, as it streamed from her hands, its rays penetrated our hearts and the innermost depths of our souls, making us see ourselves in God. ... Then, moved by an interior impulse that was also communicated to us, we fell on our knees, repeating in our hearts:

"O most Holy Trinity, I adore you! My God, my God, I love you in the most Blessed Sacrament."

After a few moments, Our Lady spoke again:

"Pray the Rosary every day, in order to obtain peace for the world, and the end of the war."

Then she began to rise serenely, going up towards the east, until she disappeared in the immensity of space.[170]

Second Apparition, June 13, 1917: The second message spoke of the importance of the daily Rosary, and explicitly introduced the wish of Jesus for a worldwide devotion to the Immaculate Heart of Mary, joined to the promise of eternal salvation for all who will embrace it:

> As soon as Jacinta, Francisco, and I had finished praying the Rosary, with a number of other people who were present, we saw once more the flash reflecting the light which was approaching (which we called lightning). The next moment, Our Lady was there on the holm-oak, exactly the same as in May.
>
> "What do you want of me?" I asked.
>
> "I wish you to come here on the 13th of next month, to pray the Rosary every day, and to learn to read. Later, I will tell you what I want."
>
> I asked for the cure of a sick person.
>
> "If he is converted, he will be cured during the year."
>
> "I would like to ask you to take us to heaven."
>
> "Yes. I will take Jacinta and Francisco soon. But you are to stay here for some time longer. Jesus wishes to

---

[170] *Ibid.*, Fourth Memoir, pp. 156-160.

make use of you to make me known and loved. He wants to establish in the world devotion to my Immaculate Heart. I promise salvation to those who embrace it, and those souls will be loved by God like flowers placed by me to adorn his throne."[171]

"Am I to stay here alone?" I asked, sadly.

"No, my daughter. Are you suffering a great deal? Do not lose heart. I will never forsake you. My Immaculate Heart will be your refuge and the way that will lead you to God."

As Our Lady spoke these last words, she opened her hands and for the second time, she communicated to us the rays of that same immense light. We saw ourselves in this light, as it were, immersed in God. Jacinta and Francisco seemed to be in that part of the light which rose towards heaven, and I in that which was poured out on the earth. In front of the palm of Our Lady's right hand was a heart encircled by thorns which pierced it. We understood that this was the Immaculate Heart of Mary, outraged by the sins of humanity, and seeking reparation.[172]

Third Apparition, July 13, 1917: The July 13 Fatima apparition constituted arguably the single-most important apparition and concomitant message in the overall Marian revelation to the modern world.[173] It revealed a vision of hell; the end of World War I, but the conditional beginning of a second world war; the rise of communism and numerous upcoming (though conditional) trials for the world, the Church and the Holy Father. The Lady subsequently offered the supernatural remedy through consecration to the Immaculate Heart of Mary and through the First Saturday Communions of Reparation,

---

[171] This last line was omitted in Lucia's final account of the 1917 apparitions, but appears in other earlier accounts as it is cited in this text. Cf. *Memoirs*, p. 187, Footnote 14.

[172] *Ibid.*, Fourth Memoir, pp. 160-161.

[173] Particularly in light of its revelation of the "triumph" of the Immaculate Heart of Mary, a triumph for which the previous apparitions of the Marian age seek to prepare for, and which subsequent approved apparitions seek to fulfill.

which would lead to the "Triumph of the Immaculate Heart of Mary" and an eventual global "era of peace":

> A few moments after arriving at the Cova da Iria, near the holm-oak, where a large number of people were praying the Rosary, we saw the flash of light once more, and a moment later Our Lady appeared on the holm-oak.
>
> "What do you want of me?" I asked.
>
> "I want you to come here on the 13th of next month, to continue to pray the Rosary every day in honor of Our Lady of the Rosary, in order to obtain peace for the world and the end of the war, because only she can help you."
>
> "I would like to ask you to tell us who you are, and to work a miracle so that everybody will believe that you are appearing to us."
>
> "Continue to come here every month. In October, I will tell you who I am and what I want, and I will perform a miracle for all to see and believe."
>
> I then made some requests, but I cannot recall now just what they were. What I do remember is that Our Lady said it was necessary for such people to pray the Rosary in order to obtain these graces during the year. And she continued:
>
> "Sacrifice yourselves for sinners, and say many times, especially whenever you make some sacrifice: O Jesus, it is for love of you, for the conversion of sinners, and in reparation for the sins committed against the Immaculate Heart of Mary."
>
> As Our Lady spoke these last words, she opened her hands once more, as she had done during the two previous months. The rays of light seemed to penetrate the earth, and we saw, as it were, a sea of fire. Plunged in this fire were demons and souls in human form, like transparent burning embers, all blackened or burnished bronze, floating about in the conflagration, now raised into the air by the flames that issued from within themselves together with great clouds of smoke,

now falling back on every side like sparks in huge fires, without weight or equilibrium, amid shrieks and groans of pain and despair, which horrified us and made us tremble with fear. (It must have been this sight which caused me to cry out, as people say they heard me.) The demons could be distinguished by their terrifying and repellent likeness to frightful and unknown animals, black and transparent like burning coals. Terrified and as if to plead for succor, we looked up at Our Lady, who said to us, so kindly and so sadly:

"You have seen hell where the souls of poor sinners go. To save them, God wishes to establish in the world devotion to my Immaculate Heart. If what I say to you is done, many souls will be saved and there will be peace. The war is going to end; but if people do not cease offending God, a worse one will break out during the pontificate of Pius XI. When you see a night illumined by an unknown light, know that this is the great sign given you by God that he is about to punish the world for its crimes, by means of war, famine, and persecutions of the Church and of the Holy Father.

"To prevent this, I shall come to ask for the consecration of Russia to my Immaculate Heart, and the Communion of Reparation on the First Saturdays. If my requests are heeded, Russia will be converted, and there will be peace; if not, she will spread her errors throughout the world, causing wars and persecutions of the Church. The good will be martyred, the Holy Father will have much to suffer, various nations will be annihilated. In the end, my Immaculate Heart will triumph. The Holy Father will consecrate Russia to me, and she will be converted, and a period of peace will be granted to the world. In Portugal, the dogma of the faith will always be preserved. ... Do not tell this to anybody. Francisco, yes, you may tell him.

"When you pray the Rosary, say after each mystery: O my Jesus, forgive us, save us from the fire of hell.

Lead all souls to heaven, especially those who are most in need."[174]

After this, there was a moment of silence, and then I asked:

"Is there anything more that you want of me?"

"No, I do not want anything more of you today."

Then, as before, Our Lady began to ascend towards the east, until she finally disappeared in the immense distance of the firmament.[175]

This third message renewed the imperative to pray the Rosary each day, also prioritized through the revelation of her Fatima title of "Our Lady of the Rosary." The intention of the daily Rosary, again directed towards world peace and the end of the First World War, was accompanied by the words, "for only she can help you." The plan of world peace has been entrusted by God to the maternal mediation of Mary Immaculate, and it is seemingly God's condition for the eventual granting of the gift of world peace that mankind acknowledges this role of the Mother in the order of grace and peace.

Lucia described hell as a "sea of fire," with visual testimony to the existence of human beings in hell. The remedy for the loss of "so many" souls into hell would be the establishment of world devotion to the Immaculate Heart of Mary. This was "God's wish."

If humanity did not sufficiently cooperate with Our Lady's requests, a more severe world war would commence during the pontificate of Pope Pius XI.[176] To the objection that the Second World War (September 1, 1939-1945), actually began during the pontificate of Pope Pius XII, Sr. Lucia has responded that the war in fact began with the Nazi occupation of Austria in 1938, which took place under the pontificate of Pius XI. The promised light that would illuminate the night as a sign of the forthcoming war corresponds with the reported "aurora borealis" that lit up the European skies (and beyond) on January 25, 1938. War would be a punishment permitted by God due to sin, a just punishment because

---

[174] The present English form of the prayer is: "O my Jesus, forgive us our sins, save us from the fires of hell. Lead all souls to heaven, especially those who are most in need of thy mercy."

[175] *Memoirs,* Fourth Memoir, pp. 161-166.

[176] Cf. *Memoirs*, pp. 112, 187.

the human cooperation and conversion necessary to avert justice through acceptance of divine mercy was not satisfied.[177] The potential effects of humanity's unwillingness to convert were foretold by Our Lady; they would consist in famine, the annihilation of nations, persecutions of the Church, and particular sufferings for the Holy Father. The assassination attempt and near-fatal shooting of John Paul II on the Fatima anniversary of May 13, 1981, has been commonly accepted as one fulfillment of the July 13 prophecy. The twentieth-century rise of world communism from the 1917 Russian revolution and its horrific trail of atheism, totalitarianism, and genocide, likewise fulfilled, in part, the Fatima prophecy.

Fourth Apparition, August 19, 1917: The fourth apparition did not take place on the typical thirteenth day of the month, due to the fact that civil authorities abducted the children and brought them to a nearby jail, where they threatened them with death if they would not deny the apparitions and reveal the secrets.[178] The fourth apparition eventually took place on August 19, feast of St. John Eudes, the first great theological and liturgical promoter of the Devotion to the Hearts of Jesus and Mary. The message of August 19 renewed the call of daily Rosary prayer and reparation for sinners and it requested the building of a chapel at the apparition site. The Lady also promised a miracle during the last monthly apparition. The message ended with the re-confirmation of the reality of hell and the need to sacrifice for sinners:

> I was accompanied by Francisco and his brother John. We were with the sheep in a place called Valinhos, when we felt something supernatural approaching and enveloping us. Suspecting that Our Lady was about to appear to us, and feeling sorry lest Jacinta might miss seeing her, we asked her brother to go and call her. As he was unwilling to go, I offered him two small coins, and off he ran.
>
> Meanwhile, Francisco and I saw the flash of light, which we called lightning. Jacinta arrived, and a moment later, we saw Our Lady on a holm-oak tree.

---

[177] Cf. St. Thomas Aquinas, *De Malo*, Q. 1-2.
[178] Cf. *Memoirs*, First Memoir, p. 35-37.

"What do you want of me?"

"I want you to continue going to the Cova da Iria on the 13th, and to continue praying the Rosary every day. In the last month, I will perform a miracle so that all may believe."

"What do you want done with the money that the people leave in the Cova da Iria?"

"Have two litters made. One is to be carried by you and Jacinta and two other girls dressed in white; the other one is to be carried by Francisco and three other boys. The money from the litters is for the 'festa' of Our Lady of the Rosary, and what is left over will help towards the construction of a chapel that is to be built here."

"I would like to ask you to cure some sick persons."

"Yes, I will cure some of them during the year."

Then, looking very sad, Our Lady said:

"Pray, pray very much, and make sacrifices for sinners; for many souls go to hell, because there are none to sacrifice themselves and to pray for them."

And she began to ascend as usual towards the east.[179]

Fifth Apparition, September 13, 1917: This message prepared for the final monthly apparition of October 13 by prophesying the appearances of the child Jesus, St. Joseph, Our Lady of Sorrows, and Our Lady of Mount Carmel. Our Lady thanked the children for their sacrifices, but instructed them not to continue to wear when going to bed the penitential ropes they had been placing around their waists for added sacrifices:

> At last, we arrived at the Cova da Iria, and on reaching the holm-oak we began to say the Rosary with the people. Shortly afterwards, we saw the flash of light, and then Our Lady appeared on the holm-oak.
>
> "Continue to pray the Rosary in order to obtain the end of the war. In October, Our Lord will come, as well as Our Lady of Dolors and Our Lady of Carmel. Saint Joseph will appear with the child Jesus to bless the world.

---

[179] *Memoirs*, Fourth Memoir, pp. 166-167.

God is pleased with your sacrifices. He does not want you to sleep with the rope on, but only to wear it during the daytime."

"I was told to ask you many things, the cure of some sick people, of a deaf-mute…"

"Yes, I will cure some, but not others. In October, I will perform a miracle so that all may believe."

Then Our Lady began to rise as usual, and disappeared.[180]

Sixth Apparition, October 13, 1917: The final 1917 apparition to Lucia, Jacinta, and Francisco renewed the general Fatima call to daily Rosary prayer, penance, conversion, peace, and an end to the offenses by humanity against its God. Following the message, there occurred the historically documented phenomenon referred to as the "miracle of the sun":

> We reached the holm-oak in the Cova da Iria. Once there, moved by an interior impulse, I asked the people to shut their umbrellas and say the Rosary. A little later, we saw the flash of light, and then Our Lady appeared on the holm-oak.
>
> "What do you want of me?"
>
> "I want to tell you that a chapel is to be built here in my honor. I am the Lady of the Rosary. Continue always to pray the Rosary every day. The war is going to end, and the soldiers will soon return to their homes."
>
> "I have many things to ask you: the cure of some sick persons, the conversion of sinners and other things…"
>
> "Some yes, but not others. They must amend their lives and ask forgiveness for their sins."
>
> Looking very sad, Our Lady said: "Do not offend the Lord our God any more, because he is already so much offended."
>
> Then, opening her hands, she made them reflect on the sun, and as she ascended, the reflection of her own light continued to be projected on the sun itself. …

---

[180] *Memoirs,* Fourth Memoir, p. 168.

After Our Lady had disappeared into the immense distance of the firmament, we beheld St. Joseph with the child Jesus and Our Lady robed in white with a blue mantle, beside the sun. St. Joseph and the child Jesus appeared to bless the world, for they traced the Sign of the Cross with their hands. When, a little later, this apparition disappeared, I saw Our Lord and Our Lady; it seemed to me that it was Our Lady of Dolors. Our Lord appeared to bless the world in the same manner as St. Joseph had done. This apparition also vanished, and I saw Our Lady once more, this time resembling Our Lady of Carmel.[181]

At the close of this sixth apparition, approximately 70,000 onlookers witnessed the ensuing solar miracle. Thousands of eye-witness accounts described the sun as a dull silver plate spinning around in a circular motion, "dancing in the sky."[182] Seconds later, it appeared to surge downward towards the earth, giving off various colors, and shortly before reaching the ground, it stopped in its course and returned to its original position in the sky.[183]

The three series of visions have been considered as representative of the three existing sets of Rosary mysteries: St. Joseph and the Christ child jointly blessing the world in representation of the Joyful Mysteries; Our Lady of Sorrows, a visible representation of Mary Co-redemptrix, signifying the Sorrowful Mysteries; and Our Lady of Mount Carmel, conveying devotion to the Scapular and its promise of eternal life (which Sr. Lucia later identified as a key Fatima element), signifying the Glorious Mysteries.

The Seventh Apparition, December 10, 1925: On the evening of December 10, 1925, Our Lady fulfilled her prophecy of May 13, 1917, which foretold that she would return for a seventh time. Sister Lucia of the Immaculate Heart, in her convent at Pontevedra, Spain, received the seventh apparition, which provided the specific conditions for the five First Saturday Communions of Reparation introduced in the July

---

[181] *Ibid.*, pp. 168-170.
[182] Cf. for example, F. Johnston, *Fatima: The Great Sign*, Tan, 1980, p. 53ff.
[183] *Ibid.*

13, 1917, message. Sr. Lucia gave the following account of this seventh apparition (referring to herself in the third person):

> On December 10, 1925, the most Holy Virgin appeared to her, and by her side, elevated on a luminous cloud, was a child. The most Holy Virgin rested her hand on her shoulder, and as she did so, she showed her a heart encircled by thorns, which she was holding in her hand. At the same time, the Child said:
>
> "Have compassion on the Heart of your most Holy Mother, covered with thorns, with which ungrateful men pierce it at every moment, and there is no one to make an act of reparation to remove them."
>
> Then the Holy Virgin said:
>
> "Look, my daughter, at my Heart, surrounded with thorns with which ungrateful men pierce me at every moment by their blasphemies and ingratitude. You at least try to console me, and say that I promise to assist at the hour of death, with the graces necessary for salvation, all those who, on the first Saturday of five consecutive months, shall confess, receive Holy Communion, recite five decades of the Rosary, and keep me company for fifteen minutes while meditating on the fifteen mysteries of the Rosary, with the intention of making reparation to me."[184]

The most striking element of the seventh apparition is the promise of eternal salvation given by Our Lady of Fatima for those who fulfill these four conditions on five consecutive first Saturdays: 1) receive sacramental confession; 2) receive Holy Communion; 3) pray five decades of the Rosary; and 4) "keep me company" while meditating for fifteen minutes on any number of the Rosary mysteries. Our Lady specifies that all four conditions must be offered with the specific intention of making reparation to her own Immaculate Heart.

The Second Vatican Council reminds us of the maternal function of the Mother of Jesus, that after her glorious Assumption into heaven, she "did not lay aside her saving office," but by her maternal intercession as

---

[184] *Memoirs*, Appendix I, p. 231.

Mediatrix "continues to bring us the gifts of eternal life" (*Lumen Gentium*, 62). What is required for the distribution of grace by the Mediatrix of all graces is the free cooperation of man. The four conditions of the First Saturday Fatima Devotion not only elicit the free cooperation of the individual, but also lead the believer into the heart of the Church's prayer and sacramental life. The Fatima promise for eternal salvation through the intercession of the Mother rests upon solid theological and Mariological foundations.

In a later revelation given by Jesus to Sr. Lucia on the night of May 29-30, 1930, the Fatima seer asked him a question from a priest as to why it had to be five first Saturdays instead of another number. Jesus responded by stating that this was in reparation for the five general categories of offenses committed against his Mother's Most Immaculate Heart: 1) blasphemies against the Immaculate Conception; 2) blasphemies against her virginity; 3) blasphemies against her divine motherhood, refusing at the same time to acknowledge her as Mother of men; 4) those who publicly attempt to instill in the hearts of children indifference, contempt, or even hatred of her Immaculate Heart; and 5) those who insult her directly in her venerated statues and images.[185]

Theologically intriguing are the repeated references to the ongoing "mystical suffering" of the Immaculate Heart of Mary. In the December 10, 1925, apparition, the Christ child referred to the thorns suffered by the Immaculate Heart of his Mother, which represent the offenses with which ungrateful men pierce it "at every moment." This was followed by Our Lady's own words which also referred directly to the sufferings experienced by her Heart "at every moment": "Look, my daughter, at my Heart, surrounded with thorns with which ungrateful men pierce me at every moment by their blasphemies and ingratitude." Is this simply a trans-temporal extension to Our Lady's sufferings during the time of her earthly life? Or could it refer to a special privilege granted by God to Our Lady as the Mother of the Mystical Body, to participate, in some mysterious way even after her Assumption into heaven, in the ongoing sufferings of humanity, and through the vulnerability that always seems to accompany love, to experience the rejection of her love by many of her earthly children? Certainly, the mystical tradition seems to support

---

[185] *Father Goncalves' Questions and Lucia's Answers Document*, May 30, 1930, *Documents on Fatima and the Memoirs of Sr. Lucia*, Fatima Family Apostolate, 1992, p. 246.

the concept of the ongoing sufferings of the Immaculate Heart, whether it be manifested in prophetic revelations like Fatima or in phenomena such as weeping statues and icons.[186]

Edouard Cardinal Gagnon refers to Our Lady's mysterious ongoing sufferings with her earthly children in his commentary on the coredemptive call of the Fatima message and the December 10, 1925, message:

> The Fatima call to coredemption and reparation unveils the request to offer consolation directly to Mary's most Immaculate Heart in atonement for the present pains inflicted on that maternal heart by the daily offenses of humanity. A mother's heart shares in the suffering of her children in the order of love, and hence the Savior Son initiates the call for reparation and consolation to the Heart of our universal spiritual Mother.[187]

Both the Christ child and the Immaculate Mother called for reparation and consolation from Sr. Lucia, and continue to call forth from all other Christian faithful with open hearts, loving atonement for the continuous piercing sins of a mankind who, to a significant degree, has rejected the love of its Mother. It is little wonder, then, why the First Saturday Communions of Reparation typically become a lifetime devotional practice of reparation to the Immaculate Heart for those with a full understanding of this means of consoling the Heart of the Mother.

On October 13, 1930, Dom José Alves Correia da Silva, bishop of the Diocese of Leiria, granted official approval of the Fatima apparitions.[188] Previous to this approval, the cardinal patriarch, Don Antonio Menes Belo, whose jurisdiction originally included the region of Fatima, had

---

[186] Cf. for example, the ecclesiastically approved Marian apparitions at Akita, Japan (1973-1981), where the tears which appeared on the statue 101 times were analyzed and found be of human tear composition, cf. Francis Fukushima, *Akita: Mother of God as Co-Redemptrix. Modern Miracles of Holy Eucharist*, Queenship, 1994, p. 168.

[187] Edouard Cardinal Gagnon, "Fatima and Our Lady Co-redemptrix," in *Maria, Unica Cooperatrice Alla Redenzione,* Fatima, Portugal, 2006, Academy of the Immaculate, p. 73.

[188] Pastoral Letter of Bishop Joseph Correia da Silva, October 13, *Documents on Fatima*, p. 247.

prohibited the local clergy from pilgrimaging to the apparition site or from taking part in any religious ceremony relating to Fatima.[189]

On March 25, 1984, John Paul II consecrated the world (inclusive of Russia), to the Immaculate Heart of Mary, in fulfillment of the July 13, 1917, Fatima request. That the 1984 consecration by John Paul II satisfied the Fatima request was repeatedly confirmed by Sr. Lucia in several statements after the 1984 consecration.[190] On May 13, 2000, John Paul II beatified Jacinta and Francisco Marto in Fatima.[191] At the conclusion of the beatification Mass and ceremony, Secretary of State Angelo Cardinal Sodano announced that the third and final part of the July 13, 1917, message of Fatima, widely known as the "Secret of Fatima," would soon be made public. On June 26, 2000, the Congregation for the Doctrine of the Faith, in compliance to the directive of John Paul II, released the "third secret" of Fatima, as written by Sr. Lucia:

> After the two parts which I have already explained, at the left of Our Lady and a little above, we saw an angel with a flaming sword in his left hand; flashing, it gave out flames that looked as though they would set the world on fire; but they died out in contact with the splendor that Our Lady radiated towards him from her right hand: pointing to the earth with his right hand, the angel cried out in a loud voice: "Penance, penance, penance!" And we saw in an immense light that is God: "something similar to how people appear in a mirror when they pass in front of it" a bishop dressed in white "we had the impression that it was the Holy Father." Other bishops, priests, men and women religious going up a steep mountain, at the top of which there was a big cross of rough-hewn trunks as of a cork-tree with the bark; before reaching there, the Holy Father passed through a big city half in ruins, and half trembling with

---

[189] Ibid., p. 251.

[190] Cf. Letter of Sr. Lucia, November 8, 1989, as quoted in *L'Osservatore Romano*, English edition, June 28, 2000, Special Insert, p. II; Cf. also her interview with Ricardo Cardinal Vidal of the Philippines in 1993, John Haffert, *God's Final Effort*, 101 Foundation, 1999, pp. 2, 6.

[191] Cf. *L'Osservatore Romano*, English edition, May 17, 2000, p.1.

> halting step, afflicted with pain and sorrow, he prayed for the souls of the corpses he met on his way; having reached the top of the mountain, on his knees at the foot of the big Cross he was killed by a group of soldiers who fired bullets and arrows at him, and in the same way there died one after another the other bishops, priests, men and women religious, and various lay people of different ranks and positions. Beneath the two arms of the cross there were two angels each with a crystal aspersorium in his hand, in which they gathered up the blood of the martyrs and with it sprinkled the souls that were making their way to God.[192]

On February 13, 2005, Sr. Lucia de Jesus of the Immaculate Heart died at the Carmel in Coimbra at the age of 97.[193]

What is the relevance of the Fatima message for the twenty-first century?

After the assassination attempt on the life of John Paul II, the "Fatima Pope" accentuated Fatima's relevance for contemporary humanity:

> The evangelical call to repentance and conversion, uttered in the Mother's message, remains ever relevant. It is still more relevant than it was 65 years ago.[194]

In his 2000 commentary on the third part of the Fatima message, Cardinal Joseph Ratzinger reminds us of the potential for untold human destruction that remains at our fingertips in light of our contemporary nuclear capabilities:

> Today the prospect that the world might be reduced to ashes by a sea of fire no longer seems pure fantasy: man himself, with his inventions, has forged the flaming sword.[195]

---

[192] *L'Osservatore Romano*, English edition, June 28, 2000, Special Insert, p. IV.
[193] Cf. Zenit, English edition, February 14, 2005.
[194] Pope John Paul II, homily delivered at the Fatima Shrine, *L'Osservatore Romano*, English edition, May 17, 1982.
[195] *L'Osservatore Romano*, English edition, June 28, 2000, Special Insert, p. VIII.

Since his election to the papacy, Pope Benedict XVI continues to emphasize the relevance of the Fatima message for our own times. In his May 14, 2006, commentary, he refers to the crucial historical importance of the unfolding Fatima message:

> A sure way of remaining united to Christ, as branches to the vine, is to have recourse to the intercession of Mary, whom we venerated yesterday, May 13, in a particular way, recalling the apparitions at Fatima, where she appeared on several occasions to three shepherd children, Francisco, Jacinta, and Lucia, in 1917.
>
> The message that she entrusted to them, in continuity with that of Lourdes, was a strong appeal to prayer and conversion; a truly prophetic message, considering that the twentieth century was scourged by unheard-of destruction caused by war and totalitarian regimes, as well as widespread persecution of the Church.
>
> Moreover, on May 13, 1981, 25 years ago, the Servant of God John Paul II felt that he was saved miraculously from death by the intervention of "a maternal hand"—as he himself said—and his entire pontificate was marked by what the Virgin had foretold at Fatima.
>
> Although there is no lack of anxiety and suffering, and although there are still reasons for apprehension about the future of humanity, what the "Lady in White" promised the shepherd children is consoling: "In the end, my Immaculate Heart will triumph."
>
> With this awareness, we now turn with confidence to Mary Most Holy, thanking her for her constant intercession and asking her to continue to watch over the journey of the Church and of humanity, especially families, mothers and children.[196]

Highly significant is the interpretation given by Sr. Lucia regarding the relevance of Fatima for today. In an interview given to Ricardo Cardinal Vidal of the Philippines in 1993,[197] Sr. Lucia explains that we

---

[196] Pope Benedict XVI, Regina Caeli address, May 14, 2006.
[197] Cf. Haffert, *God's Final Effort*, p. 2.

are presently living in the "third day" of the "Week of Fatima."[198] She identifies the "first day" of Fatima as the historical period during which the apparitions took place. The "second day" is the period following the apparitions, but previous to the consecration of the world to the Immaculate Heart. We are now in the "third day" of the seven days of Fatima, signifying our present period after the 1984 consecration:

> "Fatima is still in its third day. We are now in the post-consecration period. The first day was the apparition period. The second was the post apparition, pre-consecration period. The Fatima Week has not yet ended." ... "People expect things to happen immediately within their own timeframe. But Fatima is still in its third day. The triumph is an on-going process."[199]

Four "days" of Fatima, whether they represent time periods or specific events, are yet to come in the historical process of the triumph of the Immaculate Heart of Mary and its fulfillment in the promised "era of Peace." For our present generation the Fatima message is more relevant and crucial than ever.

---

[198] Cf. Haffert, *God's Final Effort*, p. 2.
[199] *Ibid.*

Contributing Authors

Fr. Stefano Manelli, F.I.

Fr. Stefano Manelli is founder and minister general of the Franciscan Friars of the Immaculate, and is a professor of Mariology at the "Immaculate Mediatrix" Theological Seminary. He is an internationally recognized Mariological scholar and has published widely in biblical, dogmatic and devotional Mariology.

Fr. Settimio M. Manelli, F.I.

Fr. Settimio Manelli is a member of the Franciscan Friars of the Immaculate. He lectures at the "Immaculate Mediatrix" Theological Seminary, the *Immaculatum*, of the Franciscans of the Immaculate, and at the Archdiocesan Seminary of Benevento, Italy.

Fr. Luigi Gambero, S.M.

Fr. Luigi Gambero is a Marianist priest and a recognized Patristics scholar. He teaches Marian Patristics at the *Marianum* in Rome and the International Marian Research Institute in Dayton, Ohio.

Fr. Manfred Hauke

Fr. Manfred Hauke, a diocesan priest from Germany, teaches at the Theological Faculty of Lugano, Switzerland. A noted and published author in a wide diversity of Theological and Mariological fields, Fr. Hauke is the president of the German Society for Mariology, a member of the "Pontificia Academia Mariana Internationalis" and is prefect of studies at the diocesan seminary San Carlo of Lugano.

Fr. Peter M. Fehlner, F.I.

Fr. Peter Damian Fehlner is a member of the Franciscan Friars of the Immaculate. He is a professor of Theology at the *Immaculatum*, the seminary of the Franciscans of the Immaculate in Frigento, Italy, and former editor of *Miles Immaculatae*, the magazine founded by St. Maximilian Kolbe.

Msgr. Arthur Burton Calkins

Msgr. Arthur Burton Calkins is an official of the Pontifical Commission "Ecclesia Dei" in Rome, and is a contributing member of the Pontifical International Marian Academy. He has published in a great number of Theological and Mariological anthologies, texts, and journals.

Fr. Paul Haffner

Fr. Paul Haffner is a priest for the Diocese of Portsmouth, England. He is professor of Sacramental Theology and Protology at Regina Apostolorum University and a lecturer at the Pontifical Gregorian University. He has published several works in Theology and Mariology.

Fr. Alessandro M. Apollonio, F.I.

Fr. Alessandro Apollonio is a member of the Franciscan Friars of the Immaculate. He is the rector of the *Immaculatum*, the friars' theological seminary in Italy. He is also the editor of the Mariological journal *Immaculata Mediatrix*.

Edward Sri, S.T.D.

Dr. Edward Sri is a professor of Theology and Scripture at the Augustine Institute in Denver, Colorado, and has authored several works on the subject of the Queen-Mother tradition.

Fr. Enrique Llamas, O.C.D.

Fr. Enrique Llamas Martínez is a Discalced Carmelite from Valdevimbre, Spain. He is president of the Spanish Mariological Society, professor emeritus of the Pontifical University of Salamanca, and author of several Mariological texts.

Fr. Neil J. Roy

Fr. Neil J. Roy, a priest with the diocese of Peterborough, Canada, is the co-founder of the Research Institute for Catholic Liturgy and editor of the liturgical journal *Antiphon: A Journal for Liturgical Renewal*.

Fr. Etienne Richer

Fr. Etienne Richer is assistant general of the Community of the Beatitudes, an international association of the faithful of pontifical right. He is a member of the French Society of Marian Studies as well as the Association of the French Catholic Writers.

Mark I. Miravalle, S.T.D.

Dr. Mark Miravalle is professor of Theology and Mariology at the Franciscan University of Steubenville and president of the international Catholic movement *Vox Populi Mariae Mediatrici* (Voice of the People for Mary Mediatrix). He has authored and edited a number of Mariological books and anthologies and is editor of the Marian online e-magazine, *Mother of All Peoples.com*.

www.ingramcontent.com/pod-product-compliance
Lightning Source LLC
Chambersburg PA
CBHW071428300426
44114CB00013B/1347